The Ecological Consequences of
Environmental Heterogeneity

Symposia of
The British Ecological Society

The Ecological Consequences of Environmental Heterogeneity

The 40th Symposium of the British Ecological Society
held at the University of Sussex
23–25 March 1999

EDITED BY

MICHAEL J. HUTCHINGS

School of Biological Sciences
University of Sussex

ELIZABETH A. JOHN

School of Biological Sciences
University of Sussex

AND

ALAN J.A. STEWART

School of Biological Sciences
University of Sussex

b
Blackwell
Science

© 2000 by
Blackwell Science Ltd
Editorial Offices:
Osney Mead, Oxford OX2 0EL
25 John Street, London WC1N 2BL
23 Ainslie Place, Edinburgh EH3 6AJ
350 Main Street, Malden
  MA 02148-5018, USA
54 University Street, Carlton
  Victoria 3053, Australia
10, rue Casimir Delavigne
  75006 Paris, France

Other Editorial Offices:
Blackwell Wissenschafts-Verlag GmbH
Kurfürstendamm 57
10707 Berlin, Germany

Blackwell Science KK
MG Kodenmacho Building
7–10 Kodenmacho Nihombashi
Chuo-ku, Tokyo 104, Japan

First published 2000

Set by Best-set Typesetter Ltd., Hong
  Kong
Printed and bound in Great Britain by
the University Press, Cambridge

The Blackwell Science logo is a
trade mark of Blackwell Science Ltd,
registered at the United Kingdom
Trade Marks Registry

A catalogue record for this title
is available from the British Library

ISBN 0-632-05713-0 Hardback
     0-632-05714-9 Paperback

Library of Congress
Cataloging-in-publication Data

British Ecological Society. Symposium
(40th : 1999 : University of Sussex)
    The ecological consequences of
environmental heterogeneity: the
40th symposium of the British
Ecological Society, held at the
University of Sussex, 23–25 March
1999 / edited by Mike J. Hutchings,
Libby A. John, and Alan J.A. Stewart.
    p. cm.
    ISBN 0-632-05713-0
    1. Ecological heterogeneity—
Congresses. I. Hutchings, M.J.
II. John, Libby A.   III. Stewart,
Alan J.A.   IV. Title.
QH541.15.E24 B75 1999
577—dc21   00-027087

DISTRIBUTORS

Marston Book Services Ltd
PO Box 269
Abingdon, Oxon OX14 4YN
(Orders: Tel: 01235 465500
         Fax: 01235 465555)

USA
Blackwell Science, Inc.
Commerce Place
350 Main Street
Malden, MA 02148-5018
(Orders: Tel: 800 759 6102
              781 388 8250
         Fax: 781 388 8255)

Canada
Login Brothers Book Company
324 Saulteaux Crescent
Winnipeg, Manitoba R3J 3T2
(Orders: Tel: 204 837 2987)

Australia
Blackwell Science Pty Ltd
54 University Street
Carlton, Victoria 3053
(Orders: Tel: 3 9347 0300
         Fax: 3 9347 5001)

For further information on
Blackwell Science, visit our website:
www.blackwell-science.com

Contents

List of contributors

J.P. Bakker
Laboratory of Plant Ecology, Centre for Ecological and Evolutionary Studies, University of Groningen, PO Box 14, 9750 Aa Haren, The Netherlands

M.R. Billingham
Oxford Forestry Institute, Department of Plant Sciences, University of Oxford, South Parks Road, Oxford OX1 3RB, UK

D.H. Boshier
Oxford Forestry Institute, Department of Plant Sciences, University of Oxford, South Parks Road, Oxford OX1 3RB, UK

D. Briese
CSIRO Division of Entomology, GPO Box 1700, CRC Weed Management Systems, Canberra, ACT 2601, Australia

J.S. Brown
Department of Biological Sciences, University of Illinois at Chicago, 845 W. Taylor Street, Chicago IL 60607, USA

M.L. Cadenasso
Institute of Ecosystem Studies, Box AB, Millbrook, NY 12545-0129, USA

J.F. Cahill Jr
Department of Biological Sciences, University of Alberta, Edmonton, Alberta, T6G 2E9, Canada

B.B. Casper
Department of Biology, University of Pennsylvania, Philadelphia, PA 19104-6018, USA

R.T. Corlett
Department of Ecology and Biodiversity, University of Hong Kong, Pokfulam Road, Hong Kong, China

C. Dytham
Department of Biology, University of York, Heslington, York YO10 5DD, UK

R.E. Feber
Wildlife Conservation Research Unit, Department of Zoology, University of Oxford, South Parks Road, Oxford OX1 3PS, UK

A. Fitter
Department of Biology, University of York, Heslington, York YO10 5DD, UK

R.E. Forkner
Department of Biology, University of Missouri, 8001 Natural Bridge Road, St. Louis, MO 63121, USA

H.C.J. Godfray
NERC Centre for Population Biology, Department of Biology, Imperial College, Silwood Park, Ascot, Berkshire SL5 7PY, UK

A. Hodge
Department of Biology, University of York, Heslington, York YO10 5DD, UK

M.J. Hutchings
School of Biological Sciences, University of Sussex, Falmer, Brighton, Sussex BN1 9QG, UK

M.D. Hunter
Institute of Ecology, University of Georgia, Athens, GA 30602-2202, USA

R.B. Jackson
Department of Biology and Nicholas School of the Environment, Duke University, Durham, NC 27708, USA

C.G. Jones
Institute of Ecosystem Studies, Box AB, Millbrook, NY 12545-0129, USA

E.A. John
School of Biological Sciences, University of Sussex, Falmer, Brighton, Sussex BN1 9QG, UK

P.J. Johnson
Wildlife Conservation Research Unit, Department of Zoology, University of Oxford, South Parks Road, Oxford OX1 3PS, UK

A.R. Kraaijeveld
NERC Centre for Population Biology, Department of Biology, Imperial College, Silwood Park, Ascot, Berkshire SL5 7PY, UK

J.H. Lawton
NERC Centre for Population Biology, Imperial College, Silwood Park, Ascot, Berkshire SL5 7PY, UK

M. Mangel
Department of Evironmental Studies, University of California, Santa Cruz, CA 95064, USA

D.W. Macdonald
Wildlife Conservation Research Unit, Department of Zoology, University of Oxford, South Parks Road, Oxford OX1 3PS, UK

J.N. McNeil
Département de biologie, Universitié Laval, Québec, G1K 7P4, Canada

C.B. Müller
NERC Centre for Population Biology, Department of Biology, Imperial College, Silwood Park, Ascot, Berkshire SL5 7PY, UK

S.T.A. Pickett
Institute of Ecosystem Studies, Box AB, Millbrook, NY 12545-0129, USA

M.E. Power
Department of Integrative Biology, University of California, Berkeley, CA 94720, USA

M.C. Press
Department of Animal and Plant Sciences, University of Sheffield, Sheffield S10 2TN, UK

W.E. Rainey
Department of Integrative Biology, University of California, Berkeley, CA 94720, USA

M. Rees
NERC Centre for Population Biology, Imperial College, Silwood Park, Ascot, Berkshire SL5
7PY, UK

D. Robinson
Department of Plant and Soil Science, University of Aberdeen, Aberdeen, AB24 3UU, UK

A. Sheppard
CSIRO Division of Entomology, GPO Box 1700, CRC Weed Management Systems, Canberra,
ACT 2601, Australia

A.J.A. Stewart
School of Biological Sciences, University of Sussex, Falmer, Brighton, Sussex BN1 9QG, UK

F.H. Tattersall
Royal Agricultural College, Cirencester, UK

L. Turnbull
Imperial College, Silwood Park, Ascot, Berkshire SL5 7PY, UK

J.R. Watling
Department of Animal and Plant Sciences, University of Sheffield, Sheffield S10 2TN, UK

J.A. Wiens
Department of Biology and Graduate Degree Program in Ecology, Colorado State University,
Fort Collins, CO 80523, USA

D.K. Wijesinghe
School of Biological Sciences, University of Sussex, Falmer, Brighton, Sussex BN1 9QG, UK

S.D. Wilson
Department of Biology, University of Regina, Regina, Saskatchewan S4S 0A2, Canada

History of the British Ecological Society

The British Ecological Society is a learned society, a registered charity and a company limited by guarantee. Established in 1913 by academics to promote and foster the study of ecology in its widest sense, the Society currently has around 5000 members spread around the world. Members include research scientists, environmental consultants, teachers, local authority ecologists, conservationists and many others with an active interest in natural history and the environment. The core activities are the publication of the results of research in ecology, the development of scientific meetings and the promotion of ecological awareness through education. The Society's mission is:

To advance and support the science of ecology and publicize the outcome of research, in order to advance knowledge, education and its application.

The Society publishes four internationally renowned journals and organizes at least two major conferences each year plus a large number of smaller meetings. It also initiates a diverse range of activities to promote awareness of ecology at the public and policy maker level in addition to developing ecology in the education system, and it provides financial support for approved ecological projects. The Society is an independent organization that receives little outside funding.

British Ecological Society
26 Blades Court
Deodar Road, Putney
London SW15 2NU
United Kingdom
Tel.: +44 (0)20 8871 9797
Fax: +44 (0) 20 8871 9779

Preface

This book comprises an introduction and eighteen chapters that represent the contents of talks given at a Symposium on The Ecological Consequences of Environmental Heterogeneity. The Symposium was held at the University of Sussex, UK, from 23 to 25 March 1999. Our intention in holding the meeting was two-fold. Firstly, we wanted to assemble a record of the progress that has been made, since the publication of seminal books on environmental heterogeneity in the early 1990s (e.g. Shorrocks & Swingland (1990) *Living in a Patchy Environment*, Oxford University Press, Oxford; Kolasa & Pickett (1991) *Ecological Heterogeneity*, Springer-Verlag, New York), in understanding its ecological effects. Secondly, we wanted to bring together plant and animal scientists, working at all scales and on all levels of organization, ranging from organisms and populations to communities, to discuss their mutual interests. Our hope was that discussion of new developments in each area of specialization would broaden minds and generate an atmosphere in which new research collaborations might be created. To the editors, it appeared that the mixture of plant and animal scientists with a common interest in the ecological consequences of environmental heterogeneity was highly beneficial, and we thank all participants in the symposium for contributing to a lively and stimulating meeting. We thank Catherine Stead, from the University of Sussex Conference Office, Philip Gassmann and David Chick from the University of Sussex Catering Services, and many student helpers for ensuring that everything ran smoothly during the meeting. We are also greatly indebted to Hazel Norman, Pauline Kemp and Amanda Thomas of the British Ecological Society for their handling of the Symposium booking arrangements and finances, and for dealing with all enquiries at the Conference desk during the meeting. Malcolm Press gave much valuable advice during the planning of this meeting and at many times since. We thank the many reviewers who helped us during the preparation of the manuscripts, and Ian Sherman, Delia Sandford and Cee Brandson of Blackwell Science, for their professionalism and friendly help in producing the book. Finally, we thank the Symposium speakers, who also wrote the chapters for this book. We greatly appreciated their commitment to the meeting and to the production of this book, and for dealing—mostly very promptly—with the numerous bothersome requests from the editors for clarification and alteration of their written texts.

Michael J. Hutchings
Elizabeth A. John
Alan J.A. Stewart

Chapter 1

The world is heterogeneous: ecological consequences of living in a patchy environment

A.J.A. Stewart, E.A. John and M.J. Hutchings

Recent years have witnessed considerable progress in addressing the question of how environmental heterogeneity impacts upon organisms and ecological processes. The principal aim of this Symposium was to gather insights from as wide a range of approaches as possible, focusing specifically on the ecological consequences of heterogeneity. Other aspects, such as the measurement and quantification of heterogeneity, were outside the scope of the meeting. This volume starts with chapters that explore how heterogeneity can be defined and categorized, together with consideration of the agents and processes that create, maintain and influence it (Wiens, Pickett *et al.*; Wilson). A series of chapters deals with impacts of heterogeneity on individual plants (Wilson, Fitter *et al.*; Hutchings *et al.*; Casper *et al.*; Watling and Press) and animals (Hunter *et al.*; Brown, Godfray *et al.*). The focus then moves to the effects of heterogeneity on population processes (Rees *et al.*), genetic structures (Boshier and Billingham) and community-level interactions (Power and Rainey). Four chapters deal with the potential impact of anthropogenically induced heterogeneity on the persistence of populations and species: from a theoretical standpoint (Dytham), with reference to tropical forests (Corlett) and temperate agricultural landscapes (Macdonald *et al.*) and with respect to the restoration of fragmented landscapes in general (Bakker). Finally, a series of common threads are drawn together, with some signposts towards future research opportunities (Lawton).

Organisms live in habitats that are highly heterogeneous, both in space and in time. Field research has often focused on the effect of heterogeneity in habitat quality on the distribution and abundance of plants and animals, whereas experimental designs have tended to emphasize the importance of minimizing variability within treatments rather than addressing its consequences directly. Modellers have tended to exclude heterogeneity in an attempt to avoid complicating the picture (Pickett *et al.*). As Wiens points out, this old paradigm of ecology made environmental homogeneity the starting assumption and 'emphasized simplicity at the expense of reality'. However, there is now a growing recognition that, far from

School of Biological Sciences, University of Sussex, Falmer, Brighton BN1 9QG, UK

being an irritating complication, heterogeneity is the norm in the natural environment and that its effects on individuals, populations and communities are therefore worthy of direct and serious study in their own right.

In the ecological context, heterogeneity is not an easy concept to define and, as
Sparrow (1999) has pointed out, researchers differ in their approach to this
problem of definition. The concept makes an explicit connection between
spatial and temporal variation in environmental constraints on the one hand
(whether these are provided by differences in soils, microclimates, organisms, etc.)
and the responses by organisms to variability in these constraints. One practical
approach defines heterogeneity as any factor that induces variation in individual
demographic rates (Rees *et al.*); this approach has the advantage that the effects
of heterogeneity are both specific and measurable. Within this definition there
are nested spatial scales at which heterogeneity can operate (e.g. site, habitat,
landscape) and to which ecological responses may differ. Rees *et al.* provide a
means of partitioning heterogeneity hierarchically, and apply mathematical
models to field data to demonstrate the implications of each category of heterogeneity for the evolution of the age at which flowering takes place in monocarpic
perennial plants. In an elegant demonstration of the potential impacts of heterogeneity on the evolution of plant life histories, they show that it is only by including
heterogeneity that realistic models can be derived. As a further consideration,
Wiens draws attention to important distinctions between the quantitative and
qualitative components of spatial variance and to whether or not the variance is
spatially explicit (i.e. whether the measure of heterogeneity incorporates the spatial
relationships between constituent patches, or is simply an aggregate property of
the area as a whole).

While environmental heterogeneity often results from variation in abiotic
factors, such as the physical and chemical properties of soils, microtopography and
microclimate, organisms themselves may create or influence abiotic heterogeneity
in a variety of ways (Pickett *et al.*; Wilson). In fact, organisms can create heterogeneity in otherwise relatively uniform environments. For example, plants may
affect heterogeneity of abiotic factors through their production of leaf litter or exudates, or through interception of light and rainfall. Similarly, there are many examples of animals both generating and maintaining environmental heterogeneity
through activities such as grazing, trampling or burrowing. Some organisms,
so-called 'ecosystem engineers', can exert far-reaching influences on whole communities and the ecological processes acting within them by altering the state,
availability, and perhaps degree of heterogeneity, of biotic or abiotic materials that
are available to other organisms (Pickett *et al.*; Lawton). A further layer of heterogeneity may be provided by stochastic or deterministic patterns of disturbance,
whether natural or anthropogenic in origin, which impact upon both the physical
environment and the organisms within it. These different sources of heterogeneity
interact in ways that are a challenge to disentangle.

Wilson explores the relationship between species diversity and heterogeneity.
While it is clear that habitat heterogeneity can enhance diversity, as exemplified by

MacArthur's familiar positive correlation between structural heterogeneity of trees and bird diversity (Lawton), the converse is less clear. Species richness in itself increases biotic heterogeneity; for instance, a species-rich plant community provides a heterogeneous habitat for phytophagous insects. However, there is a growing body of evidence that suggests that diverse communities are likely to be associated with smaller spatial and temporal fluctuations in abiotic parameters than less diverse communities†. A diverse community is likely to exploit resources in space more completely and show smaller temporal fluctuations in ecosystem processes. For instance, a diverse plant community will contain species with a range of rooting depths and phenological patterns of physiological activity, which together are likely to absorb more completely nutrients that are spatially and temporally heterogeneous. Wilson also explores the interesting and important idea that organisms control not only the degree but also the scale of heterogeneity, and that scale is an important determinant of the effects of heterogeneity on individual organisms. Thus, for example, trees may create large-scale spatial heterogeneity in water availability via hydraulic lift, making the soil environment less suitable for species that operate at a smaller scale.

Indeed, environmental heterogeneity is important for individual organisms only when it occurs at a scale to which the organism itself can respond. If the scale is greater than this, the result is merely a difference in performance between spatially separated locations. However, an important recent development has been the recognition of the importance of the opposite situation: i.e. conditions in which environmental heterogeneity occurs at a scale that is within the organism's normal ambit and to which it can respond in alternative ways. The critical question then becomes whether the ecological response (measured as change in fitness, growth, or whatever) differs as a consequence of whether the mean condition or total resource is presented homogeneously or heterogeneously.

Similar logic can be applied to considerations of temporal heterogeneity; life spans must be great enough to experience and respond to the time scale over which the heterogeneity operates. Similarly, individuals may experience changing modes of heterogeneity during their lifetime as a consequence of their own growth and development. Thus, the scale and category of heterogeneity experienced by an oak seedling will be very different to that experienced by the tree when it reaches maturity. This also applies to more mobile organisms and ones that undergo phase shifts during their lifecycle: the fine-scale heterogeneity between leaves experienced by a caterpillar will be radically different from that experienced by the nectar-feeding adult butterfly.

Our understanding of the ecological consequences of heterogeneity for individual plants, populations of plants and plant communities is developing rapidly, and a number of chapters reflect this current interest (Fitter *et al.*; Hutchings *et al.*; Casper *et al.*; Watling and Press). At first sight, plants, as relatively sessile organisms,

† See references in Chapter 19.

are less able to engage in habitat selection and foraging than the more mobile animals. However, effective habitat selection in plants is now being studied from two angles:

1 by investigating ramet position and its consequences in clonal plants (multiply rooted clonal plants can occupy more than one location, and their rhizomes and stolons effectively allow them some mobility); and

2 by investigating the ability of plants that root at a single site to respond to spatial heterogeneity (the proliferation of sections of the root system in resource-rich patches is a feature of many plants so far investigated; Fitter *et al.*; Hutchings *et al.*).

Studies to date have shown a great deal of variation in the precision with which plants are able to match the placement of resource-acquiring organs to the available resources, although in some cases the precision is quite remarkable (Hutchings *et al.*). Understanding the ecological implications of this variation is a goal of a number of current research programmes. The responses of plants to temporal heterogeneity have been studied less, but it is clear that over short time periods, such as brief sun-flecks experienced by tropical forest floor plants, there may be species-specific physiological constraints which limit the abilities of plants to respond rapidly to a short pulse of extra resource (Watling and Press).

When the performance of plants is compared in environments in which the same quantity of resources is supplied homogeneously or in various heterogeneous arrangements, it is found that some species are more productive in heterogeneous environments than in the equivalent homogeneous environment (Hutchings *et al.*). As species differ in their responses to heterogeneity of resource supply, it has been predicted that population and community structure should both respond to heterogeneity, although studies to date have not confirmed this (Casper *et al.*). So far, most studies of the effects of heterogeneity on plant performance have examined the effects of heterogeneity on biomass accumulation rather than plant fitness. A more detailed examination of the effects of heterogeneity on the latter will be an important challenge for researchers in future.

As roots of several plants tend to access the same nutrient patch in heterogeneous environments, and may travel quite some distance to do so, it might be expected that heterogeneity would lead to more intense underground competition. However, there is no evidence as yet that this is so. Casper *et al.* explore the inadequacy of most attempts to model competition among plants for dealing with heterogeneous environments, particularly underground, given that we still know very little about how most competing plants' roots are distributed within the soil with respect to each other.

One of the most stimulating aspects of the symposium was the degree to which animal and plant ecologists were able to integrate and exchange ideas, especially on issues to do with foraging and habitat selection. These areas have traditionally been regarded as the preserve of animal ecologists. The examination of plant responses to local resource heterogeneity has given plant ecologists a new insight into the dynamic nature of plant foraging and habitat choice, and an incentive to review the ways in which theories that were developed for animals could also be applied to plants.

Plants, as resources for herbivores, are intrinsically highly heterogeneous, both spatially and temporally. However, there are still many unanswered questions surrounding exactly what impact this heterogeneity has on higher trophic levels. What effect does variation in plant quality have on herbivore population densities and on the mechanisms that control them? How important is heterogeneity in resource quality as compared with the actual quantity and availability of the resource? To what extent can plants capitalize on their spatial heterogeneity and temporal unpredictability to defend themselves from attack by herbivores? Hunter *et al.* provide evidence that variation in plant quality affects two components of insect herbivore life histories: voltinism and the impact of natural enemies. It is, of course, a moot question as to whether such impacts affect the actual regulation of herbivore populations, rather than simply adjusting the equilibrium population size. However, against a historical background preoccupied with the importance of density dependent factors in population regulation, the potential for variation in plant quality to act in a density-independent (or perhaps even inversely density-dependent) manner, poses some interesting challenges for the development of population models.

At the individual level, models involving habitat selection and patch use behaviour (e.g. Charnov's marginal value theorem and the ideal free distribution) have been applied to many animals operating in heterogeneous environments. Drawing upon detailed and long-term studies on squirrels, Brown shows how the behaviour of related species responds differently to the trade-off between food consumption and predation risk. This in turn dictates spatio-temporal patterns of species in a number of ways: from how animals forage in patchy environments to the coexistence and geographical distribution of closely related and potentially competing species.

Insect parasitoids are also faced with a highly heterogeneous environment (Godfray *et al.*); their hosts are very patchily distributed in space and host densities may vary considerably between patches and over time. In response to this uncertainty, parasitoids have evolved a complex suite of behavioural traits that enable them to locate suitable patches, exploit their hosts and then depart in search of new patches in an efficient manner. At the population level, the non-random search of parasitoids between patches that are distributed across a heterogeneous landscape has long been recognized as the key to stabilizing models of host–parasitoid interactions, although whether or not density-dependent aggregation by the parasitoids is essential for stability remains controversial. In such circumstances, the spatial arrangement of parasitoids may conform to a metapopulation model, where extinction and re-colonization of local populations are dependent upon moderate, but not excessive, rates of dispersal between host patches. In this context, habitat heterogeneity is important for creating the asynchrony in dynamics between spatially separated local populations that is essential for metapopulation persistence.

Power and Rainey provide a new framework for examining the spatial sources of trophic resources, introducing the term 'resource shed' (analogous to watershed) to describe the geographical area from which an organism's resources are derived. Our ability to delimit resource sheds has far-reaching consequences for many aspects of pure and applied ecology (for instance food-web analysis and conservation biology), and is advancing rapidly with the range of stable-isotope techniques that are now available. Examination of an organism's resource shed can produce surprisingly counter-intuitive results and shows that resources can often move over large distances. For instance, riparian plants growing at high altitudes in Alaskan coastal watersheds may receive a significant input of oceanic nitrogen via a predator cache of salmon carcasses, derived from fish that had returned to the upper reaches of the stream to spawn.

Given the alarming rate of habitat destruction at a global scale, there is an urgent need for conservation biologists to provide predictions of how such large-scale anthropogenically imposed heterogeneity will affect constituent populations. The spatial pattern of modern development at a landscape level usually involves progressive habitat fragmentation, where remnant fragments of original habitat become smaller in area and increasingly isolated from each other. It is not yet clear how best to model the effects on populations of the large scale habitat heterogeneity that this creates; species-area models have now given way to models based on metapopulation structures (Dytham; Lawton). In any case, it is clear that specific predictions of the effects of habitat fragmentation across species, locations and habitat types will not be easy. As might be expected, empirical data suggest that generalist species will fare better than habitat specialists; unfortunately, the rarest species are likely to be in the latter category. Similarly, a consideration of how fragmentation affects the genetic composition of remnant populations and gene flow between them will be essential (Boshier and Billingham). More importantly however, data from highly modified tropical forests suggest that the persistence of a species in remnant fragments does not guarantee its long-term survival (Corlett); continuing loss of species even from protected habitat fragments suggests that extinction will continue long after the fragmentation has ceased. This is likely to be especially true for long-lived organisms such as trees, in which effects will take a long time to manifest themselves and population recovery rates will be slow. For this reason, Dytham warns against simplistic predictions of species loss based on area of habitat destroyed; the 'extinction debt' (Tilman *et al.* 1994), where currently surviving species are already locked into a downward spiral towards extinction, may take a long time to be paid off.

At a more local scale, the arable farmland landscape, with intensively managed fields separated by seminatural field margins, comprises a heterogeneous mosaic of habitat types. Conventional agricultural management practices impose periodic and dramatic perturbations upon this spatial structure, in the form of tilling, sowing, and harvesting operations and the application of nutrients, herbicides and pesticides. This landscape therefore provides a suitable arena in which the differential effects of environmental heterogeneity in space and time can be examined experimentally. Macdonald *et al.* demonstrate that the ecological effects of such heterogeneity (on individual species, communities and overall 'biodiversity') are both case-specific and highly scale-dependent. Thus, at one extreme, landscape-level studies show that the greater temporal stability and increased spatial heterogeneity of organic farming systems have a positive effect on population size and species richness of small mammals and selected invertebrate groups in comparison to conventional farms. At a fine scale, heterogeneity imposed by small-scale mowing experiments on field margins produces effects that interact closely with the detailed autecology of individual species.

This type of detailed knowledge will be essential for the successful restoration of semi-natural communities that have been degraded or destroyed as a result of modern agricultural practices. Bakker emphasizes that successful restoration of plant communities involves more than just the cessation of damaging practices and that it is necessary to understand the heterogeneous nature of both propagule availability and soil nutrient availability in order to predict whether restoration will succeed. He also points out the important role that vertebrate grazers can have in creating a heterogeneity of micro-sites, and patchiness in vegetation structure, which allow a diverse range of plant species to coexist in a community.

Several common threads emerge from the collection of contributions to this Symposium. Firstly, results from recent research re-emphasize what ecologists have known for many years: that heterogeneity, at a variety of spatial scales, is all-pervasive in natural environments. Ecologists can not afford to ignore such heterogeneity, even though it greatly complicates the task of untangling the various environmental influences on organisms. In order to respond, individual organisms must be able to perceive the heterogeneity; whether they are good or bad at dealing with heterogeneity will depend substantially on whether they have the phenotypic plasticity to respond to it. In fact, there are good reasons for suggesting that many species will have evolved strategies for coping with, and capitalizing upon, environmental heterogeneity as the norm in natural systems. The other side of this coin is that therefore one would expect to see, at least in some species, a reduction in performance when faced with homogeneity compared with their performance in certain types of heterogeneous environments; some single-species studies are now beginning to provide exactly this sort of evidence (Hutchings *et al.*). In fact, different species are likely to show a range of responses to heterogeneity; some will be able to respond positively to a particular form or scale of heterogeneity, whilst others will not. In this context, ability to respond to heterogeneity becomes an important species attribute that ecologists will need to consider alongside the other conventional attributes that are used to characterize species.

Secondly, while evidence is accumulating that natural heterogeneity has important effects on the performance and fitness of individual organisms, the implications of heterogeneity for populations and communities have been, as yet, less well explored. This presents an exciting challenge for the future. Amongst other factors, the amount of genetic variation will influence the degree to which organisms can respond to heterogeneity at the population level (Boshier and Billingham).

Finally, while we might expect many organisms to have evolved mechanisms for dealing with natural heterogeneity, anthropogenically imposed heterogeneity at the landscape level will have severe consequences for the long-term persistence of many species, particularly those that have high habitat specificity and limited powers of dispersal. Problems will arise for such species if the scale of habitat fragmentation is larger than the scale of heterogeneity to which the organisms are adapted. Unfortunately, these species are likely to be both rare and vulnerable and therefore the ones of greatest conservation concern.

References

Sparrow, A.D. (1999) A heterogeneity of heterogeneities. *Trends in Ecology and Evolution* **14**, 422–423.

Tilman, D., May, R.M., Lehman, C.L. & Nowak, M.A. (1994) Habitat destruction and the extinction debt. *Nature* **371**, 65–66.

Chapter 2

Ecological heterogeneity: an ontogeny of concepts and approaches

J.A. Wiens

Introduction

Heterogeneity is scarcely a new or novel concept in ecology. After all, the work of von Humboldt and other plant and animal geographers in the 19th century, which established the foundations of modern biogeography, was based on recognizing distinct patterns in the distributions of species or community types (McIntosh 1991). At finer scales, ecologists were analysing the dispersion patterns of plants well before many of today's ecologists were born, frequently documenting that the distributions of individuals departed significantly from random—there was spatial heterogeneity or pattern (Greig-Smith 1979, 1983; Dale 1999). By the middle of the century, laboratory experiments (e.g. Gause 1935; Huffaker 1958) had demonstrated that environmental heterogeneity could alter the dynamics of populations or communities. Alex Watt's Presidential Address to the British Ecological Society (1947) and, later, Elton's (1966) detailed treatment of habitat patterns in Wytham Woods showed clearly the reticulate spatial structure of natural environments and the interplay of spatial patterns with spatial processes.

An awareness of environmental heterogeneity and its consequences, then, appeared early in the history of ecology. Our current interest in heterogeneity, however, is a consequence of a relatively recent paradigm shift. Beginning in the 1950s, a view that ecological dynamics are played out in local habitats that are spatially homogeneous and temporally equilibrial rapidly gained force, and it came to dominate ecological theory and a good deal of ecological practice during the 1960s and 1970s. There were both philosophical and practical reasons for the widespread acceptance of this view. Philosophically, the notion that ecological systems could be thought of as closed and internally homogeneous fitted closely with the typological view of nature that was the foundation of community classification as well as of taxonomy (Mayr 1976; Pickett *et al.* 1994). Equilibrium thinking also accorded well with a Western world view of the balance of nature (Wiens 1984; McIntosh 1985; Pimm 1991; Wu and Loucks 1995). Practically, the assumptions of homogeneity and equilibrium provided the simplification of a more complex reality that was

Department of Biology and Graduate Degree Program in Ecology, Colorado State University, Fort Collins, CO 80523, USA

necessary for theory (especially mathematical theory) to develop. Because theory provided the framework for posing questions and testing hypotheses, however, empirical studies increasingly were designed with equilibrium and homogeneity in mind. Thus, short-term studies became the norm, and ecologists were admonished to seek homogeneous study areas to discern clear community patterns (MacArthur 1972). Ecosystem ecologists came to consider entire watersheds as internally homogeneous areas with regard to biogeochemical inputs and outputs (Bormann and Likens 1979). Ecologists conducting laboratory experiments justified their neglect of spatial and temporal variations by emphasizing that laboratory studies should address recurrent ecological processes of general significance, rather than the idiosyncratic and unique situations studied by field ecologists (Mertz and McCauley 1980; see also Lawton 1999). The new paradigm offered the prospect of far-reaching and unifying generalizations. As Cody and Diamond (1975) observed, the new paradigm 'transformed large areas of ecology into a structured, predictive science that combined powerful quantitative theories with the recognition of widespread patterns in nature.' Over time, the simplifying assumptions of homogeneity and equilibrium became widely accepted.

Just as it was theory and theoreticians who led ecology down the pathway to homogeneity and equilibrium, however, it was to a large degree theoreticians who provided the catalyst for a paradigm shift. By the mid-1960s and early 1970s, theoreticians were beginning to introduce temporal and spatial variation into their models (e.g. MacArthur and Levins 1964, 1967; Levins 1968, 1970; Horn and MacArthur 1972; Levin and Paine 1974), often with interesting results. The potential for a population to persist, for example, or the continued coexistence of competitors or of predators and prey, or the augmentation of local biodiversity, were all enhanced by the addition of spatial heterogeneity to models. By generating new predictions for field and laboratory ecologists to test, the theories focused attention once again on heterogeneity. Moreover, the incorporation of heterogeneity into theory made it an acceptable topic for ecological investigation, and challenges to the waning paradigm could now be published without the authors being labelled heretics (e.g. Van Valen and Pitelka 1974; Levin 1976; Wiens 1977, 1983; Simberloff 1980). The focus on spatial and temporal variation that had attracted the attention of an earlier generation of ecologists was renewed, setting the stage for an explosion of interest in heterogeneity and its consequences (e.g. Shorrocks and Swingland 1990; Kolasa and Pickett 1991; Levin et al. 1993; Rhodes et al. 1996; Tilman and Kareiva 1997). The recent development of perspectives on self-organizing properties of complex systems (Kauffman 1993), chaos theory (Gleick 1987) and fractals (Milne 1997) has provided fresh ways of thinking about heterogeneity in ecology. Complexity, however, is not quite the same as heterogeneity. In principle, a system could be complex but not vary in time or space—homogeneous complexity. Whether such complexity is seen as homogeneity or heterogeneity, however, depends on the scale on which it is viewed, a point to which I will return later in this chapter. In any case, we now recognize that models built on assumptions of homogeneity in space and equilibrium in time may be valuable in generating null hypotheses, but their applicability to the real world is severely limited. In a very real sense, 'heterogeneity' has become the ecologist's mantra.

There are both temporal and spatial dimensions to heterogeneity, however. Both involve uncertainty (i.e. not all times or places are the same), and temporal and spatial variations are often linked together. Variations in time ('disturbances'), for example, often create patterns of heterogeneity in space ('patch dynamics'). Nonetheless, ecologists have generally considered temporal variation separately from spatial variation (but see Naeem and Colwell 1991), perhaps because the challenges faced by organisms in dealing with temporal and spatial variation differ. Time is a stream in which there is no turning back; if conditions change, individuals must cope, move, or die. Traits such as seasonal phenology, 'boom or bust' reproduction, or sit-and-wait predation are often viewed as adaptations to the temporal variation and uncertainty of environments. Grime's (1979) definitions of plant strategies are differentiated largely in terms of temporal predictability: frequent disturbance (ruderals) *vs.* infrequent disturbance and good conditions (competitors) *vs.* infrequent disturbances but poor conditions (stress tolerators). Temporal uncertainty is especially critical to organisms that are sessile for much of their lifecycle, such as trees or barnacles. Variation in space assumes greater significance in shaping the adaptations of mobile organisms, which can move in response to temporal variations but must then confront spatial uncertainty. The evolution of behavioural traits such as habitat selection or predator search strategies (e.g. patch foraging) is often interpreted in the context of spatial heterogeneity. Some adaptive traits, such as dispersal or migration, are clearly driven by the combined effects of temporal and spatial uncertainty.

The realm of temporal and spatial heterogeneity is vast, too vast to be considered in a single chapter. In the following sections, I will emphasize spatial heterogeneity, and my primary focus will be on animals. The points I make, however, should also apply in general to temporal heterogeneity and, with minor modifications, to plants.

Forms of spatial heterogeneity

But what do we mean when we talk of 'heterogeneity'? A standard dictionary (e.g. Webster's Seventh New Collegiate Dictionary 1965, Blair 1982) defines heterogeneous as 'consisting of dissimilar constituents' or 'having widely unlike elements'. In an ecological context, heterogeneity has been defined as 'made up of a number of elements different from each other' (Art 1993) or 'having a non-uniform structure or composition' (Lincoln *et al.* 1998). Milne (1991) proposed that spatial heterogeneity is 'the complexity that results from interactions between the spatial distribution of environmental constraints and the differential responses of organisms to the constraints'.

In one way or another, all of these definitions emphasize discontinuities in space or time. Beyond that, however, they leave one with the feeling that the question 'What is heterogeneity?' hasn't really been answered. Kolasa and Rollo's (1991)

solution to this problem was to recognize various types or components of heterogeneity — roughly a dozen, by my count. But generating terms doesn't solve the
problem. To be a useful ecological concept, 'heterogeneity' must be an operational
term, something that can be measured and quantified and compared among sites
or studies.

Following the lead of Li and Reynolds (1995), I suggest that we might recognize
several forms of heterogeneity, which form a graded series from spatially implicit
to spatially explicit or locational (Fig. 2.1). The simplest expression of heterogeneity is *spatial variance*, a statistical measure of the aggregate variation among sampling points in a given area. In a homogeneous area, all points are the same, so
variance = 0. Heterogeneity, then, is indicated when variance >0; the greater the
value, the greater the heterogeneity.

Spatial variance, of course, says nothing about the spatial pattern of heterogeneity — it only indicates that not all places are the same. By this measure, environments with quite different patterns may be equally heterogeneous. But the pattern
of spatial variance is important. Are nearby points more similar to one another
than are distant points, for example? Such heterogeneity is expressed as *patterned
variance*. As with spatial variance, however, patterned variance is not spatially
explicit — we know that values of a given attribute for nearby points are statistically
correlated at some level, but the measure of spatial autocorrelation applies to the
area as a whole, not to particular locations within that area. Measures of anisotropy
will tell us whether the pattern of autocorrelation is symmetrical or has a directional component, but nothing more.

These first two forms of heterogeneity involve situations in which the properties
of the environment vary quantitatively — what Li and Reynolds (1995) call 'numer-

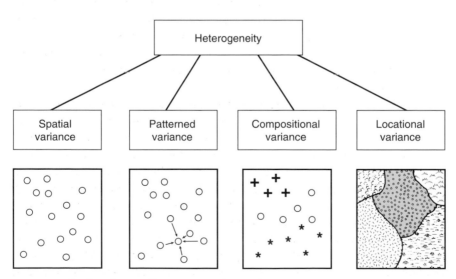

Figure 2.1 The four forms of heterogeneity (see text).

ical maps.' A third form of heterogeneity, *compositional variance*, occurs when sample points differ qualitatively as well as quantitatively. The area contains different types of entities (e.g. forests, fields, or marshes, or at a finer scale, grass clumps, shrubs, or bare ground). These types may be clustered together in space, as shown in Fig. 2.1, or dispersed in some other fashion that is reflected in measures of the spatial association or disassociation among the types (Dale 1999). Spatial clustering is recognized as 'patchiness', and the arrangement of patches in a matrix is the foundation of a good deal of patch theory. Although the patterns occupy positions in space, general measures of compositional variance, such as dispersion measures (e.g. Moran's *I*), β-diversity, or 'patchiness' (which implies bounded areas of different types), do not reference specific locations; rather, they are aggregate properties of the area as a whole. Li and Reynolds (1995) depicted such patterns through 'categorical maps', and termed the resulting heterogeneity 'complexity.' To further confuse the issue, McCoy and Bell (1991) distinguished between heterogeneity ('variation attributable to the relative abundance . . . of different structural components') and complexity ('variation attributable to the absolute abundance . . . of individual structural components'). Clearly, 'complexity' has as many meanings and nuances as 'heterogeneity', and we do not gain much by substituting one fuzzy term for another.

When compositional heterogeneity is considered in a spatially explicit way, the heterogeneity becomes expressed as *locational variance* (Fig. 2.1). Thus, if the spatial relations of patches in a matrix are specified, the variance becomes spatially referenced. Ecological landscapes, however, consist of more than patches (e.g. feeding patches or forest fragments) that are immersed in a featureless background matrix. The matrix itself has a spatial structure. Heterogeneity therefore becomes a property of the specific configuration of a landscape mosaic, and the locational relationships among the components of the mosaic can have important consequences (Turner 1989; Wiens 1995). While some of the measurable features of landscapes, such as mosaic diversity or connectivity, may reflect aggregate properties of the landscape as a whole, others (e.g. patch context, boundary form and contrast) are determined by the specific locations of elements in the mosaic (Wiens *et al.* 1993; Gustafson 1998).

These different forms of heterogeneity—spatial variance, patterned variance, compositional variance, and locational variance—represent somewhat arbitrary positions on a spectrum of ways of viewing space. At one extreme, space doesn't matter because everything is the same: space has been homogenized. At the other extreme, both what and where things are become vitally important. As I indicated earlier, the old paradigm of ecology emphasized simplicity at the expense of reality and was skewed toward the homogeneity extreme. Much of the early theory of ecology was founded on this base. With the shift to a new paradigm, ecological theory has progressively incorporated heterogeneity, but the emphasis has clearly been on the spatial, patterned, and compositional variance forms of heterogeneity. Reaction-diffusion models or epidemiological theories, for example, are based on patterned variance (spatial autocorrelation) produced by dispersal or diffusion processes (e.g. Levin 1974; Okubo 1980; Holmes 1997). A patch-matrix framework (compositional variance) has been popular in modelling foraging behaviour (e.g. MacArthur and Pianka 1966; Schmidt and Brown 1996), metapopulation dynamics (e.g. Levins 1970; Hanski 1997), population genetics (e.g. Hedrick *et al.* 1976; Hedrick and Gilpin 1997), and species interactions (e.g. Levin and Paine 1974; Hastings 1990). Indeed, island biogeography theory (MacArthur and Wilson 1967) is a form of patch-matrix theory. Perhaps because of its daunting complexity, there has been less theoretical development at the landscape extreme of the heterogeneity spectrum (Wiens 1995), although recent developments in percolation theory (Gardner *et al.* 1987; Pearson and Gardner 1997) and spatial optimization modelling (Hof and Bevers 1998) show promise.

Although not all of the forms of heterogeneity are associated with well-developed theory, they are all quantifiable, albeit not all equally so (Table 2.1). Quantification goes a long way toward making the multifarious concept of heterogeneity operational. Some measures (e.g. variance/mean ratio, mean crowding) assess only whether the spatial trend in the data from a series of samples differs from random, whereas others (e.g. semivariance, Moran's *I*) distinguish spatial patterns and describe the intensity of the patterns. Some indices quantify the spatial structure of sampled (point) data, while others characterize the geometric and spatial properties of categorical (mapped) data (Fortin 1999). Many of the indices are correlated with one another, most are bounded in some way and/or non-linear, and some produce contradictory conclusions when applied to the same data (Downing 1991; Davis 1993; Cale and Hobbs 1994; Qi and Wu 1996; Hargis *et al.* 1997). The 'perfect index' of spatial variation (Taylor 1984) has yet to be found.

Sources of heterogeneity

Understanding heterogeneity requires some consideration of how heterogeneity develops in ecological systems. At the most basic level, terrestrial and aquatic ecosystems are built upon a geophysical template that is itself heterogeneous. At fine spatial scales, for example, sites differ in microtopography and soil features. These differences create patchiness in microclimate and plant cover that in turn produce habitat heterogeneity for animals. At broader scales, patterns in bedrock geology, macrotopography, and regional climate have similar effects. Seafloor topography and ocean currents produce spatial discontinuities in marine systems (Barry and Dayton 1991).

Overlaying this geophysical templet are patterns of *disturbance*, which alter both the structure of the physical environment and the distribution of organisms over that environment (White and Harrod 1997). The list of disturbance agents and patterns is long. Landslides, hurricanes, fires, volcanic eruptions, and earthquakes are dramatic, broad-scale examples (Turner *et al.* 1997; Foster *et al.* 1998), but fine-scale disturbances such as treefall gaps (e.g. Sato and Iwasa 1993), the wind blow-outs described by Watt (1947), or fine-scale alterations of microtopography or soil-nutrient availability (Lechowicz and Bell 1991; Robertson and Gross 1994) are

Table 2.1 A sampling of measures of heterogeneity, classified according to the form(s) of heterogeneity (Fig. 2.1) that they represent

Measure	Form of variance				Reference
	Spatial	Patterned	Compositional	Locational	
Coefficient of variation (CV)	×				Downing (1991)
Variance/mean ratio	×				Downing (1991)
Mean crowding	×				Lloyd (1967)
Morisita's index	×	×			Morisita (1962)
Heterogeneity index	×	×			Wiens (1974)
Ripley's K		×			Fortin (1999)
Taylor's power law		×			Taylor et al. (1980)
Block size/variance		×			Greig-Smith (1983)
Contagion index		×			O'Neill et al. (1988); Li and Reynolds (1993)
Fractal dimension		×	×		Milne (1997)
Lacunarity		×	×		Plotnick et al. (1996)
Mean patch size		×	×		McGarigal and Marks (1995)
CV patch size		×	×		McGarigal and Marks (1995)
Correlograms (Moran's I, Geary's c)		×	×		Fortin (1999)
Join count		×	×		Cliff and Ord (1981)
Semivariance		×	×	×	Rossi et al. (1992)
Edge density		×		×	McGarigal and Marks (1995)
Mean nearest-neighbour distance		×		×	McGarigal and Marks (1995); Crist and Wiens (1996)
β-diversity			×		Caswell and Cohen (1991)
Patchiness index			×		Romme (1982)
Evenness			×		Pielou (1975)
Mosaic diversity			×		Nicholls (1994)
Patch density			×		McGarigal and Marks (1995)
Connectivity			×	×	Taylor et al. (1993)
Edge contrast index			×	×	McGarigal and Marks (1995)
Wavelet variance				×	Garcia-Moliner et al. (1993)
Proximity index				×	Gustafson and Parker (1992)

also important sources of heterogeneity that contribute to the patch dynamics of ecosystems (see Pickett and White 1985; Turner 1987; Bazzaz 1996; Pickett and Rogers 1997). Of course, in many ecosystems, anthropogenic disturbances associated with resource extraction, land use and development are increasingly the dominant forms of landscape disturbance. Rather than contributing to spatial heterogeneity, however, these activities often tend to homogenize landscape patterns, at least at fine to intermediate scales. Instead of focusing their attention on how disturbance affects particular habitat types, ecologists might do well to accept the challenge of understanding how disturbances of various sorts affect the patterns, forms and scales of spatial heterogeneity.

Organisms do more than respond to the spatial patterns of heterogeneity produced by geophysical processes and disturbances, however. In many cases, organisms alter the spatial configuration of environments, either through simple occupancy of space (e.g. trees, intertidal mussels or barnacles) or through active modification of the physical or biological structure of the environment (see Pickett *et al.* this volume). Thus, the physical and chemical properties of soil as a geophysical templet of spatial variation are themselves strongly influenced by the activity of a wide array of soil organisms (Wall and Moore 1999; Fitter *et al.*, this volume) or, at broader scales, grazing or browsing mammals such as bison (*Bison bison*), wildebeest (*Connochaetes taurinus*), or red deer (*Cervus elaphus*). Because these animals forage individually in a patchy manner and socially in large (sometimes immense) herds, they can alter vegetation stature, growth, production, species composition, and nutrient dynamics at multiple scales (Detling 1998; Knapp *et al.* 1999). 'Ecological engineers' (Lawton and Jones 1995), such as beaver (*Castor canadensis*), pocket gophers (*Thomomys* spp.), or prairie dogs (*Cynomys* spp.) have become textbook examples of the ways animals can alter the physical structure and spatial patterns of environments in fundamental ways. Less conspicuous organisms, such as harvester ants (*Pogonomyrmex* spp.) or termites (e.g. *Nasutitermes* spp.), however, may also have profound effects, but at finer scales (Fig. 2.2).

In some situations, the development of heterogeneity may be self-organizing: patchiness develops as a consequence of positive feedback dynamics. The successional patch dynamics of the *Calluna* heath described by Watt (1947) provide a classic example, as do the wave-regeneration patterns ('shimagare') of *Abies* forests in North America and Japan (Sprugel 1976; Sato and Iwasa 1993). In both of these cases, distinctive spatial patterns (vegetation bands) are produced through the interaction of physical forces (wind) with the structure and demography of the vegetation. The simulation model of Sato and Iwasa (1993) suggests that this interaction alone can generate patterned heterogeneity from an initial random distribution of individuals.

In the arid and semiarid environments of northern Australia, similar, strongly patterned heterogeneity is a consequence of the dynamics of water flow over shallow slopes. When rainfall occurs in these systems, runoff from the unvegetated interpatch areas is high and infiltration is low; when this flow meets a vegetation patch, the flow rate is reduced, infiltration is increased, and detritus and nutrients

(a)

(b)

Figure 2.2 Examples of the generation of fine-scale spatial heterogeneity by harvester ants (*Pogonomyrmex occidentalis*) in Wyoming, USA. (a) and cathedral termites (*Nasutitermes* spp.) in the Northern Territory, Australia (b). Taryn was 1.1 m tall at the time of the photographs.

carried by the flow are deposited in the patch (Fig. 2.3). Over time, the soil nutrient capital of the 'runon' patches increases, fostering plant establishment and growth (Tongway and Ludwig 1994; Ludwig *et al.* 1997). There is a scaling property to these dynamics: as the vegetation patches increase in size, the effectiveness of detritus and nutrient capture increases, and soil nitrogen concentrations increase disproportionately (Ludwig *et al.* 2000).

The self-organizing generation of patchiness is limited, as in the *Calluna* and *Abies* systems, by senescence and mortality of the plants, which itself exhibits spatial patterns. Tongway and Ludwig (1994) have shown that the runoff–runon dynamics of the Australian systems can easily be disrupted by disturbance (heavy grazing), which leads to a breakage of the vegetation pattern and an overall loss of

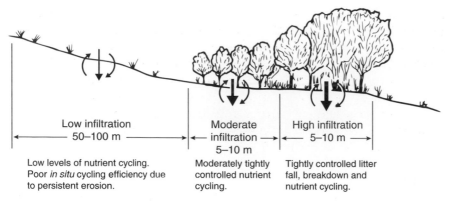

Low infiltration
50–100 m

Moderate
infiltration
5–10 m

High infiltration
5–10 m

Low levels of nutrient cycling.
Poor *in situ* cycling efficiency due
to persistent erosion.

Moderately tightly
controlled nutrient
cycling.

Tightly controlled litter
fall, breakdown and
nutrient cycling.

Figure 2.3 Diagrammatic representation of the 'runoff–runon' dynamics of water and nutrient/material flows that create self-organizing spatial patterns in the distribution of mulga woodland in Australian deserts. From Tongway and Ludwig (1994).

nutrients and materials from the system. To use their term, the system becomes 'dysfunctional'. Disturbances, physical processes, the geophysical template, and the activities of organisms all interact to produce the spatial patterns that we characterize as 'heterogeneity'.

Consequences of heterogeneity: mechanisms

Heterogeneity has ecological consequences because it affects where organisms are, and thereby what happens to them. As soon as an environment becomes heterogeneous, mating opportunities and patterns, predation risk, physiological stress, competitive interactions, foraging success, individual growth and reproduction, survival probability, and the like all differ systematically among locations (see Brown, this volume). The heterogeneous landscape mosaic may be viewed as a cost-benefit surface, with 'peaks' and 'valleys' corresponding to high-quality and poor-quality patches (Wiens 1997). Patch quality must ultimately be gauged in terms of variations in individual fitness (Van Horne 1983). At a more immediate level, however, it reflects the interplay of the distribution of resources, limiting factors, and the like (which may show varying degrees of concordance, independence, or negative covariance in space, e.g. Stuefer 1996) with the responses of organisms. Understanding how heterogeneity affects ecological systems therefore requires an understanding not only of the environmental patterns, but also of how organisms respond to the different forms of heterogeneity (the 'functional heterogeneity' of Kolasa and Rollo 1991). These responses are determined by three underlying mechanisms: movement, patch choice, and perceptual scale.

Movement is arguably the most basic of these mechanisms. Over a broad timeframe, dispersal determines how a population is structured, both demographically and genetically. At a more proximate level, movement determines the probability that an individual will encounter heterogeneity. Because of its importance in population dynamics, movement attracted the attention of theoreticians decades ago (e.g. Skellam 1951). Most models have been based on simple movement algorithms—random walks, correlated random walks or diffusion of one sort or another (Okubo 1980; Turchin 1998). These algorithms provide useful null models of movement (e.g. Crist *et al.* 1992; Johnson *et al.* 1992), but they fail to capture the elements of movement that are most likely to relate to habitat heterogeneity. Not only do organisms differ tremendously in their potential rates and patterns of movement, but movements by the same kind of organism may differ among the components of a landscape mosaic.

My colleagues and I have spent several years exploring these relations between environmental structure and individual movement in a suite of tenebrionid beetle species (*Eleodes* spp.) in simple grassland 'microlandscapes' (Wiens and Milne 1989; Crist *et al.* 1992; Wiens *et al.* 1997; McIntyre and Wiens 1999). Our observational studies have dealt primarily with compositional variance. The microlandscapes through which the beetles move are composed of mosaics of grass, cacti, small shrubs, and bare ground. We documented the movement pathways of beetles in 25 m² plots that differed in the relative degree of compositional heterogeneity, from grass-dominated to mixtures of the four landscape elements. These plots were located in larger areas (65–130 ha) that were subjected to different levels of grazing by domestic cattle, and therefore differed in compositional heterogeneity at much broader scales. The three species of beetles we considered moved at different rates, with differing tortuosity in their pathways, in plots that differed in internal heterogeneity (Fig. 2.4). However, there were also differences in movements

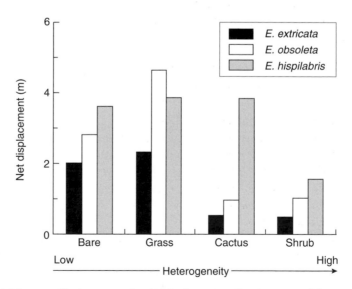

Figure 2.4 Mean net displacement after 100 5 s time steps of movements of three species of tenebrionid beetles (*Eleodes* spp.) in 25 m² plots of shortgrass steppe that differed in the dominant vegetation cover, and thus in within-plot heterogeneity. Differences between species and cover types are statistically significant ($P<0.01$, ANOVA). After Crist *et al.* (1992).

in plots of similar heterogeneity that were embedded in larger areas that differed in heterogeneity—there were broad-scale landscape influences on fine-scale movements.

We also conducted experimental studies in which we charted the movement pathways of beetles in $25\,m^2$ areas in which we created artificial landscapes of grass patches in a bare sand matrix (i.e. patterned variance). One of these experiments (Wiens *et al.* 1997) evaluated movements in mosaics containing differing amounts of grass cover (0–80%). Although the grass patches were arrayed randomly within the plot, patterned variance developed because the patches coalesced at greater coverages, as portrayed in percolation models (Gardner *et al.* 1987). Quantitative measures of movement pathways exhibited a strong threshold response to changes in grass cover and the development of patterned heterogeneity. Moreover, beetle movements within the grass patches differed in mosaics with different amounts of grass cover, suggesting that the beetles responded to the boundaries between grass and bare sand (Wiens *et al.* 1997).

This response illustrates the second behavioural mechanism contributing to organismal responses to heterogeneity: *patch choice*. Thus, while the probability that an individual will be found at a particular location within a patch is determined by the patch-specific movement characteristics, the probability that an organism will cross a patch edge and therefore occur in another element of a mosaic depends on its behavioural response to the boundary (Wiens *et al.* 1993). The reluctance or willingness of individuals to cross patch boundaries and enter markedly different areas, for example, contributes greatly to the potential effects of habitat fragmentation on population dynamics.

Different species respond to the same heterogeneous mosaic in different ways. Some of these differences are due to interspecific differences in movement characteristics or patch choice, but differences in the *perceptual scale* on which the organisms view the environment also contribute to the differential responses. The perceptual scale of an organism can be visualized in terms of the grain and extent of its responses to environmental heterogeneity (Kotliar and Wiens 1990). Grain determines the finest scale on which an organism can perceive (and thus respond to) heterogeneity of any form. Extent defines the broadest scale on which it can distinguish spatial variation of any sort. Differences in movement rates and pathways can affect perceptual scale; an organism moving rapidly across a heterogeneous mosaic covers a greater extent and resolves detail at a larger grain than does a slowly moving organism (Kolasa and Rollo 1991; Wiens 1992). With's (1994) studies of grasshopper movements through the same microlandscape mosaics in which we conducted our beetle studies demonstrate these effects. A large, rapidly moving species (*Xanthippus corallipes*) 'perceived' heterogeneity at a different scale than did a smaller, slowly moving species (*Psoloessa delicatula*) in the same environment.

Lest one think that the behavioural attributes just described apply only to animals, consider the responses of clonal plants to spatial heterogeneity in resource distribution and availability. The work of Hutchings and Wijesinghe (1997, this volume), Oborny and Cain (1997) and colleagues (see Hutchings and de Kroon 1994) has shown how different ramets of a clonal plant may specialize morphologically and physiologically on acquiring different resources from different patches in a heterogeneous habitat. Because resource acquisition from different ramets can be physiologically integrated, and resources redistributed through the plant, this 'division of labour' may enhance resource acquisition from a heterogeneous environment and lead to significantly greater plant growth than would occur were the same resources distributed homogeneously. Moreover, the capacity of the plants to respond to a patchy distribution of resources is scale-dependent; the experiments of Wijesinghe and Hutchings (1997) show that plant biomass was greater when resource patches were expressed at larger scales, and that the plants responded to environments with small-scale patchiness 'as if they were homogeneously poor'. Such systems are characterized by movement (the clonal extension of ramets), patch choice (the differential growth and resource acquisition, or 'foraging', in different kinds of patches), and perceptual scale (the differential response to patchiness at different scales).

Some insight into how such individual behavioural responses to heterogeneity may translate into population patterns comes from simulation-model studies (With and Crist 1995, 1996) that were founded on With's grasshopper work. With and Crist modelled the distribution of the two species of grasshoppers in a cell-based array of three habitat types representative of a 1-ha bird territory in the shortgrass steppe. The habitat types differed in within-habitat heterogeneity, ranging from areas with little shortgrass cover interspersed with mixtures of cactus, shrubs, midgrasses, forbs, and bare ground (very heterogeneous habitat; 27% of the cells) to areas with nearly continuous coverage of shortgrass (relatively homogeneous habitat; 8% of the cells); moderately heterogeneous habitat (65%) was intermediate between the two extremes. The probability that an individual would leave a cell of a given type was a function of its rate of movement within that habitat type. When an individual entered a cell of a different type, its transition probability then became a function of the movement pattern associated with the new habitat type. Reduced rates of movement in a particular habitat type translated into increased residence times in cells of that type. The two grasshopper species differed in movement rates within the different habitat types. *Psoloessa delicatula* had a reduced rate of movement in the homogeneous cells, which were relatively rare in the landscape. Consequently, it moved faster through >90% of the territory. On the other hand, *Xanthippus corallipes* exhibited reduced movement rates in both homogeneous and very heterogeneous cells, which together comprised 35% of the landscape. Starting with a random distribution of individuals across the territory (e.g. random emergence sites), the species developed markedly different spatial patterns (Fig. 2.5). *Xanthippus corallipes* became highly aggregated in the cells in which movement was reduced (Moran's I, $I_m = 4.1$), to the extent that most individuals were located in only 2% of the territory. *Psoloessa delicatula*, which moved rapidly through most of the landscape, continued to exhibit a random distribution ($I_m = 1.9$) and was found in 67% of the landscape. Thus, dif-

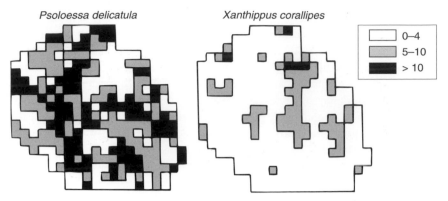

Figure 2.5 Model-generated distributions of two acridid grasshoppers (Orthoptera) within a representative 1-ha bird territory in the shortgrass steppe of north-central Colorado. Distributions were generated from an initial random distribution of individuals according to the habitat heterogeneity of each cell and movement algorithms specific to cell types that determined transition probabilities between cells or landscape elements. Each cell is 6.25×6.25 m (39.1 m^2). The key represents grasshopper density per cell. From With and Crist (1995).

ferences in grasshopper movements among the landscape elements, combined with differences between the species in patch-specific movements and the scales of landscape perception, produced patterns of spatial heterogeneity in grasshopper abundance that showed differing degrees of correspondence with the underlying pattern of the vegetation substrate. It is not difficult to imagine that, if one were to consider the birds that occupied such a territory, the distributions of the two grasshopper species would be further modified, in ways that depended on the prey preferences of the birds and the degree to which they responded to 'hot spots' of grasshopper abundance (e.g. the patches of high densities of *Xanthippus corallipes*).

Heterogeneity and scale

Heterogeneity, like everything else in ecology, is scale-dependent. A plant population that is aggregated at one scale is not aggregated at another (Greig-Smith 1979, 1983; Dale 1999), and the uniform spacing of ant colonies at the fine scale of inter-colony competition becomes random and then clumped as one expands the scale, and underlying habitat and geophysical variations assume greater importance (Fig. 2.6; Crist and Wiens 1996). Spatial variance changes systematically with scale as well. Thus, when all points are not identical but the samples are randomly distributed in space, the plot of ln variance (S^2) as a function of ln scale (n, sample size or area) is a straight line with a slope of -1. This is because S^2 is inversely proportional to n. If spatial variance is patterned, however (i.e. if spatial autocorrelation exists), the slope of the log–log plot will lie between -1 and 0 (O'Neill *et al.* 1991; Gardner

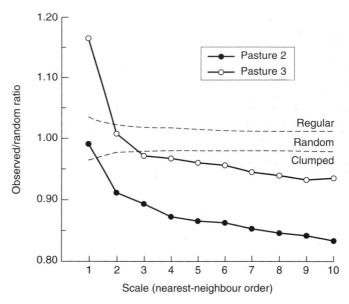

Figure 2.6 The ratio of the observed mean distance between harvester ant (*Pogonomyrmex occidentalis*) colonies in two pastures in shortgrass steppe and the distance expected from a random distribution of the same number of colonies in relation to a scale parameter (nearest neighbour order: the mean distance for the 1st, 2nd, 3rd, . . . 10th nearest neighbour colony). The dashed lines enclose the 95% confidence interval derived from 999 simulations. Values above the confidence interval indicate a regular dispersion, those below the confidence interval a clumped or aggregated dispersion. Colony density was less in pasture 2 (7.0 colonies ha^{-1}) than in pasture 3 (15.5 colonies ha^{-1}). Mean 1st nearest neighbour distances were 19.1 m in pasture 2, 11.4 m in pasture 3; mean 10th nearest neighbour distances were > 80 m in both pastures. Modified from Crist and Wiens (1996).

1998). If the scaling of heterogeneity is hierarchically structured, the ln S^2/ln n relation will exhibit scales at which the slope is < −1, interspersed with scales at which the slope approximates −1 (O'Neill *et al.* 1991).

It is not just the heterogeneity of the environment (however measured) that varies with scale. The responses of organisms to that scaled heterogeneity are also scale-dependent. Every organism 'filters' environmental heterogeneity through a grain-extent window. The dimensions and position of this window on a scale spectrum differ among species, age classes and sexes. These differences are what makes it so difficult to generalize about the effects of scale on organisms, populations, communities or ecosystems, and we do not yet have anything resembling a 'theory of scaling' to deal with them (Meentemeyer and Box 1987; Wiens 1989). One way to approach the development of scaling generalization may be through 'scaling functions' that relate scale-dependent variation in environmental patterns and heterogeneity to the scale-dependent responses of organisms based on the functional properties of those organisms (Ludwig *et al.* 2000; Wiens, in press). Following the trait-matrix approach developed by Keddy (1992) for plants and Poff (1997) for aquatic organisms, we might be able to define groups of taxa that share features of life history, behaviour, physiology, body size, trophic position and the like. Collectively, these features may dictate the size and form of the grain-extent windows through which the organisms respond to environmental scaling, and allow us to begin to lay out the dimensions on which organisms cluster in their scaling properties. This approach is as yet untried, although Holling's (1992; Holling *et al.* 1996) considerations of body-size distributions in communities provide a possible point of entry. The fact remains that scaling is an essential feature of heterogeneity, the consequences of which depend on the intersection of the scaling properties of environmental features with the scaling responses of the organisms that occupy those environments.

Conclusions

Three general principles emerge from the above deliberations about heterogeneity. The first is that different forms of heterogeneity have different properties, are measured in different ways, and may have different ecological consequences. It is therefore important that ecologists be clear, both to themselves and to others, about what they really mean when they talk of 'heterogeneity'. Because the forms of heterogeneity shown in Fig. 2.1 represent a series of increasing complexity, it is also important to determine how much of the overall texture and fabric of heterogeneity one must consider in order to draw meaningful ecological conclusions. Is it sufficient simply to assess spatial variance without reference to pattern, or pattern without respect to location? Because most environments ultimately are arrayed as spatial mosaics, does this mean that we should always deal with locational variance unless it is explicitly shown not to be important? How does the nature of the questions we ask, or the systems or scales we study, determine what forms of heterogeneity we should consider? We have no answers to these questions yet, because we have not generally considered heterogeneity in a way that leads to such questions. It is time that we did.

The second principle is that heterogeneity depends on organisms. Measuring the compositional or locational variance of an environment, as is increasingly done using remote sensing and geographic information systems (GIS), is of limited ecological value unless the measures are coupled to the responses of organisms to that variance—Kolasa and Rollo's 'functional heterogeneity'. The questions we ask in ecology (or the hypotheses we test) ultimately must relate either directly or indirectly to organisms as well as environment, and to consider one without the other is not ecology, but something else. In order to understand how organisms will respond to heterogeneity, and thus to predict the ecological consequences of heterogeneity, we must consider the behavioural mechanisms that mediate organismal responses—movement, patch choice, and perceptual scale. This requirement applies not just to animal ecologists. Plants move, via seed dispersal or clonal growth; they exhibit patch choice, through differential germination success in different patches; and they differ in the scales on which they 'perceive' or experience variations in microclimate, soil nutrient distributions, or herbivory impacts. The differences between plants and animals are perhaps not so great as we might think.

The third principle is that heterogeneity depends on scale. An environment that is heterogeneous at one scale may not be at some other scale, and what environmental heterogeneity at a given scale actually means, ecologically, depends on the scales of response of the organisms of interest. Any statements about heterogeneity, or any data documenting heterogeneity or its consequences, must be accompanied by a specification of the grain-extent range over which the statements or data apply. Without such a specification, the statements or data are of limited value in the context of a given study, much less in drawing comparisons.

These principles have clear implications. In the arena of basic ecology, they mean that simple generalizations about heterogeneity, such as 'Heterogeneity stabilizes population dynamics', or 'Heterogeneity enhances biodiversity', are meaningless oversimplifications. In the arena of applied ecology and management, they mean that attempts to attain management objectives, such as conservation of a target species or maintenance of biodiversity, by manipulating the heterogeneity of reserves or landscapes may not always produce the desired results. In both cases, it is necessary to consider the form of heterogeneity, how organisms respond to heterogeneity, and the scales of heterogeneity and organismal responses in order to derive meaningful generalizations or frame useful management policies.

My emphasis on the importance of considering both the environment and the organisms in evaluating heterogeneity and its consequences parallels Lawton's (1999) observation that ecological patterns and the laws, rules and mechanisms that underpin them are contingent on organisms and their environments. Lawton goes on to propose that all this contingency can be overwhelmingly complicated unless one focuses at a relatively simple level of ecological organization, such as populations of single species or small assemblages, or at the 'macroecological' level of large sets of species, broad spatial scales, or long time periods. At the intermediate level of communities, Lawton argues that there are so many contingencies that only idiosyncratic, situation-specific case histories and weak and fuzzy generalizations are possible. Presumably, he would draw much the same conclusion about landscape ecology, which I have argued (Wiens 1995), lacks satisfying general theory in part because of the complexity of landscape patterns and their causes and consequences (i.e. multiple contingencies). The same statements might well be made about the more complex forms of heterogeneity, whether considered in the context of single-species populations, multispecies communities, or macroecological patterns. And of course scale-dependency is nothing if not bewildering contingencies!

We should ask, however, whether we must heed Lawton's call to pay less attention to the messy, contingency-riddled world of community ecology (and, by extension, landscape ecology, spatially dependent forms of heterogeneity and scaling). Should we move on to more rewarding, less contingent areas of research, in which general patterns or 'laws' emerge more readily? Yes, general patterns *do* seem to emerge if one keeps the system simple or expands to a level at which much of the variance and detail is subsumed into broad, statistical relationships. But the complexity of those 'middle-number systems' that defy ecological generalization is also real and cannot be denied. In many ways, heterogeneity of one form or another lies at the heart of this complexity. The resurgent interest in heterogeneity and the contributions to this volume indicate that the challenge of discerning general patterns in complicated and contingent systems is indeed worthwhile. And if we fail to derive generalizations that we could call 'laws', well, then, deeper but more limited understanding of ecological patterns and processes isn't too bad.

Acknowledgments

I thank Mike Hutchings and Steward Pickett for providing the impetus to think about heterogeneity once again, Mike Hutchings and two anonymous reviewers for comments on the manuscript, Tom Crist and Kim With for inspiration, and the United States National Science Foundation and Environmental Protection Agency for supporting our seemingly arcane research on beetles, microlandscapes and scale.

References

Art, H.W. (1993) *The Dictionary of Ecology and Environmental Science.* Henry Holt, New York.

Barry, J.P. and Dayton, P.K. (1991) Physical heterogeneity and the organization of marine communities. In: *Ecological Heterogeneity* (eds J. Kolasa and S.T.A. Pickett), pp. 270–320. Springer-Verlag, New York.

Bazzaz, F.A. (1996) *Plants in Changing Environments.* Cambridge University Press, Cambridge.

Blair, D., ed. (1982) *The Pocket Macquarie Dictionary.* Jacaranda Press, Milton, Queensland, Australia.

Bormann, F.H. and Likens, G.E. (1979) Catastrophic disturbance and the steady-state in northern hardwood forests. *American Scientist* **67**, 660–669.

Cale, P.G. and Hobbs, R.J. (1994) Landscape heterogeneity indices: problems of scale and applicability, with particular reference to animal habitat description. *Pacific Conservation Biology* **1**, 183–193.

Caswell, H. and Cohen, J.E. (1991) Communities in patchy environments: a model of disturbance, competition, and heterogeneity. In: *Ecological Heterogeneity* (eds J. Kolasa and S.T.A. Pickett), pp. 97–122. Springer-Verlag, New York.

Cliff, A.D. and Ord, J.K. (1981) *Spatial Processes: Models and Applications.* Pion, London.

Cody, M.L. and Diamond, J.M., eds. (1975) *The Ecology and Evolution of Communities.* Harvard University Press, Cambridge.

Crist, T.O., Guertin, D.S., Wiens, J.A. and Milne, B.T. (1992) Animal movements in heterogeneous landscapes: an experiment with *Eleodes* beetles in shortgrass prairie. *Functional Ecology* **6**, 536–544.

Crist, T.O. and Wiens, J.A. (1996) The distribution of ant colonies in a semiarid landscape: implications for community and ecosystem processes. *Oikos* **76**, 301–311.

Dale, M.R.T. (1999) *Spatial Pattern Analysis in Plant Ecology.* Cambridge University Press, Cambridge.

Davis, F.W. (1993) Introduction to spatial statistics. In: *Patch Dynamics* (eds S.A. Levin, T.M. Powell and J.H. Steele), pp. 16–36. Springer-Verlag, Berlin.

Detling, J.K. (1998) Mammalian herbivores: ecosystem-level effects in two grassland national parks. *Wildlife Society Bulletin* **26**, 438–448.

Downing, J.A. (1991) Biological heterogeneity in aquatic ecosystems. In: *Ecological Heterogeneity* (eds J. Kolasa and S.T.A. Pickett), pp. 160–180. Springer-Verlag, New York.

Elton, C. (1966) *The Pattern of Animal Communities*. Methuen, London.

Fortin, M.-J. (1999) Spatial statistics in landscape ecology. In: *Landscape Ecological Analysis: Issues and Applications* (eds J.M. Klopatek and R.H. Gardner), pp. 253–279. Springer-Verlag, New York.

Foster, D.R., Knight, D.H. and Franklin, J.F. (1998) Landscape patterns and legacies resulting from large, infrequent forest disturbances. *Ecosystems* **1**, 497–510.

García-Moliner, G., Mason, D.M., Greene, C.H., *et al.* (1993) Description and analysis of spatial patterns. In: *Patch Dynamics* (eds S.A. Levin, T.M. Powell and J.H. Steele), pp. 70–89. Springer-Verlag, Berlin.

Gardner, R.H. (1998) Pattern, process, and the analysis of spatial scales. In: *Ecological Scale: Theory and Applications* (eds D.L. Peterson and V.T. Parker), pp. 17–34. Columbia University Press, New York.

Gardner, R.H., Milne, B.T., Turner, M.G. and O'Neill, R.V. (1987) Neutral models for the analysis of broad-scale landscape pattern. *Landscape Ecology* **1**, 19–28.

Gause, G.F. (1935) *The Struggle for Existence*. William and Wilkins, Baltimore.

Gleick, J. (1987) *Chaos: Making a New Science*. Viking, New York.

Greig-Smith, P. (1979) Patterns in vegetation. *Journal of Ecology* **67**, 755–779.

Greig-Smith, P. (1983) *Quantitative Plant Ecology*, 3rd edn. University of California Press, Berkeley.

Grime, J.P. (1979) *Plant Strategies and Vegetation Processes*. John Wiley, New York.

Gustafson, E.J. (1998) Quantifying landscape spatial pattern: What is the state of the art? *Ecosystems* **1**, 143–156.

Gustafson, E.J. and Parker, G.R. (1992) Relationship between landscape proportion and indices of landscape spatial pattern. *Landscape Ecology* **7**, 101–110.

Hanski, I. (1997) Metapopulation dynamics: from concepts and observations to predictive models. In: *Metapopulation Biology: Ecology, Genetics, and Evolution* (eds I.A. Hanski and M.E. Gilpin), pp. 69–91. Academic Press, San Diego.

Hargis, C.D., Bissonette, J.A. and David, J.L. (1997) Understanding measures of landscape pattern. In: *Wildlife and Landscape Ecology: Effects of Pattern and Scale* (ed. J.A. Bissonette), pp. 231–261. Springer-Verlag, New York.

Hastings, A. (1990) Spatial heterogeneity and ecological models. *Ecology* **71**, 426–428.

Hedrick, P.W., Ginevan, M.E. and Ewing, E.P. (1976) Genetic polymorphism in heterogeneous environments. *Annual Review of Ecology and Systematics* **7**, 1–32.

Hedrick, P.W. and Gilpin, M.E. (1997) Genetic effective size of a metapopulation. In: *Metapopulation Biology: Ecology, Genetics, and Evolution* (eds I.A. Hanski and M.E. Gilpin), pp. 166–181. Academic Press, San Diego.

Hof, J. and Bevers, M. (1998) *Spatial Optimization for Managed Ecosystems*. Columbia University Press, New York.

Holling, C.S. (1992) Cross-scale morphology, geometry and dynamics of ecosystems. *Ecological Monographs* **62**, 447–502.

Holling, C.S., Peterson, G., Marples, P., *et al.* (1996) Self-organization in ecosystems: lumpy geometries, periodicities and morphologies. In: *Global Change and Terrestrial Ecosystems* (eds B. Walker and W. Steffen), pp. 346–384. Cambridge University Press, Cambridge.

Holmes, E.E. (1997) Basic epidemiological concepts in a spatial context. In: *Spatial Ecology: the Role of Space in Population Dynamics and Interspecific Interactions* (eds D. Tilman and P. Kareiva), pp. 111–136. Princeton University Press, Princeton.

Horn, H.S. and MacArthur, R.H. (1972) Competition among fugitive species in a harlequin environment. *Ecology* **53**, 749–752.

Huffaker, C.B. (1958) Experimental studies on predation: dispersion factors and predator-prey oscillations. *Hilgardia* **27**, 343–383.

Hutchings, M.J. and de Kroon, H. (1994) Foraging in plants: the role of morphological plasticity in resource acquisition. *Advances in Ecological Research* **25**, 159–238.

Hutchings, M.J. and Wijesinghe, D.K. (1997) Patchy habitats, division of labour and growth dividends in clonal plants. *Trends in Ecology and Evolution* **12**, 390–394.

Johnson, A.R., Milne, B.T. and Wiens, J.A. (1992) Diffusion in fractal landscapes: simulations and experimental studies of tenebrionid beetle movements. *Ecology* **73**, 1968–1983.

Kauffman, S. (1993) *The Origins of Order.* Oxford University Press, New York.

Keddy, P.A. (1992) Assembly and response rules: two goals for predictive community ecology. *Journal of Vegetation Science* **3**, 157–164.

Knapp, A.K., Blair, J.M., Briggs, J.M., *et al.* (1999) The keystone role of bison in North American tallgrass prairie. *BioScience* **49**, 39–50.

Kolasa, J. and Pickett, S.T.A. (1991) *Ecological Heterogeneity.* Springer-Verlag, New York.

Kolasa, J. and Rollo, C.D. (1991) Introduction: The heterogeneity of heterogeneity: a glossary. In: *Ecological Heterogeneity* (eds J. Kolasa and S.T.A. Pickett), pp. 1–23. Springer-Verlag, New York.

Kotliar, N.B. and Wiens, J.A. (1990) Multiple scales of patchiness and patch structure: a hierarchical framework for the study of heterogeneity. *Oikos* **59**, 253–260.

Lawton, J.H. (1999) Are there general laws in ecology? *Oikos* **84**, 177–192.

Lawton, J.H. and Jones, C.G. (1995) Linking species and ecosystems: organisms as ecosystem engineers. In: *Linking Species and Ecosystems* (eds C.G. Jones and J.H. Lawton), pp. 141–150. Chapman and Hall, London.

Lechowicz, M.J. and Bell, G. (1991) The ecology and genetics of fitness in forest plants. II. Microspatial heterogeneity of the edaphic environment. *Journal of Ecology* **79**, 687–696.

Levin, S.A. (1974) Dispersion and population interactions. *American Naturalist* **108**, 207–228.

Levin, S.A. (1976) Population dynamic models in heterogeneous environments. *Annual Review of Ecology and Systematics* **7**, 287–311.

Levin, S.A. and Paine, R.T. (1974) Disturbance, patch formation, and community structure. *Proceedings of the National Academy of Sciences USA* **71**, 2744–2747.

Levin, S.A., Powell, T.M. and Steele, J.H., eds. (1993) *Patch Dynamics.* Springer-Verlag, Berlin.

Levins, R. (1968) *Evolution in Changing Environments.* Princeton University Press, Princeton.

Levins, R. (1970) Extinction. *Lecture Notes in Mathematics* **2**, 75–107.

Li, H. and Reynolds, J.F. (1993) A new contagion index to quantify spatial patterns of landscapes. *Landscape Ecology* **8**, 155–162.

Li, H. and Reynolds, J.F. (1995) On definition and quantification of heterogeneity. *Oikos* **73**, 280–284.

Lincoln, R., Boxshall, G. and Clark, P. (1998) *A Dictionary of Ecology, Evolution and Systematics*, 2nd edn. Cambridge University Press, Cambridge.

Lloyd, M. (1967) Mean crowding. *Journal of Animal Ecology* **36**, 1–30.

Ludwig, J., Tongway, D., Freudenberger, D., Noble, J. and Hodgkinson, K., eds. (1997) *Landscape Ecology: Function and Management.* CSIRO Publishing, Collingwood, VIC, Australia.

Ludwig, J.A., Wiens, J.A. and Tongway, D.J. (2000) A scaling rule for landscape patches and how it applies to conserving soil resources in tropical savannas. *Ecosystems* **3**, 84–97.

MacArthur, R.H. (1972) *Geographical Ecology.* Harper and Row, New York.

MacArthur, R.H. and Levins, R. (1964) Competition, habitat selection, and character displacement in a patchy environment. *Proceedings of the National Academy of Sciences USA* **51**, 1207–1210.

MacArthur, R.H. and Levins, R. (1967) The limiting similarity, convergence, and divergence of coexisting species. *American Naturalist* **101**, 377–385.

MacArthur, R.H. and Pianka, E.R. (1966) On optimal use of a patchy environment. *American Naturalist* **100**, 603–609.

MacArthur, R.H. and Wilson, E.O. (1967) *The Theory of Island Biogeography.* Princeton University Press, Princeton.

Mayr, E. (1976). *Evolution and the Diversity of Life.* Harvard University Press, Cambridge.

McCoy, E.D. and Bell, S.S. (1991) Habitat structure: the evolution and diversification of a complex topic. In: *Habitat Structure: the Physical Arrangement of Objects in Space* (eds S.S. Bell, E.D. McCoy and H.R. Mushinsky), pp. 3–27. Chapman and Hall, London.

McGarigal, K. and Marks, B.J. (1995) FRAGSTATS: Spatial pattern analysis program for quantifying landscape structure. *General Technical Report PNW-GTR-351.* U.S. Department of Agriculture,

Forest Service, Pacific Northwest Research Station, Portland, Oregon.

McIntosh, R.P. (1985) *The Background of Ecology.* Cambridge University Press, Cambridge.

McIntosh, R.P. (1991) Concept and terminology of homogeneity and heterogeneity in ecology. In: *Ecological Heterogeneity* (eds J. Kolasa and S.T.A. Pickett), pp. 24–46. Springer-Verlag, New York.

McIntyre, N.E. and Wiens, J.A. (1999) Interactions between landscape structure and animal behavior: the roles of heterogeneously distributed resources and food deprivation on movement patterns. *Landscape Ecology* 14, 437–447.

Meentemeyer, V. and Box, E.O. (1987) Scale effects in landscape studies. In: *Landscape Heterogeneity and Disturbance* (ed. M.G. Turner), pp. 15–34. Springer-Verlag, New York.

Mertz, D.B. and McCauley, D.E. (1980) The domain of laboratory ecology. *Synthese* 43, 95–110.

Milne, B.T. (1991) Heterogeneity as a multiscale characteristic of landscapes. *Ecological Heterogeneity* (eds J. Kolasa and S.T.A. Pickett), pp. 69–84. Springer-Verlag, New York.

Milne, B.T. (1997) Applications of fractal geometry in wildlife biology. In: *Wildlife and Landscape Ecology: Effects of Pattern and Scale* (ed. J.A. Bissonette), pp. 32–69. Springer-Verlag, New York.

Morisita, M. (1962) I_d-index, a measure of dispersion of individuals. *Researches in Population Ecology* 4, 1–7.

Naeem, S. and Colwell, R.K. (1991) Ecological consequences of heterogeneity of consumable resources. In: *Ecological Heterogeneity* (eds J. Kolasa and S.T.A. Pickett), pp. 224–255. Springer-Verlag, New York.

Nicholls, A.O. (1994) Variation in mosaic diversity in the forests of coastal northern New South Wales. *Pacific Conservation Biology* 1, 177–182.

Oborny, B. and Cain, M.L. (1997) Models of spatial spread and foraging in clonal plants. In: *The Ecology and Evolution of Clonal Plants* (eds H. de Kroon and J. van Groenendael), pp. 155–183. Backhuys Publishers, Leiden.

Okubo, A. (1980) *Diffusion and Ecological Problems.* Lecture Notes in Biomathematics 10. Springer-Verlag, Berlin.

O'Neill, R.V., Krummel, J.R., Gardner, R.H., *et al.* (1988) Indices of landscape pattern. *Landscape Ecology* 1, 153–162.

O'Neill, R.V., Gardner, R.H., Milne, B.T., Turner, M.G. and Jackson, B. (1991) Heterogeneity and spatial hierarchies. In: *Ecological Heterogeneity* (eds J. Kolasa and S.T.A. Pickett), pp. 85–96. Springer-Verlag, New York.

Pearson, S.M. and Gardner, R.H. (1997) Neutral models: useful tools for understanding landscape patterns. In: *Wildlife and Landscape Ecology: Effects of Pattern and Scale* (ed. J.A. Bissonette), pp. 215–230. Springer-Verlag, New York.

Pickett, S.T.A., Kolasa, J. and Jones, C. (1994) *Ecological Understanding.* Academic Press, San Diego.

Pickett, S.T.A. and Rogers, K.H. (1997) Patch dynamics: the transformation of landscape structure and function. In: *Wildlife and Landscape Ecology: Effects of Pattern and Scale* (ed. J.A. Bissonette), pp. 101–127. Springer-Verlag, New York.

Pickett, S.T.A. and White, P.S., eds. (1985) *The Ecology of Natural Disturbance and Patch Dynamics.* Academic Press, San Diego.

Pielou, E.C. (1975) *Ecological Diversity.* Wiley-Interscience, New York.

Pimm, S.L. (1991) *The Balance of Nature: Ecological Issues in the Conservation of Species and Communities.* University of Chicago Press, Chicago.

Plotnick, R.E., Gardner, R.H., Hargrove, W.W., Prestegaard, K. and Perlmutter, M. (1996) Lacunarity analysis: a general technique for the analysis of spatial pattern. *Physical Review E* 53, 5461–5468.

Poff, N.L. (1997) Landscape filters and species traits: towards mechanistic understanding and prediction in stream ecology. *Journal of the North American Benthological Society* 16, 391–409.

Qi, Y. and Wu, J. (1996) Effects of changing spatial resolution on the results of landscape pattern analysis using spatial autocorrelation indices. *Landscape Ecology* 11, 39–49.

Rhodes, O.E. Jr, Chesser, R.K. and Smith, M.H. (1996) *Population Dynamics in Ecological Space and Time.* University of Chicago Press, Chicago.

Robertson, G.P. and Gross, K.L. (1994) Assessing the heterogeneity of below-ground resources: quantifying pattern and scale. In: *Exploitation of*

Environmental Heterogeneity by Plants: Ecophysi-ological Processes Above- and Below-Ground (eds M.M. Caldwell and R.W. Pearcy), pp. 237–253. Academic Press, San Diego.

Romme, W.H. (1982) Fire and landscape diversity in sub-alpine forests of Yellowstone National Park. *Ecological Monographs* **52**, 199–221.

Rossi, R.E., Mulla, D.J., Journel, A.G. and Franz, E.H. (1992) Geostatistical tools for modeling and interpreting ecological spatial dependence. *Ecological Monographs* **62**, 277–314.

Sato, K. and Iwasa, Y. (1993) Modeling of wave regeneration in subalpine *Abies* forests: population dynamics with spatial structure. *Ecology* **74**, 1538–1550.

Schmidt, K.A. and Brown, J.S. (1996) Patch assessment in fox squirrels: the role of resource density, patch size, and patch boundaries. *American Naturalist* **147**, 360–380.

Shorrocks, B. and Swingland, I.R. (1990) *Living in a Patchy Environment*. Oxford University Press, Oxford.

Simberloff, D. (1980) A succession of paradigms in ecology: essentialism to materialism and probabilism. *Synthese* **43**, 3–39.

Skellam, J.G. (1951) Random dispersal in theoretical populations. *Biometrika* **38**, 196–218.

Sprugel, D.G. (1976) Dynamic structure of wave-generated *Abies balsamea* forests in the North Eastern United States. *Journal of Ecology* **64**, 889–911.

Stuefer, J.F. (1996) Potential and limitations of current concepts regarding the response of clonal plants to environmental heterogeneity. *Vegetatio* **127**, 55–70.

Taylor, L.R. (1984) Assessing and interpreting the spatial distributions of insect populations. *Annual Review of Entomology* **29**, 321–357.

Taylor, L.R., Woiwod, I.P. and Perry, J.N. (1980) Variance and the large scale spatial stability of aphids, moths and birds. *Journal of Animal Ecology* **49**, 831–854.

Taylor, P.D., Fahrig, L., Henein, K. and Merriam, G. (1993) Connectivity is a vital element of landscape structure. *Oikos* **68**, 571–573.

Tilman, D. and Kareiva, P., eds. (1997) *Spatial Ecology: the Role of Space in Population Dynamics and Interspecific Interactions*. Princeton University Press, Princeton.

Tongway, D.J. and Ludwig, J.A. (1994) Small-scale resource heterogeneity in semi-arid landscapes. *Pacific Conservation Biology* **1**, 201–208.

Turchin, P. (1998) *Quantitative Analysis of Movement. Measuring and Modeling Population Redistribution in Animals and Plants.* Sinauer Associates, Sunderland, Massachusetts.

Turner, M.G., ed. (1987) *Landscape Heterogeneity and Disturbance*. Springer-Verlag, New York.

Turner, M.G. (1989) Landscape ecology: the effect of pattern on process. *Annual Review of Ecology and Systematics* **20**, 171–197.

Turner, M.G., Dale, V.H. and Everham, E.H. III (1997) Fires, hurricanes, and volcanoes: comparing large disturbances. *BioScience* **47**, 758–768.

Van Horne, B. (1983) Density as a misleading indicator of habitat quality. *Journal of Wildlife Management* **47**, 893–901.

Van Valen, L. and Pitelka, F.A. (1974) Commentary—intellectual censorship in ecology. *Ecology* **55**, 925–926.

Wall, D.H. and Moore, J.C. (1999) Interactions underground. *BioScience* **49**, 109–117.

Watt, A.S. (1947) Pattern and process in the plant community. *Journal of Ecology* **35**, 1–22.

White, P.S. and Harrod, J. (1997) Disturbance and diversity in a landscape context. In: *Wildlife and Landscape Ecology: Effects of Pattern and Scale* (ed. J.A. Bissonette), pp. 128–159. Springer-Verlag, New York.

Wiens, J.A. (1974) Habitat heterogeneity and avian community structure in North American grasslands. *American Midland Naturalist* **91**, 195–213.

Wiens, J.A. (1977) On competition and variable environments. *American Scientist* **65**, 590–597.

Wiens, J.A. (1983) Avian community ecology: an iconoclastic view. In: *Perspectives in Ornithology* (eds A.H. Brush and G.A. Clark, Jr), pp. 355–403. Cambridge University Press, Cambridge.

Wiens, J.A. (1984) On understanding a non-equilibrium world: myth and reality in community patterns and processes. In: *Ecological Communities: Conceptual Issues and the Evidence* (eds D.R. Strong, Jr., D. Simberloff, L.G. Abele and A.B. Thistle), pp. 439–457. Princeton University Press, Princeton.

Wiens, J.A. (1989) Spatial scaling in ecology. *Functional Ecology* **3**, 385–397.

Wiens, J.A. (1992) Ecological flows across landscape boundaries: a conceptual overview. In: *Landscape Boundaries: Consequences for Biotic Diversity and Ecological Flows* (eds A.J. Hansen and F. di Castri), pp. 217–235. Springer-Verlag, New York.

Wiens, J.A. (1995) Landscape mosaics and ecological theory. In: *Mosaic Landscapes and Ecological Processes* (eds L. Hansson, L. Fahrig and G. Merriam), pp. 1–26. Chapman and Hall, London.

Wiens, J.A. (1997) The emerging role of patchiness in conservation biology. In: *Enhancing the Ecological Basis of Conservation: Heterogeneity, Ecosystem Function, and Biodiversity* (eds S.T.A. Pickett, R.S. Ostfeld, M. Shachak and G.E. Likens), pp. 93–107. Chapman and Hall, New York.

Wiens, J.A. (in press) Understanding the problem of scale in experimental ecology. In: *Scaling Relations in Experimental Ecology* (eds R.H. Gardner, M. Kemp, V. Kennedy and J. Petersen). Columbia University Press, New York.

Wiens, J.A. and Milne, B.T. (1989) Scaling of 'landscapes' in landscape ecology, or, landscape ecology from a beetle's perspective. *Landscape Ecology* **3**, 87–96.

Wiens, J.A., Schooley, R.L. and Weeks, R.D. Jr (1997) Patchy landscapes and animal movements: do beetles percolate? *Oikos* **78**, 257–264.

Wiens, J.A., Stenseth, N.C., Van Horne, B. and Ims, R.A. (1993) Ecological mechanisms and landscape ecology. *Oikos* **66**, 369–380.

Wijesinghe, D.K. and Hutchings, M.J. (1997) The effects of spatial scale of environmental heterogeneity on the growth of a clonal plant: an experimental study with *Glechoma hederacea*. *Journal of Ecology* **85**, 17–28.

With, K.A. (1994) Using fractal analysis to assess how species perceive landscape structure. *Landscape Ecology* **9**, 25–36.

With, K.A. and Crist, T.O. (1995) Critical thresholds in species responses to landscape structure. *Ecology* **76**, 2446–2459.

With, K.A. and Crist, T.O. (1996) Translating across scales: simulating species distributions as the aggregate response of individuals to heterogeneity. *Ecological Modelling* **93**, 125–137.

Wu, J. and Loucks, O.L. (1995) From balance of nature to hierarchical patch dynamics: a paradigm shift in ecology. *Quarterly Review of Biology* **70**, 439–466.

Chapter 3

Generation of heterogeneity by organisms: creation, maintenance and transformation

S.T.A. Pickett, M.L. Cadenasso and C.G. Jones

Scope and problem

The purpose of this chapter is to contribute to a general framework for understanding spatial heterogeneity generated by organisms. In particular, we hope to show how organismally generated heterogeneity differs from physical heterogeneity and how organisms create and control heterogeneity. We start with an intuitive definition of heterogeneity, as the spatial pattern of resources and environmental constraints, including other organisms, materials, energy and information (Kolasa and Rollo 1991; Pickett and Rogers 1997). Such an intuitive definition is not adequate, however, to advance the study of heterogeneity. First, following Wiens (this volume), we emphasize the locational, or spatially explicit and functional approach to heterogeneity (Kolasa and Rollo 1991). Second, our emphasis on spatial heterogeneity of resources and regulators implies a focal organism, assemblage, or process. Identifying the focus is an important step in ensuring that the study of heterogeneity moves beyond concern with just pattern of material, energy or information to consideration of the role of heterogeneity in the interactions, fluxes, and transformation in ecological systems.

Earlier syntheses of heterogeneity (Kolasa and Rollo 1991) identified needs and conditions that must be accommodated by a framework for community and landscape heterogeneity. These include the following:

1 Heterogeneity can be deterministic, random or chaotic in origin, reflecting the fact that there are many kinds of processes and agents that can generate heterogeneity and that different agents have different behaviours. Agents of heterogeneity include physical ones, such as fire and flood, and biotic ones, to be detailed later. Not all events generating heterogeneity will be readily predictable a priori, although it is possible to explain heterogeneity once it is created, and to assess its ecological effects. Our focus on organism-generated heterogeneity recognizes that it may interact with other sources of heterogeneity, such as physical disturbance or geomorphology.

2 Heterogeneity may exist on some temporal and spatial scales, but not on others. Furthermore, agents that create heterogeneity act on specific scales. However, the

Institute of Ecosystem Studies, Box AB, Millbrook NY 12545-0129, USA

effects of heterogeneity can be seen on the scale of action, or they may appear at different scales, depending on how fluxes and drivers propagate through space and time.

3 Heterogeneity may be continuous or discontinuous, and be expressed in various spatial dimensions. Gradients, patchworks, and graded patchworks are all possible types of spatial heterogeneity. Heterogeneity may be homogeneous, in which case the pattern repeats at some interval; or heterogeneous, in which case the pattern does not repeat (Hutchinson 1978).

Understanding heterogeneity requires knowledge of the organizational and scaling properties of the system of interest. Like the study of disturbance (Pickett *et al.* 1989), with which it is closely linked but not congruent, the study of heterogeneity requires careful specification of the system of interest. It is necessary to specify the parts of the system, how they are functionally connected, their hierarchical structure, their boundaries, their scales of resolution and the processes that exist within them (Jax *et al.* 1998).

The first part of this chapter develops the framework, showing key processes and controls in the role of organisms in generating heterogeneity. The processes are then placed in explicit spatial context and connected using three established or emerging areas of ecology—ecological engineering, boundary function and patch dynamics. We conclude by using patch dynamics to show links between the processes.

Components of a framework

The study of organismally generated heterogeneity in communities and landscapes can be advanced by constructing conceptual models analogous to those that have been used to improve the study of disturbance. Such models can apply to a wide range of spatial scales. The framework links the abstract, scale-independent definition of heterogeneity to specific systems and stimulates analysis of the functional significance of heterogeneity. The framework is an initial model that can be used to understand how heterogeneity is created, maintained, or transformed by organisms in ecological assemblages and landscapes. The general modelling approach we use is of ecological systems as linked *flow chains*, or chains of interaction (Shachak and Jones 1995). The model consists of an agent and a substrate (Fig. 3.1) which are both affected by a suite of controllers. The components of the model are explained in turn below.

Agents of heterogeneity

Agents of heterogeneity include physical and chemical transformations or organismal activities. Although we may use synonymous terms for activity, such as process or event, we emphasize that the creation, maintenance, or transformation of heterogeneity by any agent requires that work be done. An example of an agent of heterogeneity illustrates the key features of the concept. The digging activity of gophers creates discrete areas that differ from adjacent areas. The digging creates a

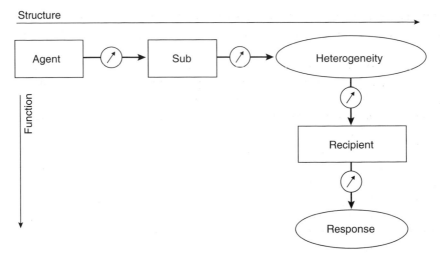

Figure 3.1 A general mechanistic model of the generation of heterogeneity. The agent, acting at specified scales, interacts with a substrate, which responds at specified scales, to generate a pattern of heterogeneity. A recipient process or organism reacts to or perceives the pattern of heterogeneity at a specified scale, to yield an ecological response, observed at a specified scale. The scaling relationships are shown by dials astride each arrow indicating an interaction. The component parts that act in the system are shown in rectangles, and the results are shown in ovals. The horizontal dimension emphasizes heterogeneity as structure, while the vertical axis emphasizes function of heterogeneity.

burrow and an adjacent mound of loose soil (Hobbs and Mooney 1985). The mounds are spatially clustered, and the volume of displaced soil in each mound is a measure of the intensity of the activity of the agent.

The substrate for heterogeneity

The second component of the model is the substrate. A substrate occupies a spatial arena specified by the researcher. Substrates have three-dimensional structure, even if they are represented on two-dimensional maps (Pickett and White 1985). Two questions must be answered about any substrate. First, how susceptible is a substrate to being altered? For example, again using gopher-generated heterogeneity, there can be contrasting soil properties in an area which differ in their ability to be dug, or in their capacity to form persistent mounds. Second, spatial distribution of the substrate will also affect how heterogeneity can be created or maintained. The substrate in some areas will resist transformation of heterogeneity, while that in other areas will be readily transformed.

Controllers in the model of heterogeneity

Controllers are the spatial dispersion of the agent and the intensity of its action, features that affect the sensitivity and dispersion of the substrate. However, additional information on controllers is needed to assess the functional effect of heterogeneity. Each of these broad categories of controllers in turn can be affected by more specific controls. Any model constructed to apply the general concept of heterogeneity in a particular system must identify the key controls on the interaction between agent and substrate. Building on the example of gopher-generated heterogeneity, the density and social structure of gopher populations control their potency as an agent of heterogeneity in specific sites (Malony 1993). On the substrate side of the interaction, soil moisture and soil texture act as controls.

Scaling in the model of heterogeneity

The model of agent, substrate and controls must be specified at a scale or a range of scales. One component of scale is the extent, or total area encompassed by the model (O'Neill *et al.* 1986). Extent is specified by the boundaries selected to describe the *arena* of interest. The second component of scale is the grain, or resolution of the extent into subsets for observation. There may of course already be heterogeneity within the extent of a substrate, such as the contrasting soil types referred to in the gopher example. It is important to match the scale of observation with the scale of heterogeneity present within an arena so that the effects of organisms can be detected and compared with those of the physical substrate.

All components of the system are potentially sensitive to scale. Agents of heterogeneity typically act over some range of scales. At scales coarser than their range, their effects may disappear or be averaged out (O'Neill *et al.* 1986). For example, gopher digging may be invisible over a region observed at a grain size of km^2. At scales finer than their range, gophers are part of the background. For example, gopher mounds embedded within an extensive burned area of prairie would not be explained by contrasts between disturbed vs. intact vegetation. Likewise, the substrate will have a scale at which it reacts to events and processes with localized effects, which are therefore capable of generating heterogeneity. This last feature indicates that substrates can be organisms, or contain organisms, and that the behaviour and range of perception of organisms can influence the existence of heterogeneity. For example, young trees free of disease may not respond to a relatively strong wind, whereas older trees that have suffered repeated wind damage, fungal attack and herbivore depredations may be damaged, broken, or uprooted by the same wind (Turner *et al.* 1998). The actual heterogeneity that appears in an arena, and the subset of that heterogeneity having an ecological function in the context of interest, both reflect scaling relationships. A single area may possess multiple heterogeneities because the patterns that appear within it may be generated by different agents, and exist on different, though perhaps linked scales (Parker and Pickett 1997).

A model of heterogeneity as a process

To identify the underlying mechanisms of organismally generated heterogeneity, we adopt the 'flow chain' approach for describing and working with state changes (Shachak and Jones 1995). This is a systems modelling approach that is appropriate

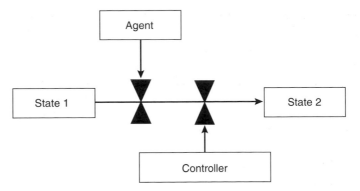

Figure 3.2 The basic flow chain for any change in physical state in an ecological system. The conversion of State 1 to an alternative, State 2, is caused by an agent acting under the influence of one or more controllers on its own activity or on the susceptibility of State 1 to alteration.

to any kind of ecological entity (not just to 'ecosystems'). The building blocks of comprehensive systems models are the specific linkages or flows that generate localized changes in state (Fig. 3.2). The components we have described combine into a general model of heterogeneity as a process (Fig. 3.1).

While heterogeneity is often initially recognized as a structure, the model is completed by assessing the response of other ecological structures or processes to the observed structural heterogeneity. Structural heterogeneity refers to the pattern of spatial variation as measured at a stated scale, while functional heterogeneity refers to the pattern to which ecological entities respond (Kolasa and Rollo 1991). More work is needed that links structural heterogeneity and functional heterogeneity into a systems model (Wiens, this volume). Aspects of such a 'systemic' approach to heterogeneity have been emphasized before (Kolasa and Rollo 1991), but the integrated understanding of heterogeneity as a process helps to assess the unique role of organisms in generating heterogeneity. Furthermore, the systemic approach accommodates the wide variety of ways in which organisms contribute to heterogeneity. Together the structural and functional aspects of heterogeneity combine into a unified ecological view of the subject.

Organisms are important agents of heterogeneity because they can react to and amplify the other components of the general model of heterogeneity. Because of their evolutionary, plastic, physiological, and often cognitive flexibility, and because of their memory and hysteresis, organisms are especially powerful nodes in any model that contains reciprocal relationships and the potential for feedback. The general model of heterogeneity falls into this category (Fig. 3.1). Although physical agents of heterogeneity are powerful and important, the reactiveness, learning and evolutionary capabilities of organisms make their role in heterogeneity particularly potent.

One of the principal reasons for focusing on organisms as agents of heterogeneity is the fact that they are subject to different energetic, material, and informational rules and constraints from abiotic factors. Most physical agents that can create heterogeneity are dissipative forces, in which stored energy is dissipated by the activity. The work done by organisms is fuelled by energy acquired by feeding and expended by focused activity, thereby increasing the efficiency of the work done. In addition, the material component of organisms that affects their role in generating heterogeneity has a different informational basis from most physical agents of heterogeneity. The mass of air moving in a windstorm or of water in a flood contains potential energy that may be dissipated. In the case of organisms as agents of heterogeneity, there are genetic controls, allometric relationships, behavioural repertoires, learning and decision-making that may yield a very different kind of heterogeneity from that produced by physical agents. Scale, intensity, localization, repetition and amplification are possible results of the features of organisms as agents of heterogeneity.

The difference between organisms and abiotic agents as generators of heterogeneity can be seen from a comparison of elephants and windstorms. Intense wind as a generator of heterogeneity is a relatively profligate agent of disturbance. Hurricanes, for example, strip forest canopies or blow down trees over broad areas if the topography is orientated so that the sites are not sheltered from the brunt of the wind (Boose *et al.* 1994). (Of course, there are heterogeneities within forests that interact with the agent.) The controls on hurricanes are often related to coarse-scale features of the habitat. Elephants, however, are influenced in their uprooting or breaking of savanna trees by peculiarly organismal behaviours. Social display, or response to browse of different qualities or availabilities, can affect the spatial arrangement of trees damaged. In addition, because elephants move about landscapes in response to resource availability, communication, population densities, and population structures, their spatial selectivity as an agent of heterogeneity is great. Such characteristics are shared by many organisms. Though both wind and elephants knock down trees, the spatial arrangement and intensity of their activities will differ greatly.

Modes of organismal contributions to heterogeneity

To identify the kinds of ecological effects that organisms have on spatial heterogeneity, we emphasize the time dimension. The conversion of one physical state to another is the basic dynamic of organisms in affecting spatial heterogeneity (Fig. 3.2). Logically, organisms can do three things to heterogeneity in an arena over time. They can:

1 create new states;
2 maintain existing states; or
3 transform existing states.

Transformation is a compound class, permitting contrasting outcomes. Transformations can yield new kinds of heterogeneity, or obliterate existing heterogeneity, resulting in more uniform environments. All three major modes by which organisms affect heterogeneity are net effects. Recognizing this makes apparent the need to identify the underlying mechanisms in flow models of heterogeneity.

In the case of the gopher mounds, the two states are intact soil and disturbed soil. The agent of state change is a digging gopher. This basic unit of interaction may seem unduly simple, but it is such simplicity that allows larger, more comprehensive systems models to be constructed, and the complex origins of heterogeneity to be separated into their component mechanisms.

A more comprehensive model, adding an important controller to the gopher example, recognizes that the change in state from intact to mounded soil at a particular spot can depend on the social organization of the animals. Social organization is a controller because gophers aggregate and thus concentrate their digging in certain areas while neglecting others (Malony 1993). Responders in the case of digging mammals may include plant species that are rare or absent from intact soil (Boeken *et al.* 1995). For example, annual plant diversity and productivity are enhanced by the digging by porcupines in the Negev Desert (Fig. 3.3).

Wind as an agent of state change also requires more comprehensive flow models,

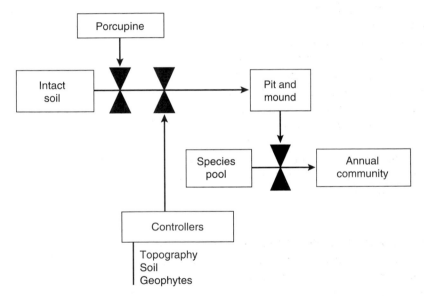

Figure 3.3 A complex flow chain model of the creation of spatial heterogeneity by desert porcupines (*Hystrix indica*). In order to indicate the ecological role of porcupines digging for the bulbs of geophytes, a minimum of two linked flow chains is required. The porcupine digging converts intact soil in specific spots to a pit and mound complex. Key controllers on the digging by porcupines are indicated. The second flow chain is of a plant species pool supplying potential colonizing annual plants vs. seed rain or seed bank, and the local enhancement of the annual community that results. For fuller understanding of the system, additional flow chains, for example, the concentration of runoff water in pits, should also be included. Based on the work of Boeken *et al.* (1995) and Boeken and Shachak (1998).

but contrasts with the agency of organisms. The basic states of interest are intact or erect trees *vs.* broken and fallen trees. Generation of a forest blowdown by an intense tornado combines the wind speed and path with the sensitivity of a stand of trees. The sensitivity of the stand is a property of the size and age of the canopy trees, whether they possess stress points as a consequence of prior disturbances, and the firmness of root anchorage. The specific damage to the stand that results from the tornado combines at least two controls (wind intensity and stand sensitivity) on the state change. Sensitivity depends on the species strategies in the system. Life history strategies determine architecture, allocation patterns, stress response, acclimatization potential and behavioural repertoire. Such organismal complexity can be reflected in flow models through feedbacks and time lags. Responders to heterogeneity created are surviving tree seedlings and saplings, annual invaders, herbivores and ecosystem processes, among others (Peterson and Pickett 1991). The functional significance of organisms to heterogeneity is due to the scale of observation, and the scales of detection and response of the organisms or other phenomena in the system.

The modelling approach we have presented has taken the intuitive definition of heterogeneity and shown it to represent a comprehensive, mechanistic, ecological system. Flow models have been introduced to show that the local transformations in physical state are the components of heterogeneity. However, such models are not spatially explicit. Knowledge of the explicit location in space of various landscape elements is a key to advancing the understanding of spatial heterogeneity (Pickett and Cadenasso 1995; Wiens, this volume). The spatial elements of an area that can be altered to produce heterogeneity must be specified and related to one another in a three-dimensional array. Without specifying the configuration of the elements, heterogeneity cannot be functionally understood. Patch dynamics is a spatially explicit approach to the ecological world (Pickett and Rogers 1997). Adding the spatial dimensions and configuration to flow models also permits the spatial controllers of changes in state to be exposed. This mechanistic enrichment of the understanding of heterogeneity is developed in the next section.

Organismal roles in heterogeneity: engineering, boundaries and patch dynamics

To this point, this chapter has laid out a framework for understanding and synthesizing the impacts of organisms on spatial heterogeneity in ecological systems. The framework consists of flow chains that identify agencies and controls on organismally generated heterogeneity. We now introduce three kinds of ecological processes that bring together a wide range of ways in which organisms affect ecological heterogeneity, namely ecological engineering, boundary function and patch dynamics. These processes provide the empirical content for the general model framework. Although ecological engineering has spatial implications, they have not been well worked out in the literature (but see Shachak and Jones 1995). We therefore include two additional processes that expose and help develop the spatial context and controllers of ecological engineering.

Ecological engineering

Ecological engineering is the direct or indirect modulation, by one kind of organism, of the availability of resources to other organisms (Jones *et al.* 1994; Lawton and Jones 1995). There are three types of ecological engineering, namely physical, chemical and transportational. The modulation therefore modifies physical, chemical or locational states of biotic or abiotic materials. Physical ecological engineering, on which we focus here, creates new habitats or physical structures composed of the engineering organisms or their parts, dead bodies, or detritus. It is these structures that directly or indirectly control the flow of resources to other organisms. Ecological engineering is the basic mechanism by which organisms affect heterogeneity.

The analysis of physical engineering by organisms is a functional, systems-orientated approach for understanding how organisms create physical structures and how these structures control the flow of resources to other organisms. For example, beaver build dams that alter hydrology, and hydrological changes affect many organisms in streams and beaver ponds (see Jones *et al.* 1994 for many other examples). The creation, maintenance or transformation of physical structure has ecological consequences because the structure directly controls or indirectly modulates the flow of resources used by other species. The resources can be energy, materials, space, information or other organisms. The effects of structure on resource availability can arise directly or indirectly. For example, beaver dams directly control the flow of water. In contrast, tree roots that bind around rocks and ameliorate the impact of hurricanes exert indirect control by modulating the impact of abiotically induced disturbance on other species (Basnet 1993).

Engineers cause physical state changes in two basic ways. Autogenic physical engineers directly transform the environment via their own structures. Endogenous processes of growth alter structure, and the structure of the organism is part of the engineered environment (e.g. a tree as living space). Allogenic physical engineers change the environment by transforming living or non-living materials from one physical state to another. The allogenic engineer does not have to be a part of the physical structure (e.g. a beaver can abandon a dam).

Systems with engineers as agents of heterogeneity exert *agent control* over other organisms in the system. Because the engineer builds the structure and the structure controls or modulates the resource, direct material or energetic participation by the engineer is not necessary for engineering effects. For example, beaver do not have to exchange energy or materials with other organisms in the system in order to affect these organisms. This is in marked contrast to biotic or abiotic resource exploitation, where energetic and material exchange is essential. However, agent control does not preclude regulation of the engineer or affected organisms by forces outside the engineering system, nor does it exclude feedbacks to the engineer from within the system. The definition of engineering is independent of the particular players and the scale of the system. For example, the same definition and general model applies to many scales, such as beaver dams, ponds in the crotches of trees, and water-filled hoof prints of cows. Nevertheless, the system model can be readily translated into the real world with real scaling properties.

System flows and controls

The physical state change is central to the system model (Fig. 3.2), because it is the physical change in the environment that enables differential control or modulation of resource flows. We take an integrated, descriptive approach to the focal physical state change. For example, a beaver dam transforms a stream to a pond, and elephants transform trees and undisturbed soil to woody debris with soil pits and mounds.

The aspects of the engineer that are central to the model are the activities that transform physical states. Elephants are complex creatures, but within the context of the agent-controlled engineering system, we are primarily concerned with factors that influence their tree-uprooting activities. The distinction between the totality of the engineer as an organism and the dimensions of the organism that are relevant to the physical state change allows for simplification, comparison and experimentation. Any living or non-living entity that causes the same physical state change will have the same consequence. From the viewpoint of tree uprooting and soil pits and mounds, elephants and wind will have much in common. However, the distinctiveness of the entities resides in the pattern of physical state changes in space and time, which are a function of the particular entity and the controllers that influence its activities. In this respect elephants and wind are very different.

The ways in which the physical state change exerts direct resource control or indirect resource modulation are functions of the structure of the system that determine the flow of resources to the other organisms. This is the interface with the recipient in the agent-substrate general model (Fig. 3.1). Direct control arises via two general paths. First, the structure created can be a resource. The size of a tree directly determines the amount of living space for other organisms. Second, the flow of the resource can be regulated by the structure. Tree structure controls throughfall and stemflow during rain events, directly controlling the distribution and abundance of water and nutrient resources for understorey plants. Indirect modulation also occurs via two paths. First, the structure acts upon other forces in the system that control resource flow. Organisms in pond sediments are affected by the hydrological control over sedimentation that is exerted by a beaver dam. Second, the structure can interact with other forces that act on the flow of resources. For example, reefs built by corals ameliorate wave action, and wave action is an important force affecting the acquisition of resources by resident coral organisms.

Ecological effects or consequences are inherent in the engineering model because physical structure acts upon resources, although the specific resources and the dependent organisms must be specified. The trivial description of heterogeneity as the spatial and temporal variance in all components (material, energy, organisms and information) is therefore excluded, and the focus is on those components that are relevant to the substrate, and subsequently, relevant to the responder in the general model.

Systems of engineers

Although there is value in constructing single species engineering models, particularly for systems in which there is an obvious and predominant engineer that builds major structures in the environment (e.g. trees, beaver, elephants or gophers), virtually all habitats are physically engineered by numerous organisms at different scales, in different ways, with different consequences (Jones *et al.* 1994; Lawton and Jones 1995). How can we deal with this complexity? There are two approaches. First, we can construct multiple, single-species models for the most important engineers and then integrate them. Integration would be accomplished by conjunction or separation of the models on the basis of similarities in the state changes, the pathways of control and modulation, the resources and the recipient organisms. This approach has the advantage of being explicit, but it results in complexity. Second, we can aggregate multiple engineers that control the same resource and recipient organisms into a single simpler model, inevitably sacrificing detail. The success of this approach would depend on the degree to which there is specification of the forces that generate distinctiveness among engineers that reside outside the model.

The general system model of flows and controls, comprising multiple engineers, is applicable to all cases of physical engineering. There is a physical state change caused by a specific set of organismal activities and there are particular pathways of control or modulation of defined resources to defined recipient organisms. The likely ecological consequences are apparent from knowledge of the resource and responders (e.g. annual plants responding to nutrient enrichment of soil *vs.* elephant-induced disturbance). Expectations for contingencies are apparent from knowledge of what influences the activities of the engineer (e.g. riparian structural influences on beaver site selection). For allogenic engineering, in which the structure has some persistence in the absence of the engineer, it is also possible to deduce the likely contingent influences (e.g. weathering of gopher mounds, or flood destruction of abandoned beaver dams).

To translate a functional model with the above characteristics into an operational, system-specific, scaled model requires integration with the boundary constraints, and ultimately the use of a patch dynamics framework. The result is an explicit, functional representation of one major way in which organisms generate resource heterogeneity. We outline this integration through the following two sections.

Ecological boundaries

The second category of process by which organisms generate spatial heterogeneity is boundary function. Boundaries are a common structure in contemporary land-scapes (Gosz 1991). Boundaries exist as discontinuities between contrasting habi-tats, and may be expressed as ecotones, gradients, or edges. For example, ecotones are compositional and architectural transitions between climatically or geologi-cally maintained vegetation or community types (Holland *et al.* 1991). The prairie-forest ecotone of North America is a clear example. The ecotone itself appears as a savanna system, with distinct composition and structure which is more than a simple blending of grassland and forest elements (Packard 1988). Gradational boundaries exist in response to transitions in soil or substrate on many scales. Edges are a particularly distinct sort of boundary over short distances. Most often they are the result of human activity, ecological engineering, or physical distur-bances. An example of a human-generated edge is the commonly encountered agricultural hedgerow, the abrupt structural contrast between agricultural fields and secondary forest, or the new edge of a forest clear cut. Biotically engineered edges include those around treefalls created by insects, buffalo wallows, or excava-tions by gophers. Physical disturbances create edges as a consequence of generating blowdowns in forest, or fire in grassland and forest, for example. As with ecological engineering, a given arena may contain boundaries to which a complex of agents contribute. For example, in East Kalimantan, Indonesia, treefall gaps are exploited and tended by villagers, conflating human and natural maintenance of the bound-ary between forest and gap, at least for a time.

Although the study of boundaries has been largely descriptive and static (Murcia 1995), they have a functional role to play in the generation of heterogeneity by organisms. Boundaries essentially control the expression of engineering over space. This process recognizes that virtually all ecological systems, be they organ-isms, populations, communities, ecosystems or landscapes, are open systems through which fluxes of matter, energy and information are crucial (Wiens 1992; Pickett and Cadenasso 1995). Boundaries are important both because they are a particular result of organismally engineered structure, and because organisms, as mobile engineers, interact with boundaries. Therefore, boundaries are part of the roster of controllers affecting the agent, the substrate, and the response to hetero-geneity (Fig. 3.1). Combining the consideration of boundaries with ecological engineering and with flux models confirms the functional role of boundaries and identifies important new research directions.

Boundaries affect heterogeneity through their division of an arena into contrast-ing types of substrate. Within an arena, organisms may concentrate their activities on one side of the boundary or the other. For example, porcupines digging for geo-phytes in the Negev Desert concentrate their activities in soil pockets located in hydrologic 'sink' areas in the landscape (Shachak and Brand 1991; Boeken *et al.* 1995). Such sink patches accumulate more runoff water from upslope, and are likely to support more or larger geophytes than non-sink areas. The boundary between parts of the desert watersheds that support higher ratios of rock to soil, *vs.* lower ratios of rock to soil is the operative transition in this case. Higher ratios of rock to soil generate greater soil moisture in the sink patches of soil (Yair and Shachak 1987).

An example of a boundary that generates organismal response that itself transforms the heterogeneity of the environment, is the creation of sodic patches in South African savanna (Rogers 1995). Generally, areas of sodic soil, which accumulate minerals and fine particles at the soil surface, support contrasting vegetation, and herbivore activities that differ from those found in the normal savanna soil. Thus there is an important biotic response to these boundaries in the savanna system. However, there is evidence that trees in the areas prone to sodic soil formation may enhance the effect by pumping mineral-laden water to the soil surface. Engineering by trees of the soil properties in the boundary area enhances the boundary formation, ultimately leading to quite distinct patches at the scale of tens of meters. This example illustrates the feedbacks between physical factors at boundaries and organism magnification of the effect through engineering. Hence, there are complex layerings of agents of heterogeneity.

Boundaries can affect the functioning of populations, landscapes and ecosystems (Pickett and Cadenasso 1995) by modulating fluxes. High elevation coniferous forest edges, and those close to extraordinary sources of atmospheric nitrogen pollution, have been shown to interact with the fluxes of nitrogen across the landscape (Draaijers *et al.* 1988, 1994). The deposition of nitrogen into edge zones of forests is substantially higher than elsewhere in the forest (Weathers *et al.* 1992, 1995; Erisman and Draaijers 1995). This raises the possibility of different effects of nutrient addition throughout the landscape as a result of the edge structure engineered by organisms, and a cascade of effects through communities and ecosystems. Weathers and Cadenasso (1996), Cadenasso (1998) and Cadenasso *et al.* (in review) have documented the enhancement of nitrogen in throughfall in forest edge zones in a low elevation, temperate deciduous system. Because earlier work on throughfall at such forest edges was conducted at high elevations, or adjacent to areas with extremely high nutrient inputs from agriculture (e.g. Erisman *et al.* 1997), it was not known whether the concentration of nutrients at edges was an unusual phenomenon. We can now appreciate it as a more general process.

A second function of edges—their ability to filter seed flux—was also examined by Cadenasso (1998). The edge between a field and secondary forest—the joint result of ecological engineering by succession of the forest and human maintenance by mowing the field—was modified by removing the lateral branches of trees, understorey trees, and shrubs from a 20-m deep zone at the forest edge. The treatment thus altered the architectural structure of the edge zone, while leaving the location of the edge unaltered. Seed flux of species characteristic of the field increased well into the forest with the modified edge compared with the forest with the intact edge. The enhancement in seed flux continued throughout the autumn seed dispersal period (Cadenasso and Pickett in press).

A third kind of flux mediated by forest edge structure is the impact of herbivores on tree seedlings. The same experimental modification of forest edge described above altered the activity and impact of herbivores (Cadenasso and Pickett 2000). In an area where voles (*Microtus pennsylvanicus*) were present in the landscape, herbivory by voles was greater in the intact than in the altered edge plots. In the same site, deer (*Odocoileus virginiancus*) and invertebrates had greater effects on seedlings in the thinned edge plots. Deer browse was greater in the forest interior than on the forest edge. This experiment illustrates a cascading effect of heterogeneity on organisms in landscapes.

The study of edges as functional features of landscape mosaics is in its infancy, and undoubtedly more examples of such organismal and ecosystem functions await discovery. The functions of edges exemplified above point to the integrated nature of landscapes, and to the potential role of engineering and organismally generated heterogeneity in them. We turn to this integration using the conceptual tool of patch dynamics.

Patch dynamics and organismal heterogeneity

Patch dynamics can serve as a spatial and temporal integrator of the role of organisms in generating, maintaining and transforming heterogeneity. Patch dynamics puts ecological engineering into a spatial context. Although the fact that engineering acts to convert one biotic or abiotic environmental state into another (Fig. 3.2), the concept only implies spatial context. Patch dynamics makes that context explicit and relates the changes in heterogeneity that might result from engineering of different locations in a landscape to one another. An example of this is the damming of streams by beaver (Naiman 1988). Dams have a finite life span, due to the exhaustion by the resident beaver of the local food supply and the accumulation of sediment behind the dams. This converts a productive area surrounding a safe pond into a poor larder with increased exposure to predators. Therefore, beaver periodically move elsewhere to establish a new dam. The temporal and spatial pattern of dam construction, pond filling, dam decline and recovery of nearby forest canopy, constitute a complex pattern of patch dynamics (Pringle *et al.* 1988; Reice *et al.* 1990). The engineering and landscape dynamics driven by the beaver, in interaction with their habitat and food, produce a shifting mosaic of habitats for fish, reptiles, waterfowl, raptors, and passerine birds, rooted aquatics, littoral marsh plants, and mesic and hydric woody plants and woodland herbs.

A second example of patch dynamics illustrates their occurrence on finer spatial scales. During postagricultural succession, spatial groupings of plant species and growth forms appear. Different patches arise and disappear through succession, or move across space in a given field (S. Bartha, unpublished; Plate 3.1 opposite p. 50). The opening and closing of canopies through succession, and the resultant shifts in availabilities of resources such as light, nutrients and water (Carson and Pickett 1990) probably cause such patch transformations. The invasion or persistence of many species through succession depends on such fine-scale patch dynamics (Carson and Peterson 1990; Armesto *et al.* 1991; Facelli and Carson 1991; Vivian-Smith 1997). In general terms, patch dynamics has been shown to be a major contributor to species coexistence and the structuring of assemblages and ecosystems in many places (Pickett and White 1985; Clark 1991; Fisher 1993; Hansson *et al.* 1995).

Not all of patch dynamics is created or driven by organisms. We note the importance of physical disturbances such as wind, fire, flood and mass movements of earth and rock (Dale *et al.* 1999). We have already noted the differences in selectivity and control of engineering by organisms, and the complementary class of disturbances by physical forces. Physical properties of sites do influence the role of organisms in patch dynamics, however. For instance, gophers in the annual grassland at Jasper Ridge, California, dig preferentially in certain locations both as a result of their own social structure, and because of the differences in soil depth from place to place in the grassland (Malony 1993).

Organisms are differentially sensitive to engineering or disturbance that initiates patch dynamics. When sensitive individuals are disproportionately clustered in landscapes, the patch dynamics are also spatially biased. For example, crown fires occurring during years having moderate conditions are controlled by fuel availability and topography (Turner and Romme 1994). More severe droughts reduce the predictability of association of fire with these controllers. The response to patch dynamics by organisms also contributes to spatial heterogeneity in Yellowstone National Park. The establishment of aspen (*Populus tremuloides*) patches in northern Yellowstone National Park was restricted to an unusually wet period after a large burn (Romme *et al.* 1995). In northeastern USA forests subject to Atlantic hurricanes, patches are preferentially opened by wind in older stands more often than in second growth stands (Foster 1988).

The subsequent dynamics of disturbed patches also reflect organismal control. Older trees are less likely to resprout after intense wind disturbance in the primary forests of the Allegheny Plateau, Pennsylvania, USA (Peterson and Pickett 1991). Biotic influences may have an additional impact after the patches were initiated by disturbance. Interactions with the large number of browsers (*Odocoileus virginianus*) in the region restricted the regeneration of certain species, notably *Tsuga canadensis* in the disturbed patch (Peterson and Pickett 1995). The engineering accomplished by organisms through the coarse woody debris left after disturbance, the propagules and surviving stems, and the modification of the soil surface through the creation of treefall pits and mounds, are all examples of the elements of heterogeneity contributed by organisms in even physically caused disturbances (Turner *et al.* 1998).

Patches may be expressed in a variety of ways. One important contrast is that between gaps formed in continuous canopies, as illustrated above, *vs.* clusters of invaders in a lower-statured matrix. Both reflect the engineering or control by organisms. In the case of some clusters, engineering results from clonal spread, for example of *Rhus typhina* in postagricultural-oldfields, where the resultant patchiness affects the invasion of *Quercus* spp. (Werner and Harbeck 1982). Initial invaders can also act as recruitment foci for plants dispersed by birds attracted to the cluster as a perch (McDonnell and Stiles 1983). Shrubs in deserts can act as 'islands of fertility' (Jackson and Caldwell 1993). For example, shrubs in the Negev

Desert accumulate loose mounds of soil that act as sinks for runoff water contributed by the impermeable microphytic crust of the matrix (Shachak and Pickett 1997). It is in such sink sites that high plant diversity and productivity is concentrated (Boeken and Shachak 1998).

Conclusions: patch dynamics and organismally-generated heterogeneity

Patch dynamics can synthesize organismal contributions to heterogeneity because the theory is so much richer now than when the concept first coalesced in the 1970s (Levins 1968; Levin 1976; Pickett and Thompson 1978). Major advances include the following points that may now be treated as principles contributing to a theory of heterogeneity (cf. Wiens, this volume).

Patch dynamics are spatially explicit. Rather than considering patches as a population characterized by averaged parameters, the configuration and geographical location of patches is an aspect of their function and dynamics. As an example, the orientation of patches affects their invasibility by migrating birds (Pearson 1993). A further example of explicit spatial effects in a patch mosaic is the preferential location of tree seedlings on the side of a forest patch nearest the presumed source of those species (Ranney and Johnson 1977). These examples show the impact of locationally specific features in a patch mosaic as controllers of response to heterogeneity created by organisms.

Patches may have different origins. Disturbance and stress are involved in the origin of many patches (Pickett *et al.* 1989). However, ecological engineering driven by organism establishment, growth and behaviour are also key agents of patch origin and patch change. Some patches may be relatively permanent on the time scales usually addressed by ecologists, since geomorphic and geological pattern is responsible for many slowly changing patches (Forman and Godron 1986). Humans are of course a major source and modifier of patches in contemporary landscapes worldwide. Patches in real mosaics will therefore often result from the engineering effects of many kinds of organisms, and the dynamics within them will be subject to a variety of controllers on subsequent organism response.

Patches have complex structure. Patches of a particular scale may be resolved into constituent patches having finer scales (Kotliar and Wiens 1990). Patches may also have either abrupt or gradual boundaries at a specified scale. Complexity within patches may result from the persistence of structural legacies or surviving propagules as a result of 'diffuse disturbance', or of low or moderate levels of disturbance at the time they are created. Such patches are especially likely to exhibit gradual boundaries. The complexity of patch structure is due in large part to the differential sensitivities of the organisms that engineered them, or the individual organisms that formed the elements of the substrate on which engineering or disturbance acted. Any heterogeneity in the substrate that existed prior to the action of an engineer or disturbance can modify the pattern of subsequent heterogeneity.

Patches are not functionally isolated from their context. The idea of a strictly contrasting matrix, which can be taken as a simple background, is rarely adequate for understanding the structure, function and dynamics of patches of interest. The island-ocean model, an extreme form of the simple contrast between patch and matrix, has been superseded in patch dynamics (Pickett and Rogers 1997). The surroundings of a focal patch or system are themselves a complex mosaic, which can control the access of engineers to the patch, or the availability of resources in it.

Patch connectivity depends on the nature of the flux through the mosaic of which the patches are a part. Percolation theory (Turner *et al.* 1994), and non-uniform flows of dispersing propagules are important features of the connectivity in mosaics. Not all aspects of connectivity are represented by obvious corridors or structural boundaries. However, the existence of boundaries or edges at various scales, and their impact on lateral flows in the landscape, becomes a crucial mechanism of organism engineering and response to heterogeneity.

In short, the principles collated above show that the study of heterogeneity has evolved from modelling as simple, two phase systems, with unrealistic assumptions of uniformity within the elements of heterogeneity, or of the uniformity of the fluxes potentially connecting them, to a more comprehensive conceptual system. The role of heterogeneity in an ecological system is determined by the interaction of an agent with a substrate, and each of these has characteristics that must be evaluated to understand the pattern of spatial differentiation and its potential effects on responders (Fig. 3.1). Organisms, or assemblages of organisms, act as agents of heterogeneity, as well as substrates in which heterogeneity can appear. Again, the organismal sensitivities and behaviours affect the susceptibility of the substrate to the action of an agent. The relationships between organisms and heterogeneity can be highlighted by using three processes. Organisms participate in ecological engineering, respond to and generate boundaries, and contribute to spatial patchiness, both as its creators and as the engines of dynamic change in the elements of heterogeneity. Finally, of course, the ecological relevance of heterogeneity as a functional feature of all scales of observation, depends on the ability of organisms to detect, access and use the resources that are associated with different elements of heterogeneity. Heterogeneity is one of the keys to the function of ecological systems and to their richness and productivity. Organisms make and maintain a vast store of the world's heterogeneity (Huston 1994; Pickett 1999).

This chapter has identified key elements that must be considered in the articulation of a theory of organismally generated heterogeneity in assemblages and landscapes. However, the conceptual principles and empirical generalizations that are emerging from ecological work need to be knitted together into a prototypical theory. This effort would link the diverse areas of study that are relevant to the generation and impact of heterogeneity in ecological systems of all scales and types.

Acknowledgments

We are grateful to the National Science Foundation (DEB 9726992) and to the Andrew W. Mellon Foundation (Mosaic Landscapes and Riparian–Upland Interactions in Kruger National Park, South Africa) for support of research contributing to this paper. This paper is a contribution to the program of the Institute of Ecosystem Studies with partial support from the Mary Flagler Cary Charitable Trust.

References

Armesto, J.J., Pickett, S.T.A. and McDonnell, M.J. (1991) Spatial heterogeneity during succession: a cyclic model of invasion and exclusion. In: *Ecological Heterogeneity* (eds J. Kolasa and S.T.A. Pickett), pp. 256–269. Springer Verlag, New York.

Basnet, K. (1993) Controls of environmental factors on patterns of montane rain forest in Puerto Rico. *Tropical Ecology* **34**, 51–63.

Boeken, B. and Shachak, M. (1998) Colonization by annual plants of an experimentally altered desert landscape: source-sink relationships. *Journal of Ecology* **86**, 804–814.

Boeken, B., Shachak, M., Gutterman, Y. and Brand, S. (1995) Patchiness and disturbance: plant community responses to porcupine diggings in the Central Negev. *Ecography* **18**, 410–422.

Boose, E.R., Foster, D.R. and Fluet, M. (1994) Hurricane impacts to tropical and temperate forest landscapes. *Ecological Monographs* **64**, 369–400.

Cadenasso, M.L. (1998) *Linking forest edge structure to edge function: an experimental and synthetic approach.* DPhil Thesis, Rutgers University, New Brunswick, New Jersey.

Cadenasso, M.L. and Pickett, S.T.A. (2000) Linking forest edge structure to edge function: mediation of herbivore damage. *Journal of Ecology* **88**, 31–44.

Cadenasso, M.L. and Pickett, S.T.A. Effects of edge structure on the flux of species into forest interiors: an experimental approach. *Conservation Biology*, in press.

Cadenasso, M.L., Pickett, S.T.A., Weathers, K.C. (in review) Effects of boundaries and edges on flux of nutrients and detritus, and organisms. In: *Food Webs at the Landscape Level: the Ecology of Trophic Flow Across Habitats* (eds G.A. Polis, M.E. Power and G.R. Huxel).

Carson, W.P. and Peterson, C.J. (1990) The role of litter in an old-field community: impact of litter quantity in different seasons on plant species richness and abundance. *Oecologia* **85**, 8–13.

Carson, W.P. and Pickett, S.T.A. (1990) Role of resources and disturbance in the organization of an old-field plant community. *Ecology* **71**, 226–238.

Clark, J.S. (1991) Disturbance and tree life history on the shifting mosaic landscape. *Journal of Ecology* **72**, 1102–1118.

Dale, V.H., Lugo, A.E., MacMahon, J.A. and Pickett, S.T.A. (1999) Ecosystem management in the context of large, infrequent disturbances. *Ecosystems* **1**, 546–557.

Draaijers, G.P.J., Ivens, W.P.M.F. and Bleuten, W. (1988) Atmospheric deposition in forest edges measured by monitoring canopy throughfall. *Water, Air, and Soil Pollution* **42**, 129–136.

Draaijers, G.P.J., Van Ek, R. and Bleuten, W. (1994) Atmospheric deposition in complex forest landscapes. *Boundary-Layer Meteorology* **69**, 343–366.

Erisman, J.W. and Draaijers, G.P.J. (1995) *Atmospheric Deposition in Relation to Acidification and Entrophication.* Elsevier, Amsterdam.

Erisman, J.W., Draaijers, G., Duyzer, J., *et al.* (1997) Particle deposition to forests — summary of results and application. *Atmospheric Environment* **31**, 321–332.

Facelli, J.M. and Carson, W.P. (1991) Heterogeneity of plant litter accumulation in successional communities. *Bulletin of the Torrey Botanical Club* **118**, 62–66.

Fisher, S.G. (1993) Pattern, process, and scale in freshwater systems: some unifying thoughts. In: *Aquatic Ecology: Scale, Pattern, and Process* (eds P.S. Giller, A.G. Hildrew and D.G. Raffaelli), pp. 575–597. Blackwell Scientific Publications, Oxford.

Forman, R.T.T. and Godron, M. (1986) *Landscape Ecology.* John Wiley, New York.

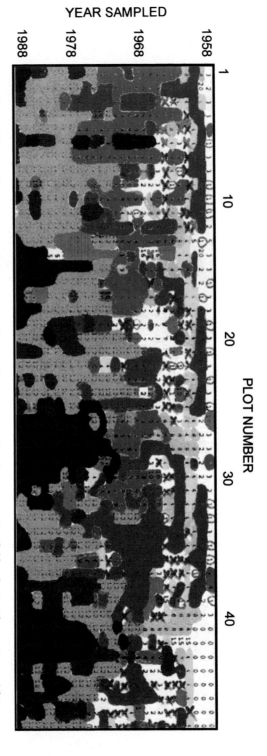

Plate 3.1 A temporal–spatial map of heterogeneity of plant functional groups in post-agricultural succession in a field at the Hutcheson Memorial Forest Center, New Jersey, USA, from 1958 to 1990. The time dimension, in years sampled since abandonment in 1958, and the spatial dimension as the linear sequence of 48 plots in the sampling grid, bound the behaviours of different functional groups based on life form and mode of spread, and key features that define successional community organization. The example shows that changes in patchiness represented by these two complex axes (note the three dimensions of space are simplified into two dimensions in the figure). Notable functional groups in late succession are turf-forming grasses (orange) clonal shrubs (blue) and forest trees (purple). Note that sampling was annual until 1980, when the field began to be sampled every other year. Full description of functional groups is beyond the scope of this paper. Unpublished data of S. Bartha, S.T.A. Pickett and M.L. Cadenasso.

Foster, D.R. (1988) Species and stand response to catastrophic wind in central New England. *Journal of Ecology* **76**, 135–151.

Gosz, J.R. (1991) Fundamental ecological characteristics of landscape boundaries. In: *Ecotones: the Role of Changing Landscape Boundaries in the Management and Restoration of Changing Environments* (eds M.M. Holland, P.G. Risser and R.J. Naiman), pp. 8–30. Chapman and Hall, New York.

Hansson, L., Fahrig, L. and Merriam, G. (eds). (1995) *Mosaic Landscapes and Ecological Processes*. Chapman and Hall, New York.

Hobbs, R.J. and Mooney, H.A. (1985) Community and population dynamics of serpentine grassland annuals in relation to gopher disturbance. *Oecologia* **67**, 342–351.

Holland, M.M., Risser, P.G. and Naiman, R.J. (eds). (1991) *Ecotones: the Role of Landscape Boundaries in the Management and Restoration of Changing Environments*. Chapman and Hall, New York.

Huston, M.A. (1994) *Biological Diversity: the Coexistence of Species in Changing Landscapes*. Cambridge University Press, New York.

Hutchinson, G.E. (1978) *An Introduction to Population Biology*. Yale University Press, New Haven.

Jackson, R.B. and Caldwell, M.M. (1993) The scale of nutrient heterogeneity around individual plants and its quantification with geostatistics. *Ecology* **74**, 612–614.

Jax, K., Jones, C. and Pickett, S.T.A. (1998) The self-identity of ecological units. *Oikos* **82**, 253–264.

Jones, C.G., Lawton, J.H. and Shachak, M. (1994) Organisms as ecosystem engineers. *Oikos* **69**, 373–386.

Kolasa, J. and Rollo, C.D. (1991) Introduction: the heterogeneity of heterogeneity: a glossary. In: *Ecological Heterogeneity* (eds J. Kolasa and S.T.A. Pickett), pp. 1–23. Springer-Verlag, New York.

Kotliar, N.B. and Wiens, J.A. (1990) Multiple scales of patchiness and patch structure: a hierarchical framework for the study of heterogeneity. *Oikos* **59**, 253–260.

Lawton, J.H. and Jones, C.G. (1995) Linking species and ecosystems: organisms as ecosystem engineers. In: *Linking Species and Ecosystems* (eds C.G. Jones and J.H. Lawton), pp. 141–150. Chapman and Hall, New York.

Levin, S.A. (1976) Population dynamic models in heterogeneous environments. *Annual Review of Ecology and Systematics* **7**, 287–310.

Levins, R. (1968) *Evolution in Changing Environments: Some Theoretical Explorations*. Princeton University Press, Princeton.

Malony, K. (1993) Determining processes through pattern: reality or fantasy. In: *Patch Dynamics* (eds S.A. Levin, T.M. Powell and J.H. Steele), pp. 62–69. Springer-Verlag, New York.

McDonnell, M.J. and Stiles, E.W. (1983) The structural complexity of old field vegetation and the recruitment of bird-dispersed plant species. *Oecologia* **56**, 109–116.

Murcia, C. (1995) Edge effects in fragmented forests: implications for conservation. *Trends in Ecology and Evolution* **10**, 58–62.

Naiman, R.J. (1988) Animal influences on ecosystem dynamics. *Bioscience* **38**, 750–752.

O'Neill, R.V., DeAngelis, D.L., Waide, J.B. and Allen, T.F.H. (1986) *A Hierarchical Concept of Ecosystems*. Princeton University Press, Princeton.

Packard, S. (1988) Just a few oddball species: restoration and the rediscovery of the tallgrass savanna. *Restoration and Management Notes* **6**, 13–20.

Parker, V.T. and Pickett, S.T.A. (1997) Historical contingency and multiple scales of dynamics within plant communities. In: *Scale Issues in Ecology* (eds D.L. Peterson and V.T. Parker), pp. 171–191. Columbia University Press, New York.

Pearson, S.M. (1993) The spatial extent and relative influence of landscape-level factors on wintering bird populations. *Landscape Ecology* **8**, 3–18.

Peterson, C.J. and Pickett, S.T.A. (1991) Treefall and resprouting following catastrophic windthrow in an old-growth hemlock-hardwoods forest. *Forest Ecology and Management* **42**, 205–217.

Peterson, C.J. and Pickett, S.T.A. (1995) Forest reorganization: a case study in an old-growth forest catastrophic blowdown. *Ecology* **76**, 763–774.

Pickett, S.T.A. (1999) Natural processes. In: *Status and Trends of the Nation's Biological Resources*, Vol. 1 (eds M.J. Mac, P.A. Opler, C.E. Puckett Haecker and P.D. Doran), pp. 11–35. US Geological Survey, Reston, Virginia.

Pickett, S.T.A. and Cadenasso, M.L. (1995) Landscape ecology: spatial heterogeneity in ecological systems. *Science* **269**, 331–334.

Pickett, S.T.A. and Rogers, K.H. (1997) Patch dynamics: the transformation of landscape structure and function. In: *Wildlife and Landscape Ecology* (ed. J.A. Bissonette), pp. 101–127. Springer-Verlag, New York.

Pickett, S.T.A. and Thompson, J.N. (1978) Patch dynamics and the design of nature reserves. *Biological Conservation* **13**, 27–37.

Pickett, S.T.A. and White, P.S., eds. (1985) *The Ecology of Natural Disturbance and Patch Dynamics.* Academic Press, Orlando, FL.

Pickett, S.T.A., Kolasa, J., Armesto, J.J. and Collins, S.L. (1989) The ecological concept of disturbance and its expression at various hierarchical levels. *Oikos* **54**, 129–136.

Pringle, C.M., Naiman, R.J., Bretschko, G., *et al.* (1988) Patch dynamics in stream ecosystems: the stream as a mosaic. *Journal of the North American Benthological Society* **7**, 503–524.

Ranney, J.W. and Johnson, W.C. (1977) Propagule dispersal among forest islands in southeastern South Dakota. *Prairie Naturalist* **9**, 17–24.

Reice, S.R., Wissmar, R.C. and Naiman, R.J. (1990) Disturbance regimes, resilience, and recovery of animal communities and habitats in lotic ecosystems. *Environmental Management* **14**, 647–659.

Rogers, K.H. (1995) Riparian wetlands. In: *Wetlands of South Africa: Their Conservation and Ecology* (ed. G.I. Cowan), pp. 41–52. Department of Environmental Affairs, Pretoria.

Romme, W.H., Turner, M.G., Wallace, L.L. and Walker, J.S. (1995) Aspen, elk, and fire in Northern Yellowstone park. *Ecology* **76**, 2097–2106.

Shachak, M. and Brand, S. (1991) Relations among spatiotemporal heterogeneity, population abundance, and variability in a desert. In: *Ecological Heterogeneity* (eds J. Kolasa and S.T.A. Pickett), pp. 202–223. Springer-Verlag, New York.

Shachak, M. and Jones, C.G. (1995) Ecological flow chains and ecological systems: concepts for linking species and ecosystem perspectives. In: *Linking Species and Ecosystems* (eds C.G. Jones and J.H .Lawton), pp. 280–294. Chapman and Hall, New York.

Shachak, M. and Pickett, S.T.A. (1997) Linking ecological understanding and application: patchiness in dryland systems. In: *The Ecological Basis of Conservation: Heterogeneity, Ecosystems, and Biodiversity* (eds S.T.A. Pickett, R.S. Ostfeld, M. Shachak and G.E. Likens), pp. 108–119. Chapman and Hall, New York.

Turner, M.G. and Romme, W.H. (1994) Landscape dynamics in crown fire ecosystems. *Landscape Ecology* **9**, 59–77.

Turner, M.G., Romme, W.H. and Gardner, R.H. (1994) Landscape disturbance models and the long-term dynamics of natural areas. *Natural Areas Journal* **14**, 3–11.

Turner, M.G., Baker, W.L., Peterson, C.J. and Peet, R.K. (1998) Factors influencing succession: lessons from large, infrequent disturbances. *Ecosystems* **1**, 511–523.

Vivian-Smith, G. (1997) *Small-scale heterogeneity, diversity and community structure in regenerating plant communities.* DPhil Thesis, Rutgers University, New Brunswick, New Jersey.

Weathers, K.C. and Cadenasso, M.L. (1996) The function of forest edges: nutrient inputs. *Bulletin of the Ecological Society of America* **77**, 471.

Weathers, K.C., Lovett, G.M. and Likens, G.E. (1992) The influence of a forest edge on cloud deposition. In: *Precipitation Scavenging and Atmosphere–Surface Exchange the Summers Volume: Applications and Appraisals*, Vol. 3 (eds S.E. Schwartz and W.G.N. Slinn), pp. 1415–1423., Washington.

Weathers, K.C., Lovett, G.M. and Likens, G.E. (1995) Cloud deposition to a spruce forest edge. *Atmospheric Environment* **29**, 665–672.

Werner, P.A. and Harbeck, A.L. (1982) The pattern of tree seedling establishment relative to staghorn sumac cover in Michigan oldfields. *American Midland Naturalist* **108**, 124–132.

Wiens, J.A. (1992) Ecological flows across landscape boundaries: a conceptual overview. In: *Landscape Boundaries*, Vol. 92 (eds F. di Castri and A.J. Hansen), pp. 216–235. Springer-Verlag, New York.

Yair, A. and Shachak, M. (1987) Studies in watershed ecology of an arid area. In: *Progress in Desert Research* (eds L. Berkofsky and M.G. Wurtele), pp. 145–193. Rowman and Littlefield, Totawa, New Jersey.

Chapter 4

Heterogeneity, diversity and scale in plant communities

S.D. Wilson

Introduction

We are at the earliest stages of measuring and understanding the relationship between heterogeneity and diversity. Environmental heterogeneity is spatial or temporal variability in resources or factors. Extensive discussion of the definitions and measurements of heterogeneity can be found elsewhere (Caldwell and Pearcy 1994; Pickett *et al.*, this volume, Weins, this volume). I distinguish two kinds of environmental heterogeneity. Abiotic heterogeneity has abiotic origins. Examples include variation in topography, slope, aspect, daily temperature, precipitation, and substrate particle sizes. Biogenic heterogeneity is caused by organisms. It may be produced by resource consumption, such as evapotranspiration, or by non-consumptive effects, such as stemflow. Biogenic heterogeneity is especially interesting because it may not only enhance abiotic heterogeneity, but it may occur even in the absence of abiotic heterogeneity.

Here I describe recent evidence concerning the relationship between heterogeneity and diversity, and show that they are not always positively correlated. Then I discuss the relative contributions of abiotic and biogenic heterogeneity to the relationship. I address the possibility that enhancement of diversity by abiotic heterogeneity entrains feedback whereby high diversity contributes to biogenic heterogeneity. Lastly, I argue that the scale of organisms is more important than diversity in affecting biogenic heterogeneity (Fig. 4.1).

Abiotic heterogeneity and diversity

Examples of diversity increasing with abiotic heterogeneity are reviewed by Huston (1994) and Rosenzweig (1995). More recent studies have also found this relationship, but those based on interpretations of natural patterns are limited by the difficulty of separating the effects of heterogeneity from those of other factors, such as sample area. For example, Caley and Schluter (1997) used published distribution maps of amphibians, birds, butterflies, corals, dragonflies, eucalypts, other trees, fish, mammals, and reptiles to determine diversity in regions of 500×500 km.

Department of Biology, University of Regina, Regina, Saskatchewan, S4S 0A2, Canada

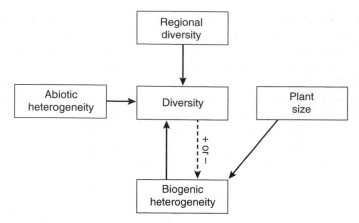

Figure 4.1 Abiotic heterogeneity has positive effects on diversity, as does regional diversity. Diversity may in turn have either positive or negative effects on biogenic heterogeneity (heterogeneity produced by organisms). Biogenic heterogeneity may have positive effects on diversity, creating the possibility of feedbacks between diversity and heterogeneity. Biogenic heterogeneity, however, is probably more strongly influenced by plant size than diversity. Solid arrows are positive effects; the dashed arrow indicates effects which may be positive or negative.

Diversity was then subsampled in areas comprising 1% and 10% of the study regions. Diversity in subsampled areas increased significantly with regional diversity, but the slope was steeper for the 10% subsample than for the 1% subsample. Thus, more species were found in large subsamples than small ones, which Caley and Schluter (1997) attributed to higher heterogeneity in the larger subsamples. On the other hand, high diversity in large samples might simply reflect the well-known positive relationship between diversity and sample area. Kohn and Walsh (1994) used path analysis to examine relationships among plant diversity, heterogeneity and the area of Scottish islands. Island size had twice the effect on richness as heterogeneity alone, but this was because island size and heterogeneity were correlated, so that heterogeneity was inseparable from the effect of island size. Similarly, Guégan *et al.* (1998) used river discharge volume as an index of fish habitat heterogeneity. All of these examples have both sample size and heterogeneity increasing together, making it difficult to separate their effects. As noted by Robertson and Gross (1994), the use of direct measures of heterogeneity would be more rigorous.

One study that explicitly measured resource heterogeneity while keeping sample area constant found results that were contrary to the usual pattern, i.e. diversity and heterogeneity were shown to be negatively related. Kleb and Wilson (1997) measured resource heterogeneity (light penetration to the soil surface and soil available N) in species-rich Saskatchewan prairie and adjacent species-poor aspen forest. Ten small (1×1 cm) samples were taken along each of 10 transects (90 cm long) in each habitat. Transects were scattered over a 4-km^2 area supporting a mix of prairie and forest. The coefficient of variation (CV) of each variable was determined for each transect, providing 10 replicate measures of CV for each habitat. Species richness was significantly higher in prairie (2.8 species per sample) than forest (1.5; $P < 0.001$), but the heterogeneity of resources was significantly higher in forest (light penetration: $CV = 100\%$; available N: 80%) than in prairie (light penetration: 60%; available N: 40%; Kleb and Wilson 1997). Thus, the relatively species-rich prairie was characterized by less heterogeneity than the species-poor forest.

Experiments can also examine heterogeneity in the absence of variation in sample area. Vivian-Smith (1997) grew mixes of wetland plants in tanks ($36 \times 52\,cm$) that contained either flat (homogeneous) or hummocky (heterogeneous) substrates. The species grown in the tanks represented a wide array of growth forms, including sedges, rushes, trees, shrubs and forbs, and were added either as seed mixes, or as seeds naturally occurring in wetland soils. Homogeneous substrates produced communities containing 2–5 species, depending on the source of propagules, whereas heterogeneous substrates supported 8–13 species. This is an unequivocal example of the direct effects of heterogeneity on diversity. Surprisingly, such examples are rare.

A field experiment in Minnesota illustrates the variability that can be found in the relationship between heterogeneity on diversity. The field containing the experiment was last farmed in 1957 and is dominated by *Schizachyrium scoparium*, a perennial C_4 grass, and cryptogamic soil (a dark surface crust of cyanobacteria and moss protonema) (Wilson and Tilman 1995). The field has nutrient-poor, sandy soil. Heterogeneity was created within plots ($5 \times 5\,m$) by assigning each plot to one of four levels of disturbance. Plots were tilled annually in late April or early May during 1988–95 to a depth of 10 cm with a rear-tined, self-propelled rototiller. Disturbance intensity varied according to the amount of bare ground produced (0%, 25%, 50%, 100%). Thus, plots with 25% bare ground were more heterogeneous than undisturbed plots, and plots with 50% bare ground were most heterogeneous. There were 4–14 replicates of each treatment. Nitrogen was applied to half of the plots as commercial solid NH_4NO_3 at $17\,g\,N\,m^{-2}\,year^{-1}$ in early May and late June each year.

In plots without added N, diversity was low in undisturbed plots, highest in plots tilled to produce 25–50% bare ground, and low in plots tilled to 100% bare ground (Fig. 4.2a). Diversity was greatest at the highest level of experimentally generated heterogeneity, i.e. bare ground of 25–50%. In contrast, undisturbed plots had no experimentally induced heterogeneity and had low richness. Highly disturbed plots started each year with little heterogeneity as they were completely tilled, and diversity was also relatively low (Fig. 4.2a). Undisturbed plots were dominated by native perennials such as *Schizachyrium scoparium*, whereas completely tilled plots contained only annuals such as *Polygonum convolvulus* and *Setaria viridis*; plots receiving intermediate levels of disturbance contained both perennials and annuals. Richness was highest at the highest levels of heterogeneity because of the coexistence of different growth forms.

In contrast to the increase in species richness with heterogeneity in unfertilized

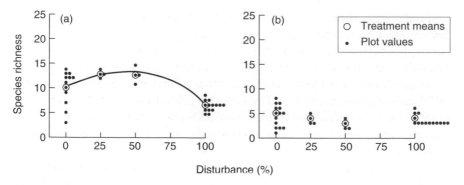

Figure 4.2 Plant species richness in Minnesota old fields after 8 years of early spring tilling to produce four intensities of disturbance (Wilson and Tilman, unpublished data). (a) Unfertilized plots. Richness varied significantly with disturbance ($P<0.001$) and was greatest at the highest level of heterogeneity, produced by 50% disturbance. (b) Plots receiving $17\,\mathrm{g\,N\,m^{-2}\,year^{-1}}$. Richness was very low regardless of disturbance.

plots, richness did not vary with disturbance in plots with added N (Fig. 4.2b). The difference in the response of diversity to heterogeneity between unfertilized and fertilized plots suggests that there are limits to the generalization that heterogeneity increases diversity. Specifically, whether or not heterogeneity increases diversity depends on other factors, such as nutrient availability.

In summary, the interpretation of field studies of heterogeneity and diversity can be hampered by indirect measures of heterogeneity. Both studies and experiments show that relationships between heterogeneity and diversity can be positive, neutral, or negative. We need to move on from the generalization that heterogeneity can increase diversity, to an understanding of the conditions under which the different aspects of the relationship—positive, neutral, or negative—are manifested.

Partitioning heterogeneity

The mechanism usually thought to cause richness to increase in response to heterogeneity is that more heterogeneity is equivalent to more niches, which allow more species to coexist (Rosenzweig 1995). A second possible mechanism, however, is that heterogeneity itself may be partitioned: some species might be favoured by relatively uniform or stable habitats, whereas others might be favoured by heterogeneous habitats (Campbell *et al.* 1991; Grime 1994). There are many examples of differences among plant species in their responses to nutrient pulses, as measured by changes in growth, resource allocation, and the placement of roots or shoots (Rorison 1987). More recent examples include both grasses and trees. Seedling growth of the south-eastern US deciduous tree *Liquidambar* responded to soil heterogeneity in pots more strongly than did that of *Pinus* (Mou *et al.* 1997). Thus, a gradient of heterogeneity might increase diversity by allowing different species to specialize on different amounts of heterogeneity.

Specifically, Grime (1994) proposed that fast-growing species should be favoured by spatial heterogeneity since they can grow into and exploit a patch. Slow-growers should be favoured by temporal heterogeneity because they can maintain tissue and wait for a pulse. Plants common in nutrient-poor habitats typically accumulate resources during the short periods when resources are available and thus may be better able to exploit temporal pulses than fast-growing plants in more fertile habitats. These ideas have been extended to explain variation in competitive effects with both resource availability and variability (Goldberg and Novoplansky 1997).

Experimental evidence, however, is conflicting. A comparison of one fast and one slow-growing British grass species showed that the slow-growing species was better at using nutrient pulses than the fast-growing species (Campbell and Grime 1989). In contrast, an early successional and relatively fast-growing *Plantago* species was better at exploiting pulses than was a later successional species (Miao and Bazzaz 1990). A review found some evidence to support Grime's ideas, but also found contradictory examples (Hutchings and de Kroon 1994). More multispecies tests are needed to determine whether growth rate is a good predictor of a plant's ability to exploit habitat heterogeneity.

Feedbacks between heterogeneity and diversity

Heterogeneity can increase biological diversity, but organisms in turn can generate heterogeneity (Fowler 1988; Pickett *et al.*, this volume), creating the possibility of positive feedback between heterogeneity and diversity (Fowler 1990; Huston 1994). Variation in competition and predation driven by variability in population size could magnify abiotic heterogeneity (Barry and Dayton 1991). For example, high plant diversity caused by abiotic heterogeneity might promote high insect diversity which might in turn further enhance plant diversity: a high diversity of specialist herbivores would presumably be more effective at reducing plant mass than would a few species of herbivores, thus decreasing competition intensity and allowing more plant species to coexist (Hunter and Price 1992).

Biogenic heterogeneity might be most important in enhancing α-diversity (within habitats) because the local scale is where plants affect and respond to abiotic conditions. In contrast, large-scale abiotic heterogeneity easily explains turnover in species composition along environmental gradients (β-diversity).

Resource uptake by plants clearly has the potential to create heterogeneity (Grime 1994), and the amount of heterogeneity produced may depend on plant diversity. For example, some growth forms are likely to be most effective at consuming soil resources, and others at consuming light, so that a highly diverse community supporting various growth forms may generate patches where different resources are limiting, creating a mosaic of contrasting competitive effects (Wilson and Tilman 1991). In contrast, a low-diversity community with only one growth form would generate only one kind of competitive effect. Evidence for this comes from competition experiments in high- and low-diversity vegetation.

The establishment of experimental gradients of N availability in high-diversity-old fields in Minnesota results in complete turnover in species composition (Tilman 1987). Quadrats (0.5×1 m) contain an average of nine plant species (Wilson and Tilman 1991). Transplants of the grass *Agropyron repens* were grown in both low and high nitrogen plots in one of three competition treatments: either without neighbours, or with only the roots of neighbours (nets tied back neighbour shoots), or with both neighbour roots and shoots. Differences between the competition treatments indicated the relative importance of root and shoot competition. In unfertilized pots, neighbour roots reduced transplant growth to the same extent as all neighbours; shoots had no effect beyond that of roots, suggesting that all competitive effects were among roots (Fig. 4.3a). With added N, however, neighbour roots had no effect on growth, but growth was decreased by shoots (Fig. 4.3a). Thus, competition shifted from roots to shoots as N increased standing crop and shade. As a result, plant competition shifted from below-to above-ground as N availability increased (Wilson and Tilman 1991), generating heterogeneity in the

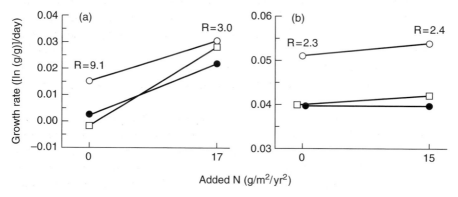

Figure 4.3 Diversity and plant competition. (a) Growth rates of transplants of the grass *Agropyron repens* in a species-rich-old field in Minnesota (data from Wilson and Tilman 1991). R: species richness in 50×100 cm quadrats. Open circles: transplants grown without neighbours; squares: transplants grown with only the roots of neighbours (nets tied back neighbour shoots); closed circles: transplants grown with both neighbour roots and shoots. Without added N, neighbour roots reduced transplant growth to about the same extent as all neighbours; shoots had no effect beyond that of roots. With added N, neighbour roots had no effect on growth, but growth was decreased by shoots. Thus, competition shifted from roots to shoots as N increased standing crop and shade, and species composition changed. (b) As above, but transplants of *Agropyron cristatum* were grown in a species-poor-old field in Saskatchewan (data from Peltzer *et al.* 1998). Competition was among roots regardless of added N, even though added N increased standing crop and shade as it did above. In this case, however, neither diversity or species composition varied with added N. Comparison of the two figures suggests that plant competition shifts from roots to shoots with increasing productivity only in species-rich vegetation with a potential for species turnover. Thus, heterogeneity in competitive effects occurred in species-rich but not in species-poor vegetation.

nature of competitive effects. In this species-rich field, experimentally created nutrient-poor patches are dominated by species which exert most of their competitive effects below-ground; nutrient-rich patches are dominated by species which exert most of their competitive effects above-ground.

In contrast, low-diversity grassland in Saskatchewan shows no change in species composition along experimental gradients of N availability comparable to those in Minnesota (Peltzer *et al.* 1998). Quadrats (0.5×1 m) contain only about two plant species. Competition experiments similar to those in the Minnesota field, using *Agropyron cristatum*, showed no shift from below- to above-ground competition as N availability increased: competition was among roots at all levels of N availability (Fig. 4.3b).

Thus, fertilization had the same ecosystem-level effects at two sites (increased standing crop and decreased light), but competition shifted from roots to shoots only at the high-diversity site where species composition also varied, and did not change at the low-diversity site without variation in species composition. The differences between the Minnesota and Saskatchewan grasslands suggest that high diversity allows not only changes in species composition, but also allows heterogeneity in the nature of competitive effects. The richer array of competitive effects in species-rich vegetation might feed back on diversity by allowing some species to succeed in patches dominated by strong competition for nutrients, and others to succeed in patches with strong competition for light. The difference between the results from Minnesota and Saskatchewan suggest a positive effect of diversity on biogenic heterogeneity.

A shift from root to shoot competition in species-rich vegetation can entrain feedbacks that further alter species composition and heterogeneity. For example, the diversity of the species-poor Saskatchewan old field described above was artificially enhanced by establishing clumps of *Symphoricarpos occidentalis*, a shrub, or *Picea glauca*, a tree (Li and Wilson 1998). Individuals of *Symphoricarpos* transplanted into the clumps had higher growth rates than those transplanted into the low-diversity background vegetation composed exclusively of grass. Similarly, individuals of *Picea* transplanted into the clumps had higher survivorship than those transplanted into the background vegetation. This facilitation by conspecific neighbours suggests that experimentally enhanced diversity promoted the invasion of grassland by trees through the creation of heterogeneity in resource availability and competitive effects. Experimental measurements of the effects of species clumps on heterogeneity should be relatively easy to do, but, apart from simulation models, are lacking (Steinberg and Kareiva 1997).

Differences among species in resource uptake could also cause diversity to increase heterogeneity. For example, the roots of five species of grasses differed significantly in the extent to which they affected the rhizome density of plants exploring potted soil (Schmid and Bazzaz 1992), presumably because the five grasses differed in their effects on soil resources. In a similar experiment, the species identity of neighbour roots had a much greater effect on the root growth of target plants than did nutrient patches (Huber-Sannwald *et al.* 1998), indicating that root growth was more strongly influenced by biogenic heterogeneity than by abiotic heterogeneity. There were also significant differences among the exploring species in their ability to grow among neighbour roots (Huber-Sannwald *et al.* 1997). Thus differences among species in the responses of their roots to neighbours, as well as differences among species in their effects on soil resources, are two other mechanisms by which increased diversity can increase heterogeneity.

Soil interactions other than competition, such as hydraulic lift, also allow diversity to increase heterogeneity. Hydraulic lift occurs when the roots of a tree or shrub raise water from deep, wet soils, and allow it to leak out into dry surface soils, creating patches of soil moisture that are used by grasses or forbs (Caldwell *et al.* 1998). A grassland with a relatively high diversity of growth forms, including trees and shrubs, will therefore have more spatial heterogeneity in soil moisture than a grassland dominated by only graminoids. Hydraulic lift also causes daily fluctuations in soil moisture (Dawson 1993), increasing temporal heterogeneity.

Diversity can also affect the heterogeneity of nutrient mineralization. The leaf litter of three tree species in North Carolina showed two-fold differences in N dynamics depending on whether the litter decomposed in mixes of all three species or in samples of litter from a single species: mixes had faster initial N release than did litter of single species (Blair *et al.* 1990). The difference between mixtures and single-species litter was probably caused by the availability of litter of differing suitability to decomposer communities. Thus, litter diversity controlled mineralization rates and potentially the temporal variability of N availability in these forests.

Alternatively, diversity might have a negative effect on resource heterogeneity because many species might exploit environmental space more effectively than few species (Tilman *et al.* 1996). In this scenario, high diversity means that resources are exploited everywhere and all the time, resulting in uniformly low availability, i.e. low heterogeneity. For example, added N was conserved more efficiently by mixes of C_3 and C_4 grasses than by separate stands in Colorado (Epstein *et al.* 1998), presumably because of complementarity in the seasons during which grasses with different photosynthetic pathways are most active: C_3 grasses in the spring and fall, and C_4 grasses in the summer. Similarly, in a dry California grassland, temporal variability in soil moisture induced by sporadic rainfall was buffered by patterns of water use that were complementary among species (Schimel *et al.* 1989). Complementarity between plants and soil microbes can decrease the temporal heterogeneity of nutrients. The early spring flush of nutrient mineralization in Michigan forests was immobilized by microbes while the plants were dormant (Zak *et al.* 1990). Thus, the coexistence of species or taxa with contrasting strategies for resource uptake can decrease heterogeneity.

Allen and Starr (1982) proposed that diversity could have either negative or positive effects on heterogeneity. A system with few connections between trophic levels might become less heterogeneous if more species are added: more species would increase connections between levels, providing alternate routes for the transfer of energy and nutrients. In contrast, a system which is already well-connected will display more biogenic heterogeneity if diversity increases and more complex connections cause time lags, cycles and chaos.

In summary, there are many ways that diversity could enhance heterogeneity, but there are few direct examples, and there are also mechanisms whereby diversity could decrease heterogeneity. The next section considers a biotic mechanism that may be more important than diversity in creating heterogeneity: the scale of the dominant organisms.

Scale, heterogeneity and diversity

The great continuum of body sizes and scales of heterogeneity makes their relationship difficult to study (Holt 1993). This problem is alleviated somewhat by considering each as a relative function of the other (Allen and Starr 1982). The response of an organism to heterogeneity depends on its size. A tree, for example, would be little affected by a 1×1 m patch because it samples a much larger area, whereas a grass could be greatly affected by a patch of that size. The tree might respond to heterogeneity characterized by a 10×10 m patch, whereas a grass would not, since the patch so greatly exceeds the sampling area of the grass, and it would merely perceive the patch as a uniform good or poor environment. The same argument holds for potential N competitors of different scales, such as a grass and a bacterium. Thus, there are differences among soil nutrient consumers (bacteria, herbs, shrubs, trees) in the patchiness they recognize (Kotliar and Wiens 1990). These diverse consumers probably all perceive similar lower scales of heterogeneity via root hairs and small bacterial cells; they differ, of course, in the extent over which they forage. An organism with large size (or mobility in the case of animals) perceives less heterogeneity than a small organism because it samples both rich and poor patches and integrates them physiologically (Huston 1994). A small organism might perceive more heterogeneity because of the fractal nature of landscapes, plants and soils (Williamson and Lawton 1991).

The effect of an organism on heterogeneity also depends on its size (Pinel-Alloul *et al.* 1988; Schlesinger *et al.* 1990; Barry and Dayton 1991; Berendse 1993; Grime 1994). Large organisms may generate large amounts of heterogeneity and, in turn, benefit from this because of their large size. Woody species with permanent, widely spread roots, for example, could average over small-scale variation, whereas a smaller plant such as a grass or forb could not. Large organisms might increase heterogeneity to a level at which they are successful but small organisms are hindered. Thus, increasing heterogeneity might be a mechanism of competitive displacement, with consequences for diversity.

Examples of the influence of organism scale on heterogeneity are few and mostly indirect. The introduction of cattle to dry grasslands in New Mexico removed grass cover and allowed runoff, increasing the spatial scale of heterogeneity as water and nutrients accumulated in low spots. These sites encouraged the increase of creosote bush (*Larrea tridentata*) which then maintained the system at this new large-scale level of heterogeneity (Schlesinger *et al.* 1990). The coefficients of variation (CV) of N and P were higher under shrubs than grasses (Schlesinger *et al.* 1996). Extensive root excavation showed an even distribution of fine roots under grassland and a patchy distribution of coarse roots under *Larrea* (Connin *et al.* 1997).

As noted above, the CVs of light and available N along 90-cm long transects were significantly higher in aspen forest than in adjacent native grassland in southern Saskatchewan (Kleb and Wilson 1997). Similar results were found for soil moisture and soil available N (sum of ammonium and nitrate) when samples of the same size (1×1 cm) were taken along the perimeter of 10-cm diameter cores. The concordance of results, of relatively high heterogeneity in forest compared with prairie for both 90 cm long transects and 10 cm diameter cores, shows that differences in heterogeneity between habitats are robust at two plant-relevant scales.

Two lines of evidence suggested that differences in heterogeneity between prairie and forest were caused by differences between the scale of trees and grasses, and did not simply reflect a preference by aspen for more heterogeneous substrates. First, only young aspen stands were sampled; tree rings, tree sizes, and published invasion rates suggest that soils currently dominated by aspens were prairie a few decades earlier (Kleb and Wilson 1997).

Second, we conducted a soil transplant experiment (Fig. 4.4). Soils cores (10 cm diameter, 15 cm deep) were moved early in the growing season from prairie to forest, and from forest to prairie. Controls (prairie to prairie, and forest to forest) were also performed to account for disturbance effects. Transplanted cores were

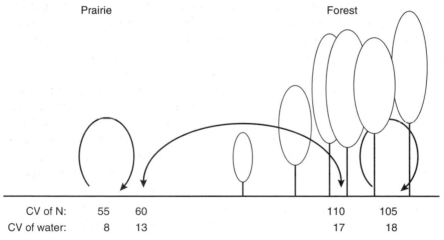

	Prairie		Forest	
CV of N:	55	60	110	105
CV of water:	8	13	17	18

Figure 4.4 The influence of prairie and forest soils on the heterogeneity (coefficient of variation, CV) of soil available N and water within 10 cm diameter tubes. Loops indicate soils transplanted back into their original habitats. The two-headed arrow indicates soils moved to the different habitat. Both resources were significantly (*P* < 0.05) more variable in forest than in prairie. Prairie soils moved to forest for five months attained the high variability of forest soils. Forest soils moved to prairie attained the low variability of prairie soils. Data from Kleb and Wilson (1997).

sampled at the end of the growing season by taking 10 samples (1×1 cm, 15 cm deep) from the perimeter of each core, and calculating the CV of soil available N and moisture in each of the 10 cores in each of the four treatments. Soils moved from prairie to forest showed significant increases in heterogeneity. Similarly, soils moved from forest to prairie showed significant decreases in heterogeneity. To a surprising degree, the heterogeneity of soils moved to the contrasting habitat achieved the heterogeneity of the new habitat (Fig. 4.4). The factors that influenced heterogeneity worked within the five-month period of the experiment. The results suggest that differences in heterogeneity between prairie and forest are caused by the vegetation that dominates them.

The high heterogeneity under invading aspen matches the predictions of Schlesinger *et al.* (1990, 1996) about the influence of large species on heterogeneity. Briggs *et al.* (1989) showed the variability of biomass was significantly greater in forest than in nearby prairie. Likewise, the CV of root mass and understory shoot mass was significantly higher in Saskatchewan forest than in prairie (Kleb and Wilson 1997). All of this suggests that differences in scale between trees and grasses contributed to the differences observed in the heterogeneity of soil resources associated with each. Woody species might have increased heterogeneity in this case because of their relatively coarse root systems.

In order to test whether root uptake contributed to differences in heterogeneity between prairie and forest, we repeated the soil transplant experiment, but with half the cores enclosed in plastic tubes to exclude roots (Wilson and Kleb 1996). The CVs of both soil N and moisture were consistently higher in cores to which roots had access, suggesting that roots contributed to spatial heterogeneity in soil resources. There was, however, no significant interaction between root exclosure and the habitat into which cores were moved. In other words, the more-patchily distributed roots in forest (Kleb and Wilson 1997) did not increase spatial heterogeneity more than the more-evenly distributed roots in prairie.

Stemflow also contributes to soil heterogeneity. Canopies of *Larrea* intercept 17% of precipitation and the resultant stemflow has ion concentrations 10 times greater than rainwater, as dryfall is washed off stems (Whitford *et al.* 1997). Stemflow results in increased soil moisture and cations around tropical tree trunks (Herwitz 1986) and different patterns above and below trunks growing on a slope in a German beech forest (Wittig and Neite 1985). The importance of stemflow to heterogeneity can be expected to increase with plant size.

Trees might also cause higher temporal variability in soil moisture than grasses, because their great shoot mass intercepts and holds rain, some of which evaporates without reaching the soil (Clark 1940). Saskatchewan aspen stands, for example, have a standing crop of about 7.5 kg/m^2 compared with 0.1 kg/m^2 in adjacent prairie (Wilson 1993). Small amounts of rainfall might result in all the water being trapped by tree canopies and evaporated without wetting the soil; the same amount of rainfall might exceed the interception ability of the grass canopy and wet the soil. Relatively large amounts of rain would penetrate the canopies of both trees and grasses. The less frequent penetration of tree canopies could alter the

63

temporal variability of soil moisture beneath trees. The temporal variability of soil moisture beneath trees might also be increased by their relatively large mass producing higher rates of evapotranspiration.

Evidence for higher temporal variability under woody plants was found in a successional study of heath in the UK. The amount of rain collected beneath an early successional heath with little cover of the shrub *Calluna* had an among-month CV of 28%. In contrast, rain collected from a more mature heath dominated by *Calluna* had a CV of 65% (Barclay-Estrup 1971; data taken from Fig. 12a). The difference between successional stages presumably reflects greater interception in plots with more shrub cover.

We explored the influence of scale on the temporal heterogeneity of soil moisture by growing single-species stands (1.4×1.4 m) of five grasses and five woody species for 3 years in a Saskatchewan old-field (Peltzer and Wilson, unpublished data). Plots without any vegetation were also established in order to study the contribution of vegetation to temporal heterogeneity. Among-month CVs for soil moisture were significantly higher under woody plants than grasses (Fig. 4.5). Diversity was identical in all plots, so the results show that plant size can influence heterogeneity in the absence of variation in diversity. Interestingly, the CVs of grass plots were very similar to those of unvegetated plots, again suggesting that large plants contribute to heterogeneity; in this case, smaller grasses had no effect on temporal heterogeneity. Positive correlations between body size and heterogeneity have also been noted in freshwater (Pinel-Alloul *et al.* 1988) and marine systems (Barry and Dayton 1991).

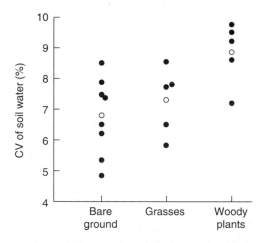

Figure 4.5 Among-month variability in soil water in three-year-old plots containing bare ground, single-species stands of grasses, or single-species stands of woody plants. Woody plants increased temporal variability more than grasses (Peltzer and Wilson, unpublished data). Dots are individual plots in the case of bare ground, and represent separate species for grasses and woody plants. Open circles are means.

The scale of biogenic heterogeneity should also vary with plant size. The scale of heterogeneity, however, is not necessarily linked to the amount of heterogeneity (Miller *et al.* 1995; Weins, this volume). Two habitats with similar patch sizes would have similar scales of heterogeneity, but could differ in the amount of heterogeneity if there is strong contrast between patch quality in one habitat but not the other. Alternatively patch size might be large in one habitat and small in another, but differences between patch types would be equal in both habitats, so that they differ in the scale but not the amount of heterogeneity.

The difference in size between grasses and aspen trees suggests that the habitats dominated by each might differ in the scale of heterogeneity. Kleb and Wilson (1999) further examined the 90-cm transects in both prairie and forest described above by taking a second series of 10 samples (each 1×1 cm) along each transect. Each sample in this second series was paired with one transect sample, but offset by a distance of 0, 1, 2, 4, 8, 16, 32, 64, 128 or 256 cm, at right angles to the transect. Offset distances were assigned randomly along the transect. The same variables that were measured along the transect were also measured in the second series. For each variable and each distance, we calculated the coefficient of correlation between the first and second series of samples, using each transect as a replicate. If spatially dependent variation occurred in the 0–256 cm range examined, then pairs of samples close together should be highly positively correlated (i.e. $r=1$), whereas samples further apart should be uncorrelated ($r=0$). We tested whether correlation coefficients decreased with increasing distance between paired samples (Bell and Lechowicz 1991). Correlation coefficients decreased significantly with increasing distance for several variables in the prairie transects, but in only one case in the forest transects. This suggests that the scale of heterogeneity in prairie tended to fall within the range examined (0–256 cm), but that heterogeneity in forest occurred at larger scales. Thus, both the scale and amount (Fig. 4.4) of heterogeneity were greater in forest than prairie.

The effects of organism size on spatial heterogeneity might be influenced by temporal heterogeneity. For example, the relatively high heterogeneity of soil resources under trees relative to grasses in Saskatchewan (Fig. 4.4) could reflect either spatial or temporal causes. High heterogeneity in forest might occur because of differences in the scale of roots of woody and grassy vegetation (e.g. Connin *et al.* 1997). Alternatively, high spatial variability could be caused by high temporal variability in the production and decomposition of tree roots. Although direct comparisons are lacking, a review suggests that root turnover in trees is generally higher than that in grasses, by as much as four-fold (Wilson 1998). The effect of high rates of root production and decomposition on a one-time sample of spatial heterogeneity would be to enhance it.

In summary, there is growing evidence that both the amount and scale of biogenic heterogeneity is strongly influenced by organism scale. Future studies will determine the generality of this influence, and the mechanisms through which organism scale controls heterogeneity.

Future directions

Direct, replicated measures of heterogeneity and diversity under a variety of conditions would allow quantification of the relationship between them. Heterogeneity measurements should be relatively fast and simple so that broad ranges of the independent variables can be examined with good representation at all levels. Measuring coefficients of variation at plant-relevant scales is one such approach (Kleb and Wilson 1997). In contrast, geostatistical analyses such as semivariograms are very sample-intensive and, while they provide much information about the sampled area, they make extensive comparisons among treatments of particular interest relatively expensive.

Direct measurements of heterogeneity might allow us to address relatively straightforward, but currently unanswered, questions about the relationship between heterogeneity and diversity: under what conditions is it positive, neutral or negative? What is the slope of the positive relationships, where they exist? What is the intercept when heterogeneity is zero? How do the slope and intercept vary? Is the exponential phase of a possibly sigmoid relationship between diversity and heterogeneity the result of positive feedbacks? Is an asymptotic relationship the result of negative feedbacks? Such measurements would also force us to consider what aspects of heterogeneity are being considered: scale, variability, or contrast.

While niche-partitioning is well-documented, the possibility that species partition heterogeneity needs more comparative measurements. Do species from rich and poor habitats really fall out as separate groups in the way they partition heterogeneity? Or will the consideration of many species simply reveal a continuum of responses only weakly related to life-history?

Experiments could also address the effect of diversity on heterogeneity. The extensive theoretical and modelling literature on diversity and heterogeneity (e.g. Allen and Starr 1982; Ricklefs and Schluter 1993; Huston and DeAngelis 1994; Tilman and Kareiva 1997) is a rich source of ideas for experiments. Do initially homogeneous mixes of species produce clumps in a uniform environment? Do the clumps produce abiotic heterogeneity? Do the clumps retain diversity longer than mixes? Answers to all of these questions require more direct measurements of heterogeneity, in both natural and experimental communities.

Acknowledgments

I thank D. MacDonald for library work, S. James for indexing, D. Peltzer for data help, H. Hager, L. Heidinga, M. Hutchings, E. John, M. Köchy, D. Peltzer, A. Stewart and an anonymous reviewer for comments, and the Natural Sciences and Engineering Research Council of Canada for support.

References

Allen, T.F.H. and Starr, T.B. (1982) *Hierarchy: Perspectives for Ecological Complexity*. University of Chicago Press, Chicago.

Barclay-Estrup, P. (1971) The description and interpretation of cyclical processes in a heath community. III. Micro-climate in relation to the *Calluna* cycle. *Journal of Ecology* **59**, 143–166.

Barry, J.P. and Dayton, P.K. (1991) Physical heterogeneity and the organization of marine communities. In: *Ecological Heterogeneity* (eds J. Kolasa and S.T.A. Pickett), pp. 270–320. Springer-Verlag, New York.

Bell, G. and Lechowicz, M.J. (1991) The ecology and genetics of fitness in forest plants. I. Environmental heterogeneity measured by explant traits. *Journal of Ecology* **79**, 663–685.

Berendse, F. (1993) Ecosystem stability, competition, and nutrient cycling. In: *Biodiversity and Ecosystem Function* (eds E.-D. Schultze and H.A. Mooney), pp. 409–431. Springer-Verlag, Berlin.

Blair, J.M., Parmalee, R.W. and Beare, M.H. (1990) Decay rates, nitrogen fluxes, and decomposer communities of single- and mixed-species foliar litter. *Ecology* **71**, 1976–1985.

Briggs, J.M., Seastedt, T.R. and Gibson, D.J. (1989) Comparative analysis of temporal and spatial variability in above-ground production in a Kansas forest and prairie. *Holarctic Ecology* **12**, 130–136.

Caldwell, M.M., Dawson, T.E. and Richards, J.H. (1998) Hydraulic lift: consequences of water efflux from the roots of plants. *Oecologia* **113**, 151–161.

Caldwell, M.M. and Pearcy, R.W. (1994) *Exploitation of environmental heterogeneity by plants. Ecophysiological Processes Above and Below Ground*. Academic Press, New York.

Caley, M.J. and Schluter, D. (1997) The relationship between local and regional diversity. *Ecology* **78**, 70–80.

Campbell, B.D. and Grime, J.P. (1989) A comparative study of plant responsiveness to the duration of episodes of mineral nutrient enrichment. *New Phytologist* **112**, 261–267.

Campbell, B.D., Grime, J.P. and Mackey, J.M.L. (1991) A tradeoff between scale and precision in resource foraging. *Oecologia* **87**, 532–538.

Clark, O.R. (1940) Interception of rainfall by prairie grasses, weeds, and certain crop plants. *Ecological Monographs* **10**, 243–277.

Connin, S.L., Virginia, R.A. and Chamberlain, C.P. (1997) Carbon isotopes reveal soil organic matter dynamics following arid land shrub expansion. *Oecologia* **110**, 374–386.

Dawson, T.E. (1993) Hydraulic lift and water use by plants: implications for water balance, performance and plant–plant interactions. *Oecologia* **95**, 565–574.

Epstein, H.E., Burke, I.C. and Mosier, A.R. (1998) Plant effects on spatial and temporal patterns of nitrogen cycling in shortgrass steppe. *Ecosystems* **1**, 374–385.

Fowler, N.L. (1988) The effects of environmental heterogeneity in space and time on the regulation of populations and communities. In: *Plant Population Ecology, 28th Symposium of the British Ecological Society* (eds A.J. Davy, M.J. Hutchings and A.R. Watkinson), pp. 249–269. Blackwell Scientific Publications, Oxford.

Fowler, N.L. (1990) Disorderliness in plant communities: comparisons, causes, and consequences. In: *Perspectives in Plant Competition* (eds J.B. Grace and D. Tilman), pp. 291–306. Academic Press, San Diego.

Goldberg, D. and Novoplansky, A. (1997) On the relative importance of competition in unproductive environments. *Journal of Ecology* **85**, 409–418.

Grime, J.P. (1994) The role of plasticity in exploiting environmental heterogeneity. In: *Exploitation of Environmental Heterogeneity by Plants* (eds M.M. Caldwell and R.W. Pearcy), pp. 1–19. Academic Press, San Diego.

Guégan, J.-F., Lek, S. and Oberdoff, T. (1998) Energy availability and habitat heterogeneity predict global riverine fish diversity. *Nature* **391**, 382–384.

Herwitz, S.R. (1986) Episodic stemflow inputs of magnesium and potassium to a tropical forest floor during heavy rainfall events. *Oecologia* **70**, 423–425.

Holt, R.D. (1993) Ecology at the mesoscale: the influence of regional processes on local communities. In: *Species Diversity in Ecological Communities: Historical and Geographical Perspectives* (eds R.E. Ricklefs and D. Schluter), pp. 77–88. University of Chicago Press, Chicago.

Huber-Sannwald, E., Pyke, D.A. and Caldwell, M.M. (1997) Perception of neighbouring plants by rhizomes and roots: morphological manifestations of a clonal plant. *Canadian Journal of Botany* 75, 2146–2157.

Huber-Sannwald, E., Pyke, D.A., Caldwell, M.M. and Durham, S. (1998) Effects of nutrient patches and root systems on the clonal plasticity of a rhizomatous grass. *Ecology* 79, 2267–2280.

Hunter, M.D. and Price, P.W. (1992) Playing chutes and ladders: heterogeneity and the relative roles of bottom-up and top-down forces in natural communities. *Ecology* 73, 724–732.

Huston, M.A. (1994) *Biological Diversity. The Coexistence of Species on Changing Landscapes.* Cambridge University Press, Cambridge.

Huston, M.A. and DeAngelis, D.L. (1994) Competition and coexistence: the effects of resource transport and supply rates. *American Naturalist* 144, 954–977.

Hutchings, M.J. and de Kroon, M.J. (1994) Foraging in plants: the role of morphological plasticity in resource acquisition. *Advances in Ecological Research* 25, 159–238.

Kleb, H.R. and Wilson, S.D. (1997) Vegetation effects on soil resource heterogeneity in prairie and forest. *American Naturalist* 150, 283–298.

Kleb, H.R. and Wilson, S.D. (1999) Scales of heterogeneity in prairie and forest. *Canadian Journal of Botany* 77, 370–376.

Kohn, D.D. and Walsh, D.M. (1994) Plant species richness—the effect of island size and habitat diversity. *Journal of Ecology* 82, 367–377.

Kotliar, N.B. and Wiens, J.A. (1990) Multiple scales of patchiness and patch structure: a hierarchical framework for the study of heterogeneity. *Oikos* 59, 253–260.

Li, X. and Wilson, S.D. (1998) Facilitation among woody plants establishing in an old field. *Ecology* 79, 2694–2705.

Miao, S.L. and Bazzaz, F.A. (1990) Responses to nutrient pulses of two colonizers requiring different disturbance frequencies. *Ecology* 71, 2166–2178.

Miller, R.E., Version Hoeff, J.M. and Fowler, N.L. (1995) Spatial heterogeneity in eight central Texas grasslands. *Journal of Ecology* 83, 919–928.

Mou, P., Mitchell, R.J. and Jones, R.H. (1997) Root distribution of two tree species under a heterogeneous nutrient environment. *Journal of Applied Ecology* 34, 645–656.

Peltzer, D.A., Wilson, S.D. and Gerry, A.K. (1998) Competition intensity along a productivity gradient in a low-diversity grassland. *American Naturalist* 151, 465–476.

Pinel-Alloul, B., Downing, J.A., Perusse, M. and Codin-Blumer, G. (1988) Spatial heterogeneity in freshwater zooplankton: variation with body size, depth, and scale. *Ecology* 69, 1393–1400.

Ricklefs, R.E. and Schluter, D. (1993) Species diversity in ecological communities. In: *Historical and Geographical Perspectives.* University of Chicago Press, Chicago.

Robertson, G.P. and Gross, K.L. (1994) Assessing the heterogeneity of belowground resources: quantifying pattern and scale. In: *Exploitation of Environmental Heterogeneity by Plants* (eds M.M. Caldwell and R.W. Pearcy), pp. 237–253. Academic Press, San Diego.

Rorison, I.H. (1987) Mineral nutrition in time and space. *New Phytologist* 106 (Suppl.), 79–92.

Rosenzweig, M.L. (1995) *Species Diversity in Space and Time.* Cambridge University Press, New York.

Schimel, J.P., Jackson, L.E. and Firestone, M.K. (1989) Spatial and temporal effects on plant-microbe competition for inorganic nitrogen in a California annual grassland. *Soil Biology and Biochemistry* 21, 1059–1066.

Schlesinger, W.H., Raikes, J.A., Hartley, A.E. and Cross, A.F. (1996) On the spatial pattern of soil nutrients in desert ecosystems. *Ecology* 77, 364–374.

Schlesinger, W.H., Reynolds, J.F., Cunningham, G.L. *et al.* (1990) Biological feedbacks in global desertification. *Science* 247, 1043–1048.

Schmid, B. and Bazzaz, F.A. (1992) Growth and responses of rhizomatous plants to fertilizer application and interference. *Oikos* 65, 13–24.

Steinberg, E.K. and Kareiva, P. (1997) Challenges and opportunities for empirical evaluation of 'spatial theory'. In: *Spatial Ecology: the Role of Space in Population Dynamics and Interspecific Interactions* (eds D. Tilman and P. Kareiva), pp. 318–331. Princeton University Press, Princeton.

Tilman, D. (1987) Secondary succession and the pattern of plant dominance along experimental nitrogen gradients. *Ecological Monographs* **57**, 189–214.

Tilman, D. and Kareiva, P. (1998) *Spatial Ecology. The Role of Space in Population Dynamics and Interspecific Interactions*. Princeton University Press, Princeton.

Tilman, D., Wedin, D. and Knops, J. (1996) Productivity and sustainability influenced by biodiversity in grassland ecosystems. *Nature* **379**, 718–720.

Vivian-Smith, G. (1997) Microtopographic heterogeneity and floristic diversity in experimental wetland communities. *Journal of Ecology* **85**, 71–82.

Whitford, W.G., Anderson, J. and Rice, P.M. (1997) Stemflow contributions to the 'fertile island' effect in creosotebush, *Larrea tridentata. Journal of Arid Environments* **35**, 451–457.

Williamson, M.H. and Lawton, J.H. (1991) Fractal geometry of ecological habitats. In: *Habitat Structure: the Physical Arrangement of Objects in Space* (eds S.S. Bell, E.D. McCoy and H.R. Mushinsky), pp. 69–86. Chapman and Hall, London.

Wilson, S.D. (1993) Belowground competition in forest and prairie. *Oikos* **68**, 146–150.

Wilson, S.D. (1998) Competition between grasses and woody plants. In: *Population Biology of Grasses* (ed. G.P. Cheplick), pp. 231–254. Cambridge University Press, Cambridge.

Wilson, S.D. and Kleb, H.R. (1996) The influence of prairie and forest vegetation on soil moisture and available nitrogen. *American Midland Naturalist* **136**, 222–231.

Wilson, S.D. and Tilman, D. (1991) Components of plant competition along an experimental gradient of nitrogen availability. *Ecology* **72**, 1050–1065.

Wilson, S.D. and Tilman, D. (1995) Competitive responses of eight old-field plant species in four environments. *Ecology* **76**, 1169–1180.

Wittig, R. and Neite, H. (1985) Acid indicators around the trunk base of *Fagus sylvatica* in limestone and loess beechwoods: distribution pattern and phytosociological problems. *Vegetatio* **64**, 113–119.

Zak, D.R., Groffman, P.M., Pregitzer, K.S., Christensen, S. and Tiedje, J.M. (1990) The vernal dam: plant-microbe competition for nitrogen in northern hardwood forests. *Ecology* **71**, 651–656.

Chapter 5

Plant response to patchy soils

A. Fitter[1], A. Hodge[1] and D. Robinson[2]

Heterogeneity in soils

Soils are inherently patchy because they are physically the most complex of all environments, comprising solid, liquid and gas phases. The solid phase is of particular importance in determining the nature of soil heterogeneity. Most inputs to soil (including those derived from the parent material and from organic sources) are in solid form. The movement of materials in the solid phase is very much slower than their movement in fluids, which limits the extent to which local variations will disperse over time.

For nutrient ions, the difference in mobility can easily be quantified: all ions diffuse at approximately the same rate (diffusion coefficients, D, $\sim 10^{-9} \, m^2 \, s^{-1}$) in free solution. In soil, however, the ions in solution interact with charged surfaces that restrict their mobility. For some ions, this effect is rather slight. Nitrates are universally soluble in water, and so the only restraints on nitrate diffusion are physical ones relating to the longer pathway that ions must follow in a soil compared with water. The diffusion coefficient for nitrate in soil is therefore around $10^{-10} \, m^2 \, s^{-1}$. Phosphate ions, in contrast, form insoluble complexes with most of the abundant cations in soil, notably Al^{3+}, Fe^{3+} and Ca^{2+}. Consequently, diffusion of phosphate is far slower, $\sim 10^{-13}$–$10^{-15} \, m^2 \, s^{-1}$ (Tinker and Nye 2000). The distance that an ion diffuses in a given time is proportional to $\sqrt{D}$ and because nitrate ions therefore diffuse about 100 times faster in soil than phosphate ions, the distribution of phosphate in soil will be inherently more patchy than that of nitrate. Since roots can absorb only those ions that are transported to them by diffusion and mass flow (Tinker and Nye 2000) these differences in mobility have large consequences for plant nutrition.

The solid phase of soils also creates heterogeneity from inputs. Leaf litter falls to, and accumulates on, the surface of many soils; animal activity may spread it more evenly. Roots die where they are produced; although they are already widely dispersed through soil (but predominantly in the surface layers in most soils: Jackson *et al.* 1996), on a fine scale they also generate heterogeneity. Although we know that this patchiness exists, and although we understand (and can predict) aspects of it for many soils, our knowledge tends to be confined to the coarser scales of heterogeneity. Fine scale patchiness, created by dying roots or animals in soil, is much less

[1]*Department of Biology, University of York, Heslington, York YO10 5YW, UK;* [2]*Department of Plant and Soil Science, University of Aberdeen, Aberdeen AB24 3MM, UK*

well characterized, and will clearly not be random. Roots, for example, are distributed throughout the soil in a fashion determined by the architecture of the root system. Architecture is, in turn, constrained developmentally but with considerable plasticity induced by local environmental stimuli.

Geostatistical techniques have been used to map the distributions of various nutrients in soil at cm scales and above. For example, Jackson and Caldwell (1993) found that the concentration of extractable P varied by 40% in a 50×50 cm area of sagebrush steppe. Within that area, patches (< 10 cm diameter) were found in which P was significantly more concentrated than the mean for the plot. At the same site, patches of soil nitrate and ammonium were evident at larger spatial scales, their concentrations showing strong spatial patterns at distances within 1 m and varying by ~100–400%. This variation probably reflects the microbial transformations (e.g. nitrification, denitrification, immobilization) within, and physical transport (i.e. diffusion and mass flow) from, microsites where ammonium and nitrate are formed (see below). None of the microbial processes measured by Jackson and Caldwell (nitrification potential, net N mineralization and CO_2 production) showed strong spatial patterns, even when measured at the smallest scales (10–50 cm). This implies that such processes may require even finer sampling scales (~1 cm or less) to detect their spatial variations. Because they are laborious, geostatistical techniques do not allow nutrient distributions to be mapped with very fine spatial and temporal resolution. It is likely that much of the dynamic behaviour of soil nutrients at scales relevant to microbes and roots is being missed (e.g. Stark and Hart 1997).

Although many studies have followed nutrient concentrations in soil through time, few have continued beyond one year. This is an essential requirement if a seasonal, as opposed to a simply temporal, pattern is to be revealed. Farley and Fitter (1999a) followed nitrate and phosphate concentrations in a woodland soil over 2 years. They found that although there was an element of seasonality in the variation, it was much less conspicuous than the non-seasonal component of the variation (Fig. 5.1). In effect, the temporal pattern was unpredictable. Not only did concentrations differ between years by a large amount, but also the timing and magnitude of peak concentrations were different in each year. These findings are consistent with the temporal variation in soil properties (i.e. soil moisture, extractable ammonium-N and N mineralization rates) measured by Ehrenfeld et al. (1997). These investigators proposed that heterogeneity in soil-plant systems should be considered as four-dimensional, continuously changing horizontally and vertically with time. Plants must be morphologically and physiologically responsive to such variations in nutrient availability if they are to optimize nutrient capture.

The complexity of the spatial and temporal patterns of nutrient availability is encapsulated in a simple classification of patches proposed by Fitter (1994). Variation in patch characteristics can be apparent in space or in time, and can be measured as extent (size or duration), number (abundance or frequency) and distribution (pattern or predictability). In addition, patches will vary in concentration

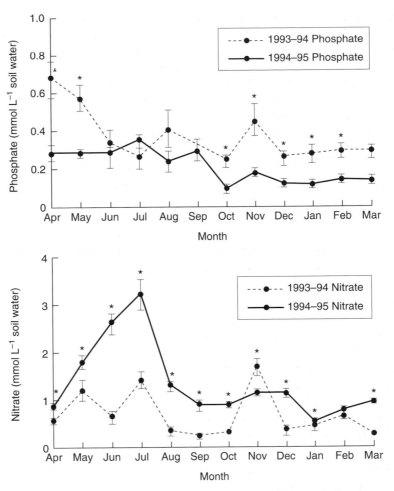

Figure 5.1 Variation in soil nitrate and phosphate concentrations over a 2-year period at a woodland site in N Yorkshire, UK. Concentrations were estimated by water extraction of soil cores sampled at monthly intervals from a regular grid within a nested series of quadrats. Months where significant ($P < 0.05$) differences between years occurred are shown by an asterisk. From Farley and Fitter (1999a), with kind permission from Blackwell Science Ltd.

(intensity) and in the nature of the materials that make up the patch (complexity, quality). Evidently no single pattern of behaviour in plants will be optimal for the exploitation of all patches.

Organic matter decomposition and the generation of heterogeneity

Soil organic matter (SOM) is decomposed by microbes. Rates of C and N release depend on the biochemical capabilities and immediate C and N demands of active microbes. They depend also on the composition of the organic substrates to which microbes have access. Generally, substrates rich in N compared with C (i.e. with a C:N ratio <10) release N more rapidly than C, causing the C:N ratio of the remaining substrate to increase. If C:N>~25, microbes are more N-limited, and they immobilize labile N rather than release it. Qualitatively similar arguments apply to the release of other nutrients (e.g. P) from SOM (see Swift *et al.* 1979).

SOM comprises a multitude of substrates in various stages of decomposition, and soil microbial floras include an equally bewildering array of species and functional groups (Coleman *et al.* 1994). Despite this complexity, Nicolardot *et al.* (1995) proposed that C and N mineralization from plant residues added to soil could be described by a simple equation which assumes that the residues are composed of only 'labile' and 'recalcitrant' fractions:

$$y = A[1 - \exp(-kt)] + bt$$

where y is the cumulative amount of substrate C or N released up to time t, A is the initial size of the labile fraction of C or N, k the mineralization constant of that fraction, and b the mineralization constant of the recalcitrant fraction. For N in herbaceous plant residues, typically $A \sim 30\%$ of total N initially in the residue, $k \sim 0.1\,d^{-1}$ and $b \sim 5 \times 10^{-4}\,d^{-1}$ (Nicolardot *et al.* 1995). Decomposition usually proceeds by an initial, rapid mineralization of N (and C), followed by much slower release as the substrate comes to consist almost entirely of recalcitrant materials. The parameters A, k and b will vary with residue type (e.g. animal or vegetable, herbaceous or woody, live or dead). They will vary also with local environmental factors (e.g. soil structure, moisture, O_2 and temperature, all of which are likely to be correlated to various extents: Jackson and Caldwell 1993). Such variation could easily create a dynamic mosaic of microsites, some of which will be decomposition 'hotspots', while others will be less active. Geostatistical surveys capture only the coarser products of such mosaics as distributions of SOM and nutrients (see p. 72).

The responses of root systems to nutrient patches

The standard view is that root systems respond to patchiness by proliferation of laterals. This response, known for over a century (see Fitter 1987), is exemplified by the dramatic images of barley (*Hordeum vulgare*) root proliferation produced by Malcolm Drew and colleagues (Drew *et al.* 1973; Drew and Saker 1975, 1978; Drew 1975; Fig. 5.2). Those experiments demonstrated that barley responded to a localized supply of nitrate, ammonium or phosphate (but not potassium) by increasing the number of primary lateral roots per unit length of axis. Those laterals became longer and, in turn, carried more secondary laterals compared with plants receiving a uniform supply of nutrients.

In such experiments, the plants were grown in water culture, with a 100-fold concentration difference between background and patch, and the differential supply was maintained continuously. These technical points are important. The

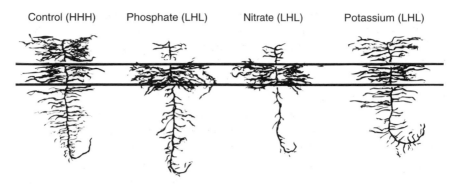

Figure 5.2 The proliferation of primary and secondary laterals by barley (*Hordeum vulgare*) when grown in water culture with a 100-fold greater concentration of various nutrient ions supplied to the middle zone of the axis. Abbreviations: H, high; L, low, which refer to the nutrient concentrations experienced by the top, middle and bottom of the root system, respectively. From Drew (1975), with kind permission from the trustees of the *New Phytologist*.

experimental conditions used by Drew (and many others) were ideal for demonstrating the occurrence of and potential for root proliferation *in vitro*. They were, however, inappropriate to reveal how root proliferation might contribute to uptake from nutrient-rich patches in soil, where the complex interactions among soil physics, chemistry and microbiology are dominant. An ecologist needs to seek generality and realism in experiments, and experimental explorations of the ecological significance of root proliferation were relatively slow to appear.

From such experiments, however, it is now clear that not all plants show the same responses to nutrient-rich patches as does the archetypal root proliferator, barley. For example, Campbell *et al.* (1991) used eight plant species that differed markedly in size, growth rate, habitat preference and competitive dominance when grown in mixed communities. When grown as isolated plants, competitively dominant species placed absolutely more root material into nutrient-rich patches than subordinate species. This placement in nutrient-rich patches represented, however, a relatively smaller fraction of the root system of the dominant species. Campbell *et al.* (1991) suggested that this demonstrated a trade-off between the scale and precision of root placement. Hutchings, Wijesinghe and John (this volume) discuss new interpretations of these data. Here, we note that the data of Campbell *et al.* (1991) clearly demonstrate that not all plant species show the same proliferation response, a point emphasized in Robinson's (1994) survey of the literature on proliferation responses.

If patches vary in certain ways (Fitter 1994), and if not all plant species respond similarly to local nutrient enrichments, different responses to patches of various types are to be expected. Remarkably, this expectation has rarely been tested. Farley and Fitter (1999b) examined proliferation responses of roots of seven plant species chosen because they coexisted at a single site and would therefore encounter a

Table 5.1 Summary of responses of co-existing woodland species to localized nutrient enhancement (from Farley and Fitter 1999b)

	Response to local nutrient enrichment			Responsiveness to patch	
Species	Proliferation	Change in SRL*	Change in branching	Size	Concentration
Silene dioica	✓	✓	✓		✓
Stachys sylvatica	(✓)	(✓)	✓		
Veronica montana	✓		✓		✓
Ajuga reptans	✓	✓	✓		
Glechoma hederacea	✓			✓	

✓ Statistically significant response shown; (✓) large numerical response in mean value but not statistically significant because of high variation between replicates.
Two species (*Viola riviniana* and *Oxalis acetosella*) showed none of these responses; both are probably dependent on mycorrhizal fungi for nutrient acquisition.
* SRL: specific root length (root length/root dry weight).

similar suite of patch characteristics. The plants were offered patches of soil or a soil/sand mixture (so creating variation in patch quality) set in a background of sand. The patches varied in size (40, 70 and 160 cm³), but the probability of encounter was the same for all patches. Only five of the seven species proliferated roots in patches. The two that did not (*Oxalis acetosella* and *Viola riviniana*) had the smallest root systems and thickest roots of the group. There was also evidence that their nutrient uptake depended on mycorrhizal associations to a greater extent than in the other species. Of the remaining five, all showed a proliferation response, but each did so in a unique fashion (Table 5.1). One species (*Glechoma hederacea*) was sensitive to the size of the patch and two other species (*Silene dioica* and *Veronica montana*) responded to patch quality. *G. hederacea* has previously been shown to respond to the spatial scale (Wijesinghe and Hutchings 1997) and the quality (Birch and Hutchings 1994; Wijesinghe and Hutchings 1999, Hutchings, Wijesinghe and John, this volume) of the patch encountered. The nature of the proliferation response detected by Farley and Fitter (1999b) also differed between species. Two species changed specific root length (length of root per unit weight of root) on encountering the patches, with finer roots in the patch. Four showed a change in branching pattern, becoming less herringbone in architecture in the patch, as predicted by theoretical models (Fitter *et al.* 1991).

Local root proliferation in an N-starved plant may be controlled by the root system architecture and the consequent economics of root growth. Farley and Fitter's (1999b) finding that the two least-responsive species had the thickest roots implies that the root growth of those species would be most costly in terms of resource allocation. Another coarse-rooted species, *Ajuga reptans*, responded by a large change in specific root length achieved by the growth of much finer roots than it normally produced. Architectural constraints such as these must be the basis of much variation in root plasticity, but they remain to be elucidated fully.

Such idiosyncrasy of response means that it will be exceptionally difficult to predict the effect of complex variation in patch attributes, such as occurs naturally in soils, on species mixtures. At the same time, this opens up obvious opportunities for species' coexistence and niche differentiation. These would arise from differential responses to a range of spatial and temporal patchiness. Species that respond weakly to nutrient-rich patches by proliferation may do so more strongly by physiological changes (for example, up-regulation of transporters).

Ecological significance of root proliferation in nitrogen-rich patches

The problem

Since plant species show idiosyncratic responses to local nutrient enrichment, one would imagine that it would be simple to demonstrate the intuitively obvious benefits of the response. The identification of a gene (*ANR1*) in *Arabidopsis thaliana* that controls one facet of the proliferation response (lateral elongation) in N-starved plants supplied locally with nitrate (Zhang and Forde 1998) offers an opportunity to manipulate the response. Paradoxically, three recent studies have demonstrated that root proliferation is quite unrelated to N capture. Van Vuuren *et al.* (1996) grew wheat (*Triticum aestivum*) roots through a patch of decomposing ^{15}N-labelled ryegrass leaves in otherwise N-deficient soil. The root systems showed a classic proliferation response, but only after the N released from the patch had largely been absorbed by the existing roots (Fig. 5.3). Increasing the amount of root in such a situation will not increase N capture. The mobility of nitrate in soil is such that single roots can deplete large soil volumes. All the nitrate in a 10-cm diameter patch should be able to diffuse to a single root in 5 days. Unsurprisingly, when roots did eventually proliferate (after 22–28 days), the N inflow (uptake rate per unit root length) declined markedly. Robinson (1996), in a commentary on this, asked 'Why do plants bother?'

Fransen *et al.* (1998) and Hodge *et al.* (1998) each compared the responses of five grasses to soil heterogeneity but used different species. Fransen *et al.* (1998) created heterogeneity by comparing different mixtures of soil and sand; Hodge *et al.* (1998) used the decomposing ryegrass leaves technique of van Vuuren *et al.* (1996). In each case some species proliferated roots more than others, but in neither did this difference in proliferation bear any relation to N capture (Fig. 5.4).

These results give added weight to Robinson's (1996) question. Plants proliferate roots markedly, some much more than others, to a localized supply of nitrate, and there is at least one gene that directly controls this response. Yet on theoretical and experimental grounds this response can be shown to be unable to increase N capture. Zhang and Forde (1998) suggested that this may be because nitrate acts as a general signal for improved soil nutrient status, although that would

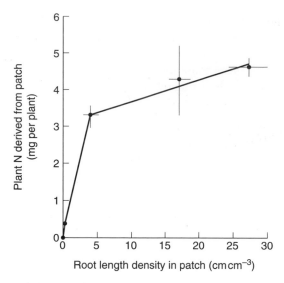

Figure 5.3 Nitrogen (N) capture by wheat roots from a patch of decomposing ryegrass leaves is not linearly related to root length density in the patch, because root proliferation occurred after the majority of plant N uptake. Lines illustrate fitted linear regressions to each phase of the relation, i.e. for root length density (RLD) $< 5\,\text{cm cm}^{-3}$, $N=0.7756$ $\text{RLD}+0.0474$, $R^2=0.999$; for $\text{RLD}>5\,\text{cm cm}^{-3}$, $N=0.0593\,\text{RLD}+3.118$, $R^2=0.963$. From van Vuuren *et al.* (1996), with kind permission from Kluwer Academic Publishers.

not explain why roots also respond specifically to ammonium and phosphate (Drew 1975).

Soil chemistry

The proliferation response to nitrate may be beneficial in terms of increasing the capture of ions other than nitrate. In any nutrient patch, it is inevitable that the concentrations of one ion will be coupled electrochemically to those of others, although the strength of such couplings depends on soil type. For example, Yanai *et al.* (1996) found that increases in nitrate concentration were accompanied by increases in Ca^{2+}, Mg^{2+}, Na^+, K^+ and H^+ concentrations in the soil solution, but by a decrease in phosphate concentration. Therefore, a localized, nitrate-induced root proliferation could engineer an increased uptake of any of these, if not of N. However, the question remains: why should an N-starved plant benefit by having access to more cations when it would still be N-starved?

Cui and Caldwell (1998) investigated the effects of patch composition on the capacities of a grass (*Agropyron desertorum*) and a shrub (*Artemisia tridentata*) to capture N and P from patches of KNO_3 and NaH_2PO_4. Both species captured similar amounts of N (11–21% of the original patch N) whether the patches were added to soil singly (KNO_3 or NaH_2PO_4) or jointly (KNO_3 *plus* NaH_2PO_4). *A. desertorum* captured similar amounts of P irrespective of patch composition.

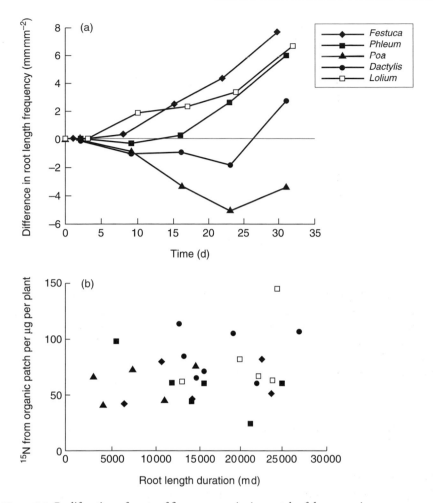

Figure 5.4 Proliferation of roots of five grass species in a patch of decomposing ryegrass material varies greatly in timing and extent. (a) Data are means of patch treatment — control values of root length visible against a glass sheet. However N capture is unrelated to proliferation. (b) Raw data for each species are shown; root length duration is the integral of root length over time. From Hodge *et al.* (1998) with kind permission from the trustees of the *New Phytologist*.

A. tridentata, by contrast, captured more P (per plant and per unit root length) from the single NaH_2PO_4 patch than from the mixed patch (although no plant captured more than 1% of the original patch P by the end of the 60-day experiment). This experiment suggests that plants can apparently 'integrate' some of the effects of nutrient (especially nitrate) patchiness. Much more information is needed, however, for the ecological implications of responses to chemically complex patches to be understood fully.

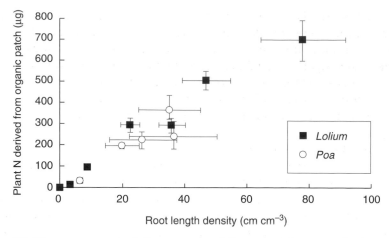

Figure 5.5 Nitrogen capture by *Lolium perenne* and *Poa pratensis* from a patch of decomposing ryegrass is a simple function of root length when the plants are grown in competition. Points shown are means ($n=4$) $\pm$ SE bars of plants harvested with time. From Hodge *et al.* (1999a) with kind permission from Blackwell Science Ltd.

Plant–plant competition for N

A simpler explanation arises from the recognition that plants have evolved in competitive communities. A single root may be able to absorb all the nitrate in a small patch within a few days, so that extra roots represent cost without benefit. During competition, however, N capture by any one root system is proportional to its fraction of total root length in the patch (Robinson *et al.* 1999). Then, proliferation yields a return in terms of N uptake. This was demonstrated by Hodge *et al.* (1999a) when they compared the strongly proliferating *Lolium perenne* with the slow-to-proliferate *Poa pratensis* grown with their roots in the same patch of decomposing organic matter. In monoculture these species captured similar amounts of N from such a patch (Hodge *et al.* 1998). In competition, *L. perenne* captured more N than *P. pratensis*, exactly in proportion to its root length (Fig. 5.5).

A similar conclusion was reached by Cahill and Casper (1999) who examined the responses of *Artemisia artemisiifolia* and *Phytolacca americana* grown individually or in combination. They found that the responses of these species to the patches, and their respective N captures, depended on whether neighbouring plants were present. This echoes Robinson *et al.*'s (1999) conclusion that the functional significance of responses to nutrient patches (and, probably, of *any* phenotypic response to the environment) is context-dependent. Measurements on isolated individuals are invaluable to appreciate the phenomenology of a response, but can mislead if extrapolated to predict interactions among individuals.

This finding leads to a fundamental re-examination of proliferation responses in relation to other potential nutrient sinks, including microbes as well as other plants (see Robinson 1994; Robinson and van Vuuren 1998). Most work on root proliferation has used inorganic nutrients to create patches, or has maintained a continuous supply of nutrients, or both. Such patches do not resemble conditions in soil. There, most heterogeneity is created by spatial and temporal patterns of organic matter inputs and by the complexity arising from that pattern caused by microbial activity (see above). The decomposition of organic matter creates new compounds that may have their own unique behaviour and dynamics, and requires plant roots to acquire nutrient ions in competition with microbes.

Plant–microbe competition for N

Micro-organisms are generally considered to be more effective competitors for N than plant roots because they can proliferate much faster in response to prevailing soil conditions. Studies on short-term (24-hour) partitioning of inorganic N additions between micro-organisms and plants in a Californian annual grassland both in the spring (Jackson *et al.* 1989) and autumn (Schimel *et al.* 1989) support this widely held view. In the longer term, however, microbial turnover may release N for plant uptake. Additionally, if patches recur frequently, plant roots may be preadapted to a new pulse by their response to a previous one.

Hodge *et al.* (1999b) investigated this aspect by adding a simple organic patch ($^{15}N/^{13}C$ dual-labelled L-lysine) to a *Lolium perenne* sward. The L-lysine was added either as a single addition of 5 mL ('patch' treatment) or as a series of smaller (1 mL) additions at 7-day intervals for 5 weeks ('pulse' treatment). If microbial competition was a major constraint on plant N capture, there should be a difference in plant uptake between these two treatments. The expectation was that the single patch would overwhelm microbial capacity, leaving lysine available for plant uptake, while the pulses would more closely match microbial capacity, ensuring that roots obtain N only after its processing by the microbial biomass. Uptake of N was monitored by sequential harvests of single shoots from the sward. The different methods of patch application had no effect on either the rate of capture or total N capture by the plants (Fig. 5.6). This suggests that plant characteristics rather than the microbial behaviour were controlling N uptake by the plants. Further, no ^{13}C excess was detected in the plant tissue, suggesting that microbial mineralization of the added substrate was occurring prior to plant uptake (cf. Näsholm *et al.* 1998). Roots must therefore have been competing effectively with the microbial biomass for the released inorganic N, and not for the lysine itself. Indeed by the final harvest (35 days) the *L. perenne* sward had captured 57% (patch) and 61% (pulse) of the total N added.

The concentration of N in the patch should therefore not affect the capture of N by a plant. Hodge *et al.* (1999c) investigated the response of *L. perenne* roots, plant N capture and soil microbial activity (in terms of protozoan biomass as a surrogate for microbial biomass: Andren *et al.* 1988) after addition of L-lysine patches of contrasting concentrations. Three treatments provided the same quantity of N (5.6 mg) but at different concentrations. The other two treatments provided five times (1 M × 1 mL) or one-fifth (40 mM × 1 mL) as much N but at the same concentration as one of the other treatments. Root production and mortality in the patch

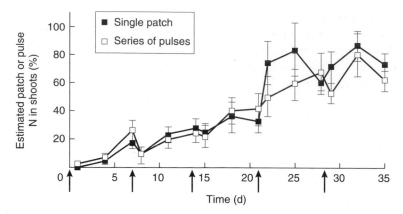

Figure 5.6 Nitrogen capture by *Lolium perenne* from a patch of 1 mmol of the amino acid L-lysine is unaffected by supplying the lysine as a single patch or as a series of pulses at 7-day intervals (indicated by arrows) offering the same total N application. From Hodge *et al.* (1999b) with kind permission from Elsevier Science.

addition zone was followed *in situ* using mini-rhizotron tubes. Despite distinct patterns of root births and deaths between treatments, absolute N capture was a function of the amount of N added irrespective of patch size but relative N capture by *L. perenne* was patch-dependent. Marked root proliferation occurred only in the 1 M patch. However, roots captured significantly less (~29%) of the N available from this patch than from the other four treatments (40–47%) where N capture did not differ significantly. Because protozoan biomass was greatest in the 1 M patch, the roots probably had to capture that N against strong microbial competition. Root proliferation may have increased their ability to achieve this. These data support the view of Robinson and van Vuuren (1998) that the circumstances in which a plant responds to a locally available nutrient supply are as important as the response itself.

Whether plants or microbes ultimately capture more N from an N-rich patch will depend on circumstances including the C:N ratio of the patch. The studies by Hodge *et al.* (1999b,c) discussed above show that when a patch of low C:N ratio is available, plants can compete effectively with micro-organisms for N. Plant N acquisition from more complex patches (i.e. those with higher C:N ratio) is generally smaller, at least over short time periods. For example, when *L. perenne* shoot material was added as a patch to soil supporting *Poa pratensis*, *Phleum pratense*, *Dactylis glomerata*, *Festuca arundinacea* or *L. perenne* seedlings, N capture 39 days after patch addition was only 3–5% of the total added (Hodge *et al.* 1998). Other values reported for N capture from organic residues vary widely (≈5–55%) and are mostly from longer time periods (i.e. over several growing seasons: Yaacob and Blair 1980; Azam *et al.* 1985; Müller and Sundman 1988; Ta and Faris 1990; Nicolardot *et al.* 1995).

Effects of mycorrhizas

In N-rich patches it seems that roots are more effective competitors with microbes than is generally assumed. Most root systems have an additional mechanism of nutrient acquisition, namely mycorrhizas. The effect of mycorrhizal colonization on root proliferation and patch exploitation has received little attention despite the importance and near-ubiquity of this association. Like roots, many fungi can proliferate in nutrient-rich patches often at the expense of growth in nutrient-poor regions (e.g. St John et al. 1983; Joner and Jakobsen 1995; Ritz et al. 1996). Thus, colonization by mycorrhizal fungi may negate the requirement for the root system to proliferate. It could, in theory, be more cost-effective in terms of carbon use for fungal hyphae to proliferate instead (Fitter 1991). Proliferation of ectomycorrhizal fungal hyphae in organic patches was demonstrated by Bending and Read (1995). However, because only the fungal hyphae and not the colonized roots reached the patch zones, the subsequent impact of mycorrhizal colonization on root proliferation could not be assessed. Proliferation by arbuscular mycorrhizal roots of *Agropyron desertorum* occurred in nutrient-rich patches (Cui and Caldwell 1996). Proliferation by non-mycorrhizal roots was greater (~22%) but this difference was only weakly significant ($P=0.07$).

Mycorrhizal colonization declines in nutrient-rich plants (Sanders 1975; Thomson et al. 1986), suggesting that local colonization should also decline in nutrient-rich patches. This hypothesis was tested by Duke et al. (1994) by adding large volumes (300 mL) of nutrient-rich solution (containing KH_2PO_4 and NH_4NO_3) as patches of ~1000 cm^3 to field-grown *Agropyron desertorum* and *Artemisia tridentata*. Fewer arbuscules, the putative organ of nutrient exchange between symbionts, were found in roots within the nutrient-enriched zones, although this response was significant only for *A. desertorum*. The frequency of vesicles and overall root colonization was not significantly different in either species. Duke et al. (1994) concluded that root proliferation and alterations in nutrient uptake kinetics were more important than mycorrhizal colonization for the exploitation of transient patches. The generality of these findings needs to be investigated however. In particular, the response of the extra-radical mycelium is unknown.

In summary, a clear effect of mycorrhizal colonization on root proliferation in patches has still to be demonstrated, as have any subsequent effects on nutrient capture from those patches.

Ecological consequences of soil heterogeneity

Demographic effects of fine-scale soil heterogeneity

Few studies have explored the consequences of nutrient-rich soil patches for plant populations. Those few have found surprisingly subtle effects that seem to be negligible at the population level, despite individuals within the population showing the kinds of responses to patches described above.

Casper and Cahill (1996, 1998) reported that soil nutrient heterogeneity had no effect on the productivity or population structure of *Abutilon theophrasti* mono-cultures. Similarly, Morris (1996) showed that a localized nutrient enrichment had no effect on density-dependent mortality (i.e. self-thinning) in *Ocimum basilicum* monocultures. In each of these studies, individual plants responded morphologi-cally by changing relative leaf and root growth and, in the case of *A. theophrasti*, by root proliferation within patches (Casper and Cahill 1998).

The lack of effect of nutrient patchiness at the population level could suggest that the plasticity of *O. basilicum* and *A. theophrasti* in response to soil heterogene-ity compensated fully for the spatial patchiness of nutrients. If true, that would be evidence for the adaptiveness of phenotypic plasticity to soil heterogeneity. To confirm this suggestion, however, measurements of nutrient capture from the uniform and localized supplies would be required, but none were made in any of these studies. The definitive experiments combining effects of patches on nutrient capture and demography have yet to be done.

Casper and Cahill (1996) commented: 'Soil heterogeneity had its strongest effect on individuals [of *A. theophrasti* within a monoculture] ... [it] influenced whether particular individuals were destined to be dominant or subordinate within the population but had little effect on overall population structure.' Soil het-erogeneity might therefore act as a random 'sorting' mechanism among neigh-bouring individuals, allowing certain of them to grow faster and bigger than others and, presumably, to increase their fitness correspondingly. But as a constraint on the productivity of natural vegetation, fine scale soil heterogeneity may be less important than once thought, perhaps because plants have the capacity to respond so strongly to such heterogeneity and therefore compensate for it.

Soil heterogeneity at ecological scales

At a coarse scale, soil heterogeneity (in terms of chemical and physical properties) clearly influences vegetation patterns, an effect easily seen where calcareous and acidic soils are juxtaposed, for example. Such patterns are documented by a wealth of observations in diverse ecosystems and from long-term ecological experiments (see, for example, Tilman 1982). The unanswered question is whether the finer scale spatial and temporal heterogeneity described in this chapter can have a similar but subtler impact.

There is an extensive literature from the 1950s and 1960s in which the variance in the distribution of soil and plant parameters was related to the scale over which the variation was measured. The technique of plotting variance (as mean square) against spatial scale ('block size') was described in detail in two classic textbooks of the period (Greig-Smith 1964; Kershaw 1964). There was often an excellent relationship between the scale at which variation in some soil factor was expressed and that at which a particular plant species showed pattern (e.g. Fig. 5.7).

Other studies have shown that vertical heterogeneity of soil horizons, which occurs to some extent in all soils, can affect community structure by promoting the coexistence of species. Berendse (1981) and Fitter (1982) each grew plants in

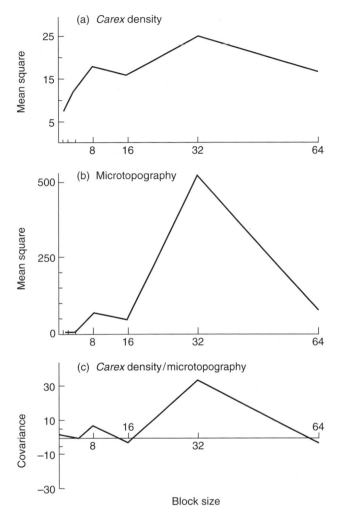

Figure 5.7 The pattern of the distribution of *Carex bigelowii* is on the same scale as that of the topography of a *Rhacomitrium* heath in Iceland, as shown by covariance of the two parameters at a given sampling scale. From Kershaw (1962), with kind permission from Blackwell Science Ltd.

competition on either a homogeneous soil or a soil with distinct upper and lower layers. Berendse (1981) allowed the grass *Anthoxanthum odoratum*, which has most roots in the top 10 cm of soil, to compete with *Plantago lanceolata*, which roots down to 50 cm. The two species coexisted best where the soil was vertically heterogeneous. When Fitter (1982) provided two contrasting soils, one acidic and one calcareous, in heterogeneous and homogeneous mixtures, the heterogeneous arrangement always resulted in higher diversity than the homogeneous soil. The increased diversity brought about by providing a calcareous layer beneath the acid layer might be explained by the more favourable conditions provided by the

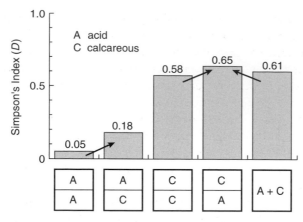

Figure 5.8 Species diversity in an artificial grassland community, composed of *Festuca rubra, Holcus lanatus, Lolium perenne, Plantago lanceolata* and *Poa trivialis,* increases when two distinct soil layers are used as opposed to a uniform soil. Diversity is measured by Simpson's index of dominance. *A* refers to an acid soil (pH 3.8) and *C* to a calcareous soil (pH 6.8); *P. trivialis* did not survive when the upper layer was acid. When the acid soil was underlain by a calcareous soil (*A/C*), diversity is greater than for a uniformly acid soil (*A/A*). Similarly when the calcareous soil is underlain by an acid soil (*C/A*), diversity is greater than with either a uniform calcareous soil (*C/C*) or a uniform mixture of the two soils (*A+C*) (redrawn from Fitter 1982).

former. However, the same result occurred when the calcareous layer was on top and the acid layer was beneath, compared with an all-calcareous soil (Fig. 5.8). The calcareous-over-acid arrangement also produced higher diversity than a uniform mixture of the two soils. Heterogeneity can therefore directly promote coexistence.

Spatial patterns, whether horizontal or vertical in soil, should create potential opportunities for niche differentiation and coexistence. There is some theoretical support for this. Tilman's (1982) equilibrium models of interspecific competition predict an increase in the number of coexisting species resulting from greater spatial heterogeneity, especially if resources are generally scarce in the habitat. Experimental support for this kind of prediction is usually sought from long-term ecological experiments, such as the Rothamsted Park Grass Experiment (PGE). Fertiliser applications, or the lack of them, cause dramatic changes in species composition. For example, PGE plots that receive P fertiliser contain fewer species, on average, than those which receive no P fertiliser (Wilson *et al.* 1996). An inevitable consequence of adding P will be to mask the innate patchiness of P distribution in topsoil, as described earlier. One reason for the greater species diversity in the less-fertile plots may be the greater (supposed) soil heterogeneity in those plots, although this cause-and-effect sequence has yet to be proven.

The effects of temporal variations in soil heterogeneity are much less well described, however. These are potentially more interesting than spatial heterogeneity. Temporal variations lead to disequilibria at a point in space and to the possibility of coexistence of species which could not coexist if competition was allowed to proceed. For example, if some plants are effective at exploiting patches and colleagues are not, then the transient appearance of a nutrient-rich patch will give the first type a temporary advantage, whereas a period without enrichment would favour the second type. To understand how important such temporal disequilibrium might be in structuring plant communities would require many more measurements of temporal patterns of soil heterogeneity at small spatial scales in the field. Almost by definition, equilibrium models are unlikely to provide many useful clues about effects of temporal soil heterogeneity on plant communities.

A more promising approach may lie in the application of cellular automata (e.g. Colasanti and Hunt 1997). In these models, dynamic changes in plant community structure can be mapped onto a digital 'environment' containing patches with defined attributes (e.g. quality, distribution and durability). Plants with contrasting phenotypes (e.g. plastic *vs.* static, fast *vs.* slow growth) can then exploit those patches and the potential consequences for the community can be explored. We suspect, however, that such models will realize their full value only when they can draw upon a more detailed body of information from experiments on real plant communities.

Acknowledgments

Angela Hodge is funded by the BBSRC. The Scottish Crop Research Institute receives grant-in-aid from the Scottish Office Agriculture, Fisheries and Environment Department. Work described here was funded by the Natural Environment Research Council and Biotechnology and Biological Sciences Research Council.

References

Andren, O., Paustian, K. and Rosswall, T. (1988) Soil biotic interactions in the functioning of agroecosystems. *Agriculture, Ecosystems and Environment* **24**, 57–67.

Azam, F., Malik, K.A. and Sajjad, M.I. (1985) Transformations in soil and availability to plants of ^{15}N applied as inorganic fertilizer and legume residues. *Plant and Soil* **86**, 3–13.

Bending, G.D. and Read, D.J. (1995) The structure and function of the vegetative mycelium of ectomycorrhizal plants. V. Foraging behaviour and translocation of nutrients from exploited litter. *New Phytologist* **130**, 401–409.

Berendse, F. (1981) Competition between plants with different rooting depths. II. Pot experiments. *Oecologia* **48**, 334–341.

Birch, C.P.D. and Hutchings, M.J. (1994) Exploitation of patchily distributed soil resources by the clonal herb *Glechoma hederacea. Journal of Ecology* **82**, 653–664.

Cahill, J.F. and Casper, B.B. (1999) Growth consequences of soil nutrient heterogeneity for two old-field herbs, *Ambrosia artemisiifolia* and *Phytolacca americana,* grown individually and in combination. *Annals of Botany* **83**, 471–478.

Campbell, B.D., Grime, J.P. and Mackey, J.M.L. (1991) A trade-off between scale and precision in resource foraging. *Oecologia* **87**, 532–538.

Casper, B.B. and Cahill, J.F. (1996) Limited effects of soil nutrient heterogeneity on populations of *Abutilon theophrasti* (Malvaceae). *American Journal of Botany* **83**, 333–341.

Casper, B.B. and Cahill, J.F. (1998) Population-level responses to nutrient heterogeneity and density by *Abutilon theophrasti* (Malvaceae): an experimental neighborhood approach. *American Journal of Botany* **85**, 1680–1687.

Colasanti, R.L. and Hunt, R. (1997) Resource dynamics and plant growth: a self assembling model for individuals, populations and communities. *Functional Ecology* **11**, 133–145.

Coleman, D.C., Dighton, J., Ritz, K. and Giller, K.E. (1994) Perspectives on the compositional and functional analysis of soil communities. In: *Beyond the Biomass* (eds K. Ritz, J. Dighton and K.E. Giller), pp. 261–271. Wiley, Chichester.

Cui, M. and Caldwell, M.M. (1996) Facilitation of plant phosphate acquisition by arbuscular mycorrhizas from enriched soil patches I. Roots and hyphae exploiting the same soil volume. *New Phytologist* **133**, 453–460.

Cui, M. and Caldwell, M.M. (1998) Nitrate and phosphate uptake by *Agropyron desertorum* and *Artemisia tridentata* from soil patches with balanced and unbalanced nitrate and phosphate supply. *New Phytologist* **139**, 267–272.

Drew, M.C. (1975) Comparison of the effects of a localized supply of phosphate, nitrate, ammonium and potassium on the growth of the seminal root system, and the shoot, in barley. *New Phytologist* **75**, 479–490.

Drew, M.C., Saker, L.R. and Ashley, T.W. (1973) Nutrient supply and the growth of the seminal root system in barley. I. The effect of nitrate concentration on the growth of axes and laterals. *Journal of Experimental Botany* **24**, 1189–1202.

Drew, M.C. and Saker, L.R. (1975) Nutrient supply and the growth of the seminal root system in barley. II. Localized, compensatory increases in lateral root growth and rates of nitrate uptake when nitrate supply is restricted to only part of the root system. *Journal of Experimental Botany* **26**, 79–90.

Drew, M.C. and Saker, L.R. (1978) Nutrient supply and the growth of the seminal root system in barley. III. Compensatory increases in growth of lateral roots and in rates of phosphate uptake in response to a localised supply of phosphate. *Journal of Experimental Botany* **29**, 435–451.

Duke, S.E., Jackson, R.B. and Caldwell, M.M. (1994) Local reduction of mycorrhizal arbuscule frequency in enriched soil microsites. *Canadian Journal of Botany* **72**, 998–1001.

Ehrenfeld, J.G., Han, X., Parsons, W.F.J. and Zhu, W. (1997) On the nature of environmental gradients: temporal and spatial variability of soils and vegetation in the New Jersey Pinelands. *Journal of Ecology* **85**, 785–798.

Farley, R.A. and Fitter, A.H. (1999a) The patchy nature of soil at a woodland site at scales applicable to plant root foraging. *Journal of Ecology* **87**, 688–696.

Farley, R.A. and Fitter, A.H. (1999b) The response of seven co-occurring woodland perennials to localized nutrient-rich patches. *Journal of Ecology* **87**, 849–859.

Fitter, A.H. (1982) Influence of soil heterogeneity on the co-existence of grassland species. *Journal of Ecology* **70**, 139–148.

Fitter, A.H. (1987) An architectural approach to the comparative ecology of plant root systems. *New Phytologist* **106** (Suppl.), 61–77.

Fitter, A.H. (1991) Costs and benefits of mycorrhizas: implications for functioning under natural conditions. *Experientia* **47**, 350–355.

Fitter, A.H. (1994) Architecture and biomass allocation as components of the plastic response of root systems to soil heterogeneity. In: *Exploitation of Environmental Heterogeneity by Plants* (eds M.M. Caldwell and R.M. Pearcy), pp. 305–323. Academic Press, New York, USA.

Fitter, A.H., Strickland, T.R., Harvey, M.L. and Wilson, G.W. (1991) Architectural analysis of plant root systems 1. Architectural correlates of exploitation efficiency. *New Phytologist* **118**, 375–382.

Fransen, B., de Kroon, H. and Berendse, F. (1998) Root morphological plasticity and nutrient acquisition of perennial grass species from habitats of different nutrient availability. *Oecologia* **115**, 351–358.

Greig-Smith, P. (1964) *Quantitative Plant Ecology*, 2nd edn. Butterworths, London.

Hodge, A., Stewart, J., Robinson, D., Griffiths, B.S. and Fitter, A.H. (1998) Root proliferation, soil fauna and plant nitrogen capture from nutrient-rich patches in soil. *New Phytologist* **139**, 479–494.

Hodge, A., Robinson, D., Griffiths, B.S. and Fitter, A.H. (1999a) Why plants bother: root proliferation results in increased nitrogen capture from an organic patch when two grasses compete. *Plant, Cell and Environment* **22**, 811–820.

Hodge, A., Stewart, J., Robinson, D., Griffiths, B.S. and Fitter, A.H. (1999b) Plant, soil fauna and microbial responses to N-rich organic patches of contrasting temporal availability. *Soil Biology and Biochemistry* **31**, 1517–1530.

Hodge, A., Robinson, D., Griffiths, B.S. and Fitter, A.H. (1999c) Nitrogen capture by plants grown in N-rich organic patches of contrasting size and strength. *Journal of Experimental Botany* **50**, 1243–1252.

Jackson, L.E., Schimel, J.P. and Firestone, M.K. (1989) Short-term partitioning of ammonium and nitrate between plants and microbes in an annual grassland. *Soil Biology and Biochemistry* **21**, 409–415.

Jackson, R.B. and Caldwell, M.M. (1993) Geostatistical patterns of soil heterogeneity around individual perennial plants. *Journal of Ecology* **81**, 683–692.

Jackson, R.B., Canadell, J., Ehleringer, J.R., Mooney, H.A., Sala, O.E. and Schulze, E.D. (1996) A global analysis of root distributions for terrestrial biomes. *Oecologia* **108**, 389–411.

Joner, E.J. and Jakobsen, I. (1995) Growth and extracellular phosphatase activity of arbuscular mycorrhizal hyphae as influenced by soil organic matter. *Soil Biology and Biochemistry* **27**, 1153–1159.

Kershaw, K.A. (1962) Quantitative ecological studies from Landmannahellir, Iceland. III. The variation in performance of *Carex bigelowii*. *Journal of Ecology* **50**, 393–399.

Kershaw, K.A. (1964) *Quantitative and Dynamic Ecology*. Arnold, London.

Morris, E.C. (1996) Effect of localized placement of nutrients on root competition in self-thinning populations. *Annals of Botany* **78**, 353–364.

Müller, M.M. and Sundman, V. (1988) The fate of nitrogen (^{15}N) released from different plant materials during decomposition under field conditions. *Plant and Soil* **105**, 133–139.

Näsholm, T., Ekblad, A., Nordin, A., Giesler, R., Högberg, M. and Högberg, P. (1998) Boreal forest plants take up organic nitrogen. *Nature* **392**, 914–916.

Nicolardot, B., Denys, D., Lagacherie, B., Cheneby, D. and Mariotti, M. (1995) Decomposition of ^{15}N-labelled catch crop residues in soil: evalua-

tion of N mineralization and plant-N uptake potentials under controlled conditions. *European Journal of Soil Science* **46**, 115–123.

Ritz, K., Millar, S.M. and Crawford, J.W. (1996) Detailed visualisation of hyphal distribution in fungal mycelia growing in heterogeneous nutritional environments. *Journal of Microbiological Methods* **25**, 23–28.

Robinson, D. (1994) The responses of plants to non-uniform supplies of nutrients. *New Phytologist* **127**, 635–674.

Robinson, D. (1996) Resource capture by localized root proliferation: why do plants bother? *Annals of Botany* **77**, 179–185.

Robinson, D. and van Vuuren, M.M.I. (1998) Responses of wild plants to nutrient patches in relation to growth rate and life-form. In: *Inherent Variation in Plant Growth. Physiological Mechanisms and Ecological Consequences* (eds H. Lambers, H. Poorter, H. and M.M.I. van Vuuren), pp. 237–257. Backhuys, Netherlands.

Robinson, D., Hodge, A., Griffiths, B.S. and Fitter, A.H. (1999) Plant root proliferation in nitrogen-rich patches confers competitive advantage. *Proceedings of the Royal Society, Biological Sciences* **266**, 431–435.

Sanders, F.E. (1975) The effect of foliar-applied phosphate on the mycorrhizal infections of onion roots. In: *Endomycorrhizas* (eds F.E. Sanders, B. Mosse and P.B. Tinker), pp. 261–276. Academic Press, London, UK.

Schimel, J.P., Jackson, L.E. and Firestone, M.K. (1989) Spatial and temporal effects on plant-microbial competition for inorganic nitrogen in a California annual grassland. *Soil Biology and Biochemistry* **21**, 1059–1066.

Stark, J.M. and Hart, S.C. (1997) High rates of nitrification and nitrate turnover in undisturbed coniferous forests. *Nature* **385**, 61–64.

St John, T.V., Coleman, D.C. and Reid, C.P.P. (1983) Growth and spatial distribution of nutrient-absorbing organs: selective exploitation of soil heterogeneity. *Plant and Soil* **71**, 487–493.

Swift, M.J., Heal, O.W. and Anderson, J.M. (1979) *Decomposition in Terrestrial Ecosystems*. Blackwell Scientific Publications, Oxford.

Ta, T.C. and Faris, M.A. (1990) Availability of N from ^{15}N-labelled alfalfa residues to three succeeding barley crops under different field conditions. *Soil Biology and Biochemistry* **22**, 835–838.

Thomson, B.D., Robson, A.D. and Abbott, L.K. (1986) Effects of phosphorus on the formation of mycorrhizas by *Gigaspora calospora* and *Glomus fasciculatum* in relation to root carbo-hydrates. *New Phytologist* **103**, 751–765.

Tilman, D. (1982) *Resource Competition and Com-munity Structure*. Princeton University Press, Princeton.

Tinker, P.B. and Nye, P.H. (2000) *Solute Movement in the Mizosphere*. Oxford University Press, Oxford.

van Vuuren, M.M.I., Robinson, D. and Griffiths, B.S. (1996) Nutrient inflow and root prolifera-tion during the exploitation of a temporally and spatially discrete source of nitrogen in soil. *Plant and Soil* **178**, 185–192.

Wijesinghe, D.K. and Hutchings, M.J. (1997) The effects of spatial scale of environmental hetero-geneity on the growth of a clonal plant: an experimental study with *Glechoma hederacea*. *Journal of Ecology* **85**, 17–28.

Wijesinghe, D.K. and Hutchings, M.J. (1999) The effects of environmental heterogeneity on the performance of *Glechoma hederacea*: the interac-tions between patch contrast and patch scale. *Journal of Ecology* **87**, 860–872.

Wilson, J.B., Wells, T.C.E., Trueman, I.C., *et al.* (1996) Are there assembly rules for plant species abundance? An investigation in relation to soil resources and successional trends. *Journal of Ecology* **84**, 527–538.

Yaacob, O. and Blair, G.J. (1980) Mineralization of ^{15}N-labelled legume residues in soils with differ-ent nitrogen contents and its uptake by rhodes grass. *Plant and Soil* **57**, 237–248.

Yanai, J., Linehan, D.J., Robinson, D., *et al.* (1996) Effects of inorganic nitrogen application on the dynamics of the soil solution composition in the root zone of maize in a Scottish soil. *Plant and Soil* **180**, 1–9.

Zhang, H. and Forde, B.G. (1998) An *Arabidopsis* MADS box gene that controls nutrient-induced changes in root architecture. *Science* **279**, 407–409.

Chapter 6

The effects of heterogeneous nutrient supply on plant performance: a survey of responses, with special reference to clonal herbs

M.J. Hutchings, D.K. Wijesinghe and E.A. John

Introduction

All natural environments are heterogeneous (Caldwell and Pearcy 1994). Consequently their ability to provide essential resources varies in space and time. Many animal species make clear choices, based on assessment of local habitat quality, about locations in which it will be most profitable to invest effort in acquiring resources. Plants make similar choices, but the length of time that they take to move between patches, and to exploit the resources within patches, makes the process of site selection less obvious. This may be why study of these activities and their consequences is much less advanced for plants than for animals. Nevertheless, this aspect of plant behaviour is important because habitat quality often varies significantly at scales small enough to affect different parts of the same plant in different ways at the same time, and over short enough periods to affect the same part of a plant in different ways at different times (e.g. Kotliar and Wiens 1990; Lechowicz and Bell 1991; Jackson and Caldwell 1993a,b; Stuefer 1996).

Most ecological experiments on plants are conducted under uniform conditions. However, plants grow in heterogeneous environments, and may function differently under such conditions than under homogeneous conditions providing equal quantities of resource. Only recently have the effects of providing resources to plants in homogeneous and heterogeneous configurations been compared. Several studies have now shown that different facets of environmental heterogeneity can affect plant behaviour and performance in distinct ways. If co-occurring species perceive and respond differently to given types of heterogeneity, this may affect their interactions, and ultimately influence community composition. Thus, the effects of heterogeneity on plants and their interactions are important subjects for ecologists to study. In this paper we review information about the effects of environmental heterogeneity on patch selection by plants and on plant performance, using studies in which soil nutrient distribution is spatially heterogeneous. The consequences of morphological responses to heterogeneity are emphasized. Where possible, we compare the effects on performance of:

School of Biological Sciences, University of Sussex, Falmer, Brighton, Sussex, BN1 9QG, UK

1 homogeneous and heterogeneous nutrient supply;

2 different heterogeneous configurations of resource supply. Although it is obvious that the quantity of resources given to a plant affects its performance, a major aim of this paper is to demonstrate that performance can also be affected by providing the same quantity of resource in different spatial patterns.

Proliferation of roots in response to heterogeneity in soil nutrient availability

Proliferation of roots in response to localized nutrient enrichment is common, although in some cases there is little or no response (Robinson 1994). When proliferation occurs, such responses are usually confined to the part of the root system that is exposed to soil enrichment. Timing of root proliferation often differs between species (Caldwell 1994; Hodge *et al.* 1998; Fitter, this volume; but see Larigauderie and Richards 1994), and its extent depends on several factors, including the concentration of nutrients in the patch, the nutritional status of the plant, the presence or absence of mycorrhiza and the presence and identity of neighbouring species (Caldwell 1994). The exact morphological response may also depend on the nutrients supplied. For example, the amount to which main root axes and first- and second-order laterals of barley proliferated in response to nutrient enrichment was dependent on whether nitrate or phosphate was supplied. Potassium had little effect on root growth (Drew *et al.* 1973; Drew 1975; Drew and Saker 1978). Significantly, localized root proliferation enabled barley plants with only a few percent of their seminal root exposed to nutrient-rich soil to achieve whole plant relative growth rates similar to those of plants with all of their root system exposed to soil containing the same nutrient concentration (Drew and Saker 1975). Thus, for plants with a heterogeneous soil nutrient supply, highly localized root proliferation in response to local enrichment permitted disproportionate growth from the amount of resource supplied.

Differential root growth between soils of different nutrient status

When part of a root system proliferates in response to local nutrient enrichment, this is often (but not always—see Robinson 1994) accompanied by reduced growth of other parts of the root system in nutrient-poor patches (Fitter 1994). Gersani and Sachs (1992) examined this phenomenon in pea (*Pisum sativum*) plants with their root systems divided between substrates that differed in nutrient supply. Local root development, measured as dry weight, depended on relative rather than absolute nutrient supply, with roots in a given quality of substrate growing faster when other roots on the same plant were in low rather than high nutrient conditions. Overall, the total number of root primordia produced was approximately constant in all treatments, but when nutrient supply to the two halves of the root system differed, primordia were less abundant in the low nutrient substrate and more abundant in the high nutrient substrate. As the nutrient concentrations diverged, so did the number of primordia on each half of the root system. Gersani and Sachs (1992) interpreted these results as showing that development of the entire root system was coordinated, with trade-offs occurring that increased root growth in favourable patches at the expense of root growth elsewhere. As a consequence, the distribution of roots in soil patches of different quality was optimized. However, Robinson (1994) concluded that invoking such trade-offs to explain root distribution between patches of soil of contrasting quality was over-simplistic.

Although the relationships between root distribution and nutrient availability can undoubtedly be complex, later work (Gersani *et al.* 1998) provided further evidence that the ratio of weights of roots produced by plants in patches of different quality was closely related to the ratio of resources in each patch. Isolated pea plants (referred to as 'fence-sitters'), were established with their root systems divided between two pots of vermiculite. When both pots contained the same amount of nutrients, each part of the root system developed equally, whereas when one pot contained twice as many nutrients as the other, the ratio of root weights in the two pots was not significantly different from 2:1. Further experiments were performed in which one of the two pots contained 0–5 competing pea plants as well as part of the root system of the fence-sitter. At harvest, the roots of the fence-sitter were carefully separated from those of the competitors, so that the weights of its roots in both pots could be accurately determined. The total weight of the root system of the fence-sitter did not change significantly with number of competitors, but the weight of its roots in the two pots varied inversely, decreasing in the pot with competitors as number of competitors increased, and increasing in the other pot (Fig. 6.1). Thus, the fence-sitter compensated for competition for nutrients in one pot by developing a greater fraction of its root system in a location where there was no competition. These results suggest that there is strong coordination of root system development in pea, and that the plant is able to exert considerable control over the locations in which it develops its roots. The ideal free distribution model of density-dependent habitat selection (Fretwell 1972) and the habitat-matching rule (Pulliam and Caraco 1984) predict that effort should be invested in harvesting resources from different patches in proportion to the availability of resources in each patch. This prediction has been verified in several studies on animals (e.g. Parker 1978; Milinski 1979; Harper 1982). An equivalent prediction for a plant is that biomass of roots located in each patch should be proportional to the abundance of resources in each patch. The results of Gersani *et al.* (1998) for the fence-sitter plants match this prediction.

The consequences, both for the fence-sitter of being able to exercise differential root growth in pots containing different amounts of nutrients, and for the competitors of being confined to homogeneous environments with limited nutrient supply, are important. As the combined density of the competitors and fence-sitter increased, the fitness (measured as fruit dry weight) of the competitors declined. This can be attributed at least in part to a fall in nutrient availability per plant. In contrast, the fitness of the fence-sitters did not change as density of competitors

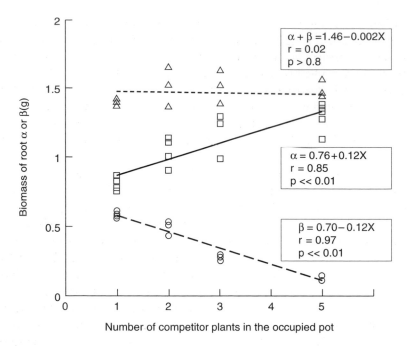

Figure 6.1 The biomass of the roots of a 'fence-sitter' pea plant located in a pot lacking competitors (□) or containing 1–5 competitor pea plants (○), and the total root biomass of the fence-sitter (△). The substrate in both pots was watered with nutrient solution of the same strength. From Gersani *et al.* (1998), with kind permission of Kluwer Academic Publishers.

increased. Fitness was buffered against reduced nutrient availability from the pot with competitors because the plant transferred its nutrient acquisition activities to the competition-free pot, where nutrients remained available in abundance. Thus, despite relative immobility, active responses of these plants to environmental heterogeneity maximized their resource capture and maintained their fitness.

Responses to heterogeneous soils with free root movement between patches

Non-clonal plants

Most nutrients that become available to plants under field conditions arise from particulate organic matter, and are more spatially aggregated than nutrients supplied in liquid form. Soil substrates have complex physical properties, and contain microbial communities that compete with higher plants for nutrients (e.g. Fitter *et al.*, this volume). In recognition of these facts, many ecological studies of plant responses to heterogeneity in nutrient supply now use slow-release fertilizer pellets or soil-based substrates instead of the nutrient solutions and sand culture which were often used in the past (Robinson 1994). Although nutrient supply is difficult to control in soil, and nutrient patches less easy to define and maintain, plant responses to heterogeneity observed in such substrates may more closely resemble plant behaviour under field conditions. Many recent studies of the effects of heterogeneous nutrient supply on plants have also used designs that eliminate physical barriers to free root movement between patches of different quality. Interest now centres not only on whether roots proliferate in response to patchy nutrient supply, but on whether there are consequences at the whole plant level, and if so, how they are generated.

An example of this approach is provided by a study of Mou *et al.* (1997). The consequences were compared of supplying the same quantity of nutrients homogeneously or heterogeneously to potted sweetgum (*Liquidambar styraciflua*) and loblolly pine (*Pinus taeda*) seedlings. Nutrients were supplied as slow-release fertilizer distributed either uniformly over the whole surface, or over one quarter of the surface, of the pots. There were no barriers to root growth within the pots. The plants were either grown in full sunlight or shaded to 30% of full sunlight. Under heterogeneous conditions, both species, but especially sweetgum, concentrated their roots in the enriched quarter of the pot. Both species produced thinner fine roots, with greater root lengths between lateral branches and more higher-order laterals in the nutrient-rich patch than in the nutrient-poor part of the heterogeneous treatment. Overall, total biomass of plants, and growth of above- and below-ground plant parts, was unaffected by the pattern of nutrient supply in full light. In contrast, when plants were grown in shade, their total biomass, above-ground biomass, leaf biomass and plant height were all lower when fertilizer was heterogeneously rather than homogeneously distributed. It was speculated that this could have been caused by the need in heterogeneous conditions to translocate nutrients internally to plant parts located in nutrient-poor soil, and that the energetic cost of this translocation was reflected in lower growth under shaded (carbon-limited) conditions. Whereas sweetgum was more plastic in its root development in response to pattern of nutrient supply in full light, both species were equally plastic in shade. It was concluded that the outcome of competition between the two species would be affected by the spatial pattern of nutrients in the soil, and further modified by decline in light availability during succession.

Einsmann *et al.* (1999) have recently examined the relationships between spatial heterogeneity in soil nutrient supply, root placement and performance for a group of 10 species native to the warm temperate coastal forests of South Carolina. Again, the experimental design added a fixed quantity of nutrients as slow-release fertilizer in different spatial configurations to a sand substrate. Several morphological attributes of the root systems were quantified, and correlations between these attributes were also sought. Whereas root placement, measured by fine root biomass distribution, was uniform under homogeneous conditions, several species produced significantly more roots in nutrient-rich than nutrient-poor patches when nutrient supply was heterogeneous (i.e. they exhibited precision in root placement, Fig. 6.2). Four species were sensitive to scale of heterogeneity, and all

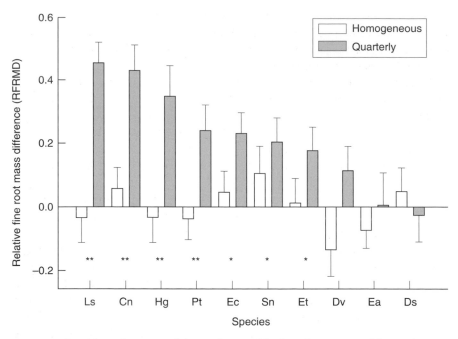

Figure 6.2 Precision of root growth in nutrient-enriched patches, measured for 10 plant species. Precision is expressed as relative fine root mass difference (RFRMD: fine root mass density in one quarter of a pot–fine root mass density in the opposite quarter of the pot/total root mass in the pot). In the homogeneous treatment the two opposite quarters of the pot received equal amounts of fertilizer. In the case of quarterly fertilized pots, opposite quarters of the pots either received or did not receive fertilizer. No species showed preferential proliferation in either pot quarter in the homogeneous treatment. **Indicates that species showed significant preferential root location in the fertilized patch (i.e. asymmetrical root development, or *precision*), and that RFRMD in the quarterly fertilized treatment differed significantly from its value in the homogeneous treatment. *Indicates that species showed significant preferential root location in the fertilized patch, but that RFRMD was not significantly different in the quarterly and homogeneous treatments. (For details of analysis see Einsmann *et al.* 1999.) Key to species acronyms: Ls: *Liquidambar styraciflua* L. (deciduous tree, Hamamelidaceae); Cn: *Chamaecrista nictitans* (L.) Moench. (annual herb, Fabaceae); Hg: *Hypericum gentianoides* L. (annual herb, Hypericaceae); Pt: *Pinus taeda* L. (evergreen tree, Pinaceae); Ec: *Erigeron canadensis* L. (annual herb, Asteraceae); Sn: *Solidago nemoralis* Aiton. (perennial herb, Asteraceae); Et: *Elephantopus tomentosus* L. (perennial herb, Asteraceae); Dv: *Diospyros virginiana* L. (deciduous tree, Ebenaceae); Ea: *Euonymus americanus* L. (deciduous shrub, Celastraceae); Ds: *Desmodium strictum* (Pursh) DC (perennial herb, Fabaceae).

four produced significantly more biomass when the nutrients were concentrated in smaller patches than when nutrients were in larger patches or homogeneously distributed. The correlation between precision and sensitivity was poor, however, showing that there is not always a link between root proliferation in nutrient-rich patches and yield enhancement in heterogeneous conditions. Some species that were sensitive to scale of heterogeneity did not show precision in root placement, demonstrating that greater growth in heterogeneous conditions can be caused by factors other than morphological responses.

A major aim of Einsmann *et al.* (1999) was to test Campbell *et al.*'s (1991) hypothesis that there is a negative relationship between the scale (i.e. size) of species' root systems and their precision in placing roots in the higher quality patches of heterogeneous soils. Campbell *et al.* assessed the competitiveness of eight herbaceous species on the basis of their percentage contribution to total yield when grown in a mixture. Subsequently, each species was grown individually at the centre of arenas divided into four quadrants. Opposing pairs of quadrants received either high or low nutrient (or light) supply. After two weeks, plants were harvested and root (and shoot) biomass increment in each quadrant, and total root (or shoot) biomass were determined. A positive relationship was observed between absolute root (and shoot) biomass increment in the resource-rich quadrants and percentage contribution to the mixture. Thus, the most competitive species with the largest root (and shoot) systems would dominate the resource-rich patches. However, less competitive species placed a higher *proportion* of their root (and shoot) biomass increments in the resource-rich quadrants. Thus, although the scale of their growth was small, subordinate species were better at selecting resource-rich patches for placement of their roots and leaves (i.e. scale and precision were negatively correlated).

This observation is appealing because it may help to explain the persistence of subordinate species in plant communities. The eight species studied by Campbell *et al.* (1991) were, however, 'common British herbaceous species, widely contrasted in morphology and ecology' (Grime 1994), rather than naturally co-occurring dominants and subordinates. The species selected by Einsmann *et al.* (1999) represented vegetation types along a successional sequence. This group of species exhibited *positive* correlations between scale (measured in terms of root mass density and root length density) and precision of root placement, and when the six herbaceous species in the sample were considered by themselves, the correlation based on root length density was almost significant (Pearson correlation coefficient = +0.76, $P = 0.08$). Different experimental procedures and methods of measuring scale and precision may have contributed to the difference between these sets of results (Einsmann *et al.* 1999), but further studies are clearly needed before we can accept the generality of the hypothesis that there is a negative correlation between the scale of a species' root system and the precision with which its roots are placed in high quality patches of soil.

Clonal plants

Most studies of plant responses to heterogeneous soil nutrient supply, including several cited above, have been conducted on fast growing, nutrient-demanding species in which roots develop at a single location. However, there has also been much recent interest in the responses of clonal species, in which roots can emerge from many separate locations on horizontally orientated stems. Clonal species are important components of many natural plant communities, and many can establish as persistent monocultures. Genets of many clonal species can be extremely long-lived and occupy very large areas (Cook 1983). Many clones spread laterally by generating an indeterminate number of simple reiterated structures (ramets) at intervals on branched stems. Ramets may bear leaves and roots. The resource-acquiring organs of a single clone may therefore be widely distributed in space and time.

The ramets of clonal species are physiologically integrated, at least at a local scale. Integration is essential when ramet growth begins, because very young ramets cannot initially photosynthesize or acquire soil-based resources. However, they may continue to receive considerable quantities of resources from older ramets, even after leaves and roots have developed. The amount received depends on local conditions. For example, resource import may increase if a ramet is shaded or defoliated. In most clonal species resource movement is mainly acropetal (i.e. towards growing apices), but resources can move in either direction, depending on whether younger or older ramets are in need of support (Marshall 1990).

Because natural environments are spatially and temporally heterogeneous, connected ramets of widely spreading (and long-lived) clonal plants will often occupy sites providing different growing conditions. Physiological integration can prolong the survival of ramets located in sites with lethal shortages of one or more essential resources, sometimes for very long periods (Alpert and Mooney 1986; Lau and Young 1988; Tissue and Nobel 1988). Wijesinghe and Handel (1994) demonstrated the importance at the whole clone level of physiological integration for relieving individual ramets from the effects of locally adverse conditions. They grew *Potentilla simplex* in five types of environment with different levels of nutrient supply. The environments were lines of pots in which ramets on the stolons of *P. simplex* could root. Either 0, 25, 50, 75 or 100% of the pots received nutrients while the remaining pots did not. In the three intermediate treatments the pots receiving nutrients were chosen randomly. Various measurements of the relative heterogeneity of the environments showed that the most heterogeneous treatment was that with 50% enrichment and that those with 25 and 75% enrichment were of intermediate heterogeneity (Wijesinghe and Handel 1994). In each environment the yield of intact clones was compared with that of clones in which the stolon internodes between ramets were severed.

Yield of intact and severed clones increased as total nutrient supply increased (Fig. 6.3). There was also a strong interaction between nutrient supply and presence/absence of ramet connections. Clone yield was not reduced by severing in the homogeneous environments, but in the most heterogeneous environment (50% enrichment) the yield of the severed clones was 35% less than that of the intact clones. Corresponding yield reductions in the 25% and 75% enriched treatments were 6% and 16%, respectively. Thus, in the heterogeneous treatments, connected clones produced higher total yields than severed clones receiving the same amount of nutrients. The intact clones in the 50% enriched treatment also achieved 80% of

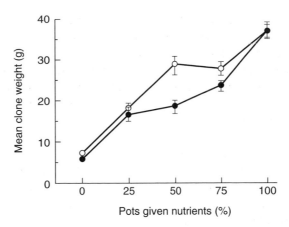

Figure 6.3 Mean (±SE) weights of clones of *Potentilla simplex* when ramets were connected to their neighbours (○) and when ramets were severed from each other (●). The percentage of pots given nutrients is shown on the horizontal axis. The treatment with 50% enrichment is the most heterogeneous. From Wijesinghe and Handel (1994).

the yield of intact clones in the homogeneous treatment with *all* pots containing nutrients. Thus, integration enabled *P. simplex* to achieve a disproportionately high yield from the nutrients available in this heterogeneous environment.

Other studies of the effects of heterogeneous resource supply on clonal species have produced similar results. Some have provided resources other than nutrients in heterogeneous supply. For example, Stuefer *et al.* (1994) compared the growth of connected pairs of ramets of *Potentilla reptans* and *P. anserina* in homogeneous (both ramets in either light or shade) or heterogeneous conditions (one ramet in light, the other in shade). Yields were greater (significantly so for *P. reptans*) in the heterogeneous treatment than in either homogeneous treatment, even though clones in the unshaded homogeneous treatment received most light. As expected, shaded ramets grew more when connected to unshaded ramets, but unshaded ramets *also* benefited when connected to shaded ramets. It was hypothesized that in the heterogeneous treatment the unshaded ramets had specialized to acquire locally abundant light while the shaded ramets had specialized to acquire water. Although uniformly supplied, water may have been more limiting to parts of the clone in light than to parts in shade. Localized morphological specializations in the clones in heterogeneous conditions would allow efficient acquisition of each resource from sites where it was abundant. Reciprocal translocation of resources from ramets in sites of abundance to ramets in sites of shortage would then enhance growth of the whole system. Analysis of biomass allocation patterns supported this hypothesis. For example, root:shoot (R:S) ratios of unshaded clone parts were lower when they were connected to shaded than unshaded parts, probably because some of their water demand could be met by translocation from the connected shaded part. Clearly, if this interpretation is correct, any costs of resource translocation (see Mou *et al.* 1997) were outweighed by the benefits to the whole clone. Local morphological specialization did not occur in the clones in the homogeneous treatments. Instead, acquisition of the uniformly limiting resource was promoted by development of higher R:S ratio throughout all parts of clones grown in homogeneous light than in clones grown in homogeneous shade.

A further experiment confirmed this interpretation (Stuefer *et al.* 1996). In homogeneous conditions, two-ramet clonal fragments of *Trifolium repens* developed low R:S ratios when shaded, and high R:S ratios when water was scarce. These changes promoted acquisition of the scarce resource. However, when half of the clone received high light and little water and the other half received low light and ample water, the part in high light developed a low R:S ratio and the part receiving abundant water developed a high R:S ratio (i.e. changes opposite to those shown by plants that root at a single position (e.g. Aung 1974; Hunt and Nicholls 1986) and of clones growing in homogeneous conditions (Slade and Hutchings 1987b; Alpert and Stuefer 1997)). These changes parallel the localized root proliferation in response to nutrient enrichment that are shown by many non-clonal species, in that they promote acquisition of locally abundant resources. If connected ramets are physiologically integrated, these modifications would be predicted on economic grounds (Bloom *et al.* 1985; Stuefer *et al.* 1996), because resource acquisition costs are lowest when resources are plentiful. Although different essential resources often exhibit negative spatial covariance in abundance (Schlesinger *et al.* 1991; Alpert and Mooney 1996; Stuefer 1996), the needs of the whole system can be satisfied by exchange of different resources from ramets in sites of abundance to ramets in sites of shortage. Such specialization and sharing has been described as division of labour (Stuefer 1997; Alpert and Stuefer 1997). Its effect in the case of *Trifolium repens* was that yield and ramet production were significantly greater in heterogeneous conditions than in either set of homogeneous conditions (Stuefer *et al.* 1996).

Detailed observation of the course of ramet development in a clonal species grown under heterogeneous conditions has revealed another aspect of this R:S response. Birch and Hutchings (1994) carried out an experiment in which the stoloniferous clonal species *Glechoma hederacea* was grown under either homogeneous or heterogeneous conditions, and the age at which each ramet began to root was recorded. (An arbitrary stage in ramet development was selected as the point at which ramet growth began, and ramets were aged from the time they reached this point. This is an application of the plastochron concept—see Erickson and Michelini 1957; Lamoreaux *et al.* 1978; Birch and Hutchings 1992.) When *G. hederacea* was grown in homogeneous conditions there was no variation in the age at which ramets began to root. In heterogeneous conditions, however, the age at which rooting began showed significant variation. Ramets located in nutrient-rich patches rooted several days earlier in their growth than those in nutrient-poor patches. These groups of ramets began rooting significantly earlier and later, respectively, than ramets of clones in homogeneous conditions. Thus, under heterogeneous conditions, ramets located in nutrient-rich soil accessed nutrients very rapidly in comparison with those located where nutrients were scarce.

Thus, developing ramets at the tips of stolons extending across the soil surface appear to sense soil quality, perhaps via their root initials. How this is done, and how perception of soil quality alters ramet ontogeny, is not known, although much progress is currently being made towards answering these questions (Zhang *et al.* 1999). Root growth anchors the ramet to the soil surface, so that any subsequent elongation of the stolon internode proximal to the ramet will not change the ramet's position. Roots elongate exponentially in *G. hederacea* (Birch and Hutchings 1994), and therefore the earlier rooting of ramets located in nutrient-rich patches leads to a high local R : S ratio, greater nutrient (and water) acquisition, and greater clone growth. Moreover, ramets in nutrient-poor patches develop a low R : S ratio because of their delayed rooting and thus at least in relative terms, specialize more in photosynthesis than in acquiring soil-based resources. Because of these localized morphological specializations it might be expected that clone yield in heterogeneous conditions would exceed that in homogeneous conditions even if resource supply were identical overall.

Birch and Hutchings (1994) tested this prediction using *Glechoma hederacea*. Large boxes were set up with a fixed quantity of nutrients either distributed homogeneously, or with half of these nutrients located in a central circle in the box that covered 10% of its area. Plants started growth as a single ramet placed half-way along one side of the box, with a single stolon growing towards the box centre. Thus, compared with the clones in the homogeneous treatment, those in the heterogeneous treatment began growth in nutrient-poor conditions that prevailed over 90% of the area of the boxes. As described above, when nutrients were heterogeneously distributed, the times at which ramets rooted, and their local R : S ratios, were sensitive to local soil nutrient status. Consequently, although clones in the heterogeneous treatment started growth under relatively disadvantageous conditions, earlier root growth of their ramets in the nutrient-rich patch resulted in them developing significantly more root biomass by harvest than the clones in the homogeneous treatment. This allowed earlier and more exhaustive exploitation of nutrients by clones in the heterogeneous treatment. At harvest, over 80% of the roots of the clones in the heterogeneous treatment were recovered from the central circle (i.e. from 10% of the soil by area and volume) whereas the corresponding value in the homogeneous treatment was only 15%. The production of a large root biomass where nutrients were abundant enabled the clones in the heterogeneous treatment to overcome the disadvantage of beginning growth in relatively nutrient-poor soil. By harvest they had produced 2.5 times as much biomass as the clones in homogeneous conditions, even though both were provided with the same quantity of nutrients. Roots made up 13% of all clone biomass in the patchy treatment, but only 7% in the homogeneous treatment.

The recognition that a fixed quantity of resource can be more beneficial to a clonal plant when provided heterogeneously rather than homogeneously, prompted further experiments to examine the specific effects of different aspects of heterogeneity on yield. To study the effects of patch size, Wijesinghe and Hutchings (1997) grew *G. hederacea* in boxes with their surfaces divided into equal-sized patches. Half of the patches contained nutrient-rich soil and half nutrient-poor soil, and each soil type covered half of the box surface. Individual patches were either few in number and large, or small and numerous (Fig. 6.4a). The total area of good and bad patches, and the concentration of nutrients in all patches of a given type (i.e. high- or low-nutrient status), was identical in all treatments. Thus, the only difference between treatments was the size and number of good and poor patches.

Both the root biomass of the whole clone (Fig. 6.4b) and the proportion of these roots located in rich patches declined as patch size decreased (Fig. 6.4c). Consequently, acquisition of nutrients depended strongly on scale of heterogeneity, and yield was significantly affected by patch scale (Fig. 6.4d). The highest mean yield (although this was not significantly more than in treatments T1, T3 and T4) was achieved with patches 25×25 cm in size. When patches were very small, the ability of *G. hederacea* to exploit them for nutrients appeared to be constrained by the speed with which its morphology adjusted to local conditions, as predicted by Oborny (1994). Morphological changes in response to patch quality, are very abrupt when *G. hederacea* moves from low- to high-nutrient patches, but much slower when the reverse transition is made (Slade and Hutchings 1987a). Thus, the ability of *G. hederacea* to match its morphology to local conditions becomes progressively more limited as patch scale declines (see Ackerly (1997) for a similar analysis of the effects of duration of light and dark periods on the ability of plants to achieve morphological matching). *G. hederacea* is either unable to perceive nutrients in very small patches, or unable to respond to them. In these conditions it produces few roots in rich and poor patches, as if the environment is uniformly poor in quality (Fig. 6.4b). This supports Oborny's (1994) prediction that growth of clonal plants will be greater in environments where offspring and parent ramets occupy patches of similar quality than in environments where the quality of patches occupied by consecutively produced ramets is different. The failure of clone biomass to continue to increase at the largest patch scales (Fig. 6.4d) again indicates that the plant, or physiologically integrated substructures within it, does not develop the appropriate responses to acquire resources efficiently from nutrient-rich patches when the environment is perceived as homogeneous. Yield appears to be maximized when the plant receives a given quantity of nutrients in a configuration that can be perceived as spatially heterogeneous.

A more complex study of the effect of soil nutrient heterogeneity on performance of a clonal species examined the effects of *contrast* in patch quality, at two patch scales (Wijesinghe and Hutchings 1999). *G. hederacea* clones were subjected to six levels of contrast in patch quality, ranging from extreme heterogeneity to homogeneity. Patches in the most heterogeneous treatment (0:100) consisted either entirely of sand or entirely of potting compost. In the homogeneous treatment (50:50) all 'patches' contained equal quantities of sand and compost,

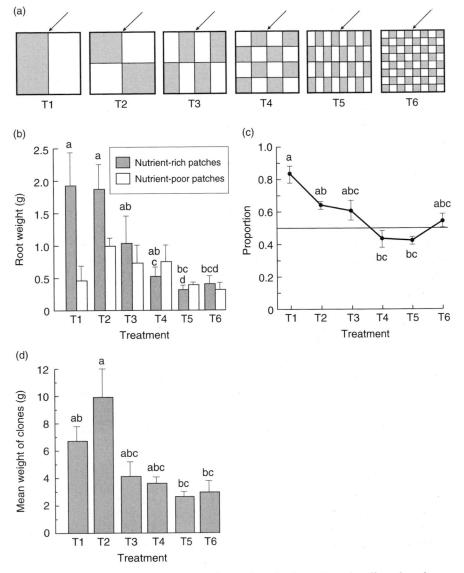

Figure 6.4 (a) Diagram of six treatments (T1–T6) used to investigate the effect of patch scale on the growth of *Glechoma hederacea* clones. The boxes are 50×50 cm in area. The same quantity of nutrients was provided in all treatments. In every treatment half of the soil volume and surface area of the growing arena was nutrient-rich and half was nutrient-poor. Clones began growth as a single ramet placed half-way along the upper edge of the growth arenas (indicated by arrows), with one stolon initially growing into nutrient-rich soil and one stolon initially growing into nutrient-poor soil. (b) The biomass of roots of *Glechoma hederacea* that were located in nutrient-rich (shaded bars) and nutrient-poor (open bars) patches in six experimental treatments with different patch scales. (c) The proportion of the roots located in nutrient-rich patches. (d) The biomass produced by *G. hederacea* clones in each treatment. The values given are means (±SE). Means with different letters above the error bars differ significantly (Bonferroni multiple-means comparison test, *P*<0.05). From Wijesinghe and Hutchings (1997).

thoroughly mixed together. Four intermediate heterogeneous treatments were created between these extremes, by mixing sand and compost in the ratios 10:90, 20:80, 30:70, 40:60. The large and small patch scales corresponded to treatments T2 and T4, respectively, as used in the experiment described above (Fig. 6.4a). As before, total nutrient availability, and the total area and proportion of the box surface consisting of rich and poor patches, was constant between treatments.

Again, root production depended on the form of heterogeneity. Significantly more root biomass was produced, both in rich and poor patches, when patch scale was large than when it was small. At both patch scales, root biomass fell in the rich patches and increased in the poor patches as contrast declined (Fig. 6.5a). Roots were evenly distributed throughout the homogeneous (50:50) environment, but as contrast increased a progressively higher proportion of the roots were located in the rich patches (Fig. 6.5b). The proportion of roots located in the nutrient-rich patches was not significantly different at any level of contrast at either scale. It is notable that the proportion of the roots located in patches of different quality in the different treatments closely matched the proportion of the nutrients available in those patches (cf. the results of Gersani *et al.* (1998) for a non-clonal species), implying that *G. hederacea* is very flexible and effective in foraging (Hutchings and de Kroon 1994) for nutrients in heterogeneous environments (Fig. 6.5b,c). The only case where this was not true was the most contrasting treatment, where lateral growth of stolons placed some ramets in low quality patches containing virtually no nutrients. A significantly lower proportion of clone root biomass was found in nutrient-rich patches in this treatment, than would be predicted if the habitat-matching rule is upheld (Fretwell 1972; Pulliam and Caraco 1984). R:S ratio also differed in different quality patches. It was higher in the richer patches at both scales, and as contrast increased, differences in R:S ratio became more pronounced. Moreover, the differences in R:S ratios in high and low quality patches were greater with larger patch sizes at all levels of contrast, implying that *G. hederacea* specializes more in response to patch quality at some scales of patchiness than at others (Fig. 6.5d). Once again, these responses to heterogeneity affected clone yield. Similar yields were achieved at both scales when contrast was low, but yields diverged as contrast increased. When the ratio of patch quality was 2:1 or greater, yield was significantly greater in the large scale environments (Fig. 6.6).

Variation in ability of *G. hederacea* to match its morphology to local patch conditions again contributed to the differences in performance when nutrients were provided in different configurations. Differences in the rates at which clone morphology adjusts when the environment changes from resource-rich to resource-poor and vice versa (Slade and Hutchings 1987a; Ackerly 1997), and the influence that this has on performance in heterogeneous environments with small spatial or short temporal scale, have already been mentioned. In addition, however, contrast in patch quality appears to affect the ease with which morphological transitions are made. For example, if spatial or temporal variation in resource abundance is low, morphology does not exhibit strong local specialization and little morphological adjustment is necessary as patch boundaries are crossed. All resources are acquired

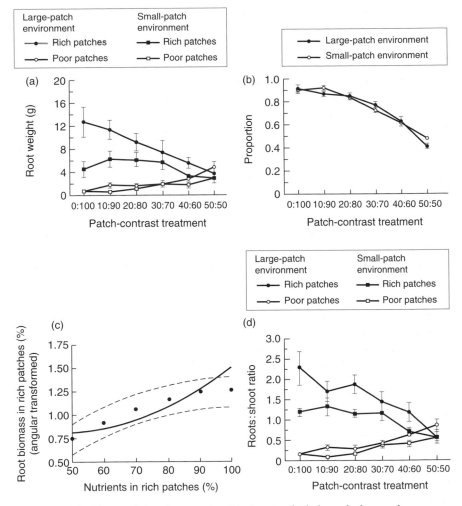

Figure 6.5 The biomass (a) and proportion (b) of roots of *Glechoma hederacea* clones located in rich and poor patches of experimental treatments with six levels of patch contrast and two patch scales. The values given are means (±SE). (c) The relationship between the percentage of clone root biomass in rich patches (angular transformed) and the percentage of the total nutrient supply in rich patches. Results from the two patch scales were pooled because there was no significant difference in proportions between them. The dots indicate a quadratic relationship between the plotted variables based on the observed data ($Y = -0.74 + 0.039X - 0.0002X^2$, $F_{2,57} = 174.48$, $P < 0.0001$) and the broken lines are the 95% confidence limits for this regression. The solid curve shows the expected percentage of root biomass in the rich patches if there were a precise match between root placement and nutrient availability in patches. (d) Mean (±SE) root:shoot ratio of clone parts located in rich and poor patches in the large- and small-patch environments at different patch contrasts. From Wijesinghe and Hutchings (1999).

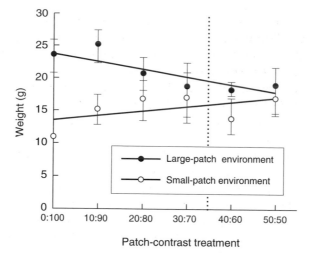

Figure 6.6 The relationship between patch contrast and whole clone biomass for *Glechoma hederacea* in large- and small-patch environments. Mean (±SE) biomass values are shown for each treatment. Linear regressions, fitted to all data points, were Y = 24.09 − 0.133X for the large-patch treatment and Y = 13.56 + 0.062X for the small-patch treatment. Values of the dependent variable (clone weight) to the left of the vertical broken line were significantly different for the two patch size treatments (Johnson–Neyman technique, P=0.05). From Wijesinghe and Hutchings (1999).

with moderate efficiency from the whole habitat and patch scale becomes virtually irrelevant. If patch contrast is high, however, patch scale becomes important. When patches are small, carryover effects prevent suitable morphological changes being completed before the plant moves beyond the boundaries of each patch (because of the time lag between assessment of patch quality and a developmental response to it taking place (Oborny 1994)). Efficient exploitation of local growing conditions can not be achieved, and yield is low. If patches are larger, however, carryover effects can dissipate before each patch is vacated, so that at least some ramets in each patch develop the appropriate morphology for exploiting local conditions. Because some patches contain resources in abundance, morphological specialization promotes efficient resource acquisition, resulting in high yield being achieved (Fig. 6.6).

Conclusion

The studies described here demonstrate that plant performance is strongly influenced by spatial habitat heterogeneity and that different resource configurations can significantly alter yield, and presumably also alter resource acquisition. This has been known for some time. For example, phosphate uptake by plants is increased when it is concentrated in a small fraction of the rooting volume rather than uniformly distributed throughout the rooting volume (Anghinoni and Barber 1980; Kovar and Barber 1989; Jackson and Caldwell 1996). Because the natural environment is characterized by heterogeneity at spatial and temporal scales that are relevant to plants (e.g. Turkington and Harper 1979; Pearcy 1983; Chazdon *et al.* 1988; Lechowicz and Bell 1991) it may not be surprising that heterogeneous conditions can support greater growth than homogeneous conditions. There are at least two circumstances, the first impinging on economic costs and benefits, the second on pure ecology, where more attention to the possible effects of environmental heterogeneity on plant performance may be beneficial. First, routine cultivation practices, such as fertilization and ploughing, tend to homogenize the environment. These practices may constrain the yields of crops of economic importance. In comparison, judicious use of heterogeneous spatial or temporal patterns of application of the same quantity of fertilizer could result in greater yields. Alternatively, the same yield might be achieved from lower levels of resource provision, thus cutting costs and reducing the impact of excessive fertilizer application on the environment. This is an area that might repay further research, but more information is certainly needed about all facets of spatial and temporal heterogeneity in different habitats, and about the types of heterogeneity to which different types of plants can respond.

Second, conditions in ecological experiments on plants are usually made as homogeneous as possible. However, if plant growth under heterogeneous conditions differs from growth under homogeneous conditions, this practice may strongly affect both the outcome of interactions between species, and community structure and composition. These possibilities merit more study. More elaborate experiments should be conducted to determine the effects of competition between plants in heterogeneous conditions. Experiments should also be performed with more than one variable having a patchy distribution, to determine whether positive and negative covariation in resource abundance in space has different consequences for plant growth. Little is known about the effects of temporal heterogeneity in resource supply on plant growth, although studies are now in progress. The time is right for plant ecology and physiology to move beyond their current crude understanding of the effects of resource supply on plant performance. Thorough study of the effects of spatial and temporal heterogeneity in resource provision on the perception of habitat quality by plants, and on its consequences for resource exploitation and growth, should be an urgent priority.

Acknowledgments
We are grateful to Rob Jackson, Jun Suzuki and an anonymous referee for their helpful and constructive comments on an earlier draft of this paper. Part of the work described in this paper was undertaken during the tenure of grants GR3/8843 (ML4) and GR3/11069 awarded by the Natural Environment Research Council, UK.

References

Ackerley, D. (1997) Allocation, leaf display, and growth in fluctuating light environments. In: *Plant Resource Allocation* (eds F.A. Bazzaz and J. Grace), pp. 231–264. Academic Press, San Diego.

Alpert, P. and Mooney, H.A. (1986) Resource sharing among ramets in the clonal herb *Fragaria chiloensis. Oecologia* 70, 227–233.

Alpert, P. and Mooney, H.A. (1996) Resource heterogeneity generated by shrubs and topography on coastal sand dunes. *Vegetatio* 122, 83–93.

Alpert, P. and Stuefer, J.F. (1997) Division of labour in clonal plants. In: *The Ecology and Evolution of Clonal Plants* (eds H. de Kroon and J. van Groenendael), pp. 137–154. Backhuys Publishers, Leiden, The Netherlands.

Anghinoni, I. and Barber, S.A. (1980) Phosphorus application rate and distribution in the soil and phosphorus uptake by corn. *Soil Science Society of America Journal* 44, 1041–1044.

Aung, L.G. (1974) Root-shoot relationships. In: *The Plant Root and its Environment* (ed. E.W. Carson), pp. 29–61. University Press of Virginia, Charlottesville, Virginia.

Birch, C.P.D. and Hutchings, M.J. (1992) Stolon growth and branching in *Glechoma hederacea* L: an application of a plastochron index. *New Phytologist* 122, 545–551.

Birch, C.P.D. and Hutchings, M.J. (1994) Exploitation of patchily distributed resources by the clonal herb *Glechoma hederacea. Journal of Ecology* 82, 653–664.

Bloom, A.J., Chapin, F.S. III and Mooney, H.A. (1985) Resource limitation in plants—an economic analogy. *Annual Review of Ecology and Systematics* 16, 363–392.

Caldwell, M.M. (1994) Exploiting nutrients in fertile soil microsites. In: *Exploitation of Environmental Heterogeneity in Plants: Ecophysiological Processes Above- and Belowground* (eds M.M. Caldwell and R.W. Pearcy), pp. 325–347. Academic Press, San Diego.

Caldwell, M.M. and Pearcy, R.W. (1994) (eds). *Exploitation of Environmental Heterogeneity in Plants: Ecophysiological Processes Above- and Belowground.* Academic Press, San Diego.

Campbell, B.D., Grime, J.P. and Mackey, J.M.L. (1991) A trade-off between scale and precision in resource foraging. *Oecologia* 87, 532–538.

Chazdon, R.L., Williams, K. and Field, C.B. (1988) Interactions between crown structure and light environment in five rainforest *Piper* species. *American Journal of Botany* 75, 1459–1471.

Cook, R.E. (1983) Clonal plant populations. *American Scientist* 71, 244–253.

Drew, M.C. (1975) Comparison of the effects of a localized supply of phosphate, nitrate, ammonium and potassium on the growth of the seminal root system, and the shoot, in barley. *New Phytologist* 75, 479–490.

Drew, M.C. and Saker, L.R. (1975) Nutrient supply and the growth of the seminal root system in barley. II. Localized, compensatory increases in lateral root growth and rates of nitrate uptake, when nitrate supply is restricted to only part of the root system. *Journal of Experimental Botany* 26, 79–90.

Drew, M.C. and Saker, L.R. (1978) Nutrient supply and the growth of the seminal root system in barley. III. Compensatory increases in growth of lateral roots, and in rates of phosphate uptake, in response to a localized supply of phosphate. *Journal of Experimental Botany* 29, 435–451.

Drew, M.C., Saker, L.R. and Ashley, T.W. (1973) Nutrient supply and the growth of the seminal root system in barley. I. The effect of nitrate concentration on the growth of axes and laterals. *Journal of Experimental Botany* 24, 1189–1202.

Einsmann, J.C., Jones, R.H., Pu, M. and Mitchell, R.J. (1999) Nutrient foraging traits in ten co-occurring plant species of contrasting life forms. *Journal of Ecology* 87, 609–619.

Erickson, R.O. and Michelini, F.J. (1957) The plastochron index. *American Journal of Botany* 44, 297–305.

Fitter, A.H. (1994) Architecture and biomass allocation as components of the plastic response of root systems to soil heterogeneity. In: *Exploitation of Environmental Heterogeneity in Plants: Ecophysiological Processes Above- and Belowground* (eds M.M. Caldwell and R.W. Pearcy), pp. 305–323. Academic Press, San Diego.

Fretwell, S.D. (1972). *Populations in a Seasonal Environment.* Princeton University Press, Princeton, NJ.

Gersani, M., Abramsky, Z. and Falik, O. (1998) Density-dependent habitat selection in plants. *Evolutionary Ecology* 12, 223–234.

Gersani, M. and Sachs, T. (1992) Developmental correlations between roots in heterogeneous environments. *Plant, Cell and Environment* **15**, 463–469.

Grime, J.P. (1994) The role of plasticity in exploiting environmental heterogeneity. In: *Exploitation of Environmental Heterogeneity in Plants: Ecophysiological Processes Above- and Belowground* (eds M.M. Caldwell and R.W. Pearcy), pp. 1–19. Academic Press, San Diego.

Harper, D.G.C. (1982) Competitive foraging in mallards: 'ideal free' ducks. *Animal Behaviour* **30**, 575–584.

Hodge, A., Stewart, J., Robinson, D. and Griffiths, B.S. and Fitter, A.H. (1998) Root proliferation, soil fauna and plant nitrogen capture from nutrient-rich patches in soil. *New Phytologist* **139**, 479–494.

Hunt, R. and Nicholls, A.O. (1986) Stress and the coarse control of growth and root-shoot partitioning in herbaceous plants. *Oikos* **47**, 149–158.

Hutchings, M.J. and de Kroon, H. (1994) Foraging in plants: the role of morphological plasticity in resource acquisition. *Advances in Ecological Research* **25**, 159–238.

Jackson, R.B. and Caldwell, M.M. (1993a) The scale of nutrient heterogeneity around individual plants and its quantification with geostatistics. *Ecology* **74**, 612–614.

Jackson, R.B. and Caldwell, M.M. (1993b) Geostatistical patterns of soil heterogeneity around individual perennial plants. *Journal of Ecology* **81**, 683–692.

Jackson, R.B. and Caldwell, M.M. (1996) Integrating resource heterogeneity and plant plasticity: modelling nitrate and phosphate uptake in a patchy soil environment. *Journal of Ecology* **84**, 891–903.

Kotliar, N.B. and Wiens, J.A. (1990) Multiple scales of patchiness and patch structure: a hierarchical framework for the study of heterogeneity. *Oikos* **59**, 253–260.

Kovar, J.L. and Barber, S.A. (1989) Reasons for differences among soils in placement of phosphorus for maximum predicted uptake. *Soil Science Society of America Journal* **53**, 1733–1736.

Lamoreaux, R.J., Chaney, W.R. and Brown, K.M. (1978) The plastochron index: a review after two decades of use. *American Journal of Botany* **65**, 586–593.

Larigauderie, A. and Richards, J.H. (1994) Root proliferation characteristics of seven perennial arid-land grasses in nutrient-enriched microsites. *Oecologia* **99**, 102–111.

Lau, R.R. and Young, D.R. (1988) Influence of physiological integration on survivorship and water relations in a clonal herb. *Ecology* **69**, 215–219.

Lechowicz, M.J. and Bell, G. (1991) The ecology and genetics of fitness in forest plants. II. Microspatial heterogeneity of the edaphic environment. *Journal of Ecology* **79**, 687–696.

Marshall, C. (1990) Source-sink relations of interconnected ramets. In: *Clonal Growth in Plants— Regulation and Function* (eds J. van Groenendael and H. de Kroon), pp. 23–41. SPB Academic Publishing, The Hague.

Milinski, M. (1979) Evolutionarily stable feeding strategy in sticklebacks. *Zietschrift für Tierpsychologie* **51**, 36–40.

Mou, P., Mitchell, R.J. and Jones, R.H. (1997) Root distribution of two tree species under a heterogeneous nutrient environment. *Journal of Applied Ecology* **34**, 645–656.

Oborny, B. (1994) Growth rules in clonal plants and environmental predictability—a simulation study. *Journal of Ecology* **82**, 341–351.

Parker, G.A. (1978) Searching for mates. In: *Behavioural Ecology* (eds J.R. Krebs and N.B. Davies), pp. 214–244. Blackwell Scientific Publications, Oxford.

Pearcy, R.W. (1983) The light environment and growth of C_3 and C_4 tree species in the understory of a Hawaiian forest. *Oecologia* **58**, 19–25.

Pulliam, H.R. and Caraco, T. (1984) Living in groups: is there an optimal group size? In: *Behavioural Ecology* 2nd edn (eds J.R. Krebs and N.B. Davies), pp. 214–244. Blackwell Scientific Publications, Oxford.

Robinson, D. (1994) Tansley Review no. 73. The responses of plants to non-uniform supplies of nutrients. *New Phytologist* **127**, 635–674

Schlesinger, W.H., Reynolds, J.F., Cunningham, J.F., *et al.* (1991) Biological feedbacks in global desertification. *Science* **247**, 1043–1048.

Slade, A.J. and Hutchings, M.J. (1987a) The effects of nutrient availability on foraging in the clonal herb *Glechoma hederacea*. *Journal of Ecology* **75**, 95–112.

Slade, A.J. and Hutchings, M.J. (1987b) Clonal

integration and plasticity in foraging behaviour in *Glechoma hederacea*. *Journal of Ecology* **75**, 1023–1036.

Stuefer, J.F. (1996) Potential and limitations of current concepts regarding the response of clonal plants to environmental heterogeneity. *Vegetatio* **127**, 55–70.

Stuefer, J.F. (1997) *Division of labour in clonal plants? On the response of stoloniferous species to environmental heterogeneity.* PhD Thesis, University of Utrecht, The Netherlands.

Stuefer, J.F., de Kroon, H. and During, H.J. (1996) Exploitation of environmental heterogeneity by spatial division of labour in a clonal plant. *Functional Ecology* **10**, 328–334.

Stuefer, J.F., During, H.J. and de Kroon, H. (1994) High benefits of clonal integration in two stoloniferous species, in response to heterogeneous light environments. *Journal of Ecology* **82**, 511–518.

Tissue, D.T. and Nobel, P.S. (1988) Parent-ramet connections in *Agave deserti*: influences of carbohydrates on growth. *Oecologia* **75**, 266–271.

Turkington, R. and Harper, J.L. (1979) The growth, distribution and neighbour relations of *Trifolium repens* in a permanent pasture. I. Ordination, pattern and contact. *Journal of Ecology* **67**, 201–218.

Wijesinghe, D.K. and Handel, S.N. (1994) Advantages of clonal growth in heterogeneous habitats: an experiment with *Potentilla simplex*. *Journal of Ecology* **82**, 495–502.

Wijesinghe, D.K. and Hutchings, M.J. (1997) The effects of spatial scale of environmental heterogeneity on the growth of a clonal herb: an experimental study with *Glechoma hederacea*. *Journal of Ecology* **85**, 17–28.

Wijesinghe, D.K. and Hutchings, M.J. (1999) The effects of environmental heterogeneity on the performance of *Glechoma hederacea*: the interactions between patch contrast and patch scale. *Journal of Ecology* **87**, 860–872.

Zhang, H., Jennings, A., Barlow, P.W. and Forde, B.G. (1999) Dual pathways for regulation of root branching by nitrate. *Proceedings of the National Academy of Sciences* **96**, 6529–6534.

Chapter 7

Plant competition in spatially heterogeneous environments

B.B. Casper[1], J.F. Cahill[2], Jr and R.B. Jackson[3]

Competition among plants occurs in two physically separated spheres—above-ground and below-ground. Above-ground, plants primarily compete for light, but below-ground competition may be much more complicated, potentially involving water, space, and any of more than 20 mineral nutrients required for plant growth. Not only are soil resources diverse but they are temporally and spatially variable (Casper and Jackson 1997; Ehrenfeld *et al.* 1997), and little is known about the consequences of this heterogeneity for population or community structure. Here we consider how spatial nutrient heterogeneity at scales smaller than a plant root system might affect the outcome of plant competition. We first review spatially explicit competition models and give particular attention to how resource heterogeneity has been incorporated into them. We then discuss experiments in which we examined the consequences of nutrient heterogeneity for both intraspecific and interspecific competition. By obtaining measures of lateral root spread in populations of an annual species, we estimated the structure of the populations below-ground and how this structure changes with the spatial distribution of nutrients. Based on theory and empirical results, we propose that a probabilistic approach to modelling the below-ground neighbourhood should be incorporated into population and community models of plant competition.

Defining the neighbourhood

Plants interact and compete with specific, individual neighbours, not with entire populations or communities. That such interactions occur among specific neighbours is the basis for spatially explicit models of competition. Whether determining the number and identity of individuals influencing growth and reproduction of a target plant, or modelling resource uptake at a particular point in space, both processes require a description of the competitive 'neighbourhood'.

We adopt a common usage of 'neighbourhood', defined as the set of individuals whose zones of influence spatially overlap (e.g. Czaran and Bartha 1992). In terms

[1]*Department of Biology, University of Pennsylvania, Philadelphia, PA 19104-6018, USA;* [2]*Department of Biological Sciences, University of Alberta, Edmonton, Alberta, T6G 2E9, Cananda;* [3]*Department of Biology and Nicholas School of the Environment, Duke University, Durham, NC 27708, USA*

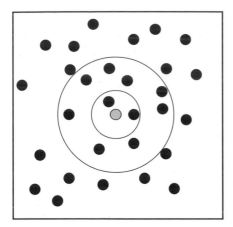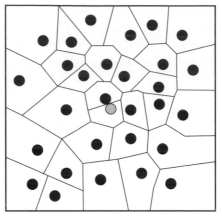

Figure 7.1 Two types of spatially explicit neighbourhood models of plant competition. In the zone of influence model, a target plant, indicated in grey, experiences competition from neighbours within some radially symmetrical area, with two possibilities shown here. The polygon model assigns space to each plant based on distances to the stems of nearest neighbours. These approaches seldom separate below-ground and above-ground plant interactions.

of space, we equate the zone of influence with the area over which a plant takes up resources, recognizing that most models do not distinguish between above-ground and below-ground neighbourhoods even though the two types may differ in size and shape. Neighbourhood predictors of plant performance, also referred to as competition indices, are based on assumptions about the neighbourhood shapes and sizes. Many predictors, likewise, do not differentiate between above- and below-ground interactions (e.g. Weiner 1982; Pacala 1987), and others typically estimate one or the other (Daniels *et al.* 1986; Nielsen and Mackenthun 1991).

Assumptions underlying neighbourhood models and predictors range from absence of overlap among zones of influence (segregation) to extensive overlap (Fig. 7.1), with zones of influence sometimes extending well beyond the canopies (Daniels *et al.* 1986). Segregated zones of influence around individual plants are modelled by allocating a polygonal area to each plant defined by lines drawn equidistant between a target plant and its adjacent neighbours (Fig. 7.1). The polygon is assumed to be the primary area available for resource uptake above- and below-ground and plant performance is often correlated with the polygonal area. In some cases, polygon areas are weighted by plant size (Mead 1966; Mithen *et al.* 1984; Daniels *et al.* 1986). Such representations, sometimes called Thiessen polygons, either preclude competition or restrict competition to adjacent neighbours. Alternatively, models can be constructed with overlapping zones of influence. Of these, some assume a fixed, radially symmetric zone of influence, while others determine the area that explains the most variation in target plant size.

Despite the importance of below-ground competition in many systems (Casper and Jackson 1997), few neighbourhood models separate competition above- and below-ground. That below-ground competition is frequently as strong or stronger than above-ground competition (Wilson 1988) is supported by data from a variety of studies, including those examining the effect of neighbours on nutrient uptake (Wilson 1988) and those using vertical tubes to exclude roots of other plants (Cook and Ratcliff 1984; Reichenberger and Pyke 1990; Wilson and Tilman 1995; Cahill 1999). While such studies document the presence of below-ground competition, they do not usually define and often restrict the area occupied by roots of competing individuals.

Recent studies have examined the plasticity and functional significance of three dimensional root structure (Tardieu 1988; McKane *et al.* 1990; Caldwell *et al.* 1991; Campbell *et al.* 1991; Brisson and Reynolds 1994; Fitter 1994; Mou *et al.* 1995), identifying changes in root growth as a function of both the biotic and abiotic environment. Many species respond to soil heterogeneity by root proliferation in high-nutrient microsites (Duncan and Ohlrogge 1958; Drew and Saker 1975; Crick and Grime 1987; Eissenstat and Caldwell 1988; Jackson and Caldwell 1989; Gross *et al.* 1993; Einsmann *et al.* 1999). Root growth may also respond to the presence of other individuals (Gersani *et al.* 1998), but the extent that root systems either intermingle or avoid each other seems to vary among species (Caldwell *et al.* 1991; Mahall and Callaway 1991; Brisson and Reynolds 1994; Schenk *et al.* 1999). Woody species may even exhibit root grafting so that roots of different individuals are physically connected (Graham and Bormann 1976).

These findings and our own experimental results with nutrient analogues discussed later in this chapter suggest that the size and shape of the rooting area, and thus a plant's below-ground zone of influence, depend on the spatial distribution of resources. Our studies demonstrate the aggregation of many root systems in nutrient patches, a response to heterogeneity that may result in larger below-ground neighbourhoods in the vicinity of a patch.

Neighbourhoods and neighbourhood models in heterogeneous environments
Spatial resource heterogeneity has the potential to change the below-ground neighbourhood, with varying consequences in different models. Polygon models that assume little or no overlap among zones of influence may have trouble incorporating competition for an enriched soil patch into their framework. For models with overlapping zones of influence, assumptions of a fixed, radially symmetric zone of influence may be incorrect, especially if more individuals access nutrient-rich soil patches than nutrient-poor ones.

Most polygon models construct a neighbourhood based on the above-ground distribution of plants. The polygons are frequently used to partition space in the model to one plant or another, often precluding direct effects of competition. Whether such neighbourhoods apply below-ground is unclear (though they seem unlikely to), and little research has addressed this issue. One interesting attempt was made by Brisson and Reynolds (1994) who excavated and mapped coarse roots (>2 mm diameter) of 32 creosote shrubs (*Larrera tridentata*) in the Chihuahuan

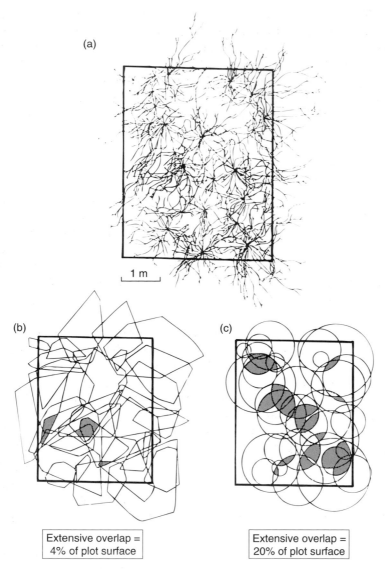

(a)

1 m

(b)

Extensive overlap =
4% of plot surface

(c)

Extensive overlap =
20% of plot surface

Figure 7.2 From Brisson and Reynolds (1994) who described the root systems of creosotebush as irregular polygons based on actual root distributions. Polygons result in less overlap among four or more plants, shown in grey, than would circular root systems with the same areas. (a) Map of excavated root system. The larger rectangle represents the plot border. (b) Map of root polygons. (c) Map of hypothetical root systems: circular in shape, centred on the plant's location and of surface area equal to their corresponding root polygon.

Desert (Fig. 7.2). They found that the root systems were shaped as irregular polygons which seemed to reflect directional growth away from the maximum competitive pressure of adjacent plants. Overlap of four or more root systems rarely occurred. The resulting irregular geometry of lateral growth filled the available soil space more effectively than would circular root systems, and the authors concluded that the root geometry of the shrubs minimized overlap among neighbours. There is also evidence that chemicals released by creosote roots may enable conspecifics to detect and avoid each other (Mahall and Callaway 1991).

Since many neighbourhood models assume that the zone of influence is circular, testing the symmetry of root distributions around individual plants, and the extent of root overlap, is important. Mou et al. (1995) found that the degree of root overlap observed in young sweet gum and loblolly pine populations grown in plots was lower than if root systems were radially symmetric. Fine root biomass was more closely correlated with concentrations of soil P and K than with above-ground biomass. The authors concluded that the distribution of fine roots in the system was a consequence of both avoiding neighbours and locating nutrient patches. They also pointed out that accurately simulating root interactions would be aided by a better understanding of root behaviour in response to heterogeneous biotic and abiotic environments.

Although some neighbourhood predictors include neighbourhood size based on the degree of overlap among canopies (Ek and Monserud 1974; Daniels et al. 1986) or root systems (Nielsen and Mackenthun 1991), other predictors take no account of mechanisms of plant interactions and are based on the assumption that all neighbours compete within a certain distance (the neighbourhood radius). These distance-based predictors assume that plants are more effective at exploiting resources close to them and that competitive effects among neighbouring plants decline with distance according to a chosen function (e.g. linear, hyperbolic, etc.; Mack and Harper 1977; Weiner 1982; Weiner 1984; Pacala and Silander 1985; Zhang and Hamill 1997). In addition, effects of neighbours are sometimes weighted by plant size (Ek and Monserud 1974; Weiner 1984) and angular dispersion (Silander and Pacala 1985; Lindquist et al. 1994) to account for asymmetric arrangements of neighbours. The latter can be important as some studies suggest that plant performance can be strongly affected by asymmetry in zones of influence around individual plants both above- and below-ground (Brisson and Reynolds 1994, 1997; Mou et al. 1995; Umeki 1997).

Neighbourhood models incorporating symmetric zones of influence vary in their ability to explain variation in plant performance. Bonan (1993) reported that published studies using this approach explained from 0 to 91% of the variation, with a mean of only 42%. In addition, he showed that curvilinear relationships between plant performance and local crowding can simply be a consequence of random, non-competitive variation among plant growth rates. Garrett and Dixon (1997) suggested that neighbourhood analyses of natural communities in heterogeneous habitats could also lead to the erroneous interpretation that plant interactions were present when plants in fact responded solely to their abiotic environment. They concluded that environmental heterogeneity rather than competition may sometimes cause correlations between the size or fecundity of individuals and the number of their competitors.

Recent models have relaxed the often unrealistic assumptions that neighbourhoods occupy circular areas, that above- and below-ground neighbourhoods are the same size, and that resources are homogeneously distributed in space. Mou *et al.* (1993) used ecological field theory to construct an individually based, spatially explicit, and resource mediated model for simulating plant interactions and examining some consequences of heterogeneity. Their model predicted individual plant response based on neighbourhood structure (the proximity of neighbouring plants), resource availability, and the basic physiology and architecture of the plants (root and crown architecture were specified separately for each individual). Starting from homogeneous soils, heterogeneity developed in the simulations over time through plant interactions and resource uptake. These simple heterogeneity simulations showed relatively small effects at the scale of populations and communities but altered growth rates of individuals dramatically. There are advantages to greater detail in models, allowing interactions among many factors to be examined, but the extra detail comes at a cost. The fairly detailed inputs in the Mou *et al.* (1993) model and its relatively small scale (a 10×10 cm grid) make it less tractable for large populations or communities. A trade-off between how much information is needed to run a given model and the scale of its predictions is apparent in all of the models we discuss.

Two relatively recent community models have examined the effect of nutrient distributions and heterogeneity on competition. Biondini and Grygiel (1994) explored the competitive ability and landscape distribution of plants as a function of the spread and density of roots and the scale of soil nitrogen availability. They began by modifying the ALLOCATE model of Tilman (1988) to include root lateral spread (RLS) and soil N, scaling for as many as 15 'species' with a range of RLS. Results varied depending on the scale of N, root attributes, and the stage of plant competition (adults vs. seedlings). Overall, plants with higher root densities and lower lateral root spread were better competitors when nitrogen was relatively common, while the opposite was true under N stress. Huston and DeAngelis (1994) incorporated soil nutrient transport rates into a community model. By relaxing the assumption of an instantly mixed and homogeneous soil pool, resource depletion could occur locally without depleting the broader soil pool substantially. Under these simulated conditions, many species could coexist in the model, even when limited by the same resource. The model also predicted that plant competition in lower fertility environments occurs primarily below-ground, while not surprisingly, competition for light is more common under high nutrient availability. The simulations also implied that light competition is more asymmetric than is below-ground competition (see also Grace 1985).

A recent analysis by Ives (1995) developed a modelling framework for measuring competition in a spatially heterogeneous environment. Two kinds of heterogeneity were considered, variation in resource quality and variation in the density and arrangement of individuals. According to the author, the first step in such an analysis is to calculate model sensitivity to a range of biologically reasonable neighbourhood sizes. If that sensitivity is low, then the size of the neighbourhood is relatively unimportant for evaluating competition. If not, then experiments are needed to determine neighbourhood size for the system of interest.

All of the above models suggest that a number of below-ground factors are important for plant competition. These include the spread and density of roots, the distribution and mobility of soil resources, and the relative importance of above- and below-ground competition. Additionally, all of these studies demonstrate the need for replacing assumptions and indirect estimates of sizes and shapes of plant neighbourhoods with actual measurements wherever possible. Better knowledge about below-ground neighbourhoods will be especially important for constructing predictive models of plant competition that include spatial nutrient heterogeneity (Pacala and Silander 1985; Biondini and Grygiel 1994). With information on actual root distributions and canopy sizes it should also be possible to examine the relative magnitude of above- and below-ground competition as factors affecting plant performance.

Potential consequences of spatial nutrient heterogeneity for competition

Plants growing without neighbours often attain greater biomass in heterogeneous soils, apparently because of their ability to exploit nutrient patches through plasticity in root morphology or physiology (Drew and Saker 1975; Lee 1982; Crick and Grime 1987; Eissenstat and Caldwell 1988; Jackson and Caldwell 1989; Gross et al. 1993; Einsmann et al. 1999). The extent to which heterogeneity improves performance may vary with the contrast, which is the difference in nutrient concentration between the patch and the background soil (Anghinoni and Barber 1980; Borkert and Barber 1985; Kotliar and Wiens 1990), or the scale of heterogeneity, as has been demonstrated for clonal plants (Hutchings et al., this volume). Differences among species in root responses to nutrient patches have led to the prediction that small-scale heterogeneity will affect the composition of plant communities (Eissenstat and Caldwell 1988; Jackson and Caldwell 1989; Jackson et al. 1990; Campbell et al. 1991; Gross et al. 1993; Fransen et al. 1998). In order to project the consequences of small-scale heterogeneity for natural systems, however, we need to understand its importance for plant performance in the presence of neighbours. Competing individuals might not respond to nutrient patches in the same way as isolated plants or physically connected ramets, and patchiness might change the magnitude or nature of the competition.

Spatial heterogeneity will alter the magnitude of below-ground competition only if changes in the spatial distribution of nutrients affects the ability of one plant to harvest nutrients at the expense of another. Thus, for heterogeneity to *increase* below-ground competition, an individual must reduce nutrient uptake by its neighbour more than it would if the two were growing on a more spatially uniform soil. This could occur through direct competition for nutrients within the patch as suggested by the work of Robinson *et al.* (1999, Fitter *et al.*, this volume) or by a plant pre-empting the soil space as might occur through allelopathy (Mahall and Calloway 1991). Schwinning and Weiner (1998) have suggested that size could confer an advantage in reaching or harvesting nutrient patches. If so, heterogeneity would result in asymmetric competition among root systems and should increase size differences among competing plants, a change from the size symmetric mode of below-ground competition typically invoked (Weiner 1990; Weiner *et al.* 1997).

We envision several ways in which nutrient heterogeneity might also affect relative plant sizes even in the absence of direct competition for soil resources. First, differences in the ability to take up nutrients from patches could mean that spatial heterogeneity simply changes the relative growth performance and above-ground competitive abilities of co-occurring species. Second, if competing plants, like isolated plants, acquire more nutrients from patches than they would under more homogeneous conditions (Fransen *et al.* 1998), then heterogeneous soils should increase overall productivity. Changes in size structure should accompany increased productivity, since skewness in size hierarchies typically increases as plants grow and compete for light (Harper 1977; Weiner and Thomas 1986). Finally, depending on distances between patches and lateral root spread, plants located on or near patches may simply have access to more nutrients than those farther away, potentially increasing inequality in plant sizes even if total productivity at the population or community level is unaffected.

Experiments examining intraspecific competition in the presence of heterogeneity

We explored these population-level responses to heterogeneity in a series of experiments with the annual *Abutilon theophrasti*, expecting that heterogeneity would increase size inequalities for the reasons just explained. In one experiment described in some detail here, we applied nutrient analogues as tracers to obtain estimates of lateral root spread and root distributions with respect to nutrient patches. We used this information to evaluate assumptions made when incorporating spatial heterogeneity into current neighbourhood models of plant competition.

We found spatial nutrient heterogeneity to have almost no effect on productivity or overall size structure of experimental populations of *A. theophrasti*, grown in a common garden plot (Casper and Cahill 1996, 1998). In one study, heterogeneity was constructed as a checkerboard of $8 \times 8 \times 10$ cm low and high nutrient patches (Casper and Cahill 1996). Heterogeneity did not change total productivity, compared with a spatially uniform distribution of nutrients, and only increased mean plant biomass in one of three planting densities. Although plants whose stems were located on high nutrient patches were larger on average than those on low nutrient patches (Fig. 7.3), maximum plant size did not differ between heterogeneous and homogeneous soils. Thus the location of plants with respect to nutrient patches influenced their size ranking within the population, but plants growing on patches

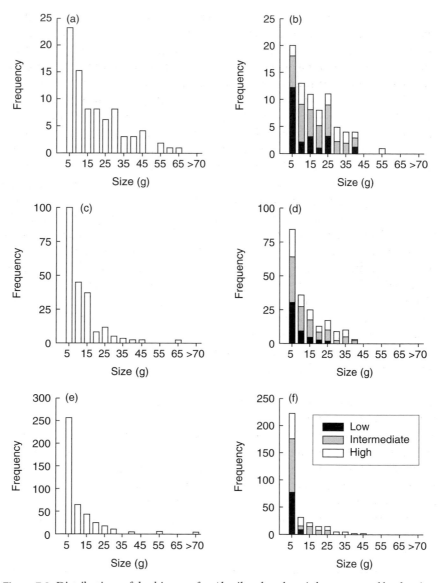

Figure 7.3 Distributions of dry biomass for *Abutilon theophrasti* plants grouped by density (30 (a and b), 60 (c and d) or 120 (e and f) plants per 72 cm×72 cm plot) and soil treatment, either a checkerboard pattern of nutrient heterogeneity (b, d and f) or homogeneous (a, c and e) soil. In the heterogeneous soil treatment, plants are further grouped by their location with respect to nutrient patches: those on high nutrient patches, low nutrient patches and the interface between the two. Biomass differed significantly (*P* < 0.02) among these locations. From Casper and Cahill (1996).

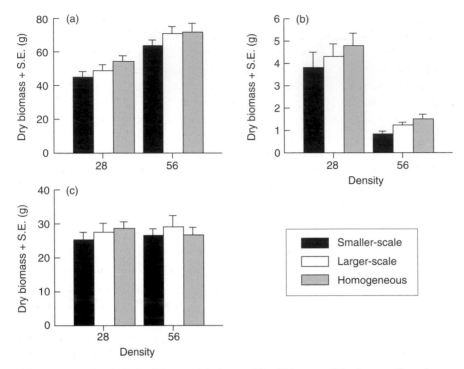

Figure 7.4 Total population biomass (a), the combined biomass of the four smallest plants (b) and the combined biomass of the four largest plants (±SE, c) for populations of *Abutilon theophrasti* growing on soil with small scale heterogeneity, large scale heterogeneity and a homogeneous treatment. Density represents the number of individuals in the 48×48 cm plots. Total population biomass differed with soil type when populations on both forms of heterogeneity were compared with the homogeneous treatment in a planned comparison (*P*<0.03). The combined biomass of the four smallest plants differed among soil treatments (*P*<0.01), but that of the four largest plants did not. From Casper and Cahill (1998).

did not perform any better and may not have acquired any more nutrients than the largest plants on homogeneous soils.

In a second experiment, we concentrated supplemental nutrients in four patches within the 0.23 m² (10 cm deep) area occupied by a population (Casper and Cahill 1998). Because patch size differed in the two heterogeneous treatments (either 8×8 ×10 cm or 16×16×10 cm) while the amount of nutrients added remained the same, the contrast between the patch and the background soil differed along with the spatial scale. In this case, heterogeneity lowered productivity slightly by decreasing the size of the smallest plants, at least in part because the most concentrated nutrients proved detrimental to plants on or near patches (Fig. 7.4). Maximum plant size was unchanged (Fig. 7.4). In a similar study involving monocultures of two grasses, biomass of *Anthoxanthum odoratum* increased in a fine scale heterogeneity treatment and the coefficient of variation increased in both the fine scale and a coarser scale treatment, but *Festuca rubra* showed no such responses to either scale of heterogeneity (Fransen *et al.* 1999).

The subtle changes in productivity and size structure in *A. theophrasti* suggest that heterogeneity has little effect on nutrient availability, the intensity of competition, or the mode of competition (symmetric or asymmetric) at the population level. The distribution of biomass among plants and the finding that rooting densities are highest on nutrient patches (Casper and Cahill 1998) suggest that many plants share the same patch, and provides no evidence that even nearby plants monopolise or exploit those patches at the expense of other individuals. Schwinning and Weiner's (1998) prediction that larger plants potentially enjoy a disproportionate advantage in patch utilization, leading to an asymmetric mode of competition and an increase in maximum plant size, is likewise unsupported.

We obtained further information regarding patch utilization by populations of *A. theophrasti* through the application of nutrient analogues as tracers to determine root locations, avoiding the difficulties associated with physically excavating roots to map them. Instead of random planting locations used in our prior studies, plants were regularly spaced, 6 cm apart (Fig. 7.5). We prepared soil to a depth of 15 cm using two different spatial distributions of nutrients. In the homogeneous nutrient treatment 33.6 g of 14–14–14 slow release N-P-K fertilizer was mixed uniformly throughout each 60×60 cm plot. In the heterogeneous soil treatment, the same quantity of fertilizer was divided among four cylindrical patches (6 cm diameter $\times$ 15 cm deep), centred on the points of tracer injection. Differences between homogeneous and heterogeneous soils in the numbers or locations of plants taking up tracer should reflect root system responses to nutrient patches. Each heterogeneous treatment was spatially paired with a homogeneous treatment; results for four replicate pairs of populations analysed for uptake of tracer are reported here. We injected nutrient analogues into the four locations where plants were omitted from the planting array 4 weeks after planting and 2 weeks prior to harvest. Each of the four — Cs, Li, Rb, Sr — was randomly assigned to a different location. (Cs and Rb are analogues for K, and Li and Sr are analogues for Na and Ca, respectively.) These tracers are naturally occurring, non-radioactive and orders of magnitude less abundant in plant tissue than N, which is sometimes employed in tracer studies. All were in the form of 0.2 M chloride salts, and a syringe was used to inject a total of 10 mL by applying 2 mL at 2 cm incremental depths, in order to achieve a nearly continuous vertical column of tracer.

At harvest, plants were identified by their location within the array and tracer concentrations were measured in tissue produced since the time of injection, based on the growth of several tagged individuals. Tracer analyses on dried material were performed by a laboratory at Pennsylvania State University using ICP spectrometry for Sr, flame emission for Li, and atomic absorption for Rb and Cs. Only Rb and Sr proved useful tracers because significant levels of Cs were not detected by the analytical procedure, and few plants apparently took up Li. Background tissue levels of each tracer were determined from the set of five plants in each population that were located farthest from the point of tracer injection. We pooled the tracer

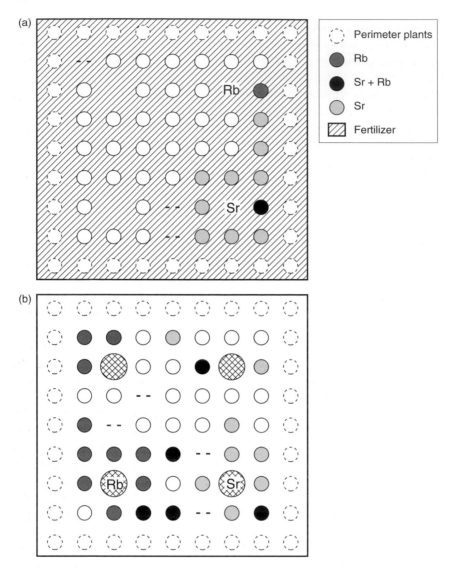

Figure 7.5 Pictorial representation of one replicate pair of soil treatment plots: the homogeneous treatment in which fertilizer was applied evenly throughout the plot (a), and the heterogeneous treatment in which fertilizer was concentrated in patches on the points of tracer injection (b). Plants, spaced 6 cm apart, are represented by circles shaded to indicate uptake elevated above background levels for Sr, Rb, or both Sr and Rb. Perimeter plants were not harvested in order to minimize edge effects, and dashes indicate plants that died or were too small for chemical analysis. Background tracer levels were determined for each pair of soil treatment plots from tracer concentrations in plants from the five locations farthest from the point of tracer injection in each of the two populations. (See text for details.) In these plots, cut-off values were 108.13 p.p.m. for Sr and 31.76 p.p.m. for Rb; tracer concentrations in plant tissues were as great as 362 p.p.m. for Sr and 1377 p.p.m. for Rb.

concentration measurements from the 10 such plants (or fewer if some died or were too small for chemical analysis) in each pair of soil treatment plots and applied a one-tailed t-test ($P < 0.01$) to establish the minimum tracer concentration to be considered elevated above background levels (Fig. 7.5). Tracers did not move significant lateral distances in the soil during the 2-week period. This was determined by injecting tracers in a second set of plots without plants and measuring uptake by negatively charged resin beads placed at 3, 6 and 10 cm from the point of injection (Casper, Jackson and Cahill, unpublished).

Results demonstrate clear population-level responses below-ground to nutrient patches. Significantly more plants took up tracer ($F = 27.341$; $P < 0.02$; mean $= 9.0$ for Sr and 7.75 for Rb on heterogeneous soil; mean $= 4.75$ for Sr and 3.75 for Rb on homogeneous soils) and in larger amounts ($F = 9.262$; $P < 0.04$; mean $= 229.78$ p.p.m. for Sr and 184.77 p.p.m. for Rb on heterogeneous soils; mean $= 165.10$ p.p.m. for Sr and 43.53 p.p.m. for Rb on homogeneous soils) when nutrient patches were centred on the points of tracer injection than when nutrients were spread uniformly throughout the population. The median distance between a plant taking up a tracer and the point of tracer injection did not differ between soil treatments. Results for one pair of populations are depicted by Fig. 7.5. Data from all eight plots are also presented graphically, with total uptake, calculated from tracer concentration and biomass produced since the time of tracer injection, graphed as a function of plant distance from tracer (Figs 7.6 and 7.7). Results corroborate our earlier conclusion that plants do not exclude neighbours from patches and show that on the contrary many individuals converge on the same patch. In the heterogeneous soil treatment tracer uptake increased with proximity to nutrient patch for Sr (Spearman's $r_s = -0.514$; $P < 0.01$; $n = 37$) but not Rb. Increased uptake of Sr probably reflects root proliferation or increased rate of uptake, typical plant responses to localized nutrients. The difference between Rb and Sr in this regard may be related to their functioning as analogues for different nutrients. The fact that Rb is an analogue for K, a component of the fertilizer patches, may have enabled us to detect root activity within patches more easily with Sr.

Besides providing information on the response of neighbouring plants to heterogeneity, tracer uptake data also illustrate lateral root spread distances, allowing estimates of the size of the zone of influence and the number of individuals making up the below-ground neighbourhood. The results provide strong evidence that a typical plant interacts with many individuals more distant than its nearest neighbour. The maximum lateral root spread detected, 32 cm, means that plants up to 64 cm apart potentially compete for soil resources. With a circular rooting area, a 32 cm rooting radius would encompass the stems of 89 individuals at the planting density used here and result in root overlap with 358 individuals! Based on the number and locations of plants taking up both tracers, it appears that root systems neither occupy a circular area nor grow in a single direction but probably have irregular shapes.

Which plants and, possibly how many, plants interact below-ground probably

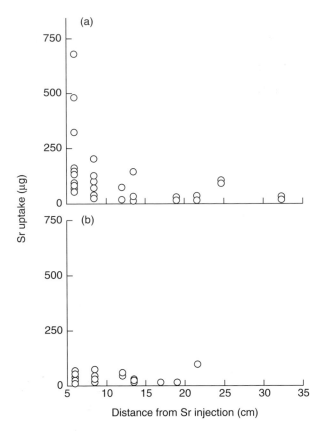

Figure 7.6 Total uptake (tissue concentration × biomass produced since the time of tracer injection) of Sr for plants with concentrations above background levels, graphed as a function of the distance of the plant from the point of tracer injection. Data are combined for all plots of the same soil treatment. More plants took up Sr in heterogeneous soils (a), and uptake decreased with distance from the point of injection. There was no such relationship in homogeneous soils (b).

changes with the spatial distribution of nutrients. We detected tracer in more individuals when it was located on a patch of nutrients, suggesting that patchiness increases the number of plants interacting at that location. However, we do not know whether plants compensate by decreasing lateral root spread in other directions. In homogeneous soils, the lack of tracer uptake by an individual may not necessarily reflect its complete absence from the point of tracer injection; its roots may have been present but poorly developed since nutrients were not locally elevated. Nevertheless, to the extent that tracer uptake is an indicator of root activity, the results suggest a potential increase in the number of competing individuals on nutrient patches.

While we have interpreted tracer uptake as evidence of the actual presence of roots in a particular location, we acknowledge that additional factors may also

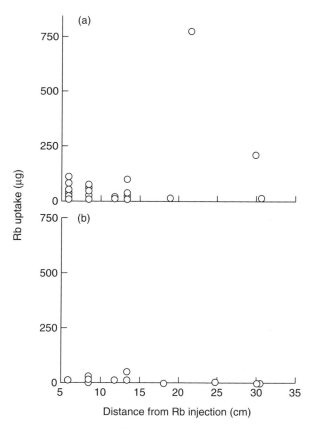

Figure 7.7 Rb uptake as a function of distance from tracer injection, presented as in Fig. 7.6. Rb uptake was independent of distance in both soil types. (a) Heterogeneous soils; (b) homogeneous soils.

contribute to functional rooting area in plants. First, *A. theophrasti* is mycorrhizal, and mycorrhizae clearly play an important role in accessing localized patches of nutrients (St. John *et al.* 1983; Allen and Allen 1990). Even if mycorrhizae serve this function in *A. theophrasti*, we feel certain that the roots themselves also respond, since rooting densities increase greatly on nutrient-enriched patches (Casper and Cahill 1998). Mycorrhizae or other biotic agents might also move tracer among plants (Chiariello *et al.* 1982; Francis *et al.* 1986; Fitter *et al.* 1998). Regardless of the tracer uptake mechanism, a major qualitative result of this study remains the same. The below-ground zone of influence in this system is extensive, and even widely separated plants potentially compete for the same pool of soil resources.

Interspecific competition in the presence of heterogeneity
Surprisingly few studies have examined the possibility that heterogeneity at scales smaller than a root system affects the outcome of interspecific competition or the

composition of plant communities. A pot experiment with *Ambrosia artemisiifolia* and *Phytolacca americana* provided no evidence that heterogeneity affects the relative performance of the two species (Cahill and Casper 1999). Although localizing nutrients in patches produced larger plants when plants were grown alone (significantly so only for *P. americana*), there was no such response when the two species were grown with intraspecific or interspecific neighbours. This was true even when patches were located closer to some plants than others. The experiment increased soil volume in proportion to the number of plants but maintained a constant number of nutrient patches, regardless of plant density. Because the contrast between the patch and background soil also remained the same, it is possible that the value of the patch—the difference in actual nutrient availability between the patch and the background soil—is diminished by the presence of neighbour roots. That is, competition among plants sharing the patch may offset the higher nutrient levels within the patch. This is consistent with the suggestion of Gersani *et al.* (1998) that plants invest in roots until the uptake rate per unit root is equal for all roots. There must also be a limit to patch contrast without a nutrient toxicity effect to the closest plants (Casper and Cahill 1998).

One other study has shown an effect of soil nutrient distributions on the relative performance of two competing perennial grasses, *A. odoratum* and *F. rubra*, but the two species performed *more* similarly with increased heterogeneity (Fransen *et al.* 1999). The amount of biomass produced by each of the species differed on homogeneous but not on heterogeneous soils, which is consistent with there being no difference between them in selective root placement within patches. Thus no study so far has shown that spatial heterogeneity increases performance differences between co-occurring species, even if the species respond differently to heterogeneity as individuals or monocultures.

Conclusions

There is no evidence to date that soil nutrient heterogeneity at scales smaller than an individual plant strongly affects the outcome of plant competition. In our experiments with *A. theophrasti*, the proximity of plants to patches sometimes determined their size ranking within populations, but overall population size structure and productivity differed very little from homogeneous soils. The enhanced growth benefits of heterogeneity shown for isolated plants may disappear in the presence of competitors. Our results also suggest that below-ground responses to heterogeneity, such as the aggregation of root systems on patches, does not necessarily affect growth performance above-ground (see also Fransen *et al.* 1998; Einsmann *et al.* 1999), perhaps because the activity of neighbour roots diminishes nutrient availability within localized patches. The long distance between some plant stems and the nutrient patches they occupied caused us to realize that lateral root spread—or the scale of foraging *sensu* Campbell *et al.* (1991)—may be an important plant trait in many heterogeneous environments. Lateral root spread should, in general, correlate with the probability or rate of patch encounter.

In addition to focusing on the consequence of heterogeneity for competition, our work also reveals a great deal about the structure of populations below-ground. For *A. theophrasti*, it appears that a model of neighbourhood competition with overlapping zones of influence is more appropriate than a polygon model (e.g. Brisson and Reynolds 1997). The extent that measures of root overlap made in either system are generalizable is yet to be determined. Lateral root system overlap may well vary with habitat characteristics or plant growth form. Plants in water-limited systems, for example, may generally exhibit less root system overlap than plants elsewhere (see Schenk *et al.* 1999), and well-developed woody root systems might grow directionally over time to avoid each other.

Several elements of plant competition models, either conceptual or quantitative, may need refinement. Our research and research by others suggests that below-ground neighbourhood size is often considerably larger than above-ground neighbourhood size and may change with the spatial distribution of nutrients. Furthermore, the zones of influence of plants are irregularly shaped and overlap extensively. There are several practical implications of these results for how the below-ground neighbourhood is included in population and community models. First, circular representations of the below-ground neighbourhood, while convenient, will be inappropriate in many cases. Second, it may be impossible to discern which individuals are interacting in the below-ground neighbourhood without direct experimentation. Fortunately, other kinds of model representations can be used productively. For example, we propose that a probabilistic approach to modelling the below-ground neighbourhood could easily be incorporated into population models. A model might assign probabilities of interaction based on distance to the soil patch (incorporating other factors, such as population density, resource of interest, etc). These probabilities can also vary depending on the soil heterogeneity in the system. This was the case in our experiments, where the introduction of soil heterogeneity increased the number of interacting individuals. Although we cannot predict precisely which individuals will interact, we can predict the likely number and their arrangement or nutrient uptake activity with distance. This probabilistic representation of the below-ground neighbourhood could be an important step forward in the development of population and community models and in our representation of the ecological consequences of soil heterogeneity.

Acknowledgments

We thank C. Hawkes, E. John, and two anonymous reviewers for helpful suggestions on the manuscript. Research described in this chapter was funded by NSF grant DEB-9708165 to B. Casper and R. Jackson.

References

Allen, E.B. and Allen, M.F. (1990) The mediation of competition by mycorrhizae in successional and patchy environments. *Perspectives on Plant Competition* (eds J.B. Grace and D. Tilman), pp. 367–389. Academic Press. San Diego, CA.

Anghinoni, I. and Barber, S.A. (1980) Phosphorus application rate and distribution within the soil and phosphorus uptake by corn. *Soil Science Society of America Journal* **44**, 1041–1044.

Biondini, M.E. and Grygiel, C.E. (1994) Landscape distribution of organisms and the scaling of soil resources. *American Naturalist* **143**, 1026–1054.

Bonan, G.B. (1993) Analysis of neighborhood competition among annual plants: implications of a plant growth model. *Ecological Modelling* **65**, 123–136.

Brisson, J. and Reynolds, J.F. (1994) The effect of neighbors on root distribution in a creosotebush (*Larrea tridentata*) population. *Ecology* **75**, 1693–1702.

Brisson, J. and Reynolds, J.F. (1997) Effects of compensatory growth on population processes: a simulation study. *Ecology* **78**, 2378–2384.

Borkert, C.M. and Barber, S.A. (1985) Soybean shoot and root growth and phosphorus concentration as affected by phosphorus placement. *Soil Science Society of America Journal* **49**, 152–155.

Cahill, J.F. Jr (1999) Fertilization effects on interactions between above- and belowground competition in an old field. *Ecology* **80**, 466–480.

Cahill, J.F. Jr and Casper, B.B. (1999) Growth consequences of soil nutrient heterogeneity for two old-field herbs, *Ambrosia artemisiifolia* and *Phytolacca americana*, grown individually and in combination. *Annals of Botany* **83**, 471–478.

Caldwell, M.M., Manwaring, J.H. and Durham, S.L. (1991) The microscale distribution of neighboring plant roots in fertile soil microsites. *Functional Ecology* **5**, 765–772.

Campbell, B.D., Grime, J.P. and Mackey, J.M.L. (1991) A trade-off between scale and precision in resource foraging. *Oecologia* **87**, 532–538.

Casper, B.B. and Cahill, J.F. Jr (1996) Limited effects of soil nutrient heterogeneity on populations of *Abutilon theophrasti* (Malvaceae). *American Journal of Botany* **83**, 333–341.

Casper, B.B. and Cahill, J.F. Jr (1998) Population level responses to nutrient heterogeneity and density by *Abutilon theophrasti* (Malvaceae): an experimental neighborhood approach. *American Journal of Botany* **85**, 1680–1687.

Casper, B.B. and Jackson, R.B. (1997) Plant competition underground. *Annual Review of Ecology and Systematics* **28**, 545–570.

Chiariello, N., Hickman, J.C. and Mooney, H.A. (1982) Endomycorrhizal role for interspecific transfer of phosphorus in a community of annual plants. *Science* **217**, 941–943.

Cook, S.J. and Ratcliff, D. (1984) A study of the effects of root and shoot competition on the growth of green panic (*Panicum maximum* var. *trichoglume*) seedlings in an existing grassland using root exclusion tubes. *Journal of Applied Ecology* **21**, 971–982.

Crick, J.C. and Grime, J.P. (1987) Morphological plasticity and mineral nutrient capture in two herbaceous species of contrasted ecology. *New Phytologist* **106**, 403–414.

Czaran, T. and Bartha, S. (1992) Spatiotemporal dynamic models of plant populations and communities. *Trends in Ecology and Evolution* **7**, 38–42.

Daniels, R.F., Burkhart, H.E. and Clason, T.R. (1986) A comparison of competition measures for predicting growth of loblolly pine trees. *Canadian Journal of Forest Research* **16**, 1230–1237.

Drew, M.C. and Saker, L.R. (1975) Nutrient supply and the growth of the seminal root system in barley. II. Localized, compensatory increases in lateral root growth and rates of nitrate uptake when nitrate supply is restricted to only part of the root system. *Journal of Experimental Botany* **26**, 79–90.

Duncan, W.G. and Ohlrogge, A.J. (1958) Principles of nutrient uptake from fertilizer bands. II. Root development in the band. *Agronomy Journal* **50**, 605–608.

Ehrenfeld, J.G., Han, X. and Parsons, W.F.J. (1997) On the nature of environmental gradients: temporal and spatial variability of soils and vegetation in the New Jersey Pinelands. *Journal of Ecology* **85**, 785–798.

Einsmann, J.C., Jones, R.H., Mou, P. and Mitchell, R.J. (1999) Nutrient foraging traits in 10 co-occurring plant species of contrasting life forms. *Journal of Ecology* **87**, 609–619.

Eissenstat, D.M. and Caldwell, M.M. (1988) Seasonal timing of root growth in favorable microsites. *Ecology* **69**, 870–873.

Ek, A.R. and Monserud, R.A. (1974) FOREST: A computer model for simulating the growth and reproduction of mixed species forest stands. *University of Wisconsin, College of Agricultural and Life Sciences Research Report* A2635, 1–14, 3 Appendices.

Fitter, A.H. (1994) Architecture and biomass allocation as components of the plastic response of root systems to soil heterogeneity. In: *Exploitation of Environmental Heterogeneity by Plants: Ecophysiological Processes Above- and Belowground* (eds M.M. Caldwell and R.W. Pearcy), pp. 305–323. Academic Press, San Diego.

Fitter, A.H., Graves, J.D. and Watkins, N.K. (1998) Carbon transfer between plants and its control in networks of arbuscular mycorrhizas. *Functional Ecology* **12**, 406–412.

Francis, R., Finlay, R.D. and Read, D.J. (1986) Vesicular-arbuscular mycorrhiza in natural vegetation systems, IV. Transfer of nutrients in inter- and intra-specific combinations of host plants. *New Phytologist* **102**, 103–111.

Fransen, B., de Kroon, H. and Berendse, F. (1998) Root morphological plasticity and nutrient acquisition of perennial grass species from habitats of different nutrient availability. *Oecologia* **115**, 351–358.

Fransen, B., de Kroon, H. and Berendse, F. (1999) Nutrient heterogeneity changes competition between populations of *Festuca rubra* L. and *Anthoxanthum odoratum* L. In: *Root foraging: the consequences for nutrient acquisition in heterogeneous environments*. PhD Thesis, Wageningen University, The Netherlands.

Garrett, K.A. and Dixon, P.M. (1997) Environmental pseudointeraction: the effects of ignoring the scale of environmental heterogeneity in competition studies. *Theoretical Population Biology* **51**, 37–48.

Gersani, M., Abramsky, Z. and Falik, O. (1998) Density-dependent habitat selection in plants. *Evolutionary Ecology* **12**, 223–234.

Grace, J.B. (1985) In search of the Holy Grail: explanations for the coexistence of plant species. *Trends in Ecology and Evolution* **10**, 263–264.

Graham, B.F. Jr and Bormann, F.H. (1976) Natural root grafts. *Botanical Review* **32**, 255–292.

Gross, K., Peters, A. and Pregitzer, K.S. (1993) Fine root growth and demographic responses to nutrient patches in four old-field plant species. *Oecologia* **95**, 61–64.

Harper, J.L. (1977) *Population Biology of Plants*. Academic Press. London.

Huston, M.A. and DeAngelis, D.L. (1994) Competition and coexistence: the effects of resource transport and supply rates. *American Naturalist* **144**, 954–977.

Ives, A.R. (1995) Measuring competition in a spatially heterogeneous environment. *American Naturalist* **146**, 911–936.

Jackson, R.B. and Caldwell, M.M. (1989) The timing and degree of root proliferation in fertile-soil microsites for three cold desert perennials. *Oecologia* **81**, 149–153.

Jackson, R.B., Manwaring, J.H. and Caldwell, M.M. (1990) Rapid physiological adjustment of roots to localized soil enrichment. *Nature* **344**, 58–60.

Kotliar, N.B. and Wiens, J.A. (1990) Multiple scales of patchiness and patch structure: a hierarchical framework for the study of heterogeneity. *Oikos* **59**, 253–260.

Lee, R.B. (1982) Selectivity and kenetics of ion uptake by barley plants following nutrient deficiency. *Annals of Botany* **50**, 429–449.

Lindquist, J., Rhode, D. and Puettmann, K.J. (1994) The influence of plant population spatial arrangement on individual plant yield. *Ecological Applications* **4**, 518–524.

Mack, R.N. and Harper, J.L. (1977) Interference in dune annuals: spatial pattern and neighborhood effects. *Journal of Ecology* **65**, 345–363.

Mahall, B.E. and Callaway, R.M. (1991) Root communication among desert shrubs. *Proceedings of the National Academy of Sciences USA* **88**, 874–876.

McKane, R.B., Grigal, D.F. and Russelle, M.P. (1990) Spatial and temporal differences in ^{15}N uptake and the organization of an old-field plant community. *Ecology* **71**, 1126–1132.

Mead, R. (1966) A relationship between individual plant-spacing and yield. *Annals of Botany* **30**, 301–309.

Mithen, R., Harper, J.L. and Weiner, J. (1984) Growth and mortality of individual plants as a function of 'available area.' *Oecologia* **62**, 57–60.

Mou, P., Jones, R.H. and Mitchell, R.J. (1995) Spatial distribution of roots in sweetgum and loblolly pine monocultures and relations with aboveground biomass and soil nutrients. *Functional Ecology* **9**, 689–699.

Mou, P., Mitchell, R.J. and Jones, R.H. (1993) Ecological field theory model: a mechanistic approach to simulate plant–plant interactions in southeastern forest ecosystems. *Canadian Journal of Forest Research* **23**, 2180–2193.

Nielsen, C.C. and Mackenthun, G. (1991) Die horizontale Variation der Feinwurzelintensität in Waldböden in Abhängigkeit von der Bestockungsdichte: Eine rechnerische Methode zur Bestimmung der 'Wurzelintensitäts-Glocke' an Einzelbäumen. *Allgemeine Forst- und Jagdzeitung* **162**, 112–119.

Pacala, S.W. (1987) Neighborhood models of plant population dynamics 3. Models with spatial heterogeneity in the physical environment. *Theoretical Population Biology* **31**, 359–392.

Pacala, S.W. and Silander, J.A. Jr (1985) Neighborhood models of plant population dynamics 1. Single-species models of annuals. *American Naturalist* **125**, 385–411.

Reichenberger, G. and Pyke, D.A. (1990) Impact of early root competition on fitness components of four semiarid species. *Oecologia* **85**, 159–166.

Robinson, D., Hodge, A., Griffiths, B.S. and Fitter, A.H. (1999) Plant root proliferation in nitrogen-rich patches confers competitive advantage. *Proceedings of the Royal Society London B* **266**, 431–435.

Schenk, H.J., Callaway, R.M. and Mahall, B.E. (1999) Spatial root segregation: are plants territorial? *Advances in Ecological Research* **28**, 145–180.

Schwinning, S. and Weiner, J. (1998) Mechanisms determining the degree of size-asymmetry in plant competition. *Oecologia* **113**, 447–455.

Silander, J.A. Jr and Pacala, S.W. (1985) Neighborhood predictors of plant performance. *Oecologia* **66**, 256–263.

St. John, C.V., Coleman, D.C. and Reid, C.P.P. (1983) Growth and spatial distribution of nutrient-absorbing organs: selective exploitation of heterogeneity. *Plant and Soil* **71**, 487–493.

Tardieu, F. (1988) Analysis of the spatial variability of maize root density II. Distances between roots. *Plant and Soil* **107**, 267–272.

Tilman, D. (1988) *Plant Strategies and the Dynamics and Structure of Plant Communities.* Princeton University Press, Princeton, NJ.

Umeki, K. (1997) Effect of crown asymmetry on size-structure dynamics of plant populations. *Annals of Botany* **79**, 631–641.

Weiner, J. (1982) A neighborhood model of annual-plant interference. *Ecology* **63**, 1237–1241.

Weiner, J. (1984) Neighborhood interference and amongst *Pinus rigida* individuals. *Journal of Ecology* **72**, 183–195.

Weiner, J. (1990) Asymmetric competition in plant populations. *Trends in Ecology and Evolution* **5**, 360–364.

Weiner, J. and Thomas, S.C. (1986) Size variability and competition in plant monocultures. *Oikos* **47**, 211–222.

Weiner, J., Wright, D.B. and Castro, S. (1997) Symmetry of belowground competition between *Kochia scoparia* individuals. *Oikos* **79**, 85–91.

Wilson, J.B. (1988) Shoot competition and root competition. *Journal of Applied Ecology* **25**, 279–296.

Wilson, S.D. and Tilman, D. (1995) Competitive responses of eight old-field plant species in four environments. *Ecology* **76**, 1169–1180.

Zhang, J. and Hamill, A.S. (1997) Seed weight, intraspecific competition, and plant performance in *Abutilon theophrasti*. *Canadian Journal of Botany* **75**, 1614–1620.

Chapter 8

Light heterogeneity in tropical rain forests: photosynthetic responses and their ecological consequences

J.R. Watling and M.C. Press

Introduction

Photosynthesis utilizes energy from sunlight to drive the conversion of inorganic carbon, either gaseous CO_2 or dissolved bicarbonate, into carbohydrates that provide the basis of all subsequent life processes. With the exception of minor contributions from some chemoautotrophic bacteria, all energy within living systems is supplied through the process of photosynthesis. In this chapter we investigate the impact that heterogeneity of light supply can have on photosynthesis, focusing on leaf level responses and discussing the functional significance of such responses for whole plants and communities. We concentrate in particular on light heterogeneity in tropical rain forests because they are perhaps the most dynamic of all terrestrial habitats with respect to light supply, both in the short-and long-term, and also because of their ecological and economic importance. Particular emphasis will be placed on the ecophysiological responses of plants in forest understoreys to short-term fluctuations in light supply, also known as sunflecks. The extent to which sunflecks can enhance growth and survival of understorey plants will be examined, followed by a discussion of the role of longer-term changes in light supply, arising from gap formation, on forest dynamics. The role of heterogeneity in light quality, while important to plant growth and development, falls beyond the scope of this chapter and thus has not been included in the following discussion (see Lee *et al.* 1996, 1997).

Spatial and temporal variation in light supply

The problems associated with heterogeneity in light supply are largely concerned with effective resource capture and efficient resource processing, in this case through the photosynthetic pathway, while simultaneously avoiding the potential consequences of exposure to too much light, which can be damaging for plants. In considering questions regarding heterogeneity in supply of any resource, it is important to examine variation at an appropriate scale—that is, one that is

Department of Animal and Plant Sciences, University of Sheffield, Sheffield S10 2TN, UK.

biologically meaningful. As well as scale, it is also important to consider variation in both spatial and temporal dimensions. Within rain forests, light varies in both the short- and long-term; rapid, short-lived increases in light supply occur in the understorey because of sunflecks, while prolonged increases result from the creation of gaps in the forest canopy.

Sunflecks

Sunflecks occur when openings in the overlying canopy permit direct sunlight to penetrate into the understorey, producing patches of high light on a background of shade. Sunflecks move across the forest floor because of the rotation of the earth, such that at any point in the understorey there will be a number of sunfleck events throughout a day (Fig. 8.1). These transient, high-light events can bring about an increase in photon flux density (PFD) by as much as two orders of magnitude above the background shade light in a matter of seconds to minutes. Because the PFD of background shade light in forest understoreys is so low, sunflecks can contribute significantly to the understorey light environment, sometimes providing as much as 80–90% of total daily PFD (Chazdon *et al.* 1996). The magnitude (PFD), duration and frequency of sunflecks are largely determined by the physical characteristics of the forest canopy, but can also be affected by wind, climate (e.g. differences between wet and dry seasons) and, in higher latitudes, by seasonal effects such as changes in the position of the sun throughout the year and leaf loss in

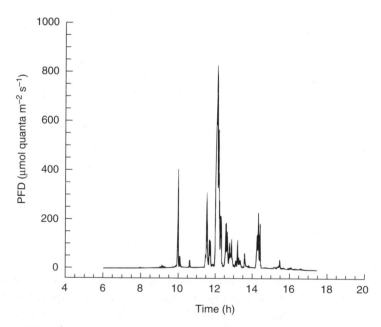

Figure 8.1 Diurnal pattern of photon flux density (PFD) in the understorey of a north-east Australian upland rain forest. Sunflecks of varying magnitude, duration and frequency can be seen.

deciduous forests in winter. Because of sunflecks, understorey light environments are highly variable, both spatially and temporally, and the efficient utilization of this heterogeneous resource is likely to be a significant determinant of survival and growth of understorey plants. Interspecific variation in the way that plants use the opportunity provided by sunflecks for enhancing carbon gain might also result in a competitive advantage for some species over others.

Gaps

Over a longer time scale, large changes in both light quantity and light quality occur as a consequence of gap creation. Gaps vary enormously in shape and size, ranging from small openings in the canopy resulting from branch falls, through larger openings from the loss of individual trees, to extensive openings caused by landslides or hurricanes. Gap creation can cause an increase in PFD of up to two orders of magnitude and there is a crude, non-linear, relationship between gap size and mean daily PFD (Brown 1993). However, gaps are highly variable environments and large spatial and temporal variations in PFD within gaps have been reported (Chazdon *et al.* 1996). Further, edge effects result in perturbation of the surrounding forest understorey light environment.

Plant responses to short-term variation in light supply

The significant contribution of sunflecks to the light environment of forest understoreys provides plants with the opportunity to enhance carbon gain and growth above that possible in the very low PFDs of the background shade light. Björkman *et al.* (1972) reported that total daily CO_2 fixation was 20% greater in the Australian understorey herb *Alocasia macrorrhiza* on clear days, when sunflecks were present, than on overcast days when there were no sunflecks. Subsequent field studies in a range of tropical and subtropical forest understoreys have indicated that sunflecks can contribute significantly to daily carbon gain in a number of species (e.g. Pearcy and Calkin 1983; Chazdon 1986; Pearcy 1987; Pfitsch and Pearcy 1989). However, this contribution is below what could be expected on the basis of the steady-state light response of understorey plants (Pfitsch and Pearcy 1989). What are the factors that determine sunfleck utilization in forest understoreys and to what extent do they vary among species?

Light interception

In order to utilize sunflecks effectively, plants must first be able to intercept them. However, most of the work carried out on light interception and absorption in understorey plants has focused on the utilization of diffuse light rather than the direct, but unpredictable, light supply in sunflecks. Leaves of many forest understorey plants have specialized features, such as convex epidermal cells, dense mono-layers of chloroplasts and increased internal reflectance, that serve to enhance light capture in contrast to features found in sun plants that serve to reduce light interception and absorption (Bone *et al.* 1985; Lee *et al.* 1990; DeLucia *et al.* 1996). Plant architecture is also important in determining efficiency of light capture in shaded understorey environments. Using computer simulations, Pearcy and Yang (1998) have shown that petiole length, leaf area and leaf divergence angles in the understorey herb *Adenocaulon bicolor* correspond with predicted values for optimum light absorption efficiency, largely through minimization of self-shading.

Despite the important contribution made by sunflecks to understorey light environments, few studies have determined how efficiently they are intercepted by plants. Beneath tall forest canopies, a greater proportion of sunflecks penetrate at steep angles than beneath shorter crop or shrub canopies. A consequence of this is that sunfleck interception in the understorey of a tall forest will be enhanced more by horizontal than vertical growth (Kohyama 1991). Thus, variation in architecture and leaf angle among understorey species could produce differences in sunfleck interception and potential carbon gain. Zipperlen and Press (1996) suggested that differences in architecture between seedlings of two dipterocarp tree species, *Dryobalanops lanceolata* and *Shorea leprosula,* may have contributed to differences in their mortality rates in the understorey. *D. lanceolata* seedlings, which had lower rates of mortality, tended to extend their branches horizontally while *S. leprosula* seedlings allocated more resources to vertical growth. The implication here is that *D. lanceolata* will be more efficient than *S. leprosula* at intercepting sunflecks. Differences in light interception efficiency arising from architectural variation have also been reported for understorey palms (Chazdon 1986) and shade-tolerant *vs.* shade intolerant saplings (King 1994).

Photosynthetic capacity
Shade plants typically have low maximum rates of photosynthesis that saturate at low photon flux densities (PFD), and this places a ceiling on their ability to utilize the light in sunflecks. For example, in two species growing in an Australian rain forest understorey (*Alocasia macrorrhiza* and *Castanospora alphandii*), 56% and 39%, respectively, of the light received over a day was excess to their photosynthetic capacity, while a pioneer species (*Omalanthus novoguineensis*), growing nearby in a small gap, was able to utilize 85% of the light it received over a day because of its higher photosynthetic capacity with respect to light (Watling 1995).

Given the relatively high levels of excess light that may be received by understorey plants as a result of sunflecks, we need to ask why they do not simply increase their photosynthetic capacity to enable them to utilize this extra light energy. There are a number of possible explanations for this apparent inefficiency. First, the higher photosynthetic capacities of sun plants are accompanied by increases in respiration rates, which could compromise the carbon balance of plants in low light. The higher respiration rates result from the greater costs of carbohydrate processing, maintenance and possibly protein turnover in sun leaves (Björkman 1981; Pearcy and Sims 1994). Of these, only maintenance is likely to be significant in low light environments as both carbohydrate processing and protein repair are a consequence of high light availability rather than high photosynthetic capacity *per se* (Pearcy and Sims 1994). The second explanation is that increases in photosynthetic capacity are usually associated with an increase in the nitrogen content of leaves (Evans 1989), making them more attractive to herbivores (Kursar and Coley 1991). Herbivore attack could lead to reductions in whole plant carbon gain through leaf loss and increased susceptibility to pathogen damage. Finally, higher photosynthetic capacity requires a concurrent increase in stomatal conductance to match the demand for CO_2 (Givnish 1988). Stomatal behaviour of many rainforest species is surprisingly conservative given the apparently high availability of water in this environment. Understorey plants tend to maintain very low rates of stomatal conductance in low light and these increase only slowly in response to increases in PFD during sunflecks (see below) (Chazdon and Pearcy 1986; Valladares *et al.* 1997; Zipperlen and Press 1997). Stomatal closure can also occur in response to increased transpiration rates during prolonged, high PFD sunflecks (Watling 1995). Maintenance of higher transpiration rates during sunflecks might require an increase in the root/shoot ratio of understorey plants. This would add to construction and maintenance costs for the whole plant, increasing respiration rates that may not be offset by increased rates of photosynthesis during sunflecks.

Variation in photosynthetic capacity among species growing in rain forest understoreys is very small, presumably because of the constraints discussed above. Thus, there appears to be very little potential for understorey plants to improve sunfleck utilization by increasing photosynthetic capacity.

Photosynthetic induction

In a study of the redwood forest understorey herb *Adenocaulon bicolor*, Pfitsch and Pearcy (1989) found that the observed daily carbon gain of plants in the field was significantly lower than that predicted on the basis of the steady-state light response curve for this species. This discrepancy largely results from delays in the response of photosynthesis to an increase in PFD. These occur because of the induction requirement for photosynthesis (reviewed in Pearcy *et al.* 1994). Leaves that have been in low light for some time and which are subsequently exposed to an increase in PFD show a gradual, rather than instantaneous, increase in the rate of photosynthesis up to the steady-state rate commensurate with the new PFD (Fig. 8.2). Photosynthetic induction is the result of light-dependent biochemical and physiological processes that activate in high light and deactivate in low light. The major biochemical limitations arise from declines, in low light, of the pool sizes of photosynthetic intermediates and the activation state of ribulose-1,5-bisphosphate carboxylase/oxygenase (Rubisco) (Seemann *et al.* 1988; Woodrow and Mott 1989). It is not entirely clear why plants modulate Rubisco activity with respect to light, but it may be important for maintaining stable concentrations of metabolites involved in regulation of other processes such as partitioning between starch and sucrose (Mott *et al.* 1997). The third, and the slowest, component of the induction response is light-activated stomatal opening, which can take anything from a few minutes to hours (Pearcy *et al.* 1994). All these process are reversed on return to low light.

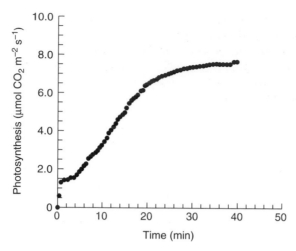

Figure 8.2 Photosynthetic induction response in *Micromelum minutum*, an Australian rain forest understorey tree. The leaf was placed in low light ($10\,\mu$mol quanta m^{-2}s^{-1}) for 2 h and then exposed to saturating PFD ($800\,\mu$mol quanta m^{-2}s^{-1}) at time 0. From Watling (1995).

The extent to which the induction response limits sunfleck utilization will depend on the induction state of a leaf, which in turn depends on the rate of induction loss and the length of the intervening low light period. Rates of induction loss have been shown to vary both between species and within species grown under different light regimes. Generally, plants grown in high light lose their induction state more rapidly than the same species grown in shade. This type of response has been reported for both a temperate species (*Fagus sylvatica*, Küppers and Schneider 1993), and for a number of tropical species (Tinoco-Ojanguren and Pearcy 1993a; Valladares *et al.* 1997; Zipperlen and Press 1997). However, in a study comparing four Australian rain forest species (Watling 1995), one species, *Castanospora alphandii*, lost induction state more slowly when grown under fluctuating light than when grown in either full sun or shade (Table 8.1). In the same study, light treatment had no effect on the rate of induction loss for the three other species, although there were significant differences in induction loss among the species. Thus, some species appear to be more plastic with respect to the rate of induction loss than others, but there also appear to be inherent differences among species that do not alter, even with a change in light environment. However, the extent to which differences among species in the rate of induction loss reflect the habitat in which those species are usually found, is not clear. Shade-tolerant species have been reported to have slower rates of induction loss than obligate sun species (Poorter and Oberbauer 1993; Ögren and Sundin 1996). This trend is supported by the results for three of the species shown in Table 8.1; the half-time for induction loss was greater in *Alocasia macrorrhiza* and *C. alphandii*, both shade-tolerant, than for *Omalanthus novoguineensis*, a shade-intolerant, pioneer species. However, the species with the fastest rate of induction loss, *Micromelum minutum*, is also a

Table 8.1 Rate of induction loss (half-time, min, $t_{1/2}$) in four Australian rain forest species, *Alocasia macrorrhiza*, *Castanospora alphandii*, *Micromelum minutum* and *Omalanthus novoguineensis*, grown under either low light (8% full sunlight), fluctuating light (natural forest understorey) or high light (full sunlight). The $t_{1/2}$ for induction loss was calculated from the initial linear relationship between induction state and time in low light ($n = 2$–3 for each species, values in parentheses are the r^2 for the fitted relationship). From Watling (1995).

Species	Low light	Fluctuating light	High light
A. macrorrhiza	18.2 (0.97)	17.5 (0.97)	18.1 (0.96)
C. alphandii	21.5 (0.95)	30.5 (0.97)	23.3 (0.98)
M. minutum	10.5 (0.96)	9.5 (0.99)	—
O. novoguineensis	11.4 (0.97)	13.4 (0.99)	12.8 (0.98)

shade-tolerant species that is most often found in forest understoreys. Thus, shade-tolerance is not necessarily accompanied by a slower rate of induction loss. Too few species have been examined to allow broad generalizations to be made on this subject.

Each component of the photosynthetic induction response has a different relaxation time in low light, and thus the contribution of each varies with time spent in low light prior to a sunfleck. Both Rubisco activation state and stomatal conductance decline more slowly, in low light, than the pools of photosynthetic intermediates and hence, limitations arising from the latter are generally only important in situations where light fluctuates rapidly, such as beneath crop canopies (Pons *et al.* 1992; Sassenrath-Cole *et al.* 1994). In rain forest understoreys, where sunflecks may be infrequent, limitations arising from Rubisco activation and stomatal opening become more important to the induction response.

Light activation of Rubisco is a complex process that involves the removal of inhibitors and the addition of a molecule of CO_2 to a lysine residue at the active site followed by the binding of Mg^{2+}, after which the enzyme is able to catalyse the fixation of CO_2 (or O_2 in photorespiration) (Miziorko and Lorimer 1983). The removal of inhibitors from Rubisco is catalysed by a second enzyme, Rubisco activase, which has been found in all plants so far examined (Portis 1992). Studies with genetically modified *Arabidopsis thaliana*, with reduced amounts of Rubisco activase, have indicated that the rate of Rubisco activation is CO_2-dependent at low CO_2 concentrations and activase-dependent at high CO_2 concentrations (Mott *et al.* 1997). Thus, rates of Rubisco activation during sunflecks could also be indirectly related to rates of stomatal conductance, as leaf internal CO_2 concentrations (Ci) will be low when stomatal conductance is also low. However, it is also possible that the higher atmospheric concentrations of CO_2 often found in rain forest understoreys (Buchmann *et al.* 1997) could enhance Ci and hence rates of Rubisco activation during sunflecks in understorey plants. If this is the case then it might be advantageous for understorey plants to have higher levels of Rubisco activase than non-understorey plants. However, the extent to which Rubisco activase content varies, either amongst species or within species grown under different light or CO_2 regimes, has not been extensively investigated. In one study where *Ocimum basilicum* (basil) and *Impatiens wallerana* (impatiens) were grown under either shade, sun or fluctuating light, both species had similar rates of Rubisco activation in all three light regimes. However, the rate at which Rubisco deactivated in low light was slower in basil grown in sun and fluctuating light than in plants grown in shade (Ernstsen *et al.* 1997). In contrast, Ögren and Sundin (1996) reported differences in Rubisco activation rate for a range of species grown under similar light conditions. They found that high-light demanding species, with inherently slow growth rates, had slower rates of Rubisco activation than either shade specialists or faster growing sun species.

In many cases the slowest component of the induction response is stomatal opening. The stomata of most plants are light-sensitive, closing in low light and opening in high light, although there are some exceptions to this pattern, such as CAM species and some hemiparasitic angiosperms. However, in most cases stomatal opening, following a period in low light, can significantly limit the rate of increase to steady-state photosynthesis by anything from a few minutes to an hour or more. Even in C_4 plants, where low Ci might be expected to be less important as a limitation to photosynthesis, slow stomatal opening can slow the induction response substantially (Frost *et al.* 1997). Very few C_4 species are found in forest understoreys, however, and those that are tend to have relatively rapid stomatal opening responses (Horton and Neufeld 1998).

Although it was initially thought that stomatal limitations to photosynthesis during the induction response were small (Chazdon and Pearcy 1986), it is now recognized that stomata, through their impact on Ci, can have a significant effect, particularly if conductance is low at the commencement of a sunfleck (Kirschbaum and Pearcy 1988; Tinoco-Ojanguren and Pearcy 1993a; Valladares *et al.* 1997). Relationships between rates of stomatal opening and closing and the frequency of sunfleck events can result in very different patterns of induction among species (Cardon *et al.* 1994). For example, some plants have symmetrical opening and closing responses, but lags in the initiation of the opening response on illumination can result in gradually declining rates of conductance in fluctuating light, such that lower rates of photosynthesis are achieved for subsequent sunflecks in a series (Fay and Knapp 1993). In contrast, stomatal closure may be slower than opening, or stomata may continue to open following a sunfleck, resulting in a higher induction state being achieved for subsequent sunflecks (Chazdon and Pearcy 1986; Tinoco-Ojanguren and Pearcy 1993a,b). Fluctuations in light and CO_2 can also initiate oscillations in stomatal conductance (Cardon *et al.* 1995). Zipperlen and Press (1997) reported that stomatal oscillations were common in seedlings of the shade-tolerant dipterocarp species *Shorea leprosula* in response to fluctuating light, and that these oscillations could enhance both the rate and the magnitude of the response of photosynthesis to sunflecks in this species.

Environmental variables such as light, vapour pressure deficit (VPD), soil moisture, temperature and CO_2 concentration can all affect stomatal behaviour and therefore can also impact on carbon gain during sunflecks. In a study of two neotropical *Piper* species, Tinoco-Ojanguren and Pearcy (1992, 1993b) examined the impact of growth irradiance and VPD on the dynamics of stomatal responses to fluctuating light. Rates of stomatal opening and closing were similar in sun and shade grown *P. aequale*, but following a light fleck, shade-grown plants had higher rates of stomatal conductance than sun-grown ones. In contrast, rates of stomatal opening and closing were faster and higher conductances were achieved in sun-grown relative to shade-grown *P. auritum*. Stomatal responses of both species were also sensitive to VPD, with high VPD inducing more rapid rates of stomatal closure following a lightfleck in *P. aequale* and lowering the maximum rate of conductance achieved by *P. auritum*. High VPD causes leaf transpiration rates to increase for a given stomatal conductance, and thus, the more conservative response of stomata to lightflecks when VPD is high is likely to improve water use efficiency. This may be more important than increasing carbon gain in regions with a distinct dry season, such as many parts of the neotropics. It has also been suggested that stomatal closure in *P. auritum* during exposure to high light and high VPD helps to prevent xylem cavitation and a subsequent loss of hydraulic conductance (Schultz and Matthews 1997). However, stomata remained open when leaf temperature was also high in *P. auritum*, presumably to maintain evaporative cooling of the leaves.

The efficiency with which a sunfleck is utilized increases with increasing induction state because of the more rapid response of photosynthesis to the change in PFD. As discussed above, the induction state is a function of the status of metabolite pools, Rubisco activation and stomatal conductance, all of which are influenced by the length of time that a leaf has been in low light. The importance of each of these components to the induction response varies among species and also with environmental conditions. Given the highly variable nature of light supply in understoreys, it is likely that the induction state of any leaf will vary from extremely low to very high throughout a day, depending on the pattern of sunflecks received and on diurnal changes in other environmental factors such as CO_2, VPD and temperature. Induction responses also vary with species and these differences are likely to affect the ability of different species to persist and grow in understorey environments. Thus they will also affect larger scale patterns of vegetation change in rain forests.

Photoinhibition

Björkman and Powles (1981) reported rapid changes in leaf angle in the redwood understorey herb *Oxalis oregana* that reduced light interception during sunflecks by as much as 80%. Photosynthetic rates in the folded leaves, however, were the same as those in leaves that had been prevented from folding, as even with such a large reduction in light interception the PFD was still at or above the light saturation point for photosynthesis in these plants (Powles and Björkman 1981).

Following the sunfleck, however, leaves that had been prevented from folding showed a 30% reduction in their photosynthetic rate in low light relative to the leaves that had been allowed to fold. Chlorophyll fluorescence measurements on these same leaves indicated that there had been a decline in the efficiency of photosystem II (PSII) in the unfolded leaves. Thus, for *O. oregana*, exposure to excess light during a sunfleck can bring about a reduction in the efficiency of light utilization following the sunfleck. However, in the field *O. oregana* avoids exposure to excess light by folding its leaves and reducing light interception. The light-dependent reduction in the quantum yield of photosynthesis that was observed in the exposed leaves of *O. oregana* is generally referred to as photoinhibition. Photoinhibition can be a consequence of either photoprotective processes that increase the proportion of absorbed light dissipated as heat, or of photodamage, or both. Shade leaves are particularly susceptible to photodamage when exposed to high light, because they have both a low capacity for photon utilization and a low capacity for photoprotection, relative to sun leaves (Demmig-Adams and Adams 1992). This can be exacerbated in understorey environments, where plants may be exposed to excess light during sunflecks, by the delay in photon utilization arising from the induction requirement of photosynthesis.

Despite the potential for photoinhibition and/or photodamage occurring during sunflecks in understorey plants, and the impact this could have on plant growth and survival, relatively few studies have investigated this aspect of light heterogeneity. Unlike *O. oregana*, most plants do not display rapid leaf movement and thus cannot avoid photodamage simply by reducing light interception. Besides, leaf folding requires energy and the benefit, in terms of avoiding photodamage, only becomes economic if sunflecks exceed $\approx 30\,\text{min}$ in length (Raven 1989). Instead, most plants depend on an equally dynamic, but internal and energetically less costly, means of photoprotection, known as the xanthophyll cycle. This involves a group of interconvertible pigments. A role for these pigments in photoprotection was first suggested by Demmig *et al.* (1987) and has since been confirmed for many species under a wide range of environmental conditions (Demmig-Adams and Adams 1992; Osmond *et al.* 1999). When leaves are in low light, the xanthophyll pigment violaxanthin predominates. However, when exposed to high light, violaxanthin is converted to antheraxanthin and zeaxanthin (Fig. 8.3). While violaxanthin functions as an accessory pigment, passing energy to chlorophyll in PSII, antheraxanthin and zeaxanthin have subtly different structures that result in them facilitating the dissipation of excess energy as heat, rather than passing it onto the PSII reaction centres (Frank *et al.* 1994). This diversion of excess light energy can help to prevent photodamage from occurring. However, it also contributes to the reduction in quantum yield of photosynthesis that is associated with photoinhibition. While this is of little consequence to carbon gain in high light, it can be a disadvantage on return to low light, hence the importance of the conversion of antheraxanthin and zeaxanthin back to violaxanthin when light is no longer present to excess (Fig. 8.3). The photoprotective function of the xanthophyll cycle is also linked to the generation of a pH gradient across the thylakoid mem-

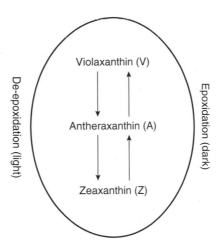

Figure 8.3 A diagrammatic representation of the xanthophyll cycle and its operation in response to changing light supply. Conversion of violaxanthin to antheraxanthin and zeaxanthin (de-epoxidation) occurs when leaves are exposed to excess light. The reverse process (epoxidation) occurs on return to low light. The presence of antheraxanthin and zeaxanthin facilitates the dissipation of excess light energy as heat.

branes on exposure to light. This serves to further modulate the dissipative capacity of the pigments in relation to light (Gilmore and Yamamoto 1993).

Thus, if the xanthophyll cycle is to provide effective protection from excess light during sunflecks it must be engaged rapidly. Equally, it should return rapidly to the non-dissipating state following a sunfleck, so that quantum efficiency is not compromised for a prolonged period in low light. Investigations of xanthophyll cycle activity in understorey plants in the field have indicated that the conversion of violaxanthin to antheraxanthin and zeaxanthin is relatively rapid on exposure to excess light, with a half-time for conversion of around 5–10 min (Watling *et al.* 1997a). However, Königer *et al.* (1995) reported that very little conversion had occurred in Panamanian understorey species during 1–2 min sunflecks. There is also evidence that plants grown in situations where sunflecks are frequent have larger pool sizes of xanthophyll pigments (on a chlorophyll basis) and therefore a greater capacity for photoprotection than the same species grown in extreme shade or constant low light (Watling 1995; Logan *et al.* 1997). In comparison with plants from gaps or plants from the rain forest canopy, however, understorey species tend to have much smaller xanthophyll pool sizes (Königer *et al.* 1995).

While the engagement of xanthophyll-mediated photoprotection occurs relatively rapidly on exposure to excess light during sunflecks, rates at which the photoprotective pigments are converted back to violaxanthin in low light have been found to vary both among species and with light environment. Following exposure to 1–2 h of high light, the return to violaxanthin was found to be slower in three species growing in a small gap in a forest in Panama than in a canopy species in the same forest exposed to high PFD for longer periods (Königer *et al.* 1995). In a study using the Australian rain forest herb *Alocasia macrorrhiza*, plants grown in high light converted antheraxanthin and zeaxanthin back into violaxanthin more rapidly than plants grown in either shade or in a rain forest understorey, following 60 min exposure to full sun (Fig. 8.4a) (Watling 1995). Similarly, following exposure to excess light during a sunfleck in the field, *A. macrorrhiza* still had high levels of antheraxanthin and zeaxanthin 60 min after the sunfleck had passed, while another understorey species, *Castanospora alphandii*, rapidly converted these pigments back to violaxanthin (Fig. 8.4b) (Watling *et al.* 1997a). In another field study, Logan *et al.* (1997) found that *Alocasia brisbanensis* also retained high levels of antheraxanthin and zeaxanthin following the first sunfleck in a day. The retention

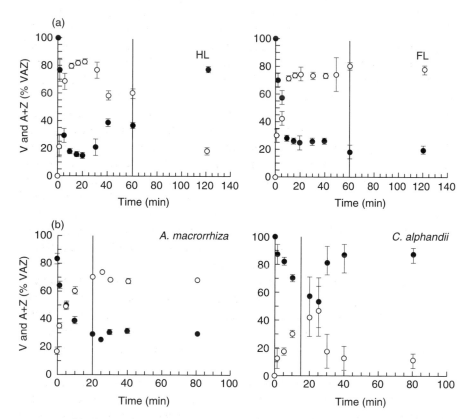

Figure 8.4 (a) The proportions of violaxanthin (V, ●) and antheraxanthin+zeaxanthin (A+Z, ○) (as a percentage of the total xanthophyll cycle pool) in leaves of *Alocasia macrorrhiza* grown in either high light (HL) or in fluctuating light in a forest understorey (FL), during and after exposure to full sun for 60 min (b) The proportions of V and A+Z during and after sunflecks in the field, for *A. macrorrhiza* and *Castanospora alphandii* growing in a rain forest understorey in north-east Australia. The vertical lines, in both figures, indicate when plants were returned to low light. Data points are means (±SE, $n=3$). (a) is from Watling (1995) and (b) is modified from Watling *et al.* (1997a).

of high levels of photoprotective pigments following sunflecks could mean that plants are better prepared for subsequent sunflecks, which often occur in clusters (Pearcy *et al.* 1994). However, it could also result in a sustained reduction in the quantum yield of photosynthesis, which could compromise carbon gain in low light.

The development of instruments for measuring chlorophyll fluorescence from leaves in the field has enabled workers to assess the extent of photoinhibition under a range of conditions including exposure to fluctuating light. Photosystem II efficiency declines rapidly in many shade-tolerant rain forest species when their leaves are exposed to even moderate PFDs, and this contrasts strongly with shade intolerant species that are able to maintain higher quantum efficiencies over the same range (Scholes *et al.* 1996). These differences are largely the result of higher photosynthetic capacities in the shade-intolerant species, whilst shade-tolerant species dissipate a much greater proportion of absorbed light thermally rather than utilizing it for photochemistry. The magnitude of photoinhibition and the rate at which it relaxes following exposure to sunflecks depend on both the period of exposure and the PFD reached during the sunflecks. Experiments with one SE Asian understorey herb, *Elatostema repens*, found both sustained photoinhibition and a reduction in net CO_2 uptake in plants exposed to a sequence of 30 min saturating ($700 \mu mol$ quanta $m^{-2} s^{-1}$), lightflecks relative to plants maintained at constant low PFD ($40 \mu mol$ quanta $m^{-2} s^{-1}$) (Le Gouallec *et al.* 1991). When the same plants were exposed to a series of low PFD ($250 \mu mol$ quanta $m^{-2} s^{-1}$) lightflecks, there was no difference in the extent of photoinhibition, and CO_2 uptake was enhanced in comparison with controls. Similarly, Watling *et al.* (1997a) found evidence of sustained reductions in quantum yield, lasting from 60 to 110 min, following exposure to high light (up to $1000 \mu mol$ quanta $m^{-2} s^{-1}$) during sunflecks in three shade-tolerant species in Australian rain forests, while Logan *et al.* (1997) found little evidence of sustained photoinhibition following low PFD (up to $250 \mu mol$ quanta $m^{-2} s^{-1}$) sunflecks in *Alocasia brisbanensis*, in the field. These data suggest that when sunflecks are at or below the light saturation point for photosynthesis, leaves can enhance carbon gain without incurring any penalty in the form of sustained photoinhibition. In contrast, exposure to light that is above saturation can lead to photoinhibition and a subsequent, but usually temporary, decline in carbon gain in low light.

The extent of foregone carbon assimilation that arises from sustained photoinhibition in understorey plants has yet to be quantified, as have any differences that exist among species in this regard. However, given the contrasting responses in relaxation of the xanthophyll pigments following sunflecks observed for *A. macrorrhiza* and *C. alphandii*, it seems likely that significant species differences will exist that could impact on survival and growth in this light-limited environment.

Whole plant responses to sunflecks

The leaf-level responses to sunflecks discussed in the preceding sections indicate that there are a number of physiological differences between species that could potentially affect their ability to either utilize sunflecks for photosynthesis, or to minimize the effects of sustained photoinhibition, and thus, to affect growth. Despite this, very few studies have attempted to quantify the contribution that sunflecks make to growth and how it varies among species. In an early field study, Pearcy (1983) was able to demonstrate a correlation between estimated exposure to sunflecks (determined from hemispherical canopy photographs) and growth of two species, *Claoxylon sandwicense* and *Euphorbia forbesii*, found in an Hawaiian forest understorey. However, in another study with the redwood understorey herb *Adenocaulon bicolor*, the experimental removal of sunflecks from plants in the field, using shadow bands, failed to show any effect on plant growth relative to plants that received sunflecks (Pfitsch and Pearcy 1992). Thus, the importance of sunflecks may be highly species- and/or environment-dependent.

The impact of specific physiological characteristics, such as the induction requirement of photosynthesis or sustained photoinhibition, on the extent to which fluctuating light is utilized for growth have been investigated more rarely. Results of experiments in which growth has been compared between plants supplied with either continuous or fluctuating light but with the same total daily PFD, have shown that growth is generally greatest under continuous light (Sims and Pearcy 1993; Wayne and Bazzaz 1993; Watling *et al.* 1997b). Furthermore, Sims and Pearcy (1993) found that growth of *A. macrorrhiza* was greater in a short lightfleck regime, with 7s lightflecks separated by 26s of low light, compared with a long lightfleck regime, where lightfleck duration was 10–12 min and flecks were separated by 48–50 min. These differences in growth were largely due to greater limitations arising from the induction requirement in the long lightfleck regime. It seems unlikely that photoinhibition would have been significant, as PFD during the lightflecks was below saturation for photosynthesis in these plants.

The work with *A. macrorrhiza* by Sims and Pearcy (1993) clearly illustrates the impact that the induction response can have on lightfleck utilization. However, it does not indicate the extent to which sunflecks might contribute to growth relative to that achieved in continuous low light, or how species might vary in this respect. Both these questions were addressed in the study of Watling *et al.* (1997b), where clear differences were observed among species in their growth responses to fluctuating light. Growth rates were similar in both continuous and fluctuating light (10 min light flecks at 50 min intervals), with the same total daily PFD, for two species, *Micromelum minutum* and *Diploglottis diphyllostegia*, implying that, for these two shade-tolerant species, limitations arising from either the induction response or sustained photoinhibition were minimal. In contrast, under the same light regimes, a third shade-tolerant species, *Alocasia macrorrhiza*, and a shade-intolerant species, *Omalanthus novoguineensis*, both had lower growth rates in fluctuating light relative to continuous light. In the same study plants were also grown in a continuous low light treatment, in which PFD was the same as that received between lightflecks by plants in the fluctuating light treatment (Fig. 8.5). Both *M. minutum* and *D. diphyllostegia* achieved greater biomass in the fluctuating light treatment than in the continuous low light treatment, indicating that they

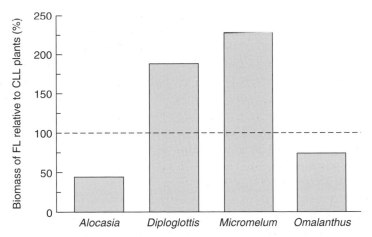

Figure 8.5 The effect of supplementary light received as lightflecks (FL) on growth of four Australian rain forest species (three shade-tolerant species, *Alocasia macrorrhiza*, *Castanospora alphandii* and *Micromelum minutum*, and one shade-intolerant species, *Omalanthus novoguineensis*) relative to plants of the same species grown in constant low light (CLL). Total daily PFDs for FL and CLL treatments were 7.02 and 4.86 mol quanta m^{-2}, respectively. From Watling *et al.* (1997b).

were able to effectively utilize the extra light received in lightflecks for growth. In contrast, neither *A. macrorrhiza* nor *O. novoguineensis* were able to enhance their growth in the fluctuating light compared with the low light treatment (Fig. 8.5). Thus, there can be significant species differences in the utilization of sunflecks for growth, and shade-tolerant species such as *A. macrorrhiza* are not always as effective in this respect as might be expected from their distribution in the wild.

Plant responses to long-term variation in light supply

The persistence of distinctive vegetation types, such as rain forests, depends largely on their regenerative capacity and this has often been linked with disturbance events (e.g. Connell 1978). Disturbance can disrupt the existing community by removing some individuals and allowing others to take their place. In social terms, disturbance is like a redistribution of wealth, with resources that were being utilized by certain individuals becoming available for others to use. The probability of success for a given individual following disturbance will depend on its ability to capture the newly available resource(s) before others. Current theories of vegetation dynamics in rain forests (and other closed forest systems) emphasize the role of gap creation in allowing the regeneration of new cohorts of tree species (e.g. Brown and Whitmore 1992). The appearance of canopy gaps creates both spatial and temporal variability in the availability of light and other resources that can affect seedling growth. Furthermore, variation in gap size, shape and orientation create differences in microclimate, both between and within gaps, that may play a role in the maintenance of high species diversity in tropical rain forests (Denslow 1987; but see Hubbell *et al.* 1999). Demographic studies have indicated that light availability can be an important factor limiting growth of forest understorey species, at the population level, in both temperate and tropical forests (Pascarella and Horvitz 1998; Valverde and Silvertown 1998). However, if light heterogeneity in forests is an important force in the maintenance of tree species diversity, there should be clear evidence of variation in ecophysiological traits and corresponding niche differentiation with respect to light, among species.

Acclimation potential

It has been estimated that 0.7–1.2% of a neotropical rain forest is converted to gaps annually and that these gaps are effectively filled in 2–3 years (Denslow 1987). Figures are similar for rain forests from other regions, except in areas that are prone to violent storms or where substrates are steep or unstable; here, canopy opening is more frequent. The rarity of gaps means that most seeds will be dispersed to understorey rather than gap sites, unless the dispersal mechanism favours gaps, and there is little evidence to support this (Schupp *et al.* 1989). Rain forest trees appear to have evolved two major strategies that enhance the probability of encountering a gap. First, there are species that produce seeds that can remain dormant in the soil for long periods, and germinate in response to conditions likely to be encountered in gaps, namely high PFD, temperature and R:FR ratios (Hopkins and Graham 1987; Vázquez-Yanes and Orozco-Segovia 1990). These are generally termed shade-intolerant species. Second are those species that produce seeds that germinate immediately, or within days of release, and generate seedling banks that can persist in the understorey for very long periods. As discussed earlier, variation in the responses of these shade-tolerant seedlings to short-term heterogeneity in light supply (sunflecks) may affect their ability to survive and grow in understorey environments and hence the probability that they will encounter a gap. Furthermore, the ability to colonize a gap successfully has been shown to be greater for larger seedlings (Brown and Whitmore 1992), and for seedlings that were present on gap formation, than for later recruits (Brokaw 1985).

Persistence in the understorey, whether through seed or seedling longevity, can increase the probability of encountering a gap. However, the ability to acclimate to the new environment created by gap formation will be an important determinant of successful gap colonization. Acclimation to an increase in light supply involves both physiological and morphological changes that result in an enhanced capacity for light utilization at the whole plant level (Pearcy and Sims 1994). Numerous studies have investigated variation in acclimation potential, with respect to light, among rain forest species (reviewed in Press *et al.* 1996). These studies indicate that there is a continuum of responses ranging from the highly plastic shade-intolerant species to shade-tolerant species with almost no ability to respond to a change in light availability. An example of this type of variability in acclimation potential is shown in Fig. 8.6, which shows photosynthetic light response curves, measured in

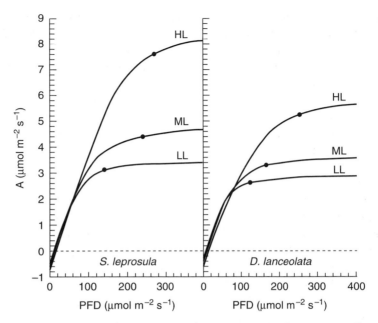

Figure 8.6 Photosynthetic acclimation in two dipterocarp species from Borneo, *Shorea leprosula* and *Dryobalanops lanceolata*. The light response of photosynthesis was measured on plants growing in three different understorey light environments in the field, with low (LL), medium (ML) or high (HL) light availability. From Zipperlen and Press (1996).

the field, for two shade-tolerant dipterocarp species growing in three different light environments. The higher photosynthetic acclimation potential of *Shorea leprosula*, relative to the more shade-tolerant *Dryobalanops lanceolata*, was also found to correspond with a trend for higher growth rates in the former in high light environments (Zipperlen and Press 1996).

It is relatively easy to demonstrate significant species differences in acclimation potential with respect to light. However, gap formation is a relatively rapid process, with plants being exposed to a sudden and prolonged increase in PFD and, under such circumstances, the rate at which different species are able to acclimate to a change in light environment is also likely to play an important role (Strauss-Debenedetti and Bazzaz 1991). Photodamage, and the potential to either avoid it or recover quickly from it, will be a significant component of this acclimation process. Kamaluddin and Grace (1992) found that shade-grown seedlings of the euphorb *Bischofia javanica* suffered sustained photoinhibition (measured as the chlorophyll fluorescence parameter Fv/Fm) and chlorophyll bleaching on exposure to high light. There was partial recovery over the following 35 days, but Fv/Fm did not return to pre-exposure values, or to values measured in new leaves produced under high light. Similar results were obtained by Lovelock *et al.* (1994) in a study of four tropical tree species from Papua New Guinea. They also recorded sustained reductions in Fv/Fm and bleaching of leaves on exposure of shade-grown seedlings to full sunlight. However, they found that both the magnitude of photoinhibition and the rate of recovery differed significantly among the species, supporting the idea that susceptibility to photodamage might play a part in determining relative success of different species in gaps. Differences in the extent of photoinhibition occurring on exposure to excess light of seedlings growing in an understorey, have also been demonstrated between plants with short- and long-lived leaves (Lovelock *et al.* 1998).

Does long-term light heterogeneity have ecological consequences?

Theories of gap-phase dynamics suggest that interactions between species variability with respect to light utilization, such as those discussed above, and spatial and temporal variation in light availability arising from gap formation, should promote species coexistence. Evidence that this does occur has been provided in one study using dendrochronological data from three tree species found in New Zealand old-growth forests (Lusk and Smith 1998). Distribution of one of the species, *Nothofagus menziesii*, was found to be clumped and to consist of even-aged groups of trees, suggesting that its regeneration may be linked to gap formation. Furthermore, examination of tree rings in adults of this species indicated that there had been continued, uninterrupted growth in more than 50% of the individuals studied, which is consistent with successful establishment in gaps. In contrast, individuals of two other species, *Dacrydium cupressinum* and *Prumnopitys ferruginea*, showed random age distributions and evidence of multiple episodes of growth release and suppression in the adult tree ring data, which is consistent with exposure to a number of gap events through time. Both these species are more shade-tolerant than *N. menziesii* and these results suggest that they may be able to survive prolonged periods beneath the canopy and pass through a number of growth release events before reaching the canopy.

Variation in dispersal, growth and survival rates of tree species below closed canopies interacts with the stochastic process of gap formation, to effectively shuffle species distributions within a forest. This can be illustrated, rather simplistically, by considering two potentially competing species, A and B, that produce overlapping seedling banks in a rain forest understorey (Fig. 8.7). Growth and survival of both species will depend on the particular combination of abiotic and biotic factors to which each is exposed, and their characteristic responses to these factors. In this case, however, we can imagine that species A has a higher survival rate, but a lower growth rate, than species B. Thus, if a gap is formed relatively soon after establishment of the seedling banks, it is likely that species B will be the superior competitor for colonization of the new space because its seedlings are larger than those of species A. However, the higher survival potential of species A gives it the advantage if gap formation does not occur until long after the time of seedling establishment. While other environmental factors are clearly also important, light plays a significant role in both seedling performance in the understorey and, seedling release on gap formation.

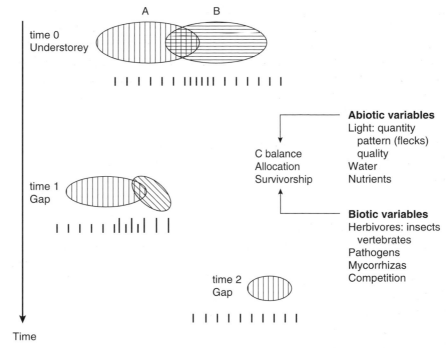

Figure 8.7 Schematic representation of the impact of abiotic and biotic variables on the performance and survivorship of two overlapping banks of seedlings in a rain forest understorey. Species A and B respond differently to the environmental variables, particularly light, and show an inverse relationship between growth and survivorship (e.g. Zipperlen and Press 1996). The size of the circles represents the number of individuals present, while the height of the lines beneath the banks represents the size of those individuals. The timing of gap creation may be critical in determining the competitive outcome of interactions in seedling banks, with infrequent gap formation favouring the success of the slower growing, but longer lived, species A.

Conclusion

In this chapter we have attempted to synthesize current knowledge of the physiological responses of plants to light heterogeneity and to discuss the role that these responses may have in determining growth and survival in forest understorey environments. On a larger scale we have also discussed the impact of light heterogeneity, and in particular the impact of gap formation, on vegetation dynamics in closed forest systems. At all scales, from the leaf to the whole plant and beyond, we have focused our attention on light energy utilization, emphasizing the importance, realized or potential, that species differences may have in determining observed distribution patterns with respect to light variability.

References

Björkman, O. (1981) Responses to different quantum flux densities. In: *Encyclopedia of Plant Physiology, Physiological Ecology,* Vol. 12A (eds O.L. Lange, P.S. Nobel, C.B. Osmond and H. Ziegler), pp. 57–102. Springer-Verlag, New York.

Björkman, O. and Powles, S.B. (1981) Leaf movement in the shade species *Oxalis oregana.* I. Response to light level and light quality. *Carnegie Institution of Washington Year Book 1980,* 59–62.

Björkman, O., Ludlow, M.M. and Morrow, P.A. (1972) Photosynthetic performance of two rain forest species in their native habitat and analysis of their gas exchange. *Carnegie Institution of Washington Year Book 1971,* 94–102.

Bone, R.A., Lee, D.W. and Norman, J.M. (1985) Epidermal cells functioning as lenses in leaves of tropical rain-forest shade plants. *Applied Optics* **24,** 1408–1412.

Brokaw, N.V.L. (1985) Gap-phase regeneration in a tropical forest. *Ecology* **66,** 682–687.

Brown, N.D. (1993) The implications of climate and gap microclimate for seedling growth conditions in a Bornean lowland rainforest. *Journal of Tropical Ecology* **9,** 153–168.

Brown, N.D. and Whitmore, T.C. (1992) Do dipterocarp seedlings really partition tropical rain forest gaps? *Philosophical Transactions of the Royal Society of London B* **335,** 369–378.

Buchmann, N., Guehl, J.-M., Barigah, T.S. and Ehleringer, J.R. (1997) Interseasonal comparison of CO_2 concentrations, isotopic composition, and carbon dynamics in an Amazonian rainforest (French Guiana). *Oecologia* **110,** 120–131.

Cardon, Z.G., Berry, J.A. and Woodrow, I.E. (1994) Dependence of the extent and direction of average stomatal response in *Zea mays* L. and *Phaseolus vulgaris* L. on the frequency of fluctuations in environmental stimuli. *Plant Physiology* **105,** 1007–1013.

Cardon, Z.G., Berry, J.A. and Woodrow, I.E. (1995) Fluctuating $[CO_2]$ drives species-specific changes in water use efficiency. *Journal of Biogeography* **22,** 203–208.

Chazdon, R.L. (1986) Light variation and carbon gain in rain forest understorey palms. *Journal of Ecology* **74,** 995–1012.

Chazdon, R.L. and Pearcy, R.W. (1986) Photosynthetic responses to light variation in rainforest species. I. Induction under constant and fluctuating light conditions. *Oecologia* **69,** 517–523.

Chazdon, R.L., Pearcy, R.W., Lee, D.W. and Fetcher, N. (1996) Photosynthetic responses of tropical forest plants to contrasting light environments. In: *Tropical Forest Plant Ecophysiology* (eds S.S. Mulkey, R.L Chazdon and A.P. Smith), pp. 5–55. Chapman and Hall, London.

Connell, J.H. (1978) Diversity in tropical rain forests and coral reefs. *Science* **199,** 1302–1310.

DeLucia, E.H., Nelson, K., Vogelmann, T.C. and Smith, W.K. (1996) Contribution of intercellular reflectance to photosynthesis in shade leaves. *Plant, Cell and Environment* **19,** 159–170.

Demmig, B., Winter, K., Krüger, A. and Czygan, F.-C. (1987) Photoinhibition and zeaxanthin formation in intact leaves. *Plant Physiology* **84,** 218–224.

Demmig-Adams, B. and Adams, W.W. III (1992) Photoprotection and other responses of plants to high light stress. *Annual Review of Plant Physiology and Plant Molecular Biology* **43,** 599–626.

Denslow, J.S. (1987) Tropical rainforest gaps and tree species diversity. *Annual Review of Ecology and Systematics* **18,** 431–451.

Ernstsen, J., Woodrow, I.E. and Mott, K.A. (1997) Responses of Rubisco activation and deactivation rates to variations in growth-light conditions. *Photosynthesis Research* **52,** 117–125.

Evans, J.R. (1989) Photosynthesis and nitrogen relationships in leaves of C_3 plants. *Oecologia* **78,** 9–19.

Fay, P.A. and Knapp, A.K. (1993) Photosynthetic and stomatal responses of *Avena sativa* (Poaceae) to variable light environment. *American Journal of Botany* **80,** 1369–1373.

Frank, H.A., Cua, A., Chynwat, B., Young, A., Gosztola, D. and Wasielewski, M.R. (1994) Photophysics of the carotenoids associated with the xanthophyll cycle in photosynthesis. *Photosynthesis Research* **41,** 389–395.

Frost, D.L., Gurney, A.L., Press, M.C. and Scholes, J.D. (1997) *Striga hermonthica* reduces photosynthesis in sorghum: the importance of stomatal limitations and a potential role for ABA? *Plant, Cell and Environment* **20,** 483–492.

Gilmore, A.M. and Yamamoto, H.Y. (1993) Biochemistry of xanthophyll-dependent nonradiative energy dissipation. In: *Photosynthetic*

Responses to the Environment, Current Topics in Plant Physiology, Vol. 8 (eds H.Y. Yamamoto and C.M. Smith), pp. 160–165. American Society of Plant Physiologists, Rockville, USA.

Givnish, T.J. (1988) Adaptation to sun and shade: a whole-plant perspective. In: *Ecology of Photosynthesis in Sun and Shade* (eds J.R. Evans, S. von Caemmerer and W.W. Adams, III), CSIRO, Australia.

Hopkins, M.S. and Graham, A.W. (1987) The viability of seeds of rainforest species after experimental soil burials under tropical wet lowland forest in north-eastern Australia. *Australian Journal of Ecology* **12**, 97–108.

Horton, J.L. and Neufeld, H.S. (1998) Photosynthetic responses of *Microstegium vimineum* (Trin.) A. Camus, a shade-tolerant, C_4 grass, to variable light environments. *Oecologia* **114**, 11–19.

Hubbell, S.P., Foster, R.B., O'Brien, S.T., *et al.* (1999) Light-gap disturbances, recruitment limitation, and tree diversity in a neotropical forest. *Science* **283**, 554–557.

Kamaluddin, M. and Grace, J. (1992) Photoinhibition and light acclimation in seedlings of *Bischofia javanica*, a tropical forest tree from Asia. *Annals of Botany* **69**, 47–52.

King, D.A. (1994) Influence of light level on the growth and morphology of saplings in a Panamanian forest. *American Journal of Botany* **81**, 948–957.

Kirschbaum, M.U.F. and Pearcy, R.W. (1988) Gas exchange analysis of the relative importance of stomatal and biochemical factors in photosynthetic induction in *Alocasia macrorrhiza*. *Plant Physiology* **86**, 782–785.

Kohyama, T. (1991) A functional model describing sapling growth under a tropical forest canopy. *Functional Ecology* **5**, 83–90.

Königer, M., Harris, G.C., Virgo, A. and Winter, K. (1995) Xanthophyll-cycle pigments and photosynthetic capacity in tropical forest species: a comparative field study on canopy, gap and understory plants. *Oecologia* **104**, 280–290.

Küppers, M. and Schneider, H. (1993) Leaf gas exchange of beech (*Fagus sylvatica* L.) seedlings in lightflecks: effects of fleck length and leaf temperature in leaves grown in deep and partial shade. *Trees* **7**, 160–168.

Kursar, T.A. and Coley, P.D. (1991) Nitrogen content and expansion rate of young leaves of rain forest species-implications for herbivory. *Biotropica* **23**, 141–150.

Kursar, T.A. and Coley, P.D. (1992) Delayed greening in tropical leaves—an antiherbivore defense. *Biotropica* **24**, 256–262.

Lee, D.W., Bone, R.A., Tarsis, S.L. and Storch, D. (1990) Correlates of leaf optical properties in tropical forest sun and extreme-shade plants. *American Journal of Botany* **77**, 370–380.

Lee, D.W., Baskaran, K., Mansor, M., Mohamad, H. and Yap, S.K. (1996) Irradiance and spectral quality affect Asian tropical rain forest tree seedling development. *Ecology* **77**, 568–580.

Lee, D.W., Oberbauer, S.F., Krishnapilay, B., Mansor, M., Mohamad, H. and Yap, S.K. (1997) Effects of irradiance and spectral quality on seedling development of two Southeast Asian *Hopea* species. *Oecologia* **110**, 1–9.

Le Gouallec, J.L., Cornic, G. and Blanc, P. (1991) Relations between sunfleck sequences and photoinhibition of photosynthesis in a tropical rain forest understory herb. *American Journal of Botany* **77**, 999–1006.

Logan, B.A., Barker, D.H., Adams, W.W. III and Demmig-Adams, B. (1997) The response of xanthophyll cycle-dependent energy dissipation in *Alocasia brisbanensis* to sunflecks in a subtropical rainforest. *Australian Journal of Plant Physiology* **24**, 27–33.

Lovelock, C.E., Jebb, M. and Osmond, C.B. (1994) Photoinhibition and recovery in tropical plant species: response to disturbance. *Oecologia* **97**, 297–307.

Lovelock, C.E., Kursar, T.A., Skillman, J.B. and Winter, K. (1998) Photoinhibition in tropical forest understorey species with short- and long-lived leaves. *Functional Ecology* **12**, 553–560.

Lusk, C.H. and Smith, B. (1998) Life history differences and tree species coexistence in an old-growth New Zealand rain forest. *Ecology* **79**, 795–806.

Miziorko, H.M. and Lorimer, G.H. (1983) Ribulose-1,5-bisphosphate carboxylase-oxygenase. *Annual Review of Biochemistry* **52**, 507–535.

Mott, K.A., Snyder, G.W. and Woodrow, I.E. (1997) Kinetics of rubisco activation as determined from gas-exchange measurements in antisense plants of *Arabidopsis thaliana* containing reduced levels of rubisco activase. *Australian Journal of Plant Physiology* **24**, 811–818.

Ögren, E. and Sundin, U. (1996) Photosynthetic responses to variable light: a comparison of species from contrasting habitats. *Oecologia* **106**, 18–27.

Osmond, C.B., Anderson, J.M., Ball, M.C. and Egerton, J.J.G. (1999) Compromising efficiency: the molecular ecology of light resource utilisation in plants. In: *Advances in Plant Physiological Ecology* (eds M.C. Press, J.D. Scholes and M. Barker), pp. 1–24. Blackwell Science, Oxford.

Pascarella, J.B. and Horvitz, C.C. (1998) Hurricane disturbance and the population dynamics of a tropical understory shrub: megamatrix elasticity analysis. *Ecology* **79**, 547–563.

Pearcy, R.W. (1983) The light environment and growth of C$_3$ and C$_4$ tree species in the understory of a Hawaiian forest. *Oecologia* **58**, 19–25.

Pearcy, R.W. (1987) Photosynthetic gas exchange responses of Australian tropical forest trees in canopy, gap and understory micro-environments. *Functional Ecology* **1**, 169–178.

Pearcy, R.W. and Calkin, H.W. (1983) Carbon dioxide exchange of C$_3$ and C$_4$ tree species in the understory of a Hawaiian forest. *Oecologia* **58**, 26–32.

Pearcy, R.W. and Sims, D.A. (1994) Photosynthetic acclimation to changing light environments: scaling from the leaf to the whole plant. In: *Exploitation of Environmental Heterogeneity by Plants* (eds M.M. Caldwell and R.W. Pearcy), pp. 145–174. Academic Press, San Diego.

Pearcy, R.W. and Yang, W. (1998) The functional morphology of light capture and carbon gain in the Redwood forest understorey plant *Adenocaulon bicolor* Hook. *Functional Ecology* **12**, 543–552.

Pearcy, R.W., Chazdon, R.L., Gross, L.J. and Mott, K.A. (1994) Photosynthetic utilization of sunflecks: a temporally patchy resource on a time scale of seconds to minutes. In: *Exploitation of Environmental Heterogeneity by Plants* (eds M.M. Caldwell and R.W. Pearcy), pp. 175–208. Academic Press, San Diego.

Pfitsch, W.A. and Pearcy, R.W. (1989) Daily carbon gain by *Adenocaulon bicolor* (Asteraceae), a redwood forest understorey herb, in relation to its light environment. *Oecologia* **80**, 471–476.

Pfitsch, W.A. and Pearcy, R.W. (1992) Growth and reproductive allocation of *Adenocaulon bicolor* following the experimental removal of sunflecks. *Ecology* **73**, 2109–2117.

Pons, T.L., Pearcy, R.W. and Seemann, J.R. (1992) Photosynthesis in flashing light in soybean leaves grown in different conditions. I. Photosynthetic induction state and regulation of ribulose-1,5-bisphosphate carboxylase activity. *Plant, Cell and Environment* **15**, 569–576.

Poorter, L. and Oberbauer, S.F. (1993) Photosynthetic induction responses of two rainforest tree species in relation to light environment. *Oecologia* **96**, 193–199.

Portis, A.R. (1992) Regulation of ribulose-1,5-bisphosphate carboxylase/oxygenase activity. *Annual Review of Plant Physiology and Plant Molecular Biology* **43**, 415–437.

Powles, S.B. and Björkman, O. (1981) Leaf movement in the shade species *Oxalis oregana*. II. Role in protection against injury by intense light. *Carnegie Institution of Washington Year Book* **1980**, 63–66.

Press, M.C., Brown, N.D., Barker, M.G. and Zipperlen, S.W. (1996) Photosynthetic responses to light in tropical rain forest tree seedlings. In: *The Ecology of Tropical Tree Seedlings, Man and the Biosphere Series*, Vol. 17 (ed. M.D. Swaine), pp. 41–54. Parthenon Publishing, Carnforth, UK.

Raven, J.A. (1989) Fight or flight—the economics of repair and avoidance of photoinhibition of photosynthesis. *Functional Ecology* **3**, 5–19.

Sassenrath-Cole, G.F., Pearcy, R.W. and Steinmaus, S. (1994) The role of enzyme activation state in limiting carbon assimilation under variable light conditions. *Photosynthesis Research* **41**, 295–302.

Scholes, J.D., Press, M.C. and Zipperlen, S.W. (1996) Differences in light energy utilisation and dissipation between dipterocarp rain forest tree seedlings. *Oecologia* **109**, 41–48.

Schultz, H.R. and Matthews, M.A. (1997) High vapour pressure deficit exacerbates xylem cavitation and photoinhibition in shade-grown *Piper auritum* HB and K during prolonged sunflecks. 1. Dynamics of plant water relations. *Oecologia* **110**, 312–319.

Schupp, E.W., Howe, H.F., Augspurger, C.K. and Levey, D.J. (1989) Arrival and survival in tropical treefall gaps. *Ecology* **71**, 504–515.

Seemann, J.R., Kirschbaum, M.U.F., Sharkey, T.D. and Pearcy, R.W. (1988) Regulation of ribulose-1,5-bisphosphate carboxylase activity in *Alocasia macrorrhiza* in response to step changes in irradiance. *Plant Physiology* **88**, 148–152.

Sims, D.A. and Pearcy, R.W. (1993) Sunfleck frequency and duration affects growth rate of the understorey plant, *Alocasia macrorrhiza*. *Functional Ecology* **7**, 683–689.

Strauss-Debenedetti, S. and Bazzaz, F.A. (1991) Plasticity and acclimation to light in tropical Moraceae of different successional positions. *Oecologia* **87**, 377–387.

Tinoco-Ojanguren, C. and Pearcy, R.W. (1992) Dynamic stomatal behaviour and its role in carbon gain during lightflecks of a gap phase and an understorey *Piper* species acclimated to high and low light. *Oecologia* **92**, 222–228.

Tinoco-Ojanguren, C. and Pearcy, R.W. (1993a) Stomatal dynamics and its importance to carbon gain in two rainforest *Piper* species. II. Stomatal versus biochemical limitations during photosynthetic induction. *Oecologia* **94**, 395–402.

Tinoco-Ojanguren, C. and Pearcy, R.W. (1993b) Stomatal dynamics and its importance to carbon gain in two rainforest *Piper* species. I. VPD effects on the transient stomatal response to lightflecks. *Oecologia* **94**, 388–394.

Valladares, F., Allen, M.T. and Pearcy, R.W. (1997) Photosynthetic responses to dynamic light under field conditions in six tropical rainforest shrubs occurring along a light gradient. *Oecologia* **111**, 505–514.

Valverde, T. and Silvertown, J. (1998) Variation in the demography of a woodland understorey herb (*Primula vulgaris*) along the forest regeneration cycle: projection matrix analysis. *Journal of Ecology* **86**, 545–562.

Vázquez-Yanes, C. and Orozco-Segovia, A. (1990) Ecological significance of light controlled seed germination in two contrasting tropical habitats. *Oecologia* **83**, 171–175.

Watling, J.R. (1995) *Sunflecks: responses of rainforest understorey plants to a fluctuating light environment.* PhD Thesis, James Cook University of North Queensland.

Watling, J.R., Robinson, S.A., Woodrow, I.E. and Osmond, C.B. (1997a) Responses of rainforest understorey plants to excess light during sunflecks. *Australian Journal of Plant Physiology* **24**, 17–25.

Watling, J.R., Ball, M.C. and Woodrow, I.E. (1997b) The utilization of lightflecks for growth in four Australian rain-forest species. *Functional Ecology* **11**, 231–239.

Wayne, P.M. and Bazzaz, F.A. (1993) Birch seedling responses to daily time courses of light in experimental forest gaps and shadehouses. *Ecology* **74**, 1502–1515.

Woodrow, I.E. and Mott, K.A. (1989) Rate limitation of non-steady-state photosynthesis by ribulose-1,5-bisphosphate carboxylase in spinach. *Australian Journal of Plant Physiology* **16**, 487–500.

Zipperlen, S.W. and Press, M.C. (1996) Photosynthesis in relation to growth and seedling ecology of two dipterocarp rain forest tree species. *Journal of Ecology* **84**, 863–876.

Zipperlen, S.W. and Press, M.C. (1997) Photosynthetic induction and stomatal oscillations in relation to the light environment of two dipterocarp rain forest tree species. *Journal of Ecology* **85**, 491–503.

Chapter 9

Heterogeneity in plant quality and its impact on the population ecology of insect herbivores

M.D. Hunter[1], R.E. Forkner[2] and J.N. McNeil[3]

Introduction

The field of insect ecology is home to a surprising paradox. When evolutionary biologists study the ecology of phytophagous insects, they often concentrate on the role of plant quality in determining the adaptive radiation, genetic variation, host preference and realized performance of insects that feed on plants (Denno and McClure 1983; Fritz and Simms 1991; Hunter *et al.* 1992; Mopper and Strauss 1998). In other words, variation in plant quality is seen as a dominant force in the evolutionary biology of phytophagous insects. In contrast, ecologists who study the population dynamics of insect herbivores generally rely on theoretical constructs that minimize the role of variation in plant quality on insect dynamics, focusing instead on the processes of predation, parasitism, disease, and competition (Varley *et al.* 1973; Hassell 1976; Anderson and May 1980; May 1981; Royama 1992). There are some notable exceptions (Foster *et al.* 1992; Rossiter 1994; Belovsky and Joern 1995) but the general absence of qualitative variation in plant quality in most insect population models is surprising because evolutionary biology and population dynamics are based on the same currencies: birth, death, and movement.

Although much in the minority, insect population models that incorporate variation in plant quality have appeared in the primary literature for some years (Fischlin and Baltensweiler 1979; Edelstein-Keshet and Rausher 1989; Foster *et al.* 1992; Frank 1993; Lundberg *et al.* 1994; Underwood 1999). What is perhaps surprising is that these models have generally failed to find a central place in our ecology textbooks, our population ecology courses, and our general theory of population dynamics. Whether the under-representation of variation in plant quality in insect population models results from 'historical inertia' or a conviction that plant quality has minimal impact upon insect herbivore population change is unclear. Evidence suggests, however, that, like natural enemies, qualitative variation within and among plants can affect insect populations in density-dependent,

[1]*Institute of Ecology, University of Georgia, Athens, GA 30602-2202, USA;* [2]*Department of Biology, University of Missouri, 8001 Natural Bridge Road, St. Louis, MO 63121, USA;* [3]*Département de biologie, Université Laval, Québec G1K 7P4, Canada*

density-independent and inverse density-dependent manners. Density-dependent effects of plant quality on insect herbivores (those with the potential to regulate populations) can occur through the limitation of edible resources (Denno *et al.* 1995) and the negative feedback associated with induced plant defences (Underwood 1999). Density-independent effects include the contributions of variation in plant quality to insect preference and performance, including voltinism, mortality and fecundity (Speight *et al.* 1999). Inverse density-dependent effects are typified by the overwhelming of plant resistance by the coordinated attack of some bark beetle species (Raffa and Berryman 1983, 1986). Finally, complex interactive effects of plant quality on the numerical and functional responses of natural enemies, so called three-trophic level interactions, are ecologically pervasive (Price *et al.* 1980) yet essentially absent from insect population models (Foster *et al.* 1992). All of these plant-based effects, whether regulatory or not, have the potential to cause profound changes in the densities of insect herbivores (Belovsky and Joern 1995; Price and Hunter 1995).

In the spirit of a recent call to re-examine the theoretical constructs of population dynamics (Cappuccino and Price 1995), this chapter explores the role of heterogeneity in plant quality in the population dynamics of phytophagous insects. We present a simple graphical model to illustrate that plant quality is central to the equilibrium dynamics of insect herbivores, even when their populations are regulated below carrying capacity by natural enemies. We then consider two empirical studies that suggest an important role for variation in plant quality in insect population dynamics. Finally, we examine some of the expected benefits that might emerge from an explicit consideration of plant quality in insect population models.

A role for variation in plant quality in affecting population equilibrium

In a simple plant–herbivore–predator system in which movement is ignored for simplicity, population equilibrium of the insect herbivore is determined by the balance of mortality and natality. If we assume that predation is density dependent up to some threshold beyond which predation is inversely density dependent (a Type III functional response) and that mortality from intraspecific competition becomes increasingly important at high density, the idealized mortality curve is cubic (Fig. 9.1a). If we also assume that variation in plant quality influences birth rate (e.g. Barbosa and Schultz 1987; Watt *et al.* 1990) which also declines with density (e.g. Rossiter *et al.* 1988; Hunter and Willmer 1989), we can envisage a series of equilibrium densities generated by the intersection of birth rates and death rates. In this scenario, variation in plant quality could emerge from differences among genotypes, populations or species of plant. The important point is that plant-mediated changes in birth rate influence population equilibrium, even when the population is regulated below carrying capacity by predation pressure (to the left of the natural enemy hump in Fig. 9.1a). For completeness, we should also note that, at high densities where the insect population escapes regulation by the

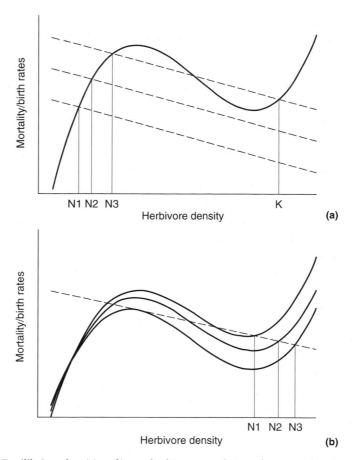

Figure 9.1 Equilibrium densities of insect herbivore populations determined by the intersection of birth rates (dotted lines) and death rates (solid lines), where N1–3 represent equilibrium densities and K represents carrying capacity. In (a), three host plants of varying quality influence equilibrium density. In (b), variation in predation pressure influences equilibrium. After Hunter (1997).

predator, changes in predation rate will still influence herbivore equilibrium, even if the predation is inversely density-dependent (Fig. 9.1b). This model, while extremely simple, can be modified to include more complex characteristics of insect population dynamics. For example, if mortality from competition is re-placed with density-dependent dispersal, the same general results emerge: spatial or temporal variation in plant quality that influences birth, death, immigration, or emigration will influence the equilibrium density around which the population will fluctuate. Likewise, changes in the shape of the natality curves (curvilinear, for example) will change equilibrium densities. From this very simple exercise, we infer that variation in resource quality (bottom-up) and variation in predation pressure (top-down) combine to determine the population dynamics of insect herbivores. As such, both should be incorporated into any theoretical framework that hopes to describe adequately insect population change.

Empirical support for the importance of plant quality in insect population dynamics

We provide two examples from our own work where variation in the quality of plants consumed by insect herbivores influences traits critical to the population dynamics of phytophagous insects. First, we describe a system in which the voltinism of the oblique-banded leafroller, *Choristoneura rosaceana* (Harris) (Lepidoptera: Tortricidae), depends upon the quality of foliage consumed by insect larvae. High quality host plants promote a bivoltine lifecycle whereas low quality host plants promote a univoltine lifecycle (Hunter and McNeil 1997). Second, we compare the relative strength of predation pressure on oak herbivores feeding on either high- or low-quality plants. By factorial manipulation of plant quality and predation pressure, we demonstrate that natural enemies have an increasing effect on oak insect populations as plant quality increases (Forkner and Hunter 2000).

Voltinism in *Choristoneura rosaceana*
Background

Diapause is an important means by which insects avoid unfavourable environmental conditions (Tauber *et al.* 1986; Danks 1987). When diapause is facultative rather than obligatory, insects have the potential to produce additional generations when conditions are favourable (Roff 1980, 1983) or enter diapause when conditions are unfavourable (Carrière *et al.* 1995). Since facultative diapause can determine the number of generations produced by a population per year, it can have profound implications for the ecology of insects, including affecting rates of population growth (Hunter and McNeil 1997).

Most studies of diapause have concentrated on the roles of photoperiod and temperature as primary cues of diapause induction (de Wilde 1962; McNeil and Rabb 1973; Tauber and Tauber 1976; Brodeur and McNeil 1989) or termination (McNeil and Fields 1985; Nakai and Takeda 1995). Other environmental factors, such as humidity (Darquenne *et al.* 1993; Lenga *et al.* 1993) or food quality (McNeil and Rabb 1973; Brodeur and McNeil 1989; Claret and Volkoff 1992; Tzanakakis and Veerman 1994), have received limited attention. Nonetheless, food has been shown to be a major factor regulating diapause for a few species of insects, particularly those that undergo aestival rather than hibernal diapause (Taper *et al.* 1986). For example, aestivation is induced by host plant maturation in the maize stem borer, *Busseola fusca* (Usua 1973), and two pyralid stalk borers of maize, *Chilo zonellus* and *C. argyrolepia* (Scheltes 1976). Although it appears to be rarer for host plant quality to dominate hibernal diapause, one well-studied example is the effect of host quality on the seasonal responses of aphids. Seasonal declines in host quality combine with photoperiod, temperature, and crowding to affect aphid morphology and, ultimately, the production of diapausing eggs (Dixon 1971; Mittler 1973; Harrewijn 1978).

It is probably more common for food quality to interact with photoperiodic and temperature responses to influence diapause than to act in isolation. For example, food constitutes one of at least four interacting determinants of diapause induction in *Hyphantria cunea* from eastern Canada (Morris 1967). Similarly, host-plant quality is one of four factors important in diapause induction in the codling moth, *Cydia pomonella*, and one of three factors affecting diapause induction in the alfalfa ladybeetle, *Subcoccinella 24-punctata*. Both of these species have a higher incidence of diapause when they are fed a non-preferred host than when they receive a pre-ferred host (Ali and Saringer 1975).

We might expect host plant quality and photoperiod to interact to determine patterns of diapause by insect herbivores. Photoperiodic induction of diapause is often restricted to specific life-stages in insects (Danilevsky 1965; Denlinger 1972; Saunders 1973; Beck 1980) and nutritional features of host-plants that result in variable growth rates may also result in variable diapause induction. For example, rapid growth on high quality plants might result in some individuals passing the critical age for diapause induction before environmental conditions, such as photoperiod, reach threshold levels that induce diapause.

We used field and laboratory experiments to examine the influence of host-plant quality on the facultative larval diapause of a polyphagous insect herbivore, *C. rosaceana*. Specifically, we addressed the following predictions:

1 the proportion of larvae entering diapause under field conditions varies among host species;

2 the quality of foliage consumed by larvae is one factor responsible for variation in diapause induction;

3 the mechanism by which host quality influences diapause induction is by influencing larval growth rate relative to changes in photoperiod.

System of study

The oblique-banded leafroller, *C. rosaceana*, is a common tortricid moth in decidu-ous woodland in much of North America and feeds on a wide variety of deciduous tree species. In the Province of Québec, Canada, *C. rosaceana* is univoltine in the north (authors' unpublished data from the Lac St-Jean region, 48°34′N; 72°14′W) and exhibits facultative bivoltinism in the south (Delisle 1992; Carrière *et al.* 1995; e.g. Parc Oka, 45°28′N; 74°05′W). Populations further south (e.g. north-eastern United States) are considered to be bivoltine, but the degree to which this voltinism is obligate or facultative has yet to be investigated. The life cycle of *C. rosaceana* in the Québec City area (46°48′N; 71°21′W), where our study was conducted, is as follows: Larvae that have overwintered as second or third instars emerge from hibernaculae following leaf-flush in spring and complete development, pupating in early June. The first adult cohort emerges in mid/late June and eggs are laid shortly thereafter. Neonates emerge after about 2 weeks, and larval dispersal on silk threads appears to be a dominant mode of dispersal and host choice (Carrière

1992). Larvae in this cohort either enter diapause (2nd or 3rd instar) until the following spring or continue development for a second generation; the progeny of any one female includes diapausing and non-diapausing individuals. Individuals that continue development produce a second cohort of adults that emerge in mid/late August. The progeny of these adults emerge and feed for a few weeks before entering diapause (2nd or 3rd instar) until the following spring.

The induction of diapause in *C. rosaceana* has been shown to depend upon temperature and photoperiod (Gangavalli and AliNiazee 1985). Specifically, 1st and 2nd instar larvae are the only stages susceptible to diapause induction. Studies of an Oregon population have shown that there is a critical photoperiod of between 14 and 15 h of light per day; at 14:10 light:dark, all larvae enter diapause. Above 15 h light per day, most larvae do not enter diapause, and continue development. The critical photoperiod can be modified slightly by altering temperature (Gangavalli and AliNiazee 1985). This study was conducted with insects reared on artificial diet. Given that, in the Québec City area, univoltine and bivoltine life-histories occur simultaneously within a year, we hypothesized that variation in plant quality could influence diapause induction and therefore voltinism.

Methods and results

In our first experiment, we enclosed eggs of *C. rosaceana* in the field on four different tree species: red maple (*Acer rubrum*), black ash (*Fraxinus nigra*), paper birch (*Betula papyrifera*), and common chokecherry (*Prunus virginiana*). All four species supported moderate to high densities of *C. rosaceana* at our field site (Sainte-Foy) just outside Québec City. Eggs, from colonies fed artificial diet for five generations, were enclosed in early July, one week after the first detection of adult males in pheromone traps. We allowed larvae to enclose and to feed for 6 weeks. After the feeding period, counts were made of individuals that had either entered diapause (2nd or 3rd instar under silk hibernacula on twigs) or continued development (pupae or adults) (methods in Hunter and McNeil 1997).

The proportion of larvae entering diapause varied among host-plant species (Fig. 9.2a). Almost all larvae entered diapause on red maple and black ash, fewer on paper birch, and fewer still on chokecherry. As predicted, host-plant species influenced diapause induction and the probability of a bivoltine life-history.

In our second experiment, we enclosed neonates on the same four host plant species under laboratory conditions. In this case, larvae were maintained at 20°C, 16:8 h light:dark. Larvae from a single egg mass were divided among hosts so that the progeny of each female were exposed to all four hosts. We had imagined that differences in diapause among host plants observed in the field experiment were the result of a photoperiod-by-growth rate interaction: larvae on high quality hosts had grown rapidly and had therefore passed the critical stage for diapause induction (1st or 2nd instar) before the reduction in day length would initiate diapause. We therefore predicted that, under constant photoperiod, there would be no differences in diapause induction among hosts.

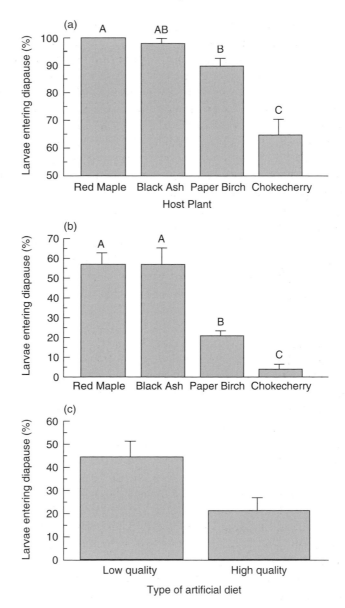

Figure 9.2 The percentage of *Choristoneura rosaceana* larvae entering diapause (a) on four host species under field conditions; (b) on four host species under laboratory conditions of constant photoperiod; and (c) on artificial diet under laboratory conditions of constant photoperiod. After Hunter and McNeil (1997); reprinted with permission.

In contrast, we observed the same qualitative pattern of diapause induction in the laboratory experiment as we had observed under field conditions: more larvae entered diapause on red maple and black ash than on either paper birch or chokecherry (Fig. 9.2b).

These results suggest that, as long as day length is sufficiently long, host plant quality has a direct impact on diapause induction. In other words, host quality has an impact on voltinism independent of any photoperiod-by-growth rate interaction. This surprising result was confirmed by a third experiment using artificial diet. In this case, we made high- and low-quality pinto bean diet (Shorey and Hale 1965) by replacing half of the pinto beans with cellulose in the low-quality diet, causing a 37% decline in nitrogen content. Again, neonates from egg masses were divided among diets and reared under constant photoperiod in the laboratory (above). More larvae entered diapause on the low quality diet than on the high-quality diet (Fig. 9.2c).

Discussion

Taken together, these results suggest that host plant quality, in this case variation among species of deciduous trees, can influence the voltinism of a polyphagous insect herbivore, *C. rosaceana*. Larvae feeding on high-quality hosts will continue development and result in a second generation. Larvae on low-quality hosts will enter diapause and exhibit a univoltine lifecycle. The progeny of a single female can enter the univoltine or bivoltine pathway, depending upon the species of plant that they encounter during neonate dispersal (Hunter and McNeil 1997).

We had initially assumed that any effects of host-plant quality on diapause induction would be due to effects on the synchrony between the sensitive stages for diapause induction (instars 1 and 2 for *C. rosaceana* (Gangavalli and AliNiazee 1985)) and changing photoperiod. However, under constant conditions of day-length and temperature on excised foliage in the laboratory, fewer larvae entered diapause on chokecherry and paper birch than on red maple and black ash. Thus, our results demonstrate that there is a direct effect of host-plant species on diapause induction that is independent of abiotic factors. Furthermore, our laboratory experiment with artificial diet further supports a direct role for nutritional quality in the initiation of diapause by *C. rosaceana*. Levels of diapause on low quality diet were twice those on high quality diet despite constant daylength and temperature. Although we do not have nutritional data for the four host plants that we used in our field and laboratory experiments, rates of larval growth and pupal mass indicated qualitative variation among the plant species that matched our diapause results (Hunter and McNeil 1997).

We might expect that host-plant quality should influence diapause in insect herbivores, given the tight links between host-plant quality, insect performance, and the population dynamics of insect herbivores (reviewed in Price and Hunter 1995). Yet despite the recognition that the number of generations per year exhibited by an insect species can be an important determinant of its ecological and evolutionary biology (Carrière *et al.* 1995), there have been too few studies of the role of host-plant quality on diapause to determine its relative importance in natural systems. Moreover, we argue that such a fundamental feature of lifehistory as voltinism is likely to have a considerable impact on population dynamics. Intrinsic rates of increase, interactions with natural enemies, and effects of the abiotic environment on population growth will all vary with the number of generations per year that an insect herbivore exhibits. We doubt that realistic predictions of *C. rosaceana* population dynamics can be achieved without explicit consideration of the effects of host plant quality on voltinism.

Top-down and bottom-up forces on oak herbivores
Background
Most ecologists now agree that both top-down and bottom-up forces (predation and resource limitation, respectively) combine to influence populations and communities of mid-trophic level species such as herbivores. Early views that focused on either natural enemies (Hairston *et al.* 1960) or plant quality (Ehrlich and Raven 1964) as dominant forces have given way to a balanced view in which the quality and quantity of primary productivity, competition and predation interact to determine patterns of herbivore abundance in space and time (Schindler 1978; Oksanen *et al.* 1981; Carpenter and Kitchell 1988; Leibold 1989; McQueen *et al.* 1992). Ecologists are now more interested in exploring the environmental conditions that determine the relative effects of top-down and bottom-up forces, and how these vary spatially and temporally (Hunter and Price 1992; Menge 1992; Power 1992a; Strong 1992; Belovsky and Joern 1995).

The relative importance of nutrient availability and predation on trophic interactions is perhaps better understood in aquatic systems than in terrestrial systems. For example, there is compelling evidence in lake systems that trophic cascades from top predators often influence all lower trophic levels (Carpenter *et al.* 1985; Carpenter and Kitchell 1988; Kurmayer and Wanzenboeck 1996). At the same time, lake productivity varies with nutrient input (Schindler 1978; Carpenter and Kitchell 1987; McQueen *et al.* 1989) and so predation and nutrients combine to determine patterns of productivity (Pinel-Alloul *et al.* 1995; Walz 1995). Spatial and temporal variation in the relative importance of top-down and bottom-up forces in lakes is now being addressed (Jassby *et al.* 1992; Ramcharan *et al.* 1995; Jeppesen *et al.* 1997; Seda and Kubecka 1997). In stream systems, there are clear differences in the relative strength of top-down and bottom-up forces among different habitats (Power 1992b). The effects of increasing resource (light) availability on primary production differs among systems with three vs. four trophic levels (Wootton and Power 1993). Bottom-up effects appear to be particularly strong in streams in which detritus (leaf litter) forms the basis of the food web (Wallace *et al.* 1997).

In marine systems, there is also evidence for combined effects of top-down and bottom-up forces on population dynamics and community structure. Although the importance of top predators in rocky intertidal habitats is a classic case (Paine 1966), bottom-up effects are also significant (Menge 1992, 1995). For example,

163

differences in rocky intertidal community structure appear to depend in part on standing stocks of nearshore phytoplankton, a bottom-up effect (Menge *et al.* 1997a). However, this bottom-up effect is mediated on shore by changes in predator–prey dynamics from the top down (Menge *et al.* 1997b). This study suggests that bottom-up forces set the stage upon which top-down forces act. Again, spatial and temporal variation is apparent. Wootton *et al.* (1996a) and Metaxas and Scheibling (1996) both found that top-down forces on phytoplankton were generally stronger than bottom-up forces in rocky intertidal systems, but that their relative contributions varied in space and time.

From where does such spatial and temporal variation arise? Recent studies have emphasized the importance of variation in weather patterns, disturbance, and nutrient subsidies on trophic interactions (Wootton *et al.* 1996b; Polis *et al.* 1997a,b; Rose and Polis 1998). For example, El Niño events can increase plant cover on coastal islands by 10–160-fold, with insect and spider densities tracking those changes (Polis *et al.* 1997a). This 'bottom-up cascade' (Hunter and Price 1992) is short-lived, however. Increases in the densities of Pompilid wasps that parasitize spiders result in spider population crashes the following year (Polis *et al.* 1998). In other words, high productivity has the ultimate effect of increasing the power of a top-down force. Other theoretical and empirical work supports this view (Oksanen *et al.* 1981; Abrams 1993; Menge *et al.* 1997b; Stiling and Rossi 1997; Fraser and Grime 1998; Fraser 1998).

In terrestrial habitats, synthesis on the relative roles of top-down and bottom-up factors on plant–insect–natural enemy systems is hampered by a general lack of factorial manipulative experiments of the type that abound in aquatic systems. There is clear evidence that both top-down (Gomez and Zamora 1994; Marquis and Whelan 1994; Moran *et al.* 1996; Schimtz *et al.* 1997) and bottom-up (Denno *et al.* 1991; Denno *et al.* 1995; Hunter and Price 1998) forces operate on insects and their host plants, but estimating their relative strengths has proven elusive (Strong 1992; Hunter *et al.* 1997). In most experiments, either predators are excluded or resources are enhanced, but rarely at the same time.

Recent studies have confirmed that predators and parasitoids can have a significant impact on insect herbivore populations. For example, Floyd (1996) reported increases in herbivore densities on creosotebush following exclusion of birds and arthropod predators. In an important study, Marquis and Whelan (1994) demonstrated that the exclusion of birds from oaks could result in increased herbivore densities, increased defoliation levels, and decreased plant growth, a trophic cascade similar to those observed in lakes (above). Similarly, Gomez and Zamora (1994) documented direct increases in plant fitness (seed number and size) as a result of the foraging by parasitoids on seed predators of the host plant. The spectacular success of some biological control programs based on the enhancement or introduction of parasitoids also demonstrates the ability of natural enemies to suppress populations of their prey and increase the growth or production of plants (Huffaker 1971; Neuenschwander *et al.* 1989; Chang 1991). Perhaps the best documented terrestrial trophic cascade is that from mantids to plants in old-field ecosystems. Increased mantid densities result in the emigration of other arthropod predators (Moran and Hurd 1994). Mantids also cause a reduction in herbivore densities through direct consumption that, in turn, reduces herbivory and increases plant biomass (Moran *et al.* 1996; Moran and Hurd 1998).

While the relative importance of predation and resource availability on populations can sometimes be inferred from sampling data (Hanks and Denno 1993; Preszler and Boecklen 1996; Hunter *et al.* 1997), the best estimates come from factorial experiments. For example, Stiling and Rossi (1997) manipulated both plant productivity (fertilization) and natural enemies (parasitoid density) to examine their relative impacts on populations of gall-making flies on sea-oxeye daisy. They found that parasitism was only a significant source of mortality on plants that had been fertilized, and concluded that bottom-up forces set the stage upon which top-down forces operate (Stiling and Rossi 1996, 1997). Similarly, working with grasses, aphids, and ladybeetle predators, Fraser and Grime (1998) have shown that a trophic cascade from ladybeetle abundance to plant biomass occurs in high nutrient treatments only. Ladybeetles have a negligible impact on aphids (and therefore grasses) in low nutrient regimes. Further manipulative experiments by Fraser (1998) have confirmed that top-down forces have their greatest impact in productive terrestrial systems supporting previous theory (Oksanen *et al.* 1981; Abrams 1993). However, other studies have found that high productivity promotes escape from top-down control and, ultimately, leads to food limitation (Belovsky and Joern 1995). More experiments in terrestrial systems, of longer duration and in a variety of habitats, are clearly required before patterns are likely to emerge. Long-term experiments would be particularly valuable to assess the strength of those factors acting to regulate insect herbivore densities from those that contribute in a density-independent fashion to major changes in equilibrium density. As Hassell *et al.* (1998) have pointed out, a combination of observation, experimentation and simulation is probably necessary to untangle the complexity of factors that act on insect herbivore population dynamics.

System of study — insects on oak
Variation in the quality of oak foliage has long been known to influence oak herbivores. Foliar tannins, nitrogen content, and leaf phenology are major determinants of the growth, reproduction and survival of oak insects (Feeny 1970; Schultz and Baldwin 1982; Du Merle and Mazet 1983; Wint 1983; West 1985; Faeth and Bultman 1986; Hunter 1987, 1990; Rossiter *et al.* 1988; 1992a; Conner *et al.* 1994). Literature reviews have established that variation in the quality of oak foliage is important for insect herbivores in leaf-mining, leaf-chewing, gall-forming and sap-sucking 'guilds' (Hunter and West 1990; Hunter 1992b, 1994). Recent studies of deme formation in oak leaf-miners strongly suggest that plant quality plays a fundamental role in the population and evolutionary ecology of this guild of oak herbivores (Mopper and Simberloff 1995; Mopper *et al.* 1995). Leaf-miners also appear to respond to changes in oak foliage quality that result from hybridization among oak species (Preszler and Boecklen 1994) or from environmental gradients

(Preszler and Boecklen 1996). In short, variation in the quality of oak foliage is a major determinant of the distribution and abundance of many oak herbivore species.

Predators can also have a dramatic impact on oak herbivore populations and subsequent levels of defoliation (Marquis and Whelan 1994). As envisioned by Price *et al.* (1980), the probability that oak herbivores succumb to a particular natural enemy varies with host plant quality (Faeth 1985; Faeth and Bultman 1986; Taper *et al.* 1986; Keating and Yendol 1987; Rossiter 1987; Hunter and Schultz 1993; Preszler and Boecklen 1994; Mopper and Simberloff 1995; Mopper *et al.* 1995). The efficacy of parasitoids (Faeth 1985; Mopper and Simberloff 1995; Preszler and Boecklen 1996) and pathogens (Taper *et al.* 1986; Hunter and Schultz 1993) can vary dramatically depending upon the quality of foliage consumed by oak herbivores. In other words, the top-down forces of natural enemies and the bottom-up forces of plant quality interact to influence oak herbivore populations and communities.

Since 1996, we have been manipulating plant quality and predation pressure in factorial experiments within an oak/insect herbivore/natural enemy system. Our initial results (Forkner and Hunter 2000) support only in part the previous factorial experiments (Stiling and Rossi 1997; Fraser and Grime 1998) described above.

Methods and results

In March of 1995, we established a plantation of 3-year-old *Quercus prinus* and one year-old *Q. rubra* saplings in Whitehall Forest, Clarke County, Georgia. We allowed the saplings to grow for one year prior to beginning experimental treatments. The plantation was a latin-square design with oak species and fertilizer treatments as the primary alternating blocks. In April and June of 1996 and 1997, we treated trees assigned to blocks receiving fertilizer with 140 g of 14–14–14 N:P:K Osmocote time-release fertilizer (approximately 40 g per square metre per year of each nutrient). This fertilization regime was similar to that used by Hunter and Schultz (1995) to generate increases in foliar nitrogen and decreases in foliar phenolics in *Q. rubra* and *Q. prinus* saplings in Pennsylvania.

In March of 1997, we chose at random 40 trees, 20 fertilized and 20 unfertilized, of each species for predator exclusion treatments. We randomly selected half of these, 10 fertilized and 10 unfertilized of each species, to serve as control trees to which birds were allowed free access. We excluded birds from the remaining 20 saplings of each species using 2 m tall cages built of nylon netting, PVC pipes and rebar, following methods in Floyd (1996). This factorial design provided 10 replicates (trees) per species per treatment. Predaceous arthropods on trees were left unmanipulated.

In May, July, and September of 1997, we counted all arthropods on each of the 80 treatment trees. Phytophagous insects were counted and assigned to one of four feeding guilds: leaf-chewers, phloem-feeders, leaf-miners and gall-formers. Arthropod predators were counted and assigned to general taxonomic groups: spiders, hymenopterans, hemipterans and Coccinellids. In addition, we measured budburst date, tree diameter, tree height, number of leaves and number of branches. In October, we measured the accumulation of insect defoliation on each sapling (Hunter 1987).

On each sampling date, we collected five leaves haphazardly from each sapling to determine the impacts of fertilization on foliar phenolics and nitrogen concentration. We measured foliar astringency, the ability of extracts to bind protein, using the radial diffusion assay (Hagerman 1987; Waterman and Mole 1994) with BSA as the standard protein. Percent dry weight carbon and nitrogen were estimated from leaf powder on a Carlo-Erba NA1500 model C/N analyser.

Fertilizer treatments increased the productivity of oak saplings (estimated as change in height, Fig. 9.3), increased foliar nitrogen concentrations (Fig. 9.4) and decreased foliar astringency (Fig. 9.5). Fertilizer addition therefore had the general effect of increasing the quality of oaks for insect herbivores by increasing productivity, increasing foliar nitrogen, and decreasing the ability of foliage extracts to bind protein.

We had predicted that predation pressure would have a greater impact on herbivores on fertilized trees than on unfertilized trees, consistent with previous empirical and theoretical studies (Oksanen *et al.* 1981; Stiling and Rossi 1997; Fraser and Grime 1998). This prediction was supported only for *Q. rubra*, and only for certain feeding guilds. For example, predation pressure caused a significant decline in total herbivore abundance on *Q. rubra*, but only on fertilized trees (Fig. 9.6a). There was no such effect on *Q. prinus*. Likewise, densities of leaf-chewing insects declined in the presence of avian predators on fertilized red oak trees, but not on unfertilized trees (Fig. 9.6b). Again, leaf-chewing insects on *Q. prinus* were unaffected by avian predators. Finally, arthropod predators declined in the presence of avian predators

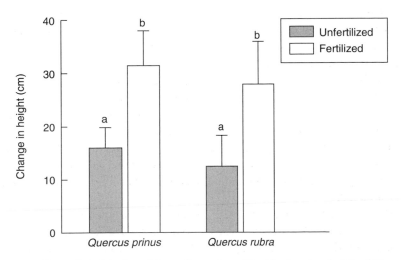

Figure 9.3 Change in height from May to September of fertilized and unfertilized *Quercus prinus* and *Q. rubra* saplings. After Forkner and Hunter (2000).

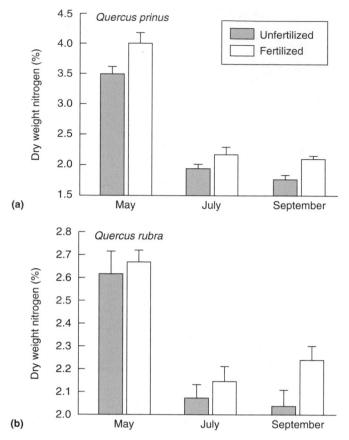

Figure 9.4 Foliar nitrogen concentrations of fertilized and unfertilized (a) *Quercus prinus*; (b) *Q. rubra* saplings. After Forkner and Hunter (2000).

on fertilized *Q. rubra*, but not on unfertilized trees. Arthropod predators were unaffected by avian predators on *Q. prinus*.

While the top-down effect of avian predators on fertilized trees can be visualized by comparing bars one and two on Fig. 9.6, the bottom-up effect of nutrient addition is represented by comparing bars one and three. In all cases, nutrient addition increased the densities of arthropods in the absence of avian predators. Leaf-mining and phloem-feeding insects were generally unaffected by avian predators or nutrient additions in any of the treatments. Arthropod predators on *Q. rubra* showed similar patterns to herbivores (Fig. 9.6c), and did not compensate for the exclusion of avian predators by maintaining lower densities of herbivores (Fig. 9.6a,b).

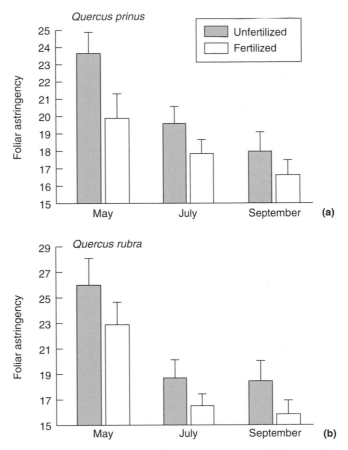

Figure 9.5 The foliar astringency of fertilized and unfertilized (a) *Quercus prinus;* (b) *Q. rubra* saplings. After Forkner and Hunter (2000).

Discussion

Previous work has established that both bottom-up (Feeny 1970; Schultz and Baldwin 1982; West 1985; Faeth and Bultman 1986; Hunter 1987; Rossiter *et al.* 1988) and top-down (Faeth 1985; Taper *et al.* 1986; Hunter and Schultz 1993; Marquis and Whelan 1994; Preszler and Boecklen 1994) forces can influence the population ecology of insect herbivores on oak. Factorial manipulations of nutrient availability and predation pressure in other terrestrial systems (Stiling and Rossi 1997; Fraser and Grime 1998; Fraser 1998) have generally supported the theory that the impact of natural enemies on herbivore populations should increase with the availability of resources for primary producers (Fretwell 1977; Oksanen *et al.* 1981). The results presented here are in partial agreement with previous work. We found that the impact of birds on some oak arthropods increased with fertilizer addition to red oak saplings. All herbivores combined, leaf-chewing

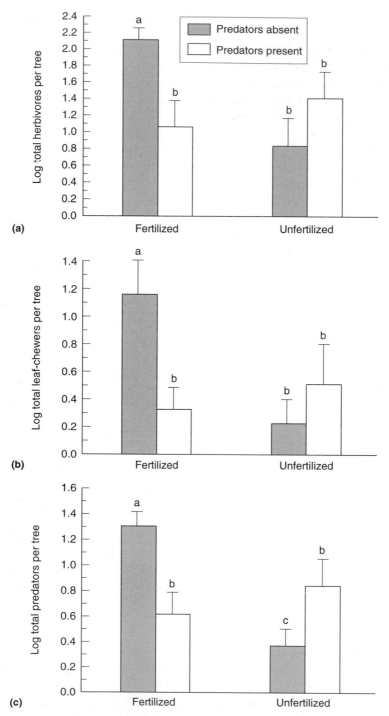

Figure 9.6 Densities of (a) total herbivores; (b) leaf-chewing insects; (c) arthropod predators on *Quercus rubra* saplings. In all cases, avian predators reduced populations of prey only on fertilized trees. Herbivores and arthropod predators were unaffected by avian predators on *Q. prinus* saplings (data not shown).

insects, and arthropod predators responded as predicted on red oak. Other herbivore guilds did not, and there was no response to our manipulations of bottom-up or top-down forces on chestnut oak.

The different responses of arthropods on the two oak species studied here are not easy to explain. Both tree species responded to fertilizer addition with increases in foliage quality (Figs 9.3–9.5) and both were exposed to the same suite of avian predators. Future work will explore both physical and chemical characteristics of the tree species and life-history differences in their arthropod faunas in an attempt to reconcile the different responses. Specifically, we need to untangle potential direct effects of trees on foraging by predators from indirect effects mediated by changes in the composition of the herbivorous insect community. At this point, we can conclude that there is no simple relationship between resource availability and predation pressure that can be generalized to the fauna of different tree species.

The impact of nutrient addition may have been conveyed to the third trophic level. The densities of predaceous arthropods were higher on fertilized red oak trees than on unfertilized trees in the absence of avian predators (Fig. 9.6c). We cannot be certain that this represents a direct effect of higher prey densities on fertilized trees (Fig. 9.6a,b) but it is consistent with previous studies suggesting that predaceous arthropods may track the densities of their prey (Hawkins 1992; Strong 1992; Polis *et al.* 1998). In addition, there were no significant correlations between our measures of tree architecture (height, diameter, number of leaves) and predator density suggesting that tree growth is not the major determinant of predaceous arthropod distribution.

In contrast to the results of Marquis and Whelan (1994) and Floyd (1996), we found no effects of bird exclusion on levels of defoliation. In our study, leaf area removed varied from about 12–25%, but did not differ among treatments. Given the rigor of the studies by Marquis and Whelan (1994) and Floyd (1996), our results appear to provide an example of spatial and temporal variation in the relative power of top-down and bottom-up forces on primary productivity (Hunter and Price 1992). Our study examined oak saplings in an old-field setting, whereas the trees examined by Marquis and Whelan (1994) were understorey oak saplings of greater age and size than those in our experiments. Future work should explore the habitat characteristics that result in strong effects of predator removal and nutrient addition on defoliation to plants.

General conclusions

We have argued here that variation in the quality of plants can have a significant impact on the population ecology of insect herbivores. Specifically, plant quality can influence both the voltinism of insects and the impact of their natural enemies. We have provided evidence that *C. rosaceana* in Québec is bivoltine on high quality plants and univoltine on low quality plants. We have described direct effects of nutrient addition on oak herbivore populations, and indirect effects mediated by increases in the power of predation pressure. Taken together, these studies suggest to us that a general theory of insect herbivore population ecology that ignores variation in plant quality will be weak at best and misleading at worst.

Variation in plant quality can act to regulate insect herbivore populations if declines in quality are dependent upon the density of the herbivore (Fischlin and Baltensweiler 1979; Edelstein-Keshet and Rausher 1989; Frank 1993; Lundberg *et al.* 1994; Underwood 1999). Because of the central importance of regulation to the study of population dynamics, such potential regulatory effects have received the most (albeit limited) attention in population models to date. Nonetheless, spatial and temporal variation in plant quality that acts in a density-independent or inverse density-dependent fashion can have dramatic effects on population dynamics. Changes in equilibrium density and the release from regulation by natural enemies are just two of the potential effects of density-independent variation in plant quality (Belovsky and Joern 1995; Fig. 9.1). Insect population models have been used extensively to explore density-independent and inverse density-dependent effects of natural enemies on population dynamics (Holling 1959, 1966; Stewart-Oaten and Murdoch 1990; Rohani *et al.* 1994; Murdoch *et al.* 1995). It would seem prudent to apply the same effort to variation in plant quality. Of particular interest, we suggest, would be to explore models that incorporate changes in the functional and numerical responses of natural enemies that are based upon spatial and temporal variation in plant quality (Price *et al.* 1980; Hunter *et al.* 1996; Eubanks and Denno 1999).

The benefits to be gained from including variation in plant quality in a general theory of herbivore population dynamics should be considerable. For example, disagreements on the factors influencing the population dynamics of certain species (Hunter *et al.* 1997; Hassell *et al.* 1998; Hunter and Price 1998; Hunter and Price 2000; Turchin and Berryman 2000) might be reconciled with modelling efforts that explicitly consider variation in plant quality. One vital and highly variable component of plant quality is defensive chemistry. We find it unfortunate that, after decades of research on the importance of plant chemistry on the birth, death and movement of insects (Rosenthal and Janzen 1979; Denno and McClure 1983; Fritz and Simms 1991; Hunter *et al.* 1992; Karban and Baldwin 1997; Mopper and Strauss 1998) we know of only one mathematical model that explicitly incorporates field-measured variation in plant chemistry in an attempt to predict population dynamics (Foster *et al.* 1992). The ecological sciences enjoy several journals dedicated to describing pervasive spatial and temporal variation in plant chemistry/quality and its effects on herbivores (e.g. *Journal of Chemical Ecology; Chemoecology; Phytochemistry*). We suggest that a realistic theory of herbivore population dynamics should embrace this variation rather than ignore it.

Acknowledgments

The research reported here was supported by NSF grant DEB-9527522 to MDH, an NSERC International Fellowship to MDH, and research grants from NSERC and FCAR to JNM. Angela Barber, Abby Feinstein, Kim Holton, Jason Leathers, Mat

Wood, Patrice-André Lefebvre, Madeleine Parent, Jacques Gobeil, and Alain Labrecque provided invaluable field and laboratory assistance. We thank Peter Price and two anonymous reviewers for constructive comments on an earlier draft of this paper.

References

Abrams, P.A. (1993) Effects of increased productivity on the abundance of trophic levels. *American Naturalist* **141**, 351–371.

Ali, M.A. and Saringer, G. (1975) Factors regulating diapause in alfalfa ladybird, *Subcoccinella 24-punctata* L. (Col., Coccinellidae). *Acta Phytopathology, Academy of Sciences of Hungary* **10**, 407–415.

Anderson. R.M. and May, R.M. (1980) Infectious diseases and population cycles of forest insects. *Science* **210**, 658–661.

Barbosa, P. and Schultz, J.C. (1987) *Insect Outbreaks*. Academic Press, San Diego.

Beck, S.D. (1980) *Insect Photoperiodism*, 2nd edn. Academic Press, New York.

Belovsky, G.E. and Joern, A. (1995) Regulation of rangeland grasshoppers: differing dominant mechanisms in space and time. In: *Population Dynamics: New Approaches and Synthesis* (eds N. Cappuccino and P.W. Price), pp. 359–386. Academic Press, San Diego.

Brodeur, J. and McNeil, J.N. (1989) Biotic and abiotic factors involved in diapause induction of the parasitoid, *Aphidius nigripes* (Hymenoptera: Aphidiidae). *Journal of Insect Physiology* **35**, 969–974.

Cappuccino, N. and Price, P.W. (1995) *Population Dynamics. New Approaches and Synthesis*. Academic Press, San Diego.

Carpenter, S.R. and Kitchell, J.F. (1987) The temporal scale of variance in lake productivity. *American Naturalist* **129**, 417–433.

Carpenter, S.R. and Kitchell, J.F. (1988) Consumer control of lake productivity. *Bioscience* **38**, 764–769.

Carpenter, S.R., Kitchell, J.F. and Hodgson, J.R. (1985) Cascading trophic interactions and lake productivity. *Bioscience* **35**, 634–639.

Carrière, Y. (1992) Larval dispersal from potential hosts within a population of a generalist herbivore, *Choristoneura rosaceana. Entomologia Experimentalis et Applicata* **65**, 11–19.

Carrière, Y., Roff, D.A. and Deland, J.-P. (1995) The joint evolution of diapause and insecticide resistance: a test of an optimality model. *Ecology* **76**, 1497–1505.

Chang, Y.C. (1991) Integrated pest management of several forest defoliators in Taiwan. *Forest Ecology and Management* **39**, 65–72.

Claret, J. and Volkoff, N. (1992) Vitamin A is essential for two processes involved in the photoperiodic reaction in *Pieris brassicae. Journal of Insect Physiology* **38**, 569–574.

Conner, E.F., Adams-Manson, R.H., Carr, T.G. and Beck, M.W. (1994) The effects of host plant phenology on the demography and population dynamics of the leaf-mining moth, *Cameraria hamadryadella* (Lepidoptera: Gracillariidae). *Ecological Entomology* **19**, 111–120.

Danilevsky, A.S. (1965) *Photoperiodism and Seasonal Development of Insects*. Oliver and Boyd, Edinburgh.

Danks, H.V. (1987) Insect dormancy: an ecological perspective. *Biological Survey of Canada Monograph Series Number 1*. Ottawa.

Darquenne, J., Elshzly, E., Tran, B. and Huignard, J. (1993) Intensity of the reproductive diapause in a strain of *Bruchus rufimanus* (Boh) (Coleoptera: Bruchidae) originating from the Merknes region of Morocco. *Acta Oecologica* **14**, 847–856.

de Wilde, J. (1962) Photoperiodism in insects and mites. *Annual Review of Entomology* **7**, 1–26.

Delisle, J. (1992) Monitoring the seasonal male flight activity of *Choristoneura rosaceana* (Lepidoptera: Tortricidae) in Eastern Canada using virgin females and several different pheromone blends. *Environmental Entomology* **21**, 1007–1012.

Denlinger, D.L. (1972) Seasonal phenology of diapause in the flesh fly *Sarcophaga bullata. Annals of the Entomological Society of America* **65**, 410–414.

Denno, R.F. and McClure, M.S. (1983) *Variable*

Plants and Herbivores in Natural and Managed Systems. Academic Press, New York.

Denno, R.F., McClure, M.S. and Ott, J.R. (1995) Interspecific interactions in phytophagous insects: Competition reexamined and resurrected. *Annual Review of Entomology* **40**, 297–331.

Denno, R.F., Roderick, G.K., Olmstead, K.L. and Dobel, H.G. (1991) Density-related migration in planthoppers (Homoptera: Delphacidae): The role of habitat persistence. *American Naturalist* **138**, 1513–1541.

Dixon, A.F.G. (1971) The 'interval timer' and photoperiod in the determination of parthenogenetic and sexual morphs in the aphid, *Drepanosiphum platanoides. Journal of Insect Physiology* **17**, 251–260.

Du Merle, P. and Mazet, R. (1983) Stades phenologiques et infestation par *Tortrix viridana* L. (Lepidoptera: Tortricidae) des bourgeons du chene pubescent et du chene vert. *Acta Oecologica* **4**, 47–53.

Edelstein-Keshet, L. and Rausher, M.D. (1989) The effects of inducible plant defences on herbivore populations. I. Mobile herbivores in continuous time. *American Naturalist*, **133**, 787–810.

Ehrlich, P.R. and Raven, P.H. (1964) Butterflies and plants: a study in coevolution. *Evolution* **18**, 586–608.

Eubanks, M.D. and Denno, R.F. (1999) The ecological consequences of variation in plants and prey for an omnivorous insect. *Ecology* **80**, 1253–1266.

Faeth, S.H. (1985) Host leaf selection by leaf miners: Interactions among three trophic levels. *Ecology* **66**, 870–875.

Faeth, S.H. and Bultman, T.L. (1986) Interacting effects of increased tannin levels on leaf mining insects. *Entomologia Experimentalis et Applicata* **40**, 297–301.

Feeny, P. (1970) Seasonal changes in oak leaf tannins and nutrients as a cause of spring feeding by winter moth caterpillars. *Ecology* **51**, 565–581.

Fischlin, A. and Baltensweiler, W. (1979) Systems analysis of the larch budmoth system. I. The larch-larch budmoth relationship. *Mitteilungen der Schweizerischen Entomologischen Gesellschaft* **52**, 273–289.

Floyd, T. (1996) Top-down impacts on creosote herbivores in a spatially and temporally complex environment. *Ecology* **77**, 1544–1555.

Forkner, R.E. and Hunter, M.D. (2000) What goes up must come down? Nutrient addition and predation pressure on oak insects. *Ecology* (in press).

Foster, M.A., Schultz, J.C. and Hunter, M.D. (1992) Modeling gypsy moth-virus–leaf chemistry interactions: implications of plant quality for pest and pathogen dynamics. *Journal of Animal Ecology* **61**, 509–520.

Frank, S.A. (1993) A model of inducible defense. *Evolution* **47**, 325–327.

Fraser, L.H. (1998) Top-down vs bottom-up control influenced by productivity in a North Derbyshire, UK, dale. *Oikos* **81**, 99–108.

Fraser, L.H. and Grime, J.P. (1998) Top-down control and its effect on the biomass and composition of three grasses at high and low soil fertility in outdoor microcosms. *Oecologia* **113**, 239–246.

Fretwell, S. (1977) The regulation of plant communities by the food chains exploiting them. *Perspectives in Biology and Medicine* **20**, 169–185.

Fritz, R.S. and Simms, E.L. (1991) *Plant Resistance to Herbivores and Pathogens: Ecology, Evolution, and Genetics.* University of Chicago Press, Chicago.

Gangavalli, R.R. and Aliniazee, M.T. (1985) Diapause induction in the oblique-banded leafroller, *Choristoneura rosaceana* (Lepidoptera: Tortricidae): Role of photoperiod and temperature. *Journal of Insect Physiology* **31**, 831–835.

Gomez, J.M. and Zamora, R. (1994) Top-down effects in a tritrophic system: Parasitoids enhance plant fitness. *Ecology* **75**, 1023–1030.

Hagerman, A.E. (1987) Radial diffusion method for determining tannin in plant extracts. *Journal of Chemical Ecology* **13**, 437–449.

Hairston, N.G., Smith, F.E. and Slobodkin, L.B. (1960) Community structure, population control and competition. *American Naturalist* **44**, 421–425.

Hanks, L.M. and Denno, R.F. (1993) Natural enemies and plant water relations influence the distribution of an armored scale insect. *Ecology* **74**, 1081–1091.

Harrewijn, P. (1978) The role of plant substances in polymorphism of the aphid *Myzus persicae. Entomologia Experimentalis et Applicata* **24**, 198–214.

Hassell, M.P. (1976) *The Dynamics of Competition and Predation*. Edward Arnold, London.

Hassell, M.P., Crawley, M.J., Godfray, H.C.J. and Lawton, J.H. (1998) Top-down versus bottom-up and the Ruritanian bean bug. *Proceedings of the National Academy of Sciences* **95**, 10661–10664.

Hawkins, B.A. (1992) Parasitoid-host food webs and donor control. *Oikos* **65**, 159–162.

Holling, C.S. (1959) Some characteristics of simple types of predation and parasitism. *Canadian Entomologist* **91**, 385–398.

Holling, C.S. (1966) The functional response of invertebrate predators to prey density. *Memoirs of the Entomological Society of Canada* **48**, 1–86.

Huffaker, C.B. (1971) *Biological Control*. Plenum, New York.

Hunter, M.D. (1987) Opposing effects of spring defoliation on late season oak caterpillars. *Ecological Entomology* **12**, 373–382.

Hunter, M.D. (1990) Differential susceptibility to variable plant phenology and its role in competition between two insect herbivores on oak. *Ecological Entomology* **15**, 401–408.

Hunter, M.D. (1992a) A variable insect–plant interaction: the relationship between tree budburst phenology and population levels of insect herbivores among trees. *Ecological Entomology* **17**, 91–95.

Hunter, M.D. (1992b) Interactions within herbivore communities mediated by the host plant: the keystone herbivore concept. In: *The Effects of Resource Distribution on Animal–Plant Interactions* (eds M.D. Hunter, T. Ohgushi and P.W. Price), pp. 287–325. Academic Press, San Diego.

Hunter, M.D. (1994) The search for pattern in pest outbreaks. In: *Individuals, Populations and Patterns in Ecology* (eds S.R. Leather, A.D. Watt, N.A.C. Kidd and K.F.A. Walters), pp. 443–448. Intercept, Andover.

Hunter, M.D. (1997) Incorporating variation in plant chemistry into a spatially-explicit ecology of phytophagous insects. In: *Forests and Insects* (eds A.D. Watt, N.E. Stork and M.D. Hunter), pp. 81–96. Chapman and Hall, London.

Hunter, M.D., Malcolm, S.B. and Hartley, S.E. (1996) Population-level variation in plant secondary chemistry and the population biology of herbivores. *Chemoecology* **7**, 45–56.

Hunter, M.D. and McNeil, J.N. (1997) Host-plant quality influences diapause and voltinism in a polyphagous insect herbivore. *Ecology* **78**, 977–986.

Hunter, M.D., Ohgushi, T. and Price, P.W. (1992) *Effects of Resource Distribution on Animal–Plant Interactions*. Academic Press, San Diego.

Hunter, M.D. and Price, P.W. (1992) Playing chutes and ladders: heterogeneity and the relative roles of bottom-up and top-down forces in natural communities. *Ecology* **73**, 724–732.

Hunter, M.D. and Price, P.W. (1998) Cycles in insect populations: Delayed density dependence or exogenous driving variables? *Ecological Entomology* **23**, 216–222.

Hunter, M.D. and Price, P.W. (2000) Detecting cycles and delayed density dependence: a reply to Turchin and Berryman. *Ecological Entomology* **25**, 122–124.

Hunter, M.D. and Schultz, J.C. (1993) Induced plant defences breached? Phytochemical induction protects an herbivore from disease. *Oecologia* **94**, 195–203.

Hunter, M.D. and Schultz, J.C. (1995) Fertilization mitigates chemical induction and herbivore response within damaged oak trees. *Ecology* **76**, 1226–1232.

Hunter, M.D., Varley, G.C. and Gradwell, G.R. (1997) Estimating the relative roles of top-down and bottom-up forces on insect herbivore populations: a classic study revisited. *Proceedings of the National Academy of Sciences* **94**, 9176–9181.

Hunter, M.D. and West, C. (1990) Variation in the effects of spring defoliation on the late season phytophagous insects of *Quercus robur*. In: *Population Dynamics of Forest Insects* (eds A.D. Watt, S.R. Leather, M.D. Hunter and N.A.C. Kidd), pp. 123–135. Intercept, Andover.

Hunter, M.D. and Willmer, P.G. (1989) The potential for interspecific competition between two abundant defoliators on oak: Leaf damage and habitat quality. *Ecological Entomology* **14**, 267–277.

Jassby, A.D., Goldman, C.R. and Powell, T.M. (1992) Trend seasonality cycle and irregular fluctuations in primary productivity at Lake Tahoe, California-Nevada, USA. *Hydrobiologia* **246**, 195–203.

Jeppesen, E., Jensen, J.P., Sondergaard, M., Lauridsen, T., Pedersen, L.J. and Jensen, L. (1997) Top-down control in freshwater lakes: The role of nutrient state, submerged macrophytes and water depth. *Hydrobiologia* **342**, 151–164.

Karban, R. and Baldwin, I.T. (1997) *Induced Responses to Herbivory*. University of Chicago Press, Chicago.

Keating, S.T. and Yendol, W.G. (1987) Influence of selected host plants on gypsy moth (Lepidoptera: Lymantriidae) larval mortality caused by a baculovirus. *Environmental Entomology* **16**, 459–462.

Kurmayer, R. and Wanzenboeck, J. (1996) Top-down effects of underyearling fish on a phytoplankton community. *Freshwater Biology* **36**, 599–609.

Leibold, M.A. (1989) Resource edibility and the effects of predators and productivity on the outcome of trophic interactions. *American Naturalist* **134**, 922–949.

Lenga, A., Glitho, I. and Huignard, J. (1993) Interactions between photoperiod, relative humidity and host-plant cues on the reproductive diapause termination in *Bruchidius atrolineatus* (Pic) (Coleoptera: Bruchidae). *Invertebrate Reproduction and Development* **24**, 87–96.

Lundberg, S., Jaremo, J. and Nilsson, P. (1994) Herbivory, inducible defence and population oscillations: a preliminary theoretical analysis. *Oikos* **71**, 537–539.

Marquis, R.J. and Whelan, C.J. (1994) Insectivorous birds increase growth of white oak through consumption of leaf-chewing insects. *Ecology* **75**, 2007–2014.

May, R.M. (1981) *Theoretical Ecology. Principles and Applications*, 2nd edn. Blackwell Scientific Publications, Oxford.

McNeil, J.N. and Fields, P.G. (1985) Seasonal diapause development and diapause termination in the European skipper, *Thymelicus lineola* (Ochs). *Journal of Insect Physiology* **31**, 467–470.

McNeil, J.N. and Rabb, R.L. (1973) Physical and physiological factions in the diapause initiation of two hyperparasitoids of the tobacco hornworm *Manduca sexta*. *Journal of Insect Physiology* **19**, 2107–2118.

McQueen, D.J., Johannes, M.R.S., Post, J.R., Stewart, T.J. and Lean, D.R.S. (1989) Bottom-up and top-down impacts on freshwater pelagic community structure. *Ecological Monographs* **59**, 289–309.

McQueen, D.J., Mills, E.L., Fourney, J.L., Johannes, M.R.S. and Post, J.R. (1992) Trophic level relationships in pelagic food webs: Comparisons derived from long-term data sets for Oneida Lake, New York, USA, and Lake St. George, Ontario, Canada. *Canadian Journal of Fisheries and Aquatic Sciences* **49**, 1588–1596.

Menge, B.A. (1992) Community regulation: under what conditions are bottom-up forces important on rocky shores? *Ecology* **73**, 755–765.

Menge, B.A. (1995) Joint 'bottom-up' and 'top-down' regulation of rocky intertidal algal beds in South Africa. *Trends in Ecology and Evolution* **10**, 431–432.

Menge, B.A., Daley, B.A., Wheeler, P.A. and Strub, P.T. (1997a) Rocky intertidal oceanography: an association between community structure and nearshore phytoplankton concentration. *Limnology and Oceanography* **42**, 57–66.

Menge, B.A., Daley, B.A., Wheeler, P.A., Dahlhoff, E., Sanford, E. and Strub, P.T. (1997b) Benthic-pelagic links and rocky intertidal communities: Bottom-up effects on top-down control? *Proceedings of the National Academy of Sciences USA* **94**, 14530–14535.

Metaxas, A. and Scheibling, R.E. (1996) Top-down and bottom-up regulation of phytoplankton assemblages in tidepools. *Marine Ecology Progress Series* **145**, 161–177.

Mittler, T.E. (1973) Aphid polymorphism as affected by diet. In: *Perspectives in Aphid Biology* (ed. A.D. Lowe), pp. 65–75. Entomological Society of New Zealand, Bulletin no. 2, Aukland.

Mopper, S., Beck, M., Simberloff, D. and Stiling, P. (1995) Local adaptation and agents of mortality in a mobile insect. *Evolution* **49**, 810–815.

Mopper, S. and Simberloff, D. (1995) Differential herbivory in an oak population: the role of plant phenology and insect performance. *Ecology* **76**, 1233–1241.

Mopper, S. and Strauss, S.Y. (1998) *Genetic Structure and Local Adaptation in Natural Insect Populations: Effects of Ecology, Life History and Behavior*. Chapman and Hall, New York.

Moran, M.D. and Hurd, L.E. (1994) Short-term responses to elevated predator densities: non-competitive intraguild interactions and behavior. *Oecologia* **98**, 269–273.

Moran, M.D. and Hurd, L.E. (1998) A trophic cascade in a diverse arthropod community caused by a generalist arthropod predator. *Oecologia* **113**, 126–132.

Moran, M.D., Rooney, T.R. and Hurd, L.E. (1996) Top-down trophic cascade from a bitrophic predator in an old-field community. *Ecology* **77**, 2219–2227.

Morris, R.F. (1967) Factors inducing diapause in *Hyphantria cunea. Canadian Entomologist* **99**, 522–528.

Murdoch, W.W., Luck, R.F., Swarbrick, S.L., Walde, S., Dickie, S.Y. and Reeve, J.D. (1995) Regulation of an insect population under biological control. *Ecology* **76**, 206–217.

Nakai, T. and Takeda, M. (1995) Temperature and photoperiodic regulation of summer diapause and reproduction in *Pyrrhalta humeralis* (Coleoptera: Chrysomelidae). *Applied Entomology and Zoology* **30**, 295–301.

Neuenschwander, P., Hammond, W.N.O., Gutierrez, A.P. *et al.* (1989) Impact assessment of the biological control of the cassava mealybug, *Phenacoccus manihoti* (Homoptera: Pseudococcidae) by the introduced parasitoid, *Epidinocarsis lopezi* (Hymenoptera: Encrytidae). *Bulletin of Entomological Research* **79**, 579–594.

Oksanen, L., Fretwell, S.D., Arruda, J. and Niemela, P. (1981) Exploitation ecosystems in gradients of primary productivity. *American Naturalist* **118**, 240–261.

Paine, R.T. (1966) Food web complexity and species diversity. *American Naturalist* **100**, 65–75.

Pinel-Alloul, B., Niyonsenga, T. and Legendre, P. (1995) Spatial and environmental components of freshwater zooplankton structure. *Ecoscience* **2**, 1–19.

Polis, G.A., Anderson, W.B. and Holt, R.D. (1997b) Toward an integration of landscape and food web ecology: The dynamics of spatially subsidized food webs. *Annual Review of Ecology and Systematics* **28**, 289–316.

Polis, G.A., Hurd, S.D., Jackson, C.T. and Sanchez-Pinero, F. (1997a) El Niño effects on the dynamics and control of an island ecosystem in the gulf of California. *Ecology* **78**, 1884–1897.

Polis, G.A., Hurd, S.D., Jackson, C.T. and Sanchez-Pinero, F. (1998) Multifactor population limitation: variable spatial and temporal control of spiders on Gulf of California Islands. *Ecology* **79**, 490–502.

Power, M.E. (1992a) Top-down and bottom-up forces in food webs: Do plants have primacy? *Ecology* **73**, 733–746.

Power, M.E. (1992b) Habitat heterogeneity and the functional significance of fish in river food webs. *Ecology* **73**, 1675–1688.

Preszler, R.W. and. Boecklen, W.J. (1994) A three-trophic-level analysis of the effects of plant hybridization on a leaf-mining moth. *Oecologia* **100**, 66–73.

Preszler, R.W. and Boecklen, W.J. (1996) The influence of elevation on tri-trophic interactions: Opposing gradients of top-down and bottom-up effects on a leaf-mining moth. *Ecoscience* **3**, 75–80.

Price, P.W., Bouton, C.E., Gross, P., McPheron, B.A., Thompson, J.N. and Weis, A.E. (1980) Interactions among three trophic levels: influence of plants on interactions between insects herbivores and natural enemies. *Annual Review of Ecology and Systematics* **11**, 41–65.

Price, P.W. and Hunter, M.D. (1995) Novelty and synthesis in the development of population dynamics. In: *Population Dynamics: New Approaches and Synthesis* (eds N. Cappuccino and P.W. Price), pp. 389–412. Academic Press, San Diego.

Ramcharan, C.W., McQueen, D.J., Demers, E., *et al.* (1995) A comparative approach to determining the role of fish predation in structuring limnetic ecosystems. *Archiv fur Hydrobiologie* **133**, 389–416.

Raffa, K.F. and Berryman, A.A. (1983) The role of host plant resistance in the colonization behavior and ecology of bark beetles. *Ecological Monographs* **53**, 27–49.

Raffa, K.F. and Berryman, A.A. (1986) A mechanistic computer model of mountain pine beetle populations interacting with lodgepole pine stands and its implications for forest managers. *Forest Science* **32**, 789–805.

Roff, D.A. (1980) Optimizing development time in a seasonal environment: the ups and downs of clinal variation. *Oecologia* **45**, 202–208.

Roff, D.A. (1983) Phenological adaptation in a seasonal environment: a theoretical perspective. In: *Diapause and Life Cycle Strategies in Insects* (eds V.K. Brown and I. Hodeck), pp. 253–270. Junk, The Hague.

Rohani, P., Godfray, H.C.J. and Hassell, M.P. (1994) Aggregation and the dynamics of host-parasitoid systems: a new discrete-generation model with within-generation redistribution. *American Naturalist* **144**, 491–509.

Rose, M.D. and Polis, G.A. (1998) The distribution and abundance of coyotes: The effects of allochthonous food subsidies from the sea. *Ecology* **79**, 998–1007.

Rosenthal, G.A. and Janzen, D.H. (1979) *Herbivores: Their Interaction with Secondary Plant Metabolites*. Academic Press, New York.

Rossiter, M.C. (1987) Use of secondary hosts by non-outbreak populations of the gypsy moth. *Ecology* **68**, 857–868.

Rossiter, M.C. (1994) Maternal effects hypothesis of herbivore outbreak. *Bioscience* **44**, 752–763.

Rossiter, M.C., Schultz, J.C. and Baldwin, I.T. (1988) Relationships among defoliation, *Q. rubra* phenolics, and gypsy moth growth and reproduction. *Ecology* **69**, 267–277.

Royama, T. (1992) *Analytical Population Dynamics*. Chapman and Hall, London.

Saunders, D.S. (1973) Thermoperiodic control of diapause in an insect: theory of internal coincidence. *Science* **181**, 358–360.

Scheltes, P. (1976) The role of graminaceous host-plants in the induction of aestivation-diapause in the larvae of *Chilo zonellus* Swinhoe and *Chilo argyrolepia* Hamps. *Symposia Biologica Hungarica* **16**, 247–253.

Schimtz, O.J., Beckerman, A.P. and O'Brien, K.M. (1997) Behaviorally mediated trophic cascades: effects of predation risk on food web interactions. *Ecology* **78**, 1388–1399.

Schindler, D.W. (1978) Factors regulating phytoplankton production and standing crop in the world's fresh-waters. *Limnology and Oceanography* **23**, 478–486.

Schultz, J.C. and Baldwin, I.T. (1982) Oak leaf quality declines in response to defoliation by gypsy moth larvae. *Science* **217**, 149–151.

Seda, J. and Kubecka, J. (1997) Long-term biomanipulation of Rimov Reservoir (Czech Republic). *Hydrobiologia* **345**, 95–108.

Shorey, H.H. and Hale, R.L. (1965) Mass-rearing of nine noctuid species on a simple artificial medium. *Journal of Economic Entomology* **58**, 522–524.

Speight, M.R., Hunter, M.D. and Watt, A.D. (1999) *Ecology of Insects: Concepts and Applications*. Blackwell Science, Oxford.

Stewart-Oaten, A. and Murdoch, W.W. (1990) Temporal consequences of spatial density dependence. *Journal of Animal Ecology* **59**, 1027–1045.

Stiling, P. and Rossi, A.M. (1996) Complex effects of genotype and environment on insect herbivores and their enemies. *Ecology* **77**, 2212–2218.

Stiling, P. and Rossi, A.M. (1997) Experimental manipulations of top-down and bottom-up factors in a tri-trophic system. *Ecology* **78**, 1602–1606.

Strong, D. (1992) Are trophic cascades all wet? Differentiation and donor-control in specious ecosystems. *Ecology* **73**, 747–754.

Taper, M.L., Zimmerman, E.R. and Case, T.J. (1986) Sources of mortality for a cynipid gall-wasp *Dryocosmus dubiosus* (Hymenoptera: Cynipidae): the importance of the tannin/fungus interaction. *Oecologia* **68**, 437–445.

Tauber, M.J. and Tauber, C.A. (1976) Larval diapause in *Chrysopa nigricornis* (Neuroptera: Chrysopidae): sensitive stages, critical photoperiod, and termination. *Entomologia Experimentalis et Applicata* **15**, 105–111.

Tauber, M.J., Tauber, C.A. and Masaki, S. (1986) *Seasonal Adaptations of Insects*. Oxford University Press, New York.

Turchin, P. and Berryman, A.A. (2000) Detecting cycles and delayed density dependence: a comment on Hunter and Price (1998) *Ecological Entomology* **25**, 119–121.

Tzanakakis, M.E. and Veerman, A. (1994) Effect of temperature on the termination of diapause in the univoltine almond seed wasp *Eurytoma amygdali*. *Entomologia Experimentalis et Applicata* **70**, 27–39.

Underwood, N. (1999) The influence of plant and herbivore characteristics on the interaction between induced resistance and herbivore population dynamics. *American Naturalist* **153**, 282–294.

Usua, E.J. (1973) Induction of diapause in the maize stemborer, *Busseola fusca*. *Entomologia Experimentalis et Applicata* **16**, 322–328.

Varley, G.C., Gradwell, G.R. and Hassell, M.P. (1973) *Insect Population Ecology: An Analytical Approach*. Blackwell Scientific Publications, Oxford.

Wallace, J.B., Eggert, S.L., Meyer, J.L. and Webster, J.R. (1997) Multiple trophic levels of a forest stream linked to terrestrial litter inputs. *Science* **277**, 102–104.

Walz, N. (1995) Rotifer populations in plankton communities: Energetics and life history strategies. *Experientia* **51**, 437–453.

Waterman, P.G. and Mole, S. (1994) *Analysis of Phenolic Plant Metabolites.* Blackwell Scientific Publications, Oxford.

Watt, A.D., Leather, S.R., Hunter, M.D. and Kidd, N.A.C. (1990) *Population Dynamics of Forest Insects.* Intercept Ltd, Andover.

West, C. (1985) Factors underlying the late seasonal appearance of the lepidopterous leaf mining guild on oak. *Ecological Entomology* **10**, 111–120.

Wint, G.R.W. (1983) The role of alternative host plant species in the life of a polyphagous moth *Operoptera brumata* (Lepidoptera: Geometridae). *Journal of Animal Ecology* **52**, 439–450.

Wootton, J.T. and Power. M.E. (1993) Productivity, consumers, and the structure of a river food chain. *Proceedings of the National Academy of Sciences USA* **90**, 1384–1387.

Wootton, J.T., Parker, M.S. and Power, M.E. (1996b) Effects of disturbance on river food webs. *Science* **273**, 1558–1561.

Wootton, J.T., Power, M.E., Paine, R.T. and Pfister, C.A. (1996a) Effects of productivity, consumers, competitors, and El Niño events on food chain patterns in a rocky intertidal community. *Proceedings of the National Academy of Sciences USA* **93**, 13855–13858.

Chapter 10

Foraging ecology of animals in response to heterogeneous environments

J.S. Brown

Introduction

Several streams flow together in this chapter. The topic concerns foraging ecology (as coined by M.L. Rosenzweig) in the context of spatial and temporal heterogeneity. Foraging ecology is a subdiscipline of evolutionary ecology that involves the study of ecological and evolutionary consequences of adaptive feeding behaviours by animals, plants and other organisms (e.g. nutrient foraging by plants through root growth and kinetics, Campbell *et al.* 1991; Birch and Hutchings 1994). In a single issue of *The American Naturalist* (1966, Vol. 100, no. 916) one can find works at or close to three intellectual headwaters that merge into foraging ecology.

Two papers (Emlen 1966; MacArthur and Pianka 1966) launched optimal foraging theory, a field that has become the *lingua franca* of feeding behaviours. Foraging theory now encompasses: the genetic, physiological, and neurological mechanisms of behaviours; the rules and models by which we understand feeding behaviours; the bases and consequences of social foraging; and foraging ecology — the subset of foraging theory that is of interest in this chapter.

Two papers (Deakin 1966; Levins and MacArthur 1966) concern the conditions under which spatial or temporal heterogeneity can maintain genetic and hence phenotypic polymorphisms (in the absence of heterosis). The combination of frequency-dependent selection of these papers (Levene 1953) and the fitness set analyses for finding the optimal phenotypes within fine-grained (small scale) or coarse-grained (large scale) environments (Levins 1962, 1968) presently find a home in evolutionary game theory and Maynard Smith and Price's (1973) concept of evolutionarily stable strategies (ESS). Models of habitat selection in response to heterogeneity (game theoretic or otherwise) consistently show how heterogeneity plus behaviours of habitat selection promote diversity (Rosenzweig 1987a, 1991). This production of diversity can occur in the context of coadaptations (Rosenzweig 1987b; Brown 1996) between behaviours and the fixed traits envisioned in Levins and MacArthur (1966) and Deakin (1966). And, this diversity can either be a polymorphism within a species or a mechanism of species coexistence.

Department of Biological Sciences, University of Illinois at Chicago, 845 W. Taylor Street, Chicago, IL, 60607, USA

A paper by Maynard Smith (1966) models the ways by which environmental heterogeneity may produce the sympatric speciation championed by Thoday and Gibson (1962, 1970). Effective ingredients for this sort of adaptive speciation include a morphological or physiological trade-off representing a range of specialist and generalist phenotypes. In conjunction with adaptive behaviours, individuals may bias their activity towards a subset of habitats. For instance, a specialist on a habitat may also selectively seek its preferred habitat to the exclusion of other habitats. A generalist may behave more opportunistically in its selection of habitats (Rosenzweig 1981). Either passive or active assortative mating may occur as individuals breed with those in close proximity. Habitat specialization, behavioural selectivity, and proximity based mating have been combined into convincing theoretical (e.g. competitive speciation, Rosenzweig 1978) and empirical (Feder *et al.* 1988; Via 1991) support for environmental heterogeneity producing adaptive speciation. Furthermore, the concept of evolutionarily stable minima from game theory (*sensu* Abrams *et al.* 1993) can permit a single species to evolve by natural selection to the valley of its frequency-dependent landscape, speciate, and then occupy the resulting two (or more, via a succession of speciation events) peaks of the ESS (Brown and Pavlovic 1992).

In this chapter, I would like to take these three threads and consider the consequence of foraging behaviour in heterogeneous environments for

1 foraging theory;
2 species coexistence; and
3 adaptive evolution and speciation.

Under foraging theory, relevant concepts include the information state of the feeding animal, the scale of heterogeneity, and whether heterogeneity is temporal or spatial. Under species coexistence, I will consider how environmental heterogeneity and feeding behaviours produce a variety of mechanisms of species coexistence. Relevant concepts include the predictability of heterogeneity in time and space; and whether heterogeneity takes the form of distinct habitats/ resources or takes the form of variability in the availability of a single resource. Under adaptive speciation, I will consider how coadaptations between behaviours and fixed morphological traits can promote or inhibit evolution and adaptive speciation in response to heterogeneity. Relevant concepts will include the scale of heterogeneity, the nature of heterogeneity (temporal vs. spatial), and adaptive dynamics along frequency-dependent adaptive landscapes (Metz *et al.* 1996).

Following these developments, I will consider two species of tree squirrels (grey squirrel, *Sciurus carolinensis*; and fox squirrel, *Sciurus niger*) that occupy wooded and woodland habitats of much of the eastern half of temperate North America. I will suggest how the almost universal foraging dilemma of balancing conflicting demands for food and safety forms the basis for understanding their use of microhabitats near and away from cover, their distributions across woodlands varying in fragmentation, their mechanism of coexistence, their distribution in human altered habitats, and their regional range limits.

Foraging ecology

Feeding involves a series of tasks. These tasks often unfold as a sequence of events starting with food item detection which includes all of the sensory and motor processes required to search for food items. Next comes prey capture which may be as simple as merely collecting a sessile prey item; or it may be as complex as stalking, attacking and subduing prey that can flee or fight. Having gained the opportunity to consume a prey item, the forager may need to identify the prey (e.g. prey recognition, Hughes 1970; Kotler and Mitchell 1995) and/or prepare the prey (e.g. prey preparation, Kaspari 1990; Barba et al. 1996) prior to consumption. Prey consumption may involve tasks of mastication, grinding, and enzymatic digestion. In general, all of the events following prey detection become various forms of 'handling time'. The two broad tasks of searching for and handling food items underpin models of diet selection (Holling 1965; Emlen 1966; Pulliam 1974). Such models do not explicitly require recourse to temporal or spatial heterogeneity, although such heterogeneity is often implicit in the assumption of a random distribution of prey items in space. Once the prey items become clumped in space (some chance aggregations will occur even if prey are randomly distributed in space), then an element of local spatial heterogeneity emerges. Spatial heterogeneity in food abundance underpins models of patch use (Charnov 1976).

Feeding behaviours and heterogeneity fit hand in glove. Most feeding behaviours are flexible and permit adaptive responses by the forager to contingencies in its feeding environment. This aspect of feeding behaviour is as important as it is self-evident. The traits under consideration include 'assess' and 'respond'. The forager may assess opportunities and hazards of its environment, and then respond by altering feeding times, distributions of activity, and feeding tactics. The adaptiveness of a particular 'assess and respond' strategy often involves assessing accurately and responding appropriately. Feeding behaviours of assess and respond are the evolutionary consequence of heterogeneity. And, the feeding behaviours in response to this heterogeneity have consequences for the ecology of the food items, the distribution and abundance of the feeding animals, and the tactics and success of the forager's predators. Heterogeneity favours flexible feeding behaviours and these feeding behaviours initiate a cascade of indirect, non-linear, and higher-order interactions that percolate through the food chain (Abrams 1984; Kotler and Holt 1989; Werner 1992).

Reasons for flexible feeding responses

Reasons for flexible responses involve arbitrage, complementarity, and bet-hedging. Arbitrage (from the field of economics) refers to profiting from the purchase and sale of goods or services as a consequence of temporal or spatial discrepancies in the prices of those goods and services. As the quality and quantity of feeding opportunities vary in time and space, a kind of natural arbitrage is probably the most important function of flexible feeding behaviours. All an animal really has to spend is time. To spend it wisely (so as to 'purchase' fitness) requires biasing feeding efforts towards profitable times and places and avoiding costly or unrewarding times and places. Animals 'buy' and 'sell' inputs into fitness by shifting time from less to more profitable activities.

These fitness inputs may be complementary. With complementary inputs, an organism may have higher fitness by including a variety of foods in its diet ('beer and pretzels', see Schmidt *et al.* 1998; Whelan *et al.* 1998) or by including a variety of habitats in its experience (Brown 1998). This occurs when different foods or habitats offer different ratios of nutrients or inputs into fitness. And these inputs either interact multiplicatively to produce fitness, or there are diminishing returns to fitness from consuming one resource without concomitant influences on the marginal value of the other resource. For instance, food and safety are generally complementary inputs into fitness (Gilliam and Fraser 1987; Brown 1988). Safety becomes increasingly valuable to an organism as it has more to lose from being killed by a predator. And safety is of little use to an animal until it achieves a sufficiently high energy state. Under the asset protection principle (*sensu* Clark 1994), an animal in a high energy state craves safety (Dill and Fraser 1984; Brown 1992; Houston *et al.* 1993).

The evolutionary need and opportunity for bet-hedging emerges from the geometric nature of fitness. Geometric means increase with the arithmetic mean but decrease with increasing temporal variability in fitness. Under bet-hedging, an organism may be willing to sacrifice arithmetic mean fitness to reduce the temporal variability in fitness. Under many circumstances, seed dormancy (Cohen 1966; Brown and Venable 1986) and animal dispersal represent bet-hedging adaptations. Holt and McPeek (1996) showed how an organism's use of a sink habitat in addition to its core habitat may be adaptive if the sink habitat has less temporal variability in fitness.

Scale

Gordon Orians (1991) writes:

> Habitat selection goes by different names on different spatial scales. On a microscale, habitat selection becomes the fine-grained theory of optimal foraging, in which foragers choose from among the various prey types they encounter at random [diet choice]. On slightly larger scales, at which different habitat patches are incorporated into the models, individuals are allowed to elect to search in patches or to pass through them without looking for prey, nest sites, or other resources [patch use]. On macroscales habitat selection converts itself into the study of emigration, immigration, and migration. (Fig. 10.1, adapted from Travis and Dytham 1999.)

The scale of temporal variability determines the extent to which an animal can expect to experience a broad range of temporal conditions within a single foraging bout, within an individual's lifetime, or among generations of the population. In general the duration and frequency of events determine the responses and consequences of temporal variability. The sudden passage of a predator through a

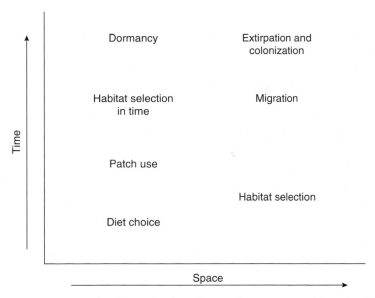

Figure 10.1 How temporal and spatial scales influence the interaction of the animal with its foraging environment. Adapted from Travis and Dytham (1999).

forager's area should elicit an immediate and sharp response from the feeding animals. However, so long as the event is of short duration and is not a harbinger of worse to come, the foragers should quickly return to their original foraging agenda. Hence, unexpected and rapid passages of a predator should have little consequence for the forager's feeding rate, its energy state, or the survivorship of its food. An increase in the actual or perceived presence of a predator for the entirety of a foraging bout can have large consequences for the forager's short-term harvest rate, its marginal value of food, and for the short-term survivorship of its food. A change in predation risk throughout the lifetime of the forager can work through feeding behaviours to represent permanent long-term changes in the abundance of food (it will generally increase), the state of the foragers (it will generally increase), and the forager's marginal valuation of food (it will generally decline).

Gerbils (*Gerbillus allenbyi* and *G. pyramidum*) in a sand dune habitat, Negev Desert, Israel respond strongly to overflights by barn owls (*Tyto alba*). They simultaneously reduce activity (hunker down) and shift habitat use to safer areas (Abramsky *et al.* 1996). Within less than 2 hours following the owls departure the gerbils have returned to their 'normal' patterns of activity and habitat use. When an owl is in close proximity for an entire night then the gerbils, throughout the night, forage less thoroughly from food patches and strongly avoid the open, risky habitat (Kotler *et al.* 1991). Even when absent, the owl's effect is still detectable on the gerbils' foraging behaviour the subsequent night. By the third night the effect has completely attenuated (Kotler 1992). In response to changes in vegetation cover, the rodents (Merriam's kangaroo rat, *Dipodomys merriami*; desert pocket mouse, *Chaetodipus penicillatus*) of a Sonoran Desert site, Arizona, USA quickly and permanently shifted their foraging behaviour and use of habitats (Rosenzweig 1973).

To illustrate how the temporal scale of heterogeneity can influence adaptive responses, imagine two populations, one which experiences temporal changes in predation at the temporal scale of foraging bouts and one which experiences these changes at the scale of generations. Let fitness be given by:

$$G = pF$$

where G is per capita growth rate, p is the individual's probability of surviving to realize fitness, and F is survivor's fitness and gives the expected fitness reward to an individual that survives predation to realize fitness. Let the survivor's fitness increase with the forager's feeding rate, f, and let the probability of surviving predation be given by:

$$P = \exp(-\mu)$$

where μ is the instantaneous risk of predation. Let both the risk of predation, μ, and feeding rate, f, be influenced by the forager's level of antipredator behaviour, u. This behaviour may be thought of as the proportion of time spent vigilant where $0 \leq u \leq 1$. Let feeding rate decline linearly with vigilance: $f = (1 - u)f_{max}$. Let predation risk decline at a diminishing rate with vigilance (Fig. 10.2): $\partial\mu/\partial u < 0$, $\partial^2\mu/\partial u^2 > 0$. Let survivor's fitness increase at a diminishing rate with feeding rate, $\partial F/\partial f > 0$, $\partial^2 F/\partial f^2 < 0$. Vigilance increases survivorship by reducing predation risk and decreases survivor's fitness through a reduction in feeding rates.

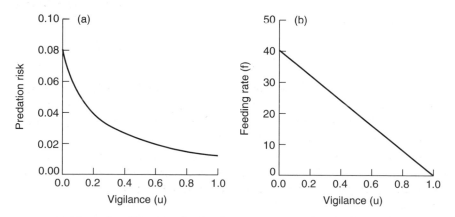

Figure 10.2 The trade-off between food and safety. These relationships assume that predation risk declines at a decelerating rate with vigilance (or some other antipredator behaviour) and that feeding rate declines linearly with vigilance (see Brown 1999 for more details). In this model, vigilance can be thought of as proportion of time spent scanning for predators.

Consider two scenarios and two extremes of information on predation risk. First consider the case where the forager has perfect knowledge of the risk of predation and assume that the temporal or spatial scale of risk is coarse-grained, so that all individuals are obliged to spend their life experiencing a particular risk regime. Let a_H and a_L be scaling factors that scale predation risk μ under high and low risk situations, respectively: $a_H > a_L$. The optimal value of vigilance under high and low risk scenarios, u_H and u_L, satisfy the following, respectively:

$$\text{high risk:} -a_H\mu'/f_{max} = (\partial F/\partial f)/F \text{ where } f_H = (1-u_H)f_{max} \qquad (10.1a)$$

$$\text{low risk:} -a_L\mu'/f_{max} = (\partial F/\partial f)/F \text{ where } f_L = (1-u_L)f_{max} \qquad (10.1b)$$

where μ' represents the derivative of predation risk with respect to vigilance.

As would be expected, the forager should be more vigilant under higher than lower risk: $u_H > u_L$. Increasing the scaling of predation risk, a, increases the optimal level of vigilance. The increase in vigilance reduces μ' and increases the right hand side of equation (10.1). The reduction in feeding rate with higher vigilance, increases the marginal value of feeding and reduces survivor's fitness.

Now consider a forager that has a fixed antipredator response to periods regardless of the actual level of predation risk. If risk level varies with time in a coarse-grained fashion, then the optimal level of vigilance should maximize geometric mean fitness across the two risk types (Brown and Venable 1986):

$$G = (p_H F)^q (p_L F)^{(1-q)} = F\exp\{-\mu[qa_H + (1-q)a_L]\} \qquad (10.1c)$$

where q is the likelihood that a temporal period exposes foragers to high predation risk.

The optimal level of vigilance of an ignorant forager, u_I (no longer conditional on actual predation risk), satisfies:

$$\text{Ignorant or unresponsive:} -[qa_H + (1-q)a_L]\mu'/f_{max} = (\partial F/\partial f)/F$$
$$\text{where } f = (1-u_I)f_{max} \qquad (10.2)$$

Obviously the optimal level of vigilance for the ignorant forager falls somewhere on the interval between what is optimal during high-risk and low-risk periods, respectively. The forager is over-vigilant during periods of low risk and over-exposed during periods of high risk (Sih 1984).

Now, consider a forager in a fine grained environment in which predation risk changes somewhat rapidly relative to the temporal scale at which the forager realizes fitness. A forager with perfect information should select u_H and u_L so as to maximize:

$$\text{fine-grained:} G = F\exp\{-[qa_H\mu_H + (1-q)a_L\mu_L]\}$$
$$\text{where } f = [q(1-u_H) + (1-q)(1-u_L)]f_{max}$$

and where μ_H and μ_L refer to predation risk evaluated at u_H and u_L, respectively.

The optimal levels of vigilance under high and low situations satisfy:

fine-grained: $-a_H\mu'_H/f_{max}=-a_L\mu'_L/f_{max}=(\partial F/\partial f)/F$

The optimal levels of vigilance under fine-grained heterogeneity will generally differ from those under coarse-grained. This is because the feeding rate determines the marginal value of feeding and survivor's fitness. The ratio of these two terms will always be highest under coarse-grained and high risk situations and lowest under coarse-grained and low risk situations. The joint value under fine-grained is intermediate. As a consequence:

$$u_H(\text{fine grained}) > u_H (\text{coarse grained}) > u_I > u_L (\text{coarse grained})$$
$$> u_L (\text{fine grained}) \tag{10.3}$$

In response to high and low risk situations, a forager in a fine-grained environment should exhibit greater extremes of vigilance behaviour than a forager in a coarse-grained environment. Interestingly, in the above model, the optimal level of vigilance of the ignorant forager, u_I, is the same under the coarse- and fine-grained scenarios.

The above model illustrates arbitrage in the context of complementary inputs into fitness. As the opportunities for safety vary in time, the organism trades off food and safety via vigilance. Food and safety are complementary. The value of survivor's fitness increases as the forager has a higher probability of surviving (asset protection principle, Clark 1994). Similarly, the value of safety increases with the survivor's fitness of the forager (Brown 1992). When the temporal variability is coarse-grained, the forager only experiences one set of circumstances. The circumstance must be endured and there is no opportunity for averaging food and safety across temporal circumstances. Under high risk the forager cannot be too vigilant as it will have little survivor's fitness to live for, and under the low risk circumstance the forager has a high survivor's fitness at risk. The fine-grained temporal heterogeneity provides an additional source of flexibility as the forager can arithmetically average food and safety across high- and low-risk periods. This permits a degree of temporal selectivity. The forager biases vigilance towards the high risk periods (u_H is higher under fine-grained then coarse-grained temporal variability) and biases feeding towards the low-risk periods (u_L is lower under fine-grained than coarse-grained variability).

In the context of light and nutrients as complementary inputs, Wijesinghe and Hutchings (1996) investigated the consequences of coarse- and fine-grained heterogeneity on a plant's investment in roots and leaves. A plant in a low light, high nutrient regime must invest heavily in leaves to secure sufficient light and requires little roots to supply the necessary nutrients; and vice-versa for high light, low nutrients. But, suppose the plant can simultaneously exploit both types of patches (high light/low nutrients and low light/high nutrient). This is exactly what the clonal plant *Glechoma hederacea* can do. The plant can now exploit this arbitrage by producing ramets with high shoot to root ratios in the high light patches and low shoot to root ratios in the high nutrient patches (Wijesinghe and Hutchings 1996, 1997, personal communication).

Abramsky *et al.* (1998) manipulated the density of competitors and predators on a population of Allenby's gerbil (*G. allenbyi*). In response to high densities of competitors (a larger gerbil species, *G. pyramidum*) or in response to several hours of flights by a trained barn owl, Allenby's gerbil shifted their activity from the half of the enclosure with high competitors and/or high predation risk to the more congenial half of the enclosure. In separate treatments, the gerbils respond strongly to both competitors and to owls (Abramsky *et al.* 1990; Rosenzweig *et al.* 1997). In combination the gerbils respond much more strongly to predation than to competition. Part of the explanation may include an extremely high cost of predation that swamps the effects of competition (Brown *et al.* 1994). Additionally, the gerbils may be balancing the opportunities and the lack of opportunities to average predation risk and competition, respectively. The predation risk is pulsed in time (within the night) and if the gerbils have some awareness of this, then there should be a very sharp contrast in the gerbils' antipredator response to the high- and low-risk periods of the night. Conversely, the competitors are present more continuously and there should be a less sharp response to the areas high and low in competition when superimposed on pulses of predation risk.

Patch use

Patch use applies to circumstances where the forager can detect and bias its effort towards spatial aggregations of resources. The forager benefits increasingly from the degree of aggregation and from its ability to detect and respond to these aggregations. At the macro-patch level, the forager may attempt to travel through areas too poor in resources to merit searching activity. In this case the forager alternates between travelling between patches and harvesting patches. The forager must be able to distinguish exploitable patches from areas unworthy of harvest. This is probably quite straightforward for a frugivorous bird exploiting patches of fruit, or browsing mammals seeking leaves from discrete shrubs. It becomes less so for an underground mammal such as a mole attempting to seek out areas with propitiously high aggregations of soil invertebrates. Having found a patch the forager must decide on how long to deplete the patch before seeking another. At a micropatch scale (Brown and Mitchell 1989), the forager may be able to detect relatively continuous variation in the abundance of food and place somewhat arbitrary boundaries around richer aggregations of food. The challenge to the forager is to place bounds on such micropatches and to bias its effort towards favourable micropatches. Branches within a tree may vary in fruit abundance and accessibility and the frugivorous bird may be able to respond to this scale of variability (Whelan 1989; Whelan and Willson 1994).

Fox squirrels are able to recognize and respond to macropatches that can vary in scale from $100\,m^2$ (Stapanian and Smith 1984) down to patches that are $0.1\,m^2$ (Brown and Morgan 1995). Steele and Weigl (1992) found that the closely related grey squirrel selects among individual conifers and then within each tree is able to select among rich and poor cones. This scaling of patch use from macro-patch to micropatch partitioning was demonstrated by Schmidt and Brown (1996). Fox squirrels could select among rich and poor patches, and within these patches they could further select among rich and poor micropatches. Squirrels became progressively better at micropatch partitioning as the contrast in micropatch quality increased, as they depleted the patch more extensively, and as micropatch boundaries were made unambiguous rather than vague.

The marginal value theorem (Charnov 1976) for patch use states that a forager should continue exploiting a depletable food patch until its harvest rate within the patch no longer exceeds the average rate of harvest that the forager can expect from travelling to and exploiting another patch. The marginal value theorem applies when the forager can accurately assess the quality of the present patch, has knowledge of the distribution of patch qualities in the environment at large, does not deplete the quality of the environment (a given patch may be depleted but the distribution of newly encountered patches remains unaffected by the forager's activity), and has maximizing average harvest rate as its objective. The optimal patch use behaviour of a forager can be generalized to consider situations where the forager may experience predation risk, may have other fitness enhancing activities, and may experience a depletion in the quality of the environment during a foraging period (Gilliam and Fraser 1987; Brown 1988). For instance, nectar resources may be highest in the morning and then decline rapidly as hummingbirds commence foraging during the day (Brown et al. 1981).

Most models of foraging under predation risk and alternative activities can be translated into a straightforward rule for patch departure. A forager should deplete a food patch until its harvest rate in the patch, H, no longer exceeds its metabolic costs, C, predation costs, P, and missed opportunity costs (MOC) of foraging (Brown 1988, 1992):

$$H = C + P + MOC \tag{10.4}$$

All of these costs and benefits can be considered in a common currency such as energy per unit time ($J s^{-1}$). For harvest rate this requires converting the rate of resource harvest into net assimilated energy. For metabolic costs this means considering the additional energetic cost of the foraging activity beyond that of remaining inactive (interestingly, the organism's basal metabolic rate is part of its missed opportunity (a negative component in this case).

The organism's missed opportunity depends upon the remaining valuable activities at the end of the period that includes time for foraging and alternative activities. Consider three likely scenarios (Brown et al. 1994; Brown 1999). In the first, the forager experiences the same C and P when travelling and when exploiting food patches. Furthermore, assume that the forager does not deplete its environment and that foraging remains a valuable activity throughout the time period. In this case, MOC equals the forager's average harvest rate (averaged over time spent travelling to and harvesting patches) minus $(P + C)$. This results in the marginal value theorem for when a forager should leave a patch:

$$H = AHR \tag{10.5a}$$

where AHR is the average harvest rate and H is the quitting harvest rate within each patch.

In the second scenario, the forager eventually runs out of useful activities and spends some of its time resting safely in a burrow or refuge. Let the cost of this resting activity be C_0 and assume that this activity incurs negligible risk of predation. In this case, MOC $= -C_0$. A forager should leave a patch when:

$$H = (C - C_0) + P \qquad (10.5b)$$

In the third scenario, assume that the forager eventually depletes resources to the point at which per capita growth rate equals zero, and assume that foraging remains a valuable activity. Namely, resting safely in its burrow saving energy is not a valuable activity. In this case MOC $= 0$. A forager should leave a patch when:

$$H = C + P \qquad (10.5c)$$

The MOC may or may not provide useful information on the state of the forager or the quality of its environment. And, what information is contained within the MOC depends critically on whether equation (10.5a), (10.5b) or (10.5c) applies. When a forager does not deplete its environment-wide foraging opportunities, then its patch use strategy given by equation (10.5a) provides an estimate of resource availability. As average patch quality increases the forager should use each patch less thoroughly. When resting safely in its nest becomes a valuable activity as a consequence of depleting the value of other activities (equation [10.5b]), then MOC provides no useful information on the forager's state or the quality of its foraging environment. When a population of foragers depletes resources to some subsistence level (the equilibrium of the consumer-resource theory of Tilman 1982), then the MOC vanishes. In conclusion, missed opportunity represents one of three components to the cost of foraging. However, its functional form varies widely with circumstance, and it is probably not very revealing for organisms that deplete foraging opportunities. In contrast, as we shall see, the cost of predation has a very consistent functional form and it provides a very revealing window into the animal's ecology.

The cost of predation

The predation cost is probably the most important and the most interesting component of foraging costs. Important, because it can often be very large. For gerbils in Israel the cost of predation may be 8–10 times higher than the metabolic cost of foraging. For every 10 J of energy harvested by an Allenby's gerbil, up to nine joules goes to feeding the predators in the form of enhanced growth and reproduction by gerbils. Only one joule remains available for maintaining and supporting homeostasis (Brown *et al.* 1994).

The cost of predation does not just include the risk of predation. It also includes survivor's fitness, F, and the marginal value of energy (or other inputs into fitness), $\partial F/\partial f$. The relationship of risk of predation, survivor's fitness, and marginal value of energy provide a mathematical expression for fear. The equation of fear is given by (Brown 1988, 1992):

$$P = \mu F / (\partial F / \partial f)$$

It is possible to double the cost of predation to a forager by either doubling the actual risk of predation, doubling the forager's survivor's fitness, or by doubling the marginal value of energy to the forager. The cost of predation, more so than other foraging costs, integrates all aspects of the forager's prospects, well-being, and environment.

In a heterogeneous environment, a forager should demand a higher quitting harvest rate, H, from risky than from safe patches (Sih 1980; Werner *et al.* 1983; Abrahams and Dill 1989; Nonacs and Dill 1990). A forager with a higher survivor's fitness has more to lose from predation than a forager with a lower survivor's fitness. Hence, quitting harvest rate should increase with survivor's fitness. Clark (1994) has referred to this as the asset protection principle. A forager that has a higher marginal value of energy should have a lower quitting harvest rate than one with a lower marginal value of energy (McNamara and Houston 1986; Lima 1988; Brown *et al.* 1992).

Patch use and 'giving-up densities'

In most depletable food patches, the forager's harvest rate is influenced by the amount of food remaining in the patch. This means that the food left behind by a forager within a food patch provides a surrogate for its quitting harvest rate. I will refer to the food remaining in a food patch after a forager abandons the patch as its giving-up density (GUD). The giving-up density can be the foliage left behind on a shrub by a browsing animal (Astrom *et al.* 1990; Shipley *et al.* 1999). It may be the partial consumption of a food item such as lions leaving behind less desirable portions of a carcass. It may be the number of insects remaining on leaves after an insect gleaning bird has foraged its way through a tree canopy (e.g. warblers; Whelan 1989). In all of these cases, the GUD can provide valuable insights into the forager's state and the forager's environment. Figure 10.3 shows how the environment-wide availability of food, the food quality, predation risk, survivor's fitness, and the marginal value of energy influence the GUD.

Ecological consequences of the forager's patch use strategy

The patch use rule given by equation (10.4) presupposes that the forager can accurately assess patch quality. Most patch use strategies can be lumped into three broad categories: fixed time, fixed amount, and fixed quitting harvest rate. If a forager is unable to estimate patch quality then its best option is to devote the same amount of search effort to each encountered food patch, regardless of the quality (Iwasa *et al.* 1981). If foods are distributed randomly within the patch, then a constant proportion of food items will be harvested from each patch. In the Sonoran Desert of Arizona, Gambel's quail (*Callipepla gambelii*) and mourning dove (*Zenaida macrour*) searching for seeds seem to use a fixed time strategy (Valone

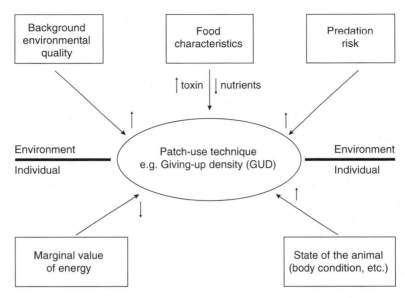

Figure 10.3 The ways in which properties of the individual and properties of the environment influence the forager's giving-up density (GUD) in depletable food patches.

and Brown 1989), as do crested larks (*Galerida cristata*) in the Negev Desert of Israel (Garb *et al.* 2000).

If a forager becomes sated during the exploitation of a patch, then its best strategy may be a fixed amount strategy. In this case a forager harvests no more than a fixed number of food items from a patch. This strategy can occur in foragers that take at most one item per patch (e.g. cave beetles seeking cave cricket eggs; Griffith and Brown 1992). Such a forager will harvest a smaller proportion of food from richer patches.

Most foragers probably make more or less accurate assessments of patch quality and subsequently bias their search effort towards richer patches. Such foragers use a fixed quitting harvest rate rule for when to leave the patch. If the forager is prescient and has near perfect knowledge of patch quality then it will in fact leave each patch at the same quitting harvest rate given by equation (10.4). More likely, foragers estimate patch quality based on sensory cues (e.g. a bird viewing the abundance of fruit on various trees, or a rodent using olfaction to smell seeds) and on experience gained from the current and previous patches (Wildhaber *et al.* 1994; Adler and Kotar 1999). Such foragers may use a Bayesian strategy for updating their estimate of patch quality based on experience in this and other patches. In striving for a fixed quitting harvest rate, a Bayesian forager will tend to (but not necessarily) over-utilize poor patches and under-utilize rich patches (e.g. kangaroo rats, Valone and Brown 1989; woodpeckers, Olsson 1998). A Bayesian forager will generally harvest a higher proportion of food from rich than from poor patches, but there will be a positive relationship between GUDs and patch quality (Rodriguez-

Girones and Vasquez 1997; Olsson 1998). The tendency for foraging animals to over-utilize poorer patches and habitats and under-utilize the richer ones is wide-spread (Kennedy and Gray 1993) and may reflect foragers with useful yet imperfect information.

Habitat use

A forager using a fixed quitting harvest rate strategy will tend to spend more time in habitats with higher food abundance than those with lower abundance. Predation risk should also alter patch use behaviours. All else equal, a forager should have a higher GUD in the risky habitat. Vegetation cover ('bush' vs. 'open' microhabitats) often correlates strongly with patch use and GUDs (e.g. aquatic systems; Persson 1991; Persson and Eklov 1995). Fox squirrels, grey squirrels, and chipmunks within the United States (Bowers *et al.* 1993; Brown and Morgan 1995) have lower GUDs near trees and vegetation cover than away from them. In deserts, many rodents have lower GUDs in the bush than open microhabitat (e.g. pocket mice, Brown 1989a; gerbils, Kotler *et al.* 1991; Indian crested porcupine, Brown and Alkon 1990).

Merriam's kangaroo rat provides an exception. Its use of the bush vs. open microhabitat depends upon the relative contribution of snakes and owls to preda-tion risk. At a site in California where rattlesnakes were the predominate predator, kangaroo rats had lower GUDs in the open than bush microhabitat (Bouskila 1995). At a Sonoran Desert site, kangaroo rats had lower GUDs in the bush than the open during the winter and then higher GUDs in the bush during the summer (Fig. 10.4; Brown 1989a). Rattlesnakes predominated among predators during the summer while owls predominated during the winter months.

The response of birds to cover probably depends upon escape tactic. Northern bobwhites (*Colinus virginianus*) that escape predators by fleeing towards cover have lower GUDs in the bush than open microhabitat (Kohlmann and Risenhoover 1996). Crested larks exhibit the opposite. They have lower GUDs in the open than bush microhabitat. Crested larks escape by taking flight and moving ≈ 50–$100\,\mathrm{m}$ before landing again on the ground or on a small shrub (Brown *et al.* 1997).

Diet selection

The distribution and abundance of a forager's food can strongly influence its diet (e.g. wood bison, *Bison bison*; Larter and Gates 1991). A food item may be over-represented in a forager's diet because:

1 it occurs in a favourable habitat;
2 it occurs at high abundance within its patches;
3 it is easy to find; and
4 it is highly preferred (Brown and Morgan 1995).

Consider each of these in turn. If food A occurs in a safe habitat and food B occurs in a risky habitat, then the forager for reasons of safety may bias its diet towards food A. Fox squirrels had a higher selectivity for granulated peanuts relative to

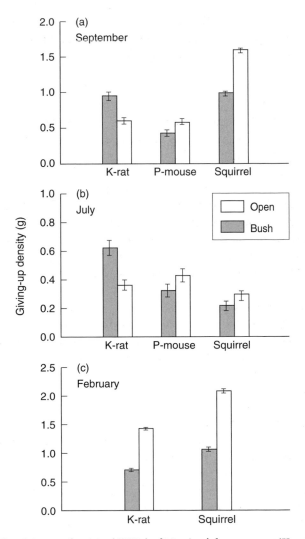

Figure 10.4 The giving-up densities (GUDs) of Merriam's kangaroo rat (K-rat), Arizona pocket mouse (P-mouse), and round-tailed ground squirrel (Squirrel) at different seasons of the year and by microhabitat (bush and open). Food patches consisted of metal trays filled with 3 g of millet seeds mixed into 3 L of sifted soil. As an indicator of higher predation risk, GUDs were generally higher in the open microhabitat. In July, however, kangaroo rats indicated a higher perceived predation risk in the bush microhabitat; probably as a result of predation risk from rattlesnakes. GUDs are also a measure of foraging efficiency. A low GUD provides one measure of interspecific competitive ability. There is a seasonal rotation in which species has the lowest GUD: pocket mice in September, squirrels in July and kangaroo rats in February (Brown 1989a).

sunflower seeds when the peanuts were placed near trees and sunflower seeds away from trees. This apparent preference switched as soon as sunflower seeds were near trees and the peanuts were placed away from trees.

If food A and food B occur in separate patches, the forager may have an apparent preference for whichever food occurs at high abundance within its patches. Fox squirrels bias their effort towards patches with high food abundance (Morgan *et al.* 1997). In this way, squirrels will appear to prefer peanuts over sunflower seeds when food patches with peanuts have much more food than patches with sunflower seeds. This apparent preference switches when patches with sunflower seeds have much more food than patches with peanuts.

If food A and food B occur together within food patches, then the forager may appear to prefer the food that is easiest to find. Fox squirrels, presumably because of olfaction, have an easier time finding the granulated peanuts than finding the sunflower seeds when they are buried in sand within the food patches. When both sunflower seeds and peanuts are mixed together in the sand of a patch, the squirrels will disproportionately harvest the peanuts when they forage the patch to a low GUD. However, when lightly foraged (high GUD), the fox squirrels disproportionately harvest the sunflower seeds. This occurs, because sunflower seeds offer higher reward per unit handling time, and sunflower are selectively harvested when they occur at high abundance (Brown and Morgan 1995).

Indirect effects among a forager's prey

The spatial distribution of a forager's prey may introduce indirect effects among prey species mediated through the forager's patch use behaviour. Adding a second prey to a food patch will increase its quality and likely cause the forager to spend more time harvesting the patch (short-term apparent competition, Holt and Kotler 1987). By adding a second prey species to the food patch, a higher proportion of the original prey species will be harvested. When the forager uses a fixed quitting harvest rate strategy for leaving patches, then prey species will interact negatively via the forager's behaviour. In fox squirrels, peanuts suffer a higher mortality rate when they co-occur with sunflower in the patch than when peanuts and sunflower occur in separate patches. Adding sunflower to a patch with peanuts increases peanut mortality (Fig. 10.5). Similarly adding peanut to a patch with sunflower increases sunflower seeds mortality (Brown and Morgan 1995). Schmitt (1987) found that gastropods and bivalves interacted via short-term apparent competition as a consequence of the foraging behaviour of lobster and octopus.

When prey co-occur within food patches, then a fixed quitting harvest rate strategy results in short-term apparent competition among prey species. A fixed time strategy results in no indirect effect among prey species. And, a fixed amount strategy results in a short-term indirect mutualism among prey species (Brown and Mitchell 1989).

When prey species occur in separate patches, then the presence of a second prey is likely to result in a short-term indirect mutualism even if the forager uses a fixed quitting harvest rate strategy. The presence of the other prey species

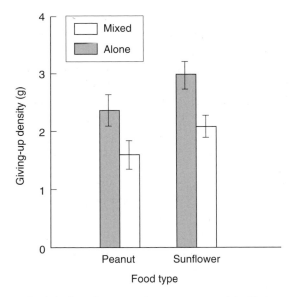

Figure 10.5 Fox squirrels induce short-term 'apparent competition' between peanut and sunflower 'prey'. Experimental food patches consisted of mixing peanuts and/or sunflower seeds into 4 L of sifted sand. GUDs provide a measure of those seeds that 'survived' the day's foraging. GUDs on sunflower and peanut were higher when the seed types occurred in separate patches. When sunflower seeds and peanuts were mixed together in the same patch, the squirrels responded to these food patches by devoting more search time and reducing the GUDs of each food type to a lower level. The presence of sunflower in a patch with peanuts causes more peanuts to be harvested and *vice-versa* for the presence of peanuts in a food patch with sunflower (Brown and Morgan 1995).

should increase the forager's overall harvest rate. If the forager harvests patches according to the marginal value theorem then it will leave all patches at a higher GUD. Or, if the forager experiences a cost of predation, then the forager's higher harvest rate should increase GUDs via an increased cost of predation (F should increase and $\partial F/\partial f$ should decline with a higher feeding rate). The increase in GUDs means that prey experience lower mortality in the presence of patches with the other prey.

Indirect effects among a forager's predators

A forager's behaviour in a heterogeneous environment can create behavioural indirect effects among its predators. Predator facilitation (Charnov *et al.* 1976) occurs when the forager's fear response to one predator makes it more susceptible to the hunting tactics of another predator species. The response of kangaroo rats to owls and snakes suggests predator facilitation. Kangaroo rats prefer the open microhabitat in response to snakes and the bush microhabitat in response to owls. Kotler *et al.* (1992, 1993a) tested for this possibility with gerbils in an aviary within which the presence and absence of barn owls or snakes was manipulated. In

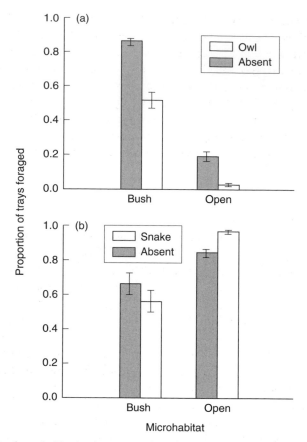

Figure 10.6 Predator facilitation between owls and snakes preying upon gerbils (*G. pyramidum*). In the first experiment (above) within an aviary, the presence or absence of owls was varied randomly from night to night. Gerbils responded by biasing their activity (proportion of food patches foraged) towards the bush microhabitat, and this bias intensified with the actual presence of owls during the night. In the second experiment (below), the presence or absence of snakes was varied randomly from night to night. Gerbils responded by biasing activity towards the open microhabitat. And, the actual presence of snakes during the night caused a decline in activity in the bush microhabitat and an increase in activity in the open (Kotler *et al.* 1993a).

response to owls, gerbils shifted foraging behaviour away from the open towards the bush microhabitat, and *vice-versa* for snakes. At first glance, owls and snakes may appear to be competitors for gerbils. In fact, owls and snakes are indirect mutualists via the gerbils' fear responses (Fig. 10.6). Owls drive gerbils into the fangs of snakes and snakes drive gerbils into the talons of owls (Kotler *et al.* 1992).

Suppose two predator's have similar hunting tactics and suppose that a given fear response by the prey is appropriate in reducing risk from both predators. These two predators may have both a negative direct interaction via resource competition, and also a negative indirect effect via the prey's fear responses. For example, the increase of tigers (*Panthera tigris*) in the Royal Bardia National Park, Nepal has been associated with a sharp decline in leopards (*P. pardus*) (Stoen and Wegge 1996). The leopards may have lost thrice as a consequence of the tigers. First, the tigers may compete directly with the leopard for prey such as nilgai antelope (*Boselaphus tragocamelus*). Second, the nilgai may have become harder to catch as they shifted their activity away from risky habitats in response to the presence of highly lethal tigers. Third, intraguild predation and interference from tigers may have hampered the hunting effectiveness of leopards as the leopards must watch their backs.

Mechanisms of coexistence

The behavioural responses of foragers to temporal and spatial variability in prey, resources or foraging habitats can facilitate several different mechanisms of coexistence (Holt 1984; Kotler and Brown 1988, 1999; Vincent *et al.* 1996). A mechanism of coexistence requires an axis of environmental heterogeneity and an appropriate trade-off among the species exploiting or tolerating the axis. The trade-off requires that each species has some region along the axis such that it is better than the other species at exploiting or tolerating the region (Tilman 1982; Brown 1989a).

A central tenet of ecology is that habitat heterogeneity promotes diversity (MacArthur 1958). If no species can simultaneously be best at all habitats, then spatial (and temporal) heterogeneity supports biodiversity. Some important aspects of habitat heterogeneity include the scale of heterogeneity and whether heterogeneity is a fixed property of the environment (giving rise to habitat partitioning) or variability in the abundance of a single resource (giving rise to variance partitioning).

In general, it is easier to promote diversity with coarse-grained heterogeneity than with fine-grained (Levins 1968; Brew 1982; Vincent *et al.* 1996). Density-dependent habitat selection (Fretwell and Lucas 1970; Fretwell 1972) in coarse-grained environments tends to greatly reduce interspecific interactions while intensifying intraspecific interactions (Rosenzweig 1981). This phenomenon can be seen with the aid of isolegs which give all combinations of the abundance of species 1 and species 2 such that a given species is indifferent between using both habitats opportunistically or using just one habitat selectively. As can be seen in Fig. 10.7, the isolegs create kinks in each species zero-growth isocline (combinations of species 1's and species 2's population sizes such that a given species has zero growth rate). Under coarse-grained habitat selection, the point of intersection of the two species' isoclines occurs in the region where each species is selective on a different habitat. This point is the ghost of competition past (Connell 1980). At this point, the two species are entirely segregated and no longer interact. Pimm *et al.* (1985) measured the isolegs of two hummingbird species. Abramsky *et al.* (1990, 1991) derived the isolegs and the isoclines for two gerbil species inhabiting sand dunes in the Negev desert.

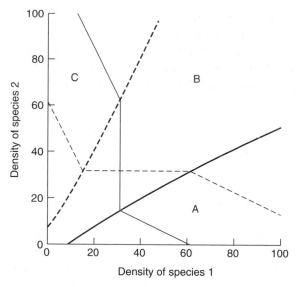

Figure 10.7 Schematic diagram showing the arrangement of isolegs (positively sloped lines) and zero-growth isoclines (negatively sloped lines with kinks) for species 1 (solid lines) and species 2 (dashed lines). The two species are assumed to compete for resources in two habitats (coarse-grained heterogeneity). Under the assumption that species 1 prefers habitat 1, species 1 only resides in habitat 1 above its isoleg and occupies both habitats below its isoleg. Under the assumption that species 2 prefers habitat 2 (distinct preference habitat selection), species 2 resides only in habitat 2 below its isoleg and resides in both habitats above its isoleg. In region A, species 1 uses both habitats and species 2 only uses habitat 2. The isoclines have negative slope because the two species compete for resources in habitat 2. In region C, species 2 uses both habitats and species 1 only uses habitat 1. Again, the isoclines have negative slopes in this region as the species compete in habitat 1. In region B, species 1 only uses habitat 1 and species 2 only uses habitat 2. Because the two species do not actually co-occur within the same habitat in region B, species 1's and species 2's isoclines become vertical and horizontal, respectively. At the intersection of the two species' isoclines, the ghost of competition past, there is no direct competition (Rosenzweig 1981).

Two sympatric and closely related species of insect-feeding bats may represent the ghost of competition past. For *Myotis myotis* and *Myotis blythii*, feeding habitats are largely species-specific. Despite easy access to each others' foraging habitats, *M. myotis* restricted foraging to meadows, mown lawns and forests without tall grass or undergrowth; and *M. blythii* restricted foraging to meadows and pastures with tall grass (Arlettaz 1999).

This mechanism can occur in time as individuals travel from night to night or from day to day by remaining inactive. In a typical woodland community of the midwestern United States (e.g. Morton Arboretum, Lisle, Illinois, USA) diurnal rodents such as fox squirrels, grey squirrels and chipmunks (*Tamias striatus*) face red-tailed hawks (*Buteo jamaicensis*), while nocturnal white-footed mice (*Peromyscus leucopus*) and flying squirrels (*Glaucomys volans*) face great-horned owls (*Buteo virginianus*). In this way, competition between hawks and owls is greatly reduced from what would occur if hawks and owls distributed their activity independently of day and night. While the occasional grey or fox squirrel shows up in the diet of the owl and the occasional white-footed mouse in the talons of the hawk, only the meadow vole (*Microtus pennsylvanicus*) which is active anytime day or night strongly connects the owl and the hawk as resource competitors.

Fine-grained heterogeneity in habitats or resource types offers fewer opportunities for coexistence based on a trade-off among foraging species with respect to habitat-specific aptitudes (Vincent *et al.* 1996). As the habitat becomes more fine-grained, each species is encouraged to behave more opportunistically and the region of the state space in which each species selects an exclusive habitat becomes smaller, and eventually the region may disappear entirely (Brown and Rosenzweig 1986). The increased overlap in habitat use increases interspecific competition which reduces the range of conditions under which coexistence is possible. However, fine-grained variability in heterogeneity promotes new opportunities for mechanisms of coexistence.

Variability in the abundance of a resource may be the axis of environmental heterogeneity that can promote the coexistence of 'cream skimmer' and 'crumb picker' species. The cream skimmer is a species that is able to move quickly or inexpensively among patches. This allows it to concentrate on rich patches. The crumb picker may not be able to move around as quickly or efficiently but it compensates by being a more efficient forager (=lower GUD, Brown 1989b) and harvesting each patch to a lower abundance of resources. Wing-loading in Hawaiian honeycreepers may represent such a trade-off where the two species with low wing-loading are more efficient while the species with the very high wing-loading is able to move quickly among flowering trees (Pimm and Pimm 1982). Brown (1989a) found this mechanism between a kangaroo rat (*D. merriami*) species (crumb picker) and a squirrel species (cream skimmer; Harris antelope squirrel, *Ammospermophilus harrisi*) in the Sonoran desert.

In some environments, particularly those with pulsed productivity, the temporal decline in environment-wide resource availability may provide a mechanism of coexistence. The cream-skimmer must be able to defend resources from the crumb-picker while they are abundant, and/or be able to remain dormant less expensively than the crumb-picker. The crumb-picker must have a higher foraging efficiency and be able to forage profitably to a lower GUD (Brown 1989b). On some sand dune habitats of the Negev Desert, seed resource renewed nightly as a consequence of afternoon winds uncovering and burying seeds. The larger gerbil, *G. pyramidum*, is able to dominate the early portions of the night. This happens to be the period when seed abundances are highest. But, *G. allenbyi*, the smaller gerbil, has the lower GUD (Brown *et al.* 1994) and is able to continue foraging even after the larger species has ceased being active (Kotler *et al.* 1993b; Ziv *et al.* 1993). Schaffer *et al.* (1979) found that degree of sociality among three bee species represented a trade-off between speed and efficiency of exploiting nectar resources.

Seasonal diet switching by the predators can also promote coexistence, so long as the predators use an adaptive feeding strategy of focusing on the most abundant or promising prey. Hamback (1998) discusses such a model in the context of grey-sided voles promoting the coexistence of two species of arctic dwarf shrubs. Brown (1989a) found that the seasonal and non-synchronous changes in the abundance of rattlesnakes, owls, and diurnal birds of prey promoted the coexistence of Merriam's kangaroo rat, Arizona pocket mouse (*Perognathus amplus*), and round-tailed ground squirrel (*Spermophilus tereticaudus*). The kangaroo rat was the most efficient forager and had the lowest GUD during the winter and spring when diurnal hawks and owls were abundant but rattlesnakes were dormant. The pocket mouse had the lowest GUD of the three rodent species during the autumn when rattlesnakes were active. And, the squirrel had the lowest GUD during the summer when diurnal hawks were mostly absent (Fig. 10.4). In these two examples, coexistence resulted from the conjunction of seasonality (productivity in Hamback 1998; or predator abundances in Brown 1989a) with the optimal feeding behaviours of predator and prey, respectively.

Guerra and Vickery (1998) tested among five mechanisms of coexistence and found that eastern chipmunks coexisted with red squirrels (*Tamaisciurus hudsonicus*) via spatial and temporal habitat selection. Chipmunks had the lower GUD of the two species during the summer in all forest patches, and in the spring chipmunks had the lower GUD in the mixed forest. Red squirrels had exclusive use of all habitats during the winter (chipmunks are inactive) and had the lower GUD during the spring in the coniferous forest patches.

Similarly, it is generally easier to promote diversity under qualitative rather than quantitative niche axes (Rosenzweig 1991). A qualitative niche axis is one in which the different species differ in their relative ranking of habitat preferences. Each species actually prefers a unique portion of the axes. A food and safety axis in which one habitat is safe but poorer in food resources and the other habitat is risky but rich in food offers qualitatively different opportunities and hazards (Grand and Dill 1999). A quantitative niche axis is one in which the magnitude of some factor (such as productivity, precipitation, etc) varies in a manner such that all species share the same preference ranking of habitats. Brown (1996) modelled simultaneously changes in scale and productivity of three distinct habitats. As expected, increasing the scale of habitat heterogeneity promoted diversity and the ghost of competition past. Varying productivity, by making some habitats more productive than others (quantitative niche axes) promoted diversity in which the community of species exhibited nested niches. Simultaneously varying habitat-specific productivities and habitat-specific scales produced centrifugal community organizations in which several species shared a common core habitat but then diverged with respect to their secondary habitat preferences (Rosenzweig and Abramsky 1986).

Habitat selection, coevolution and speciation

Density-dependent habitat selection considers the simultaneous effects of habitat type (or quality) and density on the fitness (or success) of an individual within that habitat. In general, fitness increases with the productivity of the habitat and declines with the density of individuals using the habitat. In response, individuals should distribute themselves among habitats in a way that equalizes fitness opportunities among habitats (e.g. ideal free distribution, Fretwell and Lucas 1970). Hence, the number of individuals using one habitat should not be independent of those in another. Furthermore, the relationship between the abundance of individuals within one habitat and those in another provides valuable information on quantitative and qualitative differences among habitats (McNamara and Houston 1990). Morris (1988, 1989) has defined the 'isodar' as the relationship between the numbers of individuals in one habitat vs. those in another habitat. In general this relationship is positive (Fig. 10.8). In a coarse-grained environment, the slope is proportional to the ratio of productivities between the two habitats. The intercept indicates qualitative differences among habitats. A positive intercept indicating that habitat 2 is qualitatively preferred to habitat 1, perhaps because habitat 2 is safer from predation (Morris 1994, 1999; Moody et al. 1996; Brown 1998).

As shown in isodars, the habitat selection behaviour of individuals determines their exposure to habitats. This exposure becomes the ecological context to which subsequent morphological and physiological evolution should occur (Matsuda and Namba 1989). For instance, if an individual and its descendants selectively use just a single habitat then they should evolve the appropriate morphological and physiological specializations. There will be a coadaptation between an individual's behaviour and its fixed traits. Rosenzweig (1987b) found that two habitats could promote the evolution of

1 a single species behaving opportunistically;

2 two specialist species each behaving selectively towards its own respective habitat;

3 one specialist species behaving selectively and a generalist species behaving opportunistically.

With three habitats the number of possible combinations of species increases to 10 and includes a variety of one, two and three species communities with varying degrees of coadaptations between behaviours of habitat selection and fixed traits of habitat specialization (Brown 1996).

The interaction of behaviours and morphological evolution can create limitations on, and opportunities for, adaptive evolution. For instance, selective behaviours remove the opportunity for natural selection to promote traits that enhance abilities on habitats that are not currently in the population's repertoire (Rosenzweig 1987b). The positive evolutionary feedback between selective behaviours and specialization promotes niche conservatism (Holt and Gaines 1992; Holt and Gomulkiewicz 1997). It is hard for natural selection to evolve an opportunistic generalist species from a selective specialist (Holt 1996). On the

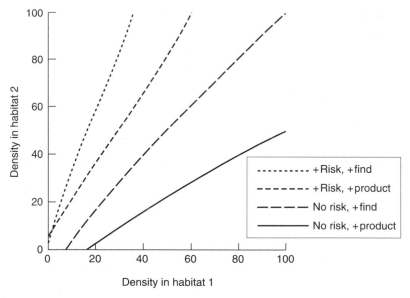

Figure 10.8 Schematic diagram showing isodars under the four combinations generated by having no predation risk (No risk) vs. higher predation risk in habitat 1 (+Risk), and having higher productivity in habitat 1 (+Product) vs. a higher encounter rate on food in habitat 1 (+find). The isodars give the combinations of population sizes in the two habitats that should result from density-dependent habitat selection. When there is no predation risk, then the isodar shows the distribution of individuals among habitats that equalizes fitness. When there is predation risk an individual should use a mix of both habitats as a way of balancing food and safety as complementary inputs into fitness. Under habitat differences in predation risk, the isodar shows the optimal proportion of an individual's activity within each habitat. A higher productivity in habitat 1 (solid line) insures a strong bias of activity towards habitat 1, regardless of population size. A higher encounter probability on food in habitat 1, causes a biased distribution towards habitat 1 at small population sizes, but this bias disappears at high population sizes. A higher predation risk in habitat 1 has the large effect of biasing the population's distribution towards habitat 2 despite a lower productivity and encounter probability, respectively, in habit 2 (Morris 1988, 1999; Brown 1998).

other hand, it is relatively easier to evolve selective specialists from an opportunistic generalist. Figure 10.9 illustrates how adaptive speciation can produce two specialist species from a single generalist species. The single opportunistic generalist evolves to the peak of its adaptive landscape. The value of the individual's fixed trait represents a compromise between aptitudes on the respective habitats. Under coarse-grained heterogeneity, the adaptive surfaces for the two selective behaviours intersect each other at the peak of the opportunist's landscape. This forms a 'V' in the landscape at the optimal strategy for the opportunistic generalist. In a manner analogous to the adaptive speciation envisioned in Maynard Smith (1966), Bush

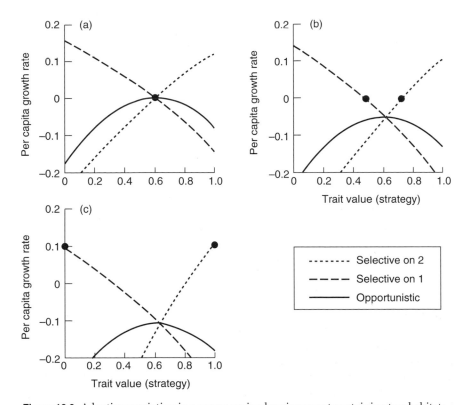

Figure 10.9 Adaptive speciation in a coarse-grained environment containing two habitats. Each graph shows the configuration of the adaptive landscapes of individuals: (i) using both habitat types opportunistically (solid line); (ii) using habitat 1 selectively (dashed line); and (iii) using habitat 2 selectively (dotted line). Each landscape plots per capita growth rate as a function of some fixed morphological or physiological trait. The trait is assumed to vary from 0 to 1 and represent a trade-off between aptitude in habitat 1 (a trait value of 0 = the extreme habitat 1 specialist) and aptitude in habitat 2 (a trait value of 1 = the extreme habitat 2 specialist). (a) The configuration of landscapes when the population consists of opportunistic individuals that possess their optimal value of the trait (given opportunistic behaviour) in a population that has grown to its ecological equilibrium (hence, per capita growth rate equals 0). At this optimal value (population shown by the large dot), each individual has the same fitness whether it is opportunistic or selective (consequence of individuals equalizing fitness opportunities between the two habitats). This is why the landscapes for the two selective behaviours intersect at the ESS of the opportunistic individuals. But, each selective type can have still higher fitness by exhibiting a trait with more extreme specialization on habitat 1 or 2, respectively. (b) The configuration of landscapes, when the opportunistic type is allowed to speciate adaptively into the two selective types. Once both behaviourally selective types exist in the population, individuals of each type begin to diverge towards lower and higher trait values. These transitional values are shown by the large dots. (c) The eventual ESS community of a habitat 1 specialist (trait value of 0) and a habitat 2 specialist (trait value of 1). Each specialist species behaves selectively towards its respective habitat.

(1969), and Rosenzweig (1978), selection favours individuals that behave selectively. Once an individual shows even a partial selectivity towards one of the habitats then selection favours a more specialist morphology. Evolution will proceed until the community consists of two specialist species behaving selectively. This can promote short-term or permanent divergence in habitat use and/or foraging tactics (e.g. brook char, *Salvelinus fontinalis*, McLaughlin *et al.* 1999). Rice and Salt (1990) have been able to produce this speciation in laboratory experiments with *Drosophila*. The laboratory environment offered two distinct habitats that promoted the evolution and speciation of two selective 'species' from a single ancestral population. Via (1991) provides an example of this phenomenon with pea aphids (*Acyrthosiphon pisum*) specializing on clover or alfalfa, and Feder *et al.* (1988) found this with apple maggot flies (*Rhagoletis pomonella*) that have speciated to occupy hawthorn trees and apple trees, respectively.

Squirrels as an example

Fox squirrels and grey squirrels inhabiting the central to eastern portions of North America illustrate beautifully the ecological consequences of foraging in heterogeneous environments. The fox squirrel is larger, less aggressive in intra- and interference, found in more open habitats, and has a range that extends farther west. The grey squirrel is smaller, more aggressive, found in deep woods, and has a range that extends farther north (Brown and Yeager 1945; Nixon *et al.* 1968; Brown and Batzli 1984).

Let us start with their foraging behaviour near and away from trees. In response to predation risk, each has a higher GUD away from trees than near trees (Bowers *et al.* 1993; Brown and Morgan 1995). This appears to be the axis of heterogeneity that promotes coexistence. Most of the characteristics of the fox squirrel seem to favour its ability to detect and avoid predation by hawks, whereas the grey squirrel's characteristics seem to make it the better resource competitor in the absence of predation. Hence, fox squirrels may be more efficient foragers than greys under high predation; and vice-versa under low predation risk. The edges of woods represent a higher risk habitat that favours fox squirrels, and the deep interior of woods may represent lower risk that favours grey squirrels. This can be seen temporally across the state of Illinois, in which fox squirrels were numerically dominant following the clearing of most of Illinois' forests. Subsequently, the frequency of grey squirrels has been increasing dramatically as reforestation takes place (Fig. 10.10; Hoffmeister 1989).

This effect of predation risk on the distribution and abundance of grey and fox squirrels may also hold in urban areas. A survey of a Chicago suburb revealed that grey squirrels had lower GUDs than fox squirrels where the two co-occurred (Fig. 10.11; Lanham 1998). Furthermore, GUDs of squirrels were highest in parts of Oak Park, IL with the highest density of cats and dogs (Fig. 10.12; Bowers and Breland 1996). And, density of cats and dogs was an excellent predictor of the predominant squirrel species. Fox squirrels predominated in the high risk areas

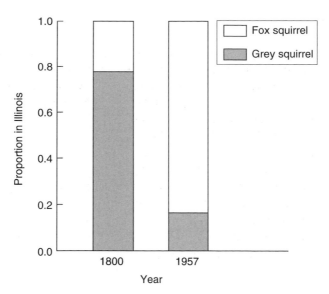

Figure 10.10 The ratio of fox squirrels to grey squirrels in Illinois. In 1800, Illinois retained most of its pre-European settlement forests. Extensive forests favoured grey squirrels over fox squirrels. By 1950, most of these presettlement forests had been cut or fragmented. Less extensive and more fragmented forests favoured fox squirrels over grey squirrels. Currently, grey squirrels are increasing relative to fox squirrels throughout much of the state (data taken from Nixon *et al.* 1978).

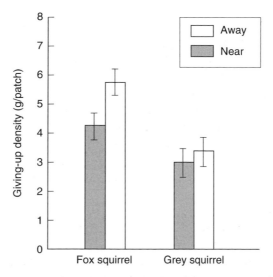

Figure 10.11 GUDs of fox squirrels and grey squirrels within backyards of the suburb of Oak Park (directly west of Chicago), Illinois, USA. Even in an urban area, squirrels have lower GUDs near trees compared to away from trees (differences in perceived predation risk). Grey squirrels occupy parts of Oak Park that have fewer cats and dogs. This relative safety is reflected in grey squirrels having a lower GUD than fox squirrels (data taken from Lanham 1998).

207

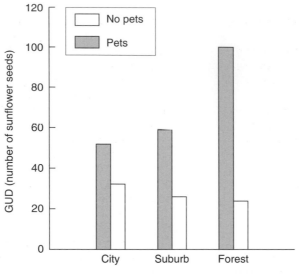

Figure 10.12 GUDs of grey squirrels across a landscape in Virginia containing city, suburb and rural forest. Regardless of the location of the homeowner's yard, grey squirrels perceived pets as a risk, and this risk was magnified in yards located within forests (adapted from fig. 2 of Bowers and Breland 1996).

while grey predominated in the areas with lower densities of cats and dogs. The same processes governing coexistence and distributions under natural situations seems to operate in towns.

Food and safety and the squirrels' foraging responses may determine the differences in their range limits. Moving west, forests become more open and presumably more risky from soaring avian predators. As a consequence, the grey squirrel drops out first and the fox squirrel's range continues further west. Moving north, winters become longer and colder necessitating larger food caches and more efficient foraging. As a consequence, the fox squirrel drops out first and the grey continues farther north and north-west.

Heterogeneity in vegetation structure and its effect on the aptitudes of soaring hawks creates heterogeneity in predation risk for squirrels. This heterogeneity in risk generates a trade-off in food and safety via higher GUDs under higher risk. This heterogeneity at the scale of forests dictates the coexistence and distribution of the two squirrel species locally. The relative abilities of the two squirrels to forage efficiently and to avoid predators dictates their regional distributions and overlap. Foraging ecology is the key to understanding the squirrels from the local scale to the regional. Presumably these profound consequences of foraging ecology hold true for most other organisms as well!

References

Abrahams, P.A. and Dill, L.M. (1989) A determination of the energetic equivalence of the risk of predation. *Ecology* **70**, 999–1007.

Abrams, P.A. (1984) Foraging time optimization and interactions within food webs. *American Naturalist* **124**, 80–96.

Abrams, P.A., Matsuda, H. and Harada, Y. (1993) Evolutionarily unstable fitness maxima and stable fitness minima of continuous traits. *Evolutionary Ecology* **7**, 465–487.

Abramsky, Z., Rosenzweig, M.L., Pinshow, B., Brown, J.S., Kotler, B.P. and Mitchell, W.A. (1990) Habitat selection: an experimental field test with two gerbil species. *Ecology* **71**, 2358–2369.

Abramsky, Z., Rosenzweig, M.L. and Pinshow, B. (1991) The shape of a gerbil isocline: an experimental field study using principles of optimal habitat selection. *Ecology* **72**, 329–340.

Abramsky, Z., Rosenzweig, M.L. and Subach, A. (1998) Do gerbils care more about competition or predation? *Oikos* **83**, 75–84.

Abramsky, Z., Strauss, E., Subach, A., Kotler, B.P. and Reichman, A. (1996) The effects of barn owls (*Tyto alba*) on the activity and microhabitat selection of *Gerbillus allenbyi* and *G. pyramidum*. *Oecologia* **105**, 313–319.

Adler, F.R. and Kotar, M. (1999) Departure time versus departure rate: How to forage optimally when you are stupid. *Evolutionary and Ecology Research* **1**, 411–421.

Arlettaz, R. (1999) Habitat selection as a major resource partitioning mechanism between two sympatric sibling bat species, *Myotis myotis* and *Myotis blythii*. *Journal of Animal Ecology* **68**, 460–471.

Astrom, M., Lundberg, P. and Danell, K. (1990) Partial prey consumption by browsers: Trees as patches. *Journal of Animal Ecology* **59**, 287–300.

Barba, E., Lopez, J.A. and Gil-Delgado, J.E. (1996) Prey preparation by adult great tits *Parus major* feeding nestlings. *Ibis* **138**, 532–538.

Birch, C.P.D. and Hutchings, M.J. (1994) Exploitation of patchily distributed resources by the clonal herb *Glechoma hederacea*. *Journal of Ecology* **82**, 653–664.

Bouskila, A. (1995) Interactions between predation risk and competition: a field study of kangaroo rats and snakes. *Ecology* **76**, 165–178.

Bowers, M.A. and Breland, B. (1996) Foraging of gray squirrels on an urban-rural gradient: use of the GUD to assess anthropogenic impact. *Ecological Applications* **6**, 1135–1142.

Bowers, M.A., Jefferson, J.L. and Kuebler, M.G. (1993) Variation in giving-up densities of chipmunks (*Tamias striatus*) and squirrels (*Sciurus carolinensis*). *Oikos* **66**, 229–236.

Brew, J.S. (1982) Niche shift and the minimization of competition. *Theoretical Population Biology* **22**, 367–381.

Brown, B.W. and Batzli, G.D. (1984) Habitat selection by fox and gray squirrels: a multivariate analysis. *Journal of Wildlife Management* **48**, 616–621.

Brown, J.H., Kodric-Brown, A., Witham, T.G. and Bond, H.W. (1981) Competition between hummingbirds and insects for the nectar of two species of shrubs. *Southwestern Naturalist* **26**, 133–145.

Brown, J.S. (1988) Patch use as an indicator of habitat preference, predation risk, and competition. *Behavioral Ecology and Sociobiology* **22**, 27–37.

Brown, J.S. (1989a) Desert rodent community structure: a test of four mechanisms of coexistence. *Ecological Monographs* **20**, 1–20.

Brown, J.S. (1989b) Coexistence on a seasonal resource. *American Naturalist* **133**, 168–182.

Brown, J.S. (1992) Patch use under predation risk. I. Models and predictions. *Annales Zoologici Fennici* **29**, 301–309.

Brown, J.S. (1996) Coevolution of community organization in three habitats. *Oikos* **75**, 193–206.

Brown, J.S. (1998) Game theory and habitat selection. In: *Game Theory and Animal Behaviour* (eds L.A. Dugatkin and H.K. Reeve), pp. 188–220. Oxford University Press, Oxford.

Brown, J.S. (1999) Vigilance, patch use and habitat selection: Foraging under predation risk. *Evolutionary Ecology Research* **1**, 49–71.

Brown, J.S. and Alkon, P.A. (1990) Testing values of crested porcupine habitats by experimental food patches. *Oecologia* **83**, 512–518.

Brown, J.S., Kotler, B.P. and Mitchell, W.A. (1997) Competition between birds and mammals: a comparison of giving-up densities between crested larks and gerbils. *Evolutionary Ecology* **11**, 757–771.

Brown, J.S., Kotler, B.P. and Valone, T.J. (1994) Foraging under predation: a comparison of energetic and predation costs in rodent communities of the Negev and Sonoran Deserts. *Australian Journal of Zoology* **42**, 435–448.

Brown, J.S. and Mitchell, W.A. (1989) Diet selection on depletable resources. *Oikos* **54**, 33–43.

Brown, J.S. and Morgan, R.A. (1995) Effects of foraging behavior and spatial scale on diet selectivity: a test with fox squirrels. *Oikos* **74**, 122–136.

Brown, J.S., Morgan, R.A. and Dow, B.D. (1992) Patch use under predation risk: II. A test with fox squirrels, *Sciurus niger. Annales Zoologici Fennici* **29**, 311–318.

Brown, J.S. and Pavlovic, N.B. (1992) Evolution in heterogeneous environments: effects of migration on habitat specialization. *Evolutionary Ecology* **6**, 360–382.

Brown, J.S. and Rosenzweig, M.L. (1986) Habitat selection in slowly regenerating environments. *Journal of Theoretical Biology* **123**, 151–171.

Brown, J.S. and Venable, D.L. (1986) Evolutionary ecology of seed bank annuals in temporally varying environments. *American Naturalist* **127**, 31–47.

Brown, L.C. and Yeager, L.E. (1945) Fox and gray squirrels in Illinois. *Illinois Natural Histology Survey* **23**, 419–436.

Bush, G.L. (1969) Sympatric host race formation and speciation in frugivorous flies of the genus *Rhagoletis. Evolution* **23**, 237–251.

Campbell, B.D., Grime, J.P., Macky, J.M.L. and Jalili, A. (1991) The quest for a mechanistic understanding of resource competition in plant communities: the role of experiments. *Functional Ecology* **5**, 241–253.

Charnov, E.L. (1976) Optimal foraging and the marginal value theorem. *Theoretical Population Biology* **9**, 129–136.

Charnov, E.L., Orians, G.H. and Hyatt, K. (1976) Ecological implications of resource depression. *American Naturalist* **110**, 247–259.

Clark, C.W. (1994) Antipredator behaviour and the asset-protection principle. *Behavioral Ecology* **5**, 159–170.

Cohen, D. (1966) Optimizing reproduction in a randomly varying environment. *Journal of Theoretical Biology* **12**, 119–129.

Connell, J.H. (1980) Diversity and the coevolution of competitors, or the ghost of competition past. *Oikos* **35**, 131–138.

Deakin, M.A.B. (1966) Sufficient conditions for genetic polymorphism. *American Naturalist* **100**, 690–692.

Dill, L.M. and Fraser, A.H.G. (1984) Risk of predation and the feeding behavior of juvenile coho salmon (*Oncorhynchus kisutch*). *Behavioral Ecology and Sociobiology* **16**, 65–71.

Emlen, J.M. (1966) The role of time and energy in food preferences. *American Naturalist* **100**, 611–618.

Feder, J.L., Chilcote, C.A. and Bush, G.L. (1988) Genetic differentiation and sympatric host races of the apple maggot fly, *Rhagoletis pomonella. Nature* **336**, 61–64.

Fretwell, S.D. (1972) *Populations in Seasonal Environments.* Princeton University Press, Princeton, New Jersey.

Fretwell, S.D. and Lucas, H.L. Jr (1970) On territorial behavior and other factors influencing habitat distribution in birds. I. Theoretical development. *Acta Biotheoretica* **19**, 16–36.

Garb, J., Kotler, B.P. and Brown, J.S. (2000) Foraging and community consequences of seed size for coexisting crested lark and Allenby's gerbil. *Oikos* **88**, 291–300.

Gilliam, J.F. and Fraser, D.F. (1987) Habitat selection under predation hazard: a test of a model with foraging minnows. *Ecology* **68**, 1856–1862.

Grand, T.C. and Dill, L.M. (1999) Predation risk, unequal competitors and the ideal free distribution. *Evolutionary Ecology Research* **1**, 389–409.

Griffith, D.M. and Brown, J.S. (1992) A null model of patch assessment with an application to a Carabid cave beetle. *Oikos* **64**, 523–526.

Guerra, B. and Vickery, W.L. (1998) How do red squirrels, *Tamiasciurus hudsonicus,* and eastern chipmunks, *Tamias striatus,* coexist? *Oikos* **83**, 139–144.

Hamback, P.A. (1998) Seasonality, optimal foraging, and prey coexistence. *American Naturalist* **152**, 881–895.

Hoffmeister, D.F. (1989) *Mammals of Illinois.* University of Illinois Press, Urbana, USA.

Holling, C.S. (1965) The functional response of predators to prey density and its role in mimicry and population regulation. *Memoirs of the Entomological Society of Canada* **45**, 1–60.

Holt, R.D. (1984) Spatial heterogeneity, indirect interactions, and the coexistence of prey species. *American Naturalist* **124**, 377–406.

Holt, R.D. (1996) Adaptive evolution in source-sink environments: direct and indirect effects of density dependence in niche evolution. *Oikos* **75**, 182–192.

Holt, R.D. and Gaines, M.S. (1992) Analysis of the adaptation in heterogeneous landscapes: implications for the evolution of fundamental niches. *Evolutionary Ecology* **6**, 433–447.

Holt, R.D. and Gomulkiewicz, R. (1997) How does immigration influence local adaptation? A re-examination of a familiar paradigm. *American Naturalist* **149**, 563–572.

Holt, R.D. and Kotler, B.P. (1987) Short-term apparent competition. *American Naturalist* **130**, 412–430.

Holt, R.D. and McPeek, M. (1996) Chaotic population dynamics favors the evolution of dispersal. *American Naturalist* **148**, 709–718.

Houston, A.I., McNamara, J.M. and Hutchinson, J.M.C. (1993) General results concerning the trade-off between gaining energy and avoiding predation. *Philosophical Transactions of the Royal Society of London B* **341**, 375–397.

Hughes, R.N. (1970) Optimal diets under the energy maximization premise: the effects of recognition time and learning. *American Naturalist* **113**, 209–221.

Iwasa, Y.M., Higashi, M. and Yamamura, N. (1981) Prey distribution as a factor determining the choice of optimal foraging strategy. *American Naturalist* **117**, 710–723.

Kaspari, M. (1990) Prey preparation and the determinants of handling time. *Animal Behavior* **40**, 118–126.

Kennedy, M. and Gray, R.D. (1993) Can ecological theory predict the distribution of foraging animals? A critical analysis of experiments on the ideal free distribution. *Oikos* **68**, 158–166.

Kohlmann, S.G. and Risenhoover, K.L. (1996) Using artificial food patches to evaluate habitat quality for granivorous birds: an application of foraging theory. *Condor* **98**, 854–857.

Kotler, B.P. (1992) Behavioral resource depression and decaying perceived predation in two species of coexisting gerbils. *Behavioral Ecology and Sociobiology* **30**, 239–244.

Kotler, B.P., Blaustein, L. and Brown, J.S. (1992) Predator facilitation: The combined effect of snakes and owls on the foraging behavior of gerbils. *Annales Zoologici Fennici* **29**, 199–206.

Kotler, B.P. and Brown, J.S. (1988) Environmental heterogeneity and the coexistence of desert rodents. *Annual Review of Ecology and Systematics* **19**, 281–307.

Kotler, B.P. and Brown, J.S. (1999) Mechanisms of coexistence of optimal foragers as determinants of the local abundance and distributions of desert granivores. *Journal of Mammalogy* **80**, 361–374.

Kotler, B.P., Brown, J.S. and Hasson, O. (1991) Owl predation on gerbils: the role of body size, illumination, and habitat structure on rates of predation. *Ecology* **71**, 2249–2260.

Kotler, B.P., Brown, J.S., Slotow, R.H., Goodfriend, W.L. and Strauss, M. (1993a) The influence of snakes on the foraging behavior of gerbils. *Oikos* **67**, 309–316.

Kotler, B.P., Brown, J.S. and Subach, A. (1993b) Mechanisms of species coexistence of optimal foragers: Temporal partitioning by two species of sand dune gerbils. *Oikos* **67**, 548–556.

Kotler, B.P. and Holt, R.D. (1989) Predation and competition: the interaction of two types of species interactions. *Oikos* **54**, 256–260.

Kotler, B.P. and Mitchell, W.A. (1995) The effect of costly information on diet choice. *Evolutionary Ecology* **9**, 18–29.

Lanham, C.R. (1998) Mechanisms of coexistence in urban fox squirrels and gray squirrels. Unpublished MSc Thesis, University of Illinois at Chicago, Chicago, USA.

Larter, N.C. and Gates, C.C. (1991) Diet and habitat selection of wood bison in relation to seasonal changes in forage quantity and quality. *Canadian Journal of Zoology* **69**, 2677–2685.

Levene, H. (1953) Genetic equilibrium when more than one ecological niche is available. *American Naturalist* **87**, 311–313.

Levins, R. (1962) Theory of fitness in a heterogeneous environment: I. The fitness set and adaptive function. *American Naturalist* **96**, 361–373.

Levins, R. (1968) *Evolution in Changing Environments*. Princeton. Princeton University Press.

Levins, R. and MacArthur, R.H. (1966) The maintenance of genetic polymorphism in a spatially heterogeneous environment: variations on a theme by Howard Levene. *American Naturalist* **100**, 585–590.

Lima, S.L. (1988) Initiation and termination of daily feeding in dark-eyed juncos: Influences of predation risk and energy reserves. *Oikos* **53**, 12–26.

MacArthur, R.H. (1958) Population ecology of some warblers of northeastern coniferous forests. *Ecology* **39**, 599–619.

MacArthur, R.H. and Pianka, E.R. (1966) On optimal use of a patchy environment. *American Naturalist* **100**, 603–610.

Matsuda, H. and Namba, T. (1989) Co-evolutionarily stable community structure in a patchy environment. *Journal of Theoretical Biology* **136**, 229–243.

Maynard Smith, J. (1966) Sympatric speciation. *American Naturalist* **100**, 637–650.

Maynard Smith, J. and Price, G.R. (1973) The logic of animal conflict. *Nature* **246**, 15–18.

McLaughlin, R.L., Ferguson, M.M. and Noakes, D.L.G. (1999) Adaptive peaks and alternative foraging tactics in brook charr: evidence of short-term divergent selection for sitting-and-waiting and actively searching. *Behavioral Ecology and Sociobiology* **45**, 386–395.

McNamara, J.M. and Houston, A.I. (1986) The common currency for behavioral decisions. *American Naturalist* **127**, 358–378.

McNamara, J.M. and Houston, A.I. (1990) State-dependent ideal free distribution. *Evolutionary Ecology* **4**, 298–311.

Metz, J.A.J., Geritz, S.A.H., Meszena, G., Jacobs, F.J.A. and van Heerwaarden, J.S. (1996) Adaptive dynamics, a geometrical study of the consequences of near faithful reproduction. In: *Stochastic and Spatial Structure of Dynamical Systems* (eds S.J. van Strien and S.M. Verduyn Lunel). Royal Academy of Arts and Sciences, Northern Holland, Amsterdam.

Moody, A.L., Houston, A.I. and McNamara, J.M. (1996) Ideal free distribution under predation risk. *Behavioral Ecology and Sociobiology* **38**, 131–143.

Morgan, R.A., Brown, J.S. and Thorson, J.M. (1997) The effect of spatial scale on the functional response of fox squirrels. *Ecology* **78**, 1087–1097.

Morris, D.W. (1988) Habitat-dependent population regulation and community structure. *Evolutionary Ecology* **2**, 253–269.

Morris, D.W. (1989) Density-dependent habitat selection: Testing the theory with fitness data. *Evolutionary Ecology* **3**, 80–94.

Morris, D.W. (1994) Habitat matching: alternatives and implications to populations and communities. *Evolutionary Ecology* **4**, 387–406.

Morris, D.W. (1999) A haunting legacy from isoclines: mammal coexistence and the ghost of competition. *Journal of Mammalogy* **80**, 375–384.

Nixon, C.M., Worley, D.M. and McClain, M.W. (1968) Food habits of squirrels in southeast Ohio. *Journal of Wildlife Management* **62**, 294–305.

Nixon, C.M., Harera, S.P. and Greenberg, R.E. (1978) Distribution and abundance of the gray squirrel in Illinois. *Illinois Natural History Survey Biology Notes* **105**, 1–55.

Nonacs, P. and Dill, L.M. (1990) Mortality risk versus food quality trade-offs in a common currency: ant patch preference. *Ecology* **71**, 1886–1892.

Olsson, O. (1998) Through the eyes of a woodpecker: Understanding habitat selection, territory quality and reproductive decisions from individual behaviour. Unpublished PhD Dissertation, Lund University, Sweden, 152.

Orians, G.H. (1991) Preface. *American Naturalist* **137**, S1–S4.

Persson, L. (1991) Behavioral response to predators reverses the outcome of competition between prey species. *Behavioral Ecology and Sociobiology* **28**, 101–105.

Persson, L. and Eklov, P. (1995) Prey refuges affecting interactions between piscivorous perch and juvenile perch and roach. *Ecology* **76**, 70–81.

Pimm, S.L. and Pimm, J.W. (1982) Resource use, competition, and resource availability in Hawaiian honeycreepers. *Ecology* **63**, 1468–1480.

Pimm, S.L., Rosenzweig, M.L. and Mitchell, W. (1985) Competition and food selection: Field tests of a theory. *Ecology* **66**, 798–807.

Pulliam, H.R. (1974) On the theory of optimal diets. *American Naturalist* **108**, 59–75.

Rice, W.R. and Salt, G.W. (1990) The evolution of reproductive isolation as a correlated character under sympatric conditions: experimental evidence. *Evolution* **44**, 1140–1152.

Rodriguez-Girones, M.A. and Vasquez, R.A. (1997) Density-dependent patch exploitation and acquisition of environmental information. *Theoretical Population Biology* **52**, 32–42.

Rosenzweig, M.L. (1973) Habitat selection experiments with a pair of coexisting heteromyid rodent species. *Ecology* **62**, 327–335.

Rosenzweig, M.L. (1978) Competitive speciation. *Biological Journal of the Linnaean Society* **10**, 275–289.

Rosenzweig, M.L. (1981) A theory of habitat selection. *Ecology* **62**, 327–335.

Rosenzweig, M.L. (1987a) Community organization from the point of view of habitat selectors. In: *Organization of Communities: Past and Present* (eds J.H.R. Gee and P.S. Giller), pp. 469–490. Blackwell Scientific Publications, Oxford.

Rosenzweig, M.L. (1987b) Habitat selection as a source of biological diversity. *Evolutionary Ecology* **1**, 315–330.

Rosenzweig, M.L. (1991) Habitat selection and population interactions. *American Naturalist* **137**, S5–S28.

Rosenzweig, M.L. and Abramsky, Z. (1986) Centrifugal community structure. *Oikos* **46**, 339–348.

Rosenzweig, M.L., Abramsky, Z. and Subach, A. (1997) Safety in numbers: sophisticated vigilance by Allenby's gerbil. *Proceedings of the National Academy of Sciences of the USA* **94**, 5713–5715.

Schaffer, W.M., Jensen, D.B., Hobbs, D.E., Gurevitch, J., Todd, J.R. and Schaffer, M.V. (1979) Competition, foraging energetics, and the cost of sociality in three species of bees. *Ecology* **60**, 976–987.

Schmidt, K.A. and Brown, J.S. (1996) Patch assessment in fox squirrels: The role of resource density, patch size and patch boundaries. *American Naturalist* **147**, 360–380.

Schmidt, K.A., Brown, J.S. and Morgan, R.A. (1998) Plant defenses as complementary resources: a test with squirrels. *Oikos* **81**, 1–13.

Schmitt, R.J. (1987) Indirect interactions between prey: apparent competition, predator aggregation, and habitat segregation. *Ecology* **68**, 1887–1897.

Shipley, L.A., Illius, A.W., Danell, K., Hobbs, N.T. and Spalinger, D.E. (1999) Predicting bite size selection of mammalian herbivores: a test of a general model of diet optimization. *Oikos* **84**, 55–68.

Sih, A. (1980) Optimal behavior: can foragers balance two conflicting demands? *Science* **210**, 1041–1043.

Sih, A. (1984) The behavioral response race between predator and prey. *American Naturalist* **123**, 143–150.

Stapanian, M.A. and Smith, C.C. (1984) Density-dependent survival of scatterhoarded nuts: an experimental approach. *Ecology* **65**, 1387–1396.

Steele, M.A. and Weigl, P.D. (1992) Energetics and patch use in the fox squirrel *Sciurus niger*: responses to variation in prey profitability and patch density. *American Midland Naturalist* **128**, 156–167.

Stoen, O.G. and Wegge, P. (1996) Prey selection and prey removal by tiger (*Panthera tigris*) during the dry season in lowland Nepal. *Mammalia* **60**, 363–373.

Thoday, J.M. and Gibson, J.B. (1962) Isolation by disruptive selection. *Nature* **193**, 1164–1166.

Thoday, J.M. and Gibson, J.B. (1970) The probability of isolation by disruptive selection. *American Naturalist* **104**, 219–230.

Tilman, D. (1982) *Resource Competition and Community Structure*. Princeton. Princeton University Press.

Travis, J.M.J. and Dytham, C. (1999) Habitat persistence, habitat availability and the evolution of dispersal. *Proceedings of the Royal Society of London B* **266**, 723–728.

Valone, T.J. and Brown, J.S. (1989) Measuring patch assessment abilities of desert granivores. *Ecology* **70**, 1800–1810.

Via, S. (1991) The genetic structure of host plant adaptation in a spatial patchwork: Demographic variability among reciprocally transplanted pea aphid clones. *Evolution* **45**, 827–852.

Vincent, T.L.S., Scheel, D., Brown, J.S. and Vincent, T.L. (1996) Trade-offs and coexistence in consumer-resource models: it all depends on what and where you eat. *American Naturalist* **148**, 1038–1058.

Werner, E.E. (1992) Individual behavior and higher-order species interactions. *American Naturalist* **140**, S5–S32.

Werner, E.E., Gilliam, J.F., Hall, D.J. and Mittlebach, G.G. (1983) An experimental test of the effects of predation risk on habitat use in fish. *Ecology* **64**, 1540–1548.

Whelan, C.J. (1989) Avian foliage structure preferences for foraging and the effect of prey biomass. *Animal Behavior* **38**, 839–846.

Whelan, C.J., Schmidt, K.A., Steele, B.B., Quinn, W.J. and Dilger, S. (1998) Are bird-consumed fruits complementary resources? *Oikos* **83**, 195–205.

Whelan, C.J. and Willson, M.F. (1994) Fruit choice in migratory North American birds: field and aviary experiments. *Oikos* **71**, 137–151.

Wijesinghe, D.K. and Hutchings, M.J. (1996) Consequences of patchy distribution of light for the growth of the clonal herb *Glechoma hederacea*. *Oikos* **77**, 137–145.

Wijesinghe, D.K. and Hutchings, M.J. (1997) The effects of spatial scale of environmental heterogeneity on the growth of a clonal plant: an experimental study with *Glechoma hederacea*. *Journal of Ecology* **85**, 17–28.

Wildhaber, M.L., Green, R.F. and Crowder, L.B. (1994) Bluegills continuously update patch giving-up times based on foraging experience. *Animal Behavior* **47**, 501–513.

Ziv, Y., Abramsky, Z., Kotler, B.P. and Subach, A. (1993) Interference competition and temporal partitioning in two gerbil species. *Oikos* **66**, 237–246.

Chapter 11

Habitat heterogeneity and the behavioural and population ecology of host–parasitoid interactions

H.C.J. Godfray, C.B. Müller and A.R. Kraaijeveld

Introduction

Parasitoids are insects whose larvae develop at the expense of other insects, their hosts. Like most true parasites, a single larval parasitoid requires only a single host on which to complete its development; but like predators, its feeding invariably leads to host death. There are three main reasons why parasitoids have attracted considerable study from ecologists. First, they are abundant members of virtually all terrestrial communities, both in terms of numbers of individuals and numbers of species. Actually we are remarkably ignorant about just how many species of parasitoids there are on earth (or even in relatively well studied areas such as the UK), but the current best guesses put the number somewhere around one million (Godfray 1994). Second, parasitoids are of major economic importance as biological control agents. Though success is far from guaranteed, in a number of cases the release of a parasitoid to control an exotic pest has been outstandingly successful with financial benefits measured in millions of dollars per annum (Mills and Getz 1996). Lastly, parasitoids have proved to be very valuable model systems for investigating more general questions concerning the evolutionary and population ecology of resource consumer systems. The trophic simplicity of the act of parasitoid oviposition — one attack leads to the conversion of one host individual into a parasitoid individual (solitary species) or parasitoid family (gregarious species) — makes this a particularly simple and tractable resource–consumer interaction for both experimental and theoretical study.

Any study of host–parasitoid interactions must take into account the huge heterogeneity of the environments they inhabit. Almost without exception, the hosts of parasitoids are distributed in a very patchy manner throughout the environment, and parasitoids must seek ways of locating and exploiting this highly dispersed resource. Habitat heterogeneity and its consequences is a *leitmotiv* running through nearly all studies of parasitoid ecology. In this chapter we shall divide parasitoid ecology into three broad areas — behavioural, population and community

NERC Centre for Population Biology, Department of Biology, Imperial College, Silwood Park, Ascot, Berkshire SL5 7PY, UK

ecology — and briefly explore how issues involving habitat heterogeneity have been treated in these separate subfields. Of the three areas, parasitoids have emerged as a major model system in behavioural ecology and population ecology, but to a much lesser degree in community ecology. In the final section we ask two questions. First, has an understanding of the behavioural ecology of parasitoids exploiting patchy environments assisted in understanding the population dynamics of the hosts and parasitoids involved? That there should be synergy between the two fields has been an article of faith of many ecologists, and was the theme underlying a British Ecological Society Symposium in 1984. Fifteen years later we ask whether this promise has been fulfilled. Second, we argue that parasitoids can be as useful a model system in community ecology as they have been in the other two subfields, and discuss the extent to which an understanding of the population dynamics of individual host–parasitoid interactions in heterogeneous environments may help explain the structure and functioning of larger assemblages and communities.

Behavioural ecology

Behavioural ecology means two things in parasitoid biology. First it refers to the investigation of the highly complex array of behaviours through which parasitoids locate and assess the quality of their hosts. Second it means behavioural ecology in the Krebs and Davies (1996) sense: the use of evolutionary thinking in understanding behavioural adaptations. One of the strengths of parasitoid behavioural ecology in its broadest sense is the interaction between the two wings of the subject.

Parasitoids are typically small insects (they actually include the smallest of all insects) that have to search in a highly complex environment for other small insects, their hosts. Moreover, their hosts are very heterogeneously distributed, and in the majority of cases they inhabit patches that are relatively short lived, necessitating the frequent discovery of new host concentrations by the parasitoid population. The most important means of locating hosts or environments where hosts are found is through chemical cues, volatile substances that can be used in locating suitable patches, and less volatile chemicals that can indicate to the parasitoid that hosts may be found in the near vicinity.

A major triumph of the first school of parasitoid behavioural ecology is the identification and study of a wide range of chemical cues used by parasitoids. In the absence of direct evidence of the presence of hosts, parasitoids will orientate towards habitats where hosts may be present. Some of the best evidence for habitat location comes from the parasitoids of *Drosophila* (Vet *et al.* 1984a,b). Different *Drosophila* species feed in a variety of habitats, for example sap fluxes, rotting fruit, decaying leaves or mushrooms, and often they have specific parasitoids that recognize and home in on volatiles produced in the appropriate habitat. Of course, cues emanating directly from the host are much more useful and a picture emerges of a state of chemical espionage or warfare between host and parasitoid, with intense selection pressure on the host to be chemically as invisible as possible, and with equivalently high selection pressure on the parasitoid to exploit all possible means of host location (Dicke and Sabelis 1988). It is relatively rare for an inactive host to produce substances that can be detected by a parasitoid, but hosts must both eat and excrete and it is often chemicals associated with mandibular and labial gland secretions, or with frass, that parasitoids have evolved to recognize (Nordlund *et al.* 1981). A relatively small number of parasitoids attack adult hosts, but some of these have evolved to locate host sex pheromones or, in the case of parasitoids attacking scolytid beetles, the aggregative pheromone used to obtain the critical mass of insects that is needed to overcome the defences of the host tree (Kennedy 1979). Sex pheromones are also used by parasitoids attacking colonial homopterans and by egg parasitoids, two situations where the presence of adults is likely to indicate the availability of hosts.

A common finding is that what has become known as the 'host–host plant' complex is more attractive to parasitoids than either the host or host plant in isolation (Turlings *et al.* 1990, 1991). This is perhaps to be expected as damaged plants mobilize a variety of wound and antipathogen compounds, and while hosts may be selected to be 'chemically silent', there will be no such constraint on the plant. Other parasitoids use volatiles emanating from host commensals such as the fungi that siricid sawflies use to digest wood (Madden 1968), again perhaps because selection for reduced volatile production is weaker or absent on host associates than on the hosts themselves. It is even possible that the plant may be actively selected to produce volatiles to attract parasitoids — on the principle that my enemy's enemy is my friend (Turlings *et al.* 1995).

A second major finding of this school of parasitoid behavioural ecology is of the importance of learning in host location (Lewis and Takasu 1990; Vet and Groenewold 1990; Vet *et al.* 1990; Turlings *et al.* 1992). Parasitoids seem to have a ranking of the cues they respond to, and the position of a specific cue can be changed by experience. Thus if a parasitoid encounters a host in an environment containing a specific volatile chemical, even a novel substance placed there by the experimenter, it will subsequently show strong orientation to that cue (Lewis and Takasu 1990). An interesting example of a related type of learning occurs just after the parasitoid emerges from its pupa or cocoon. Often, there will be remnants of the host, or material from the host environment, in the vicinity or adhering to the cocoon. Parasitoids can be seen after hatching antennating the cocoon and the surrounding area, and experiments have shown that volatile chemicals detected at this stage are then used in host location (Turlings *et al.* 1992; van Emden *et al.* 1996).

Though volatile chemicals are the most important cues used in host habitat and host detection, visual, auditory, tactile and thermal evidence have also been employed by different species of parasitoids, though they tend to be of more importance in short-range host detection rather than in coping with larger scale habitat heterogeneity (Vinson 1984). A possible and interesting exception is the long-range auditory cues used by certain tachinid flies that parasitize adult male crickets: the parasitoids use the male cricket's song in host location (Cade 1975).

The development of an evolutionary theory of the exploitation of patchy resources as part of optimal foraging theory in the 1970s had obvious interest for parasitoid biology. When should a parasitoid that has discovered a patch of hosts abandon it and begin to search for new hosts? In some cases, all hosts are easily accessible to the parasitoid which simply attacks all individuals and leaves. An example of this is the egg parasitoids that attack leafhopper eggs which are laid in a neat row on the plant and which ensure all eggs are attacked prior to dispersal (Sahad 1982; Cronin and Strong 1990a,b). But more often the hosts are harder to locate and as the parasitoid searches it experiences diminishing returns because the remaining hosts are more concealed and harder to find, or because the parasitoid wastes time re-encountering and rejecting previously parasitized individuals. This situation is not dissimilar to the classic case of a bird foraging in a patch that it depletes. For these situations, the optimal time to spend in the patch is given by Charnov's (1976) celebrated marginal value theorem: the parasitoid should leave when its marginal rate of gain of fitness drops below the best average that it could obtain in the environment (this average incorporating travel time between patches). As this average falls, because for example patches are widely dispersed and hence travel times are greater, the parasitoid should spend longer within the patch.

The qualitative predictions of patch use theory, that parasitoids should stay longer on good patches and when travel times are high, have been supported by experiments on several species of parasitoid (review in van Alphen and Vet 1986; Godfray 1994), but in no cases have there been good quantitative matches to theoretical predictions. There are several reasons for this. First, parasitoids live for a relatively short period of time and probably often only encounter a few patches in their lifetime. The marginal value theorem rests on renewal theory which assumes a very large number of patches are encountered. Second, classical patch use theory assumes the organism to be time-limited whereas some parasitoids may not be limited by time but by their egg supply. Third, parasitoids may use other information in addition to their marginal rate of host location in assessing whether it is worth remaining in the patch. Unlike conventional foragers, parasitoids re-encounter previously parasitized hosts which may influence their rate of gain of fitness, and may provide additional information about the course of patch exploitation. Lastly, many parasitoids will exploit patches in the company of conspecifics. While conventional foragers often face competition for food, an added complication in the parasitoid context is that superparasitism is possible which will have different consequences if the host was previously attacked by the same or a different individual.

The issue of whether parasitoids are time- or egg-limited has been addressed both experimentally and theoretically. For example, Driessen and Hemerik (1992) explored the behaviour of a *Drosophila* parasitoid as it foraged for hosts in a woodland environment. They attempted to measure initial egg loads, migration between patches, mortality and oviposition rates and incorporated the different measurements into a simulation to determine the distribution of egg loads at death for different individuals. They concluded that about 13% of wasps (range 3–32% in different simulations) used up all their eggs before death. Recently Rosenheim (1996), Sevenster *et al.* (1998) and Rosenheim (1999) have debated whether theoretical arguments can be used to assess the likelihood of egg or time limitation in parasitoid populations. Given a certain degree of stochasticity in the environment (which prevents a precise match of egg number with oviposition opportunities), the opposing selection forces acting on fecundity and somatic maintenance will lead to a low fraction of the population running out of eggs prior to death. This fraction is predicted to decrease even further when hosts are highly aggregated. However, even if egg exhaustion is rare, its possibility may still have a significant effect on life history evolution.

An important issue in foraging theory is the behavioural rules of thumb that foragers use to assess the right moment to leave one patch to begin to search for another. Waage (1979) was one of the first to suggest such a simple patch-leaving rule, based on experimental work with the ichneumonid wasp *Venturia canescens*, a parasitoid of stored product moths. He hypothesized that parasitoid females enter a patch with a certain motivation level, which gradually decreases over time. When this motivation level drops below a certain threshold, the parasitoid leaves the patch, but encounters with hosts result in an incremental increase in the motivation level. Such a rule leads to parasitoids spending more time on patches with high host densities (one of the predictions of patch use models), something that has been demonstrated experimentally for a range of parasitoid species (Driessen *et al.* 1995). When hosts are highly clumped, such a simple, mechanistic patch-leaving rule can indeed approach the optimal strategy closely (Iwasa *et al.* 1981). Recently, however, Driessen *et al.* (1995), working with the same parasitoid species as Waage, found that oviposition actually *decreases* the motivation level. Such a 'count-down' patch-leaving rule would be optimal in an environment where patches have uniform low host densities. A possible explanation for this discrepancy is that Waage and Driessen *et al.* were studying populations of *V. canescens* that had evolved to utilize hosts with different spatial distributions. Of course, in the most extreme case, if patches never contain more than one host, then the parasitoid should remain in the patch until it locates that host whereupon it should leave. Strand and Vinson (1982) suggested that this was the strategy of the braconid wasp, *Cardiochiles nigriceps*, a parasitoid of caterpillars of the tobacco budworm (*Heliothis virescens*) which are always solitary in nature.

Work with parasitoids has been in the vanguard of a new statistical approach for deducing patch-leaving rules. This approach treats the probability that a parasitoid leaves the patch as a problem in survival analysis (modelled using proportional hazard techniques). The wasp is assumed to enter the patch with a certain leaving tendency that may change over time and be influenced by events such as encounters with parasitized and unparasitized hosts, as well as by the time between such encounters. The analysis is a marked advance over previous *ad hoc* models as it allows different hypotheses to be tested by fully rigorous statistics. Haccou *et al.* (1991) and Hemerik *et al.* (1993) used these methods to study patch leaving rules in *Drosophila* parasitoids of the genus *Leptopilina*. They found that increasing the number and rate of encounters with unparasitized hosts strongly decreased the probability of patch leaving, and that encounters with previously parasitized hosts either had no effect on patch leaving or increased its probability. Further analyses may also need to consider the experience of the parasitoid before it enters the patch. Working with the same parasitoids, Visser *et al.* (1992) found that wasps spent longer in a patch if the previous patch it visited was of comparatively low quality. The presence of conspecifics and heterospecifics will also influence patch leaving decisions. Visser *et al.* (1990, 1992), working with *Leptopilina heterotoma*, showed that females spend more time on a patch after they have encountered other females in the environment (either on the patch itself or before entering the patch). Interestingly, females are more ready to superparasitize hosts in the presence of other females, presumably because the risks of self-superparasitism are lower. Recent work on several *Leptopilina* species has shown that females actively avoid patches with heterospecific competitors (Janssen *et al.* 1995a,b).

The main conceptual idea underlying studies of groups of foraging individuals is the ideal free distribution of Fretwell and Lucas (1970). A group of identical consumers are assumed to distribute themselves across patches that vary in resource quality, though are not depleted through foraging. At the ideal free distribution, no consumer can increase its fitness by moving to a different patch. A straight application of the ideal free distribution to parasitoid biology is not very helpful because the assumption of non-depletable patches will be seldom if ever true. Instead, a number of workers beginning with Cook and Hubbard (1977) and Comins and Hassell (1979) have modelled groups of foraging parasitoids by applying what might be called a time-varying ideal free distribution, in which parasitoids are assumed to distribute themselves across patches so that at any one time no individual can increase its fitness by moving. The models predict that all parasitoids will initially go to the best patch which they will exploit until the rate of discovery of new hosts equals that which could be expected on the second best patch, whereupon the parasitoid population divides itself between the two patches such that everyone has the same marginal rate of gain of fitness (Fig. 11.1). Exploitation continues with successively worse patches being included in the parasitoid's repertory. The picture is complicated by interference between adult searching parasitoids and by time costs for the recognition and rejection of previously parasitized hosts (both factors lead to poorer patches being attacked sooner).

Experiments to test these ideas tend to provide qualitative but not quantitative support for the models. Two of the model's main assumptions that are almost certainly normally violated in the field is that the parasitoid is omniscient and that travel time between patches is relatively negligible. The effect of relaxing these assumptions has been explored in a series of interesting simulation models by Bernstein *et al.* (1991). They considered a consumer foraging in a patchy environment that moved between patches when its resource intake rate fell below a threshold. This threshold was updated by a behavioural rule that took into account recent experience. Bernstein *et al.* (1991) found that this simple rule led to a good approx-

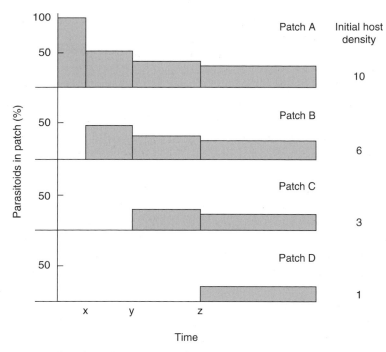

Figure 11.1 Predicted searching patterns of parasitoids in a patchy, depleting environment. Suppose the environment consists of four types of patches with initial host densities 10, 6, 3 and 1. Initially all parasitoids are selected to go to the high density patch which they deplete until its marginal rate of fitness returns equals that of the second best patch (time *x*). At this point the parasitoid population divides itself between the top two classes of patch, and depletion continues until the third best (time *y*) and worst (time *z*) patches are exploited.

imation to the time-varying ideal free distribution, as long as the environment did not deplete quickly, and as long as travel costs were not very high. This suggests that parasitoids may be quite efficient at exploiting local variations in host abundance, but may face problems when hosts vary on a wider spatial scale. Most of the models and experiments based on the ideal free distribution have been prompted by population dynamic questions, and at the end of this chapter we return to the interplay between behavioural and population ecology.

Population ecology

Population dynamicists are interested in parasitoids because of their importance in controlling and regulating host populations in the field; because of their value as biological control agents; and as model resource-consumer systems. Historically, applied entomologists studying parasitoids have been instrumental in developing some of the most fundamental concepts in the subject: for example, Howard and

Fiske's work on density dependence, and Nicholson and Bailey's introduction of difference equations for modelling coupled interactions between species.

The framework for modelling host–parasitoid interactions introduced by Nicholson and Bailey is still at the core of most present-day studies. They considered the population dynamic interaction between a host and its specialized parasitoid with discrete, synchronized generations. If parasitoids at time t (P_t) search randomly for their hosts so that the average number of times a particular host is encountered is linearly related to parasitoid density (with slope a), then the number of hosts in the next generation is simply the number in this generation multiplied by the fraction that escape parasitism (the zero term of a Poisson distribution with mean aP_t) and the fecundity of the survivors. The numbers of parasitoids in the next generation are simply the numbers of hosts this generation that succumb to parasitism multiplied by the number of parasitoids that develop per host. This model has a single outcome. Hosts and parasitoids show diverging oscillations of steadily increasing magnitude until one or both species becomes extinct. Essentially the parasitoids overexploit the host and then in the absence of oviposition sites their numbers crash; in the absence of parasitoids, host numbers recover and reach high levels, and this is followed by a further cycle of overexploitation and crash unless extinction intervenes. The simple Nicholson–Bailey model cannot explain persistent host–parasitoid interactions, at least within a single population.

The fact that what might be called the null model of host–parasitoid interactions was unstable, while such interactions patently occur and persist in the field, has lead to intensive effort to understand what processes made the latter possible. The original Nicholson–Bailey model did not incorporate a saturating functional response, but the insertion of a typical Type II functional response not only failed to stabilize the interaction, but increased its instability (Hassell and May 1973; Getz and Mills 1996). Adding direct host density dependence could stabilize the interaction, but only at levels where host plant resource depletion should be important and visible which was not the case for many persistent interactions (Beddington et al. 1978; Hassell 1978). Initially it was thought that mutual interference between searching parasitoids might be an important stabilizing process, but experimental studies suggested that in the field this would be insufficiently strong to make a difference (Hassell and Varley 1969; Hassell 1978). By the end of the 1970s, the prime candidate as the factor stabilizing host–parasitoid interactions was non-random search in a heterogeneous environment. Today, most workers in the field believe this to be correct, though our views about exactly what type of non-random search is responsible have changed substantially.

Rather than take a strictly historical viewpoint, it is useful to describe the consensus that had developed by the early 1990s about how heterogeneities in host and parasitoid distributions influence population persistence. There are three ways to break the cycle of over-exploitation and crash that renders the basic Nicholson–Bailey model unstable. The first two are to reduce the efficiency of high density populations of hosts or parasitoids by including direct density dependence acting on the host (by, for example, resource competition) or the parasitoid (by, for example, interference). The third way is to provide some sort of refuge for the host to allow it to ride out times of intense rates of parasitism. There are a number of possible ways that a refuge might arise. First, there may be an actual physical refuge. For example, a certain fraction of the host population may be unavailable to parasitoids because they are embedded too deeply in plant tissue, or have constructed too large a gall (Price and Clancy 1986). An interesting question is of course why don't all hosts protect themselves in this manner, but there may be trade-offs between concealment and other elements of fitness that prevent this from happening. Second, there may be a temporal refuge. Certain hosts may emerge before or after the parasitoid's flight period and so be protected from attack (Godfray *et al.* 1994). Third, there may be differences in the ability of hosts to protect themselves against parasitoids. Many insect hosts have a cellular immune response (encapsulation) that protects them from parasitoid and pathogen attack, though parasitoids have found numerous ways of circumventing this. There is evidence of genetic variability in host resistance, and were a certain fraction of hosts protected in this way then they could constitute a stabilizing refuge. Again, a problem is to explain why all hosts do not evolve to be resistant to parasitoids and the existence of trade-offs may be crucial here as well (Kraaijeveld and Godfray 1997). A series of recent models that have explicitly modelled both genetic and population dynamics have shown that persistent cycles in both gene frequencies and population densities can lead to persistent interactions, though this is unlikely to be a widespread and important stabilizing process (Doebeli 1997; Sasaki and Godfray 1999). Fourth, if one moves a little from the strict Nicholson–Bailey framework with discrete, synchronized generations, and allows the overlap of generations, then long-lived life history stages that are immune to parasitoid attack can act as a refuge for hosts from high parasitoid attack. The long-lived stage might be an immune adult (most parasitoids attack larvae or nymphs) or diapausing eggs or pupae (Murdoch *et al.* 1987; Ringel *et al.* 1998).

The last type of refuge is spatial and involves habitat heterogeneity. Suppose that the host population is distributed in a patchy manner across the environment, as it nearly always will be. Were certain patches not to be visited by parasitoids, or to be visited infrequently, then these would constitute a refuge in which the hosts could weather periods of high parasitoid density. A natural reason why parasitoids might visit certain patches over others is if they contained high densities of hosts. This was modelled by Hassell and May (1973, 1974) who assumed that parasitoids distributed themselves (once) across the patches at the beginning of the season in proportion to some function of host density. The resulting model was stable, so long as density-dependent aggregation was strong enough.

Some years later, Murdoch and Stewart-Oaten (1989) produced a continuous-time model of a host–parasitoid interaction in a patchy environment in which non-random parasitoid search was modelled as the covariance of the distribution of hosts and parasitoids across patches. In this model, density-dependent aggregation was destabilizing. Exactly how appropriate this model is in describing host–parasitoid interactions has been much debated (Godfray and Pacala 1992; Ives 1992; Murdoch *et al.* 1992), but it was important in highlighting the significance of the assumption of only a single episode of parasitoid dispersal in the Hassell and May models. In the latter there is a negative correlation between the number of unparasitized hosts at the beginning and end of the season; in other words initially high density patches are so over-exploited that by the end of the season they contain fewer unparasitized hosts than low density patches. If this occurs, the question is why don't parasitoids disperse from these patches to find other less-exploited patches. But if parasitoids do disperse, then the low density patches are no longer refuges and the system destabilizes. This was illustrated by Rohani *et al.* (1994) who showed how the stabilizing effect of density-dependent aggregation was lost as more and more within-generation dispersal was allowed. The Murdoch and Stewart–Oaten model effectively assumed instantaneous dispersal and hence density-dependent aggregation had no stabilizing effect. In conclusion, density-dependent aggregation can contribute to stability, but it is very unlikely to be the critical factor it was thought to be until recently.

There may be other reasons apart from host density that cause parasitoids to aggregate to certain patches over others, and as long as this leads to certain hosts enjoying a statistical refuge from parasitism then this can be important for stabilizing the interaction. The simplest conceptual way to visualize this is to assume that the probability of escaping parasitism is not the zero term of a Poisson distribution (as in the original Nicholson–Bailey model), but of a more clumped distribution where some hosts receive more than average and colleagues fewer than average attacks (Chesson and Murdoch 1986). This was first done by May (1978; see also Griffiths 1969) using the negative binomial distribution which has a 'clumping parameter', k, smaller values of which indicate greater contagion. Replacing the Poisson distribution by the negative binomial in the Nicholson–Bailey model results in a stable interaction, providing clumping is strong enough ($k < 1$).

All the types of refuge discussed so far are stabilizing because they cause some hosts to be more and others less susceptible to parasitism. This suggests that a general principle may be involved, and this was discovered by Pacala *et al.* (1990; see also Hassell *et al.* 1991; Pacala and Hassell 1991). To a good approximation, and sometimes exactly, a system will be stable provided the coefficient of variation of the risk of parasitism experienced by individual hosts is greater than 1: the $CV^2 > 1$ rule. The rule tends to work well for models that are stabilized purely through host refuges, in the broad sense, but less well when other stabilizing factors such as host density dependence or interference are present. For hosts distributed in patchy environments, it is possible to decompose the variance in risk into components due to host-density independent and host-density dependent components, and then to estimate these components from field data. The major assumptions here are that parasitoid searching within a patch can be described by the Nicholson–Bailey model, and that there is a single episode of parasitoid dispersal at the beginning of the season (see above). Even bearing these caveats in mind, it is still interesting that in the majority of cases, the greatest contribution to stability came through density-independent rather than density-dependent aggregation.

Our discussion so far of population dynamics has considered only local populations where individuals are completely mixed at least once each generation. In other words the system has no spatial memory: a knowledge of the spatial distribution of individuals this generation tells us nothing about the state of the system next generation. In the last few years there has been considerable interest in spatial population dynamics throughout population ecology including parasitoid biology, and we discuss a few of the major findings here that are most relevant to the theme of this chapter.

The simplest way to model a spatial system of interconnected populations is as a loosely connected metapopulation that recruits immigrants from and contributes emigrants to a pool of migratory individuals. As was first discussed by Nicholson and later shown formally by Reeve (1988), an ensemble of connected populations can persist even though any constituent population, if isolated from the group, is unstable. Populations that drop to very low levels or go extinct as a result of their local dynamics can be rescued by immigration from other populations. For this to work, the rates of migration must be sufficiently high that colonization of empty patches exceeds their creation through extinctions, but not so high that the populations all fluctuate in phase as a single system. Habitat heterogeneity has a critical role here in decoupling the dynamics of loosely connected populations.

A more sophisticated way to model linked populations is within an explicitly spatial framework where each population has its own x and y coordinates. Either space can be considered continuous and migration modelled by a redistribution kernel, or discrete populations can be modelled on a lattice. As before, a system that is unstable at any one site can be globally persistent because of the spatial rescue effect. However, with explicit space, patterns can be generated by the interaction between the two species. Hassell *et al.* (1991) working with a coupled map lattice found that for certain parameters spiral waves of hosts and parasitoids moved through space. Essentially these are caused by a travelling wave of parasitoids that feed off and then destroy the host population. For other parameters the coherence of the waves breaks down giving rise to patterns that appear random and which because the system is deterministic have been called spatial chaos. Similar patterns have been found in spatial host–parasitoid systems modelled in other ways, as well as in other spatial resource-consumer systems (Gurney *et al.* 1998; Wilson *et al.* 1998). Indeed, this behaviour is a general property of a broad class of spatial excitable media (Fig. 11.2).

The beautiful spiral patterns that appear on computer screens arise in systems where there is no spatial heterogeneity. We do not yet know in any general sense whether such patterns are robust to the type of spatial heterogeneity that will inescapably occur in any real field site. In fact, until recently there were virtually no examples of host–parasitoid systems in the field that had been studied within a spatial context, though the last few years have seen a number of exciting new

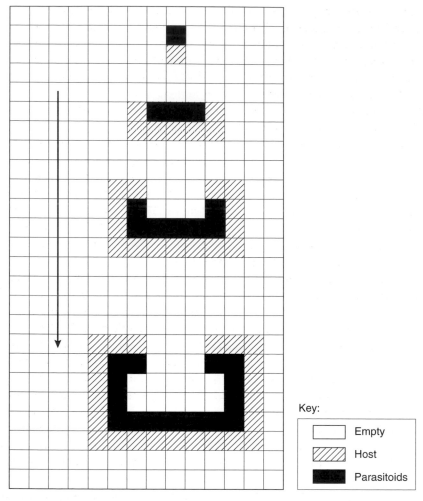

Key:

☐	Empty
▨	Host
■	Parasitoids

Figure 11.2 Schematic demonstration of the production of spatial host–parasitoid spiral waves. Suppose the environment can be represented by a square array of patches which may be occupied by hosts, by hosts and parasitoids or empty. The host population is 'chased' through space by the parasitoid population. Host populations expand in all directions where parasitoids are absent, and it is this expansion at the end of the front that causes the wave to bend and the characteristic spiral pattern to emerge. These waves can appear in any excitable media that has an 'excited' and a 'refractory' state (equivalent to locations being occupied by hosts and by hosts with parasitoids).

studies. The spatially most extensive has been Roland and Taylor's (1997) work on *Malacosoma disstria* in Canada. *M. disstria*, the forest tent caterpillar, is an outbreak pest of aspen parkland in central Canada, where it is attacked by four main species of parasitoid. A large grid of 127 sampling points within a 25×25 km study area was set up and the density of larvae and their percentage parasitism estimated at each. The pattern of parasitism was linked to the local extent of woodland, as estimated from satellite imagery. The authors found that the four species of parasitoids responded differently to both host density and to local woodland fragmentation. Moreover, parasitoid body size explained some of the differences. Large species showed positive density-dependent parasitism and their distribution was correlated with large scale measures of forest fragmentation. The smallest species showed negative density-dependent parasitism with its distribution correlated with small scale measures of forest fragmentation.

The results reported so far describe the dynamics of a single generation of moths and parasitoids, but this scale of study offers the prospect of testing some of the theory described above. One interesting result to emerge already is the spatial density dependence shown by the larger parasitoid. While it was argued above that local spatial density dependence may actually tend to destabilize an interaction if parasitoids visit many patches within a generation, large scale density of the type reported here is likely to be a strongly regulating factor as the distances involved would preclude many episodes of redistribution.

Despite their importance in current population dynamic thinking, there are rather few well-documented examples of metapopulations in the field. Perhaps the best entomological example is the population of Glanville Fritillaries (*Melitaea cinxia*) in the Åland archipelago of western Finland (Hanski *et al.* 1995). An ensemble of small populations show frequent local extinctions, but also local recolonizations. Extinctions have been shown to be correlated with population size, and most recently with the presence of a locally specific parasitoid *Cotesia melitaearum*. Cases of parasitoid, but not host, extinction, and parasitoid colonization of host patches have also been documented (Lei and Hanski 1997). The picture is complicated by the presence of other parasitoids in the system including another primary parasitoid that does best in patches where *C. melitaearum* is absent, and a polyphagous hyperparasitoid which shows a strong density-dependent response to *C. melitaearum* cocoons.

Finally, Harrison (1997) and colleagues have discovered an interesting spatial pattern involving *Orgyia vetusta*, a moth that attacks *Lupinus* sp. along the north Californian littoral. While lupin is relatively widespread in this region, persistent outbreaks of the herbivore only occur on certain patches of its host plant and these may persist for many years without spreading. Experiments have excluded differences in host plant quality leading Brodmann *et al.* (1997) to ask whether parasitoids, dispersing from the outbreak area, might cause a halo of intense parasitism ('a ring of death') in the surrounding bushes that prevents the spread of an outbreak. Experimental studies involving placing larvae in the field at varying distances from the outbreak show that indeed parasitism is highest in the areas surrounding the outbreak. However, questions remain: in particular why should parasitoids disperse away from outbreaks and so presumably lower their reproductive fitness, and why do not parasitoids reduce population densities within the outbreak? Interference between searching parasitoids is a possible answer, and one amenable to experimental investigation.

Community ecology

While parasitoids have furnished excellent model systems for studying problems in behavioural and population ecology, they have been less influential in studies of community ecology. Here we discuss only two aspects of parasitoid community ecology and how they are influenced by patchiness and habitat heterogeneity. For review and discussion of other issues in parasitoid community ecology see Godfray (1994), Hawkins (1994) and Hawkins and Sheehan (1994).

Consider first three-species communities, either two hosts attacked by a common parasitoid or two parasitoids attacking the same host. In both cases the simplest theoretical models would predict that the system would collapse into a simple two species system (Holt and Lawton 1993). The reasons for these results are related: consider a host–parasitoid system at equilibrium. By definition, both the host and the parasitoid are exactly replacing themselves. Now add another species, either a host or a parasitoid. If it is a host it will either be worse than the resident host at surviving in the face of the current equilibrium number of parasitoids, in which case it won't invade, or be better in which case it will invade. For simple host–parasitoid models, invasion will be followed by the establishment of a new equilibrium with a higher density of parasitoids (to counter the greater intrinsic growth rate of the invading host) which will lead to the exclusion of the original resident host. Similarly with an invading parasitoid, either it will not be able to maintain itself on the current equilibrium numbers of hosts and so it will not invade, or else it will be able to invade and so lead to a new equilibrium with lower densities of host and the consequent extinction of the original parasitoid. While we have explained these results in a host–parasitoid context, they are naturally corollaries of Gause's principle that nonidentical competitors cannot coexist on a single resource.

These results may be significant in understanding community structure. One species of host that feeds on a different resource from a second which it may never encounter in the field, can still be responsible for the exclusion of the latter because of indirect interactions mediated via natural enemies. This type of indirect effect has been called apparent competition because many of its community consequences are similar to those of direct competition (Holt 1977). Because of apparent competition, parasitoids may appear to be specialists, not because of any physiological or ecological constraint, but purely as a consequence of population dynamics, what Holt and Lawton (1993) have called dynamic monophagy. Similarly, hosts may evolve to avoid the depredations of parasitoids attacking other hosts, what Jeffries and Lawton (1984) called evolution into enemy-free space.

Dynamic monophagy is not the only outcome when one parasitoid attacks two hosts, otherwise the complexity of many natural communities would be hard to explain (Holt and Lawton 1993). However, for two hosts to persist, both must have mechanisms that allow them to increase in density when rare. This is a general criterion for the persistence of two competitors and much work on ecological coexistence can be applied to parasitoids. Briefly, mechanisms that allow coexistence include:

1 refuges from parasitoid attack for both species;
2 switching, in which the parasitoid concentrates its attack on the more common species of host (Murdoch 1969);
3 environmental variation that affects both host species in different manners so that each host has higher growth rates under different conditions (see Chesson and Huntly 1989 for discussion in another context, this possibility has received little study in the parasitoid literature); and
4 local instability but persistence in a metapopulation (Hassell *et al.* 1994; Comins and Hassell 1996).

Similarly for two parasitoids to coexist on the same species, interspecific competition must be less than intraspecific competition so that either parasitoid species has an advantage when rare. One way that this can be obtained is by assuming that both species have a clumped distribution across host patches, but that the two distributions are not or are only weakly correlated (in other words the host experiences independent heterogeneity of risk of attack by the two parasitoids). Such a mechanism underlies (often implicitly) the predicted coexistence of parasitoids in a number of models (Hassell and Varley 1969; May and Hassell 1981; Hogarth and Diamond 1984; Kakehashi *et al.* 1984; Godfray and Waage 1991). Interspecific competition is also less than intraspecific competition if two parasitoids have subtly different niches, attacking the host in different microhabitats (Kakehashi *et al.* 1984).

A different though related mechanism that allows coexistence is called the competition–colonization trade-off. If the host has a patchy population structure with new patches continually being colonized, then a species of parasitoid that is an inferior competitor but a superior colonizer can persist by virtue of its ability to find patches not yet discovered by the better competitor. It is interesting that soon after the competition–colonization trade-off was being introduced into mainstream population ecology (Hutchinson 1951; Skellam 1951), applied entomologists were independently developing the same ideas to explain patterns in parasitoid communities (Pschorn-Walcher and Zwölfer 1968; Zwölfer 1971). Finally, two parasitoids may coexist in a variable environment if each species is favoured under certain conditions. The variability may be caused by environmental variation, or in certain circumstances by fluctuations in host population densities that arise as part of the dynamics of the host–parasitoid interaction (Armstrong and McGehee 1980; Briggs 1993; Briggs *et al.* 1993).

Linking subfields

We conclude this chapter by commenting briefly on how studies of heterogeneity can link the three subfields we have discussed. Specifically, we ask whether consideration of the behavioural ecology of parasitoids searching in a patchy environment can assist in understanding population processes, and how might we begin to understand the population dynamics of complex communities of hosts and parasitoids.

As mentioned at the beginning of the chapter, it has long been a hope, in some quarters an article of faith, that behavioural ecological and evolutionary thinking will make a major contribution to understanding population dynamics. At one level this is a truism: the value of any host or parasitoid demographic parameter will be strongly influenced by natural selection acting on the organism, and hence at least in theory its value could be predicted by evolutionary arguments. But in practice this will be difficult, and population ecologists will make faster progress just by going out and measuring the relevant parameters. A more stringent test of the value of evolutionary thinking is thus whether it provides new information that could not be obtained, or could not be obtained easily, by simple measurements.

The foraging strategies of parasitoids searching in a patchy environment have been closely studied by behavioural ecologists, but what impact has this had on population dynamics? Rereading the classic models of parasitoid searching strategies from a contemporary viewpoint, they all seem to predict that parasitoids will act to reduce heterogeneity of risk across hosts, and hence that adaptive foraging will tend to be destabilizing. Only if there is interference between parasitoids or some other factors operating will parasitoid foraging make a modest contribution towards stability, yet it was exactly these aspects of the models that were highlighted at the time because of the prevailing view (from models without within-generation redistribution) that density-dependent aggregation by parasitoids was stabilizing. Today, it appears that the most important heterogeneities influencing host–parasitoid dynamics act at spatial scales equal to or greater than the average lifetime ambit of a parasitoid, and this makes the application of the simple models of foraging theory far harder. Perhaps a more successful application of behavioural ecology to population dynamics has involved the question of how parasitoids utilize hosts of different size (small hosts may be ignored, used as food rather than as an oviposition site, or used to produce male eggs). Evolutionary thinking has informed the construction of age-structured population models (Murdoch *et al.* 1997), and has also helped interpret the comparative dynamics of different parasitoid species (Luck 1990).

We believe that one of the greatest current challenges in host–parasitoid biology is to understand the make-up and composition of complex communities composed of many host and parasitoid species. Only a few studies have attempted to model communities of greater than three or four species (Hochberg and Hawkins 1992; Wilson *et al.* 1996) and these have shown how difficult it is to make predictions in the face of rapid parameter proliferation. It is almost certainly impossible to build inductive models of large communities, starting from scratch. Two strategies may allow progress to be made. First, models can be constructed that are tailored to real communities. Here, parasitoid workers are at an advantage: the relative simplicity of the host–parasitoid trophic link makes it possible to construct relatively large, quantitative food webs describing the interactions between the parasitoids attacking a guild of hosts (e.g. Memmott *et al.* 1994; Müller *et al.* 1999; Rott

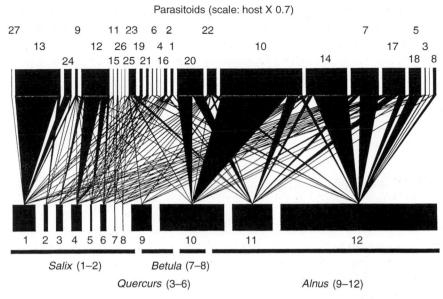

Parasitoids (scale: host X 0.7)

Figure 11.3 An example of a quantitative parasitoid web (from Rott and Godfray 2000). The web describes a community of 12 species of leaf-mining moths in the genus *Phyllonorycter* (Gracillariidae) attacking four species of tree at a single site in Silwood Park, southern England. The lowest range of bars depicts the relative abundance of the four trees (in biomass of leaves), the numbers after the tree genera referring to the identities of the leaf miners attacking the plant (all miners are monophagous). The 12 species of miners are shown in the middle range of bars and the 26 species of parasitoid in the top range, the links showing quantitative rearing records. The web summarizes four generations of wasps (over 2 years), and the estimated cumulative number of mines in the site was 12.1 million.

and Godfray 2000; Fig. 11.3). Typically such webs consist of a series of hosts that do not interact directly because they feed on different host plants, linked dynamically to different degrees by their parasitoids and possible hyperparasitoids. Comparison of such webs may reveal patterns in community structuring amenable to theoretical exploration and experimentation. Second, evolutionary arguments may be used to predict the diversity of parasitoid strategies in natural communities. This approach was pioneered by Price (1974) 25 years ago who discovered systematic patterns in parasitoid fecundity and the type of host attacked, but has received far less recent attention than it deserves. Parasitoid natural histories are not distributed randomly in trait space, and an exciting challenge for theoreticians is to try to predict the patterns that are seen in nature, and to deduce their consequences for community persistence and structure.

References

Briggs, C.J. (1993) Competition among parasitoids on a stage-structured host and its effect on host suppression. *American Naturalist* **141**, 372–393.

Briggs, C.J., Nisbet, R.M. and Murdoch, W.W. (1993) Coexistence of competing parasitoid species on a host with a variable life cycle. *Theoretical Population Biology* **44**, 341–373.

Brodmann, P.A., Wilcox, C.V. and Harrison, S. (1997) Mobile parasitoids may restrict the spatial spread of an insect outbreak. *Journal of Animal Ecology* **66**, 65–72.

Cade, W. (1975) Acoustically orienting parasitoids: fly phonotaxis to cricket song. *Science* **190**, 1312–1313.

Charnov, E.L. (1976) Optimal foraging: the marginal value theorem. *Theoretical Population Biology* **9**, 129–136.

Chesson, P.L. and Huntly, N. (1989) Short-term instabilities and long-term community dynamics. *Trends in Ecology and Evolution* **4**, 293–298.

Chesson, P.L. and Murdoch, W.W. (1986) Aggregation of risk: relationships among host–parasitoid models. *American Naturalist* **127**, 696–715.

Comins, H.N. and Hassell, M.P. (1979) The dynamics of optimally foraging predators and parasites. *Journal of Animal Ecology* **48**, 335–351.

Comins, H.N. and Hassell, M.P. (1996) Persistence of multispecies host–parasitoid interactions in spatially distributed models with local dispersal. *Journal of Theoretical Biology* **183**, 19–28.

Cook, R.M. and Hubbard, S.R. (1977) Adaptive searching strategies in insect parasitoids. *Journal of Animal Ecology* **46**, 115–125.

Cronin, J.T. and Strong, D.R. (1990a) Density-independent parasitism among host patches by *Anagrus delicatus* (Hymenoptera: Mymaridae): experimental manipulation of hosts. *Journal of Animal Ecology* **59**, 1019–1026.

Cronin, J.T. and Strong, D.R. (1990b) Biology of *Anagrus delicatus* (Hymenoptera: Mymaridae), an egg parasitoid of *Prokelesia marginata* (Hymenoptera: Delphacidae). *Annals of the Entomological Society of America* **83**, 846–854.

Dicke, M. and Sabelis, M.W. (1988) Infochemical terminology: based on cost–benefit analysis rather than origin of compounds. *Functional Ecology* **2**, 131–139.

Doebeli, M. (1997) Genetic variation and the persistence of predator–prey interactions in the Nicholson–Bailey model. *Journal of Theoretical Biology* **188**, 109–120.

Driessen, G., Bernstein, C., van Alphen, J.J.M. and Kacelnik, A. (1995) A count-down mechanism for host search in the parasitoid *Venturia canescens*. *Journal of Animal Ecology* **64**, 117–125.

Driessen, G. and Hemerik, L. (1992) The time and egg budget of *Leptopilina clavipes*, a parasitoid of larval *Drosophila*. *Ecological Entomology* **17**, 17–27.

Fretwell, S.D. and Lucas, H.J. (1970) On territorial behavior and other factors influencing habitat distribution in birds. *Acta Biotheoretica* **19**, 16–36.

Getz, W.M. and Mills, N.J. (1996) Host–parasitoid coexistence and egg-limited encounter rates. *American Naturalist* **148**, 333–347.

Godfray, H.C.J. (1994) *Parasitoids, Behavioral and Evolutionary Ecology*. Princeton University Press, Princeton, New Jersey.

Godfray, H.C.J. and Pacala, S.W. (1992) Aggregation and the population dynamics of parasitoids and predators. *American Naturalist* **140**, 30–40.

Godfray, H.C.J. and Waage, J.K. (1991) Predictive modelling in biological control: the mango mealy bug (*Rastrococcus invadens*) and its parasitoids. *Journal of Applied Ecology* **28**, 434–453.

Godfray, H.C.J., Hassell, M.P. and Holt, R.D. (1994) The population dynamic consequences of phenological asynchrony between parasitoids and their hosts. *Journal of Animal Ecology* **63**, 1–10.

Griffiths, K.J. (1969) The importance of coincidence in the functional and numerical responses of two parasites of the European pine sawfly, *Neodiprion sertifer*. *Canadian Entomologist* **101**, 673–713.

Gurney, W.S.C., Veitch, A.R., Cruickshank, I. and McGeachin, G. (1998) Circles and spirals: population persistence in a spatially explicit predator–prey model. *Ecology* **79**, 2516–2530.

Haccou, P., de Vlas, S.J., van Alphen, J.J.M. and Visser, M.E. (1991) Information processing by foragers: effects of intra-patch experience on the leaving tendency of *Leptopilina heterotoma*. *Journal of Animal Ecology* **60**, 93–106.

Hanski, I., Pakkala, T., Kuussaari, M. and Lei, G.C. (1995) Metapopulation persistence of an endangered butterfly in a fragmented landscape. *Oikos* **72**, 21–28.

Harrison, S. (1997) Persistent, localized outbreaks in the western tussock moth *Orgyia vetusta*: the roles of resource quality, predation and poor dispersal. *Ecological Entomology* **22**, 158–166.

Hassell, M.P. (1978) *The Dynamics of Arthropod Predator–Prey Systems*. Princeton University Press, Princeton, New Jersey.

Hassell, M.P., Comins, H.N. and May, R.M. (1994) Species coexistence and self-organizing spatial dynamics. *Nature* **370**, 290–292.

Hassell, M.P. and May, R.M. (1973) Stability in insect host–parasite models. *Journal of Animal Ecology* **42**, 693–726.

Hassell, M.P. and May, R.M. (1974) Aggregation of predators and insect parasites and its effect on stability. *Journal of Animal Ecology* **43**, 567–594.

Hassell, M.P., Pacala, S.W., May, R.M. and Chesson, P.L. (1991) The persistence of host–parasitoid associations in patchy environments. I. A general criterion. *American Naturalist* **138**, 568–583.

Hassell, M.P. and Varley, G.C. (1969) New inductive population model for insect parasites and its bearing on biological control. *Nature* **223**, 1133–1137.

Hawkins, B.A. (1994) *Pattern and Process in Host–Parasitoid Interactions*. Cambridge University Press, Cambridge.

Hawkins, B.A. and Sheehan, W. (1994) *Parasitoid Community Ecology*. Oxford University Press, Oxford.

Hemerik, L., Driessen, G. and Haccou, P. (1993) Effects of intra-patch experiences on patch time, search time and searching efficiency of the parasitoid *Leptopilina clavipes*. *Journal of Animal Ecology* **62**, 33–44.

Hochberg, M.E. and Hawkins, B.A. (1992) Refuges as a predictor of parasitoid diversity. *Science* **255**, 973–976.

Hogarth, W.L. and Diamond, P. (1984) Interspecific competition in larvae between entomophagous parasitoids. *American Naturalist* **124**, 552–560.

Holt, R.D. (1977) Predation, apparent competition and the structure of prey communities. *Theoretical Population Biology* **12**, 197–229.

Holt, R.D. and Lawton, J.H. (1993) Apparent competition and enemy-free space in insect host–parasitoid communities. *American Naturalist* **142**, 623–645.

Hutchinson, G.E. (1951) Copepodology for the ornithologist. *Ecology* **32**, 571–577.

Ives, A.R. (1992) Density-dependent and density-independent parasitoid aggregation in model host–parasitoid systems. *American Naturalist* **140**, 912–937.

Iwasa, Y., Higashi, M. and Yamamura, N. (1981) Prey distribution as a factor determining the choice of optimal foraging strategy. *American Naturalist* **117**, 710–723.

Janssen, A., van Alphen, J.J.M., Sabelis, M.W. and Bakker, K. (1995a) Odour-mediated avoidance of competition in *Drosophila* parasitoids: the ghost of competition past. *Oikos* **73**, 356–366.

Janssen, A., van Alphen, J.J.M., Sabelis, M.W. and Bakker, K. (1995b) Specificity of odour-mediated avoidance of competition in *Drosophila* parasitoids. *Behavioural Ecology and Sociobiology* **36**, 229–235.

Jeffries, M.J. and Lawton, J.H. (1984) Enemy free space and the structure of ecological communities. *Biological Journal of the Linnaean Society* **23**, 269–286.

Kakehashi, M., Suzuki, Y. and Iwasa, Y. (1984) Niche overlap of parasitoids in host–parasitoid systems: its consequence to single versus multiple introduction controversy in biological control. *Journal of Applied Ecology* **21**, 115–131.

Kennedy, B.H. (1979) The effect of multilure on parasites of the European elm bark beetle, *Scolytus multistriatus. Bulletin of the Entomological Society of America* **25**, 116–118.

Kraaijeveld, A.R. and Godfray, H.C.J. (1997) Trade off between parasitoid resistance and larval competitive ability in *Drosophila melanogaster*. *Nature* **389**, 278–280.

Krebs, J.R. and Davies, N.B. (1996) *An Introduction to Behavioural Ecology*. Blackwell Scientific Publications, Oxford.

Lei, G.C. and Hanski, I. (1997) Metapopulation structure of *Cotesia melitaearum*, a specialist parasitoid of the butterfly *Melitaea cinxia*. *Oikos* **78**, 91–100.

Lewis, W.J. and Takasu, K. (1990) Use of learned odours by a parasitic wasp in accordance with host and food needs. *Nature* **348**, 635–636.

Luck, R.F. (1990) Evaluation of natural enemies for biological control: a behavioral approach. *Trends in Ecology and Evolution* **5**, 196–199.

Madden, J.L. (1968) Behavioural responses of parasites to the symbiotic fungus associated with *Sirex noctilio* F. *Nature* **218**, 189–190.

May, R.M. (1978) Host–parasitoid systems in patchy environments: a phenomenological model. *Journal of Animal Ecology* **47**, 833–843.

May, R.M. and Hassell, M.P. (1981) The dynamics of multiparasitoid–host interactions. *American Naturalist* **117**, 234–261.

Memmott, J., Godfray, H.C.J. and Gauld, I.D. (1994) The structure of a tropical host–parasitoid community. *Journal of Animal Ecology* **63**, 521–540.

Mills, N.J. and Getz, W.M. (1996) Modelling the biological control of insect pests: a review of host–parasitoid models. *Ecological Modelling* **92**, 121–143.

Müller, C.B., Adriaanse, I.C.T., Belshaw, R. and Godfray, H.C.J. (1999) The structure of an aphid–parasitoid community. *Journal of Animal Ecology* **68**, 346–370.

Murdoch, W.W. (1969) Switching in general predators: experiments on predator specificity and stability of prey populations. *Ecological Monographs* **39**, 335–354.

Murdoch, W.W. and Stewart-Oaten, A. (1989) Aggregation by parasitoids and predators: effects on equilibrium and stability. *American Naturalist* **133**, 288–310.

Murdoch, W.W., Nisbet, R.M., Blythe, S.P., Gurney, W.S.C. and Reeve, J.D. (1987) An invulnerable age class and stability in delay-differential parasitoid-host models. *American Naturalist* **129**, 263–282.

Murdoch, W.W., Briggs, C.J., Nisbet, R.M., Gurney, W.S.C. and Stewart-Oaten, A. (1992) Aggregation and stability in metapopulation models. *American Naturalist* **140**, 41–58.

Murdoch, W.W., Briggs, C.J. and Nisbet, R.M. (1997) Dynamical effects of host size- and parasitoid state-dependent attacks by parasitoids. *Journal of Animal Ecology* **66**, 542–556.

Nordlund, D.A., Jones, R.L. and Lewis, W.J. (1981) *Semiochemicals, Their Role in Pest Control.* John Wiley, New York.

Pacala, S.W., Hassell, M.P. and May, R.M. (1990) Host–parasitoid associations in patchy environments. *Nature* **344**, 150–153.

Pacala, S.W. and Hassell, M.P. (1991) The persistence of host–parasitoid associations in patchy environments. II. Evaluation of field data. *American Naturalist* **138**, 584–605.

Price, P.W. (1974) Strategies for egg production. *Evolution* **28**, 76–84.

Price, P.W. and Clancy, K.M. (1986) Interactions among three trophic levels: gall size and parasitoid attack. *Ecology* **67**, 1593–1600.

Pschorn-Walcher, H. and Zwölfer, H. (1968) Konkurrenzerscheinungen in Parasitenkomplexen als Problem der biologischen Schädlingsbekampfung. *Anzeiger für Schädlingskunde* **41**, 71–76.

Reeve, J.D. (1988) Environmental variability, migration, and persistence in host–parasitoid systems. *American Naturalist* **132**, 810–836.

Ringel, M.S., Rees, M. and Godfray, H.C.J. (1998) The evolution of diapause in a coupled host–parasitoid system. *Journal of Theoretical Biology* **194**, 195–204.

Rohani, P., Godfray, H.C.J. and Hassell, M.P. (1994) Aggregation and the dynamics of host–parasitoid systems—a discrete-generation model with within-generation redistribution. *American Naturalist* **144**, 491–509.

Roland, J. and Taylor, P.D. (1997) Insect parasitoid species respond to forest structure at different spatial scales. *Nature* **386**, 710–713.

Rosenheim, J.A. (1996) An evolutionary argument for egg limitation. *Evolution* **50**, 2089–2094.

Rosenheim, J.A. (1999) The relative contributions of time and eggs to the cost of reproduction. *Evolution* **53**, 376–385.

Rott, A. and Godfray, H.C.J. (2000) The structure of a leafminer-parasitoid community. *Journal of Animal Ecology* **69**, 274–289.

Sahad, K.A. (1982) Biology and morphology of *Gonatocerus* sp. (Hymenoptera, Mymaridae), an egg parasitoid of the green rice leafhopper *Nephottetix cincticeps* Uhler (Homoptera, Deltocephalidae). I. Biology. *Kontyû* **50**, 467–476.

Sasaki, A. and Godfray, H.C.J. (1999) A model for the coevolution of resistance and virulence in coupled host–parasitoid interactions. *Proceedings of the Royal Society London B* **266**, 455–463.

Sevenster, J.G., Ellers, J. and Driessen, G. (1998) An evolutionary argument for time limitation. *Evolution* **52**, 1241–1244.

Skellam, J.G. (1951) Random dispersal in theoretical populations. *Biometrika* **38**, 196–218.

Strand, M.R. and Vinson, S.B. (1982) Behavioural

response of the parasitoid, *Cardiochiles nigriceps* to a kairomone. *Entomologia Experimentalis et Applicata* **31**, 308–315.

Turlings, T.C.J., Tumlinson, J.H. and Lewis, W.J. (1990) Exploitation of herbivore-induced plant odours by host seeking parasitic wasps. *Science* **250**, 1251–1253.

Turlings, T.C.J., Tumlinson, J.H., Eller, F.J. and Lewis, W.J. (1991) Larval-damaged plants: source of volatile synomones that guide the parasitoid *Cotesia marginiventris* to the microhabitat of its host. *Entomologia Experimentalis et Applicata* **58**, 75–82.

Turlings, T.C.J., Wäckers, F.L., Vet, L.E.M., Lewis, W.J. and Tumlinson, J.H. (1992) Learning of host-location cues by hymenopterous parasitoids. In: *Insect Learning: Ecological and Evolutionary Perspectives* (eds A.C. Lewis and D.R. Papaj), pp. 51–78. Chapman and Hall, New York.

Turlings, T.C.J., Loughrin, J.H., McCall, P.J., Rose, U.S.R., Lewis, W.J. and Tumlinson, J.H. (1995) How caterpillar-damaged plants protect themselves by attracting parasitic wasps. *Proceedings of the National Academy of Sciences USA* **92**, 4169–4174.

van Alphen, J.J.M. and Vet, L.E.M. (1986) An evolutionary approach to host finding and selection. In: *Insect Parasitoids* (eds J. K. Waage and D. Greathead), pp. 23–61. Academic Press, London.

van Emden, H.F., Sponagl, B., Baker, T., Ganguly, S. and Douloumpaka, S. (1996) Hopkins' 'host selection principle', another nail in its coffin. *Physiological Entomology* **21**, 325–328.

Vet, L.E.M. and Groenewold, A.W. (1990) Semiochemicals and learning in parasitoids. *Journal of Chemical Ecology* **16**, 3119–3135.

Vet, L.E.M., Janse, C.J., van Achterberg, C. and van Alphen, J.J.M. (1984a) Microhabitat location and niche segregation in two sibling species of drosophilid parasitoids: *Asobara tabida* (Nees) and *A. rufescens* (Foerster) (Braconidae: Alysiinae). *Oecologia* **61**, 182–188.

Vet, L.E.M., Meyer, M., Bakker, K. and van Alphen, J.J.M. (1984b) Intra- and interspecific host discrimination in *Asobara* (Hymenoptera) larval endoparasitoids of Drosophilidae: comparison between closely related and less closely related species. *Animal Behaviour* **32**, 871–874.

Vet, L.E.M., Lewis, W.J., Papaj, D.R. and van Lenteren, J.C. (1990) A variable response model for parasitoid foraging behavior. *Journal of Insect Behaviour* **3**, 471–491.

Vinson, S.B. (1984) How parasitoids locate their hosts: a case of insect espionage. In: *Insect Communication* (ed. T. Lewis), pp. 325–348. Academic Press, London.

Visser, M.E., van Alphen, J.J.M. and Nell, H.W. (1990) Adaptive superparasitism and patch time allocation in solitary parasitoids: the influence of the number of parasitoids depleting the patch. *Behaviour* **114**, 21–36.

Visser, M.E., van Alphen, J.J.M. and Nell, H.W. (1992) Adaptive superparasitism and patch time allocation in solitary parasitoids: the influence of pre-patch experience. *Behavioural Ecology and Sociobiology* **31**, 163–171.

Waage, J.K. (1979) Foraging for patchily distributed hosts by the parasitoid *Nemeritis canescens*. *Journal of Animal Ecology* **48**, 353–371.

Wilson, H.B., Hassell, M.P. and Godfray, H.C.J. (1996) Host–parasitoid food webs: dynamics, persistence, and invasion. *American Naturalist* **148**, 787–806.

Wilson, H.B., Godfray, H.C.J., Hassell, M.P. and Pacala, S.W. (1998) Deterministic and stochastic host–parasitoid dynamics of in spatially-extended systems. In: *Modelling Spatiotemporal Dynamics in Ecology* (eds J. Bascompte and R.V. Sole), pp. 63–82. Springer-Verlag, Berlin.

Zwölfer, H. (1971) The structure and effect of parasite complexes attacking phytophagous host insects. *Proceedings Advanced Study Institute: Dynamics and Numbers of Populations (Oosterbeek, 1970)*, 405–418.

Chapter 12

The effects of heterogeneity on dispersal and colonization in plants

M. Rees[1], M. Mangel[2], L. Turnbull[1], A. Sheppard[3] and D. Briese[3]

Introduction

Heterogeneity, in its various guises, is a ubiquitous feature of ecological systems. To see this, one need only look at any published experimental study, where complex statistical analyses are used to disentangle the signal, generated by the experimental treatments, from the universally present heterogeneity or 'noise'. This noise is often seen as problematic, complicating analyses and making inference difficult. However, ecologists have recently started viewing the noise as an intrinsic property of the system rather than a complication to be ignored or averaged over. For example, Rees *et al.* (1996) found that changes in population size in a guild of winter annuals were influenced by previous population sizes, and the spatial distribution of the populations. Thus, heterogeneity in the spatial distribution of competitors influenced the observed population sizes in this guild.

Studies of heterogeneity fall into two broad categories: the first asks what are the potential effects of heterogeneity, while the second attempts to evaluate the actual impact of heterogeneity. In this chapter, we illustrate both these approaches. We start with general definitions of dispersal and heterogeneity, and then look at how dispersal can generate a heterogeneous distribution of competitors. The consequences of this heterogeneity for community structure are then explored. We then turn our attention to how heterogeneity can influence dispersal. We illustrate this by analysing how heterogeneity influences the reproductive decisions in monocarpic plants and how this in turn results in temporal dispersal. In each case we show how the interplay between the development of simple general models and data leads to the development of new, more complex models, and greater understanding of natural systems.

[1] *Imperial College, Silwood Park, Ascot, Berks, SL5 7PY, UK;* [2] *Department of Environmental Studies, University of California, Santa Cruz, CA 95064, USA and T.H. Huxley School of Environment, Earth Sciences and Engineering, Imperial College, London, SW7 2AZ, UK;* [3] *CSIRO Division of Entomology, GPO Box 1700, CRC Weed Management Systems, Canberra, ACT 2601, Australia*

What is dispersal?

We define dispersal to be any demographic process that results in members of a cohort experiencing different environments. Dispersal is one process that exposes organisms to heterogeneity, see below, and can occur in both time and space (Harper 1977). In addition to the usual processes that result in dispersal, namely seed movement, dormancy and clonal growth, this definition includes repeated reproduction and delayed reproduction in monocarpic plants. Both the latter processes result in members of a cohort experiencing different environments, and so can be considered as types of temporal dispersal. For example, reproduction in a single cohort of *Carlina vulgaris*, a monocarpic perennial, at an unproductive site in the Netherlands was spread over at least a 7-year period (Klinkhamer *et al.* 1996). Because each of these processes performs a similar population dynamic function we would expect trade-offs to exist between the different types of dispersal (Venable and Brown 1988; Rees 1994) and this is indeed the case (Rees 1993; Rees 1996).

What is heterogeneity?

Heterogeneity is defined as any factor that can cause variation in individual demographic rates, and may have a biotic or an abiotic origin. Clearly, this is a very broad definition including such factors as genetic differences, variation caused by the predators or pathogens, and spatial and temporal variation in the abiotic and biotic environment. This definition is similar to that of Milne (1991), see Wiens, this volume. However, Milne (1991) suggests that heterogeneity is the complexity caused by the spatial distribution of constraints and organisms' responses to them, whereas we prefer to focus on the demography. In this way, the magnitude of different forms of heterogeneity, and their potential effects, can be quantified. Different types of heterogeneity can often be arranged in a hierarchical way, see also chapters by Wiens and Pickett. For example, within an area, all habitats might experience common yearly influences caused by the weather. Then there might be habitat-specific heterogeneity caused by local conditions unique to a given habitat. In addition to this, individuals within a habitat might experience individual-specific heterogeneity related to their position or genetic makeup, and there might be non-specific heterogeneity, associated with chance events that affect individuals in a way unrelated to their identity. This simple hierarchical organization of heterogeneity will be discussed further, and methods for quantifying the different components presented in later sections.

Evolution and ecological consequences of seed dispersal

There is a large and growing literature on the evolution and ecological implications of spatial seed dispersal (Hamilton and May 1977; Comins *et al.* 1980; Bulmer 1984; Levin *et al.* 1984; Comins and Noble 1985; Pacala and Silander 1985; Pacala 1986a,b; Klinkhamer *et al.* 1987b; Pacala 1987; Venable and Brown 1988; Venable and Brown 1993; Tilman 1994; Dytham 1995; Watkinson and Sutherland 1995; Tilman et al. 1997; Pacala and Rees 1998). In order to understand the role of spatial dispersal several studies have used a phenomenological approach, replacing explicit models of dispersal with aggregated probability distributions, such as the negative binomial distribution (Atkinson and Shorrocks 1981; Ives and May 1985). A partial justification for this approach is given by simulation studies which show aggregated distributions can be generated by local dispersal (Pacala and Silander 1985). However, local dispersal will generally result in positive covariance between parents and offspring, a complication we ignore in the model discussed below. The use of aggregated distributions has the advantage of analytical tractability but, as in any abstraction of this type, there is a potential difficulty with linking the aggregated distribution with a biological generative mechanism (May 1978).

Here we illustrate some of the potential difficulties of using this approach. Consider two species of annual plant competing for microsites, the first is the competitive dominant and excludes the second from any microsites where they both occur. Both species have identical dispersal mechanisms and the resulting distribution of seeds can be described by independent negative binomial distributions with a common aggregation parameter, κ. As κ becomes smaller so the distribution becomes more aggregated. The dynamics of the first species can be described using a simple equation of the form

$$p_1(t+1) = 1 - \left(1 + \frac{F_1 p_1(t)}{\kappa}\right)^{-\kappa},$$
(12.1)

where $p_1(t)$ is the proportion of sites occupied by species 1 in year t and F_1 is the per microsite fecundity of species 1. Providing $F_1 > 1$ this model has a single, globally stable equilibrium, p_1^*; this follows from the fact that $dp_1(t+1)/dp_1(t)$ is strictly positive.

The dynamics of the second species can be described by

$$p_2(t+1) = (1 - p_1(t))\left(1 - \left(1 + \frac{F_2 p_2(t)}{\kappa}\right)^{-\kappa}\right)$$
(12.2)

where the subscript 2 refers to the second species. The equation has two parts: the first is the free space left by the first species; the second the fraction of sites colonized by species 2. For coexistence, species 2 must be able to invade once species 1 has reached equilibrium, p_1^*. This leads to the condition:

$$F_2\left(1 - p_1^*\right) > 1.$$
(12.3)

We note two things from this:

1 Invasion of species 2 is independent of its spatial distribution, and hence dispersal characteristics.

2 Invasion, and hence coexistence, becomes easier as F_1 and κ become smaller, as decreases in these parameters lead to lower p_1^*.

The first of these results has been noted by several authors (Atkinson and

Shorrocks 1981; Ives and May 1985; Silvertown and Smith 1989; Rees and Long 1992) and is intuitively surprising, as one would expect dispersal to influence the success of an invading species. Further insight into this model can be obtained by considering the special case $\kappa = 1$, which gives $p_1^* = 1 - 1/F_1$ and leads to the simple invasion condition,

$$F_2 > F_1. \tag{12.4}$$

From which we conclude that for values of $\kappa < 1$ the critical value of F_2 is less than F_1, (Fig. 12.1). How can an inferior competitor, which loses in competition whenever it co-occurs with species 1, and has identical patterns of dispersal invade species 1 when it has a lower fecundity? To understand this apparent paradox, consider the invasion condition, equation (12.3). This states that the probability species 2 finds an empty site, $1 - p_1^*$, multiplied by species 2's fecundity, F_2, must be greater than unity. This implicitly assumes that species 2 samples the habitat at random, which in turn implies that species 2 has global dispersal. The apparent paradox is therefore generated by unwittingly making species 2 a better disperser than species 1. In fact, the model has become an example of a competition–colonization trade-off (Skellam 1951; Levins and Culver 1971; Tilman 1994). Note this is not an explicit assumption of the model but an implicit assumption of the invasion analysis. The difficulties in interpreting these models have been discussed by several authors (Green 1986; Chesson 1991; Remer and Heard 1998).

There are several examples where the outcome of competition, between species with finite dispersal, is not correctly predicted by a simple invasion analysis, which

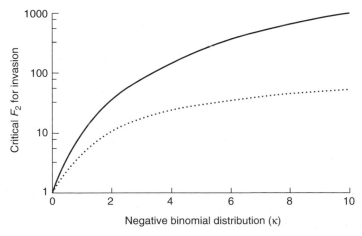

Figure 12.1 The critical value of F_2 required for invasion as a function of the negative binomial parameter, κ, of species 1, the competetive dominant. At values of $\kappa < 1$ invasion by an inferior competitor with fecundity less than the superior competitor is possible. Solid curve, $F_1 = 10$, dotted curve, $F_1 = 5$.

assumes that species sample the habitat at random, see Pacala (1986b). To predict the outcome of competition correctly we need to understand the dynamics of spatial pattern formation. The use of moment-closure methods permits this to be done (Pacala and Levin 1997). Moment closure is a mathematical technique used to derive equations for the spatial moments of a system. In biological terms, these are equations for the average density of competitors, their variances and covariances (Pacala and Levin 1997; Bolker and Pacala 1999). The invasion criterion for interspecific competition models takes the following form (Bolker and Pacala 1999),

$$\text{Spatial invasion rate} = \text{growth rate at low densities} - \text{intraspecific clustering} \\ + \text{interspecific clustering} + \text{spatial segregation.} \quad (12.5)$$

The first term gives the non-spatial invasion rate (i.e. equation [12.3] in the previous model), the second term is negative, because when a species forms clusters intraspecific competition will operate, even at low densities, so slowing the rate of invasion. The last two terms represent the effects of interspecific clustering and segregation; both of these reduce interspecific competition so increasing the invasion rate (Bolker and Pacala 1999).

In these models, long-range dispersal of the inferior competitor does not always promote coexistence. If growth is sufficient to allow gaps to be fully exploited then long-range dispersal aids coexistence, whereas short-range dispersal makes coexistence more difficult. However, if local population growth is necessary for exploiting gaps then short-range dispersal of the inferior competitor may favour coexistence. In this case, short-range dispersal allows rapid population growth in gaps, resulting in a greater number of seeds dispersing although the proportion dispersing is smaller (Pacala and Levin 1997; Bolker and Pacala 1999).

Clearly, when using simple phenomenological models, great care is required in linking biological mechanisms with the simple descriptive functions used in model formulation. Invasion analyses of such models also need to be interpreted with caution.

Much of the recent work on dispersal has focused on the competition–colonization trade-off, and how systems where diversity is maintained by this mechanism respond to habitat destruction (Dytham 1994; Tilman et al. 1994; Moilanen and Hanski 1995). This simple model is particularly attractive because the coexistence mechanism operates in a homogeneous world, so there is no need to invoke environmental heterogeneity, and each species is characterized by just three parameters; one for dispersal, one for mortality and a position in the competitive hierarchy. Coexistence occurs because the good competitors are also the worst colonizers and so, although superior competitors always exclude inferior competitors when they co-occur, the superior competitors fail to colonize all sites and so leave space to be exploited by the inferior competitors. If this mechanism allowed coexistence in natural systems then community ecology would be much simpler as one would no longer need to worry about complex, high dimensional niche axes. Several field systems appear to conform to this simple model (Tilman 1994; Rees 1995; Rees *et al.* 1996; Turnbull *et al.*, in press, b).

Tests of the competition–colonization mechanism of coexistence are possible using seed sowing experiments (Tilman 1994; Pacala and Rees 1998; Turnbull *et al.*, in press, a). By sowing saturating densities of all species, one removes all colonization limitation from the system and diversity should collapse leaving the best competitor growing in isolation. Turnbull *et al.* (in press, b) tested this idea using a guild of co-occurring annual species growing in limestone grassland in south Wales. Previous studies of similar annual plant guilds suggested that small-seeded species produced more seeds per plant but were inferior competitors (Rees 1995; Rees *et al.* 1996); this generates a competition–colonization trade-off, which could be important in maintaining diversity. Turnbull *et al.* (in press, b) showed that large-seeded species do indeed produce fewer seeds per plant and so have lower colonization potential than small-seeded species (Fig. 12.2). In an experiment where seeds of all species were added to quadrats in equal numbers, the large-seeded species were found to dominate the community when sowing density was high (Fig. 12.3). This is consistent with the idea that large-seed size confers a competitive advantage, as assumed by the competition–colonization model. However, even at the highest sowing density the inferior competitors were not excluded from the system suggesting the presence of species-specific niches.

How does the presence of species-specific niches affect the predictions of the simple competition–colonization model? This question was addressed by Pacala and Rees (1998) who modified the standard model (Levins and Culver 1971) to allow finite rates of competitive exclusions: the standard model assumes instanta-

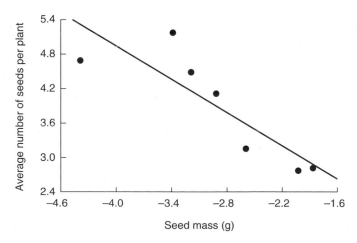

Figure 12.2 Relationship between average seed output per plant for seven co-occurring annual plants species and average seed mass; both axes are log scales. The fitted line is $y = 1.10 – 0.96x$, $r^2 = 0.74$. The species are, in order of decreasing seed mass, *Aphanes microcarpa*, *Myosotis ramosissima*, *Veronica arvensis*, *Arenaria serpyllifolia*, *Cerastium diffusum*, *Cerastium globmeratum* and *Saxifraga tridactylites*. Redrawn from Turnbull *et al.* (1999b).

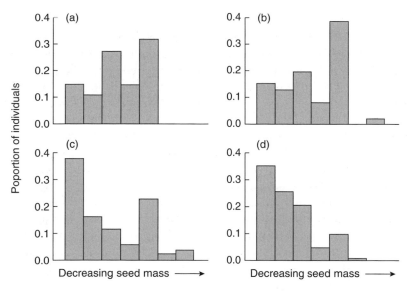

Figure 12.3 Impact of increased sowing density (equal numbers of all species) on community composition in a guild of co-occurring annual species. (a) No seeds sown, (b) 10 seeds sown, (c) 50 seeds sown and (d) 200 seeds sown. At low sowing densities there is no relationship between seed weight, a surrogate for competitive ability and composition, whereas at high sowing density the large-seeded species dominate the community. Redrawn for Turnbull *et al.* (1999b).

neous exclusion of competitively inferior species. By allowing finite rates of competitive exclusion, Pacala and Rees (1998) incorporate a successional niche whereby early successional species, which are poor competitors, can dominate recently disturbed sites although they are ultimately excluded by the late successional species. In this model, adding saturating densities of seeds to all sites does not cause a collapse of diversity because the early successional species is able to reproduce in recently disturbed sites, regardless of the abundance of the late successional, superior competitor.

Pacala and Rees (1998) suggest that by combining seed sowing and competitor removal experiments, the relative importance of the competition–colonization and niche mechanisms can be assessed. In addition, they argue that in many systems where disturbances are of small spatial extent, the niche mechanism will be more important than competition–colonization. This is because late successional, superior competitors eventually occupy almost all sites. Disturbed areas therefore always contain propagules of the superior competitor, making it impossible for the early successional, poor competitor to persist. The seed sowing experiments of Crawley *et al.* (unpublished) have shown that when saturating densities of all species are sown in a mesic grassland it is the early successional forbs that increase in abundance, not the late successional species, as predicted by the competition–colonization model. This suggests that early successional species are more recruitment limited than late successional species, making coexistence via the competition–colonization trade-off impossible.

The distinction between the niche and competition–colonization hypotheses is important, in part because the two hypotheses have strikingly different management implications. In systems where diversity is maintained by the competition–colonization mechanism even small amounts of habitat destruction lead to extinction of late-successional species (Nee and May 1992). The reason is that rare, late-successional species are near the brink of extinction because of their poor colonizing ability. Any habitat destruction causes them to waste seeds that disperse into unsuitable areas. This small loss of colonizing ability pushes rare late-successional species to extinction. In contrast, because species can coexist even when all sites are colonized when there is a successional niche, small amounts of habitat loss may not result in any extinctions. However, when there is recruitment limitation, resulting in failure to colonize some sites, habitat destruction can result in extinction of either early or late successional species depending on which is more recruitment limited (Pacala and Rees 1998).

Spatial seed dispersal can evolve in response to a range of different types of environmental heterogeneity (Venable and Brown 1993). Not all types of heterogeneity favour the evolution of dispersal, for example, if the habitat consists of a fixed mosaic of habitat patches then no dispersal from the parental site is the evolutionarily stable strategy (ESS) (Hastings 1983). This occurs because dispersal results in net movement of seeds from good patches to bad ones so lowering fitness and selecting against dispersal. Dispersal can evolve as a bet hedging strategy only when there is global temporal variation in reproductive success. Here dispersal reduces the variance in reproductive success, which increases the geometric mean fitness (Levin *et al.* 1984). In a temporally stable environment, dispersal can evolve to reduce the effects of local crowding, and this requires spatial variation in the quality of the environment but no global temporal variation (Venable and Brown 1993). Finally, if there is genetic structure, dispersal can evolve as a way of reducing competition between relatives (Hamilton and May 1977; Comins *et al.* 1980). When there is temporal variation in the environment, either local or global, the pattern of variation, whether it shows positive or negative covariation, also becomes important and can lead to the evolution of multiple dispersal types (Ludwig and Levin 1991). Olivieri *et al.* (1995) put these ideas in a successional framework and show that there are conflicting selection pressures within and between populations (demes). Within population selection favours low dispersal, while between population selection favours migrants, and this can lead to the coexistence of genotypes with different dispersal rates.

How will habitat destruction influence the evolution of dispersal and population persistence? Increasing urbanization and conversion of natural habitats to agriculture creates areas which are permanently unsuitable for population growth. This situation is analogous to the colonization of oceanic islands, where each population is surrounded by large areas of unsuitable habitat. This can lead to rapid evolution resulting in reduced dispersal ability (Cody and Overton 1996). This in turn makes the populations more isolated, resulting in habitat specialization, and reducing the likelihood of metapopulation persistence. This topic is explored further by Dytham (this volume).

Evolution and ecological consequences of delayed and repeated reproduction

Both delayed reproduction in monocarpic plants and repeated reproduction in iteroparous species result in offspring experiencing different environments and so both processes can be considered forms of dispersal. The ages at flowering of individuals of *Onopordum illyricum* and *Carlina vulgaris* are shown in Fig. 12.4; clearly there is considerable variation in the age at which individuals flower resulting in individuals within a cohort, experiencing very different environments. These data pose two evolutionary questions: (i) Why do plants wait to flower, and a corollary of this, can we predict the optimal age at flowering; and (ii) Why is there such a large spread in the timing of reproduction? This section will be devoted to monocarpic plants simply because the fitness consequences of delayed reproduction are simpler to quantify in species that reproduce only once. In species with multiple reproductive episodes there are additional problems associated with quantifying the costs of reproduction and possible effects of mast seeding. Having said this,

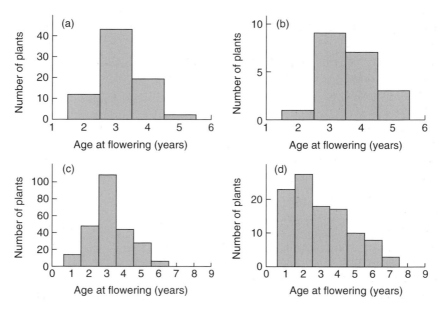

Figure 12.4 Age at flowering in monocarpic perennials. In all cases there is considerable spread in the timing of the reproduction. (a) and (b) *Onopordum illyricum* at two sites in the south of France ((a) Viols and (b) La Crau; see Rees *et al.* (1999)). (c) and (d) *Carlina vulgaris* at two sites. (c) *Salix* vegetation in the Meijendal dune system, the Netherlands (Klinkhamer *et al.* 1996) and (d) chalk grassland at Castle Hill National Nature Reserve, near Brighton. Data kindly supplied by Peter Grubb.

many of the ideas developed for monocarpic plants are directly applicable to iteroparous species, see Charnov (1993).

The main deterministic selective forces influencing delayed reproduction in monocarpic plants are:
1 Increased mortality as a result of delaying reproduction;
2 Increased reproduction, as a result of growth.

These selective forces underpin the simple growth models used to predict the evolutionarily stable size and age at reproduction; this approach has an extensive pedigree in the animal literature (Roff 1984; Roff 1986; Roff 1992; Stearns 1992; Charnov 1993; Mangel 1996). We now outline these simple models, and assess their ability to predict patterns of flowering observed in the field.

Simple models ignoring heterogeneity

We assume that size on a log scale, $L(t)$, at time t can be described by a 3-parameter von Bertalanffy equation:

$$L(t) = L_\infty (1 - \exp(-k(t - t_0))), \tag{12.6}$$

where L_∞ is the maximum possible size, k is a rate parameter and t_0 is the hypothetical (negative) age at which size would be zero. An important assumption implicit in this equation is that all individuals grow along a deterministic trajectory so that age and size are interchangeable. This could only be true if there is no heterogeneity in the environment. We assume a constant rate of mortality m, so the probability an individual survives to age t is $\exp(-mt)$. The probability a seed becomes an established plant is p. Finally, we assume that the seed production of an individual of size $L(t)$, is an exponential function of plant size, namely:

$$seeds = \exp(A + BL(t)), \tag{12.7}$$

where A and B are allometric parameters relating log-seed set to log-size (van der Meijden and van de Waals-Kooi 1979; Samson and Werk 1986; Rees and Crawley 1989). Combining these formulae, we obtain an expression for the expected number of offspring produced by an individual that reproduces at age t,

$$R_0 = p\exp(-mt)\exp[A + BL_\infty (1 - \exp(-k(t - t_0)))]. \tag{12.8}$$

R_0 consists of two components: the first is the probability an individual survives to age t, and the second is the seed production of a plant of size $L(t)$ We can calculate the ESS flowering time, $\tilde{t}$, by solving $\partial R_0 / \partial t = 0$ which gives:

$$\tilde{t} = \frac{\ln\left(\dfrac{BkL_\infty}{m}\right)}{k} + t_0, \tag{12.9}$$

and substituting this into equation (12.6) we find the ESS flowering size,

$$\tilde{L} = \text{Asymptotic size} - \text{mortality term}$$

$$= L_\infty - \frac{m}{Bk}. \tag{12.10}$$

Evolutionary stability occurs if $\partial R_0/\partial^2$ evaluated at $\hat{t}$ is negative; which is always true in this case. In calculating the ESS in this way we are assuming that density dependence acts at the seedling stage (Charnov 1993; Kawecki 1993), which is a reasonable assumption for many plant species. As expected the ESS flowering size increases with the asymptotic length, and decreases with increasing mortality. The mortality term is, however, offset by the growth rate, k, and the slope of the fecundity relationship, B. In these simple models all forms of heterogeneity are assumed to be unimportant. We now ask, how well do these models describe actual flowering strategies?

Case studies ignoring heterogeneity
Rees *et al.* (1999) used the simple growth models, described above, to explore size-dependent flowering in *Onopordum illyricum* growing in the south of France. Using long-term demographic data, from two field sites, we parameterized the simple growth models and predicted the average size at flowering should be $\approx 1000\,cm^2$. At both sites, the prediction error was greater than 50%; the plants actually flowered at sizes approximately double the model predictions. Clearly, this approach, which ignores all forms of heterogeneity, does not accurately describe the flowering strategies of plants in the field.

Oenothera glazioviana is a monocarpic plant that often occurs in sand dune areas, and its demography has been extensively studied by Kachi and Hirose (Kachi and Hirose 1983; Kachi 1983; Kachi and Hirose 1985). For an *Oenothera* rosette relative growth rate (RGR), is given by:

$$\text{RGR} = \frac{L(t+1)-L(t)}{\Delta t} = -0.65L(t)+0.96+\varepsilon_{i,t}, \tag{12.11}$$

where $L(t)$ is log rosette diameter in May, $\Delta t = 1$ year, and $\varepsilon_{i,t}$ is a standard normal deviate with mean zero and standard deviation, $\sigma_{i,t}=0.45$; this represents the residual scatter about the regression line. The probability of flowering is given by:

$$p(\text{flowering}) = 1.1L(t)-2.29, \tag{12.12}$$

and the survivorship of vegetative rosettes by:

$$p(\text{rosette survival}) = 0.17L(t)+0.36, \tag{12.13}$$

where the probability of rosette survival has an upper asymptote of 0.7. The number of seeds produced as a function of rosette diameter is given by:

$$\text{seeds} = \exp(2.22L(t)+1.035). \tag{12.14}$$

Note, the parameters in Kachi and Hirose (1985) are given for log to the base 10 and we have converted to natural logarithms by dividing by $\ln(10)$. The number of recruits was independent of seed production suggesting density dependence acts on seedlings (Fig. 12.5). With these assumptions, we can implement the flow chart given in Kachi and Hirose (1985), their Fig. 1, using an individual-based approach. We used output from the simulation model to parameterize a von

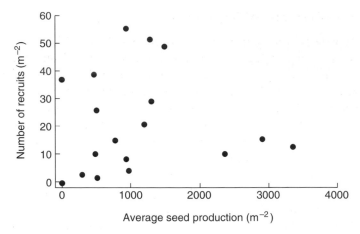

Figure 12.5 Relationship between the number of new *Oenothera* recruits and the previous years' seed production (data from Kachi (1983)). There is no significant relationship between seed production and subsequent recruitment (linear regression $F_{1,16}=0.001$, $p>0.1$).

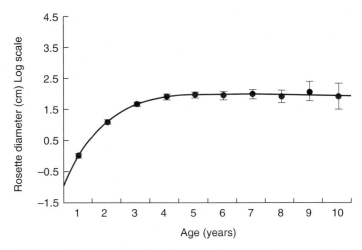

Figure 12.6 Relationship between predicted rosette diameter and plant age. The solid circles are means of data generated from an individual-based simulation, using the parameterized growth equation of Kachi and Hirose (1985), see text for details. The fitted line is a 3-parameter von Bertalanffy equation. Estimated parameters $L_\infty=2.17$, $k=0.72$ and $t_0=1.05$. $r^2=0.53$. The vertical bars are 2 standard errors.

Bertalanffy growth model (equation 12.6), see Fig. 12.6. As in the Kachi and Hirose (1985) simulation, plant size reached an asymptote of ≈ 9 cm rosette diameter. We also used the simulation model to estimate the probability of a plant surviving to age t, this probability is accurately described ($r^2=0.99$, $n=9$) by:

$$p(\text{survival to age } t) = 0.57\exp(-0.54t). \qquad (12.15)$$

Substituting the parameter estimates into equations 12.9 and 12.10 we obtain, $\tilde{t} = 3.6$ years and $\tilde{L} = 1.84$ (log scale) which corresponds to a diameter of 6.3 cm. Average size at flowering is ≈ 18 cm (Kachi and Hirose 1983), with a median flowering size of 14 cm. The ESS prediction is considerably lower than the observed values, and indeed is smaller than the smallest flowering size ever observed. *O. glazioviana* takes between 3 and 6 years to flower in rough agreement with the theoretical prediction (Hirose and Kachi 1982). Clearly, as in *Onopordum*, the simple growth model approach has failed to capture the important evolutionary trade-offs that determine flowering size in *Oenothera*.

We also applied this approach to the long-term data set on *Carlina vulgaris* collected by Peter Grubb (Rees *et al.* in preparation). In this study, the fate of over 1000 individuals was followed over an 18-year period. All individuals were sized and whether they flowered or died recorded. Using these data, we parameterized the simple growth and survival models described above. The fitted relationships and parameter estimates are given in Fig. 12.7. We do not have good data on reproductive allocation and so have assumed constant proportional reproductive allocation; this corresponds to $B=1$ in equation (12.7). This provides a good description of reproductive allocation in several monocarpic species (Reinartz 1984a; de Jong *et al.* 1989; Klinkhamer and de Jong 1993). Using these parameter estimates, we predicted that plants should flower at 7 mm, whereas the average size of flowering plants was 49.5 mm (Fig. 12.8). The model predictions are smaller than the smallest size ever observed flowering in an 18-year study (Rees *et al.* in preparation). As in the other species this simple approach, which ignores all forms of heterogeneity, considerably underestimates the size at flowering. The main

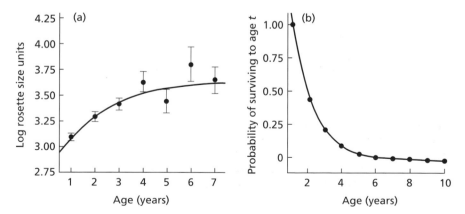

Figure 12.7 Age-specific demography of *Carlina vulgaris*. (a) Rosette diameter as a function of plant age. The line is the fitted von Bertalanffy growth curve; the vertical bars are standard error. Parameter estimates $L_\infty = 3.68$, $k = 0.45$ and $t_0 = -3$. (b) The probability a rosette survives to age t; the line is the fitted function $p\exp(-mt)$ where t is plant age. Parameter estimates $p = 2.18$ and $m = 0.74$. Data kindly supplied by Peter Grubb.

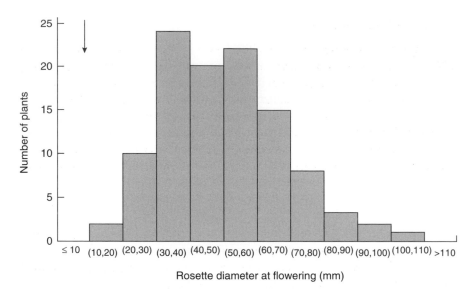

Figure 12.8 Size distribution of flowering plants in *Carlina vulgaris*. The arrow indicates the predicted size at flowering assuming there is no heterogeneity in the system. Data kindly supplied by Peter Grubb.

reason these models make predictions far too small is that the asymptotic size predicted by the growth models is too small. In order to predict the flowering strategies observed in field populations, we need to understand how various forms of heterogeneity influence flowering decisions, and then quantify these sources of heterogeneity. Once quantified, we can use modelling approaches to determine whether the measured levels of heterogeneity are sufficient to explain the observed pattern of flowering.

Analytical models exploring the effects of heterogeneity
In order to begin to understand the effects of heterogeneity it is useful to classify different types of heterogeneity; the different forms of heterogeneity should ideally be easily estimated from field data. In this way, the impact of various forms of heterogeneity on population dynamics and evolution can be explored. Three types of heterogeneity are considered:
1 *non-specific heterogeneity* where individuals experience different environments in different years;
2 *individual-specific heterogeneity* where individuals experience different environments but the effects are constant throughout their lifetime; and
3 *temporal heterogeneity* where all individuals experience the same environment in a given year but the effects vary between years.
This simple classification requires some explanation, consider the following simple model for plant growth:

$$L_i(t+1) = a_g + b_g L_i(t) + \varepsilon_{i,t} \qquad (12.16)$$

where a_g and b_g are parameters, $L_i(t)$ is the log size of plant i at time t and $\varepsilon_{i,t}$ follows a Normal distribution with mean zero and variance $\sigma_{i,t}^2$. Therefore, in each year, each plant grows according to a linear model and each receives a different value of $\varepsilon_{i,t}$. This is an example of non-specific heterogeneity. Note, because the expected values (averages) of a_g, b_g and and $\varepsilon_{i,t}$ do not vary with time there is no temporal heterogeneity in this model. Also as each individual gets a new value of $\varepsilon_{i,t}$ in each time interval there is no individual-specific heterogeneity. We can include individual-specific heterogeneity by adding a new error term to the model, so we have:

$$L_i(t+1) = a_g + b_g L_i(t) + \varepsilon_{i,t} + \varepsilon_i. \qquad (12.17)$$

In this model, each individual has its own growth intercept given by $a_g + \varepsilon_i$, and this does not vary from year to year. Again, because the expected values of the model parameters do not vary between years there is no temporal heterogeneity. The final model includes temporal heterogeneity, and so we have

$$L_i(t+1) = a_g + b_g L_i(t) + \varepsilon_{i,t} + \varepsilon_i + \varepsilon_t, \qquad (12.18)$$

where the term ε_t represents temporal variation in the intercept of the growth equation; that is the intercept of individual i in any particular year is $a_g + \varepsilon_i + \varepsilon_t$. These different forms of heterogeneity can be quantified using linear mixed models (Venables and Ripley 1997); see Rees *et al.* (1999) for a biological example of this approach.

For a plant to grow, we require that $a_g > 0$ and for it to achieve an asymptotic size, $b_g < 1$. In that case the asymptotic size, on a log scale, is found by setting $\tilde{L}_i = a_g + b_g \tilde{L}_i + \varepsilon_i$, so that:

$$\tilde{L}_i = \frac{a_g + \varepsilon_i}{(1 - b_g)}. \qquad (12.19)$$

Averaging over individuals, we find the average asymptotic size in the population, $\tilde{L} = a_g/(1 - b_g)$. This assumes the average value of ε_i is zero.

How do these different forms of heterogeneity influence the evolution of size-dependent flowering? The effects of individual-specific and non-specific heterogeneity can be explored analytically using the one-year look-ahead approach developed in Rees *et al.* (1999). This approach leads to a switching value L_s. Plants with $L(t) > L_s$ are predicted to reproduce in year t, whereas those with $L(t) < L_s$ are predicted to continue to grow. We compare reproduction given the current size, $L(t)$, with the expected reproduction in the next year, taking growth and survival into account. The switch value will be the size that makes these equal. It should be realized that this approach is only approximate because growth opportunities more than one-year ahead will influence the optimal switch value. However, comparing this approach with a dynamic state variable model indicates that the error involved is generally less than 10% (Rees *et al.* 1999). We assume that mortality is independent of plant size, which is a reasonable assumption for large-sized individuals, and that seed production is described by equation (12.7). Non-specific heterogeneity in growth is described by equation (12.16), and this leads to the following equation, which the switching value satisfies

$$\exp(A+BL_s) = \int f(\varepsilon_{i,t})\exp(-d_0 + A + B(a_g + b_g L_s + \varepsilon_{i,t}))d\varepsilon_{i,t} \tag{12.20}$$

where $f(\varepsilon_{i,t})$ denotes the probability density function for $\varepsilon_{i,t}$ and $\exp(-d_0)$ is the probability of survival. The term on the left-hand side of equation represents current reproduction and the term on the right-hand side expected future reproduction, taking growth and survival into account. The integral on the right-hand side can be evaluated by completing the square in the Gaussian integral, remembering that $\varepsilon_{i,t}$ follows a Normal distribution (see Hilborn and Mangel (1997) page 75) and is:

$$\int f(\varepsilon_{i,t})\exp(B\varepsilon_{i,t})d\varepsilon_{i,t} = \exp(B^2\sigma_{i,t}^2/2). \tag{12.21}$$

Making this substitution and solving for L_s gives:

$$L_s = \text{Asymptotic size} + \text{variance term} - \text{mortality term}$$

$$= \frac{a_g}{1-b_g} + \frac{B\sigma_{i,t}^2}{2(1-b_g)} - \frac{d_0}{B(1-b_g)} \tag{12.22}$$

The dependence of the switching value on d_0 is intuitive and sensible: as the chance of mortality increases, the payoff from immediate reproduction is greater than the payoff from waiting, and thus we predict a decrease in the switching value. That it scales by $B(1-b_g)$ could not be anticipated without analysis. Furthermore, and perhaps more importantly, equation (12.22) demonstrates that non-specific heterogeneity in growth is important for the switching value. In particular, because the variance term is always positive, as variability increases, the predicted size at switching increases.

Assuming there is no variance in growth ($\sigma_{i,t}^2=0$) gives:

$$L_s = \frac{a_g}{1-b_g} - \frac{d_0}{B(1-b_g)}, \tag{12.23}$$

which is the same form as the ESS prediction derived from the von Bertalanffy growth model with $L_\infty = a_g/(1-b_g)$, $m=d_0$ and $k=(1-b_g)$, see equation (12.10) (Charnov 1993; Mangel 1996).

We can also incorporate individual-specific heterogeneity into this framework, which leads to the following equation for the switching value:

$$\exp(A+BL_s) = \iint f(\varepsilon_{i,t})f(\varepsilon_i)\exp(-d_0 + A + B(a_g + b_g L_s + \varepsilon_{i,t} + \varepsilon_i))d\varepsilon_{i,t}d\varepsilon_i$$

$$= \frac{a_g}{1-b_g} + \frac{B(\sigma_{i,t}^2 + \sigma_i^2)}{2(1-b_g)} - \frac{d_0}{B(1-b_g)} \tag{12.24}$$

where σ_i^2 is the variance of the individual-specific heterogeneity distribution, which is also assumed to follow a Normal distribution. As with non-specific heterogeneity, this form of heterogeneity increases the predicted switching value. Both these models assume that plants have no information on the heterogeneity in the system. If plants had complete information on their individual-specific heterogeneity then we would expect individuals to flower at different sizes, and the switching value for an individual would be:

$$L_{s,i} = \frac{a_g + \varepsilon_i}{1 - b_g} + \frac{B\sigma_{i,t}^2}{2(1 - b_g)} - \frac{d_0}{B(1 - b_g)}.$$

(12.25)

Note, however, that when plants have complete information on individual-specific heterogeneity then the average switch value, $\tilde{L}_s$, does not change:

$$\tilde{L}_s = \int f(\varepsilon_i) \left(\frac{a_g + \varepsilon_i}{1 - b_g} + \frac{B\sigma_{i,t}^2}{2(1 - b_g)} - \frac{d_0}{B(1 - b_g)} \right) d\varepsilon_i$$

$$= \frac{a_g}{1 - b_g} + \frac{B\sigma_{i,t}^2}{2(1 - b_g)} - \frac{d_0}{B(1 - b_g)}$$

(12.26)

These models illustrate how individual-specific and non-specific heterogeneity influence the reproductive decisions of monocarpic plants. If plants have no information on the heterogeneity in growth, then the optimal switch value, L_S, generally increases with increasing heterogeneity, equation (12.24). In this model, there is an optimal switch value and any variation about this is maladaptive. When plants have information on the heterogeneity acting on them and can adjust their switch value appropriately, either through a phenotypic or genetic response, then the optimal switch value varies from individual to individual, but the population average value does not change, equation (12.26).

In natural populations the relationship between the probability of flowering and plant size is often relatively shallow, with substantial overlap between the size distributions of flowering and non-flowering plants (Werner 1975; Baskin and Baskin 1979; van der Meijden and van de Waals-Kooi 1979; Gross 1981; Hirose and Kachi 1982; van Baalen and Prins 1983; Reinartz 1984b; Wesselingh et al. 1993; Bullock et al. 1994; Klinkhamer et al. 1996). It has been suggested that this overlap results from the additional factors, weakly correlated with size, influencing the control of flowering (de Jong et al. 1986). However, this would lead to equal within-population variance in flowering size and the data in Wesselingh et al. (1993) contradicts this idea. For example, in populations of Cynoglossum officinale from botanical gardens, there was virtually no overlap in the distributions of flowering and non-flowering plants, whilst in natural populations there was considerable overlap (Wesselingh et al. 1993). Weak selection against large threshold sizes for flowering is another possible explanation. A third possible explanation is that the graded response of flowering to plant size is a consequence of an adaptive response to spatially or temporally varying selection pressures. This adaptive response could either have a phenotypic or genetic basis; however, it should be noted that selection experiments have shown there is substantial genetic variance in the threshold size for flowering (Wesselingh and de Jong 1995; Wesselingh and Klinkhamer 1996).

We cannot explore the effects of temporal heterogeneity using the one-year look-ahead approach, as the geometric mean fitness is the appropriate fitness measure and individual optimization fails (Metz *et al.* 1992; McNamara *et al.* 1995). However, simulation studies, using an individual-based model incorporating a simple genetic algorithm, have shown that temporal heterogeneity in the growth equation makes delaying reproduction more risky, and this selects for smaller sizes at flowering (Rees *et al.* 1999).

Case studies including heterogeneity

In order to explore the discrepancy between the analytical predictions of the growth models and the field data, we developed a range of models that allow heterogeneity to be incorporated. Specifically, we used the one-year look-ahead approach, a dynamic state variable model (Mangel and Clark 1988; Mangel and Ludwig 1992), and an individual-based simulation, which incorporated a simple genetic algorithm and so allows the flowering strategy to evolve.

For *Oenothera glazioviana*, we modified the one-year look-ahead approach to use the parameterized functions for growth, survival and flowering, see equations (12.11), (12.12), (12.13) and (12.14) (Kachi and Hirose 1985). For this species, we only have information on non-specific heterogeneity, $\varepsilon_{i,p}$ in the growth equation. Using the published parameter values gives a predicted switch value, L_s, of 2.78, which using forward iteration (Mangel and Clark 1988), corresponds to an average size at flowering of 24 cm. The one-year look-ahead is 'myopic' in the sense that it ignores all growth opportunities except for those in the following year. For example, in small plants, the expected seed production from waiting 2 years may be greater than from waiting one year because of the stochastic variation in growth. So for a given plant size, the optimal decision based on the one year look-ahead might be to flower, whereas using a 2-year look-ahead the optimal decision might be to wait. We therefore require a technique that allows growth opportunities several years ahead to influence the optimal flowering strategy. Dynamic state variable (DSV) models allow this type of calculation to be easily performed (Mangel and Clark 1988; Mangel and Ludwig 1992). In this model, we assume that there is a terminal time, T, at which the plant must reproduce; the time T can be interpreted alternatively as the time of reproductive senescence or the time at which successional changes make reproduction mandatory, see Rees *et al.* (1999) for details of model construction. The DSV model allows the calculation of switch values, L_s, allowing for growth opportunities several years ahead. The approach calculates the optimal decision at time $T-1$, and then works backward in time and in this way allows for growth opportunities several years ahead. The DSV and one-year look-ahead approaches agree at time $T-1$ because there is only a single growth opportunity at this time. The DSV solutions are age-dependent although mortality up to time T is age-independent (Fig. 12.9). However, when there is little variance about the growth curve, the flowering strategy is age-independent. The DSV model predicts, using forward iteration, an average size at flowering of 26 cm; clearly, the one-year look-ahead approach is a good approximation to the DSV model. If we ignore

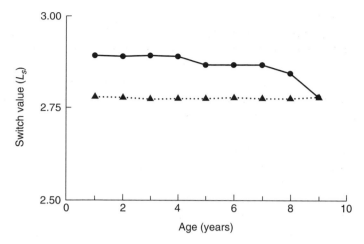

Figure 12.9 The predicted switching curve for Oenothera calculated using the DSV and one-year look-ahead models. Above the switching curve, individuals are predicted to reproduce; below it they are predicted to continue growing. The solid line is the DSV switching value; the dashed line is the one-year look-ahead switching value. As expected the two approaches give identical answers at time T-1 where there is only one year of growth possible. In this case $T = 10$, see text for other parameter values.

non-specific heterogeneity in growth, by setting $\varepsilon_{i,t} = 0$ in equation (12.11), then both approaches predict a switch value of 1.97, which corresponds to an average size at flowering of 7.2 cm. This is close to the prediction based on the von Bertalanffy growth model (6.3 cm). We learn two things from these models:

1 Non-specific heterogeneity about the growth curve potentially has a large effect on the predicted flowering strategy, and as anticipated from the analytical models selects for larger sizes at flowering.

2 The combination of non-specific heterogeneity about the growth curve and an upper bound on longevity results in an age-dependent flowering strategy. This is a result of varying opportunities for growth as plants approach the terminal time, T. It is not a consequence of age-dependent mortality as demonstrated by the fact that the flowering strategy is not age-dependent when growth is deterministic.

In order to explore the generality of these approaches we developed an individual-based simulation, based on the flow diagram given in Kachi and Hirose (1985). We used the simulator to explore when and at what size a plant should flower. We did this by introducing a simple genetic algorithm (GA) into the model (Sumida *et al.* 1990). In the model, each individual is characterized by its size and age, but in addition to this also has a flowering strategy. Each seed inherits its parent's flowering strategy plus a small random deviation. In all the simulations, we assumed that offspring strategies were uniformly distributed about the parental strategy with a range of ± 0.05. The number of recruits next year is independent of the seed production this year, as demonstrated by Kachi (1983) see Fig. 12.5, but the flowering strategy of each recruit is determined by a fair lottery amongst seeds.

In this way, the flowering strategies of the recruits reflect the relative reproductive success of the different flowering strategies in the population. In the GA model, the intercept in equation (12.12), which describes how the probability of flowering varies with plant size, was allowed to evolve. We explored two different scenarios: in the first, we assumed there was no scatter about the growth equation (i.e. $\varepsilon_{i,t}=0$ in equation [12.11]), which means that all plants follow a deterministic growth curve, as in the simple growth models. In the second scenario, we incorporated the non-specific heterogeneity by using the estimated error variance about the growth equation.

In the first scenario the model evolved to an intercept of 1.5, which corresponds to an average diameter at flowering of 6.7 cm and an average age at flowering of 3.6 years (Fig. 12.10). These values agree well with the analytical predictions (von Bertalanffy 6.3 cm, DSV and one-year look-ahead 7.2 cm), but are considerably less than those observed in the field. In the second scenario the model evolved to an intercept of 2.5, which is close to the estimated value of 2.3, and the average diameter at flowering was 21.8 cm, which is close to the field value of ≈ 18 cm. The age at flowering was 4.7 years, which is within the range observed in the field (3–6 years) and exactly matches the value obtained in Kachi and Hirose (1985) simulation. Using the DSV results we can calculate the intercept predicted by the GA model; we do this by setting the probability of flowering, equation (12.12), equal to 0.5, L equal to L_s and solving for the intercept. This gives a predicted intercept of 2.55 while the GA gives 2.5; the agreement between the approaches is excellent.

Clearly, the non-specific heterogeneity about the growth curve is an important aspect of *Oenothera*'s demography and has substantial implications for the evolution of size at flowering in this species.

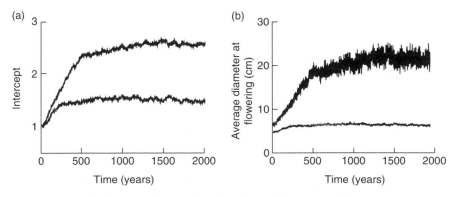

Figure 12.10 Evolutionary trajectories for *Oenothera* under two growth scenarios. (a) Evolution of the intercept of the probability of flowering equation and (b) the average size at flowering. In both panels the upper trajectory corresponds to scenario two, where there is non-specific heterogeneity in the growth equation, the lower trajectory is scenario one where there is no heterogeneity in the growth equation, see text for details. Note the non-specific heterogeneity in growth selects for substantially larger sizes at flowering, as predicted by the analytical models.

The size and age-dependent demography of *Onopordum illyricum* is described in Rees *et al.* (1999). As discussed earlier the simple growth model approach, equation (12.10), fails to describe the size-dependent flowering in this species, in fact this approach gives predictions that are 50% smaller than the average size observed in the field. Statistical analysis of the long-term population data indicated that:

1 recruitment was independent of the previous year's seed production;

2 mortality varied from year to year and was age and size-dependent; there was substantial individual-specific heterogeneity (Fig. 12.11);

3 flowering was age and size-dependent; there was little individual-specific heterogeneity, and growth varied from year to year and was age and size-dependent; there was little individual-specific heterogeneity but substantial non-specific heterogeneity.

Incorporating individual-specific and non-specific heterogeneity but excluding temporal heterogeneity into one-year look-ahead and DSV models lead to predicted sizes at flowering approximately double ($\approx 3600 \, cm^2$) those observed. Surprisingly the substantial individual-specific heterogeneity in mortality had little impact on model predictions. This occurs because over the range of sizes that plants flower: (i) the individual-specific heterogeneity, in the intercepts of the mortality curve, translates into small changes in the probability of death; and (ii) the logistic mortality curve is approximately linear (Fig. 12.11). With approximate linearity and small changes in the probability of death between individuals, the effects of individual-specific heterogeneity in the intercepts of the mortality curve are small. Using an individual-based model incorporating a genetic algorithm, we

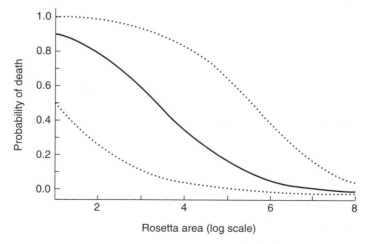

Figure 12.11 Probability of mortality in *Onopordum illyricum* for a two-year-old individual in the average environment (middle solid line) and ±3 standard deviations about the average (dotted lines about the central line). For an individual of size 4 the probability of mortality could be anything from 0.05 to 0.95, demonstrating substantial individual-specific heterogeneity. Redrawn from Rees *et al.* (1999).

studied the effects of temporal heterogeneity in growth. This model showed that temporal heterogeneity in growth selected for smaller sizes at flowering and gave predictions extremely close to the sizes at flowering observed in the field; the prediction error (predicted-observed/observed) was less than 2%. We can use this model to predict the distribution of age at flowering (Fig. 12.12). The predicted distributions are similar to those observed in the field (Fig. 12.4). The spread in the timing of reproduction is a direct consequence of the temporal and non-specific heterogencity in growth.

In this system different forms of heterogeneity select for larger or smaller sizes at flowering or have little effect. How do the various forms of heterogeneity influence population size? We assessed this by running the model ignoring the different forms of heterogeneity in turn; the model predictions are given in Table 12.1. Clearly, the heterogeneities in this system have relatively little impact on the predicted population sizes. However, heterogeneity is critical in determining the average values of the model parameters through an evolutionary response. Therefore, although the direct effects of heterogeneity on population size are small, the indirect effects through evolutionary changes in model parameters, can be large.

Discussion

In this chapter we have explored how heterogeneity may be generated by colonization limitation, resulting in not all sites being colonized, and so allowing coexistence of species that otherwise would be unable to persist together. This heterogeneity can influence the conditions for coexistence; however, simple models based on the negative binomial distribution are potentially misleading. In

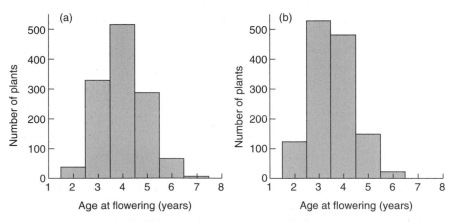

Figure 12.12 Predicted distributions of age at flowering in *Onopordum illyricum*, from an individual-based model incorporating all three types of heterogeneity. The predictions are for two sites in France, (a) La Crau and (b) Viols. In both cases, the models predict a wide range of ages at flowering. This is a consequence of the heterogeneity in growth combined with a size-dependent flowering strategy. See Rees *et al.* (1999) for details of the model.

Table 12.1 Effects of removing various forms of heterogeneity on the predicted population size based on an individual-based model of *Onopordum illyricum* at two sites. In each case, we removed the one form of heterogeneity at a time, leaving the others in the model, except where all forms of heterogeneity were removed

	La Crau	Viols
Data	176	240
Model	172	283
Temporal heterogeneity in growth	174	290
Temporal heterogeneity in mortality	148	219
Individual-specific heterogeneity in mortality	172	267
Individual-specific heterogeneity in growth	177	287
Non-specific heterogeneity in growth	179	296
All heterogeneity	152	217

these models, the condition for invasion of an inferior competitor does not depend on its spatial distribution, suggesting that dispersal does not influence community structure. This is a direct consequence of the way the invasion condition, which ensures that a species can increase when rare, is calculated. In more realistic models that consider the persistence of insects exploiting a patchy, ephemeral resource and explicitly include local movement, invasion depends on the foraging strategies of the competing species (Heard and Remer 1997; Remer and Heard 1998). These models assume that individuals have a fixed number of eggs that can be laid in clutches, and patches are visited at random (Remer and Heard 1998). If the inferior competitor lays eggs in larger clutches, its colonization potential is reduced and rapid exclusion occurs. However, if the inferior competitor lays eggs in smaller clutches than the superior competitor, then coexistence is possible. In this case, the inferior competitor has a colonization advantage that allows coexistence via the competition–colonization trade-off.

We then explored how heterogeneity can result in temporal dispersal in monocarpic plants. In these plants non-specific heterogeneity in growth results in a decoupling of age and size, and so makes size-dependent flowering strategies superior to age-dependent ones (Kachi and Hirose 1985; Rees *et al.* 1999). In agreement with this prediction, reproduction in monocarpic plants is strongly influenced by size, although in some species the flowering strategy does have an age-dependent component (Werner 1975; Baskin and Baskin 1979; van der Meijden and van de Waals-Kooi 1979; Gross 1981; Hirose and Kachi 1982; Gross and Werner 1983; Reinartz 1984b; Kachi and Hirose 1985; Klemow and Raynal 1985; de Jong *et al.* 1986; Lacey 1986; Klinkhamer *et al.* 1987a; Wesselingh *et al.* 1993; Bullock *et al.* 1994; Klinkhamer *et al.* 1996; Wesselingh and Klinkhamer 1996). However, strict biennials do occur and these species seem to have age-dependent flowering (Kelly 1985). In the strict biennial *Gentianella amarella* all surviving plants flowered in their second year, with the result that many plants flowered while very small and so failed to set seed (Kelly 1989a,b). It seems unlikely that such behaviour would be adaptively superior to a size-based flowering strategy, and Kelly suggests that these species can be considered as 'extended annuals' that occur in habitats so infertile or densely vegetated that enough reserves cannot be accumulated in one year for successful flowering (Kelly 1985). In other species with age-dependent flowering, such as bamboo, delays in reproduction have been linked with mast seeding and predator satiation (Janzen 1976).

Non-specific heterogeneity in growth means that individuals of the same age can have very different sizes and so flowering is spread through time; resulting in a form of temporal dispersal. Heterogeneity here causes temporal dispersal although it does not directly select for it. In contrast to non-specific heterogeneity, temporal heterogeneity in growth makes waiting to flower more risky so selecting for smaller sizes at flowering. In *Onopordum illyricum* both these forms of heterogeneity dramatically influence the model predictions and accurate prediction is only possible when both forms of heterogeneity are included in the model Rees *et al.* (1999).

From the various examples presented, it should be clear that the potential effects of heterogeneity on ecological systems can be substantial, however, this is not always the case, and the best way of assessing the importance of various types of heterogeneity is through the use of parameterized mathematical models. In general, heterogeneity will be important when it interacts with any non-linearity in the system, this is essentially a consequence of Jensen's inequality (Ruel and Ayres 1999). For example, say heterogeneity acts on plant size, resulting in individuals having different sizes, and the probability of dying is an exponential function of plant size L, then:

$$\text{average probability of dying} = E[\exp(-dL)]$$

$$\approx \exp(-d\overline{L}) + \frac{d^2\sigma^2 \exp(-d\overline{L})}{2} \tag{12.27}$$

where d is a parameter that determines how rapidly the probability of dying decreases with plant size, $\overline{L}$ is the average plant size and σ^2 the variance in plant size — a measure of heterogeneity. Now if heterogeneity was unimportant in the system, then we could ignore it, and work with mean plant size, $\overline{L}$. However, because the mortality function, $\exp(-dL)$, is non-linear, and has a positive second derivative, heterogeneity increases the average value of the probability of dying, as shown by equation (12.27). If the mortality function had a negative second derivative, then heterogeneity would decrease the average value. However, simply knowing there is substantial heterogeneity and that it influences demographic rates in a non-linear way does not mean that it will be important. For example, Pacala and Silander (1990) showed that plant performance was a non-linear function of the number of neighbours within a certain radius, and there was substantial variance in the number of neighbours around target plants in sown plots. But this spatial heterogeneity turned out to have little effect on the properties of this system because population size rapidly increased, and at high densities the relationship between plant performance and the number of neighbours was approximately linear (Pacala and Silander 1990). A similar effect is seen in the influence of individual-specific heterogeneity in mortality on the evolution of flowering strategies in *Onopordum illyricum* (Fig. 12.11; Rees *et al.* 1999). General discussions of the effects of heterogeneity on life-history decisions can be found in a series of paper by Real and colleagues (Lacey *et al.* 1983; Caswell and Real 1987; Real and Ellner 1992).

In summary, we have shown how dispersal may generate heterogeneity and conversely how heterogeneity can result in dispersal. Ecologists are only now starting to realize that the error terms used in their statistical analyses might be as important as the systematic parts of the model formulation (Pacala and Hassell 1991). We can no longer assume that error terms can be ignored as these provide quantitative estimates of the heterogeneity present in natural systems, and their consequences on model prediction can be substantial (Kachi and Hirose 1985; Pacala and Silander 1990; Pacala and Hassell 1991; Cain *et al.* 1995; Pacala *et al.* 1996; Rees *et al.* 1996; Wesselingh *et al.* 1997; Rees *et al.* 1999).

Acknowledgments

We should particularly like to thank Peter Grubb for access to his unpublished data.

References

Atkinson, W.D. and Shorrocks, B. (1981) Competition on a divided and ephemeral resource: a simulation model. *Journal of Animal Ecology* **50**, 461–471.

Baskin, J.M. and Baskin, C.M. (1979) Studies on the autecology and population biology of the weedy monocarpic perennial, *Pastinaca sativa. Journal of Ecology* **67**, 601–610.

Bolker, B.M. and Pacala, S.W. (1999) Spatial moment equations for plant competition: Understanding spatial strategies and the advantages of short dispersal. *American Naturalist* **153**, 575–602.

Bullock, J.M., Hill, B.C. and Silvertown, J. (1994) Demography of *Cirsium vulgare* in a grazing experiment. *Journal of Ecology* **82**, 101–111.

Bulmer, M.G. (1984) Delayed germination of seeds — Cohen's model revisited. *Theoretical Population Biology* **26**, 367–377.

Cain, M.L., Pacala, S.W., Silander, J.A. and Fortin, M.J. (1995) Neighborhood models of clonal growth in the white clover *Trifolium repens. American Naturalist* **145**, 888–917.

Caswell, H. and Real, L.A. (1987) An approach to

the perturbation analysis of optimal life histories. *Ecology* **68**, 1045–1050.

Charnov, E.L. (1993). *Life History Invariants. Some Explorations of Symmetry in Evolutionary Biology.* Oxford University Press, Oxford.

Chesson, P.L. (1991) A need for niches? *Trends in Ecology and Evolution* **6**, 26–28.

Cody, M.L. and Overton, J.M. (1996) Short-term evolution of reduced dispersal in island plant populations. *Journal of Ecology* **84**, 53–61.

Comins, H.N., Hamilton, W.D. and May, R.M. (1980) Evolutionary stable dispersal strategies. *Journal of Theoretical Biology* **82**, 205–230.

Comins, H.N. and Noble, I.R. (1985) Dispersal, variability, and transient niches. Species coexistence in a uniformly variable environment. *American Naturalist* **126**, 706–723.

de Jong, T.J., Klinkhamer, P.G.L., Geritz, S.A.H. and van der Meijden, E. (1989) Why biennials delay flowering — an optimization model and field data on *Cirsium vulgare* and *Cynoglossum officinale. Acta Botanica Neerlandica* **38**, 41–55.

de Jong, T.J., Klinkhamer, P.G.L. and Prins, A.H. (1986) Flowering behavior of the monocarpic perennial *Cynoglossum officinale* L. *New Phytologist* **103**, 219–229.

Dytham, C. (1994) Habitat destruction and competitive coexistence—a cellular-model. *Journal of Animal Ecology* **63**, 490–491.

Dytham, C. (1995) The effect of habitat destruction pattern on species persistence: a cellular model. *Oikos* **74**, 340–344.

Green, R.F. (1986) Does aggregation prevent competitive exclusion? A response to Atkinson and Shorrocks. *American Naturalist* **128**, 301–304.

Gross, K.L. (1981) Predictions of fate from rosette size in four 'biennial' plant species: *Verbascum thapsus, Oenothera biennis, Daucus carota,* and *Tragopogon dubius. Oecologia* **48**, 209–213.

Gross, R.S. and Werner, P.A. (1983) Probabilities of survival and reproduction relative to rosette size in the common burdock (*Arctium minus*, Compositae). *American Midland Naturalist* **109**, 184–193.

Hamilton, W.D. and May, R.M. (1977) Dispersal in stable habitats. *Nature* **269**, 578–581.

Harper, J.L. (1977). *Population Biology of Plants.* Academic Press, London.

Hastings, A. (1983) Can spatial variation alone lead to selection for dispersal. *Theoretical Population Biology* **24**, 244–251.

Heard, S.B. and Remer, L.C. (1997) Clutch-size behavior and coexistence in ephemeral-patch competition models. *American Naturalist* **150**, 744–770.

Hilborn, R. and Mangel, M. (1997). *The Ecological Detective. Confronting Models with Data.* Princeton University Press, Princeton, New Jersey.

Hirose, T. and Kachi, N. (1982) Critical plant size for flowering in biennials with special reference to their distribution in a sand dune system. *Oecologia* **55**, 281–284.

Ives, A.R. and May, R.M. (1985) Competition within and between species in a patchy environment: relations between microscopic and macroscopic models. *Journal of Theoretical Biology* **115**, 65–92.

Janzen, D.H. (1976) Why bamboos wait so long to flower. *Annual Review of Ecology and Systematics* **7**, 347–391.

Kachi, N. (1983) *Population dynamics and life history strategy of Oenothera erythrosepala in a sand dune system.* PhD Thesis, University of Tokyo.

Kachi, N. and Hirose, T. (1983) Bolting induction in *Oenothera erythrosepala* borbas in relation to rosette size, vernalization, and photoperiod. *Oecologia* **60**, 6–9.

Kachi, N. and Hirose, T. (1985) Population-dynamics of *Oenothera glazioviana* in a sand-dune system with special reference to the adaptive significance of size-dependent reproduction. *Journal of Ecology* **73**, 887–901.

Kawecki, T.J. (1993) Age and size at maturity in a patchy environment: fitness maximisation versus evolutionary stability. *Oikos* **66**, 309–317.

Kelly, D. (1985) On strict and facultative biennials. *Oecologia* **67**, 292–294.

Kelly, D. (1989a) Demography of short-lived plants in chalk grassland. I. Life-cycle variation in annuals and strict biennials. *Journal of Ecology* **77**, 747–769.

Kelly, D. (1989b) Demography of short-lived plants in chalk grassland. II. Control of mortality and fecundity. *Journal of Ecology* **77**, 770–784.

Klemow, K.M. and Raynal, D.J. (1985) Demography of two facultative biennial plant species in an unproductive habitat. *Journal of Ecology* **73**, 147–167.

Klinkhamer, P.G.L. and de Jong, T.J. (1993) Phenotypic gender in plants: effects of plant size and environment on allocation to seeds and flowers in *Cynoglossum officinale. Oikos* **67**, 81–86.

Klinkhamer, P.G.L., de Jong, T.J. and de Heiden, J.L.H. (1996) An 8-year study of population-dynamics and life-history variation of the biennial *Carlina vulgaris. Oikos* **75**, 259–268.

Klinkhamer, P.G.L., de Jong, T.J. and Meelis, E. (1987a) Delay of flowering in the biennial *Cirsium vulgare*: size effects and devernalization. *Oikos* **49**, 303–308.

Klinkhamer, P.G.L., de Jong, T.J., Metz, J.A.J. and Val, J. (1987b) Life-history tactics of annual organisms—the joint effects of dispersal and delayed germination. *Theoretical Population Biology* **32**, 127–156.

Lacey, E.P. (1986) The genetic and environmental-control of reproductive timing in a short-lived monocarpic species *Daucus carota* (Umbelliferae). *Journal of Ecology* **74**, 73–86.

Lacey, E.P., Real, L., Antonovics, J. and Heckel, D.G. (1983) Variance models in the study of life histories. *American Naturalist* **122**, 114–131.

Levin, S.A., Cohen, D. and Hastings, A. (1984) Dispersal strategies in patchy environments. *Theoretical Population Biology* **26**, 165–191.

Levins, R. and Culver, D. (1971) Regional coexistence of species and competition between rare species. *Proceedings of the National Academy of Sciences of the USA* **68**, 1246–1248.

Ludwig, D. and Levin, S.A. (1991) Evolutionary stability of plant-communities and the maintenance of multiple dispersal types. *Theoretical Population Biology* **40**, 285–307.

Mangel, M. (1996) Life-history invariants, age at maturity and the ferox trout. *Evolutionary Ecology* **10**, 249–263.

Mangel, M. and Clark, C.W. (1988) *Dynamic Modeling in Behavioral Ecology*. Princeton University Press, Princeton, New Jersey.

Mangel, M. and Ludwig, D. (1992) Definition and evaluation of the fitness of behavioral and developmental programs. *Annual Review of Ecology and Systematics* **23**, 507–536.

May, R.M. (1978) Host-parasitoid systems in patchy environments: a phenomenological model. *Journal of Animal Ecology* **47**, 833–843.

McNamara, J.M., Webb, J.N. and Collins, E.J. (1995) Dynamic optimization in fluctuating environments. *Proceedings of the Royal Society* **261**, 279–284.

Metz, J.A.J., Nisbet, R.M. and Geritz, S.A.H. (1992) How should we define fitness for general ecological scenarios. *Trends in Ecology and Evolution* **7**, 198–202.

Moilanen, A. and Hanski, I. (1995) Habitat destruction and coexistence of competitors in a spatially realistic metapopulation model. *Journal of Animal Ecology* **64**, 141–144.

Nee, S. and May, R.M. (1992) Dynamics of metapopulations—habitat destruction and competitive coexistence. *Journal of Animal Ecology* **61**, 37–40.

Olivieri, I., Michalakis, Y. and Gouyon, P. (1995) Metapopulation genetics and the evolution of dispersal. *American Naturalist* **146**, 202–228.

Pacala, S.W. (1986a) Neighborhood models of plant-population dynamics. 4. Single-species and models of annuals with dormant seeds. *American Naturalist* **128**, 859–878.

Pacala, S.W. (1986b) Neighborhood models of plant-population dynamics. 2. Multi-species models of annuals. *Theoretical Population Biology* **29**, 262–292.

Pacala, S.W. (1987) Neighborhood models of plant-population dynamics. 3. Models with spatial heterogeneity in the physical-environment. *Theoretical Population Biology* **31**, 359–392.

Pacala, S.W., Canham, C.D., Saponara, J., Silander, J.A., Kobe, R.K. and Ribbens, E. (1996) Forest models defined by field-measurements—estimation, error analysis and dynamics. *Ecological Monographs* **66**, 1–43.

Pacala, S.W. and Hassell, M.P. (1991) The persistence of host–parasitoid associations in patchy environments. 2. Evaluation of field data. *American Naturalist* **138**, 584–605.

Pacala, S.W. and Levin, S.A. (1997) Biologically generated spatial pattern and the coexistence of competing species. In: *Spatial Ecology. The Role of Space in Population Dynamics and Interspecific Interactions* (eds D. Tilman and P. Kareiva), pp. 204–232. Princeton University Press, Princeton.

Pacala, S.W. and Rees, M. (1998) Models suggesting field experiments to test two hypotheses explaining successional diversity. *American Naturalist* **152**, 729–737.

Pacala, S.W. and Silander, J.A. (1985) Neighborhood models of plant-population dynamics. 1. Single-species models of annuals. *American Naturalist* **125**, 385–411.

Pacala, S.W. and Silander, J.A. (1990) Field-tests of neighborhood population-dynamic models of 2 annual weed species. *Ecological Monographs* **60**, 113–134.

Real, L.A. and Ellner, S. (1992) Life-history evolution in stochastic environments—a graphical mean-variance approach. *Ecology* **73**, 1227–1236.

Rees, M. (1993) Trade-offs among dispersal strategies in British plants. *Nature* **366**, 150–152.

Rees, M. (1994) Delayed germination of seeds—a look at the effects of adult longevity, the timing of reproduction, and population age/stage structure. *American Naturalist* **144**, 43–64.

Rees, M. (1995) Community structure in sand dune annuals. Is seed weight a key quantity? *Journal of Ecology* **83**, 857–863.

Rees, M. (1996) Evolutionary ecology of seed dormancy and seed size. *Philosophical Transactions of the Royal Society of London Series B* **351**, 1299–1308.

Rees, M. and Crawley, M.J. (1989) Growth, reproduction and population-dynamics. *Functional Ecology* **3**, 645–653.

Rees, M., Grubb, P.J. and Kelly, D. (1996) Quantifying the impact of competition and spatial heterogeneity on the structure and dynamics of a four-species guild of winter annuals. *American Naturalist* 147, 1–32.

Rees, M. and Long, M.J. (1992) Germination biology and the ecology of annual plants. *American Naturalist* 139, 484–508.

Rees, M., Sheppard, A., Briese, D. and Mangel, M. (1999) Evolution of size-dependent flowering in *Onopordum illyricim*: A quantitative assessment of the role of stochastic selection pressures. *American Naturalist* 154, 628–651.

Reinartz, J.A. (1984a) Life-history variation of common mullein (*Verbascum thapsus*). 2. Plant size, biomass partitioning and morphology. *Journal of Ecology* 72, 913–925.

Reinartz, J.A. (1984b) Life-history variation of common mullein (*Verbascum thapsus*). 1. Latitudinal differences in population-dynamics and timing. *Journal of Ecology* 72, 897–912.

Remer, L.C. and Heard, S.B. (1998) Local movement and edge effects on competition and coexistence in ephemeral-patch models. *American Naturalist* 152, 896–904.

Roff, D.A. (1984) The evolution of life-history parameters in teleosts. *Canadian Journal of Fisheries and Aquatic Sciences* 41, 989–1000.

Roff, D.A. (1986) Predicting body size with life-history models. *Bioscience* 36, 316–323.

Roff, D.A. (1992) *The Evolution of Life Histories. Theory and Analysis*. Chapman and Hall., London.

Ruel, J.J. and Ayres, M.P. (1999) Jensen's inequality predicts effects of environmental variation. *Trends in Ecology and Evolution* 14, 361–366.

Samson, D.A. and Werk, K.S. (1986) Size-dependent effects in the analysis of reproductive effort. *American Naturalist* 127, 667–680.

Silvertown, J. and Smith, B. (1989) Germination and population-structure of spear thistle *Cirsium vulgare* in relation to experimentally controlled sheep grazing. *Oecologia* 81, 369–373.

Skellam (1951) Random dispersal in theoretical populations. *Biometrika* 38, 196–218.

Stearns, S.C. (1992) *The Evolution of Life Histories*. Oxford University Press, Oxford.

Sumida, B.H., Houston, A.I., McNamara, J.M. and

Hamilton, W.D. (1990) Genetic algorithms and evolution. *Journal of Theoretical Biology* 147, 59–84.

Tilman, D. (1994) Competition and biodiversity in spatially structured habitats. *Ecology* 75, 2–16.

Tilman, D., Lehman, C.L. and Yin, C.J. (1997) Habitat destruction, dispersal, and deterministic extinction in competitive communities. *American Naturalist* 149, 407–435.

Tilman, D., May, R.M., Lehman, C.L. and Nowak, M.A. (1994) Habitat destruction and the extinction debt. *Nature* 371, 65–66.

Turnbull, L.A., Rees, M. and Crawley, M.J. (1999) Seed mass and the competition/colonization trade-off: a sowing experiment. *Journal of Ecology* 87, 899–912.

Turnbull, L., Crawley, M.J. and Rees, M. (2000) Are plant populations seed-limited? A review of seed sowing experiments. *Oikos* 88, 225–238.

van Baalen, J. and Prins, E.G.M. (1983) Growth and reproduction of *Digitalis purpurea* in different stages of succession. *Oecologia* 58, 84–91.

van der Meijden, E. and van de Waals-Kooi, R.E. (1979) The population ecology of *Senecio jacobaea* in a sand dune system. I. Reproductive strategy and the biennial habit. *Journal of Ecology* 67, 131–153.

Venable, D.L. and Brown, J.S. (1988) The selective interactions of dispersal, dormancy, and seed size as adaptations for reducing risk in variable environments. *American Naturalist* 131, 360–384.

Venable, D.L. and Brown, J.S. (1993) The population-dynamic functions of seed dispersal. *Vegetatio* 108, 31–55.

Venables, W.N. and Ripley, B.D. (1997) *Modern Applied Statistics with S-PLUS*. Springer Verlag, New York.

Watkinson, A.R. and Sutherland, W.J. (1995) Sources, sinks and pseudo-sinks. *Journal of Animal Ecology* 64, 126–130.

Werner, P.A. (1975) Predictions of fate from rosette size in teasel (*Dipsacus fullonum* L.). *Oecologia* 20, 197–201.

Wesselingh, R.A. and de Jong, T.J. (1995) Bidirectional selection on threshold size for flowering in *Cynoglossum officinale* (Hounds tongue). *Heredity* 74, 415–424.

Wesselingh, R.A., de Jong, T.J., Klinkhamer, P.G.L., Vandijk, M.J. and Schlatmann, E.G.M. (1993) Geographical variation in threshold size for flowering in *Cynoglossum officinale*. *Acta Botanica Neerlandica* **42**, 81–91.

Wesselingh, R.A. and Klinkhamer, P.G.L. (1996) Threshold size for vernalization in *Senecio jacobaea*: genetic variation and response to artificial selection. *Functional Ecology* **10**, 281–288.

Wesselingh, R.A., Klinkhamer, P.G.L., DeJong, T.J. and Boorman, L.A. (1997) Threshold size for flowering in different habitats: Effects of size-dependent growth and survival. *Ecology* **78**, 2118–2132.

Chapter 13

Genetic variation and adaptation in tree populations

D.H. Boshier and M.R. Billingham

Introduction

Environmental heterogeneity occurs over a range of spatial and temporal scales, under which individuals may encounter different selection pressures, with adaptation to different localities producing a genotypic mosaic within and between populations (Levin 1988). The extent to which phenotypic patterns of variation are under genetic control, and related to the environment in which a particular population occurs, has formed fertile ground for research. Most ecologists are familiar with the classical studies in which Turesson (1922), by studying populations of several species in transplant 'common garden' experiments, demonstrated the widespread occurrence of intraspecific, habitat-related, genetic variation. Subsequent experiments by Clausen *et al.* (1940) extended study of the expression of population adaptation to environmental differences, by using climatically different sites over a range of altitudes. Discussion in the 1930s and 1940s focused on the extent to which such intraspecific variation was continuous or discontinuous. Langlet (1934) suggested that as most important habitat factors, such as temperature and rainfall, varied in a continuous fashion, continuous variation would be expected in many species. Huxley termed such character variation in relation to an environmental gradient a 'cline', and subsequent research has shown that clinal variation in phenotypic characters is also widespread (see summary in Briggs and Walters 1997).

It is not our aim therefore to repeat what is already well known, but rather to examine the influence of habitat heterogeneity on the patterns of genetic diversity and adaptation within a particular group of organisms, namely trees. Most tree species have little or no history of domestication and their more extreme life history characteristics, when compared with other plants (e.g. long lives, overlapping generations, late attainment of reproductive maturity, resulting in the accumulation of mutations and limited effective population sizes), make them of particular interest. We examine the factors influencing the spatial scale of genetic diversity and adaptation in trees, along with the sources of information and their experimental limitations. For trees, such knowledge is important, not

Oxford Forestry Institute, Department of Plant Sciences, University of Oxford, South Parks Road, Oxford, OX1 3RB, UK

only in understanding evolutionary and ecological processes, but also increasingly for the purposes of conservation (e.g. sampling for *ex situ* collections, priority setting for genetic reserves, sourcing of material for use in ecological restoration), production (plantations for a variety of products) and future adaptability to changing environmental conditions. We therefore also consider the possible impacts of human disturbance on such patterns, particularly with regard to the future stability of tree populations and their ability to adapt to environmental change.

Genetic diversity in trees

The primary factors that shape genetic variability within tree species are, as for other plants, breeding system, natural selection, genetic drift, and gene flow. Trees have a diverse array of breeding systems that influence their reproduction and levels of genetic diversity, and hence their evolution. Such systems are themselves controlled genetically and therefore may not be constant, but have the flexibility to respond to changing conditions. Thus, at any moment the genetic status of a plant population results from a combination of factors such as history, spatial distribution, flowering phenology, breeding system, pollination and seed dispersal patterns. Many tree species have wide geographical distributions across which environmental heterogeneity is assumed to have led to genetic differentiation of populations adapted to local conditions. Research on trees has largely focused on species of commercial interest, and consequently much information is limited to coniferous taxa of the northern temperate forests (Muona 1990; Hamrick 1992). A recent increase in the number of studies of tropical species has started to redress the balance, by investigating a range of taxa which are more representative of the diversity of reproductive attributes found in trees.

There are two main sources of information on patterns of genetic variation, levels of gene flow and adaptation in trees. Firstly, over the last 30 years, genetic markers such as allozymes, and more recently a variety of DNA markers, have permitted direct study of the distribution of genetic diversity within and between populations. Additionally, in conjunction with field observations of factors such as stand size, density, spatial distribution, and flowering phenology, they have allowed estimates of mating system and gene flow to be made (e.g. Brown 1990). Secondly, field experiments, mainly in the form of provenance and progeny trials, have provided estimates of levels and distribution of quantitative genetic variation, heritability of particular traits, and the extent of genotype–environment interaction. In the following sections we review the information provided by each of these methods, the limitations of field experimentation to date, and discuss how a full understanding of genetic variation and adaptation to the environment actually requires a unified use of a range of experimental approaches.

Information from molecular markers

Mating systems

The genetic structure of tree species, both within and between populations, is dependent, to some extent, on the mating system, i.e. whether the species is predominantly selfing, outcrossing, or has a mixed mating system. The interplay between gene flow and selection is also critical to patterns of genetic variation and any adaptation to environmental heterogeneity. Gene flow may counteract even fairly strong levels of selection, preventing the formation of locally adapted populations. Views of the extent of gene flow in plants have differed, with plant biologists, on the basis of studies of herbaceous plants, traditionally arguing that it is much too restricted to homogenize anything but local gene pools (e.g. Levin and Kerster 1974). From the low density of many tropical rain forest tree species it was, however, assumed that pollinator movement and hence pollen flow was restricted, and that most trees were self-pollinated and consequently inbred (Corner 1954; Federov 1966). Subsequent work, based primarily on hand pollination studies of self- and cross-compatibility and observations of pollinator behaviour, indicated strong barriers to selfing and resulted in the conclusion that tropical trees are predominantly outcrossed (Janzen 1971; Bawa 1974; Zapata and Arroyo 1978; Bawa *et al.* 1985). Estimates of mating in tropical trees generally indicate high levels of outcrossing[1] ($t_m > 0.9$), with few of the species studied so far appearing to have truly mixed mating systems (see review in Boshier, 2000). Similarly, evidence from temperate conifers suggests that accumulated long-distance dispersal of small amounts of pollen is considerable so that the potential for gene flow between nearby populations is great (Muona 1990). Outcrossing rates in conifers are generally greater than 0.85, despite the lack of self incompatibility mechanisms in these species. The spatial separation of male and female cones on individual trees, combined with high genetic loads reducing seed set when inbreeding occurs, is effective at reducing the incidence of selfing.

Impacts of density and flowering on mating

Any form of spatial or temporal isolation which is effective in restricting gene flow between populations of a species may facilitate the independent response of populations to local selective influences. Environmental control of phenology may impose some restriction on gene exchange between subpopulations. Thus, occupation of a heterogeneous habitat may fragment a plant population into partly isolated breeding groups by breaking down the synchrony of flowering. Differences between, and annual variation in, mating patterns for individual trees of several neotropical tree species have been reported to be consistent with changes in local flowering densities and in the spatial patterns of flowering individuals (Murawski and Hamrick 1991). Species occurring at low densities appeared to combine

---

[1]Outcrossing rates (t_m) theoretically range from 0 (complete selfing) to 1.0 (outcrossed to a random sample of the population's pollen pool).

significant levels of biparental mating with long distance gene flow, whereas higher density species showed more random mating, generally over shorter distances. *Cavanillesia platanifolia*, a self compatible tree species, showed year to year variation in outcrossing rate, with lower outcrossing levels apparently related to lower flowering densities (Murawski *et al.* 1990; Murawski and Hamrick 1992). Similarly, increased levels of inbreeding were found in some low density conifer stands when compared with high density stands, and in small, isolated populations (e.g. *Pinus ponderosa*, Farris and Mitton 1984; *Larix laricina*, Knowles *et al.* 1987), presumably because of the increased proportion of self pollen in the pollen cloud reaching any one tree. Mating patterns in three neotropical species (*Calophyllum longifolium, Spondias mombin, Turpinia occidentalis*) that naturally occur at low densities, were strongly affected by the spatial distribution of reproductive trees, although they still showed high levels of outcrossing (Stacy *et al.* 1996). Where trees were clumped, the majority of matings were with near neighbours, whereas evenly spaced trees exhibited a large proportion of matings over several hundred metres and well beyond the nearest reproductive neighbours (Stacy *et al.* 1996).

Genetic structure within populations

Genetic structuring (non-random distribution of alleles in space) within tree populations is typical, particularly for those taxa with wind-dispersed seed. Near neighbours usually have more alleles in common than more widely separated individuals, even when occupying relatively homogeneous habitats (Linhart 1989; Ledig 1992; Moran 1992; Hamrick *et al.* 1993). Furthermore, in natural populations of *Eucalyptus* spp. such neighbourhood 'family' groups appeared to consistently lead to a degree of effective selfing, with outcrossing rates averaging about 0.75 (Eldridge *et al.* 1993). However, although pollen dispersal has a leptokurtic distribution in many tree species, its dispersal range is much more extensive (direct estimates showing high rates of pollen flow from several hundred metres to kilometres away) than that of the localized genetic structure, and little or no inbreeding has been found (e.g. *Banksia brownii* (Sampson *et al.* 1994), *Cordia alliodora* (Boshier *et al.* 1995a,b), *Pinus attenuata* (Burczyk *et al.* 1996)). In neotropical tree populations two trends are apparent in the mating patterns observed. Firstly, individual trees appear to receive pollen from relatively few pollen donors, but the genetic composition of the pollen received varies greatly from tree to tree. Secondly, although a high proportion of fertilization is effected by nearest neighbours, a significant proportion of dispersed pollen moves over relatively long distances (Hamrick 1992). These trends explain the relatively small differences in allele frequencies between stands of trees separated by distances of one to several kilometres.

Genetic structure between populations

Compared to annual or herbaceous plants, trees generally exhibit relatively high levels of genetic diversity at the individual tree, population and taxon levels

(Hamrick *et al.* 1992; Hamrick and Nason 2000). Both the mean level of heterozygosity and proportion of polymorphic loci are high, with most alleles (typically 70–80%) common across most populations (Loveless 1992; Hamrick 1992; Moran 1992; Müller-Starck *et al.* 1992). The few notable exceptions, such as the genetically depauperate, but geographically widespread *Pinus resinosa*, which appears to have experienced a genetic bottleneck during the last glaciation (Mosseler 1992), illustrate how historical factors also influence levels of genetic diversity.

As for other plant groups, high levels of genetic diversity are generally found in predominantly outcrossing tree taxa, with most of the genetic variation found within, rather than between populations (typically >0.1 $G_{ST}<0.2$;[2] Hamrick 1992). In contrast, inbred species show lower levels of within tree and population diversity, and greater interpopulation genetic variation. However, species with disjunct distributions (e.g. *Acacia mangium, Eucalyptus caesia, E. pulverulenta*, Moran *et al.* 1989; Moran 1992) typically show high differentiation between populations ($G_{ST}>$ 0.3, Moran 1992). Many widespread species show a hierarchical ordering of population structure, with a larger proportion of the variation occurring between regions (sometimes corresponding to recognizable geographical regions), than between populations within regions (e.g. *A. mangium* (Butcher *et al.* 1998), *Casuarina cunninghamiana, E. delegatensis* (Moran 1992), *Cedrela odorata* (Gillies *et al.* 1997). Many tree species show low levels of population differentiation (G_{ST} values 0.1–0.2, Hamrick *et al.* 1992) suggesting extensive gene flow in forest trees. Indirect estimates of gene flow (*Nm*: number of migrants per generation, where N is the population size and m the rate of migration) from such population differentiation studies show this to be the case, with values of $Nm>1.0$. Such values are generally considered high enough to counteract the effect of genetic drift (Scott Mills and Allendorf 1996). In contrast, values for many herbaceous species are well below 1.0 (Hamrick and Nason 2000).

Gene flow via pollen or seed?

Gene flow in plants occurs through pollen and/or seed dispersal and the relative extent of each influences local genetic structure, levels of inbreeding, and connectivity/differentiation between populations. Direct comparisons of the ratio of gene flow via pollen: gene flow via seeds in seven tree species, using differences in the inheritance patterns of molecular markers, gave ratios from 1.8 for the animal-pollinated, wind-dispersed *Eucalyptus nitens* to 500 for the wind-pollinated, gravity/secondary animal-dispersed *Quercus petraea* (El Mousadik and Petit 1996; Hamrick and Nason 2000). Direct measures of pollen and seed dispersal show similar patterns (e.g. Boshier *et al.* 1995b). Despite earlier suggestions that insect pollination may limit pollen flow in comparison with wind pollination, such that seed dispersal would become a relatively more important factor in insect-

---

[2] G_{ST} indicates the proportion of genetic variation owing to differences between populations.

pollinated species (e.g. Heslop-Harrison 1964), pollen dispersal generally appears to be the dominant component of gene flow in trees.

Information from field experiments

Field tests to determine levels of quantitative genetic variation, genotype–environment interaction and genetic adaptation to environmental heterogeneity in populations fall into one of two types, namely common garden or reciprocal transplant designs. Common garden trials test the performance of seedlings/adults from a number of sources at one or more environmentally different sites. In some cases the environment may be artificially controlled or manipulated to study the response of the seed sources to a particular variable such as temperature, water or soil pH. In reciprocal transplant experiments the fitness of 'home' and 'away' genotypes is tested at all of the sites from which they originate (Primack and Kang 1989). For trees, most information has been derived from provenance trials carried out by foresters to identify seed sources suitable for planting at particular locations. Although planting sites are sometimes within the natural range of the seed collections (e.g. Schmidtling 1994; Alía *et al.* 1997), they are generally outside this range (e.g. Birks and Barnes 1990) and as such these trials generally fit the common garden category.

Provenance trials

In his review 'Two hundred years' genecology', Langlet (1971) noted that the study of intraspecific variation and adaptation of populations to environmental heterogeneity began at a much earlier date than Turesson's introduction of the term genecology in 1922. Linnaeus reported as early as 1759 that yew trees brought to Scandinavia from France were less winter hardy than indigenous Swedish yews, and Langlet (1971) highlighted information from often overlooked forestry provenance trial work. Commercial tree species, unlike agronomic crops, generally have long rotation times, little history of domestication, and are often planted in 'natural' settings where genetic diversity is important for adaptability, and increased productivity. Therefore applied forestry research has the potential to inform about patterns of variation in response to habitat heterogeneity, although the wider importance or usefulness of such research has often been ignored by other biologists, perhaps through ignorance, or because forest scientists did not initially consider it important to discuss the general biological aspects of their research. Research through extensive provenance trials has provided information about levels and patterns of genetic variation and adaptive differentiation for a wide variety of temperate and tropical tree species, and although more work has been done on temperate conifers, the coverage of species is much wider than for molecular studies. As revealed in molecular studies, the largest proportion of genetic diversity in provenance trials is due to differences between trees within populations, rather than to differences between populations. Nevertheless, as illustrated below, although proportionately small in many species, the differences

between populations appear to be of major significance for adaptation or production (e.g. Eldridge *et al.* 1993).

Temperate zone trees
Evidence for adaptive variation over short distances, in response to features such as
aspect and altitude, has consistently emerged from provenance trials of temperate
tree species (e.g. Adams and Campbell 1981). The degree of risk in transplanting
across a species' distribution is correlated more with environmental changes than
with the geographical distance moved (Adams and Campbell 1981). There are
often differences between provenances from warmer and colder climates, the
former showing adaptation to the longer growing season in lower latitudes, but
suffering from early or late frosts when moved too far into higher latitudes. For
example, when transplanted north of their site of origin, loblolly pine seed sources
from warmer southern USA climates grew for a longer period in the autumn than
those from colder northern climates (Jayawickrama *et al.* 1995). Thus, loblolly pine
seed sources that were moved north a modest distance grew quicker than local
sources, but if moved too far north they suffered from early frosts, performing less
well than local sources (Wells and Wakeley 1966).

Patterns of genetic variation revealed by morphological traits and molecular
markers may differ for the same species, however. In some species there may be
large differences at the molecular level (e.g. because of genetic drift), but few
significant adaptive differences. In other cases there may be adaptive differences
between populations, but no molecular differences owing to the neutral nature of
the markers. For example, over its north to south range (approximately 1000 km),
populations of Scots pine (*Pinus sylvestris*) in Finland show high levels of heterozygosity (using a range of molecular markers) and low levels (2%) of differentiation
(Hedrick and Savoleinen 1996). In contrast, in common garden and transplant
experiments the northern and southern populations are highly differentiated with
respect to a number of traits that confer adaptation to the severe conditions (e.g.
date of first budset — 34% north–south differentiation; Karhu *et al.* 1996). Furthermore, transplant experiments performed in Sweden showed that survival of
seedlings is reduced by 7% per degree increase in latitude and by 16% per 100 m
increase in altitude (Persson and Stahl 1990). Over a 450 m altitudinal transect on
Mount Wellington in Tasmania, *Eucalyptus urnigera* showed a complete change
from non-glaucous to glaucous leaved individuals in the adult population, indicating a change in the selection pressure (Barber and Jackson 1957; Barber 1965).
Analysis of *E. urnigera* progeny from trees of known elevation under common
garden conditions showed the cline to be less steep than in the adult population,
indicating that strong selection (in this case death) can create population differentiation over short distances even in the face of considerable gene flow. Theoretical
models confirm that very strong environmental variation (hence selection pressure), may produce clines over short distances despite continued high levels of gene
flow. The width of the cline found in *E. urnigera* accorded well with model-based
predictions (May *et al.* 1974).

Tropical species

As in temperate tree species, most morphological genetic variation in tropical trees occurs within rather than between provenances. In contrast to temperate trees, there is little evidence from provenance trials for adaptive variation over very short distances. In most of the species studied, ranking reversals (adaptation) or significant genotype–environment interactions only occur in response to large environmental site differences (e.g. dry/wet zones, alkaline/acidic soils). For example, international provenance trials revealed large differences between coastal and inland provenances of *Pinus caribaea* var. *hondurensis* (Gibson *et al.* 1983). In particular, the coastal provenances showed greater stability when exposed to cyclones in Queensland, presumably as a result of selection in response to the higher frequency of hurricanes in the coastal region of its natural distribution in Central America (Nikles *et al.* 1983). Similarly, the superior growth of *P. caribaea* var. *bahamensis* on alkaline soils presumably reflects the karstic coral reef-based soils of its origin. In contrast, the island population of *P. caribaea* var. *hondurensis* from Guanaja exhibits very different growth characteristics from other coastal populations, possibly reflecting genetic drift (Gibson *et al.* 1983; Birks and Barnes 1990). Furthermore, trials of *Eucalyptus camaldulensis*, a species distributed throughout dry regions of Australia, illustrated the finding that provenances from climates with winter rainfall show poor growth in climates with summer rainfall, and vice versa (Eldridge *et al.* 1993). In some species, however, particular provenances show superior growth over a whole range of sites (e.g. Retalhuleu *Gliricidia sepium*, Dunsdon and Simons 1996), while for others only larger regions show consistent superiority, although different provenances from within the superior region perform better on different sites (e.g. *P. caribaea*, Birks and Barnes 1990).

Reciprocal transplant experiments

Direct testing for localized adaptation to environmental heterogeneity requires reciprocal transplant experiments, in which it is assumed that when home genotypes have higher fitness, differential selection has led to adaptation to local conditions (Primack and Kang 1989). Where such localized adaptation exists, genotypes perform differently between environments and a significant genotype–environment interaction results. Reciprocal transplant experiments have clear attractions; by subjecting the plants to more natural conditions than those of most common garden or tolerance tests, it is possible to examine responses to natural environmental processes, including competition with the native flora at each site. Most reciprocal transplant experiments have been conducted on grasses, herb and shrub species (e.g. Davies and Snaydon 1976; Schemske 1984; Waser and Price 1985; McGraw 1987; Kindell *et al.* 1996). In the species examined to date, localized adaptation appears to be the rule rather than the exception, with all but one study (Platenkamp 1990) identifying localized adaptation at the finest scale examined (ranging from 20 m to 8 km). The extent and scale at which adaptation occurs in trees is uncertain however, as few truly reciprocal transplant experiments

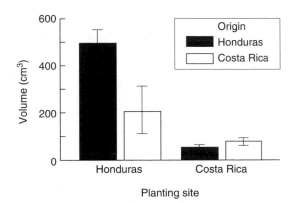

Figure 13.1 Reciprocal differences in growth of *Swietenia humilis* saplings in a reciprocal transplant experiment showing localized adaptation over 400 km in Central America (mean volume at 2 years of age, bars indicate one standard error of mean. Site×origin interaction significant at $p < 0.013$, $n = 58$ and 179 for the Honduras and Costa Rica sites respectively).

have been undertaken on trees. Sork *et al.* (1993) and Rice *et al.* (1997) have reciprocally transplanted tree species in sufficient numbers to directly test for localized adaptation, and some other small-scale experiments have been carried out (e.g. Green 1969; Augspurger and Kitajima 1992). Sork *et al.* (1993) found that when seed of *Quercus rubra* was reciprocally transplanted between north-, south-west-, and west-facing slopes (each over a 1 ha area) the native seedlings suffered significantly less leaf damage due to herbivory than alien seedlings. In contrast, Rice *et al.* (1997), failed to find evidence for localized adaptation in *Q. douglasii*.

We have tested for localized adaptation in the neotropical tree species *Swietenia humilis*, using reciprocal transplant experiments with seed and seedlings over fine (1 km) and coarse (up to 400 km) spatial scales (Billingham and Boshier, in preparation). Results to date from seedling transplantation experiments suggest that selection has led to localized adaptation over distances of more than 50 km, but are inconclusive at the finest scale. At 2 years of age, seedlings of Honduran origin outranked those of Costa Rican origin for volume, when planted in Honduras. However, when planted in Costa Rica, the seedlings of Costa Rican origin had a greater volume (Fig. 13.1). Similar reciprocal differences were also found for two Costa Rican populations separated by 55 km. At a finer scale (1 km), the local seedlings (Las Tablas Plain, Honduras) outperformed the seedlings from one kilometre away (Cerro Jiote, Honduras), but also performed slightly better when planted at the Cerro Jiote site. Seed germination and seedling survival failed to show any such reciprocal differences over 400 km, with the Honduran material showing higher values at both the Honduran and Costa Rican sites. However, the initial year of the study was particularly dry (an El Niño year), and more similar to the climatic conditions of the Honduran sites than to the Costa Rican conditions.

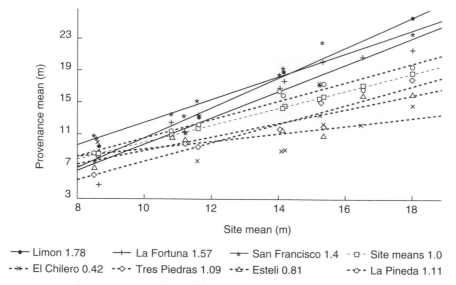

—•— Limon 1.78   —+— La Fortuna 1.57   —⋆— San Francisco 1.4   -□- Site means 1.0
-⋇- El Chilero 0.42   -◇- Tres Piedras 1.09   -△- Esteli 0.81   -○- La Pineda 1.11

Figure 13.2 Joint regression analysis of height of seven provenances of *Cordia alliodora* at twelve sites; differences between provenances are quantified with respect to their deviation from the joint regression line (dotted line=site mean), while the gradients (after each provenance name) provide a measure of the stability of the phenotypic performance of the provenances over the range of sites (solid lines: Caribbean watershed provenances; dashed lines: Pacific watershed provenances; see Boshier and Henson, 1997 for full discussion).

Combining field and laboratory research — *Cordia alliodora*

Research on the neotropical tree *Cordia alliodora* (Boshier 1984, 1995; Boshier *et al.* 1995a,b; Chase *et al.* 1995; Boshier and Henson 1997) illustrates how field and laboratory studies can combine to indicate possible influences of habitat heterogeneity on patterns of genetic variation and adaptation. Within its natural distribution in Central America, populations of *C. alliodora* from the seasonally dry Pacific coast show strong phenotypic differences from those found on the wetter Caribbean watershed. The Pacific provenances have smaller, more sinuous trees with a coarser, thicker bark, whereas the Caribbean watershed provenances are taller and straighter, with a smooth thin bark. An international provenance trial over a range of environments confirmed the stability of these differences and their genetic basis (Boshier and Henson 1997). The Caribbean provenances had greater volumes and straighter trees at all sites, including seasonally dry sites more typical of the Pacific provenances (Fig. 13.2). Levels of genetic variation (heterozygosity, measured by allozymes) showed a statistically significant negative relationship with mean annual rainfall (Chase *et al.* 1995; Fig. 13.3) consistent with the separation of provenances by phenotype and provenance trial results. This may reflect greater levels of environmental heterogeneity in the highly seasonal and annually variable climate of the Pacific dry forest. There was, however, no relationship between the groupings produced using genetic distance, and geo-

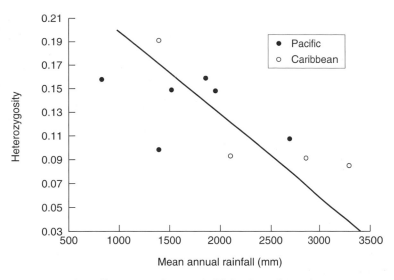

Figure 13.3 Regression of heterozygosity on rainfall for Central American provenances of *Cordia alliodora*, location identified by watershed, i.e. Pacific or Caribbean (from Chase *et al.* 1995).

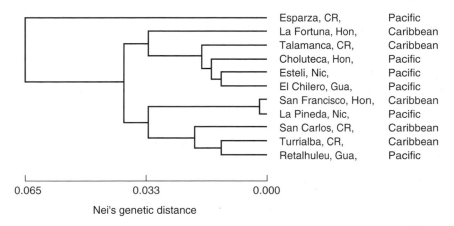

Figure 13.4 Genetic distance among Central American populations of *Cordia alliodora*, location identified by watershed, i.e. Pacific or Caribbean (based on Nei's genetic distance; from Chase *et al.* 1995). CR, Costa Rica; Gua, Guatemala; Hon, Honduras; Nic, Nicaragua.

graphical separation of the populations (Fig. 13.4). The genetic similarity of some wet and dry zone populations, in contrast to very dissimilar levels of heterozygosity, and the large differences in quantitative characters between wet and dry zone provenances in trials (Boshier and Henson 1997) may reflect both adaptation and the species' evolutionary history. Following the Pleiocene, as the Central American Caribbean watershed became wetter (Prance 1974), *C. alliodora* may have adapted in form and growth to the wetter climate, but suffered a reduction in occurrence that is now evident in its low frequency in undisturbed lowland wet forest, when compared with dry forest. Such a contraction in population size, followed by a more recent expansion through human disturbance, would be expected to randomize the patterns of genetic diversity through bottleneck and founder effects.

Limitations of field trials

Although provenance trials and reciprocal transplant experiments are useful sources of evidence for adaptive variation they also have inherent limitations. Provenance trials essentially look at production variables of interest to foresters, and may not study traits that are particularly related to fitness, such as survival or reproduction. In particular they are poor at informing about survival at the seed/seedling phase at which the highest mortality risk, and therefore the greater opportunity for selection, is likely to occur. Thus, the superior growth of the Caribbean provenances of *C. alliodora* may be useful in successful plantation establishment using robust nursery stock, but these populations may be poorly adapted to survive the initial natural establishment phase via seed. Indeed, nursery data showed that the Pacific provenances germinated and grew more rapidly up to about six months of age, suggesting a strategy more suited to survival under the seasonally dry Pacific conditions (Fig. 13.5, Boshier 1984).

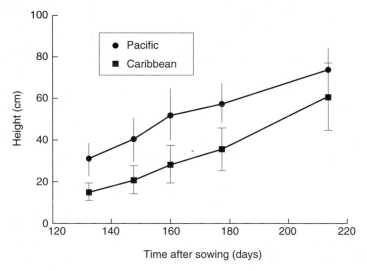

Figure 13.5 Height differences between Pacific and Caribbean watershed provenances of *Cordia alliodora* in the nursery 4–7 months after sowing (error bars = 1 standard error of the mean, based on > 5 provenances per watershed and 18 plants per provenance). Days to first germination: Pacific = 11.7 ± 1.7, n = 25 seed lots; Caribbean = 16.5 ± 0.3, n = 28 (adapted from Boshier 1984).

Reciprocal transplant trials involving seed-established material do not, however, directly compare previously selected populations, as in the case where adult individuals are directly transplanted. As seed composition is affected by patterns of pollen flow, the detection of local adaptation may be buffered by the extent of pollen flow from differing environments. Such a buffering effect may be considerable when populations vary over a short distance, or where pollen flow is altered as a result of human intervention. In Honduras, under fragmentation of the forest, the pattern of pollen flow in *Swietenia humilis* changed, with two sites studied for localized adaptation receiving different percentages (38% and 68% from > 1.2 km and > 900 m, respectively) of pollen from sources external to the fragments, compared to 36% from sources > 600 m distant in an 'undisturbed' plot (White and Boshier, in press).

Adaptive effects may not appear until trees are older, and may depend on the onset of competition or the occurrence of extreme and infrequent climatic events. In a *Pinus ponderosa* seed source study, reciprocal differences in growth were found, with individuals collected from the elevational zones corresponding approximately to each of the plantation sites outperforming those collected from other elevations. However, these differences did not become apparent until the trees were 20 years of age. This coincided with the onset of intense competition between trees for soil moisture (Namkoong and Conkle 1976). Similarly, for Douglas Fir in the north-west USA, reduced fitness of introduced seed sources (exhibited as higher mortality and slower growth), did not become apparent in a provenance trial until after the trees were 30 years old (Silen 1978). In forestry, the low chances of encountering a rare extreme environmental event (e.g. a one in 20-year frost) may not limit production under short rotations, although such occasional events may be influential in adaptation of natural populations. With much research funded only on a short-term basis, the potential to overlook important long-term adaptation in trees is great, given their long lifecycles. Experiments are also usually only established in a single year, which may not be typical of the conditions at a particular site, while the environment may subsequently alter, such that the site no longer provides the conditions under which the trees evolved. Given their long life and the rapid changes to habitats that can occur under conditions of deforestation and fragmentation, this is particularly likely to be a problem in studying trees.

Common garden trials, in looking for adaptation to environmental factors, face the problem of preconceived human notions of the factors that are most influential in determining adaptation (Antonovics *et al.* 1988). The testing of populations on exotic sites may obscure genetically determined differences in the capacity to adapt to environments. Conversely it may reveal hitherto unsuspected genetic variation in quantitative traits that is not adaptive in the environmental conditions under which it originally evolved. Certain populations of *Pinus caribaea* var. *hondurensis* produce 'fox tails' (excessively long internodes, without branching) when grown in particular exotic environments, but these never occur within its natural distribution (Birks and Barnes 1990). Similarly, in cultivation a population may show differences from plants from other habitats, but the differences need not relate to its adaptive capacities, as traits may differ between populations without being adaptive. The production objectives of forestry also often produce certain biases that limit the usefulness of provenance trials in making generalizations about localized adaptation. Seed collections often avoid poorly formed or diseased trees, creating an inherent bias in the sampling of populations. Highly diverse tropical forests, where competition between tree species is intense, present more complex conditions for the evaluation of adaptation than the less diverse temperate conifer-ous forests. Adaptations to the conditions in such forests are not evaluated in normal provenance trials. Furthermore, the type of species studied is also often restricted to fast growing or long lived pioneers, so that we know little about shade tolerant, slow growing climax tropical tree species.

As scales of gene flow and relevant environmental heterogeneity differ between species, there is no 'correct' or single natural scale which should be examined (Levin 1992). The method of sampling, and extent of habitat heterogeneity, inevitably influence the scale over which genetic variation and adaptation are found to occur. Widely spaced samples from extreme habitats may show 'ecotypic' variation, whereas samples taken at regular points along environmental gradients show clinal variation. Transplants of *Impatiens pallida* placed into the same and similar natural hardwood forest populations in Quebec showed effects of environ-mental heterogeneity over scales of 1–10 m (Bell *et al.* 1991). The dominant tree species, *Fagus grandifolia* and *Acer saccharum*, are, however, unlikely to respond over such short distances, given their size, spatial distribution and dispersal strate-gies, and possible responses to environmental heterogeneity should be examined over larger distances in trees. Within highly diverse forests, such as the tropics, reciprocal transplant studies over short distances (e.g. < 1 km) present sampling problems associated with the wide dispersion of individuals, environmental heterogeneity, high genetic variability of many tree species and the need for sample sizes sufficient to detect statistically significant differences. Given the evidence for extensive gene flow in trees, however, high selection pressures will be required to produce adaptive variation over such short distances.

Management and conservation of trees

Given the current dramatic human impacts on forest ecosystems it is important to consider some of their possible consequences for the genetic diversity of tree popu-lations and how these may impact on their adaptability in the immediate and long term. The dangers of inbreeding in many tree species are clear. Trees generally carry heavy genetic loads (deleterious recessive alleles, e.g. Williams and Savolainen 1996), such that inbreeding, and in particular selfing, may lead to reduced fertility, slower growth in progeny and increased susceptibility to pests or diseases (e.g. Park and Fowler 1982; Sim 1984; Griffin 1991). The poor growth on anything other than highly fertile agricultural soils, and susceptibility to pest attacks, of the selfed tree *Leucaena leucocephala*, show the limitations of this genetically depauperate material (Hughes 1998). Furthermore, the loss of a large part of the remnant mainland population of *Pinus radiata* to pitch canker and urban development, coupled with pollen contamination from urban tree plantings, illustrate the type of threats to native tree populations (Eldridge 1995, 1998). The maintenance of genetic variation, conferring adaptability to a range of environmental conditions over both space and time, should be an important part of any conservation effort involving trees. Reducing the possibility of inbreeding in naturally outcrossing tree species is important, while maintenance of breeding system flexibility will be a priority for species that naturally combine outcrossing and inbreeding.

Knowledge of the effects of human disturbances (e.g. harvesting and fragmentation) on tree gene pools is relatively poor, although predictions of impacts, such as losses of genetic diversity through increased levels of inbreeding and subsequent reductions in fitness and adaptability abound (e.g. Young *et al.* 1996). Identifying the circumstances under which inbreeding or variation in mating patterns occur naturally is important for understanding how human, or other disturbances, may impact on the genetic integrity of populations. While many populations of a large number of tree species appear to be predominantly outcrossed, variation among trees within a population may be high, with a number of factors leading to this variation (see 'Impacts of density and flowering on mating', page 269). Increases in inbreeding will be particularly dependent on the presence and strength of a species' incompatibility mechanism. Self incompatible species which show highly asynchronous population flowering may be more susceptible to reductions in population size, both in terms of compatible pollination and reduced diversity (e.g. *Shorea siamensis*, Ghazoul *et al.* 1998). Tree species with specialist pollinators are more likely to face threats from reductions in both pollinator and tree numbers, where successful pollination may become a limiting factor (Compton *et al.* 1994; Ghazoul *et al.* 1998). In contrast, species with unspecialized pollination syndromes are only likely to suffer problems when there is a general loss of pollinator fauna in an area. However, any increased levels of inbreeding may be unimportant from an evolutionary viewpoint, as inbred individuals may be selected against at various stages of the lifecycle. They may, however, be critical in terms of the levels of diversity that are sampled for *ex situ* conservation, tree breeding or plantation programmes.

There are potential dangers from fragmentation in isolating the resultant patches of forest and exposing populations to loss of genetic diversity through founder effects, limited gene flow, inbreeding and genetic drift (Young *et al.* 1996). Forest fragmentation has, however, been shown to lead to increased levels of pollen flow between remnant patches in both tropical (e.g. White and Boshier, in press) and temperate (e.g. Young *et al.* 1993) tree species. Our own studies of *Bombacopsis quinata* and *Swietenia humilis*, have shown no evidence for increased levels of inbreeding within fragments compared to undisturbed forest, with both species still showing high levels of outcrossing (t_m not significantly different from 1.0), even in the smallest fragments (White and Boshier, in press; Boshier and Billingham, unpublished data). In contrast to the prediction that spatially isolated trees are more likely to deviate from random mating and receive pollen from fewer donors (Murawski and Hamrick 1991), even 'isolated' trees in pastures were found to be outcrossing, with a wide array of pollen donors from across the fragmented populations. In contrast to other predictions and some studies (e.g. Ghazoul *et al.* 1998) both species also showed increases in seed production with an increasing degree of disturbance (Boshier, unpublished data). Increased levels of gene flow raise the converse possibility of outbreeding depression from the break up of co-adapted allelic complexes, or dilution of adapted alleles (Ledig 1992). Hardner *et al.* (1998), having selfed individuals of *Eucalyptus globulus* ssp. *globulus* and crossed individuals at distances ranging from 21 m up to 100 km away, failed to find evidence for such outbreeding depression. Our own studies (Billingham and Boshier, unpublished data), testing for outbreeding depression in *B. quinata* at distances up to 1800 km, suggest that such negative effects may only occur at extreme distances. The genetic impacts of fragmentation and management are undoubtedly complex. There will clearly be some distance beyond which genetic isolation will occur (differing for species and pollinators and depending on the specificity of the tree-pollinator relationship) which may be followed by losses in genetic diversity, and associated problems, such as inbreeding depression and limitations to future adaptation. Pollination for some tree species will occur over considerably greater distances and more frequently than has generally been considered.

A key current issue is ecosystem restoration, where the importance of using local seed sources is often stressed (Linhart 1995). A crucial question is again one of the scale over which adaptation occurs, and therefore how 'local' should be defined. As we have already seen, the scale over which species show adaptation to their environment will inevitably depend on the degree of habitat heterogeneity, in particular the specific habitat characteristics which affect a species, and the interaction with gene flow. Both field, greenhouse and laboratory studies in the north-west USA, using a range of conifer species, show that a significant proportion (typically 25–45%) of the genetic variation within populations is accounted for by climatic (e.g. mean annual rainfall and temperature) or location (e.g. latitude, altitude, slope aspect, distance from ocean) variables that reflect a range of environmental factors specific to each location. Much subsequent work has gone into the integration of information (models developed using regression, principal components and classification analysis) to assess the relative risks of moving seed from one location to another, the development of seed zones (e.g. Campbell and Sugano 1993; Sorensen 1994), and Genetic Management Resource Units (GMRUs; Millar and Westfall 1992). By contrast, similar information collected within Britain is very scarce. The UK woodland grant scheme states that 'where nature conservation is an important aim, this will normally mean that you should use the species which are, or might have been, native to the site' (Forestry Authority 1993). A review of information from British provenance trials (Worrell 1992) shows that British material is adapted to British conditions, whereas material introduced into Britain from continental Europe often suffers from the late spring frosts typical of the British climate. However, virtually nothing is known about the extent of adaptive variation within Britain (Ennos *et al.* 1998), so that discussion about suitable seed sources often emphasizes 'local' in a very narrow sense, rather than being based on sound evidence for the scale over which adaptation occurs.

Consequences for longer term adaptation have also been addressed by Mátyás (1996) and Schmidtling (1994, 1997), who advocated the use of old provenance trials to study the possible impact of climate change on tree growth. Some researchers have predicted productivity increases in boreal forests in response to global warming. However, their models assume genetic adaptation of the trees to the new climate (e.g. Kauppi and Posch 1988). Growth of Norway spruce (*Picea abies*), loblolly pine (*Pinus taeda*), and other southern USA pines in provenance tests was interpreted using regression models relating growth to temperature variables (Schmidtling 1994, 1997). Data from different plantings were combined by expressing growth as a percentage deviation from that of the local seed source, and expressing temperature at the site of each seed source as a deviation from that at the planting site. The loblolly and spruce models predicted losses of about 5–10% in height growth relative to that expected from a genetically adapted source, given a 4°C mean temperature increase (Fig. 13.6). Results showed that although rises in

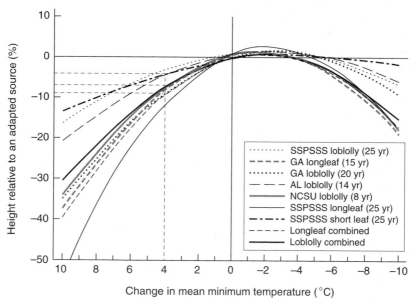

Figure 13.6 Old provenance trials as indicators of possible impacts of climate change on tree growth. Graphs show height deviation from local sources *vs.* change in mean minimum temperature (source to planting site) for three southern pine species (from Schmidtling 1997). The loblolly and spruce models predict losses of about 5–10% in height growth relative to that expected from a genetically adapted source, given a 4°C mean temperature increase. Reproduced with permission from *Ecological Issues and Environmental Impact Assessment.* ©1997, Gulf Publishing Company, Honston, Texas, 800-231-6275. All rights reserved.

temperatures may lead to growth increases, the increase would be considerably less than expected unless a genetically adapted source has time to evolve, migrate or is planted by forest managers. Given the rate at which climatic change may occur, the ability of tree species to respond by migration or selection may be limited.

As has been shown, the relationships between genetic diversity, habitat hetero-geneity and the scale of adaptation in trees are complex, and involve a variety of factors. Human disturbances add further complications, of which the nature and implications for management and conservation, are not fully understood. Despite the practical difficulties and expense associated with experimentation on trees, there is a clear need for more studies that examine genetic adaptation within complex forest environments. Future studies need to look at, amongst other issues

1 adaptation over a greater ecological range and reproductive variety of species;

2 adaptation over a mosaic of spatial scales—in tropical trees such work should focus particularly on areas where abrupt habitat changes occur within the range of pollen dispersal;

3 adaptation at the seed/seedling phase, particularly under conditions of natural regeneration with intra- and interspecific competition.

However, given the extent of human disturbance of forests it is clear that tree populations with sufficient genetic diversity must be conserved, so that they continue to adapt to whatever future conditions they may experience.

Acknowledgments

We thank MINAE and CONSEFORH/COHDEFOR for facilitating fieldwork in Costa Rica and Honduras, respectively. We would like to thank two anonymous reviewers for their incisive and helpful comments. This paper is an output from research projects funded by the Department for International Development of the United Kingdom. The Department for International Development can accept no responsibility for any information provided, or views expressed. Projects R5729, R6516 Forestry Research Programme.

References

Adams, T. and Campbell, R.K. (1981) Genetic adaptation and seed source specificity. In: *Reforestation of Skeletal Soils: Proceedings of a Workshop*, 17–19 November 1981, Medford, OR. (eds S.D. Hobbs and O.T. Helgerson), pp. 78–85. Corvallis, OR: Forest Research Laboratory, Oregon State University.

Alía, R., Moro, J. and Denis, J.B. (1997) Perfor-mance of *Pinus pinaster* provenances in Spain: interpretation of the genotype by environment interaction. *Canadian Journal of Forest Research* **27**, 1548–1559.

Antonovics, J., Ellstrand, N.C. and Brandon, R.N. (1988) Genetic variation and environmental variation: expectations and experiments. In: *Plant Evolutionary Biology* (eds L.D. Gottlieb and S.K. Jain), pp. 275–303. Chapman and Hall, London.

Augspurger, C.K. and Kitajima, K. (1992) Experimental studies of seedling recruitment from contrasting seed distributions. *Ecology* **73**, 1270–1284.

Barber, H.N. (1965) Selection in natural popula-tions. *Heredity* **20**, 551–572.

Barber, H.N. and Jackson, W.D. (1957) Natural selection in action in *Eucalyptus*. *Nature* **179**, 1267–1269.

Bawa, K.S. (1974) Breeding systems of tree species of a lowland tropical community. *Evolution* **28**, 85–92.

Bawa, K.S., Perry, D.R. and Beach, J.H. (1985) Reproductive biology of tropical lowland rainforest trees 1. Sexual systems and incompatibility mechanisms. *American Journal of Botany* **72**, 331–345.

Bell, G., Lechowicz, M.J. and Schoen, D.J. (1991) The ecology and genetics of fitness in forest plants. III. Environmental variance in natural populations of *Impatiens pallida*. *Journal of Ecology* **79**, 697–713.

Birks, J. and Barnes, R.D. (1990) Provenance variation in *Pinus caribaea*, *P. oocarpa* and *P. patula* ssp. *tecunumanii*. Tropical Forestry Papers No. 21, Oxford Forestry Institute, Oxford.

Boshier, D.H. (1984) The international provenance trial of *Cordia alliodora* (R. and P.) Oken in Costa Rica. In: *Provenance and Genetic Improvement Strategies in Tropical Forest Trees* (eds R.D. Barnes and G.L. Gibson), pp. 168–185. Commonwealth Forestry Institute, Oxford and Forest Research Centre, Harare.

Boshier, D.H. (1995) Incompatibility in *Cordia alliodora* (Boraginaceae), a neotropical tree. *Canadian Journal of Botany* **73**, 445–456.

Boshier, D.H. (2000) Mating systems. In: *Forest Conservation Genetics: Principles and Practice* (eds A. Young, D.H. Boshier and T. Boyle). CSIRO, Australia, pp. 63–79.

Boshier, D.H. and Henson, M. (1997) Genetic variation. In: *Cordia alliodora: Genetics and Tree Improvement* (eds D.H. Boshier and A.T. Lamb), pp. 39–65. Tropical Forestry Papers No 36, Oxford Forestry Institute, Oxford.

Boshier, D.H., Chase, M.R. and Bawa, K.S. (1995a) Population genetics of *Cordia alliodora* (Boraginaceae), a neotropical tree. 2. Mating system. *American Journal of Botany* **82**, 476–483.

Boshier, D.H., Chase, M.R. and Bawa, K.S. (1995b) Population genetics of *Cordia alliodora* (Boraginaceae), a neotropical tree. 3. Gene flow, neighbourhood, and population substructure. *American Journal of Botany* **82**, 484–490.

Briggs, D. and Walters, S.M. (1997) *Plant Variation and Evolution*, 3rd edn. Cambridge University Press.

Brown, A.H.D. (1990) Genetic characterization of plant mating systems. In: *Plant Population Genetics, Breeding, and Genetic Resources* (eds A.H.D. Brown, M.T. Clegg, A.L. Kahler and B.S. Weir), pp. 145–162. Sinauer Associates, Sunderland, MA.

Burczyk, J., Adams, T.W. and Shimuzu, J.Y. (1996) Mating patterns and pollen dispersal in a natural knobcone pine (*Pinus attenuata*) stand. *Heredity* **77**, 251–260.

Butcher, P.A., Moran, G.F. and Perkins, H.D. (1998) RFLP diversity in the nuclear genome of *Acacia mangium*. *Heredity* **81**, 205–213.

Campbell, R.K. and Sugano, A.I. (1993) *Genetic variation and seed zones of Douglas-Fir in the Siskiyou National Forest*. Research Paper PNW-RP-461. U.S. Department of Agriculture, Forest Service, Pacific Northwest Research Station, Portland, OR.

Chase, M.R., Boshier, D.H. and Bawa, K.S. (1995) Population genetics of *Cordia alliodora* (Boraginaceae), a neotropical tree. 1. Genetic variation in natural populations. *American Journal of Botany* **82**, 468–475.

Clausen, J., Keck, D.D. and Hiesey, W.M. (1940) *Experimental studies on the nature of species. I. Effect of varied environments on western North American plants*. Publication No. 520, Carnegie Institute, Washington.

Compton, S.G., Ross, S.J. and Thornton, I.W.B. (1994) Pollinator limitation of fig tree reproduction on the island of Anak Krakatau (Indonesia). *Biotropica* **26**, 180–186.

Corner, E.J.H. (1954) The evolution of tropical forests. In: *Evolution as a Process* (eds J. Huxley, A.C. Hardy and E.C. Ford). Allen and Unwin, London.

Davies, M.S. and Snaydon, R.W. (1976) Rapid population differentiation in a mosaic environment. III. Measures of selection pressures. *Heredity* **36**, 59–66.

Dunsdon, A.J. and Simons, A.J. (1996) Provenance and progeny trials. In: *Gliricidia sepium: Genetic Resources for Farmers*. (eds J.L. Stewart, G.E. Allison and A.J. Simons), pp. 93–118. Tropical Forestry Papers No. 33, Oxford Forestry Institute, Oxford.

Eldridge, K.G. (1995) Pitch canker: assessing the risk to Australia. *Institute of Foresters of Australia Newsletter* **36** (6), 9–13.

Eldridge, K.G. (1998) Californian radiata pine seed in store: what to do with it? CSIRO Forestry and Forest Products. Client Report No. 389, Canberra, Australia.

Eldridge, K.G., Davidson, J., Harwood, C. and van Wyk, G. (1993) *Eucalypt Domestication and Breeding.* Clarendon Press, Oxford.

El Mousadik, A. and Petit, R.J. (1996) Chloroplast DNA phylogeography of the argan tree of Morocco. *Molecular Ecology* **5**, 547–555.

Ennos, R.A., Worrell, R. and Malcolm, D.C. (1998) The genetic management of native species in Scotland. *Forestry* **71**, 1–23.

Farris, M.A. and Mitton, J.B. (1984) Population density, outcrossing rate, and heterozygote superiority in ponderosa pine. *Evolution* **38**, 1151–1154.

Federov, A.A. (1966) The structure of the tropical rain forest and speciation in the humid tropics. *Journal of Ecology* **54**, 1–11.

Forestry Authority (1993) *Woodlands Grant Scheme: Grants for Planting Trees and Looking After Woodland.* Forestry Authority, Forest Research Station, Alice Holt Lodge, Wrecclesham, Farnham, Surrey.

Ghazoul, J., Liston, K.A. and Boyle, T.J.B. (1998) Disturbance induced density-dependent seed set in *Shorea siamensis* (Dipterocarparceae), a tropical forest tree. *Journal of Ecology* **86**, 462–473.

Gibson, G.L., Barnes, R.D. and Berrington, J. (1983) Provenance productivity in *Pinus caribaea* and its interaction with environment. *Commonwealth Forestry Review* **62**, 93–106.

Gillies, A.C.M., Cornelius, J.P., Newton, A.C. *et al.* (1997) Genetic variation in Costa Rican populations of the tropical timber species *Cedrela odorata* L., assessed using RAPDs. *Molecular Ecology* **6**, 1133–1145.

Green, J.W. (1969) Temperature responses in altitudinal populations of *Eucalyptus pauciflora* Sieb. ex Spreng. *New Phytologist* **68**, 399–410.

Griffin, A.R. (1991) Effects of inbreeding on growth of forest trees and implications for management of seed supplies for plantation programmes. In: *Reproductive Ecology of Tropical Forest Plants* (eds K.S. Bawa and M. Hadley), pp. 355–374. Man and the Biosphere Series, Volume 7.

Hamrick, J.L. (1992) Distribution of genetic diversity in tropical tree populations: implications for the conservation of genetic resources. In: *Resolving Tropical Forest Resource Concerns Through Tree Improvement, Gene Conservation and Domestication of New Species* (eds C.C. Lambeth and W. Dvorak), pp. 74–82. Proceedings of the IUFRO Conference, Cartagena-Cali, Colombia, October 1992, CAMCORE, North Carolina State University, Raleigh, NC.

Hamrick, J.L., Godt, M.J.W. and Sherman-Broyles, S.L. (1992) Factors influencing levels of genetic diversity on woody plant species. *New Forests* **6**, 95–124.

Hamrick, J.L., Murawski, D.A. and Nason, J.D. (1993) The influence of seed dispersal mechanisms on the genetic structure of tropical tree populations. *Vegetatio* **107/108**, 281–297.

Hamrick, J.L. and Nason, J. (2000) Gene flow in forest trees. In: *Forest Conservation Genetics: Principles and Practice* (eds A. Young, D.H. Boshier and T.J. Boyle), CSIRO, Australia, 81–90.

Hardner, C.M., Potts, B.M. and Gore, P.L. (1998) The relationship between cross success and spatial proximity of *Eucalyptus globulus* ssp. *globulus* parents. *Evolution* **52**, 614–618.

Hedrick, P.W. and Savoleinen, O. (1996) Molecular and adaptive variation: a perspective for endangered plants. In: *Southwestern Rare and Endangered Plants: Proceedings of the Second Conference* (eds J. Maschinski, H.D. Hammond and L. Holter), pp. 92–102. General Technical Report RM-GTR-283. U.S. Department of Agriculture, Forest Service, Rocky Mountain and Range Experiment Station, Fort Collins, CO.

Heslop-Harrison, J. (1964) Forty years of genecology. *Advances in Ecological Research* **2**, 159–247.

Hughes, C.E. (1998) *Leucaena Genetic Resources Handbook.* Tropical Forestry Papers No. 37, Oxford Forestry Institute, Oxford, 274 pp.

Janzen, D.H. (1971) Euglossine bees as long-distance pollinators of tropical plants. *Science* **171**, 203–205.

Jayawickrama, K.J.S., McKeand, S.E. and Jett, J.B. (1995) Phenological variation in height and diameter growth in provenances and families of loblolly pine. *Proceedings of the 23rd Southern Forest Tree Improvement Conference.* Asheville, NC, June 1995, pp. 33–47.

Karhu, A., Hurme, P., Karjalainen, M. *et al.* (1996) Do molecular markers reflect patterns of differentiation in adaptive traits? *Theoretical and Applied Genetics* **93**, 215–221.

Kauppi, P. and Posch, M. (1988) A case study of the effects of CO_2-induced climatic warming on forest growth and the forest sector: A. Productivity reactions of northern boreal forests. In: *Impact of Climatic Variations on Agriculture, Vol 1: Assessment in Cool Temperature Regions* (eds M.L. Parry, T.R. Carter and N.T. Konijn), pp. 183–194. Kluwer Academic Publishers.

Kindell, C.E., Winn, A.A. and Miller, T.E. (1996) The effects of surrounding vegetation and transplant age on the detection of local adaptation in the perennial grass *Aristida stricta*. *Journal of Ecology* **84**, 745–754.

Knowles, P., Furnier, G.R., Aleksiuk, M.A. and Perry, D.J. (1987) Significant levels of self-fertilization in natural populations of tamarack. *Canadian Journal of Botany* **65**, 1087–1091.

Langlet, O. (1934) Om variationen hos tallen *Pinus sylvestris* och dess samband med climatet. *Meddelanden Från Statens Skogsförsöksanstalt* **27**, 87–93.

Langlet, O. (1971) Two hundred years' genecology. *Taxon* **20**, 653–722.

Ledig, F.T. (1992) Human impacts on genetic diversity in forest ecosystems. *Oikos* **63**, 87–108.

Levin, D.A. (1988) Local differentiation and the breeding structure of plant populations. In: *Plant Evolutionary Biology* (eds L.D. Gottlieb and S.K. Jain) pp. 305–329. Chapman and Hall, New York.

Levin, D.A. (1992) The problem of pattern and scale in ecology. *Ecology* **73**, 1943–1967.

Levin, D.A. and Kerster, H.W. (1974) Gene flow in seed plants. *Evolutionary Biology* **7**, 139–220.

Linhart, Y.B. (1989) Interactions between genetic and ecological patchiness in forest trees and their dependent species. In: *The Evolutionary Ecology of Plants* (eds J.H. Bock and Y.B. Linhart), pp. 393–430. Westview Press, Boulder, Colorado.

Linhart, Y. (1995) Restoration, revegetation, and the importance of genetic and evolutionary perspectives. In: *Proceedings: Wildland Shrub and Arid Land Restoration Symposium.* October 19–21 1993, Las Vegas. (Compilers B.A. Roundy, E.D. McArthur, J.S. Haley and D.K. Mann),

pp. 271–287. General Technical Report INT-GTR-315, US Department of Agriculture, Forest Service, Intermountain Research Station, Ogden, UT.

Loveless, M.D. (1992) Isozyme variation in tropical trees: patterns of genetic organization. *New Forests* **6**, 67–94.

Mátyás, C. (1996) Climatic adaptation of trees: rediscovering provenance tests. *Euphytica* **92**, 45–54.

May, R., Endler, J.A. and McMurtrie, R.E. (1974) Gene frequency clines in the presence of selection opposed by gene flow. *American Naturalist* **109**, 659–676.

McGraw, J.B. (1987) Experimental ecology of *Dryas octopetala* ecotypes. *Oecologia* **73**, 465–468.

Millar, C. and Westfall, R. (1992) Allozyme markers in forest genetic conservation. *New Forests* **6**, 347–371.

Moran, G.F. (1992) Patterns of genetic diversity in Australian tree species. *New Forests* **6**, 49–66.

Moran, G.F., Muona, O. and Bell, J.C. (1989) *Acacia mangium*: a tropical forest tree of the coastal lowlands with low genetic diversity. *Evolution* **43**, 231–235.

Mosseler, A. (1992) Life history and genetic diversity in red pine: implications for gene conservation in forestry. *Forestry Chronicle* **68**, 701–708.

Müller-Starck, G., Baradet, P. and Bergmann, F. (1992) Genetic variation within European tree species. *New Forests* **6**, 23–48.

Muona, O. (1990) Population genetics in forest tree improvement In: *Plant Population Genetics, Breeding, and Genetic Resources* (eds A.H.D. Brown, M.T. Clegg, A.L. Kahler and B.S. Weir), pp. 282–298. Sinauer Associates, Sunderland, MA.

Murawski, D.A. and Hamrick, J.L. (1991) The effect of the density of flowering individuals on the mating systems of nine tropical tree species. *Heredity* **67**, 167–174.

Murawski, D.A. and Hamrick, J.L. (1992) The mating system of *Cavanillesia platanifolia* under extremes of flowering tree density: a test of predictions. *Biotropica* **24**, 99–101.

Murawski, D.A., Hamrick, J.L., Hubbell, S.P. and Foster, R.B. (1990) Mating systems of two Bombacaceous trees of a neotropical moist forest. *Oecologia* **82**, 501–506.

Namkoong, G. and Conkle, M.T. (1976) Time trends in genetic control of height growth in ponderosa pine. *Forest Science* **22**, 2–12.

Nikles, D.G., Spidy, T., Rider, E.J. *et al.* (1983) Genetic variation in windfirmness among provenances of *Pinus caribaea* Mor. var. *hondurensis* Barr. and Golf. in Queensland. *Silvicultura* **8**, 126–130.

Park, Y.S. and Fowler, D.P. (1982) Effects of inbreeding and natural variances in a natural population of tamarack (*Larix laricina* (Du Roi) K. Koch) in eastern Canada. *Silvae Genetica* **31**, 21–26.

Persson, B. and Stahl, E.G. (1990) Survival and yield of *Pinus sylvestris* L. as related to provenance transfer and spacing at high altitudes in northern Sweden. *Scandinavian Journal of Forestry Research* **5**, 381–395.

Platenkamp, G.A.J. (1990) Phenotypic plasticity and genetic differentiation in the demography of the grass *Anthoxanthum odoratum*. *Journal of Ecology* **78**, 772–788.

Prance, G. (1974) Phytogeographic support for the theory of Pleistocene forest refuges in the Amazon Basin, based on evidence from distribution patterns in Caryocaraceae, Chrysobalanaceae, Dichapetalaceae, and Lecythidaceae. *Acta Amazonica* **3**, 5–28.

Primack, R.B. and Kang, H. (1989) Measuring fitness and natural selection in wild plant populations. *Annual Review of Ecology and Systematics* **20**, 367–396.

Rice, K.J., Richards, J.H. and Matzner, S.L. (1997) Patterns and process of adaptation in blue oak seedlings. USDA Forest Service General Technical Report PSW-GTR-160. U.S. Department of Agriculture, Forest Service, Intermountain Research Station, Ogden, UT.

Sampson, J.F., Collins, B.G. and Coates, D.J. (1994) Mixed mating in *Banksia brownii* Baxter ex R. Br. (Proteaceae). *Australian Journal of Botany* **42**, 103–111.

Schemske, D.W. (1984) Population structure and local selection in *Impatiens pallida* (Balsaminaceae), a selfing annual. *Evolution* **38**, 817–832.

Schmidtling, R.C. (1994) Use of provenance tests to predict response to climatic change: loblolly pine and Norway spruce. *Tree Physiology* **14**, 805–817.

Schmidtling, R.C. (1997) Using provenance tests to predict response to climatic change In: *Ecological Issues and Environmental Impact Assessment* (ed. P.N. Cheremisinoff), pp. 633–654. Gulf Publishing, Houston, TX.

Scott Mills, L. and Allendorf, F.W. (1996) The one-migrant-per-generation rule in conservation and management. *Conservation Biology* **10**, 1509–1518.

Silen, R.R. (1978) Genetics of Douglas-fir. USDA Forest Service Research Paper WO-35, 34 pp.

Sim, B.L. (1984) The genetic base of *Acacia mangium* Willd. in Sabah. In: *Provenance and Genetic Improvement Strategies in Tropical Forest Trees* (eds R.D. Barnes and G.L. Gibson), pp. 597–603. Commonwealth Forestry Institute, Oxford and Forest Research Centre, Harare.

Sorensen, F.C. (1994) *Genetic Variation and Seed Transfer Guidelines for Ponderosa Pine in Central Oregon*. Research Paper, PNW-RP-472. U.S. Department of Agriculture, Forest Service, Pacific Northwest Research Station, Portland, OR, 24 pp.

Sork, V.L., Sork, K.A. and Hochwender, C. (1993) Evidence for local adaptation in closely adjacent subpopulations of northern red oak (*Quercus rubra* L.) expressed as resistance to leaf herbivores. *American Naturalist* **142**, 928–936.

Stacy, E.A., Hamrick, J.L., Nason, J.D., Hubbell, S.P., Foster, R.B. and Condit, R. (1996) Pollen dispersal in low density populations of three neotropical tree species. *American Naturalist* **148**, 275–298.

Turesson, G. (1922) The genotypical response of the plant species to the habitat. *Hereditas* **3**, 211–350.

Waser, N.M. and Price, M.V. (1985) Reciprocal transplant experiments with *Delphinium nelsonii* (Ranunculaceae): evidence for local adaptation. *American Journal of Botany* **72**, 1726–1732.

Wells, O.O. and Wakeley, P.C. (1966) Geographic variation in survival, growth, and fusiform rust infection of planted loblolly pine. *Forest Science Monograph*, No. 11.

White, G.M. and Boshier, D.H. (2000) Fragmentation in Central American dry forests — genetic impacts on *Swietenia humilis*. In: *Genetics, Demography and the Viability of Fragmented Populations* (eds A.G. Young and G. Clarke). Cambridge University Press, Cambridge (in press).

Williams, C.G. and Savolainen, O. (1996) Inbreeding depression in conifers: implications for breeding strategy. *Forest Science* **42**, 102–117.

Worrell, R. (1992) A comparison between European continental and British provenances of some British native trees: growth, survival and stem form. *Forestry* **65**, 253–280.

Young, A., Boyle, T. and Brown, T. (1996) The population genetic consequences of habitat fragmentation for plants. *Trends in Ecology and Evolution* **11**, 413–418.

Young, A.G., Merriam, H.G. and Warwick, S.I. (1993) The effects of forest fragmentation on genetic variation in *Acer saccharum* Marsh. (sugar maple) populations. *Heredity* **71**, 277–289.

Zapata, T.R. and Arroyo, M.T.K. (1978) Plant reproductive ecology of a secondary deciduous tropical forest in Venezuela. *Biotropica* **10**, 221–230.

Chapter 14
Food webs and resource sheds: towards spatially delimiting trophic interactions

M.E. Power and W.E. Rainey

Introduction

Ecologists are bringing more spatial realism to theoretical and data-based studies of food webs, but we are still impeded by our ignorance of movements of consumers and their resources in the real world (e.g. Okubo 1980). These movements determine the fate of populations and the nature of their interactions. They also bear upon applied concerns, such as species habitat requirements (Schell *et al.* 1988; Wennergren *et al.* 1995), or their roles in contaminant transport (Rau *et al.* 1981; Jackson and Schindler 1996; Jackson 1997).

In the course of grappling with spatial dynamics of consumers and resources in the real world, it would be useful to know more about consumer 'resource sheds': source areas for resources consumed by individuals during their lifetimes. (Autotrophs are included here as consumers in the sense that they consume photons and molecules.) In this paper, we will develop this idea, which borrows from concepts developed by Cousins (1990, 1996) and Polis *et al.* (1997). Resource sheds can be spatially bounded, sometimes by abrupt thresholds, other times by diffusive gradients, which are often but not always related to physical heterogeneity in the environment. Using case histories of organisms we have studied in river and watershed food webs of Northern California, as well as published studies from other ecosystems, we will explore how resource sheds may be determined both by physical features of a landscape and by attributes of consumers or resources. We then present a simple model to describe and interpret landscape variation in fluxes of emerging river insects consumed by spiders, lizards, frogs, birds, and bats in the surrounding old growth conifer forest.

The watershed—resource shed analogy

Promoting the notion of a 'resource shed' (such as photon sheds, or nitrogen sheds) might violate Paine's (1996) dictum: 'Thou shalt not commit jargon.' However, there are several reasons for doing so. First, the term efficiently communicates, and focuses attention on a useful concept. This concept is similar but not equivalent to Cousins' 'Ecosystem Trophic Module' (also known as ecotrophic

Department of Integrative Biology, University of California, Berkeley, CA 94720, USA

modules). Cousins's (1990) ecotrophic modules are home ranges or foraging territories of the largest predator in ecosystems, or a social group of that species. He has
made a strong case that these areas can be used as quantifiable, spatially delineated
ecosystem boundaries that are functionally more meaningful than boundaries
drawn by discontinuities in physical features or vegetation (Cousins 1990, 1996).
Cousins (1990) emphasizes that only the behaviour of top predators (or their social
groups) determines the spatial extent of his ecotrophic modules. Our notion
of resource sheds differs in that movements of either consumers or resources
can determine these source areas (as reviewed in Polis *et al.* 1997). Physical
processes that advect or concentrate resources or consumers can also influence the
boundaries, sizes, shapes, and positions of resource sheds.

Second, a meaning of 'shed', as a verb, is to impart or release; give or send forth.
Shed derives from the Old English scead, 'to divide' (Webster 1989). Therefore
the meaning—a division of landscape that imparts resources to a consumer—is
etymologically appropriate.

A third reason for using this term is that it is closely analogous to the familiar
'watershed' as used in American English. In a river network, every cross-section
of every channel has upstream a drainage area feeding it water. If water flows
past a cross-section, it entered the system (most likely, fell as precipitation on
the Earth's surface) somewhere within this spatially defined watershed. Not all the
precipitation that falls within a watershed will flow past the channel cross-section.
For example some will evaporate back to the atmosphere before reaching the
channel. Likewise, an organism will not capture all of the resources in its resource
shed.

Drainage networks in watersheds and food webs in resource sheds are both hierarchical, although in the food web, the hierarchy is somewhat distorted by
omnivory. In river networks, water flows from small tributaries with small watersheds to larger main stems whose watersheds encompass those of the tributaries.
Similarly, resource sheds of predators contain those of their prey, and are similarly
nested as one traces energy flow up the food chain (Fig. 14.1).

In fact, the boundaries of watersheds are slightly indeterminate. Although most
precipitation reaching channels falls inside the topographic drainage divide, some
may be carried over the divide by wind or avalanches, or under the divide via frac-
tures in bedrock. For similar reasons, defining 'entry' is more straightforward for
some resources than others. Photons that hit the Earth are either absorbed by photosynthetic or accessory pigments, or converted immediately to heat. Because
photon effects in food webs lack history, photon sheds for autotrophs are straightforward (in theory, if not in practice) to delineate. Source areas for elemental
resources (e.g. C, N) are more difficult to demarcate because, over time, they
undergo chemical transformations and lateral fluxes through ecosystems. In a
sunny short grass prairie, intense root competition from neighbouring plants may
restrict the nitrogen shed for an annual herb to miniscule soil pockets around its
rhizosphere. A tree in a flooded forest, on the other hand, might derive water-borne
nitrogen from a source area equivalent to much of the watershed upstream. Coast

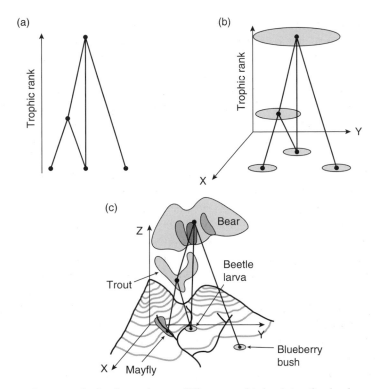

Figure 14.1 Resource sheds of organisms at different trophic levels in a food web, modified from Holt (1996). (a) Food web with no spatial or temporal context (b) and (c) Food web showing source areas for various trophic positions. In all figures, the z axis designates trophic rank with producer or decomposer species at the bottom level, intermediate consumers above them, and top predators in the uppermost positions. In (b), Holt uses the x and y axes to designate the spatial coordinates of landscape patches (the ovals) 'pertinent to the population dynamics' (Holt 1996, p. 314) of the web members. In (c), we have modified his diagram to project the landscape of a hypothetical western North American forest food web. Topographic elevation as well as trophic rank increases up the z axis. Shading indicates source areas for trophic resources for organisms, with more darkly shaded areas designating areas from which most fluxes to particular consumers derive.

redwoods (*Sequoia sempervirens*) in California derive much of their nitrogen from marine fog (T. Dawson, unpublished data) as do nitrogen-limited forests in southern Chile (Weathers and Likens 1997). When lateral fluxes of resources are extensive, delineating shed boundaries may require arbitrary cutoffs along the tails of two probability densities: (i) the probability that a given resource unit (e.g. a nitrogen atom) in the body of a consumer entered the ecosystem within radius x from that consumer (or the most frequently occupied site in its home range); and (ii) the (much lower) probability that a resource unit within radius x of the consumer (or the site) will eventually become incorporated into its body. Again, we might define 'entry' of the resource unit as its assimilation into producer or decomposer biomass that is eventually transferred along food chains to the consumer in question. For some purposes, however, it might be useful to look further back in time, and upstream along biogeochemical flow paths conveying resources, particularly to sites where isotopic fractionation processes have occurred that can fingerprint sources. For example, if volatilized NH_3 from pig sewage triggers *Pfisteria piscicida* blooms in coastal lagoons off the south-eastern United States (Burkholder *et al.* 1992), it would be of considerable interest to delineate the nitrogen shed feeding this dinoflagellate population.

The time dimension

Watersheds have storage elements (off river lakes, landslide deposits) that retain water or sediment for various lengths of time. Consumers also store resources for various lengths of time in tissues with different turnover rates. For example, vertebrate ear bones may retain for a lifetime atoms acquired during an animal's first days, while atoms in epithelial tissue may be completely exchanged within a few weeks. A consumer's conserved tissues therefore derive from its entire lifetime resource shed (and possibly part of its mother's resource shed, if maternal endowments were substantial). More labile tissues derive from those portions of the resource sheds used by the organism in its more recent past (Fry and Arnold 1982; Fig. 14.2). In resource sheds, as in watersheds (Dietrich *et al.* 1982), the source area expands with the time interval over which elements are acquired.

  In addition, the consumer may pick up resources of different ages as it forages. A wood-boring beetle consumes contemporary tissues as it enters through the bark and attacks the cambium. Then it may work its way inward to ingest wood laid down during decades or centuries past. The tree itself may have absorbed young, surficial water while a seedling, then taken up deeper, older groundwater as it grew longer roots (Dawson and Ehleringer 1991). (The water's age is referenced with respect to when it first entered the biosphere as precipitation.)

Limits of the analogy

Considering mobile consumers may push the watershed–resource shed analogy to its breaking point. Unlike recipient channel cross sections or catchment areas, mobile consumers go and get resources, or pick them up over the course of other movements. Tracers have proven invaluable to researchers attempting to keep track of movements of consumers and fluxes of resources, in situations (which are more the rule than the exception) in which direct observations of foraging and fluxes are rare or impossible.

Using tracers to delimit resource sheds

Stable and radioactive isotopes, along with distinctive, persistent molecules like organochlorines or stable lipid residues, are proving increasingly useful in revealing spatial and temporal dimensions of resource sheds. Radioactive ^{14}C, used

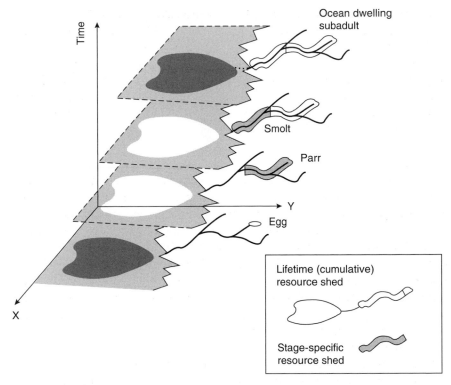

Figure 14.2 Ontogenetic changes in the nitrogen shed of a salmon. Here, the *x* and *y* axes indicate plan-view map coordinates (e.g. of the western coast of North America and a coastal river drainage). The darkened patches designate areas from which the organism derives resources over short time-scales (days or weeks). Tissues with short turnover times (e.g. epithelium) would be built of these resources. The light patches designate source areas for resources accumulated over longer time scales. Tissues with long turnover times (e.g. ear bones) would conserve resources from these areas. The nitrogen shed for a salmon egg corresponds to its mother's habitat, rather than its own habitat.

widely as a dating tool (Aitken 1990), can also serve as a source marker for food web studies. For migrating animals, ^{14}C has been used to determine when, and therefore where, certain resources were acquired (Schell and Ziemann 1988; Schell *et al.* 1988). Applications of stable isotopes have been well-reviewed elsewhere (Rundel *et al.* 1988). There are many sources of variation for stable isotope composition of biological tissues (multiple potential sources and various physical and physiological fractionation processes), and consequently many opportunities for misinterpreting them. Nevertheless, technical innovations, diligence and clever detective work by ecologists are gradually turning more of this noise into signal, as sources of spatial and temporal variation in isotopes are identified (e.g. Schell *et al.* 1988; Finlay *et al.* 1999).

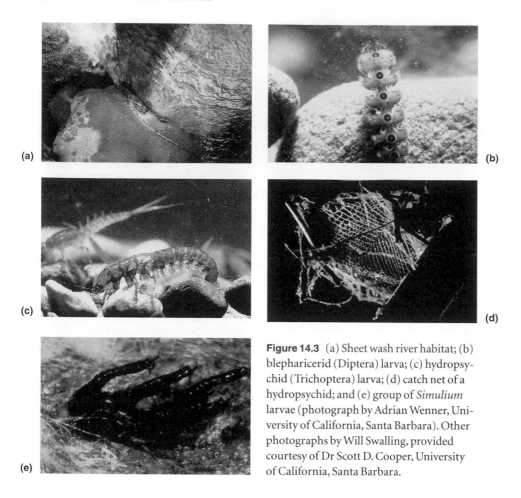

(a)

(b)

(c)

(d)

(e)

Figure 14.3 (a) Sheet wash river habitat; (b) blepharicerid (Diptera) larva; (c) hydropsychid (Trichoptera) larva; (d) catch net of a hydropsychid; and (e) group of *Simulium* larvae (photograph by Adrian Wenner, University of California, Santa Barbara). Other photographs by Will Swalling, provided courtesy of Dr Scott D. Cooper, University of California, Santa Barbara.

Case histories

Four case histories illustrate the use of isotopic tracers and the roles of consumers, resources and environments in delineating resource sheds for stream-dwelling insects (Finlay *et al.* 1999), forest trees (Simard *et al.* 1997), migratory Bowhead whales (Schell *et al.* 1988) and riparian plants (Ben-David *et al.* 1997a).

Carbon sheds of co-occurring stream insects

Defining resource sheds is somewhat simpler if consumers are sessile, or nearly so. Small (1–10 mm long) larval stream-dwelling insects (Blephariceridae, Simuliidae, Hydropsychidae) live in close proximity in fast-flowing habitats, such as sheet wash over boulders (Fig. 14.3). Blepharicerid larvae (Diptera) use ventral sucker disks to cling to rock surfaces, which they graze. Hydropsychid caddisflies (Trichoptera) capture drifting food particles in funnel-shaped webs attached to substrates. Simuliid (blackfly) larvae (Diptera) affix their posteriors to substrates with glue and silk, and filter particles with their cephalic crown appendages. These larvae are all considered primary consumers, feeding on algae and detrital organic matter. Their primary food sources are not obvious, however, from either gut contents or behavioural observations.

Carbon isotope analysis revealed surprising differentiation in the diets of these co-occurring insects (Finlay *et al.* 1999). Jacques Finlay discovered that in sunlit, productive rivers, velocity strongly influences the ^{13}C composition of primary producers, and of the primary consumers that feed on them. CO_2 diffuses much more slowly in water than air. Algae preferentially take up lighter ^{12}C isotopes when supply is not limiting (Keeley and Sandquist 1992). When CO_2 supply is low relative to demand, however, algae take up more ^{13}C. Finlay found a strong relationship between flow velocity and the ^{13}C composition of benthic algae in three productive rivers of northern California, with more ^{13}C enrichment ($\delta\,^{13}C$ of -22 to -13) in slow-flow (pool) habitats. In fast flowing riffles where delivery of CO_2 to algae is rapid, algal $\delta\,^{13}C$ ranged from -24 to -32, with some samples even more depleted than the average for terrestrial vegetation ($\delta\,^{13}C$ of -27). Blepharicerids had similarly depleted ^{13}C signatures ($\delta\,^{13}C$ of -26), indicating that they were largely built of local sheet flow algae. Hydropsychids and simuliids, in contrast, had the ^{13}C-enriched signals characterizing pool-derived algae. Despite the fact that these insects occur within millimeters of each other, their carbon signatures differ markedly, indicating that the surface-scraping blepharicerids are deriving their carbon from local riffle algae, and the filtering insects are deriving most of their carbon from algal production in pools upstream. Knowledge of these differences in resource sheds could lead to predictions about the relative dominance of these taxa in rivers where geomorphology, water management, or land management (e.g. timber harvest) changed the amount and local productivity of pool vs. riffle habitats. In regions where simuliids are pests of livestock or vectors of human disease (e.g. onchocerciasis, or river blindness (Desowitz 1981)), such information could be of practical use.

Carbon sheds of forest trees

Many terrestrial plants are linked underground by networks of mycorrhizae, or 'fungus-root' symbioses, which spatially expand the underground foraging volumes of individual plants. Simard *et al.* (1997) showed that different species of forest trees that share fungal symbionts are trophically connected by ectomycorrhizae. These investigators labelled birch (*Betula papyrifera*) and Douglas fir (*Pseudotsuga menzies*) with ^{14}C or ^{13}C, respectively. They switched the isotopes given to each species to check for differential isotope mobility, and found none. They also checked for indirect transfer of the label through soil fluxes of gaseous CO_2, sloughed root or fungal cells, or root exudates, by measuring uptake of the label by adjacent cedar, *Thuja plicata*, which are colonized by endomycorrhizae, and do not share in the ectomycorrhizal networks of birch and fir. Uptake of label by cedar was relatively small, showing that the carbon was moving primarily through ectomycorrhizal hyphae. (Robinson and Fitter (1999) and Fitter *et al.* (1999), however, have pointed out that appropriate controls for the possibility of carbon transfer via soil were not used.) These pioneering double label studies showed a substantial net transfer of carbon from birch to fir through fungal hyphae. Two-year-old Douglas fir acquired 3–10% of the total carbon transferred, a net carbon gain of 6% over what trees acquired by photosynthesis alone. Hence, the carbon shed of a tree can be expanded by underground mycorrhizal networks. The flow of carbon down source-sink gradients suggests that shaded individuals can be subsidized by sunlit trees, offsetting site-related growth advantages of the latter. This finding has implications for forest management and interpretation of species interactions over the course of succession.

Carbon sheds for migratory whales

Schell and colleagues (Schell *et al.* 1988) have used stable and radioactive isotope analysis to glean information on feeding grounds of Bowhead whales that would have been impossible to learn from field observations. Bowhead whales winter on the ice edge of the Western Bering Sea, then migrate north through the Bering Straight and the Chukchi Sea to spend summers in the Eastern Beaufort Sea. They feed throughout the course of this migration, filtering zooplankton on plates of keratinous baleen attached to their upper jaw. Zooplankton from the Bering Sea are depleted in ^{13}C, because of upwellings from deep ocean water, the import of terrestrial carbon from the Mackenzie River, or both. As the whales move east, they encounter zooplankton that are more enriched in heavy carbon. By looking at changes in stable isotopes along the length of baleen from five whales, Schell and colleagues were able to detect regular cycles of ^{13}C peaks and troughs, which reflected annual movements of the whales from summer feeding grounds in the Beaufort Sea to wintering grounds in the Bering Sea. The time period of cycles in ^{13}C content was deduced by analysis of ^{14}C along the baleen plate. The authors traced ^{14}C content from the young growing edge of the baleen plate of a whale killed in 1971 back towards the distal, older end of the plate, fitting the baleen ^{14}C to the radiocarbon content predicted in marine biota after atmospheric weapons tests in the early 1960s. The good fit of the ^{14}C baleen data to year-by-year predictions confirmed that the ^{13}C cycles were annual, and also supported the hypothesis that Bowhead baleen grew continuously. Their analysis sheds light on the relative importance to whales of foraging grounds in the Bering and Beaufort Seas. Before their study, the conventional wisdom was that Bowhead whales made most of their growth during summer feeding in the Beaufort Sea, and lived off stored fat while wintering in the Western Bering Sea. Cycles of ^{13}C, however, showed wider valleys than peaks, indicating that most bowhead growth occurred during winter feeding in the Western Bering Sea, where ^{13}C was depleted. This finding is of critical conservation importance for the much reduced whale population, given plans for renewed indigenous hunting and potential oil drilling off the coast of Alaska. Schell *et al.* (1988) point out that other keratinous structures like horns, claws, or antlers could be used to reconstruct regional feeding histories in other vertebrates.

Nitrogen sheds for riparian plants

A growing number of studies are documenting that salmonid migrations import marine carbon and nitrogen (which are enriched in ^{13}C and ^{15}N relative to terrestrial C and N) to freshwater macroinvertebrates and fish (Cederholm *et al.* 1989; Kline *et al.* 1993; Bilby *et al.* 1996), terrestrial mammals (Ben-David *et al.* 1997a,b), and even riparian plants (Ben-David *et al.* 1998) high in coastal watersheds. Ben-David and colleagues sampled ^{15}N content in vegetation growing in areas with contrasting flood regimes and predator activity along six streams with salmon runs in the Tongass National Forest in South-west Alaska. They hypothesized that three possible pathways could convey marine nitrogen to riparian vegetation: deposition of salmon carcasses on floodplains during receding floods, dissolved nitrogen in stream water, and transport of salmon carcasses by predators that carry and cache them well upslope from the river. In four of five plant species sampled, ^{15}N was enriched where predators were active in conveying and caching salmon carcasses. Three of the five plant species (blueberry (*Vaccinium* spp.); Devil's club (*Oplopanax horridus*); and spruce (*Picea sitchensis*)), all showed nitrogen enrichment near the river, which declined sharply with distance from the channel and elevation. This trend was absent in skunk cabbage (*Lysichitum americanum*), which grew in moist swales filled with decaying leaves. The authors conjectured that plants in these microhabitats might not be nitrogen-limited. Small mammals (deer mice, shrews, voles, and squirrels) sampled along these elevational gradients showed the same ^{15}N enrichment patterns as the plants. If these small mammals had been eating salmon carcasses, their ^{13}C would also be enriched. That this was not the case indicated that the marine derived ^{15}N entered these small mammals through herbivory on the plants that drew their CO_2 from the air.

Shapes, sizes, and boundaries of resource

Some resource sheds are simple discrete patches (e.g. photon sheds for intertidal limpets or sessile scraping stream insects). In some cases, their boundaries are sharpened by predator-induced resource avoidance (Sih 1982; Power 1984; Power *et al.* 1989; Lima and Dill 1990), intra- or interspecific territoriality (Ben-David *et al.* 1997b; Carpenter and MacMillen 1976; Berry and Playford 1992), or physical constraints on the consumer (e.g. the 60 m limit on diving depth by sea otters (VanBlaricom and Estes 1988)). Many resource sheds, however, involve complex networks of structures or flow paths that convey or expose resources to consumers from dispersed or distant sources. The tracer studies reviewed above illustrate how movements of consumers (e.g. Bowhead whales), physical advection of resources (e.g. pool-produced algae for riffle-dwelling filter feeders), or vectoring of resources by other organisms (e.g. mycorrhizal networks or migrating salmon) can shape and expand resource sheds of organisms to a counter-intuitive extent. Resources can either move 'down diffusion gradients' (from areas of high to low concentration), or 'up gradient', to become collected and concentrated. The diffusion case occurs in the mycorrhizal hyphal network supplying nutrients and carbon supplements to forest trees (Simard *et al.* 1997). Both resources flow down chemical source-sink gradients (e.g. from sunlit birch to shaded Douglas fir), so that the 'poor get richer' due to the flux. Simard *et al.* suggest that by evening out site-related competitive advantages of trees, this flux may stabilize forests against species loss. Increasing dominance of Douglas fir throughout coastal forests of the Pacific North-west as a result of fire suppression, however, suggests that acting as a resource sink is a successful physiological adaptation for this species rather than the consequence of being a poor competitor.

While the diffusion flow path seems consistent with chemical thermodynamics, the advection-concentration path often occurs in nature due to gravity. Fluids and particles move downslope and concentrate in low points on landscapes. Lowland rivers, lakes, estuaries and coastal lagoons become enriched as they receive and store nutrients from watersheds upslope. This process can be dramatically acceler-ated by timber harvest, agriculture, and concentrated livestock, resulting in eutrophication and serious harm to local economies, ecosystems, and human health (Carpenter *et al.* 1998 and references therein).

The vectoring of river or marine resources upslope by migrating fish or foraging bats, eagles, bears, or other mobile top predators is notable because it counters, at least locally, the otherwise dominant tendency for nutrients to be shed down hill. For example, certain California bats feed almost exclusively over quiet, lowland water, but roost in large, thermally stable structures (massive trees or rock forma-tions) that tend to occur high in landscapes (Rainey *et al.* 1992). As these bats migrate between nocturnal feeding areas and their day roosts, they convey nutri-ents from agriculturally enriched lowland rivers upslope, sometimes tens of kilo-metres, to nutrient-poor chaparral or forest ridge habitats (Rainey *et al.* 1992; Power *et al.*, in press). These localized nutrient 'resets' (translocations of nutrients lost from watersheds back upslope) occur on even larger scales with anadromous salmon supplying marine nitrogen to blueberries growing along Alaska streams (Ben-David *et al.* 1998).

On a more modest scale, river-derived nitrogen and carbon can move back upslope by biological diffusion (*sensu* Okubo 1980). After aquatic insects emerge from productive rivers in northern California, they diffuse laterally into less pro-ductive forested watersheds, their flux decreasing exponentially with distance from the river (Fig. 14.4, Power *et al.*, in press). What factors influence the magnitude of this flux, and its lateral decay rate?

Controls on fluxes of aquatic insects available to watershed consumers

We have been studying the importance of emerged aquatic insects to terrestrial consumers (various spiders, lizards, birds and bats) in the watershed of the South Fork Eel River, in north-western California (39°44′N; 123°39′W). We sample emergence with floating traps set on the water surface (Fig. 14.5). We sample lateral penetration of insects into the surrounding old-growth conifer forest by harvesting insects from sticky and pitfall traps deployed from the river to the ridge (typically only 200–300 m away from the river, as the terrain is steep in this canyon-bound

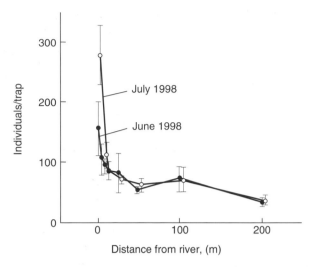

Figure 14.4 Exponentially decreasing insect abundance with distance from the river. June 1998 and July 1998 sticky trap data with Stickum Special R on clear acetate sheets rolled into cylinders and deployed ≈ 1 m off the ground. Points are averages of means of three sites (averaged from three transects per site); lines show 2 SE.

Figure 14.5 Traps sampling emergence of insects (B_0) from the South Fork Eel River.

river). Descriptions of the site and the study are given in Power (1990) and Power *et al.* (in press), respectively.

Consistently, we find that the flux of aquatic insects declines exponentially as one moves inland from the river, typically so steeply that within 10 m, the flux is less than half of its value at the river's edge. The flux of these emerged insects past a point at distance x (m) from the river, B_x (g m^{-2} d^{-1}), depends on the rate of emergence of insects from the river channel reach supplying this flux (B_0 (g m^{-2} d^{-1}) and the flux decay coefficient, ϕ, (m^{-1}), so that

$$B_x = B_0\, e^{-\phi x} \tag{14.1}$$

If emergence is measured, ϕ is the only free parameter in equation (14.1). If $\phi = 0$, the emergence flux passing up through the water surface does not decay at all as it

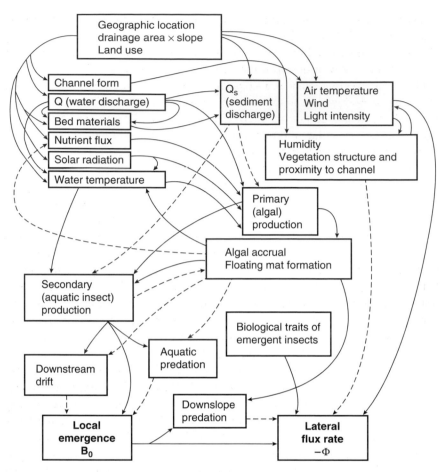

Figure 14.6 Causality flow chart linking landscape position, environment and biology to emergence rates (B_0) and lateral insect flux into the forest ($-\phi$). Dashed arrows indicate reduction of downstream by upstream entities.

moves laterally through the watershed. If ϕ=infinity, the emerged insects concentrate directly over the water, and do not move laterally away from the river. Fitting equation (14.1) with representative data from our summer 1998 emergence and river-to-ridge watershed sticky trap transects gives preliminary estimates of ϕ=0.010 m^{-1} in early June, and ϕ=0.016 m^{-1} in mid-July, when emergence from the river is greater and, in the watershed, soil moisture and insect densities are both lower (Fig. 14.4).

To predict how fluxes of aquatic insect resources may change across sites or under different environmental conditions, we need to unpack and examine some of the ecological variables aggregated into the two parameters of equation (14.1) (Fig. 14.6). Rates of emergence B_0, will depend on local aquatic insect production, and how much of this emerges locally. Secondary production of aquatic insects in our largely algal-based river food web depends on local primary production (and food quality) of algae, and temperature (see Benke (1984, 1993), and Sweeney (1984) for more general reviews). The proportion of insects that emerge, rather than drift downstream or end up in aquatic predators, is heavily influenced by habitat structures that retain and refuge aquatic insects. In the South Fork Eel River and its more productive tributaries, floating algal mats play a major role in enhancing local aquatic insect production, retaining it locally, and diverting it away from aquatic consumers and out into the watershed (Power 1990). Floating algal mats (Fig. 14.7) provide safe oviposition sites for female aquatic insects, and sun-warmed, food-rich incubators for larvae. The mats (made up largely of the macroalga *Cladophora glomerata* in our system) filter and accumulate organic seston from the river, and become overgrown with nutritious diatom epiphytes. During the afternoon, they commonly become more than 8°C warmer than the surrounding water. They are cooler than the water by night (diel air temperatures fluctuate with 2–3 times the amplitude of river temperatures during the summer), but temperature variation itself can hasten the development of aquatic insects (e.g. Huffaker 1944; Sweeney and Schnack 1977; Gresens 1997). The importance to terrestrial consumers of floating algal mats as hot spots of insect emergence is easily demonstrated by the numerical responses of cursorial wolf spiders (Lycosidae) to river margins where mats occur naturally or have been experimentally introduced (Power *et al.*, in press, Parker and Power 1993).

The rate at which flux declines laterally as emerged insects move into the forest, ϕ, is controlled by many factors. These include (i) the behaviour of the adult insects (densities and positions of swarming aggregations—some mayflies swarm directly over the water, while some chironomids may fly well upslope to swarm over landmark trees (M. Butler, personal communication); (ii) their active and passive responses to environmental conditions (temperature, wind, air humidity, light, and vegetative clutter); and (iii) downslope interception of insects by intervening terrestrial predators. At the South Fork Eel, emerging insects suffer nocturnal depredation by bats (W.E. Rainey, unpublished data) and tetragnathid spiders that line the river channel (A. Smyth, unpublished data), and diurnal losses to birds, lizards (J. Sabo, unpublished data), and adult odonates that also concentrate their hunting along the river channel.

Consumers of river-derived insects

Resource shed estimation for a stationary watershed consumer

Emerging aquatic insects are tracked and consumed by a variety of terrestrial predators (Jackson and Fisher 1986; Gray 1989; Power *et al.*, in press; Henschel *et al.*, in press). At our study sites along the South Fork Eel River and its tributaries, bats, lizards, and most spiders (lycosids, tetragnathids) concentrate their foraging activities around the river channel, particularly during the summer drought when forest, meadow and chaparral habitats upslope become dry and less productive. One common consumer, however, does not numerically track river-derived insect prey. The filmy dome spider, *Neriene radiata* (Linyphiidae) (Fig. 14.8) is common

(a)

(b)

(c)

Figure 14.7 Floating algal mats in the South Fork Eel River. (a) Mats accumulate in slack water areas and around emergent rocks in riffles. (b) Close-up of a mat showing ceratopogonid (Diptera) egg masses (black spots) with a predatory water strider (*Gerris remigis*) who will probably consume a very small fraction of the mat's insect emergence. (c) Floating mat shown with a basking aquatic garter snake (*Thamnophis couchi*). Predation risk from these piscivores may deter Eel River fish from foraging in floating algal mats.

throughout the forested watershed around the South Fork Eel River, wherever the vegetation provides sufficiently stiff branches to support its elaborate web in areas with some cover from wind (S. Khandwala and M.E. Power, personal observations). This spider invests so much silk in its web that it moves very infrequently

Figure 14.8 Michael S. Parker (Southern Oregon University) contemplating a cluster of filmy dome spiders (*Neriene radiata*) in the South Fork Eel watershed.

(M.S. Parker, personal observations). It therefore serves as a nearly sessile point sampler of prey flux. During a year of high filmy dome spider abundance, Michael Parker found that spiders along the river margin spun smaller webs, and had fatter abdomens and longer times to starvation in experiments. Spiders several hundred meters back from the river spun much larger webs, were thinner, and starved faster (Parker, unpublished data, discussed in Power *et al.*, in press). These findings are consistent with results from stable isotope analysis. The ^{13}C content of filmy dome spiders suggests that they may derive at least half of their carbon from river-derived prey, even when located hundreds of m back from the river (J.C. Finlay, unpublished data).

   With some simplifying assumptions, isotope analysis could be used to test the usefulness of equation (14.1) in delineating the 'aquatic insect shed' for filmy dome spiders at various positions along the river and into its watershed (Fig. 14.8). As reviewed above, the carbon of insects feeding on pool-grown algae is enriched in ^{13}C, while the carbon of insects feeding on riffle algae is considerably depleted (Finlay *et al.* 1999). Jacques Finlay has pointed out that this isotopic distinction should be maintained in consumers that are close to the river, but should blur in more distant consumers that intercept both pool and riffle prey that mix as they diffuse away from the river. If we assume that

1 pools and riffles are point sources of prey;
2 the flux gradient is maintained as a steady state;

3 insects from both sources become well-mixed as they move laterally; and
4 they are intercepted in proportion to their local abundance,
we should be able to predict the fraction of pool- *vs.* riffle-fed prey in the diet of a
spider as a function of its distance from the river, and its longitudinal position relative to the riffle and pool sources (Fig. 14.9). If prey from other habitats are not
important carbon sources for spiders, the fraction of river- vs. pool-derived prey in
their diets can be calculated from simple mixing models (Fry and Sherr 1988).
These mixing model predictions can be calibrated with field measurements of
emergence and lateral flux of insect prey. Deviations of observation isotopic ratios
from predictions could reveal flaws in our parameter estimation for the flux-
determined resource shed geometry, or in our four assumptions.

Mobile watershed consumers of river-derived insects

In contrast to filmy dome spiders, the more mobile consumers of river-derived
insects that we are studying (bats, lizards, lycosid and tetragnathid spiders) numerically track high concentrations of emerging prey (W.E. Rainey, J. Sabo, K. Marsee,
and A. Smyth, unpublished data; Power *et al.* in review). We can reformulate equation (14.1) to describe the degree to which collective consumption rates of predators at distance x from the river (C_x ($g\,m^{-2}\,d^{-1}$)) as

$$C_x = C_0\,e^{-\eta\,x} \tag{14.2}$$

where C_0 ($g\,m^{-2}\,d^{-1}$), is the collective consumption rate (predator density $\times$ per
capita biomass consumption rate) of predators feeding directly over the river, and
η (m^{-1}), describes the change in their collective consumption rate with distance
from the river. If η is less than ϕ, predators are less aggregated around the river
than their prey (Fig. 14.10a). This sets up concentric changes in predator:prey
ratios that create spatial 'death halos' discovered in the lupine-western tussock
moth-parasitoid system by Maron and Harrison (1997). This situation would
favour evolution by emerging insects to swarm and search for mates directly over
the river (e.g. mayflies). If η is greater than ϕ, predators are more aggregated
around the river than are their prey (Fig. 14.10b). In this case, selection would
favour emerging insects that quickly moved laterally into the watershed, away from
the danger zone (as some chironomids with 'hill topping' lekking behaviour do).
The impact of predators on the behaviour and life history traits of emerging
aquatic insects has been discussed by Edmunds and Edmunds (1979), Butler
(1984), and Flecker *et al.* (1988).

Fitting acoustic data on bat collective foraging activity in mid-July gives preliminary estimates of $\eta = 0.070, 0.026$, and 0.014 for three different river reaches which
differ in channel width and cross-valley profiles. These estimates suggest that bats
are over-aggregated in the first two reaches, and well-matched to insect flux densities in the third (recall that $\phi = 0.016$ in mid-July). In general, insect fluxes and
predator tracking abilities will change in ways that may be partially predictable
from fixed site characteristics as we move downstream from the headwaters of a
river system (Figs 14.6; 14.11). Can we predict how thresholds or gradients in

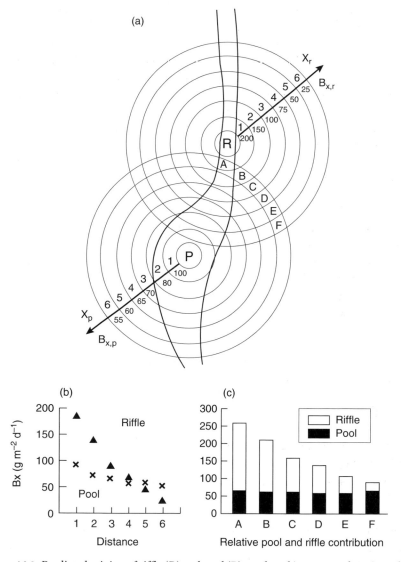

Figure 14.9 Predicted mixing of riffle (R) and pool (P) produced insects as a function of distance from the river. We assume that riffle emergence is higher than pool emergence (as our sampling has indicated, and as predicted by other studies demonstrating higher productivity of riffle areas). Lateral flux of insects is assumed to attenuate more rapidly in riffles, however, because they are often located in narrower, more confined reaches of the river channel. B_x represents the biomass flux of insects at distance x from the emergence source. In (a) emergence sources are depicted as points, which might be a good approximation if most emergence derives from discrete small patches of floating algae. In other cases, emergence sources might better be depicted as stream reaches, and the two-dimensional projection of the flux on to the habitat surface would shift from circular to oval. (b) Shows the decline in Bx with distance from the point source and (c) shows the relative contribution to Bx from riffle and pool insects at points A–F indicated in (a).

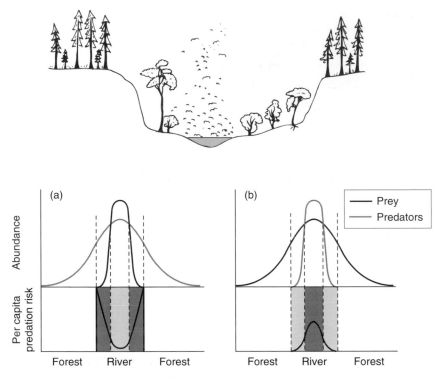

Figure 14.10 Predator tracking (collective consumption) superimposed on emergent insect flux distributions, and resulting spatial patterns of predation risk. (a) Predators are less aggregated than their prey, and potentially generate lateral 'death halos' (Maron and Harrison 1997), selecting for limited lateral prey dispersal. (b) Predators are more aggregated than their prey, potentially selecting for rapid lateral prey dispersal.

environmental conditions along river networks will influence resource fluxes and consequent interactions at different landscape positions?

Longitudinal changes along river networks

Stream drainage networks begin some distance down from the watershed divide, where the downslope flux of water and sediment first cuts a distinct channel head into the hillside. The position of the channel head can move up and downslope with changes in rainfall or sediment discharge (Montgomery and Dietrich 1988). The upstream limit for production of aquatic insects begins downstream from the channel head, where surface water is retained long enough for taxa to complete their larval lives. Clearly, this boundary will also change with precipitation regime, and the permeability of the bed and the surrounding watershed (Hynes 1975). Downstream, channels collect discharge from larger drainage areas and their slopes decrease. They widen, deepen, and flow faster according to empirical rules of hydraulic geometry (Leopold *et al.* 1964) that relate channel width, depth, and

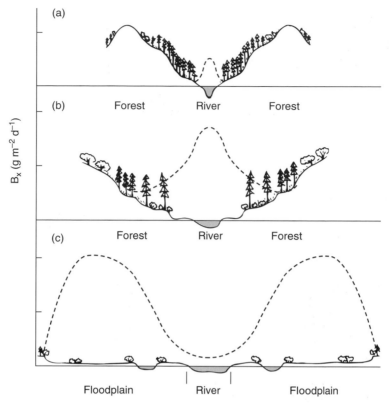

Figure 14.11 Cross sections through a river at its (a) headwaters; (b) middle reaches; and (c) lowland reaches with floodplains, with predicted patterns of emergence and lateral fluxes of aquatic insects from these positions.

velocity to discharge, which scales with drainage area. Width : depth ratios increase and channels change from cascades and stepped pools in narrow gorges, to meandering pools and riffles in middle reaches, to broad floodplains with off-river water bodies in the lowlands. Corresponding to these slope and drainage area-driven changes, bed materials change from boulders and bedrock in headwaters to cobbles and gravel in mid-reaches to fine sand and silt near river mouths (Leopold *et al.* 1964; Montgomery and Buffington 1997; Fig. 14.11). Disturbance regimes related to sediment transport change from rare (few or none per millennium) but catastrophic debris slides in headwaters to bed scouring floods in middle reaches that move cobbles and gravels as frequently as several times per year to chronic sand and silt transport in lowland rivers (Dietrich and Dunne 1978; Benda and Dunne 1990).

   Are these geomorphically predictable changes in habitat structure and physical processes useful in predicting resource fluxes and delimiting boundaries of resource (emerged insect) sheds? If algal productivity and standing crops (e.g. floating mats) are major controls on aquatic insect emergence, we can predict that

B_0 will increase abruptly downstream after channel and valley walls widen enough for river beds to receive enough sunlight to support macroalgal growth (Vannote *et al.* 1980). Positions of these transitions can be predicted for specific watersheds by the application of solar radiation models to high resolution digital elevation data from laser altimetry (D. Allen, unpublished data). Downstream from middle reaches, attached algal production will decrease as stable bedrock, boulder, and cobble substrates give way to finer gravels and sand or silt, on which attached algae are frequently silted or chronically abraded. Water column turbidity increases, decreasing benthic algal productivity (Vannote *et al.* 1980). If, however, lowland rivers have access to their floodplains (increasingly uncommon in the Northern Hemisphere), aquatic insect production will be supported by periphyton on emergent and floating macrophytes and semiaquatic floodplain vegetation (e.g. Forsberg 1993). The emergence of insects from lowland river reaches will depend on floodplain characteristics (morphology, especially of off-river water bodies; hydrologic cycles; extent and type of vegetation (Junk 1973, 1970; Junk *et al.* 1989; Power 1995; Power *et al.* 1995)), and are likely to be higher over inundated floodplains and off-river water bodies than over the main channel (Fig. 14.11c).

The lateral fluxes of insects into watersheds will also be influenced by longitudinal position in the drainage network (Fig. 14.11), although the net influences are perhaps less clear than for emergence. Near the headwaters, lateral penetration of emergence to the watershed is probably reduced. Because insects will be less active in the cool gorges, they will be physically confined by steep channel walls, and sheltered there from winds that might otherwise advect them away from the channel. Emerged insects (e.g. adult chironomids) near headwaters are commonly seen in swarms within dark, cave-like air pockets under large boulders, hovering over the surface of small pools. In lower, more open river reaches, insects are denser and warmer, both factors which might enhance their lateral diffusion (Okubo 1980). Wider channels will also be windier, so that insects could be advected laterally, or might leave open channel areas to avoid displacement or desiccation. Where, as at the Eel River, flow is seasonal, there would be less vegetative structure next to the stream to interfere with flight and offer resting perches. Lateral fluxes in lower reaches could be diminished, however, if predators aggregating to these more productive feeding grounds can deplete their prey, or if ovipositing females are strongly attracted to algal mats or still water surfaces (Horvath 1995).

Conclusion

Although landscape control on species distributions has been a venerable focus in the literature in ecology (Elton 1927; Shelford 1932; Holridge 1967), there is still considerable scope for research on the degree to which fixed site characteristics allow partial prediction of ecological processes (Brown 1995; Wiley *et al.* 1990, 1997; Wiens *et al.* this volume). River networks exhibit, and impose, partially predictable features and regimes on landscapes, which influence resource sheds, such as the source areas supplying emergent insects to terrestrial insectivores. Resource supplies and physical conditions in turn constrain the interactions of consumers and their effects on ecosystems and communities.

Environmental heterogeneity is usually viewed as a fact of life that complicates or thwarts our ability to apply predictive models to ecological interactions. It is certainly the case that the uplift of a mountain range or the conversion of warm and cold oceanic circulations are historically determined, idiosyncratic phenomena that interfere with the ability of ecologists to apply general models ubiquitously. In non-theoretical applications, however, reading landscapes has long helped humans predict specific distributions and behaviours of organisms. Spear fishermen knew where and when to wait for migrating salmon to swim up a waterfall. Trappers could predict which foot of which sex of beaver would be caught in traps positioned in marshes around their lodges. As we struggle to merge the general dynamics of theoretical spatial ecology with the static description of landscape ecology, we will probably enjoy at least modest success by tailoring dynamic models of fluxes and interactions to boundary conditions and parameter constraints imposed by a partially ordered physical world.

Acknowledgments

We would like to thank Jacques Finlay and Gilbert Cabana for enlightening us about the use of stable isotopes in ecology, Bob Holt, Libby John and an anonymous reviewer for their helpful ideas and comments, and Terry Chapin for his early unflagging encouragement. This research was funded by the National Science Foundation (DEB–961517) and the Water Resources Center of California (WRC-895). The University of California Natural Reserve System, by providing a site protected for field research at the Angelo Coast Range Reserve, has made much of our work possible.

References

Aitken, M.J. (1990) *Science-Based Dating in Archaeology*. Longman, London.

Benda, L. and Dunne, T. (1990) Predicting deposition of debris flows in mountain channels. *Canadian Geotechnical Journal* 27, 409–417.

Ben-David, M., Flynn, R.W. and Schell, D.M. (1997a) Annual and seasonal changes in diets of martens: evidence from stable isotope analysis. *Oecologia* 111, 280–291.

Ben-David, M., Hanley, T.A., Klein, D.R. and Schell, D.M. (1997b) Seasonal changes in diets of coastal and riverine mink: the role of spawning Pacific salmon. *Canadian Journal of Zoology* 75, 803–811.

Ben-David, M., Hanley, T.A. and Schell, D.M. (1998) Fertilization of terrestrial vegetation by spawning Pacific salmon: The role of flooding and predator activity. *Oikos* 83, 47–55.

Benke, A.C. (1984) Secondary production of aquatic insects. In: *The Ecology of Aquatic Insects* (eds V.H. Resh and D.M. Rosenberg), pp. 289–322. Plenum, New York.

Benke, A.C. (1993) Concepts and patterns for invertebrate production in running waters. *Internationale Vereinigung für Theoretische und Angewandte Limnologie, Verhandlungen* 25, 15–38.

Berry, P.F. and Playford, P.E. (1992) Territoriality in a subtropical kyphosid fish associated with macroalgal polygons on reef platforms at

Rottnest Island, Western Australia. *Journal of the Royal Society of Western Australia* **75**, 67–73.

Bilby, R.E., Fransen, B.R. and Bisson, P.A. (1996) Incorporation of nitrogen and carbon from spawning coho salmon into the trophic system of small streams: Evidence from stable isotopes. *Canadian Journal of Fisheries and Aquatic Sciences* **53**, 164–173.

Brown, J.H. (1995) *Macroecology.* University of Chicago Press, Chicago.

Burkholder, J.M., Noga, E.J., Hobbs, C.W., Glasgow, H.B. Jr and Smith, S.A. (1992) New 'phantom' dinoflagellate is the causative agent of major estuarine fish kills. *Nature* **358**, 407–410.

Butler, M.G. (1984) Life histories of aquatic insects. In: *The Ecology of Aquatic Insects* (eds V.H. Resh and D.M. Rosenberg), pp. 24–55. Plenum, New York.

Carpenter, F.L. and MacMillen, R.E. (1976) Threshold model of feeding territoriality and test with a Hawaiian honeycreeper. *Science* **194**, 639–642.

Carpenter, S.R., Caraco, N.F., Correll, D.L., Howarth, R.W., Sharpley, A.N. and Smith, V.H. (1998) Nonpoint pollution of surface waters with phosphorus and nitrogen. *Ecological Applications* **8**, 559–568.

Cederholm, C.J., Houston, D.B., Cole, D.L. and Scarlett, W.J. (1989) Fate of coho salmon (*Oncorhynchus kisutch*) carcasses in spawning streams. *Canadian Journal of Fisheries and Aquatic Sciences* **46**, 1347–1355.

Cousins, S.H. (1990) Countable ecosystems deriving from a new food web entity. *Oikos* **57**, 270–275.

Cousins, S.H. (1996) Food webs: From the Lindeman paradigm to a taxonomic general theory. In: *Food Webs. Integration of Patterns and Dynamics* (eds G.A. Polis and K.O. Winemiller), pp. 243–251. Chapman and Hill, New York.

Dawson, T.E. and Ehleringer, J.R. (1991) Streamside trees that do not use stream water. *Nature* **350**, 335–337.

Desowitz, R.S. (1981) *New Guinea Tapeworms and Jewish Grandmothers.* Avon Books, New York.

Dietrich, W.E. and Dunne, T. (1978) Sediment budget for a small catchment in mountainous terrain. *Zeitschrift Fur Geomorphogie Supplement* **29**, 191–206.

Dietrich, W.E., Dunne, T., Humphrey, N.F. and Reid, L.M. (1982) Construction of sediment budgets for drainage basins, *United States Forest Service General Technical Report*, PNW-141. 5–23.

Edmunds, G.F. Jr and Edmunds, C.H. (1979) Predation, climate, and emergence and mating of mayflies. In: *Advances in Ephemeroptera Biology* (eds J.F. Flannagan and K.E. Marshall), pp. 277–285. Plenum Press, New York.

Elton, C. (1927) *Animal Ecology.* Sidgwick and Jackson, London.

Finlay, J.C., Power, M.E. and Cabana, G. (1999) Effects of water velocity on algal carbon isotope rations: implications for river food web studies. *Limnology and Oceanography* **44**, 1198–1203.

Fitter, A.H., Hodge, A., Daniell, T.J. and Robinson, D. (1999) Resource sharing in plant fungus communities: did the carbon move for you? *Trends in Ecology and Evolution* **14**, 70.

Flecker, A.S., Allan, J.D. and McClintock, N.L. (1988) Swarming and sexual selection in a Rocky Mountain mayfly. *Holarctic Ecology* **11**, 280–285.

Forsberg, B.R. (1993) Autotrophic carbon sources for Amazon fish? *Ecology* **74**, 643–652.

Fry, B. and Arnold, C. (1982) Rapid 13C/12C turnover during growth of brown shrimp (*Penaeus aztecus*). *Oecologia* **54**, 200–204.

Fry, B. and Sherr, E.B. (1988) d13C measurements as indicators of carbon flow in marine and freshwater ecosystems. In: *Stable Isotopes in Ecological Research* (eds P.W. Rundel, J.R. Ehleringer and K.A. Nagy), pp. 196–229. Springer, Berlin.

Gray, L.J. (1989) Emergence production and export of aquatic insects from a tallgrass prairie stream. *Southwestern Naturalist* **34**, 313–318.

Gresens, S.E. (1997) Interactive effects of diet and thermal regime on growth of the midge *Pseudochironomus richardsoni* Malloch. *Freshwater Biology* **38**, 365–373.

Henschel, J.R., Mahsberg, D. and Stumpf, H. (in press) Spatial subsidies: the influence of river insects on spider predation of terrestrial insects. In: *Review for Food Webs and Landscapes* (eds G.A. Polis and M.E. Power). University of Chicago Press, Chicago.

Holridge, L.R. (1967) *Life zone ecology.* Tropical Science Center, San Jose, Costa Rica.

Holt, R.D. (1996) Food webs in space: an island biogeographic perspective. In: *Food Webs* (eds.

G.A. Polis and K.O. Winemiller) Chapman and Hall, New York.

Horvath, G. (1995) Reflection-polarization patterns at flat water surfaces and their relevance for insect polarization vision. *Journal of Theoretical Biology* **175**, 27–37.

Huffaker, C.B. (1944) The temperature relations of the immature stages of the malarial mosquito, *Anopheles quadrimaculatus* Say, with a comparison of the developmental power of constant and variable temperatures in insect metabolism. *Annals of the Entomological Society of America* **37**, 1–27.

Hynes, H.B.N. (1975) The stream and its valley. *Internationale Vereinigung für Theoretische und Angewandte Limnologie, Verhandlungen* **19**, 1–15.

Jackson, J.K. and Fisher, S.G. (1986) Secondary production, emergence, and export of aquatic insects of a Sonoran Desert stream. *Ecology* **67**, 629–638.

Jackson, L.J. (1997) Piscivores, predation, and PCBs in Lake Ontario's pelagic food web. *Ecological Applications* **7**, 991–1001.

Jackson, L.J. and Schindler, D.E. (1996) Field estimates of net trophic transfer of PCBs from prey fishes to Lake Michigan salmonids. *Environmental Science and Technology* **30**, 1861–1865.

Junk, W.J. (1970) Investigations on the ecology and production-biology of the 'floating meadow' (Paspalo-Echinochloetum) on the Middle Amazon. I. The floating vegetation and its ecology. *Amazoniana* **2**, 449–495.

Junk, W.J. (1973) Investigations on the ecology and production-biology of the 'floating meadow' (Paspalo-Echinochloetum) on the Middle Amazon. II. The aquatic fauna in the root zone of floating vegetation. *Amazoniana* **4**, 9–102.

Junk, W.J., Bayley, P.B. and Sparks, R.E. (1989) The flood pulse concept. In: *Proceedings of the International Large Rivers Symposium, 106* (ed. D.P. Dodge), pp. 110–127. Canadian Special Publications in Fisheries and Aquatic Sciences, Ottawa, Ontario.

Keeley, J.E. and Sandquist, D.R. (1992) Carbon: freshwater plants. *Plant and Cell Environment* **15**, 1021–1035.

Kline, T.C., Goering, J.J., Mathisen, O.A. and Poe, P.H. (1993) Recycling of elements transported upstream by runs of Pacific salmon. II. d15N and d13C evidence in the Kvichak River, Bristol Bay, Southwestern Alaska. *Canadian Journal of Fisheries and Aquatic Sciences* **50**, 2350–2365.

Leopold, L.B., Wolman, M.G. and Miller, J.P. (1964) *Fluvial Processes in Geomorphology.* Freeman, San Francisco.

Lima, S.L. and Dill, L.M. (1990) Behavioral decisions made under the risk of predation: a review and prospectus. *Canadian Journal of Zoology* **68**, 619–640.

Maron, J.L. and Harrison, S. (1997) Spatial pattern formation in an insect host parasitoid system. *Science* **278**, 1619–1621.

Montgomery, D.R. and Buffington, J.S. (1997) Channel-reach morphology in mountain drainage basins. *Geological Society of America Bulletin* **109**, 596–611.

Montgomery, D.R. and Dietrich, W.E. (1988) Where do channels begin?. *Nature* **336**, 232–234.

Okubo, A. (1980) *Diffusion and Ecological Problems: Mathematical Models.* Springer-Verlag, Berlin.

Paine, R.T. (1996) Preface. In: *Food Webs. Integration of Patterns and Dynamics* (eds G.A. Polis and K.O. Winemiller), pp. ix–x. Chapman and Hill, New York.

Parker, M.S. and Power, M.E. (1993) Algal-mediated differences in aquatic insect emergence and the effect on a terrestrial predator. *Bulletin of the North American Benthological Society* **10**, 171.

Polis, G.A., Anderson, W.B. and Holt, R.D. (1997) Toward an integration of landscape and food web ecology: The dynamics of spatially subsidized food webs. *Annual Review of Ecology and Systematics* **28**, 289–316.

Power, M.E. (1984) Depth distributions of armored catfish: predator-induced resource avoidance?. *Ecology* **65**, 523–528.

Power, M.E. (1990) Benthic turfs versus floating mats of algae in river food webs. *Oikos* **58**, 67–79.

Power, M.E. (1995) Floods, food chains, and ecosystem processes in rivers. In: *Linking Species and Ecosystems* (eds C.G. Jones and J.H. Lawton), pp. 52–60. Chapman and Hall, New York.

Power, M.E., Dudley, T.L. and Cooper, S.D. (1989) Grazing catfish, fishing birds, and attached algae in a Panamanian stream. *Environmental Biology of Fishes* **26**, 285–294.

Power, M.E., Parker, G., Dietrich, W.E. and Sun, A. (1995) How does floodplain width affect floodplain river ecology? An exploration using simulations. *Geomorphology. Special Issue on Biogeomorphology* **13**, 301–317.

Power, M.E., Rainey, W.E., Parker, M.S., *et al.* (in press) River to watershed subsidies in an old-growth conifer forest. In: *Review for Food Webs and Landscapes* (eds G.A. Polis, G. Huxel and M.E. Power). University Press, Chicago.

Rainey, W.E., Pierson, E.D., Colberg, M. and Barclay, J.H. (1992) Bats in hollow redwoods: seasonal use and role in nutrient transfer into old growth communities. *Bat Research News* **33**, 71.

Rau, G.H., Sweeney, R.E., Kaplan, I.R., Mearns, A.J. and Young, D.R. (1981) Differences in animal 13C, 15N, and D abundance between a polluted and an unpolluted coastal site: likely indicators of sewage uptake by a marine food web. *Estuarine Coastal Shelf Science* **13**, 701–707.

Robinson, D. and Fitter, A.H. (1999) The magnitude and control of carbon transfer between plants linked by a common mycorrhizal network. *Journal of Experimental Botany* **50**, 9–13.

Rundel, P.W., Ehleringer, J.R. and Nagy, K.A. (1988) *Stable Isotopes in Ecological Research.* Springer, Berlin.

Schell, D.M., Saupe, S.M. and Haubenstock, N. (1988) Natural isotope abundances in Bowhead whale (*Balaena mysticetus*) Baleen: Markers of aging and habitat usage. In: *Stable Isotopes in Ecological Research* (eds P.W. Rundel, J.R. Ehleringer and K.A. Nagy), pp. 260–269. Springer-Verlag, Berlin.

Schell, D.M. and Ziemann, P.J. (1988) Natural carbon isotope tracers in Arctic aquatic food webs. In: *Stable Isotopes in Ecological Research* (eds P.W. Rundel, J.R. Ehleringer and K.A. Nagy), pp. 230–251. Springer, Berlin.

Shelford, V.E. (1932) Life zones, modern ecology and the failure of temperature summing. *Wilson Bulletin* **44**, 144–157.

Sih, A. (1982) Foraging strategies and the avoidance of predation by an aquatic insect, *Notonecta hoffmani. Ecology* **63**, 786–796.

Simard, S.W., Perry, D.A., Jones, M.D., Myroid, D.D., Durall, D. and Molina, R. (1997) Net transfer of carbon between ectomycorrhizal tree species in the field. *Nature* **388**, 579–582.

Sweeney, B.W. (1984) Factors influencing life-history patterns of aquatic insects. In: *The Ecology of Aquatic Insects* (eds V.H. Resh and D.M. Rosenberg), pp. 56–100. Plenum, New York.

Sweeney, B.W. and Schnack, J.A. (1977) Egg development, growth, and metabolism of *Sigara alternata* (Say) (Hemiptera: Corixidae) in fluctuating thermal environments. *Ecology* **58**, 265–277.

VanBlaricom, G.R. and Estes, J.A., eds. (1988) *The Community Ecology of Sea Otters.* Springer-Verlag, Berlin.

Vannote, R.L., Minshall, G.W., Cummins, K.W., Sedell, J.R. and Cushing, C.E. (1980) The river continuum concept. *Canadian Journal of Fisheries and Aquatic Sciences* **37**, 130–137.

Webster (1989) *Webster's Encyclopedic Unabridged Dictionary of the English Language.* Portland House, New York.

Weathers, K.C. and Likens, G.E. (1997) Clouds in southern Chile: an important source of nitrogen to nitrogen-limited ecosystems. *Environmental Science and Technology* **31**, 210–213.

Wennergren, U., Ruckelshaus, M. and Kareiva, P. (1995) The promise and limitations of spatial models in conservation biology. *Oikos* **75**, 349–356.

Wiley, M.J., Kohler, S.L. and Seelbach, P.W. (1997) Reconciling landscape and local views of aquatic communities: Lessons from Michigan trout streams. *Freshwater Biology* **37**, 133–148.

Wiley, M.J., Osborne, L.L. and Larimore, R.W. (1990) Longitudinal structure of an agricultural prairie river system and its relationship to current stream ecosystem theory. *Canadian Journal of Fisheries and Aquatic Science* **47**, 373–384.

Chapter 15

Habitat destruction and extinctions: predictions from metapopulation models

C. Dytham

Introduction

Human activity is the primary agent of habitat destruction on Earth. Humans destroy habitats both directly through forest clearance or wetland drainage and indirectly through pollution or over-fishing. The effects of natural agents of habitat destruction, physical and biological, are now dwarfed by our activities.

Species are being lost at an unprecedented rate and it must be accepted that the major cause of species extinctions is habitat destruction (e.g. Glowka *et al.* 1994; Heywood 1995; Primack 1998). If we are concerned about species extinctions then the biome where we should concentrate our attentions is that with the highest species diversity: tropical forest (e.g. Whitmore and Sayer 1992). Concern about the ecological consequences of tropical deforestation is something that has been voiced for a long time now (e.g. Soulé and Wilcox 1980). The problem has not gone away even if there is some evidence that the rate of deforestation is declining in some countries (FAO 1998). This slight reduction in rate is more likely to be the result of the global economic recession of the 1990s than any environmental awakening.

One estimate of the scale of destruction is 13 million hectares per year in global net loss of forest cover (FAO 1998). This is probably a conservative estimate because it is based on satellite images where canopy coverage needs to fall to around 20% before the forest is counted as having been lost and also, the loss of tropical forest is off-set by afforestation outside the tropics. A loss of 13 million ha/yr translates to 1000 ha (or $10 \, km^2$) in just over 40 minutes. Forest fires have been worse in recent years. In 1997 and 1998 there were extensive fires in lowland moist forest that have not burned in recorded history. Huge areas of Indonesia have been devastated as have large areas of Brazil. Data are unreliable, but it is estimated that 2 million hectares of rainforest burned in Brazil in 1997 and estimates for 1998 are even higher.

The root cause of the problem is global growth, both economic and demographic. In many parts of the world the human population is growing at over 3% per year. The pressure on land and resources will intensify, leading to continued habitat degradation and destruction on a massive scale.

Department of Biology, University of York, Heslington, York YO10 5DD, UK

Estimating the cost of habitat loss

A quantification of the cost of habitat loss is often asked for. There is a debate about how we value our natural assets, but for the purpose of this paper I will only count the cost in the simplest terms: how many species were there before habitat destruction and how many afterwards? This measure of the cost of habitat destruction as the net loss of species is easy to grasp, if difficult to measure. It excludes any value associated with loss of ecosystem functions, retention of soil, carbon storage, existence values, etc., that are all important but difficult properties to quantify.

The question asked by a politician or developer may be something like this: 'If we take a nature reserve and remove half of its area, what proportion of the resident species will we lose?'. Of course the answer is not a simple one. It depends on some consideration of the variability of terrain in the original reserve, the types of habitat bordering the reserve, its shape, history, current management and many other features. When pushed for an answer, ecologists resort to back of the envelope calculations derived from species–area relationships. The answer that has seeped into the political and media psyche is that when half of a nature reserve is destroyed we will lose about 15% of the species. So, if nature reserves are cut in half, on average, some 85% of the species will remain. This logic can be extended so that if a further 50% loss of habitat occurs there will be a further 15% loss of the remaining species. So, losing 75% of the original area of the reserve costs the local extinction of less than 30% of the species. A staggering 90% of habitat destroyed will only result in a 50% loss of species. This level of species loss might be considered a small price to pay for progress.

Species–area relationships have had a long history. The simple observation that more species are found as larger areas are sampled was noted in the nineteenth century. A plot of species against area gives a curve but a plot of log area sampled and log number of species usually generates a fairly good straight line. This relationship can then be used to make predictions about the effects of habitat loss.

There has been much debate about the slopes of log species–log area relationships (e.g. Williams 1964; Usher 1979; Hart and Horwitz 1991). There are some general patterns. For example, samples of different sizes on mainlands nearly always have a relationship with a lower slope than when the samples are islands in an archipelago. Unfortunately, the straight-line log species–log area relationship arises largely because of a sampling artefact. As larger areas are sampled, more individuals are sampled. More individuals will inevitably lead to more species being recorded. There is a second sampling artefact because larger areas will contain more habitats and therefore add more species. The problems of using species–area relationships to make predictions about the consequences of habitat loss are discussed at length in Rosenzweig (1995).

The real cost?

I think that a different question was answered when the loss of species was estimated by using a species–area relationship. Destruction of half of the remaining downland on the South Downs of England might remove about 15% of the species at one stroke. This instant loss of species is only the start of the process of loss, and some species surviving the initial destruction will become extinct at some time in the future. A major component of these future extinctions is a metapopulation effect. Although the idea is not new, it fell to David Tilman and colleagues (Tilman *et al.* 1994) to coin the excellent term 'extinction debt' to describe the continuing loss of species following a habitat destruction event. So the true cost in number of species lost will be paid as the initial loss of species and then the extinction debt. Rosenzweig (1995) argues that area is the primary determinant of species diversity and fears that 50% of habitat lost may well result, in the long term, in a 50% loss of species while a 90% loss of habitat will lead to a 90% loss of species.

In this paper I consider the metapopulation effect on future extinctions, although there are clearly several other processes at work in addition to the sampling effect of the species–area relationship that are only partially incorporated into the metapopulation paradigm. For example, across a species' range there will be areas at the periphery (sinks) where the net reproductive rate does not replace losses from the population due to death or emigration (generation growth rate, $R < 1$ or intrinsic rate of increase, $r < 0$) and the local populations are maintained by immigration from a core area (sources). If the habitat supporting the core is destroyed or degraded then habitat remaining at the periphery will not support the persistence of local populations (e.g. Lawton 1994). Another problem for large-bodied species (the 'charismatic megafauna') may be range-size limitations for species that require large, continuous home ranges that are unavailable in fragmented landscapes. Furthermore, populations in fragmented or degraded habitats will tend to be smaller than those in more continuous habitats. Stochastic extinctions are more likely in small populations. There are also long-term, genetic consequences of inbreeding in small populations and the Allee effect (reduced survival or fecundity at low density) may also cause local extinction especially where habitat quality, rather than extent, is reduced. There is a growing realization that the Allee effect (reduced survival or reproductive rate at low density) has been overlooked as a force in evolutionary ecology (e.g. Courchamp *et al.* 1999; Stephens and Sutherland 1999).

Modelling destruction and extinction

I will consider how metapopulation models can be used to predict the effects of habitat loss on species persistence, by covering three approaches to modelling space: implicit, explicit and realistic. Then I will consider how population-based models can be used to predict extinction thresholds. It should also be noted that many more people now have access to computers powerful enough to consider quite complex individual-based and spatially extended models (e.g. Judson 1994; Travis and Dytham 1998), although I do not cover individual-based models here.

The Levins metapopulation model

This is a spatially implicit population-level model. It was suggested by Levins at the end of the 1960s and was originally proposed as a model to predict the number of agricultural fields that would be infested by an insect pest (Levins 1969). The model describes a very large number of fields that can be in one of two states: occupied by the pest or unoccupied by the pest. Only two parameters are needed to model the change in proportion of fields that are infested, namely extinction rate in occupied patches (i.e. the chance of a patch going from an occupied to an unoccupied state) and the colonization rate (i.e. the chance of a patch sending out a propagule that might turn another patch from an unoccupied to an occupied state). The rate of change in the proportion of occupied patches can be simply expressed:

$$\mathrm{d}p/\mathrm{d}t = cp(1-p) - ep \tag{15.1}$$

where p is the proportion of patches that are occupied, e is the extinction rate and c is the colonization rate. Local extinction is quite a straightforward process. Only occupied patches can be affected and where it occurs a population in a patch goes from being present to absent. Colonization is more complex. Colonization propagules have to leave occupied patches (cp), find unoccupied ones ($1-p$) and then establish a population. This is a multistage process, comprising dispersal, arrival, survival and establishment, that is simplified to the term: $cp(1-p)$. Ims and Yoccoz (1997) consider some of the problems associated with measuring movements between habitat patches.

This model makes some interesting assumptions about how populations persist. First, provided that $e > 0$, it assumes that populations in all patches will inevitably suffer local extinction. This implies that if an organism exists as a metapopulation, protection of a single site is certain to fail as a long-term conservation method.

The Levins model is an extremely simplified representation of a complex set of processes and many enhancements or adjustments can be made to make it more realistic, for example, 'rescue' effects where colonists save occupied patches from extinction (see, e.g. Hanski 1997).

The equilibrium proportion of patches occupied in the basic Levins model is:

$$\hat{p} = 1 \, e/c \tag{15.2}$$

The (meta)population will persist (i.e. have an equilibrium occupancy greater than zero), so long as the colonization rate exceeds the extinction rate ($c > e$). An important message of the Levins model, and one that is still rather overlooked, is that it predicts that a proportion of perfectly acceptable patches (e/c) will be unoccupied. In other words, if a patch (or area) does not support a population this is not necessarily an indication of the unsuitability of the patch.

The critical difference between the Levins metapopulation model and the island biogeography model (MacArthur and Wilson 1967) is the absence of a mainland in the former. The MacArthur-Wilson model assumes that there is a mainland supporting populations of a large pool of species. These mainland populations disperse colonists to the islands as propagule rain. The propagules then develop into local, island populations. In contrast, in the Levins model all patches are equal and there is no permanent source of propagules. All colonization events originate internally. This is certainly a paradigm shift.

Habitat destruction in a Levins model

A simple, perhaps simplistic, modification of the Levins model is to imagine that the very large number of patches available for colonization is reduced from one to a proportion 'h' or habitable (Nee and May 1992). So instead of colonists arriving at just empty patches they can only establish in empty, habitable patches. There is a slight change to the model:

$$dp/dt = cp(h-p) - ep \tag{15.3a}$$

This might also be re-framed to consider the proportion of habitat destroyed 'd' rather than the proportion that is habitable:

$$dp/dt = cp(1-d-p) - ep \tag{15.3b}$$

The equilibrium proportion of patches occupied for equation (15.3) is:

$$\hat{p} = h - e/c \tag{15.4}$$

This changes the requirement for persistence of the metapopulation somewhat, adding the further hurdle that e/c must be less than the proportion of habitable patches, h. For example, if $h=1$, $e=0.05$ and $c=0.2$ then 75% of all patches should be occupied at equilibrium. If the habitability, h, is reduced to 0.6, then only 35% of the original patches should be occupied (see Fig. 15.1).

I certainly do not advocate using this approach as a tool for predicting extinction thresholds in anything but the broadest of terms. The model is too coarse and over-simplified to be applied to individual species. Hanski (1997) identifies and discusses several shortcomings of the model.

The implication of the Levins model is that for the 50% habitat loss = 15% species loss approximation derived from the species–area relationship to be true, we have to assume that 85% of species have an occupancy of original patches of 50% or more before the destruction event. For the prediction of 90% habitat loss = 50% species loss to be true, half of all species need to have an occupancy of original patches greater than 90%. Here we have a problem, as it is almost impossible to measure the proportion of patches occupied because of the difficulty of distinguishing those patches that are empty but suitable from those that are empty and unsuitable (see Shorrocks and Bingley (1990) for a discussion of a similar problem). If we assume that species occupancies are evenly spread from 0% to 100%, then 50% habitat loss will lead to 50% species loss and 90% habitat loss will lead to 90% species loss. However, there is no reason to believe that occupancy is evenly spread. Indeed, this is extremely unlikely to be the case. However it might be closer to the truth than the assumption that half of all species have a predestruction occupancy greater than 90%.

There are problems in translating the Levins model to the real world. The gross assumption of identical habitat patches is impossible to reconcile with real

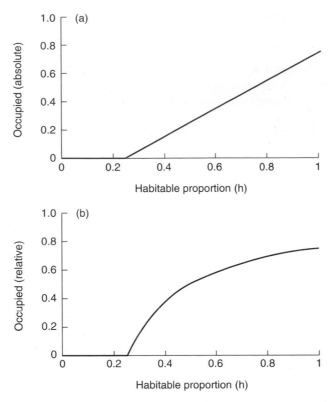

Figure 15.1 Habitat destruction is applied in a simple Levins model. As habitat is destroyed the proportion of the original habitat patches that remain habitable (*h*) is reduced. In (a) the occupancy is shown as the proportion of the original patches that are occupied. As habitat is destroyed (*h* reduced) the proportion of the original patches that are occupied falls. In this case of local extinction rate (*e*)=0.05 and colonization rate (*c*)=0.2 the metapopulation extinction threshold is reached when 25% of the habitat patches remains. The same result can be expressed in a different way, as the proportion of the remaining habitat that is occupied (b) This gives a slightly different picture, and is perhaps the one that more closely relates to ecological surveys—who looks in destroyed habitats? The proportion of patches occupied appears to fall slowly with the initial habitat destruction and then declines rapidly to extinction.

populations. It is difficult to obtain field data for *e*- and *c*-values, and the unoccupied, but suitable, patches require a great deal of long-term study to identify.

The modified Levins model in equations (15.3a) and (15.3b) assumes that *e* and *c* do not change as the habitat is destroyed. A further modification makes the extinction rate dependent on the scale of habitat destruction. It is quite likely that local extinction will be more probable as regional destruction worsens, perhaps due to general degradation of habitat. This modification is effectively adding an Allee effect (survival is reduced as the occupied patches become less dense) and

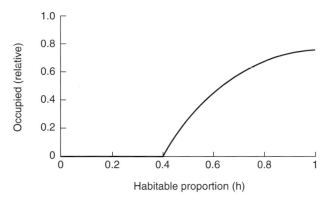

Figure 15.2 This is a slightly modified version of Fig. 15.1(a). In this example, extinction rate increases slightly as more habitat is destroyed. The prediction of the persistence point (extinction threshold) changes from 25% to 40% habitat remaining.

obviously makes extinction more likely. The consequences of the Allee effect on spatially structured populations may be dire for species reduced by hunting or habitat deterioration whether the effect operates within habitat patches or between them (Amarasekare 1998). Figure 15.2 shows the effect of a slight increase in extinction rate as habitat is destroyed.

Extinctions in a stochastic Levins model

The beguiling simplicity of the Levins model can be converted into simulation models with only a few lines of code. The e and c values become per-patch probabilities rather than overall rates and a finite number of patches can be used rather than an assumption of a very large (effectively infinite) number of patches. Stochastic versions of the Levins model have variable occupancy (see Fig. 15.3).

The profound difference between the deterministic and stochastic versions of the model is that in the deterministic model, global extinction is impossible while the persistence criteria are met, whereas in the stochastic model extinction is quite possible. Indeed, extinction is inevitable, given a long enough time series, whenever $e > 0$. As Fig. 15.4 shows, even in a fairly large system (16 900 patches), when the predicted patch occupancy of a Levins model is 17%, only a small proportion of the stochastic metapopulations survive for 2000 iterations. Clearly, in a stochastic Levins model the persistence criterion of $c/e > 1$ is insufficient to avoid extinction.

Relaxation and extinction debts

One of the most important features of the Levins model and its variants is that the equilibrium level of patch occupancy is not reached instantly. At the community level this delay is often called relaxation (although the model considers just one species within the community). As the persistence requirements and predicted occupancy are based on the e/c ratio, if there are two species with different

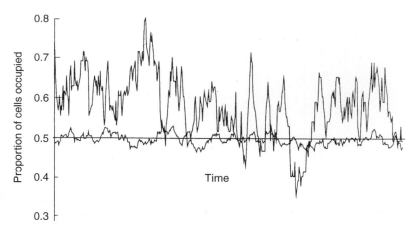

Figure 15.3 Two realizations of a stochastic Levins model (e=0.1, c=0.2). The straight line is the predicted occupancy of the Levins model (0.5 or 50% of patches). The highly fluctuating solid line is the occupancy in an arena of 100 cells and the less variable line is the occupancy in an area with 2500 cells. Both stochastic realizations have colonists with global dispersal.

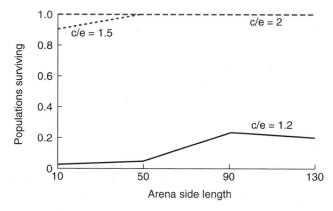

Figure 15.4 The proportion of realizations of a stochastic Levins model where metapopulations persist for 2000 generations in different sized arenas for three c/e ratios. In all cases there would be no extinction in a deterministic Levins model as $c > e$. When the colonization rate is double the extinction rate (c/e=2) all stochastic metapopulations persist but when c/e=1.2, less than 25% of metapopulations persist for 2000 generations. All arenas are square, so a side length of 50 gives 2500 patches.

extinction rates (e) the Levins model predicts that they will have the same occupancy if they have correspondingly different colonization rates (c). So, a species with e=0.4 and c=0.8 will have the same patch occupancy level at equilibrium as a species with e=0.005 and c=0.01 (in both cases e/c=0.5, giving an equilibrium patch occupancy of 50%). However, if there is a habitat destruction event that

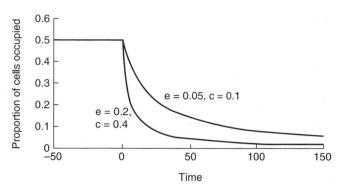

Figure 15.5 In this deterministic Levins model there is a habitat destruction event at time zero with half of the habitat removed ($h=0.5$). Two metapopulations with the same e/c ratio both have equilibrium occupancy of 0.5 before the destruction event. One has $e=0.05$ and $c=0.1$ while the other has $e=0.2$ and $c=0.4$. Although they both have the same equilibrium occupancy of 0 (i.e. extinction) after the habitat destruction event the species with high e and c moves more quickly towards the new equilibrium point.

changes the equilibrium occupancy, the first species will move towards the new equilibrium level more quickly than the second (Fig. 15.5). If the new equilibrium is zero occupancy or below, this means that the species with a higher local extinction rate will become regionally extinct first.

While we do not really know extinction and colonization rates for many species other than a few butterflies (see Thomas and Hanski 1997), we can assume that trees are likely to have lower extinction and colonization rates than annual plants. There are probably thousands of species of tropical tree that already have equilibrium patch occupancy levels of zero and are heading for extinction, but might take hundreds of years to actually go extinct. This is the essence of the extinction debt (Tilman *et al.* 1994). These trees and their associated fauna may be already doomed to extinction, existing now as the 'living dead' (Janzen and Martin 1982). An excellent example of relaxation can be found in Corlett (this volume).

Estimates of future losses due to relaxation are sobering. Hanski and Kuussaari (1995) estimated that over 10% of resident butterfly species in Finland were heading for extinction, while an experimental study of 18 grassland species (Eriksson and Kiviniemi 1999) showed that eight (44%) appeared to be below the occupancy threshold and were declining to extinction.

Spatially explicit metapopulation models

There are many approaches to a spatially explicit version of the Levins model. The models of Hanski and co-workers, using the incidence function approach, allow for variation in patch quality as well as being spatially explicit (e.g. Hanski 1997). Incidence function uses a Markov chain model and assigns different values of e and c for each patch generating state transition probabilities (i.e. chance of a particular patch going from occupied to unoccupied or vice versa). These extinction and colonization rates are based on the size and/or quality of the habitat patch and the spatial arrangement of other patches. A simpler approach is to play out the Levins model on a large grid of patches with only local colonization allowed (e.g. Dytham 1994; 1995a,b; Bascompte and Solé 1996; Ives et al. 1998). Once such a grid of patches is held as a matrix, different spatial patterns of destruction can be applied. The patterns of destruction can be generated at random, which captures the spirit of the parameter 'h' in equations (15.3) and (15.4), they can use patterns generated by fractal algorithms (Hill and Caswell 1999; With and King 1999), or they can use plausible scenarios such as gradients of habitat loss or the restriction of habitat destruction to patches that are adjacent to roads (as in Fig. 15.6).

The striking result of these different patterns of habitat loss is that the extinction threshold for the loss along roads is much lower than if habitat loss is spread randomly across the landscape (Fig. 15.7). This result is general for a range of patterns using this type of model with local (i.e. short-range) dispersal. If the pattern of habitat loss is more clumped than random then, on average, a colonist is more likely to reach a suitable patch of habitat than if habitat is lost at random. Consequently extinction thresholds are lowered. We might interpret this as good news, as the majority of habitat loss across the world is highly aggregated. It must be noted that this is somewhat reminiscent of the argument for large reserves in the SLOSS (single large or several small) debate over optimal designs for nature reserves. I have been considering here models where patches are only of two types: suitable and destroyed. Supporters of the several small reserves argument would rightly point out that not all suitable patches are equal in quality and that the highest quality patches should be conserved to minimize the chance of species extinction (i.e. identify and conserve the core habitat). However, in a spatially explicit metapopulation model with local dispersal, few large reserves are considerably better than many smaller reserves of the same total area.

Spatially realistic metapopulation models

The move from spatially explicit models to spatially realistic ones is quite a small jump. Geographical information systems (GIS) as a tool for processing images from aerial photographs or satellites are now widely available. This allows us to generate realistic landscape patterns for use in the spatially explicit models. For example, Ives et al. (1998) used landscapes derived from land-cover maps in their simulation model. Figure 15.8 is derived from a LANDSAT image of the Vale of York using GIS, and shows the areas of woodland. The Vale of York was once heavily wooded but it is immediately obvious that there is rather little woodland left. In fact woodland has been reduced to only about 3% of the landscape, with the bulk of the rest either agricultural land or urban development. A species using only the woodland as suitable habitat in this landscape is likely to become extinct rapidly. However, there are four ways that a metapopulation of a woodland species might persist in such a highly fragmented landscape:

1 A generalist species would be able to survive in more than the woodland frag-

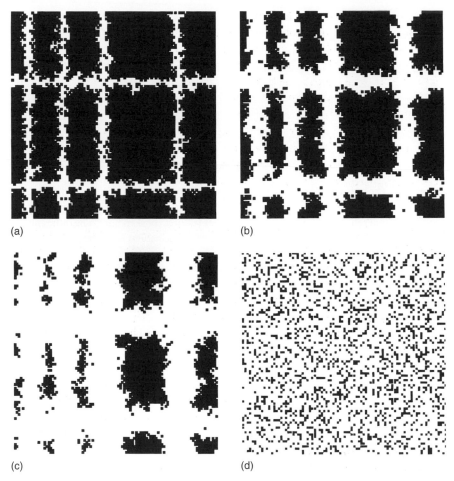

(a)

(b)

(c)

(d)

Figure 15.6 Simulated patterns of habitat destruction. Habitat destruction patterns are not random. In (a) 25% of the habitat has been removed (white) along linear features (e.g. logging access roads in a rain forest). Further destruction is constrained to be adjacent to existing destruction. In (b) the habitat destruction is 50% and in (c) it is 75%. A random pattern of habitat destruction is shown for comparison (d). Although the scale of destruction is the same in (c) and (d) the remaining habitat forms blocks in (c) and does not in (d). Other patterns of habitat destruction are considered in Dytham 1995b.

ments because it would perceive a landscape with more than just 3% available habitat. Suburban gardens, parks, verges, etc. might all provide suitable habitat.

2 A very high colonization rate can allow persistence to very low habitat availability. High colonization rates may be achieved through a high reproductive rate (increasing the number of potential colonists), a high establishment probability, an ability to detect an available habitat patch at a distance and move through the matrix habitat towards it, or by using a combination of strategies (see model by

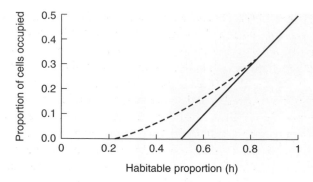

Figure 15.7 The mean proportion of patches occupied in 10 realizations of a stochastic Levins model of 10 000 patches with local dispersal (e/c=0.5). Habitat destruction is applied either at random (solid line) or along linear features (broken line). The difference in occupancy only becomes apparent after about 25% of the habitat is destroyed.

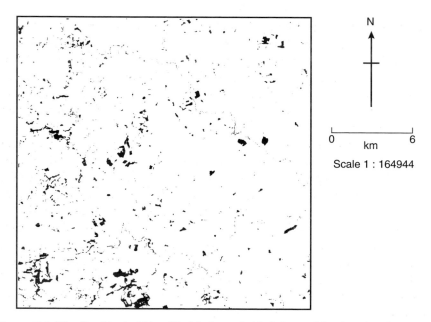

Figure 15.8 Woodland in the Vale of York is shown in black (part of the city of York appears in the SE corner of the map and part of Harrogate in the west). Area shown is 22×22 km and comprises pixels of 35×35 m (approx.). The proportion of the area that is woodland is around 3%. Woodland pixels are not randomly distributed across the landscape but are aggregated at several scales. This image was derived by GIS processing of a LANDSAT image by David Murrell.

Bevers and Flather 1999). These characteristics are often associated with fugitive or ruderal species, or successful invaders (Williamson 1996). Self fertilization or vegetative reproduction will also augment colonization rates as the Allee effect associated with mate-finding or pollen limitation in small propagules is removed.

3 Have a very low local extinction rate. However, without some colonization ability this characteristic will do little more than postpone extinction.

4 Receive 'propagule rain' from a mainland, increasing the colonization rate generated within the metapopulation itself. This essentially recaptures the MacArthur and Wilson (1967) theory of island biogeography with the fragments of woodland becoming islands in an archipelago. Of course, for some species, the 'propagule rain' in a landscape such as the Vale of York may appear in the form of human activity, such as tree planting. Translocations of populations may also fall into this category.

Without at least one of the above the species will fade inexorably to regional extinction unless saved by human intervention.

Challenges and shortcomings of metapopulation modelling

I have only considered models based on very simple metapopulation concepts. In these models, patches are arranged in a matrix, all suitable habitats are equal, dispersal is either global or local and destroyed habitats are useless. Clearly this is a massive oversimplification of reality. There are, however, several areas where progress is being made towards making metapopulation modelling a predictive tool in conservation ecology.

• The realization that the matrix between the suitable habitats is something other than useless habitat 'desert' is an important one. A whole science of landscape ecology is growing up as a consequence of the increased availability of satellite images. The pattern of different habitats in the matrix, their quality and permeability (how easy they are to cross) will have to be incorporated into future models (see Forman 1995; Harrison and Fahrig 1995; or Wiens 1997 for reviews). For example, the woodland species in the Vale of York may be able to exploit suburban gardens, hedgerows and even some agricultural crops as well as the woodland. Unfortunately this realization makes modelling infinitely more complex, as instead of dividing the habitat into the two categories of 'suitable' and 'not suitable' we have to consider the individual properties of every patch.

• Real values for the basic parameters of the model need to be gathered. Shifting patterns of annual patch occupancy for several species of butterfly with highly specific food requirements have provided some estimates (reviewed by Thomas and Hanski 1997), but information on many more species is sorely needed.

• Relaxing the assumption of even-sized and evenly spaced patches in the model is well advanced theoretically (see Hanski 1997; Cantrell *et al.* 1998). What is needed is more information on the size, shape and quality of all the patches, both occupied and unoccupied but suitable for a given species, that can be found in a landscape (e.g. Honnay *et al.* 1999). Acquisition of this information is possible for some species (e.g. butterflies restricted to few host plants) but difficult for most.

• Dispersal between patches is central to metapopulation dynamics. All colonization events are the result of a successful dispersal event by an individual or group of individuals. The crude assumptions of global or local dispersal are now being replaced by a clearer understanding of the evolution of dispersal strategies (e.g. Olivieri *et al.* 1995; Ruxton 1996; Dieckmann *et al.* 1999; Travis and Dytham 1999). For example, the realization that dispersal strategies are likely to be density-dependent (Denno *et al.* 1991; Travis *et al.* 1999) has important implications for the conservation of species existing in a metapopulation. There is now a desire to accumulate information about dispersal, in the real world, that is not biased by over-recording of short-range movements.

Conclusions

The last 20 years has seen continuing destruction of tropical forests and degradation and encroachment on habitats elsewhere. Sometime in late 1999 the Earth's human population exceeded six billion. It is likely to reach seven billion before 2013. This rate of growth in the global human population may be declining slightly but it is still staggering. Every 45 minutes about 12 000 people are born and 5000 die. This is a global human population increase of around a quarter of a million people each day. This expanding population needs more resources to support it. Many resources such as firewood, charcoal, timber, agricultural land and paper are found in tropical forests. Because of this pressure, forests are being lost at more than 20 hectares each minute (FAO 1998). There are undoubtedly hundreds of thousands of species that are already committed to extinction. Continued habitat destruction dooms more species daily.

This was Paul Ehrlich's word of caution for conservationists in 1980:
... you will be confronted by ... politicians, economists, engineers and
developers asking you to be 'reasonable', 'responsible' and to make
compromises.... Remember always that these people are the enemy, ... out
for your blood and that of your children (Ehrlich 1980).
Very few have heeded him and those who have are considered antediluvian crackpots and troublemakers. Ecologists still need to keep their minds on the problem of mass extinction and do what they can to raise awareness of the menace of habitat destruction amongst policy makers.

Priorities for the future

The effects of past destruction will continue to be felt hundreds of years into the future. Habitat destruction is now, and will remain, the dominant agent of extinction on the planet. The drastic, catastrophic and perhaps fatal violence done to the world's biota by continuing habitat destruction is a far more pressing problem to ecologists than anything caused by global environmental change, pollution, hunting or trade. We can already offer solutions of vast reserves, environmental restoration and trade embargoes but we must first prove that the problem is real and the consequences dire before we can expect any implementation.

Acknowledgments

Thanks to David Murrell for the GIS image and comments on the manuscript and to Mike Hutchings for inviting me to such an excellent symposium. The manuscript was considerably improved by Mike Hutchings and two anonymous referees. Permission to use the Landsat image was kindly given by the National Remote Sensing Centre.

References

Amarasekare, P. (1998) Allee effects in metapopulation dynamics. *American Naturalist* **152**, 298–302.

Bascompte, J. and Solé, R.V. (1996) Habitat fragmentation and extinction thresholds in spatially explicit models. *Journal of Animal Ecology* **65**, 465–473.

Bevers, M. and Flather, C.H. (1999) Numerically exploring habitat fragmentation effects on populations using cell-based coupled map lattices. *Theoretical Population Biology* **55**, 61–76.

Cantrell, R.S., Cosner, C. and Fagan, W.F. (1998) Competitive reversals inside ecological reserves: the role of external habitat degradation. *Journal of Mathematical Biology* **37**, 491–533.

Courchamp, F., Clutton-Brock, T. and Grenfell, B. (1999) Inverse density dependence and the Allee effect. *Trends in Ecology and Evolution* **14**, 405–410.

Denno, R.F., Roderick, G.K., Olmstead, K.L. and Dobel, H.G. (1991) Density-related migration in planthoppers (*Homoptera: Delphacidae*): the role of habitat persistence. *American Naturalist* **138**, 1513–1541.

Dieckmann, U., O'Hara, B. and Weisser, W. (1999) The evolutionary ecology of dispersal. *Trends in Ecology and Evolution* **14**, 88–90.

Dytham, C. (1994) Habitat destruction and competitive coexistence: a cellular model. *Journal of Animal Ecology* **63**, 490–491.

Dytham, C. (1995a) Competitive coexistence and empty patches in spatially explicit metapopulation models. *Journal of Animal Ecology* **64**, 145–146.

Dytham, C. (1995b) The effect of habitat destruction pattern on species persistence: a cellular model. *Oikos* **74**, 340–344.

Ehrlich, P.R. (1980) The strategy of conservation, 1980–2000. In: *Conservation Biology, an Evolutionary-Ecological Perspective* (eds M.E. Soulé and B.A. Wilcox), pp. 329–344. Sinauer Associates, Sunderland, Mass.

Eriksson, O. and Kiviniemi, K. (1999) Site occupancy, recruitment and extinction thresholds in grassland plants: an experimental study. *Biological Conservation* **87**, 319–325.

FAO (Food and Agriculture Organization of the United Nations) (1998) *State of the World's Forests 1997.* FAO, Rome.

Forman, R.T.T. (1995) *Land Mosaics, the Ecology of Landscapes and Regions.* Cambridge University Press, Cambridge.

Glowka, L., Burhenne-Gulimin, F. and Synge, H. (1994) *A Guide to the Convention on Biological Diversity.* IUCN — The World Conservation Union, Gland.

Hanski, I.A. (1997) Metapopulation dynamics: from concepts and observations to predictive models. In: *Metapopulation Biology: Ecology, Genetics, and Evolution* (eds I.A. Hanski and M.E. Gilpin), pp. 69–91. Academic Press, San Diego.

Hanski, I. and Kuussaari, M. (1995) Butterfly metapopulation dynamics. In: *Population Dynamics: New Approaches and Synthesis* (ed. N. Cappuccino, and P.W. Price), pp. 142–172. Academic Press, San Diego.

Harrison, S., Fahrig, L. (1995) Landscape pattern and population conservation. In: *Mosaic Land-*

scapes and Ecological Processes (ed. Hansson *et al.*), pp. 293–308, Chapman and Hall, London.

Hart, D.D. and Horwitz, R.J. (1991) Habitat diversity and the species–area relationship: alternative models and tests. In: *Habitat Structure: the Physical Arrangement of Objects in Space* (eds S.S. Bell, E.D. McCoy and H.R. Mushinsky), pp. 47–68. Chapman and Hall, London.

Heywood, V.H., ed. (1995) *Global Biodiversity and Assessment.* Cambridge University Press, New York.

Hill, M.F. and Caswell, H. (1999) Habitat fragmentation and extinction thresholds on fractal landscapes. *Ecology Letters* 2, 121–127.

Honnay, O., Hermy, M. and Coppin, P. (1999) Effects of area, age and diversity of forest patches in Belgium on plant species richness, and implications for conservation and reforestation. *Biological Conservation* 87, 73–84.

Ims, R.A. and Yoccoz, N.G. (1997) Studying transfer processes in metapopulations: emigration, migration and colonization. In: *Metapopulation Biology: Ecology, Genetics, and Evolution* (eds I.A. Hanski and M.E. Gilpin), pp. 247–266. Academic Press, San Diego.

Ives, A.R., Turner, M.G. and Pearson, S.M. (1998) Local explanations of landscape patterns: can analytical approaches approximate simulation models of spatial processes? *Ecosystems* 1, 35–51.

Janzen, D.H. and Martin, P.S. (1982) Neotropical anachronisms — the fruits the gomphotheres ate. *Science* 215, 19–27.

Judson, O.P. (1994) The rise of the individual-based model. *Trends in Ecology and Evolution* 9, 9–14.

Lawton, J.H. (1994) Population dynamic principles. In: *Extinction Rates* (eds J.H. Lawton and R.M. May), pp. 147–163. Oxford University Press, Oxford.

Levins, R. (1969) Some demographic and genetic consequences of environmental heterogeneity for biological control. *Bulletin of the Entomological Society of America* 15, 237–240.

MacArthur, R.H. and Wilson, E.O. (1967) *The Theory of Island Biogeography.* Princeton University Press, Princeton.

Nee, S. and May, R.M. (1992) Patch removal favours inferior competitors. *Journal of Animal Ecology* 61, 37–40.

Olivieri, I., Michalakis, Y. and Gouyon, P. (1995)

Metapopulation genetics and the evolution of dispersal. *American Naturalist* 146, 202–227.

Primack, R.B. (1998) *Essentials of Conservation Biology,* 2nd edn. Sinauer Associates, Sunderland, Mass.

Rosenzweig, M.L. (1995) *Species Diversity in Space and Time.* Cambridge University Press, Cambridge.

Ruxton, G.D. (1996) Dispersal and chaos in spatially structured models: an individual-level approach. *Journal of Animal Ecology* 65, 161–169.

Shorrocks, B. and Bingley, M. (1990) The problem with zeroes: why don't drosophilids lay eggs. *Oecologia* 85, 150–152.

Soulé, M.E. and Wilcox, B.A. (1980) *Conservation Biology, an Evolutionary-Ecological Perspective.* Sinauer Associates, Sunderland, Mass.

Stephens, P.A. and Sutherland, W.J. (1999) Consequences of the Allee effect for behaviour, ecology and conservation. *Trends in Ecology and Evolution* 14, 401–405.

Thomas, C.D. and Hanski, I.A. (1997) Butterfly metapopulations. In: *Metapopulation Biology: Ecology, Genetics, and Evolution* (eds I.A. Hanski and M.E. Gilpin), pp. 359–386. Academic Press, San Diego.

Tilman, D., May, R.M., Lehman, C.L. and Nowak, M.A. (1994) Habitat destruction and the extinction debt. *Nature* 371, 65.

Travis, J.M.J. and Dytham, C. (1998) The evolution of dispersal in a metapopulation: a spatially explicit, individual-based model. *Proceedings of the Royal Society of London, Series B* 265, 17–23.

Travis, J.M.J. and Dytham, C. (1999) Habitat persistence, habitat availability and the evolution of dispersal. *Proceedings of the Royal Society of London, Series B* 266, 723–729.

Travis, J.M.J., Murrell, D.J. and Dytham, C. (1999) The evolution of density-dependent dispersal. *Proceedings of the Royal Society of London, Series B* 266, 1837–1842.

Usher, M.B. (1979) Changes in the species–area relation of higher plants on nature reserves. *Journal of Applied Ecology* 16, 213–215.

Whitmore, T.C. and Sayer, J.A., eds. (1992) *Tropical Deforestation and Species Extinction.* Chapman and Hall, London.

Wiens, J.A. (1997) Metapopulation dynamics and landscape ecology. In: *Metapopulation Biology:*

Ecology, Genetics, and Evolution (eds I.A. Hanski and M.E. Gilpin), pp. 43–62. Academic Press, San Diego.

Williams, C.B. (1964) *Patterns in the Balance of Nature*. Academic Press, London.

Williamson, M. (1996). *Biological Invasions*. Chapman and Hall, London.

With, K.A. and King, A.W. (1999) Extinction thresholds for species in fractal landscapes. *Conservation Biology* **13**, 314–326.

Chapter 16
Environmental heterogeneity and species survival in degraded tropical landscapes

R.T. Corlett

The final decades of the second millennium have seen a big increase in rates of deforestation in the humid tropics, primarily as a result of agricultural expansion (Whitmore and Sayer 1992). Vast tracts of continuous forest have been reduced to tiny fragments scattered in a non-forest matrix. There is now a large and growing literature on the biological changes in such tropical forest fragments (Laurance and Bierregaard 1997; Laurance 1999). In much of the tropics, however, the process of deforestation and fragmentation on the pioneer front of human expansion will be a more or less short-lived stage in the transformation of a forested landscape with a sparse human population into a human-dominated cultural landscape with little or no forest. In this transformation, species loss from fragments is only one way in which the biota changes, and the ability to persist in fragments is no guarantee of long-term survival (Dytham, this volume).

From an ecological viewpoint, this transformation can be seen as 'landscape degradation'—a decrease in biomass, biodiversity, structural complexity and soil fertility. Although pathways and rates of degradation vary, three general stages can be recognized: a deforestation-fragmentation stage, which leaves forest fragments in a non-forest matrix, a stage of rapid changes in both the fragments and the matrix, resulting in a net loss of species, and a final stage in which degraded tropical landscapes approach the long-term stability shown by human-dominated landscapes outside the tropics. The aims of this paper are to describe the major processes at each stage, determine species characteristics which favour persistence in the landscape, and make suggestions for reducing species losses. I start with a review of the relevant literature, and follow this by two case studies from tropical East Asia.

Stage 1: Deforestation–fragmentation

Forest clearance may not leave forest fragments where it is done by large land owners in topography that is favourable for agricultural mechanization. In most cases, however, there are sites which escape immediate clearance because they are too steep, swampy, infertile or inaccessible for farming. Deforestation also tends to

Department of Ecology and Biodiversity, University of Hong Kong, Pokfulam Road, Hong Kong, China

spread contagiously, so that more remote areas survive longer (Dytham, this volume). Land tenure and legal restrictions may also prevent complete clearance, although Brazilian laws requiring settlers to keep half their land under forest have not been effectively enforced (Fujisaka *et al.* 1998). Forest patches may also be retained for positive reasons: as sources of timber and firewood, as shelters for cattle, as protection for freshwater springs (Ferrari and Diego 1995), as scenic reserves (Laurance 1997), as sacred forests (Wiersum 1997), or for other conservation purposes.

The surviving forest fragments represent a biased sample of the original landscape mosaic, in which the communities of fertile soils on farmable topography are usually under-represented or absent (e.g. Laurance 1997). No study has attempted to quantify the species loss resulting from this sampling bias, but it must be substantial, particularly in highly heterogeneous landscapes and for species with specialized habitat requirements. Moreover, many species of plants and animals have low densities in all habitats and may therefore be absent from the fragment sample simply by chance. Laurance *et al.* (1999) show, with a simple model, that density has an overriding influence on the susceptibility of plant species to clearing, with rare species (<1 tree ha^{-1}) becoming extremely vulnerable at high ($>95\%$) levels of clearance. This model, in which the distributions of both species and clearances are random, appears robust on the scale at which it was tested (9 ha), but non-randomness in both plant distributions and clearance patterns is likely to become more significant at larger scales.

Stage 2: Species loss

Changes in the species composition of fragments

The most comprehensive study of the biological changes in recently isolated forest fragments is the Biological Dynamics of Forest Fragments Project (BDFFP) in Central Amazonia, where 10 forest blocks of various sizes (1–100 ha) were isolated in pasture between 1980 and 1984 (Bierregaard and Stouffer 1997) (Table 16.1). In contrast to most real world fragments, hunting and other forms of exploitation are prevented, the experimental site is surrounded by a very large area of continuous primary forest, isolation distances are small, and unplanned secondary vegetation has reconnected some fragments to the forest. Despite this, there have already been large changes in the communities of primates (Lovejoy *et al.* 1986), insectivorous birds (Stouffer and Bierregaard 1995b), termites (De Souza and Brown 1994), beetles (Didham 1997), ants (Carvalho and Vasconcelos 1999; Gascon *et al.* 1999) and butterflies (Brown and Hutchings 1997). Many species were lost from the fragments but, in the case of the beetles and butterflies, this was compensated by an increase in the diversity and abundance of species invading from disturbed areas outside. Unexpectedly, isolated fragments had more diverse frog (Tocher *et al.* 1997) and small mammal (Malcolm 1997) faunas, while understorey hummingbirds showed little change (Stouffer and Bierregaard 1995a). The fragments have

Table 16.1 The effects of 7–16 years of isolation on the biota of forest fragments in Central Amazonia that were experimentally created as part of the Biological Dynamics of Forest Fragments Project, and the fragment sizes in which the effects were observed. Area and edge effects are not distinguished in this table

Group	Forest Fragment Sizes (ha)	Effects	Source
Trees	1, 10, 100	Fewer taxa of shade-tolerant, mature-phase seedlings	Benitez-Malvido (1998)
	1, 10, 100	Increased mortality of Myrtaceae near edges	Ferreira and Laurance (1997)
Palms	1, 10	Fewer seedling taxa	Scariot (1999)
Beetles	1, 10, 100	Changes in species composition of leaf-litter fauna	Didham (1997)
Termites	1, 10	Fewer species	De Souza and Brown (1994)
Ants	1, 10, 100	Fewer species	Gascon *et al.* (1999); Carvalho and Vasconcelos (1999)
Butterflies	1, 10, 100	Fewer forest interior species but more edge species	Brown and Hutchings (1997)
Frogs	1, 10, 100	More species as a result of invasions from matrix	Tocher *et al.* (1997)
Mammals	1, 10	Increased abundance and diversity of small mammals	Malcolm (1997)
	1, 10, 100	Fewer primate species	Lovejoy *et al.* (1986)
Birds	1, 10	Little change in understorey hummingbirds	Stouffer and Bierregaard (1995a)
	1, 10	Decline in abundance and species richness of understorey insectivores	Stouffer and Bierregaard (1995b)

also undergone large changes in forest structure and dynamics, with increases in tree mortality near the margins (Ferreira and Laurance 1997), elevated rates of tree recruitment (Laurance *et al.* 1998), but a decline in the abundance of seedlings of shade-tolerant, mature-phase trees (Benitez-Malvido 1998) and palms (Scariot 1999).

Studies elsewhere on a wide range of organisms have confirmed the main lessons of the BDFFP, namely that recently isolated forest fragments within the range of sizes most commonly left in agricultural landscapes (< 500 ha) undergo rapid biological changes, including the loss of many forest species, and the invasion of some species from the matrix. However, the details of these changes are site- and taxon-specific, and few strong generalizations have emerged. A major problem is that the proximate mechanisms for species loss are still largely unknown in most cases (Turner 1996). Moreover, few studies have attempted to separate the influences of fragment area, isolation, edge effects and other potentially significant factors (Didham 1997) (Fig. 16.1). Robust predictions await a better understanding of the processes involved.

The situation in almost all real fragments is further complicated by continued human impacts. Hunting of larger vertebrates and collection of firewood and small timber are the most widespread impacts, but a great variety of different forest products are exploited in various parts of the world. Fires started in the matrix open up the dense wall of vegetation which seals the edges of older fragments and can greatly increase the penetration distance of physical edge effects (Didham and Lawton 1999). These human activities may do more to accelerate species loss from fragments than the internal biological processes which have received most attention (Terborgh 1992; Chiarello 1999).

Few generalizations on the vulnerability of species in unexploited fragments have received widespread empirical support. An exception, is that species which can utilize matrix habitats are less vulnerable than species which are confined within fragment boundaries (Laurance 1997; Estrada *et al.* 1994; Stouffer and Bierregaard 1995b; Gascon *et al.* 1999). An example of this idea is the suggestion that nocturnal organisms (moths, bats, small mammals) may be less vulnerable than diurnal organisms (butterflies, birds), because of the greatly reduced contrast

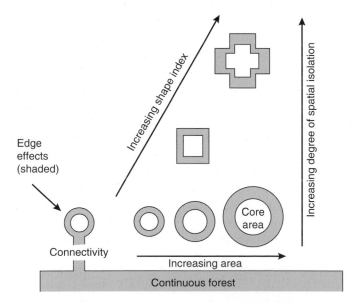

Figure 16.1 Diagrammatic representation of five potentially important processes operating on organisms in forest fragments: area effects, measured by either total fragment area or interior core area; edge effects; shape effects; isolation effects; and connectivity. From Didham (1997), with kind permission of Kluwer Academic Publishers.

between forest and non-forest environments at night (Daily and Ehrlich 1996). Canopy specialists also tend to be more likely to cross open spaces than understorey species, presumably because they are adapted to a more open environment (Johns 1991; Cosson *et al.* 1999).

Another widely supported generalization is the greater vulnerability of species with large area requirements, including large carnivores (e.g. Estrada *et al.* 1994; Laurance 1997; Chiarello 1999) and frugivores (Christiansen and Pitter 1997; Chiarello 1999; Renjifo 1999). However, such species may persist if they can cross the non-forest matrix and if the total area of forest habitat remaining in the landscape is adequate (Johns 1991), and can provide important genetic and ecological links between fragments (Laurance 1999). Species with specialized food or habitat requirements may also be unable to meet their needs in small fragments (Willis 1979; Estrada *et al.* 1994; Christiansen and Pitter 1997). Species which are rare in continuous forest may be more vulnerable to extinction in fragments (e.g. Newmark 1991), but there are also examples of common species being lost, and also of rare species becoming common because of a positive response to edge or matrix environments (Laurance 1997).

There appears to be a rapid initial loss of vulnerable species from fragments, followed by a decline in extinction rates (Laurance 1997). When losses to date were expressed as a fraction of eventual losses, avifaunal relaxation in 1000 ha African forest fragments approximated to an exponential decay, with a half-life of 25–100 years (Brooks *et al.* 1999). However, even small, unprotected fragments (< 100 ha) can retain populations of forest-dependent vertebrates for > 50 years (Newmark 1991; Christiansen and Pitter 1997; Corlett and Turner 1997).

In general, fragments of different areas tend to support nested subsets of the faunas of larger fragments (Patterson 1987; Chiarello 1999). Observations on recently isolated fragments suggest that selective, area-dependent extinction is the main process responsible for this pattern, although active selection of larger fragments by mobile species and the nesting of habitats may also contribute, and probably become more important in older fragments where the most vulnerable species have been lost. Although it has not been tested quantitatively, nesting is not obvious for fragment floras, where many forest species persist, apparently at random, in those fragments in which they were originally isolated (S.C. Thomas, personal communication). Plants also appear to have much lower long-term extinction rates in fragments than animals (Corlett and Turner 1997), with long-lived species, such as trees, persisting longer than shrubs, herbs and epiphytes (Turner *et al.* 1996). The proportions of vertebrate-dispersed, understorey and shade-tolerant woody species declined with fragment size in long-isolated forest fragments in south-eastern Brazil (Tabarelli *et al.* 1999), but it is not clear how much this resulted from local extinctions and how much from the addition of ruderal species. The high floristic diversity of some natural forest fragments near the climatic limit of forest, although a very different situation, also suggests that rapid floristic impoverishment is not an inevitable consequence of fragmentation (Kellman *et al.* 1998).

Both the empirical and the theoretical literature have concentrated on within-fragment processes, but continued erosion and loss of fragments may be a more important cause of species loss in many areas. As with the initial deforestation-fragmentation stage, this is likely to be a non-random process, with relatively accessible and agriculturally useful forest areas being lost first. This will sharpen the initial sampling bias, favouring the survival of species which occur on the least valuable land.

Changes in the matrix

Post-clearance changes in the matrix between fragments have received less attention than changes in the fragments themselves, but may be of greater long-term significance in the control of landscape-level biodiversity in permanently settled areas. Matrix communities start with low plant and animal diversity immediately after clearance, because of the paucity of species tolerant of non-forest environments in a largely forested landscape. Pastures in recently deforested areas have much less diverse faunas than natural savannas (Lavelle *et al.* 1989; Eggleton *et al.* 1996). Matrix diversity typically increases with time, however, as open-country species in adjacent regions expand their distributions (e.g. Stouffer and Bierregaard 1995a; Lawton *et al.* 1998; Gascon *et al.* 1999; Renjifo 1999; Vasconcelos 1999; Wells 1999). The biotas of anthropogenic open habitats in forest climates are therefore dominated by widespread species (e.g. Holloway *et al.* 1992).

Matrix heterogeneity also tends to increase with time as the postclearance flush in soil fertility is exhausted. Neither pasture nor cultivation are continuously sustainable on most deforested sites and, over a decade or so, the matrix develops into a mosaic of patches consisting of various stages of regrowth after abandonment. Some patches may be abandoned permanently and develop into secondary forest, while others are cleared again and re-used. The rate at which woody vegetation develops on cleared sites is inversely related to the duration and intensity of disturbance (Nepstad *et al.* 1996; Hughes *et al.* 1999). Except on lightly used sites, where many species may develop from root sprouts, woody succession depends on seed dispersal and may be further limited by seed predation, competition with non-woody vegetation, and a range of abiotic factors (Nepstad *et al.* 1996; Holl 1998). All these processes are highly selective and only a subset of the mature forest flora occurs in secondary forests even after several decades (Finegan 1996; Turner *et al.* 1997; Ferreira and Prance 1999). In contrast, where there is mature forest nearby, at least some elements of the primary forest fauna may recover in less than 25 years (Raman *et al.* 1998; Vasconcelos 1999).

Even narrow strips of woody regrowth along streams and fences can support some forest species, providing additional habitat as well as links between isolated forest patches (Estrada *et al.* 1993, 1994, 1998; Crome *et al.* 1994; Warketin *et al.* 1995; Laurance 1997). Scattered shrubs and trees—particularly if they provide fleshy fruits—make grasslands more attractive to small, frugivorous forest birds, thus accelerating forest succession (Da Silva *et al.* 1996; Duncan and Chapman 1999; Petit *et al.* 1999). Larger patches of secondary forest provide habitat for many forest species. Agricultural vegetation which includes trees can also provide additional habitat for the more tolerant species, and corridors or stepping stones for others (Estrada *et al.* 1993, 1994, 1998, 1999; Petit *et al.* 1999). Traditional, multi-species agroforests, which often retain a canopy of native forest trees over the planted crop, or acquire a native understorey below it, can support a diverse flora and fauna, including many species which are absent from tree-less vegetation (Alger and Caldas 1994; Thiollay 1995; Moguel and Toledo 1999). Crops with planted shade trees are less attractive to forest animals and industrial monoculture plantations even less so, but any form of woody vegetation is likely to facilitate movements of some forest species across the deforested landscape (Estrada *et al.* 1998) and reduce edge effects in forest fragments (Mesquita *et al.* 1999).

Stage 3: Towards stability?

The ecology of highly degraded landscapes in the humid tropics has received so little attention (but see Case Study 2, below) that any discussion of processes and their consequences for species survival must be largely speculative. In long-settled, human-dominated landscapes, primary forest fragments have often been eliminated, or else survive only as tiny, disturbed remnants in topographically protected sites which are too small to maintain a forest interior microclimate. Permanent agriculture is confined to the most favourable areas and the rest of the landscape is abandoned, or subject to light grazing or intermittent cultivation. In these circumstances, the survival of any forest-dependent elements of the original biota must depend largely on the extent of forest-like agricultural or secondary habitats.

Case study 1: Singapore

Singapore (Figs 16.2, 16.3) is the best-documented example of the long-term effects of tropical forest fragmentation, but it is not ideal as a case study. Firstly, the earliest reliable records for most groups of organisms come from the late nineteenth century, after the major period of deforestation and fragmentation, which followed the founding of the colony in 1819. Secondly, Singapore is itself an island, with an original land area of $540\,km^2$, separated from the Malay Peninsula by a minimum water gap of 0.6 km. Both tigers and elephants have swum these straits in recent times but the water is probably an effective barrier to many organisms. Thus there is an island effect which complicates the identification of human impacts. Species for which there are no good nineteenth century records (such as gibbons) must be assumed to have always been absent, but there are a number of less conspicuous birds and mammals for which this assumption may not be justified, resulting in a probable underestimate of the number of species lost.

In Singapore's equatorial climate (Fig. 16.4), forest is the natural vegetation everywhere except coastal cliffs and beaches. Much of the initial clearance was for the cultivation of gambier (*Uncaria gambir*) and the growers moved on when the soil and firewood supplies were exhausted. Cantley (1884) described the results of this 'reckless, migratory cultivation':

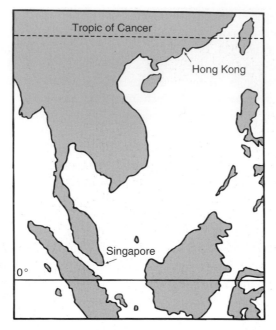

Figure 16.2 Tropical East Asia, showing the locations of Singapore and Hong Kong.

Such Crown forests as remain uncut are widely distributed in isolated patches over the island. These forest patches or clumps are of various sizes, from half an acre or so to about 25 acres (10 ha), and of no particular shape; their distance from each other may average a quarter of a mile (0.4 km) though often exceeding a mile (1.6 km). The interspace is generally waste grassland, which supports, as a rule, only the strongly growing grass known locally as 'lalang' (*Imperata cylindrica*).

The only primary forest fragments which have survived until today are now included within the 2100 ha of nature reserves in the centre of the island (Fig. 16.3: Corlett 1999). These fragments range in size from less than a hectare to about 40 ha and include approximately 190 ha of dry land primary forest and 80 ha of fresh-water swamp forest. They are now embedded in a matrix of secondary forest, which covers a total area of 1560 ha, but has been re-fragmented by reservoirs, roads and recreational facilities.

Vascular plants

Although forest covers less than 4% of modern Singapore, it contains 73.5% of its recorded vascular plant flora (Turner 1994). Turner *et al.* (1994) estimate that 29% of Singapore's recorded forest flora of 1674 species has been lost since the late nineteenth century. This is certainly an underestimate of the total loss resulting from deforestation and fragmentation, since the forest areas available to late nineteenth

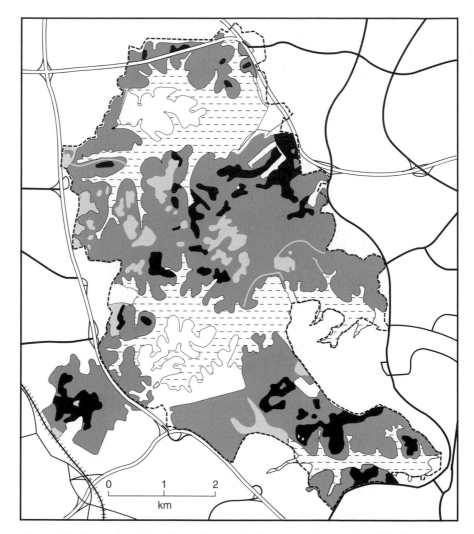

Figure 16.3 Vegetation of the Nature Reserves in Singapore: primary forest (black), secondary forest (dark grey), and non-forest vegetation within the reserves (light grey). The remainder of the area mapped is either roads, reservoirs (dashed) or non-forest vegetation and urban areas outside the reserves (white). Information and map provided by the National Parks Board, Singapore.

century botanical collectors were already a non-random sample of the original forest habitat mosaic. Most recorded extinctions were probably a result of the continued clearance of forest fragments outside the central protected area and there is no direct evidence for plant species loss from surviving fragments. Initial results from a 2-ha permanent plot in the largest surviving fragment, on Bukit Timah Hill, suggest that forest structure, plant diversity and recruitment are similar to much larger forest areas in Malaysia (Ercelawn *et al.* 1998). The one suggestion of a

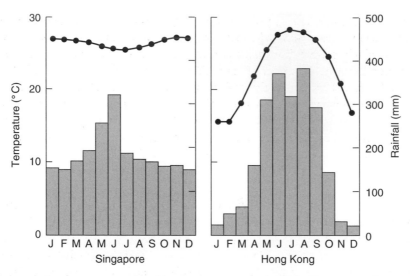

Figure 16.4 Long-term mean monthly temperature and rainfall for Singapore and Hong Kong.

fragmentation effect is the low recruitment rate for the diverse and abundant tree family Myristicaceae, which is dependent for seed dispersal on locally extinct, large avian frugivores. Although some areas of secondary forest may be more than a hundred years old, they are still structurally and floristically distinct from, and much less diverse than, the primary forest fragments (Corlett 1991; Turner *et al.* 1997). The inland, non-forest flora of Singapore is relatively impoverished (only 15.5% of the total flora: Turner 1994) and shows almost no overlap with the forest flora.

Birds

At least 70 resident forest bird species have been lost from Singapore since records began (Lim 1999). Many additional species which occur in the nearest forest areas in Malaysia are not recorded from Singapore, but it is impossible now to assess whether this is a result of an island effect or local extinction before reliable records started. It is also difficult to assess the proportion of the current forest avifauna that consists of survivors from the primeval avifauna, since several species which range throughout the forest in Singapore are confined to edge and secondary habitats in Malaysia (Hails 1987). A minimum estimate for the extinction rate is 50%, while taking the most pessimistic assumption — that Singapore's resident forest avifauna was once similar to that a few kilometres to the north — raises this to about 70%. Species loss has been selective both taxonomically and ecologically. All pheasants (Phasianidae), hornbills (Bucerotidae), trogons (Trogonidae) and broadbills (Eurylaimidae) have gone, all but one barbet (Megalaimidae), and more than half the woodpeckers (Picidae), bulbuls (Pycnonotidae) and babblers (Timaliini) (Lim

1999). Ecologically, large-gaped frugivores, large species in general, and forest interior specialists have suffered most. The surviving avifauna consists largely of species which tolerate disturbed and marginal habitats in Malaysia (Wells 1999), although there are a number of surprising presences and absences (Hails 1987). Several species have extremely small population sizes and at least 12 species are considered endangered in Singapore (Lim 1999). Only four forest species have adapted to non-forest conditions and the other open-country birds seem to be mostly either of coastal origin or invaders — spontaneous or human-introduced — from drier, more open parts of the region (Hails 1987).

Mammals

At least 24 forest mammal species have been lost from the main island of Singapore since the nineteenth century (Yang *et al.* 1990; Teo and Rajathurai 1999). Unfortunately, nineteenth century records are clearly incomplete — since some species which must have been present were not recorded — and also unreliable, with some records based on specimens that were probably acquired in the market. There is also a problem with some recent records, which may be of escaped or released animals. Various assumptions on the validity of past and present records give a range of estimates of the percentage of species lost, from 41 to 48%. Even if all records are accepted, however, Singapore's forests supported only about half as many species as those in adjacent parts of Malaysia, suggesting either a strong island effect or many early, unrecorded losses.

As with the birds, species loss has been selective both taxonomically and ecologically: all four (or five) cats (Felidae), more than half the civets (Viverridae), and four out of five ungulates (Artiodactyla) are missing, but less than half the bats and the rodents. The missing species are often the largest in the taxon or guild. Like the birds, the surviving mammal species are largely those which tolerate disturbed or marginal forest habitats in Malaysia. Some of these species have attained extremely high densities in comparison with Malaysian forests (Teo and Rajathurai 1999). Most striking is the overwhelming dominance of the night-time forest floor by the Singapore Rat, *Rattus annandalei,* which is not a primary forest species in Malaysia. In contrast, several surviving species have very small population sizes, including endemic subspecies of the Banded Langur (*Presbytis femoralis*), with an estimated 15–23 individuals, and the Cream-coloured Giant Squirrel (*Ratufa affinis*), with 4–5 individuals. In total, 19 forest mammal species are considered to be endangered in Singapore (Teo and Rajathurai 1999).

Amphibians and reptiles

All 20 reliably recorded forest frogs are still extant (Lim and Lim 1992; Teo and Rajathurai 1999). Most of these are restricted to forest. Reptiles are more difficult to survey and recent records are incomplete (Lim and Lim 1992; Teo and Rajathurai 1999). However, two-thirds of the approximately 90 reliably recorded forest reptile species have been seen recently, suggesting that extinctions, if any, are few.

Freshwater fish

Of the 61 native species of freshwater fish recorded from Singapore, 26 (43%) are now locally extinct (Ng and Lim 1999). A total of 21 of the 35 extant, native freshwater fish species in Singapore are confined to forest and 17 of these are considered endangered.

Dragonflies

A recent survey recorded 79 odonate species within the nature reserves, although not all live in the forest (Murphy 1999). All but one of the nine forest species collected by A.R. Wallace in 1854, when the forest was already fragmented but much more extensive, were recorded. Four more species reliably recorded by later collectors were not seen and may be locally extinct. The other previously recorded species which were not seen are either nocturnal or high-flying, and could easily have been missed.

Butterflies

Out of a total of 381 species of butterfly reliably recorded from Singapore, 145 (38%) have not been recorded recently (Khew and Neo 1999). Almost all the losses are forest species, while a number of the survivors are wholly or largely confined to non-forest habitats. Thus the percentage loss for the forest fauna is probably higher, although this may be at least partly balanced by recent under-recording of inconspicuous and taxonomically difficult groups.

Other taxa

Published and unpublished information on the distributions of other taxonomic groups within Singapore, including water beetles (Balke *et al.* 1999), semi-aquatic bugs (Yang *et al.* 1999), stick insects (Seow-Choen 1999), termites (D.H. Murphy, personal communication), freshwater prawns and crabs (Ng 1999), and bryophytes (B. Tan, personal communication), all show the same basic pattern, with most of Singapore's extant biota found in the limited area of forest habitats, among which the primary forest remnants are most diverse.

Case study 2: Hong Kong

Although Hong Kong and Singapore have very different climates and topography, they are comparable in their very similar histories of biological exploration and the low percentage of forest remaining in the period when systematic records first became available. The 1100 km² Hong Kong Special Administrative Region includes a section of the South China coastal region as well as adjacent islands, so island effects do not complicate interpretation (Fig. 16.5). However, Hong Kong is only 130 km south of the Tropic of Cancer and has a distinctly subtropical climate (Fig. 16.4). Species in many taxonomic groups reach their present-day northern limits at 20–30°N in South China, complicating the identification of human impacts on the biota. Deforestation of coastal South China started at least 1000 years ago and was near complete by the seventeenth century (Corlett 1997), so

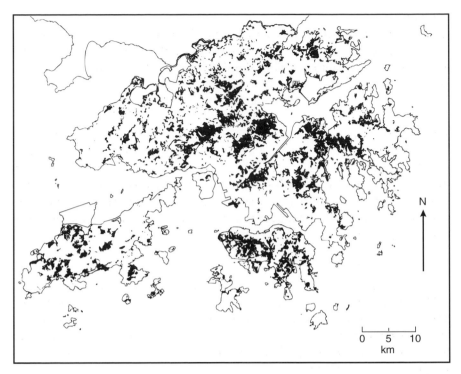

Figure 16.5 The current forest cover of Hong Kong (black), consisting mostly of secondary forest and plantations < 50 years old.

there is neither a baseline for comparison with the present day nor a deforestation history.

In the mid-nineteenth century, when studies on Hong Kong's flora and fauna started, forest covered only 2–5% of the land area (Corlett and Turner 1997). All flat land was cultivated and the hills were covered in grass, with a few scattered shrubs and stunted pine trees. Forest patches — mostly less than 10 ha in area but some considerably larger — were preserved near villages for reasons of *feng shui*, the Chinese system for determining favourable locations for settlements. At higher altitudes, there were numerous tiny forest patches in deep ravines and similar sites protected by topography from fire and cutting. It is not clear whether any of these areas were primary forest, but some sites were probably never completely cleared. Today, secondary forests up to 50 years old cover about 10% of the land area (Zhuang and Corlett 1997), with an additional 5% under plantations, largely of exotic species. Although grassland is still the most extensive non-forest vegetation type, it is increasingly being replaced by secondary shrublands in fire-protected areas.

Vascular plants
Approximately half of Hong Kong's total recorded flora of around 2000 species

belongs to the regional forest flora, although many of these species also occur in secondary shrublands or as isolated individuals in fire-protected microsites. Out of 381 tree species (potential maximum height >5 m) recorded since the mid-nineteenth century, only 23 (6%) have not been recorded in the last decade (Zhuang *et al.* 1997). However, more than half the surviving forest flora of Hong Kong is considered rare or very rare, and many species, with very varied biology, are confined to upland streamsides, cliffs and ridge-tops, where they may have persisted through the deforestation of Hong Kong.

Birds

Hong Kong has lost only one well-established species, the Ring-necked Pheasant (*Phasianus colchicus*) since reliable records began in 1860. This species is unlikely to have been present in the primeval, forested landscape. Earlier extinctions of forest birds must be inferred from comparisons with larger, older forest areas in the adjacent Guangdong Province (Cheng 1987; Lewthwaite 1996). Excluding recently established species, the most striking absences are all the forest pheasants, all the woodpeckers (although several are occasional visitors), and almost all the babblers. Hong Kong's forests are also deficient in forest raptors, cuckoos, owls, bulbuls and tits (M.R. Leven, personal communication). As in Singapore, the missing forest resident species are mostly large and/or forest interior specialists. Hornbills, broadbills and trogons are absent but, apart from a single species of trogon, these families are also missing from forest areas in Guangdong, whether through human impact or for climatic reasons, cannot now be determined. The survivors are all habitat generalists which can persist in shrubland and other non-forest vegetation. In the largest forest area in Hong Kong (460 ha), the great tit (*Parus major*), light-vented bulbul (*Pycnonotus sinensis*), and Japanese white-eye (*Zosterops japonica*) — all three of which also occur in urban parks and gardens — make up 65% of the mean total bird density (Kwok and Corlett 1999).

In striking contrast to Singapore, Hong Kong's forest avifauna has shown a real increase over the last few decades, with the addition of at least 25 species (M.R. Leven, personal communication). The 11 most vagile of these species seem to have arrived as natural colonists of Hong Kong's expanding secondary forest area, while the remaining 15 — which are mostly weakly flying babblers and laughingthrushes, and not all within their natural ranges — have apparently established from escaped or released cage-birds. Recent additions to the resident forest avifauna include the commonest forest bulbul in Guangdong (chestnut bulbul, *Hemixos castanonotus*), the commonest laughingthrush (greater-necklaced laughingthrush, *Garrulax pectoralis*), and the most abundant forest babbler (grey-cheeked fulvetta, *Alcippe morrisonia*).

Mammals

Mammalian species losses since the nineteenth century — the tiger, leopard, large Indian civet, badger, fox and dhole — are all carnivores and probably all these losses are the result of hunting and trapping. Comparisons with current and historically recorded mammal distributions in Guangdong (Corbet and Hill 1992) suggest that many additional species were lost earlier. Elephants, rhinos (apparently *Dicerorhinus sumatrensis*: Liu 1998) and gibbons have disappeared from Guangdong in historical times, but the mammal fauna of the larger, older forest areas is still considerably richer than that of Hong Kong. Hong Kong had no primates or squirrels until the recent successful introduction of macaques (*Macaca mulatta*, which is within its natural range, and *M. fascicularis*, which is not) and the tree squirrel, *Callosciurus erythraeus* (two, non-local subspecies) (Dudgeon and Corlett 1994). The missing species are almost all forest-dependent, while none of the remaining species need forest to survive, although the barking deer (*Muntiacus reevesi*) is usually recorded in or near forest patches.

Amphibians and reptiles

Excluding several doubtful records, there have been no local extinctions among Hong Kong's 23 recorded amphibian species since the nineteenth century and only one probable extinction, the common water monitor (*Varanus salvator*), which was exploited for food, among the 67 non-marine reptiles (Bogadek and Lau 1997).

Freshwater fish

Thirty-three primary freshwater fish species have been reliably recorded in Hong Kong since the nineteenth century (Chong and Dudgeon 1992; Dudgeon, personal communication). Three species are probably locally extinct as a result of the increasing degradation of lowland streams. No fish species seems to be strictly forest-dependent but several are confined to upland streams, which are usually shaded by trees or shrubs.

Dragonflies

There are recent records of all but five (5%) of the 108 dragonfly species recorded in Hong Kong (Wilson 1997). Although a number of species are confined to forest, the sites with the highest diversity are not forested.

Butterflies

There are recent records for almost all of the 231 butterfly species recorded in Hong Kong (Bascombe *et al.* 1999; R. Kendrick, personal communication). Local butterfly diversities are highest in forest edges and few species are confined to forest interior habitats. However, several forest species have become (re)established in Hong Kong since the 1950s and there has been a real increase in both total and forest butterfly diversity (Bascombe *et al.* 1999).

Other taxa

Recent, unpublished survey data are also available for ants, spiders, moths, land snails, bryophytes and various groups of aquatic insects. Preliminary analyses show that, as with the animal groups considered above, neither the habitat types nor the actual locations with highest diversity coincide for different taxonomic groups, although there are some areas which are relatively rich in most groups.

Discussion

The concentration of research effort on the fate of organisms in recently isolated forest fragments has tended to obscure the role of other mechanisms, including fragment loss and matrix processes, in controlling which species survived in degraded tropical landscapes. This bias may be justified by the current importance of forest fragments in delaying deforestation-related extinctions (Turner and Corlett 1996), but it does not permit predictions about the long-term fate of tropical forest biotas in human-dominated landscapes.

In Singapore, the primary forest fragments, which have now been isolated for 130–160 years, are in very good condition botanically, but local extinctions in most groups of animals have been high and losses have continued since the incorporation of all surviving fragments in protected areas nearly 50 years ago. The high proportion of critically endangered species among the survivors suggests that these high extinction rates will continue. However, for all groups of organisms for which there are adequate data, the larger fragments are still the most diverse sites in Singapore, so the diversity hotspots for all taxa approximately coincide.

In Hong Kong, after several hundred years of intense human impact, the spatial distribution of much of the forest flora still shows an apparent imprint of deforestation history, but patterns of diversity for animal taxa reflect current or recent-historical environmental heterogeneity. Thus the diversity hotspots for different taxa do not coincide. The percentage of species lost since records began has been much lower in all groups than in Singapore for the same period (Table 16.2), and, unlike Singapore, most losses can be attributed to specific human impacts: hunting, water pollution and development of lowland habitats. With the possible exception of the forest flora, the Hong Kong biota thus seems to have attained the long-term stability seen in human-dominated landscapes outside the tropics—but at much higher levels of diversity. For most major groups of organisms for which we have data, Hong Kong supports more species than the whole of the United Kingdom (Table 16.3). There has been a real increase in forest diversity over the last few decades for the most mobile groups studied—the birds, the butterflies and, probably, the dragonflies—suggesting that Hong Kong's forests are currently undersaturated in species.

All stages of the degradation process favour vagile habitat generalists, which can move between widely separated habitat patches, do not have specialized requirements for recruitment, and are not exploited. However, as long as primary forest fragments maintain their structural integrity, at least some non-vagile, forest-dependent species persist. No such animal species are known to have persisted in Hong Kong, where no primary forest areas appear to have survived intact, but the forest flora still includes several hundred species which are confined to sites that have probably never been completely cleared, and have been unable to expand into

Table 16.2 Percentage loss of reliably-recorded species since records began in the 19th century in Singapore and Hong Kong. The Singapore figures refer to the forest biota only, except for butterflies and freshwater fish (the whole of Singapore) and dragonflies (the Nature Reserves). The Hong Kong figures refer to the whole of Hong Kong, except for vascular plants (the forest flora). There have been no losses of forest-dependent animals in Hong Kong over this period, although many species must have been lost during deforestation, several centuries before records began

Group	Singapore	Hong Kong
Vascular plants	>30%	<6%
Dragonflies	5–10%	<5%
Butterflies	40%	<3%
Amphibians	0%	0%
Reptiles	0–30%	1%
Mammals	40–50%	12%
Birds	>50%	<1%

Table 16.3 Numbers of species recorded in Hong Kong ($1100\,km^2$) and the UK ($244\,000\,km^2$) for selected groups of organisms (from various sources)

Group	HK species	UK species
Bryophytes	330	1000
Pteridophytes	220	80
Flowering plants	1930	1400
Amphibians	23	6
Reptiles	67	6
Breeding birds	134	210
Total birds	500	500
Mammals	50	48
Butterflies	231	62
Dragonflies	108	51
Ants	160	43

secondary woody habitats. This reflects what appears to be a fundamental difference between the ways in which plants and animals are affected by landscape degradation. Plants persist longer in forest fragments, and are far less sensitive to fragment area than most animals, but plant diversity recovers more slowly during forest succession on degraded and/or isolated sites. There are also, apparently, large differences between higher animal taxa in their vulnerability to fragmentation, such as the unexpected resilience of forest frog communities.

In general, there seems to be a rapid loss of vulnerable species during the early stages of landscape degradation, followed by a decline in local extinction rates. Because the loss of primary forest species is partly compensated by an increase in widespread matrix species, the 'quality' of landscape-level diversity declines more quickly than the quantity. Long-term survival of forest-adapted species in human-dominated landscapes depends on the maintenance of heterogeneous landscapes which include areas dominated by woody plants. Traditional patterns of land-use have often resulted in such landscapes, in which a significant fraction of the forest biota can survive, but, in many parts of the tropics, the rapid industrialization of agriculture is creating uniform monocultures, which support few or no forest species.

Implications for conservation management
Successful conservation management is site-, species- and situation-specific, but general recommendations can be useful where, as in much of the humid tropics, local information is insufficient. At the deforestation-fragmentation stage, more forest species could be retained if the forest fragments sampled the full range of environments, rather than just those that are least useful for agriculture. More animal species will survive for longer if the fragments are large and connected, and the persistence of some species will require very large fragments (>20 000 ha), in which any exploitation of forest products is managed for sustainability. Although it may often be impractical to enforce this prescription on peasant farmers, it should be possible in the case of the large-scale commercial clearances which account for an increasing proportion of tropical deforestation.

After the initial clearance stage, as many as possible of the surviving forest fragments should be protected from clearance and disturbance. Large fragments should have priority but even the smallest, most disturbed fragments may have unique plant species. Planted or regenerated buffer zones around fragments will help to maintain the forest interior environment and minimize edge effects. The planting or regeneration of strips or stepping stones of woody vegetation in the matrix should promote dispersal movements between fragments and thus help mobile species with large area requirements. Reforestation on any scale can also provide additional habitat for the more tolerant forest species. None of this will be possible, however, without control of fires, which may be the single most important management activity in drought-susceptible areas (Laurance and Fearnside 1999; Taylor *et al.* 1999).

In the most degraded landscapes, problems and solutions are qualitatively similar to those of human-dominated landscapes outside the tropics (e.g. Thomas *et al.* 1997), although the problems are quantitatively increased by the much higher diversity. The priorities are the maintenance of landscape heterogeneity, the establishment of a protected area system which covers the full range of habitats, including non-forest ones, and the protection of endangered species outside this area. Where local social and economic conditions permit, the restoration of at least some components of the primeval forest diversity may be possible. The success of the many, unplanned animal (re)introductions in Hong Kong, without an active habitat creation and reintroduction program, shows the potential of this approach.

In most of the tropics, preserving large areas of pristine forest will be impossible and native biodiversity will only survive, if at all, in a landscape-level mosaic of primary and secondary forests, plantations, agriculture and human habitations. Current evidence suggests that relatively small changes in clearance patterns, and in the subsequent management of agroecosystems and abandoned land, can permit the survival of species which would otherwise be lost from such landscapes. The earlier such changes begin the better.

Acknowledgments

Thanks are due to more people in both Hong Kong and Singapore than I can acknowledge individually, for comments, suggestions and access to unpublished data, but I am particularly grateful to Ian Turner, Michael Leven and David Dudgeon.

References

Alger, K. and Caldas, M. (1994) The declining cocoa economy and the Atlantic forest of southern Bahia, Brazil: conservation attitudes of cocoa planters. *Environmentalist* **14**, 107–119.

Balke, M., Hendrich, L. and Yang, C.M. (1999) Water beetles (Insecta: Coleoptera) in the nature reserves of Singapore. *Gardens' Bulletin, Singapore* **49**, 147–159.

Bascombe, M.J., Johnston, G. and Bascombe, F.S. (1999) *The Butterflies of Hong Kong.* Academic Press, London.

Benitez-Malvido, J. (1998) Impact of forest fragmentation on seedling abundance in a tropical rain forest. *Conservation Biology* **12**, 380–389.

Bierregaard, R.O. and Stouffer, P.C. (1997) Understorey birds and dynamic habitat mosaics in Amazonian fragments. In: *Tropical Forest Remnants: Ecology, Management, and Conservation of Fragmented Communities* (eds W.F. Laurance and R.O. Bierregaard), pp. 138–155. University of Chicago Press, Chicago.

Bogadek, A. and Lau, M.W.N. (1997) A revised checklist of Hong Kong amphibians and reptiles. *Memoirs of the Hong Kong Natural History Society* **21**, 173–187.

Brooks, T.M., Pimm, S.L. and Oyugi, J.O. (1999) Time lag between deforestation and bird extinction in tropical forest fragments. *Conservation Biology* **13**, 1140–1150.

Brown, K.S. and Hutchings, R.W. (1997) Disturbance, fragmentation, and the dynamics of diversity in Amazonian forest butterflies. In:

Tropical Forest Remnants: Ecology, Management, and Conservation of Fragmented Communities (eds W.F. Laurance and R.O. Bierregaard), pp. 91–110. University of Chicago Press, Chicago.

Cantley, N. (1884) *Report on the Forests of the Straits Settlements.* Singapore Printing Office, Singapore.

Carvalho, K.S. and Vasconcelos, H.L. (1999) Forest fragmentation in central Amazonia and its effects on litter-dwelling ants. *Biological Conservation* **91**, 151–157.

Cheng, T.S. (1987). *A Synopsis of the Avifauna of China.* Science Press, Beijing.

Chiarello, A.G. (1999) Effects of fragmentation of the Atlantic forest on mammal communities in south-eastern Brazil. *Biological Conservation* **89**, 71–82.

Christiansen, M.B. and Pitter, E. (1997) Species loss in a forest bird community near Lagoa Santa in Southeastern Brazil. *Biological Conservation* **80**, 23–32.

Chong, D.H. and Dudgeon, D. (1992) Hong Kong stream fishes: an annotated checklist with remarks on conservation status. *Memoirs of the Hong Kong Natural History Society* **19**, 79–112.

Corbet, G.B. and Hill, J.E. (1992) *The Mammals of the Indomalayan Region: a Systematic Review.* Oxford University Press, Oxford.

Corlett, R.T. (1991) Plant succession on degraded land in Singapore. *Journal of Tropical Forest Science* **4**, 151–161.

Corlett, R.T. (1997) Human impact on the flora of Hong Kong Island. In: *The Changing Face of East Asia During the Tertiary and Quaternary* (ed. N. Jablonski), pp. 400–412. Centre of Asian Studies, Hong Kong.

Corlett, R.T. (1999) The vegetation in the nature reserves of Singapore. *Gardens' Bulletin, Singapore* 49, 147–159.

Corlett, R.T. and Turner, I.M. (1997) Long-term survival in tropical forest remnants in Singapore and Hong Kong. In: *Tropical Forest Remnants: Ecology, Management and Conservation of Fragmented Communities* (eds W.F. Laurance and R.O. Bierregaard), pp. 333–345, University of Chicago Press, Chicago.

Cosson, J.F., Pons, J.M. and Masson, D. (1999) Effects of forest fragmentation on frugivorous and nectarivorous bats in French Guiana. *Journal of Tropical Ecology* 15, 515–534.

Crome, F., Isaacs, J. and Moore, L. (1994) The utility to birds and mammals of remnant riparian vegetation and associated windbreaks in the tropical Queensland uplands. *Pacific Conservation Biology* 1, 328–343.

Daily, G.C. and Ehrlich, P.R. (1996) Nocturnality and species survival. *Proceedings of the National Academy of Sciences USA* 93, 11709–11712.

Da Silva, J.M.C., Uhl, C. and Murray, G. (1996) Plant succession, landscape management, and the ecology of frugivorous birds in abandoned Amazonian pasture. *Conservation Biology* 10, 491–503.

De Souza, O.F.F. and Brown, V.K. (1994) Effects of habitat fragmentation on Amazonian termite communities. *Journal of Tropical Ecology* 10, 197–206.

Didham, R.K. (1997) An overview of invertebrate responses to forest fragmentation. In: *Forests and Insects* (eds A.D. Watt, N.E. Stork and M.D. Hunter), pp. 303–315. Chapman and Hall, London.

Didham, R.K. and Lawton, J.G. (1999) Edge structure determines the magnitude of changes in microclimate and vegetation structure in tropical forest fragments. *Biotropica* 31, 17–30.

Dudgeon, D. and Corlett, R.T. (1994) *Hills and Streams: an Ecology of Hong Kong.* Hong Kong University Press, Hong Kong.

Duncan, R.S. and Chapman, C.A. (1999) Seed dispersal and potential forest succession in abandoned agriculture in tropical Africa. *Ecological Applications* 9, 998–1008.

Eggleton, P., Bignell, D.E., Sands, W.A., *et al.* (1996) The diversity, abundance and biomass of termites under differing levels of disturbance in the Mbamayo Forest Reserve, southern Cameroon. *Philosophical Transactions of the Royal Society of London B*, 351, 51–68.

Ercelawn, A.C., LaFrankie, J.V., Lum, S.K.Y. and Lee, S.K. (1998) Short-term recruitment of trees in a forest fragment in Singapore. *Tropics* 8, 105–115.

Estrada, A., Coates-Estrada, R. and Meritt, D. (1993) Bat species richness and abundance in tropical rain forest fragments and in agricultural habitats at Los Tuxtlas, Mexico. *Ecography* 16, 309–318.

Estrada, A., Coates-Estrada, R. and Meritt, D. (1994) Non flying mammals and landscape changes in the tropical rain forest region of Los Tuxtlas, Mexico. *Ecography* 17, 229–241.

Estrada, A., Coates-Estrada, R., Dadda, A.A. and Cammarano, P. (1998) Dung and carrion beetles in tropical rain forest fragments and agricultural habitats at Los Tuxtlas, Mexico. *Journal of Tropical Ecology* 14, 577–593.

Estrada, A., Anzures, D. and Coates-Estrada, R. (1999) Tropical rain forest fragmentation, howler monkeys (*Allouatta palliata*), and dung beetles at Los Tuxtlas, Mexico. *American Journal of Primatology* 28, 253–262.

Ferrari, S.F. and Diego, V.H. (1995) Habitat fragmentation and primate conservation in the Atlantic forest of eastern Minas Gerais, Brazil. *Oryx* 29, 192–196.

Ferreira, L.V. and Laurance, W.F. (1997) Effects of forest fragmentation on mortality and damage of selected trees in Central Amazonia. *Conservation Biology* 11, 797–901.

Ferreira, L.V. and Prance, G.T. (1999) Ecosystem recovery in terra firme forests after cutting and burning: a comparison on species richness, floristic composition and forest structure in the Jau National Park, Amazonia. *Botanical Journal of the Linnean Society* 130, 97–110.

Finegan, B. (1996) Pattern and process in neotropical secondary rain forests: the first 100 years of succession. *Trends in Ecology and Evolution* 11, 119–124.

Fujisaka, S., Escobar, G. and Veneklaas, E. (1998)

Plant community diversity relative to human land uses in an Amazon forest colony. *Biodiversity and Conservation* **7**, 41–57.

Gascon, C., Lovejoy, T.E., Bierregaard, R.O., *et al.* (1999) Matrix habitat and species richness in tropical forest remnants. *Biological Conservation* **91**, 223–229.

Hails, C. (1987) *Birds of Singapore*. Times Editions, Singapore.

Holl, K.D. (1998) Do bird perching structures elevate seed rain and seedling establishment in abandoned tropical pasture? *Restoration Ecology* **6**, 253–261.

Holloway, J.D., Kirk-Spriggs, A.H. and Ken, C.V. (1992) The responses of some rain forest insect groups to logging and conversion to plantation. *Philosophical Transactions of the Royal Society of London B*, **335**, 425–436.

Hughes, R.F., Kauffman, J.B. and Jaramillo, V.J. (1999) Biomass, carbon, and nutrient dynamics of secondary forests in a humid tropical region of Mexico. *Ecology* **80**, 1892–1907.

Johns, A.D. (1991) Responses of Amazonian rain forest birds to habitat modification. *Journal of Tropical Ecology* **7**, 417–437.

Kellman, M., Tackaberry, R. and Rigg, L. (1998) Structure and function in two tropical gallery forest communities: implications for forest conservation in fragmented systems. *Journal of Applied Ecology* **35**, 195–206.

Khew, S.K. and Neo, S.S.H. (1999) Butterfly biodiversity in Singapore with particular reference to the Central Catchment Area Nature Reserve. *Gardens' Bulletin, Singapore* **49**, 273–296.

Kwok, H.K. and Corlett, R.T. (1999) Seasonality of a forest bird community in Hong Kong, South China. *Ibis* **141**, 70–79.

Laurance, W.F. (1997) Responses of mammals to rainforest fragmentation in tropical Queensland: a review and synthesis. *Wildlife Research* **24**, 603–612.

Laurance, W.F. (1999) Introduction and synthesis. *Biological Conservation* **91**, 101–107.

Laurance, W.F. and Bierregaard, R.O. (1997) *Tropical Forest Remnants: Ecology, Management and Conservation of Fragmented Communities*. University of Chicago Press, Chicago.

Laurance, W.F., Ferreira, L.S., Rankin de Merona, J.M., Laurance, S.G., Hutchings, R.W. and Lovejoy, T.E. (1998) Effects of forest fragmentation on recruitment patterns in Amazonian tree communities. *Conservation Biology* **12**, 460–464.

Laurance, W.F. and Fearnside, P.M. (1999) Amazon burning. *Trends in Ecology and Evolution* **14**, 457.

Laurance, W.F., Gascon, C. and Rankin de Merona, J.M. (1999) Predicting effects of habitat destruction on plant communities: a test of a model using Amazonian trees. *Ecological Applications* **9**, 548–554.

Lavelle, P., Barois, I., Martin, A., Zaidi, Z. and Schaefer, R. (1989) Management of earthworm populations in agro-ecosystems: a possible way to maintain soil quality. In: *Ecology of Arable Land* (eds M. Clarholm and L. Bergstrom), pp. 109–122. Kluwer Academic, Dordrecht.

Lawton, J.H., Bignell, D.E., Bolton, B. *et al.* (1998) Biodiversity inventories, indicator taxa and effects of habitat modification in tropical forest. *Nature* **391**, 72–75.

Lewthwaite, R.W. (1996) Forest birds of Southeast China: observations during 1984–96. *Hong Kong Bird Report* **1995**, 150–203.

Lim, K.K.P. and Lim, F.L.K. (1992) *A Guide to the Amphibians and Reptiles of Singapore*. Singapore Science Centre, Singapore.

Lim, K.S. (1999) Bird biodiversity in the nature reserves of Singapore. *Gardens' Bulletin, Singapore* **49**, 225–244.

Liu, H. (1998) The change of geographical distribution of two Asian species of rhinoceros in Holocene. *Journal of Chinese Geography* **8**, 83–88.

Lovejoy, T.E., Bierregaard, R.O., Rylands, A.B., *et al.* (1986) Edge and other effects of isolation on Amazonian forest fragments. In: *Conservation Biology: the Science of Scarcity and Diversity* (ed. M.E. Soulé), pp. 257–285. Sinauer Associates, Sunderland, Mass.

Malcolm, J.R. (1997) Biomass and diversity of small mammals in Amazonian forest fragments. In: *Tropical Forest Remnants: Ecology, Management and Conservation of Fragmented Communities* (eds W.F. Laurance and R.O. Bierregaard), pp. 207–221. University of Chicago Press, Chicago.

Mesquita, R.C.G., Delamonica, P. and Laurance, W.F. (1999) Effect of surrounding vegetation on edge-related tree mortality in Amazonian forest fragments. *Biological Conservation* **91**, 129–134.

Moguel, P. and Toledo, V.M. (1999) Biodiversity

conservation in traditional coffee systems of Mexico. *Conservation Biology* **13**, 11–21.

Murphy, D.H. (1999) Odonate diversity in the nature reserves of Singapore. *Gardens' Bulletin, Singapore* **49**, 333–352.

Nepstad, D.C., Moutinho, P.R., Uhl, C., Vieira, I.C. and da Silva, J.M.C. (1996) The ecological importance of forest remnants in an Eastern Amazonian frontier landscape. In: *Forest Patches in Tropical Landscapes* (eds J. Schelhas. and R. Greenberg), pp. 133–150. Island Press, Washington, D.C.

Newmark, W.D. (1991) Tropical forest fragmentation and the local extinction of understorey birds in the eastern Usambara Mountains, Tanzania. *Conservation Biology* **5**, 67–78.

Ng, P.K.L. (1999) The conservation status of freshwater prawns and crabs in Singapore with emphasis on the nature reserves. *Gardens' Bulletin, Singapore* **49**, 267–272.

Ng, P.K.L. and Lim, K.K.P. (1999) The diversity and conservation status of fishes in the nature reserves of Singapore. *Gardens' Bulletin, Singapore* **49**, 245–265.

Patterson, B.D. (1987) The principle of nested subsets and its implications for biological conservation. *Conservation Biology* **1**, 323–334.

Petit, L.J., Petit, D.R., Christian, D.G. and Powell, H.D.W. (1999) Bird communities of natural and modified habitats in Panama. *Ecography* **22**, 292–304.

Raman, T.R.S., Rawat, G.S. and Johnsingh, A.J.T. (1998) Recovery of tropical rainforest avifauna in relation to vegetation succession following shifting cultivation in Mizoram, north-east India. *Journal of Applied Ecology* **35**, 214–231.

Renjifo, L.M. (1999) Composition changes in a subandean avifauna after long-term forest fragmentation. *Conservation Biology* **13**, 1124–1139.

Scariot, A. (1999) Forest fragmentation effects on palm diversity in central Amazonia. *Journal of Ecology* **87**, 66–76.

Seow-Choen, F. (1999) Stick and leaf insect (Phasmida: Insecta) biodiversity in the nature reserves of Singapore. *Gardens' Bulletin, Singapore* **49**, 297–312.

Stouffer, P.C. and Bierregaard, R.O. (1995a) Effects of forest fragmentation on understorey hum-

mingbirds in Amazonian Brazil. *Conservation Biology* **9**, 1085–1094.

Stouffer, P.C. and Bierregaard, R.O. (1995b) Use of Amazonian forest fragments by understorey insectivorous birds. *Ecology* **76**, 2429–2445.

Tabarelli, M., Mantovani, W. and Peres, C.A. (1999) Effects of habitat fragmentation on plant guild structure in the montane Atlantic forest of southeastern Brazil. *Biological Conservation* **91**, 119–127.

Taylor, D., Saksena, P., Sanderson, P.G. and Kucera, K. (1999) Environmental change and rain forests on the Sunda shelf of Southeast Asia: drought, fire and the biological cooling of biodiversity hotspots. *Biodiversity and Conservation* **8**, 1159–1177.

Teo, R.C.H. and Rajathurai, S. (1999) Mammals, reptiles and amphibians of the nature reserves in Singapore—diversity, abundance and distribution. *Gardens' Bulletin, Singapore* **49**, 353–425.

Terborgh, J. (1992) Maintenance of diversity in tropical forests. *Biotropica* **24**, 283–292.

Thiollay, J.M. (1995) The role of traditional agroforests in the conservation of rain forest bird diversity in Sumatra. *Conservation Biology* **9**, 335–353.

Thomas, R.C., Kirby, K.J. and Reid, C.M. (1997) The conservation of a fragmented ecosystem within a cultural landscape—the case of ancient woodland in England. *Biological Conservation* **82**, 243–252.

Tocher, M.D., Gascon, C. and Zimmerman, B.L. (1997) Fragmentation effects on a Central Amazonian frog community: a ten-year study. In: *Tropical Forest Remnants: Ecology, Management and Conservation of Fragmented Communities* (eds W.F. Laurance and R.O. Bierregaard), pp. 124–137. University of Chicago Press, Chicago.

Turner, I.M. (1994) The taxonomy and ecology of the vascular plant flora of Singapore: a statistical analysis. *Botanical Journal of the Linnean Society* **114**, 215–227.

Turner, I.M. (1996) Species loss in fragments of tropical rain forest: a review of the evidence. *Journal of Applied Ecology* **33**, 200–209.

Turner, I.M. and Corlett, R.T. (1996) The conservation value of small, isolated fragments of lowland tropical rain forest. *Trends in Ecology and Evolution* **11**, 330–333.

Turner, I.M., Tan, H.T.W., Wee, Y.C., Ibrahim, A.B., Chew, P.T. and Corlett, R.T. (1994) A study of plant species extinction in Singapore: lessons for the conservation of tropical biodiversity. *Conservation Biology* **8**, 705–712.

Turner, I.M., Chua, K.S., Ong, J.S.Y., Soong, B.C. and Tan, H.T.W. (1996) A century of plant species loss from an isolated fragment of lowland tropical rain forest. *Conservation Biology* **10**, 1229–1244.

Turner, I.M., Wong, Y.K., Chew, P.T. and Ibrahim, A.B. (1997) The species richness of primary and old secondary tropical forest in Singapore. *Biodiversity and Conservation* **6**, 537–543.

Vasconcelos, H.L. (1999) Effects of disturbance on the structure of ground-foraging ant communities in central Amazonia. *Biodiversity and Conservation* **8**, 409–420.

Warkentin, I.G., Greenberg, R. and Ortiz, J.S. (1995) Songbird use of gallery woodlands in recently cleared and older settled landscapes of the Selva Lacandora, Chiapas, Mexico. *Conservation Biology* **9**, 1095–1106.

Wells, D.R. (1999) *The Birds of the Thai-Malay Peninsula*, Vol. 1, *Non-Passerines*. Academic Press, London.

Whitmore, T.C. and Sayer, J.A. (1992) *Tropical Deforestation and Species Extinction*. Chapman and Hall, London.

Wiersum, K.F. (1997) Indigenous exploitation and management of tropical forest resources: an evolutionary continuum in forest–people interactions. *Agriculture, Ecosystems and Environment* **63**, 1–16.

Willis, E.O. (1979) The composition of avian communities in remanescent woodlots in southern Brazil. *Papeis Avulsos de Zoologia* **33**, 1–25.

Wilson, K.D.P. (1997) An annotated checklist of the Hong Kong dragonflies with recommendations for their conservation. *Memoirs of the Hong Kong Natural History Society* **21**, 1–68.

Yang, C.M., Lua, H.K. and Yeo, K.L. (1999) Semi-aquatic bug (Heteroptera: Gerromorpha) fauna in the nature reserves of Singapore. *Gardens' Bulletin, Singapore* **49**, 313–319.

Yang, C.M., Yong, K. and Lim, K.K.P. (1990) Wild mammals of Singapore. In: *Essays in Zoology* (eds L.M. Chou and P.K.L. Ng), pp. 1–23. Department of Zoology, National University of Singapore, Singapore.

Zhuang, X. and Corlett, R.T. (1997) Forest and forest succession in Hong Kong, China. *Journal of Tropical Ecology* **14**, 857–866.

Zhuang, X., Xing, F. and Corlett, R.T. (1997) The tree flora of Hong Kong: distribution and status. *Memoirs of the Hong Kong Natural History Society* **21**, 69–126.

Chapter 17

Ecological experiments in farmland conservation

D.W. Macdonald, R.E. Feber, F.H. Tattersall[1] and P.J. Johnson

Introduction

Heterogeneity, while having a clear intuitive meaning, is, in the ecological sense, a more elusive concept. While there is no such thing as a homogeneous habitat—even a bacterial suspension in a test tube experiences a discontinuity between the glass of the tube and the water in it (Begon *et al.* 1996)—there is no obvious way to characterize this type of variation in natural habitats. Attempts have been made to create formal frameworks for habitat structure which incorporate heterogeneity as one of their elements. Although these models are arguably only partially successful, they serve as a useful framework around which to consider the ecological significance of habitat heterogeneity, and related concepts, in the agricultural landscape.

McCoy and Bell (1991) saw heterogeneity as a measure of variation in the abundance (per unit area or volume) of different structural elements. In this model, heterogeneity is explicitly dependent upon the scale of measurement. Similarly, Addicott *et al.* (1987) considered heterogeneity to be an aspect of environmental patterning—the 'patchiness' of a habitat, where patches are defined by environmental discontinuities, provided that these are relevant to the organism in question. Heterogeneity and division are then two qualitatively different aspects of spatial patterning in this scheme: 'division' the separation of similar patches in space, and 'heterogeneity' the diversity of patch types. Scale effects are increasingly being recognized as important. Levin (1992) argued that pattern and scale is 'the central problem' in ecology. Wiens (this volume) reviews current ideas of heterogeneity in ecology and the 'overarching effects of scale'.

These models also recognize the importance of time as an aspect of heterogeneity. The duration of different patches is likely to be important to many organisms. It is therefore possible to visualize a series of continua in these dimensions with undivided homogeneous habitats, stable over time at one end, to divided and heterogeneous habitats with strong temporal dynamics at the other.

Farmland, particularly that under arable cultivation in temperate regions, is in many respects at this latter end of the continuum. Firstly, at the farm scale, the discontinuities between patch types are very distinct. Field boundary habitats,

Wildlife Conservation Research Unit, Department of Zoology, University of Oxford, South Parks Road, Oxford OX13PS, UK; [1] *Royal Agricultural College, Cirencester, UK*

particularly hedgerows, are very clearly delineated. Other uncropped habitats are also well defined, whether they are islands of woodland, or patches of scrub or ponds. From its appearance from the air (on a human scale), arable farmland has frequently been likened to a 'mosaic' or 'patchwork' (e.g. Doncaster and Krebs 1993).

Secondly, the major part of the surface area of the farm, the crop, is subject to severe perturbations in the form of sowing, harvesting, cultivation and the application of pesticides and fertilizers. The abruptness and severity of these changes uniquely characterizes arable farmland.

There is an increasing body of literature on the effect of patch fragmentation, isolation and metapopulation dynamics (e.g. Hanski 1997). The extent to which these processes are relevant to the fauna of farmland is largely unknown. Aside from its potential theoretical value as a testbed for questions related to environmental disturbance and patchiness, farmland is also the focus of interest for purely conservation motives (Macdonald and Smith 1990). The protection and, increasingly, the restoration and enhancement of biodiversity on farmland is undeniably a pressing concern for environmentalists at the start of the 21st century. Using the UK as an example, three compelling arguments can be advanced in support of this notion. Firstly, most of the landscape of the UK is made up of farmland. The Countryside Survey of 1990 (Anonymous 1993) estimated that more than 60% of the land surface was either tilled land, managed grassland or rough grassland of some kind. In purely quantitative terms, then, conservation on farmland is an important issue. Secondly, many species of plant, and some invertebrates, are restricted to farmland (Donald 1998). Charlock (*Sinapsis arvensis*), for example, is a weed of arable crops that is rarely found elsewhere (Mellanby 1981). While the detail of these points applies only to the UK, the broader picture is in many ways similar to that in Europe and North America.

Finally, there is abundant evidence that modern farming methods have had, and are continuing to have, adverse effects on a wide variety of taxa. The evidence is particularly strong for birds. Fuller *et al.* (1995) reported that 24 out of 28 farmland species had reduced range sizes compared with 1970. Where individual species have been the subject of close scrutiny, decline has been steepest in regions where intensive agriculture is most prevalent (Chamberlain and Crick 1999). Many species of arable weed have also declined dramatically since the 1960s (Wilson 1992). The less comprehensive long-term evidence for trends in invertebrate numbers also suggests an overall picture of decline for many groups, including spiders, moths and polyphagous predators (Donald 1998). The abundance of beneficial invertebrates in cereal crops sampled in Sussex dropped sharply around the mid-1970s (Aebischer 1991).

The factors that have been implicated as responsible for this general pattern of declining biodiversity are mainly associated with modern intensive agriculture, and also reduce the heterogeneity of the 'farmscape' at some level. Some have a direct negative impact on the local abundance of specific habitats. For example, the removal of hedgerows and ponds to enlarge field sizes in the interests of productivity is among these. Hedgerow removal is particularly well documented (e.g. Barr *et al.* 1993). While this may be less severe in recent years than in the 1970s, there is evidence that a substantial minority of farmers continued to remove hedgerows in the 1990s (Macdonald and Johnson 2000; from 1997, hedgerows have had limited legal protection). Increased herbicide application is also a conspicuous feature of modern agriculture. The absence of broad spectrum herbicide use at the crop edge results in increases in the numbers of many species of broad leaved weeds including several rare arable plants (Sotherton 1991). In addition, spray drift can affect plants in the field boundary (Marrs *et al.* 1991). While herbicides are intended to have a direct impact on botanical diversity, there are likely to be longer term effects on invertebrates and birds (Campbell *et al.* 1997). Higher inputs of fertilizer also reduce botanical diversity; many species of dicotyledenous herb are unable to compete at high soil nutrient levels, and the result is a much impoverished flora (Wilson 1999).

As well as these local direct influences within individual habitats, overall policy at the farm level has also reduced the variety of different habitats available. Recent intensification has tended to polarize cropping patterns. Crop rotations are a less prominent feature of conventional arable farming and crop diversity is generally lower on conventional modern farms. An individual farm is therefore likely to support a narrower range of structural and habitat diversity for flora and fauna to exploit (Gardner and Brown 1998).

Recent years, however, have seen a shift in agricultural policy in Europe. Current policies aimed at the national and global protection of biodiversity specifically include directives concerning agricultural, including arable, habitats (Anonymous 1994). Underpinning these changes is a burgeoning wealth of data on methods of creating and managing farmland habitats for the enhancement of biodiversity, driven by opportunities such as the introduction of set-aside (see Clarke 1992; Firbank 1998), the development of agri-environment schemes (e.g. Mitchell, 1999), as well as increasing attention on quantified species declines (e.g. Sotherton 1991; Fuller *et al.* 1995). Although they are wide-ranging, these studies share a common underlying theme: how can we manipulate environmental heterogeneity to promote biodiversity on farmland?

In this paper we synthesize the findings of a series of experiments in arable farmland. We consider how environmental heterogeneity affects biodiversity. In particular, we consider the effect of scale. Farmland is particularly amenable to a manipulative approach as many of the processes with the potential to impact on wildlife—such as harvest, spraying with pesticide and crop-type—are already under human control. The experiments under consideration range from farm-scale observational studies to radio-tracking studies of individual animals.

Habitat heterogeneity on farmland—a view from three levels

The observations brought together here are derived from several groups of experiments in the agricultural landscape. Three groups of invertebrates (butterflies, spiders and beetles), and small mammals are considered. These were chosen for several reasons: they represent different levels in the food-chain, they span a wide range of mobilities and they are ubiquitous on farmland. We also make use of some observations concerning other groups.

Heterogeneity at the landscape level: butterflies, spiders and small mammals on organic and conventional farms

Our first study compares the biodiversity of arable farms under organic and conventional management. From this perspective we can evaluate how the abundance of different groups is affected by the complex of factors that are associated with these different landscape-level regimes. We ask if any differences are mediated by the effect of the different management regimes on aspects of the structural heterogeneity of the landscape.

Butterflies

Because butterflies respond rapidly to changes in plant communities (Feber *et al.* 1996) and are sensitive to the presence of structural features in the landscape, including field boundaries (Dover 1996), they are very useful indicators of habitat quality on farmland.

The spatial and temporal variability of farmland makes it difficult for populations of the less mobile butterfly species to persist, since they are unable to respond to the changing distribution of often scarce resources. In intensively farmed landscapes, the general reduction in plant diversity in hedge bottoms (Barr *et al.* 1993) and grasslands (Fuller 1987; Barr *et al.* 1993) has reduced the range and abundance of foodplants for many species (Feber and Smith 1995). Butterflies in hedgerows are also susceptible to spray drift from insecticides (Cilgi and Jepson 1995). Organic farming systems, by contrast, adhere to standards which prohibit the use of artificial pesticides and fertilizers and which encourage sympathetic habitat management. They rely, for example, on nitrogen-building leys to increase soil fertility, and on natural predators to control pests (Lampkin 1990). It is therefore feasible that these different farming systems support different butterfly populations. This hypothesis was tested by surveying butterflies and habitats on pairs of organic and conventional farms in southern England between 1994 and 1996.

Butterflies were recorded at each site at approximately fortnightly intervals between April and September using a modified transect recording method, described in Feber *et al.* 1997. The overall pattern of butterfly abundance was clear, and strikingly consistent between years, despite an annual variation in butterfly abundance. Our results showed that butterfly abundance per kilometre per farm, averaged over the season, was significantly higher on organically managed farms than on conventionally managed farms in all 3 years of the study (Fig. 17.1 shows the pattern for 1994 and 1995).

Most butterfly species had higher abundances of individuals recorded on organic than on conventional farmland in most years, significantly so for three species, *Ochlodes venata* (the large skipper), *Polyommatus icarus* (the common

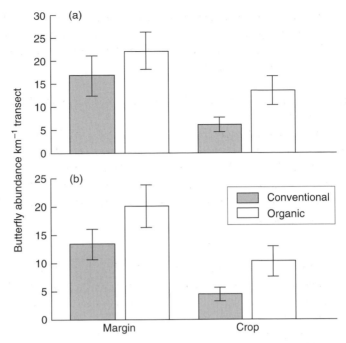

Figure 17.1 Butterfly abundance on organic and conventional systems in (a) 1994 and (b) 1995. Butterflies were significantly more abundant on organic systems in both years ($F_{1,7}=9.22$, $P<0.05$ and $F_{1,9}=31.5$, $P<0.001$, respectively).

blue) and *Maniola jurtina* (the meadow brown). These species have typically 'closed' populations and are less mobile. Some species which are highly mobile, for example the large and small white butterflies, were not found in increased abundance on organic farms (see also Feber *et al.* 1997).

In all 3 years of our study, we found that more butterflies were recorded on the uncropped field boundaries than the crop edge in both organic and conventional systems. However, although butterflies on intensively farmed arable land have been shown to be largely restricted to field boundaries (Dover 1990), we found in our comparison of organic and conventional systems that differences between butterfly abundances attributable to the system were found not only for the uncropped margin habitat, but also for the crop edge and that the difference between use of crop and boundary habitats was greater on conventional than on organic farms. System effects were therefore likely to stem from differences in management of both the uncropped margin and the cropped habitats.

Organic farms had larger hedgerows (Fig. 17.2) and a tendency for more perennial species of plant at the field boundary than conventional farms, and they also differed in terms of cropping regime. Grass-clover leys are important for maintaining fertility within organic rotations and the increased proportion of grassland within organic farms is likely to have benefits for butterflies. Common, but not

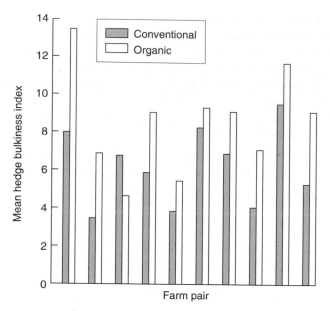

Figure 17.2 Hedgerow size on organic and conventional farms. Hedgerows were significantly bulkier (where bulkiness was defined as the mean product of height and width) on the organic farms (paired *t*-test, d.f. = 10, P=0.005).

highly mobile, butterfly species, such as *M. jurtina* (meadow brown) and *Pyronia tithonus* (gatekeeper), require grassy swards in which to overwinter in their larval stage (Emmet and Heath 1990) and so grass leys, depending on their species composition, can provide valuable breeding habitat. Our results suggested that the greater temporal stability resulting from the maintenance of grass leys which are in place for two or more years, and the presence of more perennial field edge plant communities, combined with an increase in spatial heterogeneity at a landscape level sustained a greater diversity and abundance of butterflies on organic farms. Those benefits derived from different patterns of cropping cannot readily be recreated under conventional systems, but other studies suggest that restoration of vegetation at the field margin and its protection from damaging operations, can have substantial benefits for biodiversity within non-organic systems (Feber *et al.* 1997).

Spiders

Detecting significant effects of farming system at the field, rather than the farm, scale can be very difficult, particularly where abundances of individuals are low. Spiders occur in much greater abundance than butterflies on arable land. We tested whether an effect of farming system could be detected on spider abundance and species richness by sampling surface-active spiders from winter wheat fields on three pairs of organic and conventional farms in southern England in May and

June 1995. A number of vegetational characteristics were also measured in each field. The methodology is described in full in Feber *et al.* (1998).

Significantly more spiders, and more species of spider, were captured from the organic fields. Furthermore, our analyses suggested that spider communities as a whole differed between the contrasting management systems. While we could not interpret this difference in terms of the ecological characteristics of the species involved, vegetational data suggested that, on a local scale within each field, there were differences associated with the contrasting farming systems which were likely to have had a measurable impact on the spider communities. A number of vegetation variables differed significantly between organic and conventional systems. In particular, understorey vegetation (both grasses and forbs) was substantially more abundant on organic fields, and the crop was less dense (Fig. 17.3).

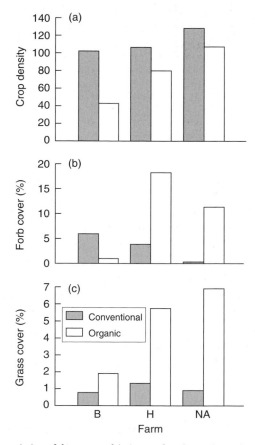

Figure 17.3 Characteristics of the cropped (winter wheat) area in spring on organic and conventional farms. Crop density was significantly lower on organic fields at Broadfield (B) and Harnhill (H), *t*-tests, $P < 0.001$ and $P < 0.05$, respectively. Forb cover was significantly higher on organic fields at Harnhill and North Aston (NA), *t*-tests, $P < 0.05$. Grass cover was significantly higher at North Aston, *t*-test, $P < 0.05$.

In both months, there were significant positive relationships between the abundance of spiders and the percentage cover of forbs and grasses within the crop. These relationships were significant both overall, and within each management system. Similarly, the species richness of catches tended to be positively associated with the percentage cover of forb and grass species within the crop. Web-building spiders are sensitive to changes in vegetation density (Topping 1993), biomass (Rypstra and Carter 1995), structure (Asteraki *et al.* 1992; Alderweireldt 1994) and height (Smith *et al.* 1993); in addition, understorey vegetation assumes increasing importance as senescence occurs in the lower leaves of the wheat stems (Sunderland *et al.* 1986). Habitats with a greater degree of architectural complexity provide more niches for web-building forms (Gibson *et al.* 1992) resulting in greater abundance and diversity. The growth of understorey vegetation may also increase the abundance of prey items for polyphageous predators. Thus within-crop structural heterogeneity may be one mechanism by which the observed farm-scale differences in spider communities were mediated.

Wood mice, Apodemus sylvaticus

The most commonly perceived difference between organic and conventional farming systems is in the level of agrochemical inputs. However, the lack of these inputs in organic systems has implications for other aspects of farm management which might impact on wildlife. An example of this is sowing date. Conventional farmers are able to use fertilizers to maintain artificially high soil nitrogen levels over winter, and can take advantage of a longer growing period, sowing their crops in the autumn. Organic farmers cannot compensate for excess losses of soil nitrogen, and may need to wait for more favourable sowing conditions in the spring (Lampkin 1990). By summer, wheat sward height remains significantly lower in spring sown organic than winter sown conventional wheat in southern England (Field 1998). Abundance of wood mice in cereal fields in May and June is positively correlated with sward height (Fig.17.4), and this may account for the finding that there are fewer mice in spring sown organic wheat than in conventional winter wheat fields (Field 1998). Paired comparisons of 12 organic and 12 conventional fields revealed mean May/June densities equivalent to 1.3/ha and 3.4/ha, respectively.

The studies described so far have compared organic and conventional farming systems to illustrate how heterogeneity within each farming system may affect faunal populations at a landscape level. Because organic and conventional farms differ in a variety of complex ways, it is difficult to identify which of these have direct impacts on biodiversity. To do this, it is necessary to focus at a smaller scale.

In the next two sections we look first at how small mammals and invertebrates use the various cropped and uncropped habitats available on farmland (heterogeneity at the farm level); and second at how they respond to the management which results in variations within these habitats (heterogeneity at the habitat level).

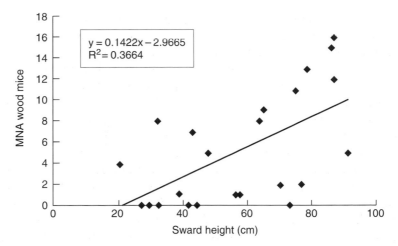

Figure 17.4 Wood mouse abundance and sward height. There was a positive relationship between sward height (cm) and wood mouse abundance (MNA); the trendline shows linear regression ($F_{1,22} = 12.7$, $P = 0.002$).

Heterogeneity at the farm level

At the farm level, the type of heterogeneity we are considering is that which is most apparent to the human observer; the clear division of the landscape into patches of different crop types, separated by field boundaries of various structures.

On arable farms, the boundary is a much more stable habitat than the cropped area. For many species it may provide a refuge from the management practices associated with cultivation. Mellanby (1981) described how the role of the field boundary as a refuge for small mammals could occasionally be observed. The subterranean runs of moles are destroyed by ploughing, and many moles are probably killed, with others escaping to hedges and ditch banks. In spring, mole runs can be traced from field boundaries to the outer edges of the crop, while locations further into the crop remain mole-free. How general are patterns like these?

Wood mice

Wood mice are found throughout the full range of habitats available on farmland, raising interesting questions about how animals choose to use an apparently heterogeneous habitat. The human eye can perceive several major habitat types on farmland—cropped areas (e.g. wheat, barley and oil-seed rape), hedgerow, field margins, set-aside and patches of farm woodland. Are these broad categories ecologically meaningful to a mouse? We looked at this question at both the population and at the individual level.

Wood mice populations were monitored by live-trapping in eight standardized 0.36 ha grids covering four habitats (set-aside field, hedgerow with margin, crop and woodland) at each of two sites at monthly intervals for 2 years. If wood mice do not respond to these broad habitat categories we would have expected to see no

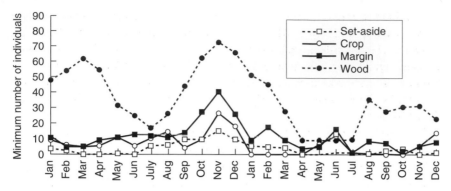

Figure 17.5 Wood mouse abundance in different habitats on farmland.

consistent differences in abundance. However, there were clear differences in abundance in different habitats, with set-aside fields having the fewest and woodland consistently having the most individuals, but also the greatest fluctuations (Fig. 17.5). In summer, when woodland abundances were at their lowest, they were similar to, or even exceeded by crop and hedgerow abundances. Wood mice remained in the crop after harvest and over winter, sometimes at high densities.

The large-scale movements of wood mice make them a particularly useful model for studying individual response to habitat heterogeneity at different scales (Todd *et al.* 2000). The 'choice' made by an individual wood mouse in how to react to the array of habitat patches available to it can be thought of as a two-level process. Firstly, a mouse has to 'decide' where to place its home range in the landscape. If the observed patchiness of crop types and field boundaries is of no relevance, two consequences would be expected to follow. Firstly, that home ranges would appear to be placed at random with respect to these habitat patches. Secondly, that the use of space by a mouse within its selected range would also appear to be independent of the composition of its home range. That is, it would neither be attracted to nor avoid any of the patch-types occurring within its 'selected' range.

Studies of radio-tracked wood mouse individuals at two sites, Wytham (Oxfordshire) and Eysey (Wiltshire), showed that the behaviour of wood mice was consistent with neither of these predictions (Macdonald *et al.* 1998; Macdonald *et al.* 2000; Tew *et al.* 2000; Todd *et al.* 2000). Time of year had a large impact on how wood mice were affected by patch types. In summer, ranges were relatively large and at Wytham there was a tendency for them to include less oilseed rape in their ranges than would be expected if mice were not selective. Within their ranges, there was a highly significant tendency for the mice to prefer patch types in the rank order hedgerow first, followed by wheat, barley and lastly rape. At Eysey, the available habitats were used randomly in summer. At this time male wood mice have very large home ranges (averaging more than 1.5 ha), which overlap with other males and females, while females have smaller ranges (averaging 0.5 ha) which are exclusive of other females.

After harvest and over winter, however, both males and females had small (about 0.2 ha), overlapping ranges which, with respect to occurrence in the landscape, contained significantly more hedgerow than any other habitat. There were no statistically significant preferences between any of the three arable crops at Wytham (Todd *et al.* 2000). At Eysey, set-aside field margins were consistently avoided relative to other habitats (Fig. 17.6), significantly so after the crop was harvested and the set-aside cut.

These patterns of habitat use are probably a response to seasonal disturbance and availability of cover in the crop fields and set-aside (Tattersall *et al.* 1997, 1999). Once cut, set-aside no longer provides much cover, and wood-mice would be particularly exposed to the predators which favour hunting along field edges. Harvest is an even more marked and traumatic period of disruption for arable wildlife, when the crop is removed from the fields and the ground prepared for sowing. Harvest itself has little direct impact on mice living in fields, but surviving mice inhabit a vastly changed landscape, as the standing cereal crop is replaced by open fields of stubble. Tew and Macdonald (1993) showed that the removal of cover afforded by the crop greatly increased predation pressure on the mice, and, after

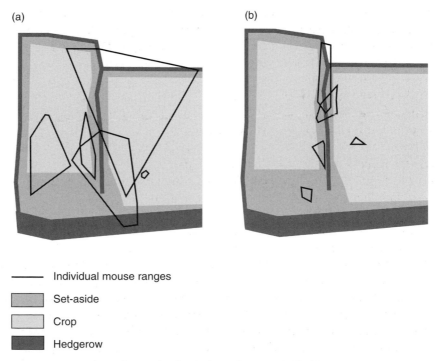

(a) (b)

——— Individual mouse ranges

  Set-aside

  Crop

  Hedgerow

Figure 17.6 Range boundaries of individual wood mice (a) before, and (b) after harvesting. When both sexes were considered together, habitats were use at random before harvest, but after harvest hedgerows were used more than expected and margins less than expected (*P*=0.005).

harvest, mice either left the fields or reduced their activity. After harvest, mice remaining in the fields became less active above ground, moved more slowly, less frequently and for shorter distances.

Wood mice clearly do respond to their environment at the level of the broad habitat categories that we outlined at the beginning of this section, but not all the time. Temporal habitat heterogeneity is a major influence on habitat choice, but is modified by changes in population density, breeding behaviour and social toler-ance. It is simplistic to assume that animals choose where to live purely on the basis of the attractiveness of the vegetative habitat.

Invertebrates

There is also evidence that the crop and margin-level patches influence the distri-bution of invertebrates. We have two sets of data supporting this. At Wytham we sampled invertebrates using suction sampling at two locations in the crop adjacent to extended field margins. At Cirencester, we sampled using the same methods in field boundaries, and at several locations into adjacent set-aside. The details of the methodology are given in full in Smith *et al.* (1993) and Gates *et al.* (1997), respec-tively. As for small mammals, the status of the crop appeared to be influential. In the Wytham spring samples, spiders, for example, were significantly more abun-dant closest to the boundary, and relatively scarce in the crop. Later in the year, just before harvest, abundance in the margin and crop were much more similar, and not statistically significantly different (Fig. 17.7).

At Cirencester, in suction samples collected in June, we found that several

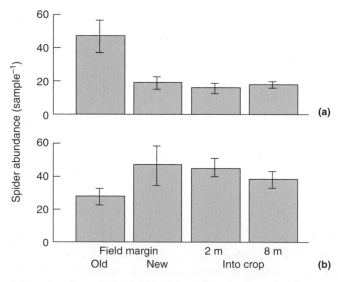

Figure 17.7 Spider abundance in the field margin and cropped area in (a) May and (b) July. In May, spiders were significantly more abundant in the original margin ($F_{3,100}=12.47$, $P<0.001$). In July, abundance did not differ significantly ($F_{3,59}=1.43$, $P=0.246$).

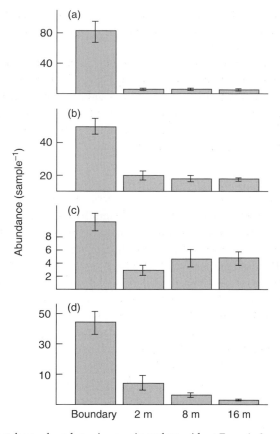

Figure 17.8 Invertebrate abundance in margin and set aside at Eysey in June 1995. For all groups, abundance in the boundary was significantly higher than in the set-aside; ANOVA results: (a) Auchenorrhyncha, $F_{3,35} = 63.8$; (b) Araneae, $F_{3,35} = 18.1$; (c) Carabidae, $F_{3,35} = 10.9$; (d) Heteroptera, $F_{3,35} = 8.9$; all, $P < 0.05$.

important groups were significantly more abundant in the boundary samples. The set-aside, in this case consisting of a sparse covering of low vegetation and comprising relatively few plant species, plainly constituted an unattractive habitat by comparison with the adjacent boundary, and its dense species-rich vegetation (Fig. 17.8).

Heterogeneity within farm-level habitat patches

At this point we shift our perspective further down the spatial scale and consider what elements of habitat heterogeneity within hedgerows and the major farmland habitat patches are linked to biodiversity. In the terminology of Addicott *et al.* (1987), this represents a change of focus of interest between the two qualitatively different types of patterning. We move from the *division* between patches (crops and boundaries) to the *heterogeneity* within them.

369

The studies in question were established largely from a conservation standpoint, given the background of overall decline described above.

Small mammals

From the above, we might conclude that wood mice, while showing a tendency to avoid including oilseed rape within their ranges, do not seem to use any crop types above others within their ranges. Does this mean then that they treat arable fields within their ranges as homogeneous? If we examine their use of space within these patches at a finer scale, we can show that wood mice are able to respond to micro-habitat variability within crops, such as the presence of weedy areas.

The positions of mice radio-tracked before harvest were marked. Positions of two categories of interest were identified; (a) 'stationary', where the mouse did not change location but stayed active for > 10 min; and (b) 'travelling', positions that the mouse passed through but did not pause at (recorded at hourly intervals). In addition, a set of sites was selected at random within each home range. At each position the presence of floral species within a 25×25 cm central quadrat, and in two adjoining quadrats, was determined, and the seed bank sampled. The composition of the vegetation and seed bank composition of these sites was then compared according to location-type, mouse sex and year.

Twelve plant species were sufficiently abundant for analysis, and eight of these were more abundant at stationary positions than at travelling or random ones. In contrast, bare soil was less abundant at stationary positions. Places where mice were feeding (active but stationary) were characterized by annual weed species such as cleavers *Galium aparine*, chickweed *Stellaria media*, black grass *Alopecurus myosuroides* and barren brome *Bromus sterilis*, and bare ground was absent. Of these, *Galium aparine* and *Alopecurus myosuroides* were significantly more abundant at these locations. There was no effect of the seed bank on microhabitat selection by wood mice. Assuming that vegetative growth is easier for mice to perceive and quantify than the relatively hidden seed bank, an efficient strategy for finding seeds might be to forage in or near patches of weeds, particularly if those weeds are themselves seeding. Such a strategy would enhance the chances of finding insect prey and would ensure that only the freshest seeds are eaten (Todd *et al.* 2000). Wood mice are capable of sophisticated response patterns to food availability; Plesner Jensen (1993) showed that, given a choice, they will include food items with high sugar content at the beginning of a night's foraging, changing to carbohydrate-rich items as the night progresses.

These data demonstrate that although wood mice did not differentiate between superficially homogeneous crop types, within the crops there was hidden heterogeneity in the form of small patches of weeds and bare earth between which the mice did differentiate. This heterogeneity arises through uneven herbicide application, germination from the seed bank and competition with the crop. However, farmers can also take specific action to promote heterogeneity within a habitat, usually for conservation or environmental reasons. We illustrate this with two examples in which action has been taken to increase food and cover.

Wood mice on arable land feed on many of the plants and invertebrates which have been shown to benefit from a selective reduction of herbicides applied to the outer edges of cereal crops ('conservation' headlands; Sotherton 1991). A reduction in herbicide applications to headlands should therefore create localized food-rich patches for wood mice. Tew *et al.* (1992) experimentally manipulated herbicides on winter wheat and found that radio-tracked wood mice were able to detect, exploit and benefit from food-rich patches resulting from selectively sprayed conservation headlands.

Plesner Jensen and Honess (1995) demonstrated that fewer small mammals were captured in plots of short (5 cm) grass than in tall (60 cm) grass, which provided them with cover from predators. Farmers are allowed to leave part of their set-aside uncut, and we created alternate cut and uncut patches of set-aside, 50 m long and 6 m wide, adjacent to hedgerow to test the hypothesis that wood mice would favour areas of longer vegetation. Radio-tracking after harvest, we found that wood mice strongly avoided the cut set-aside, and preferred the uncut patches (Macdonald *et al.* 1998).

In the same way that food-rich patches can be created for wood-mice in arable crops by modifying pesticide use, so too can uncropped field boundary habitats be manipulated for enhancement of biodiversity on farmland. Simple methods for restoring and managing field boundary swards could potentially result in radical improvements in habitat quality for wildlife on farmland. In experiments at Wytham, we quantified the effects of different field margin management regimes on botanical and invertebrate diversity.

Habitat heterogeneity and conservation management of field margins

Field margins around arable fields were extended in width from 0.5 m to 2 m by fallowing arable strips. The fallowed strips were divided into 50 m long plots, and were either left to regenerate naturally, or were sown with a grass and wild flower seed mixture. Plots were managed by mowing using one of three regimes (mown in summer, mown in spring and summer, mown in spring and autumn), by spraying with a broad-spectrum herbicide once-annually, or were left unmanaged. Plots were monitored over a nine year period for the diversity of plants and invertebrates (including Araneae, Auchenorrhyncha, Heteroptera and Lepidoptera (butterflies only)). The experiment is described in full in Smith *et al.* (1993).

The management regimes were expected to result in habitats with very different heterogeneity characteristics. For example, mowing causes a short-term catastrophic removal of architectural complexity in the habitat but will, however, provoke new sward growth, altering the habitat at ground level. Similarly, spraying with herbicide affects the structural heterogeneity of the sward, although not with immediate effect, and reduces the botanical species diversity of the sward over the longer term (Smith *et al.* 1994). Leaving plots unmanaged would allow an uninterrupted process of succession, eventually leading to the development of scrub. This generally involves directional changes in habitat structure, normally increases (Brown 1991).

371

Our results showed that all of the mowing regimes caused an immediate reduction in the abundance of all the groups of invertebrates monitored, as expected. However, there were some clear differences in how the habitat recovered, in terms of the invertebrate faunas they supported. The mowing regimes differed both in the size and in the persistence of their effects. Figure 17.9 shows how butterflies were affected by the summer cutting. Margins that were left uncut in summer provided a continuous supply of nectar, and undisturbed sites for oviposition. If plots were instead cut in spring and autumn, then the abundance and species richness of butterflies could not be distinguished from that on uncut plots, at least over the first five years of the experiment (Feber *et al.* 1996).

Summer cutting, as well as removing nectar sources, caused a more persistent loss of the habitat architecture. Vegetation height was consistently significantly lower on these plots (Smith *et al.* 1993). Figure 17.10 illustrates how this is likely to have affected the abundance of spiders.

There was a clear tendency for spider abundance to recover more quickly on plots cut in spring and autumn compared with those cut in summer (Baines *et al.* 1998). The Auchenorrhyncha did not show such clear differences in their sensitivity to these cutting regimes, probably because of their less immediate dependence on vegetation structure.

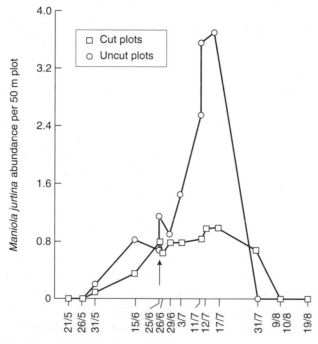

Figure 17.9 The effect of summer cutting of field margins on the abundance of meadow brown butterflies, *Maniola jurtina*, at Wytham in 1995. The arrow denotes the approximate timing of the summer cut. Butterflies were significantly less abundant on plots cut in summer (squares) compared with uncut plots (circles) ($F_{1,49}$, $P<0.001$).

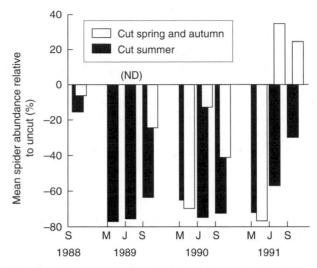

Figure 17.10 The effect of summer cutting of field margins on the abundance of spiders, compared with cutting in spring and autumn. M = May, J = July, S = September. ND signifies 'no data'.

We also have indirect evidence that small mammals were influenced by the cutting regimes. Trays containing seeds of three common arable weeds were placed on cut and uncut swards. These were either left open or caged to protect them from predators. It was found that the depletion of seeds in the open trays, relative to the caged trays, was consistently higher on the uncut swards (Povey *et al.* 1993).

One of the possible strategies for improving the conservation value of newly restored arable field margins, whilst at the same time controlling weeds (Watt *et al.* 1990; Smith *et al.* 1993) might be to sow them with a wild-flower seed mixture. In our experiment, where a relatively complex mixture was sown, plant species richness was higher on the sown than naturally regenerated plots, and this effect persisted for several years after the sowing (Smith *et al.* 1993, 1997).

Several invertebrate groups benefited from sowing. The abundance and species richness of both spiders and the Auchenorrhyncha (Fig. 17.11) were consistently higher on sown plots. It seems likely from the biologies of these two groups that the positive effect of sowing was mediated via two different aspects of habitat heterogeneity. Spiders are almost universally carnivorous, and many are specialized web-builders. Sown plots were likely to provide a more heterogeneous habitat architecture, within which web-building niches were consequently more diverse. A combined measure of vegetation height and density, obtained using a modified sward stick (Anonymous 1986), was consistently greater on sown than unsown plots.

Auchenorrhyncha, while probably benefiting in some ways from enhanced physical heterogeneity of the habitat (Denno 1994) are likely to be more directly dependent on the plant species composition of a habitat. While the group is

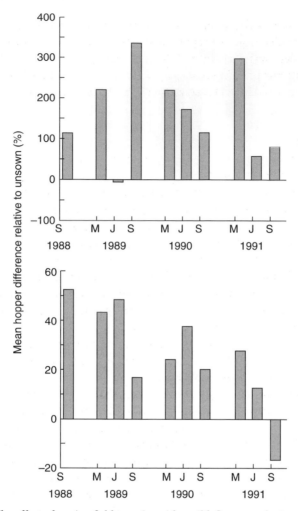

Figure 17.11 The effect of sowing field margins with a wild-flower seed mixture on the abundance (above) and species richness (below) of Auchenorhyncha. Sown plots had more individuals and species of Auchenorhyncha ($P<0.05$ for both). M = May, J = July, S = September.

considered to have rather generalized phytophagous habits (Morris 1971), the majority of British species in grassland habitats are known to prefer grasses to other vegetation and some feed exclusively on grasses (Morris 1990). Phytophagous groups may in general show a more direct link with plant species diversity rather than structural complexity. We know that the sown margins in our experiment contained significantly more grass species compared with unsown (Smith *et al.* 1993).

Evidence that spiders and Auchenorrhyncha were responding to different aspects of the changes in habitat heterogeneity resulting from the different management regimes was provided by their responses to herbicide spraying. While Auchenorrhyncha showed a rapid but short-lived decline following spraying, the effect of spiders was very delayed. This is exactly what we would expect if the spiders were principally influenced by structure, as the sprayed, but dead, vegetation stems remained intact for some time after the herbicide application.

Conclusion

At the time of writing, farming in the EU is entering a phase of upheaval, which may have far-reaching implications for the conservation of biodiversity in the farming landscape. The reforms to the Common Agricultural Policy which will emerge from this phase of upheaval may provide opportunities to reverse many of the declines in wildlife for which farming practices of recent decades have been held responsible. Policy makers are placing increasing emphasis on high environmental standards as an integral part of the future of British farming. And increasingly, 'biodiversity' is a term in the mainstream vocabulary at all levels of environmental management, where a few years earlier it was largely confined to the lobbying of marginal pressure groups. Indeed, parties to the Convention on Biological Diversity including the individual member states of the EU are obliged to develop national strategies for the conservation and sustainable use of biological diversity (Anonymous 1998). The ideal is to integrate conservation needs with the new EU measures for rural development.

It seems unlikely that the potential of these changes to benefit the environment can be fully exploited without being informed at every step by the scientific background. Without detailed knowledge of the ways in which individual farming practices affect the flora and fauna of farmland, policy will inevitably flounder. We believe that studies such as those outlined above form the starting points from which to expand knowledge of the interrelationships between farming practice, habitat heterogeneity over a range of scales, and the distribution and abundance of the animals and plants inhabiting the rural landscape.

The practical priorities on the agenda for research into conservation on farmland need not, however, be tied to short-term issues related either to the inevitable vagaries of policy, or to the changing detail of farming management on the ground. Research to date has provided evidence of the ways in which biodiversity at the landscape scale is an emergent property of processes at smaller scales. For example, we have presented evidence that weedy hot-spots in an apparently homogeneous crop may benefit small mammals. This almost certainly has knock-on benefits further up the food chain. Similarly, appropriately managed hedgerows and field margins support large invertebrate populations, and insectivorous birds benefit. The focus for the future should be to identify and to integrate key observations over the range of relevant scales, and to move towards holistic and predictive models of farmland biodiversity. The adoption of a range of approaches, from large scale manipulative experiments to detailed autecological studies, remains the strategy most likely to be successful in achieving this aim (Macdonald and Smith 1991).

References

Addicott, J.F., Aho J.M., Antolin, D.K., Padilla, D.K., Richardson, J.S. and Soluk, D.A. (1987) Ecological neighborhoods: scaling environmental patterns. *Oikos* **49**, 340–346.

Aebischer, N.J. (1991) 20 years of monitoring invertebrates and weeds in cereal fields in Suffolk. In: *The Ecology of Temperate Cereal Fields. The 32nd Symposium of the British Ecological Society* (eds L.G. Firbank, N. Carter, J.F. Darbyshire and G.R. Potts.), pp. 305–331. Blackwell Scientific Publications, Oxford.

Alderweireldt, M. (1994) Prey selection and prey capture strategies of linyphiid spiders in high input agricultural fields. *Bulletin of the British Arachnological Society* **9**, 300–308.

Anonymous (1986) *The Management of Chalk Grassland for Butterflies.* Focus on Nature Conservation No. 17. Nature Conservation Council, Peterborough.

Anonymous (1993) Countryside survey 1990. *Summary Report.* Department of the Environment, London.

Anonymous (1994) *Biodiversity: the UK Action Plan.* HMSO, London.

Anonymous (1998) Briefing Note. Conference on Biodiversity and a sustainable Countryside. Department of the Environment, Transport and the Regions. http://www.wildlife-countryside.detr.gov.uk/biodiversity/bground.html.

Asteraki, E.J., Hanks, C.B. and Clements, R.O. (1992) The impact of the chemical removal of the hedge-base flora on the community structure of carabid beetles (Col. Carabidae) and spiders (Araneae) of the field and hedge bottom. *Journal of Applied Entomology* **113**, 398–406.

Baines, M., Hambler, C., Johnson, P.J., Macdonald, D.W. and Smith, H. (1998) The effects of arable field margin management on the abundance and species richness of Araneae (spiders). *Ecography* **21**, 74–86.

Barr, C.J., Bunce, R.G.H., Clarke, R.T., *et al.* (1993) *Countryside Survey 1990. Main Report.* Department of the Environment, London.

Begon, M., Harper, J.L. and Townsend, C.R. (1996) *Ecology. Individuals, Populations and Communities,* 3rd edn. Blackwell Science, Oxford.

Brown, V.K. (1991) The effects of changes in habitat structure during succession in terrestrial communities. In. *Habitat Structure: the Physical Arrangement of Objects in Space* (eds S.S. Bell, E.D. McCoy and H.R. Mishinsky), pp. 141–167. Chapman and Hall, London.

Campbell, L.H., Avery, M.I., Donald, P., Evans, A.D., Green, R.E. and Wilson, J.D. (1997) *A. Review of the Indirect Effects of Pesticides on Birds.* JNCC report No. 227. Joint Nature Conservation Committee, Peterborough.

Chamberlain, D.C. and Crick, H.Q.P. (1999) Population declines and reproductive performance of skylarks *Alauda arvensis* in different regions and habitats of the United Kingdom. *Ibis* **141**, 38–51.

Cilgi, T. and Jepson, P.C. (1995) The risks posed by deltamethrin drift to hedgerow butterflies. *Environmental Pollution* **87**, 1–9.

Clarke, J. (ed.) (1992) *Set-aside.* BCPC Monograph No. 50. BCPC Publications, Farnham.

Denno, R.F. (1994) Influence of habitat structure on the abundance and diversity of plant hoppers. In. *Planthoppers: Their Ecology and Management* (eds R.F. Denno and T.J. Perfect), pp. 140–159. Chapman and Hall, New York.

Donald, P. (1998) Changes in the abundance of invertebrates and plants on British farmland. *British Wildlife* **10**, 279–288.

Doncaster, C.P.D. and Krebs, J.R. (1993) The wider countryside — principles underlying the responses of mammals to heterogenous environments. *Mammal Review* **23**, 113–120.

Dover, J.W. (1990) Butterflies and wildlife corridors. *Game Conservancy Review* **21**, 62–64.

Dover, J.W. (1996) Factors affecting the distribution of satyrid butterflies on arable farmland. *Journal of Applied Ecology* **33**, 723–734.

Emmet, A.M. and Heath, J., eds. (1990) *The Moths and Butterflies of Great Britain and Ireland,* Vol. 7. Part I. Harley Books, Colchester.

Feber. R.E., Bell, J., Johnson, P.J., Firbank, L.G. and Macdonald, D.W. (1998) The effects of organic farming on surface-active spider assemblages in wheat in southern England, U.K. *Journal of Arachnology* **26**, 190–202.

Feber, R.E., Firbank, L.G., Johnson, P.J. and Macdonald, D.W. (1997) The effects of organic farming on pest and non-pest butterfly abundance. *Agriculture, Ecosystems and Environment* **64**, 133–139.

Feber, R.E., Johnson, P.J., Smith, H., Baines, M. and Macdonald, D.W. (1995) The effects of arable field margin management on the abundance of beneficial arthropods. In: *Integrated Crop Protection— Towards Sustainability?* BCPC Symposium Proceedings No. 63. (eds R. McKinley and D. Atkinson), pp. 163–170. British Crop Protection Council Publications, Farnham.

Feber, R.E., Smith, H. and Macdonald, D.W. (1996) The effects on butterfly abundance of the management of uncropped edges of arable fields. *Journal of Applied Ecology* **33**, 1191–1205.

Feber, R.E. and Smith, H. (1995) Butterfly conservation on arable farmland. In: *Ecology and Conservation of Butterflies* (ed. A.S. Pullin), pp. 84–97. Chapman and Hall, London.

Field, J. (1998) *Small mammal abundance in organic and intensive farmland in Gloucestershire and Wiltshire, UK.* MSc Thesis, University of Reading, UK.

Firbank, L.G. (ed.) (1998) *The agronomic and environmental evaluation of set-aside under the EC Arable Area Payments Scheme.* Report to the Ministry of Agriculture, Fisheries and Food. Institute of Terrestrial Ecology, Grange-over-Sands.

Fuller, R.M. (1987) The changing extent and conservation interest of lowland grasslands in England and Wales: a review of grassland surveys 1930–84. *Biological Conservation* **40**, 281–300.

Fuller, R.J., Gregory, R.D., Gibbons, D.W., *et al.* (1995) Population declines and range contractions among lowland farmland birds in Britain. *Conservation Biology* **9**, 1425–1441.

Gardner, S.M. and Brown, R.W. (1998) *Review of the comparative effects of organic farming on biodiversity.* MAFF, London.

Gates, S., Feber, R.E., Macdonald, D.W., Hart, B.J., Tattersall, F.H. and Manley, W.J. (1997) Invertebrate populations of field boundaries and set-aside land. *Aspects of Applied Biology* **50**, 313–322.

Gibson, C.W.D., Hambler, C. and Brown, V.K. (1992) Changes in spider (Araneae) assemblages in relation to succession and grazing management. *Journal of Applied Ecology* **29**, 132–142.

Hanski, I. (1997) Habitat destruction and metapopulation dynamics. In: *The Ecological Basis of Conservation: Heterogeneity, Ecosystems and Biodiversity* (eds S.T.A. Pickett, R.S. Ostfeld,

M. Shachak. and G.E. Likens), pp. 217–227. Chapman and Hall, New York.

Lampkin, N. (1990) *Organic Farming.* Farming Press Books, Ipswich.

Levin, S.A. (1992) The problem of pattern and scale in ecology. *Ecology* **43**, 1943–1967.

Macdonald, D.W., Tew, T.E., Todd, I.A., Garner, J.P. and Johnson, P. (2000) Arable habitat use by wood mice (*Apodemus sylvaticus*). 3. A farm-scale experiment on the effects of crop rotation. *Journal of Zoology* **250**, 313–320.

Macdonald, D.W., Hart, B.J., Tattersall, F.H., Johnson, P.J., Manley, W.J. and Feber, R.E. (1998) *The Effects of Shape, Location, and Management of Set-Aside on Invertebrates and Small Mammals.* A Report to the Ministry of Agriculture, Fisheries and Food. MAFF, London.

Macdonald, D.W. and Johnson, P.J. (2000) Farmers and the custody of the countryside. *Biological Conservation* **94**, 221–234.

Macdonald, D.W. and Smith, H. (1990) Dispersal, dispersion and conservation in the agricultural ecosystem. In. *Species Dispersal in Agricultural Habitats* (eds R.G.H. Bunce and D.C. Howard), pp. 18–64. Belhaven Press, London.

Macdonald, D.W. and Smith, H. (1991) New perspectives on agroecology. Between theory and practice in the agricultural ecosystem. In: *The Ecology of Temperate Cereal Fields. The 32nd Symposium of the British Ecological Society* (eds L.G. Firbank, N. Carter, J.F. Darbyshire and G.R. Potts), pp. 413–448. Blackwell Scientific Publications, Oxford.

Marrs, R.H., Frost, A.J. and Plant, R.A. (1991) Effects of herbicide spray drift on selected species of nature conservation interest—the effects of plant age and surrounding vegetation structure. *Environmental Pollution* **69**, 223–235.

McCoy, E.D. and Bell, S.S. (1991) Habitat structure. the evolution and diversification of a complex topic. In: *Habitat Structure: The Physical Arrangement of Objects in Space* (eds S.S. Bell, E.D. McCoy and H.R. Mishinsky), pp. 4–22. Chapman and Hall, London.

Mellanby, K. (1981) *Farming and Wildlife.* Collins, London.

Mitchell, K. (1999) European policies for field margins and buffer zones. *Aspects of Applied Biology* **54**, 13–18.

Morris, M.G. (1971) The management of grassland

for the conservation of invertebrate animals. In: *The Scientific Management of Plant and Animal Communities for Conservation* (eds E. Duffey and A.S. Watt), pp. 527–552. 11th Symposium of the British Ecological Society. Blackwell Scientific Publications, Oxford.

Morris, M.G. (1990) The Hemiptera of two sown calcareous grasslands. I. Colonization and early succession. *Journal of Applied Ecology* **27**, 367–378.

Plesner Jensen, S. (1993) Temporal changes in food preferences of wood mice, *Apodemus sylvaticus,* L. *Oecologia* **94**, 76–82.

Plesner Jensen, S. and Honess, P. (1995) The influence of moonlight on vegetation height preference and trappability of small mammals. *Mammalia* **59**, 35–42.

Povey, F.D., Smith, H. and Watt, T. (1993) Predation of annual grass weed seeds in arable field margins. *Annals of Applied Biology* **122**, 323–328.

Rypstra, A.L. and Carter, P.E. (1995) The web-spider communities of soybean agroecosystems in southwestern Ohio. *Journal of Arachnology* **23**, 135–144.

Smith, H., Feber, R.E., Johnson, P.J., *et al.* (1993) *The Conservation Management of Arable Field Margins.* English Nature Science No. 18. English Nature, Peterborough.

Smith, H., Feber, R.E. and Macdonald, D.W. (1994) The role of wildlife seed mixtures in field margin restoration. In: *Field Margins—Integrating Agriculture and Conservation* (ed. N.D. Boatman), pp. 289–294. BCPC Monograph No. 58. BCPC Publications, Farnham.

Smith, H. and Macdonald, D.W. (1989) Secondary succession on extended arable field margins: its manipulation for wildlife benefit and weed control. In: *Brighton Crop Protection Conference: Weeds.* pp. 1063–1068. British Crop Protection Council Publications, Farnham.

Smith, H., McCallum, K. and Macdonald, D.W. (1997) Experimental comparison of the nature conservation value, productivity and ease of management of a conventional and a more species-rich grass ley. *Journal of Applied Ecology* **34**, 53–64.

Sotherton, N.W. (1991) Conservation headlands. a practical combination of intensive cereal farming and conservation. In: *The Ecology of*

Temperate Cereal Fields (eds L.G. Firbank, N. Carter, J.F. Darbyshire and G.R. Potts), pp. 373–397. Blackwell Scientific Publications, Oxford.

Sunderland, K.D., Fraser, A.M. and Dixon, A.F.G. (1986) Field and laboratory studies on money spiders (Linyphiidae) as predators of cereal crops. *Journal of Applied Ecology* **23**, 433–447.

Tattersall, F.H., Macdonald, D.W., Manley, W., Gates, S. and Hart, B. (1997) Small mammals on one year set-aside. *Acta Theriologica* **42** (3), 329–334.

Tattersall, F.H., Hart, B.J., Manley, W.E., Macdonald, D.W. and Feber, R.E. (1999) Small mammals on set aside blocks and margins. *Aspects of Applied Biology* **54**, 163–170.

Tew, T.E., Macdonald, D.W. and Rands, M.R.W. (1992) Herbicide application affects microhabitat use by arable wood mice (*Apodemus sylvaticus*). *Journal of Applied Ecology* **29**, 532–539.

Tew, T.E. and Macdonald, D.W. (1993) The effects of harvest on arable field mice, *Apodemus sylvaticus. Biological Conservation* **65**, 279–283.

Tew, T.E., Todd, I.A. and Macdonald, D.W. (2000) Arable habitat use by wood mice (*Apodemus sylvaticus*). 2 Microhabitat. *Journal of Zoology* **250**, 305–311.

Todd, I.A., Tew, T.E. and Macdonald, D.W. (2000) Arable habitat use by wood mice (*Apodemus sylvaticus*). 1 Macrohabitat. *Journal of Zoology* **250**, 299–303.

Topping, C.J. (1993) Behavioural responses of three linyphiid samples to pitfall traps. *Entomologia Experimentalis et Applicata* **68**, 287–293.

Watt, T.A., Smith, H. and Macdonald, D.W. (1990) The control of annual grass weeds in fallowed field margins managed to encourage wildlife. In: *Integrated Weed Management in Cereals.* Proceedings of the European Weed Research Society Symposium, Helsinki 1990, pp. 187–196.

Wilson, P.J. (1992) The natural regeneration of vegetation under set-aside in southern England. In: *Set-aside.* BCPC Monograph No. 50. British Crop Protection Council Publications, Farnham.

Wilson, P.J. (1999) The effect of nitrogen on populations of rare arable plants in Britain. *Aspects of Applied Biology* **55**, 93–100.

Chapter 18

Environmental heterogeneity: effects on plants in restoration ecology

J.P. Bakker

Introduction

Species-rich grassland plant communities are found in environments with moderate above-ground standing crop including litter (Grime 1979). Few plant species are found in environments with very low standing crop including litter, e.g. environments characterized by drought stress, low temperatures or very low nutrient availability. Only a few plant species that are good competitors for light are found in environments with high standing crop including litter. High standing crop can be caused by high nutrient availability and/or litter accumulation, if the above-ground biomass is not removed by cutting or grazing. Species-rich grassland communities with relatively low levels of nutrient availability can be maintained by infrequent cutting. However, annual or more frequent cuts are needed in grasslands with higher levels of nutrient availability (Huston 1979; Peet *et al.* 1983). Long-term, unchanged land use might contribute to high species numbers, as plants could have established in the past and have adapted to the prevailing regime (Naveh and Whittaker 1980; Peet *et al.* 1983). Indeed, the relationship between species richness and standing crop including litter, holds only for 'saturated' communities (Grime 1979), in which characteristic species are present in the neighbourhood, and propagule dispersal is no problem.

Species-rich grassland communities are thought to have resulted from low intensity farming systems (Beaufoy *et al.* 1994; Bignal and McCracken 1996). Low-intensity farming systems have been transformed over the last decades in one of two ways. They have either been intensified by drainage and high fertilizer inputs, or abandoned. Both changes have resulted in a dramatic decrease in species richness. The relationship between species richness and standing crop including litter (Grime 1979), suggests that the restoration of species richness to productive communities can be achieved by reducing community productivity and removing accumulated litter, provided the species lost are still present somewhere.

In this chapter I will address the extent to which species-rich grassland communities can be restored from species-poor communities. This issue will be related to environmental heterogeneity in both abiotic conditions and propagule availability.

Laboratory of Plant Ecology, Centre for Ecological and Evolutionary Studies, University of Groningen, PO Box 14, 9750 Aa Haren, The Netherlands

Is restoration a matter of just reduction of nutrient levels? Why is restoration not equally successful for all plant species?

Restoration experiments

Many studies have been published recently on the effects of nature restoration experiments on abiotic factors (Galatowitsch and Van Der Valk 1996; Pfadenhauer and Klötzli 1996). Such studies deal with reducing nutrient availability (Marrs 1993; Aerts *et al.* 1995; Koerselman and Verhoeven 1995), rewetting (De Mars *et al.* 1996; Oomes *et al.* 1996; Van Duren *et al.* 1998), and liming (Bellemakers *et al.* 1996; De Graaf *et al.* 1998). Based on the relationship between abiotic factors and the occurrence of species in the established vegetation (Ellenberg *et al.* 1991), it may be predicted where, for instance, species-rich forests have the best chance to be found in about 25 years (Witte 1998). A problem is that such studies do not seem to take into account limiting factors such as seed banks and the dispersal of target species (Burke and Grime 1996; Bekker *et al.* 1997; Handel 1997; Tilman 1997; Bakker and Berendse 1999). A theoretical study on the feasibility of restoring target communities in a Dutch brook valley system on the Pleistocene sandy plateau of Drenthe did include these constraints. The outcome of the study was, that after 100 years, 51% of the target species would establish in species-rich grassland, 38% in heathland, 8% in arable field, and 16% in species-rich woodland (Prins *et al.* 1998). However, some projects aimed at nature restoration by the removal of top soil (and hence large amounts of nutrients) did lead to the establishment of Red List-species from a buried persistent seed bank, for instance in heathland pools (Bellemakers *et al.* 1996; Roelofs *et al.* 1996).

Heterogeneity in abiotic conditions

Heterogeneity in nutrient availability with hay-making

The gradual increase in nutrient input to grasslands in recent decades means that fields where fertilizer application was ceased in 1945 received much fewer nutrients overall than fields where fertilizer application was terminated recently. In order to account for this 'fertilization history' effect, the cumulative N input per field since 1945 for each year until 1990 was calculated, using information on average N input and the duration of restoration management (Bakker and Olff 1995). A field acquired in 1945 only subsequently received N from atmospheric deposition, while fields acquired later received more N, as fertilizer application continued for longer. From these cumulative N inputs the estimated offtake of N by cutting was subtracted, resulting in a 'cumulative N balance' (CNB). The N offtake was estimated from data on biomass and N content of biomass given by Olff and Bakker (1991) for different fields. It was found that the field acquired in 1945 had a negative CNB (more offtake than input) over the whole period, while the CNB of the field acquired in 1971 became negative in 1990, and it will take many years before the balance for fields acquired more recently will become negative. Indeed, the peak standing crop of the grass-dominated parts (not the *Juncus acutiflorus*-dominated parts) was clearly lower in fields which had been longer under restoration management than in fields that had recently been acquired (Bakker and Olff 1995).

The decrease in total above-ground biomass during restoration management by hay-making could be caused by nutrient limitation and changes in nutrient supply within a field. This hypothesis was tested by growing intact sods from fields with various fertilizer histories in the glasshouse on nutrient solutions from which various nutrients were omitted (Van Der Woude *et al.* 1994; Pegtel *et al.* 1996; Van Duren *et al.* 1997). The effect of omitting all nutrients simultaneously resulted in the largest cumulative (summed over all harvests) yield reduction in sods from all fields. However, there were substantial differences in the effect of the other treatments. Both early and recently acquired fields were limited by both N and K. The effect of omitting K was larger in earlier acquired fields than in later acquired fields. Furthermore, in the field acquired in 1971 the effect of omitting P was significant, and the magnitude of this effect was greater in the field acquired in 1945. This means that the type of nutrient limitation changed from both N and K in recently acquired fields, to simultaneous N, P and K limitation in earlier acquired fields. In the field acquired in 1945, the effect of omitting N, P or K was almost as large as omitting N, P and K simultaneously. Changes in nutrient concentrations in the various plant species in different fields support the results of the glasshouse experiment reported above (Bakker and Olff 1995).

Plant biodiversity under hay-making
The cumulative nitrogen balance (CNB) accounted better for the number of species per plot than did the number of years without fertilizer application (15% improvement in explained variance). The number of species per plot decreased strongly when the CNB was positive. For negative values of CNB the number of species tended to increase (Bakker and Olff 1995).

In a field of 0.5 ha acquired in 1971, nine cutting regimes were imposed after the cessation of fertilizer application (Bakker 1989). The field was subdivided in sections of 50×10 m each. These sections each harboured two permanent plots $(2 \times 2$ m) for recording the vegetation $(n=2)$, whereas above-ground biomass was recorded in 10 plots $(20 \times 20$ cm) $(n=10)$. We compared the effects of annual hay-making in July, annual hay-making in September, bi-annual hay-making in July and September, and hay-making every second year in September. In 1971, the vegetation was characterized by *Agrostis stolonifera*, *Alopecurus geniculatus*, *Lolium perenne*, *Poa trivialis* and *Ranunculus repens*. These species indicate nutrient-rich soil conditions (Klapp 1965; Ellenberg *et al.* 1991). After 24 years species indicating mesotrophic soil conditions, such as *Holcus lanatus*, *Festuca rubra*, *Agrostis capillaris*, *Anthoxanthum odoratum*, *Rumex acetosa*, *Rhinanthus angustifolius* and *Plantago lanceolata* had established, as well as some species indicating nutrient-poor soil conditions, such as *Hypochaeris radicata*. It was hypothesized that, due to the removal of cuttings, impoverishment of the soil would take place according to the ranking: September hay-making every second year < September hay-making

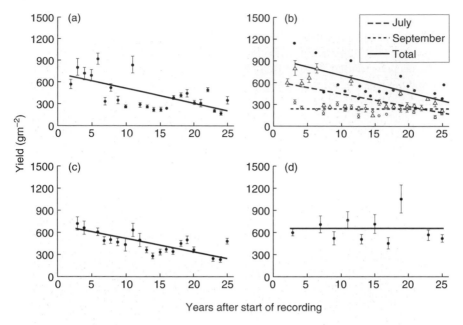

Figure 18.1 Average ($n=10$) yield ($g\,m^{-2}$) within sections with different cutting regimes within one field, where application of fertilizers ceased in 1971. (a) Hay-making in July; (b) hay-making in July and September; (c) hay-making in September; (d) hay-making in September every second year.

every year < July hay-making every year < July and September hay-making every year (Fig. 18.1). Indeed the proportion of species indicating nutrient-rich soil conditions remained at 50% with hay-making every second year, whereas it decreased to 20% with two annual cuttings, and was intermediate with cutting either in July or September (Fig. 18.2). After 24 years the average number of plant species $4\,m^{-2}$ remained 10 with hay-making every second year, increased to 14 with annual September hay-making, nearly doubled after 20 years with July hay-making, but decreased in the last two years. It rapidly more than doubled with cutting in both July and September, but started to decline again after 15 years (Fig. 18.3).

An adjacent field with similar hydrological and soil conditions was acquired in 1967 and cut for hay in July every year without fertilizer application. Over about 20 years the yield decreased from 600 to under $300\,g\,m^{-2}$, the proportion of species indicating nutrient poor soil conditions increased from 20 to 50%, and the average number of species $4\,m^{-2}$ decreased from 15 to 10. The comparison of the fields acquired in 1967 and 1971 demonstrates the importance of the history of fertilizer applications. It took the field acquired in 1971, and which had received fertilizer applications for five extra years, over 20 years to reach the proportion of species indicating nutrient-poor soil conditions and the number of species that were present in the 1967 field immediately after cessation of fertilizer applications.

We can conclude from the above studies on the effects of hay-making that the

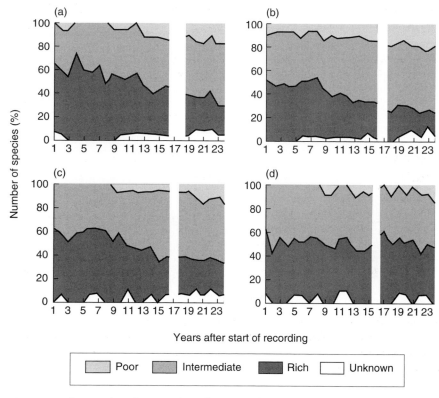

Figure 18.2 Average (*n*=2) proportion of species indicating nutrient-poor, intermediate and nutrient-rich soil conditions in sections with different cutting regimes within one field, where application of fertilizers ceased in 1971. (a) Hay-making July; (b) hay-making July and September; (c) hay-making September; (d) hay-making September every second year.

above-ground biomass can be reduced after the cessation of fertilizer application. This reduction coincides with an increase in species numbers: the more biomass is removed, the higher the number of species gets. However, after some time, with high biomass removal, the number of species decreases again. The proportion of species indicating nutrient-rich soil conditions decreases, whereas the proportion of species indicating nutrient-poor soil conditions does not increase. Most species in the latter category only occur in fields with a longer non-fertilization history. Both the history of fertilizer application and the current cutting regime determine the composition of the plant community.

Heterogeneity under grazing

In small experimental paddocks a uniform grazing intensity across the entire paddock can be achieved by grazing to a certain sward height. In larger paddocks or entire fenced-in areas grazed for nature conservation purposes, the vegetation will include plant communities with different species composition. Patterns in grazing intensity may be due to heterogeneity in abiotic conditions and plant characteris-

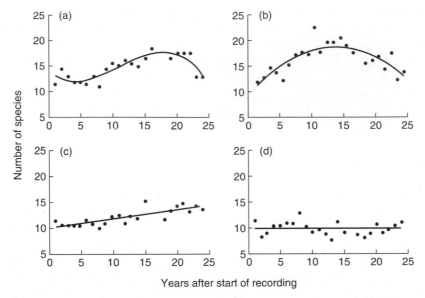

Figure 18.3 Average ($n=2$) number of species $4\,m^{-2}$ in sections within one field with different cutting regimes, where application of fertilizers ceased in 1971. (a) Hay-making July; (b) hay-making July and September; (c) hay-making September; (d) hay-making September every second year.

tics, causing selection by the herbivores (WallisDeVries 1998). Charles *et al.* (1977) found in Scottish uplands that deer preferred feeding on grasslands rather than heaths and bogs. Wielgolaski (1975) and Job and Taylor (1978) reached similar conclusions for upland sheep grazing. Thalen *et al.* (1987) reported a pattern of terrain-use by ponies 4 years after they started year-round grazing in a 100-ha mosaic of *Pinus* plantation, heathland and abandoned arable fields in the Netherlands. I conclude that the observed large-scale patterns of grazing intensity are controlled by the patterns of plant communities, which in turn are caused by abiotic conditions.

At an intermediate spatial scale, vegetation patterns may be induced by differences in local grazing intensity, often on more or less homogeneous substrate. Man-made salt marshes have developed from accretion works, and are characterized by a relatively flat topography and by a dense artificial drainage system. The gradients in grazer utilization found in salt-marsh areas over a gradient of over 500 m (Kiehl *et al.* 1996) were apparently caused by the position of fresh water points for the grazing animals. Rosén (1973) described a gradient in plant communities in a 400-m transect starting at an animal shelter on the alvar of Öland, Sweden. Only a few ruderals occurred close to the shelter, mosses were found from 70 m from the shelter onwards, whereas lichens occurred from 200 m. Total species richness reached a maximum at 100 m from the shelter.

Apart from macro-patterns at the plant community level, grazing selectivity may result in a small-scale mosaic or micropattern. An initially uniform *Holcus lanatus* community on sandy soil that was no longer fertilized at the 'Westerholt' in the Netherlands remained similar for several years under a hay-making regime. With grazing a mosaic of taller tufts interspersed with shorter vegetation developed. The diameter of the tufts ranged from 0.5 m to a maximum of 3 m (Bakker *et al.* 1984). Hunter (1962) and Nicholson *et al.* (1970) found micropatterns in upland vegetation stands in the UK due to the avoidance of certain plant species by the grazers. They described the development of *Nardus stricta* tussocks in a *Nardus stricta/Festuca ovina/Molinia caerulea/Anthoxanthum odoratum* sward under grazing with a stocking density of 2–5 sheep/ha. Single plants or clumps of *Anthoxanthum odoratum* or young *Molinia caerulea* shoots provided loci that were initially moderately grazed. While grazing increased around the edges of these patches, material tended to be taken less selectively and then the initially grazed spots expanded outwards producing a patchwork of short-tufted areas. The close-grazed areas eventually coalesced and grazing pressure over the entire area became relatively uniform, except for isolated areas that were partly rejected— usually *Nardus stricta* tussocks. An experiment in paddocks (12.6 ha) in native mixed-grass prairie in Kansas, USA, compared seasonal cattle grazing lasting 150 days at 0.7 animal ha^{-1} with intensive early stocking for the first 75 days only at 2.1 animals ha^{-1} for two consecutive seasons. Intensive early stocking resulted in heavily grazed areas and undergrazed patches. Seasonal grazing at the lower stocking rate, however, resulted in re-establishment of heavily grazed patches (mean vegetation height of 4.6 cm, biomass of 700 kg ha^{-1}, in contrast to mean vegetation height of 13 cm, with a biomass of 2450 kg ha^{-1} in undergrazed patches) in the second year. Of points undergrazed in the first year 86% remained undergrazed in the second year, and hence locations of patches in two consecutive years were significantly associated (Ring *et al.* 1985). Such stable structural patterns are a prerequisite for the development of various plant communities at a small scale. Different species will establish in short and tall patches, respectively. Hence diversity will increase.

The relationship between large- and small-scale vegetation patterns may be illustrated by an example of wet heathland, dominated by *Erica tetralix* and *Molinia caerulea*, and grazed for decades by sheep in the large (1300 ha) nature reserve of Dwingelose Heide, in the Netherlands. Several hundred sheep leave their shelter in the morning and return in the afternoon, tended by a herdsman. The first study site was at a distance of 150 m from the shelter and was heavily grazed and trampled by sheep. *Molinia caerulea* covered 85%, *Erica tetralix* 1%, the mean canopy height was 4 cm, litter was lacking, 90% of incoming light reached the soil, and there was little spatial pattern to light interception. The second study site at 1000 m from the shelter and intermediately grazed by sheep, had *Erica tetralix* cover of 55% and *Molinia caerulea* cover of 35%. The mean canopy height was 15 cm, litter thickness was 2 cm, 15% of incoming light reached the soil, and a small scale spatial pattern of light interception was found. The third study site was at 2000 m from the shelter and hardly grazed by sheep. *Molinia caerulea* covered 50%, *Sphagnum* spp. 30% and *Erica tetralix* 1%. The mean canopy height was 25 cm with large variations, litter thickness was 7 cm, 15% of incoming light reached the soil, and a large-scale pattern of light interception was found (Bakker 1998). Apparently long-term grazing has resulted in different plant communities at a large scale and hence enhanced diversity.

Different plant communities at various spatial scales are not only created by herbivores removing biomass. The voiding of dung and urine by grazing animals results in the transport of nutrients, and affects nutrient cycling and hence soil conditions. Dung can enhance plant production. Experiments suggested that intermediate levels of grazing pressure by Lesser Snowgeese resulted in the greatest enhancement of plant production in extremely nutrient-poor subarctic salt marshes (Hik and Jefferies 1990) due to more rapid cycling of nutrients released from the faeces of the geese. However, recent studies in temperate salt marshes that are more nutrient-rich than subarctic marshes, as a result of marine sedimentation, found higher N-mineralization rates in areas from which small herbivores (Van Wijnen et al. 1999) or sheep (Vivier 1997) were excluded for a few years, than in grazed areas. The cessation of grazing resulted in the accumulation of easily decomposable litter that enhanced nutrient availability. Nevertheless, the decomposition of litter is slower than that of faeces (Perkins et al. 1978). Hence, grazing enhances nutrient cycling, sometimes up to tenfold, of N (Floate 1970), P (Harrison 1978), Ca, Mg, Mn and P (Bülow-Olsen 1980). However, this enhancement occurs only locally due to the concentration of nutrients by faeces, and so does not contradict the finding that grazing prevents litter accumulation and hence a lower nutrient availability in grazed areas over a large scale.

Selective foraging on palatable plant species with low amounts of poorly decaying components such as lignin, will leave patches of unpalatable plant species, where the release of limiting nutrients by decomposers is low (Jefferies 1999). Thus, grazing may create a more heterogeneous nutrient supply. The different C/N ratios of the dominant plant species and their subsequent rates of decomposition, as well as changes in soil aeration resulting from soil compaction by grazers, may lead to differences in soil conditions (Miles 1987). The short and tall patches of vegetation created by grazing animals can differ in species composition (Silvertown et al. 1994). The resulting stable patterns in community structure may lead to a wider range of plants at a small scale and a variety of different plant communities at a larger scale.

The introduction of grazing in previously abandoned areas results at many study sites in an increase in the number of different plant communities and plant species (Bakker 1998). However, grazing does not always increase plant diversity. Extensive grazing may result in locally ungrazed areas within the fence, and a subsequent increase of tall herbs in wet sites, or litter accumulation in dry sites, associated with a decrease in species richness in the locally ungrazed sites. Species richness in the entire area may remain high (Bakker 1998). Grazing in a previously abandoned salt marsh resulted in an increase in the number of species, and in the higher salt marsh with low salinity soil, led to a higher species richness than haymaking (Bakker 1989; Bakker et al. 1997a), though it took 5 years before the species number in the grazed sites exceeded that in the mown sites. Cattle-grazing can prevent competitive exclusion of small-statured species (Olff and Ritchie 1998). However, in a low salt marsh with high salinity soil, cattle grazing resulted in a lower species number than the high salt marsh (Bakker 1989; Olff and Ritchie 1998). Plants on high salinity soils are small-statured and water-stressed. This stress factor may relax competitive interactions, as resource supply rates exceed demands, and the biomass reductions of dominant species have little consequences for subordinate species. Salinity stress also improves forage quality by preventing 'dilution' of nitrogen in plant biomass, with the result being that plants in saline parts of the salt marsh are heavily fed upon. This may even cause excessive damage to certain species, which also reduces diversity (Olff and Ritchie 1998). Compaction of wet soils at the lower salt marsh and trampling by large herbivores may also reduce plant diversity (Bakker 1989).

Conclusions

A survey of 281 fields in various European countries revealed a relationship between soil extractable P and K and plant diversity (Janssens et al. 1998). Fields with over 5 mg P $100\,g^{-1}$ dry soil, do not contain over 20 species $100\,m^{-2}$ (Fig. 18.4). The highest numbers of species of over $50\,100\,m^{-2}$ were found below the optimum content of the soil for growing crops (5–8 mg P $100\,g^{-1}$ soil). For K, the highest numbers of species were found at 20 mg K $100\,g^{-1}$ soil, which corresponds to an optimum content of the soil for growing crops. Hence, high K contents are compatible with high plant biodiversity.

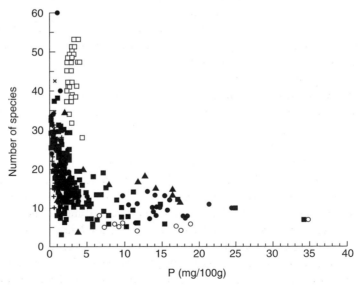

Figure 18.4 Number of species $100\,m^{-2}$ at various concentrations of extractable phosphorus in 281 fields in different West-European countries (after Janssens et al. 1998).

Patterns in nutrient availability often vary both in space and time, and small differences may have large consequences in the ecophysiological response and competitive abilities of plant species (Tilman 1988; Wedin and Tilman 1990; Grime 1994). Nevertheless the spatial scale and the degree of spatial heterogeneity in soil and how they might differ among communities are poorly understood (Ozinga *et al.* 1997). Further understanding of the mechanisms involved in the fine-tuned balance between competition and coexistence in plant communities depends on further bridging the gap in knowledge between the levels of study of the individual plant and the plant community. Multiple limitation by N, K and P, measured at the plant community level, may contribute to species richness only if the component plant species are, indeed, differently limited by these nutrients. Further experiments are necessary.

It can be concluded from the cutting experiments that plant biodiversity may increase after the decrease of available N and K, and concomitant decline of above-ground biomass, and become highest at very low levels of P availability. Restoration succession proceeds from initially little nutrient limitation (and probably light limitation under fertilized conditions) to multiple nutrient limitation, and increased species diversity. The mechanisms linking multiple nutrient limitation and increased diversity need to be further studied.

The example of decreasing species richness after long-term hay-making twice a year (Fig. 18.3), shows that there is not always a negative relationship between above-ground biomass and species richness. Other authors show very low species numbers in nutrient-poor soil conditions and a lack of species characteristic of those conditions (Van der Woude *et al.* 1994; Pegtel *et al.* 1996). In some cases, it has also been shown that despite a decrease in above-ground standing crop, the number of species did not increase (Oomes and Mooi 1985; Berendse *et al.* 1992). Apparently other limiting factors in the restoration of plant biodiversity have to be considered (Bakker and Berendse 1999). Heterogeneity in propagule availability is one of the candidates.

Heterogeneity in propagule availability

Soil seed banks

Heterogeneity in soil seed banks is a well-known phenomenon. Repeated sampling at intervals of weeks over two years clearly demonstrated heterogeneity in time, as viable seeds of some species were only present for a few months each year (Thompson and Grime 1979). These species were classified as having a transient seed bank. Species with viable seeds throughout the year and hence surviving over one year were classified as having a persistent seed bank (Thompson and Grime 1979). Later studies demonstrated heterogeneity in space by examining the distribution of viable seeds in different soil layers. Seeds of some species were only present in the upper layer or more abundant in the upper than in deeper soil layers. Again these species were classified as having a transient seed bank. If they were long lived, they might have been transported into deeper soil layers by soil animals. When viable seeds were found throughout the year in deeper soil layers, the species were regarded as having a persistent seed bank (Thompson *et al.* 1997), under the assumption that it takes time for seeds to become buried in the soil. Species with more seeds in the deeper than in the upper soil layer are classified as having a long-term persistent seed bank. Because soil biota can move seeds around, this assumption still needs experimental testing (Willems and Huijsmans 1994).

The number of viable seeds of dry alvar grassland species in Sweden declined after *Juniperus communis* encroachment (Bakker *et al.* 1996), as did that of heath-land species in England after shrub and forest encroachment (Mitchell *et al.* 1998). The number of viable seeds of *Linum catharticum* and *Oxytropis campestris* in the Swedish alvar decreased after 55 years of abandonment of the formerly grazed alvar, the number of seeds of *Calluna vulgaris* and *Helianthemum nummularium* declined after 80 years. The heathland study showed that at sites that were heath-land 20–50 years ago, there was a reduction in the viable seed bank of *Calluna vulgaris* and *Erica* spp. to 10–20% of that under heathland. This shows that long-term persistent seeds do not survive indefinitely. A study in different European grass-lands revealed that sites with a short period of agricultural intensification have the best chance for restoration purposes (Bekker *et al.* 1997).

If it is known when a species disappeared from the established vegetation in per-manent plot records (Thompson *et al.* 1997) or from the period of forest planta-tion (Poschlod and Jackel 1993), a minimum potential longevity may be estimated. I concluded that heterogeneity in the distribution in space and time of viable seeds, together with the relationship with the established vegetation seem powerful tools in the classification of soil seed banks, and the understanding of their subsequent utility for restoration.

In restoration practices only long-term persistent seeds are a source from which regeneration can take place. It is therefore important to detect viable seeds before restoration practices are carried out in order to find out whether target species are present. Soil sampling easily reveals the abundant species but not the rare species, because of the heterogeneity of the latter. The soil coring method is nevertheless very useful in detecting large seed banks of non-target species such as *Juncus* spp. that might establish after top soil removal and outcompete target species. A special case of heterogeneity of the seed bank is the occurrence of viable seeds only in deeper soil layers after reclamation by deep-ploughing in the past (Ter Heerdt *et al.* 1997).

The classification of species to seed bank types lacks consistency for most species (Thompson *et al.* 1997). The same species can be classified both as persistent and transient according to different records. In order to compare the longevity of indi-vidual species, a longevity-index (LI) was estimated as $LI = (SP + LP)/(T + SP + LP)$, where $(SP + LP)$ represents the total number of short-term + long-term persistent records, and $(T + SP + LP)$ the total number of transient + short-term + long-term persistent records in the database of Thompson *et al.* (1997). The longevity-index ranges from 0 (strictly transient) to 1 (strictly persistent) (Bekker *et al.* 1998a;

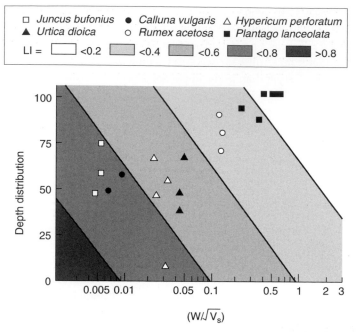

Figure 18.5 The relationship between depth distribution (number of seeds in the upper layer as percentage of the total found in the first two layers), seed size (including weight [W] and variance of shape [Vs]) and seed longevity (see text) of six individual species (after Bekker *et al.* 1998).

Thompson *et al.* 1998). It may represent the best standard for seed longevity available at present. A predictor of seed longevity may be the weight and shape of seeds. Light and round seeds tend to be classified as persistent, whereas heavy and flat or long seeds tend to be classified as transient (Thompson *et al.* 1993). The heterogeneity of seed longevity of individual species is also assessed by relating mass and shape of seeds to the depth distribution (number of seeds in the upper layer as percentage of the total found in the first two layers). Seeds of individual species from various sites in Europe do not reveal a fixed longevity-index, but occur in a range of the longevity-index (Fig. 18.5) (Bekker *et al.* 1998a).

Why do individual species vary in their longevity-index? A 3-year experiment with different groundwater levels in large soil cores (48 cm diameter, 40 cm deep) (mesocosms), demonstrated that the anoxic conditions in the high water level treatment were beneficial to the survival of species of wet grassland communities. Seeds of species of dry grassland survived better under oxic conditions (Bekker *et al.* 1998b). A burial experiment in the field revealed site effects on individual fen meadow species after 2 years. Effects of fertilizer application have not yet been detected (Bekker *et al.* 1998c). It seems that heterogeneity in soil conditions may be responsible for the discrepancies found in seed longevity. However, further experimental evidence is needed.

Table 18.1 Presence (+) and absence (−) of plant species in the established vegetation and their abundance in the seed bank at two depths in a fen meadow cut for hay in July. The meadow was fertilized until three years before sampling. *Juncus acutiflorus* is the only target species present in the seed bank

	Established vegetation	Seed bank seeds m^{-2}	
		0–5 cm	5–10 cm
Holcus lanatus	+	5710	1448
Ranunculus repens	+	3820	3025
Cardamine pratensis	+	2480	30
Juncus bufonius/J. effusus	−	12230	9140
Glyceria fluitans	−	470	770
Juncus acutiflorus	−	230	630
Stellaria uliginosa	−	120	120
Lythrum portula	−	55	55
Gnaphalium uliginosum	−	30	30

Propagule availability

A case study will be used to illustrate the relationship between the established vegetation and propagule availability in restoration management. The effects of cessation of fertilizer application and cutting for hay in brook valley grasslands in the Netherlands were previously shown in both permanent plots and on a chronosequence (Bakker and Olff 1995). From studies of hydrological factors at the landscape level (Grootjans 1980), restoration at the wet sites was expected to result in a Junco-Molinion with abundant *Juncus acutiflorus*, a plant community that occurred before agricultural intensification. In two fields in the chronosequence the soil seed bank was sampled. Three years after the start of restoration no target species were found in the established vegetation, and only *Juncus acutiflorus* and pioneer species (known for their long-term persistent seed bank) were present in the seed bank (Table 18.1). Twenty-three years later there were more target species in both the established vegetation and the seed bank. Their higher abundance in the upper than in the deeper soil layer indeed suggests a transient/short-term persistent character (Table 18.2). This suggests that the composition of the seed bank follows that of the established vegetation and not the other way round.

It is now known that the aforementioned target species were introduced by haymaking machinery; mowing machines are also sowing machines (Strykstra *et al.* 1997). The species originated from the local species pool (Zobel *et al.* 1998) in adjacent fields in the brook valley system. Not all species were transported in similar amounts. Seeds of tall plant species were particularly dispersed on the cloth of the machine, but within fields. More important was the catcher, by which seeds were dispersed between fields. An important point of species heterogeneity is the period

Table 18.2 Presence and absence of plant species in the established vegetation and their abundance in the seed bank at two depths in a fen meadow cut for hay in July. The meadow was fertilized until 26 years before sampling. The group of species starting with *Juncus acutiflorus* represents target species

	Established vegetation	Seed bank seeds m^{-2}	
		0–5 cm	5–10 cm
Holcus lanatus	+	1 290	50
Ranunculus repens	+	780	3 095
Juncus bufonius/J. effusus	–	32 870	37 910
Glyceria fluitans	–	250	2 740
Juncus acutiflorus	+	5 020	6 130
Myosotis palustris	+	70	180
Lychnis flos-cuculi	+	135	80
Anthoxanthum odoratum	+	620	90
Caltha palustris	+	95	85
Plantago lanceolata	+	765	0
Cynosurus cristatus	+	0	0

Table 18.3 Occurrence of seeds gram^{-1} dust collected in July from the cloth and the catcher of hay-making machinery. The second group of species is tall and is more found at the cloth (30 cm above soil level) than at the catcher (at soil level). The third group of species has already shed their seeds, or is just about to flower (*Juncus acutiflorus*)

	occurrence in the vegetation	cloth (seed gram^{-1})	catcher (seeds gram^{-1})
Anthoxanthum odoratum	abundant	20	24
Rhinanthus angustifolius	abundant	18	36
Dactylorhiza majalis	rare	5	95
Rumex obtusifolius	abundant	13	1
Cynosurus cristatus	abundant	16	1
Deschampsia cespitosa	abundant	154	94
Ranunculus repens	abundant	1	0
Caltha palustris	frequent	0	0
Juncus acutiflorus	abundant	0	0

of seed ripening: some species had already dropped their seeds at the cutting period in early July, whereas others were about to flower (Table 18.3).

Hay-making without fertilizer application may decrease the above-ground standing crop, as mentioned above. After 19 years this leads to a more open canopy with only a few dense patches, whereas a dense closed canopy is typical of the first few years of restoration management (Olff *et al.* 1994). The more open canopy may provide safe sites for the establishment of newly arrived species transported by hay-making machinery. Extensive grazing may create heterogeneity of the canopy at the scale of the landscape (Bakker 1998; Olff *et al.* 1999), the stand (Berg *et al.* 1997; Bakker 1998) or the individual plant (Olff *et al.* 1999). Grazing may therefore be more effective in creating heterogeneity of the canopy than hay-making.

Older studies on the dispersal of propagules focused on weeds in agricultural systems. Recently, studies on dispersal in the framework of nature conservation and restoration have been published. These include endozoochory (Welch 1985; Fischer *et al.* 1995; Malo and Suárez 1995), and exozoochory by hooves (Fischer *et al.* 1995) and fur (Fischer *et al.* 1996; Kiviniemi 1996). Olff and Ritchie (1998) stress the importance of propagule availability in relation to the effects of grazing on diversity. Bonn and Poschlod (1998) recently reviewed propagule dispersal.

As shown above, target species can find a safe site to establish under certain circumstances. Safe sites are not fixed positions in a landscape or stand of vegetation. Long-term permanent plot records show that many species are always present at the m² scale but not at the cm² scale in dry alvar grasslands (Van Der Maarel and Sykes 1993). They jump around within larger plots that may provide heterogeneous conditions in the structure of the canopy and/or the availability of propagules. Ehrlén and Van Groenendael (1998) proposed a trade-off between dispersability and seed longevity. They noticed that morphological adaptations for dispersal are less common in species that better tolerate stress, that are better competitors or possess seed dormancy. Such patterns suggest that species that are good survivors as adult plants may have a limited ability to colonize new patches and vice versa. Differences in colonization capacity imply that restoration of plant biodiversity should not only focus on conditions within patches, but also consider the (heterogeneous) spatial arrangement of patches in order to enable plants to bridge gaps in space and time.

Conclusions

Spatio-temporal analyses elucidate the framework in which plant communities exist in a distinct land unit. The chronosequence in the very species-rich dry Alvar grassland communities at Öland (Sweden) revealed the spatio-temporal relationship between the grassland communities that have been grazed for many centuries, and the ones that have been abandoned or cultivated. After two centuries of arable field exploitation only a few dry grassland species were present in the soil seed bank (Bakker *et al.* 1997b). Many dry grassland species returned within decades of cessation of arable field exploitation, probably by zoochory through livestock that had free access to the former arable fields (Fig. 18.6). Abandonment of grazing in the dry grasslands resulted in dense Juniper scrub within 100 years, and a decrease in the number of dry grassland species, both in the established vegetation and the soil seed bank (Bakker *et al.* 1996). In further studies germination strategies should be taken into account once a seed has arrived at the target site (Olff *et al.* 1994). Small

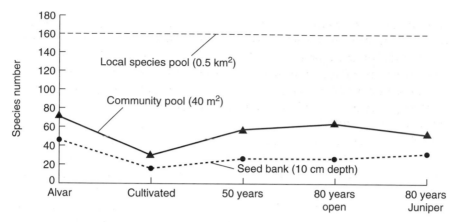

Figure 18.6 The number of species in the local species pool, the community pool and the soil seed bank in the Avenetum community (dry calcareous grasslands) near Dröstorp at Öland (Sweden) in the time series undisturbed alvar, cultivated field and various years of abandonment from cultivation.

scale heterogeneity in the target sites may strongly affect the chances of plants finding a safe site.

It is clear now that defining target communities for a certain target area should include knowledge of the established vegetation, the soil seed bank, the rate of dispersal from outside the target area, and the possibilities for newly arrived species to establish. Species that are potentially capable of existing in a certain community are referred to as a 'species pool' (Eriksson 1993). According to spatial scale three hierarchical levels of species pool are distinguished (Pärtel *et al.* 1996; Zobel 1997; Zobel *et al.* 1998): regional species pool (the set of species occurring in a reasonably large part of the earth with a more or less uniform physiography and climate), local species pool (set of species occurring in the landscape type, e.g. river valley, forest complex) and community pool (species occurring in the target community).

Perspectives

Knowledge of both abiotic conditions and species traits is needed to predict the effects of restoration on plant biodiversity. An example is shown in an integrated study in the Netherlands. We tested whether species-rich fen meadows suffering from drainage and subsequent acidification could be restored by flooding in the winter and spring periods. Sod cutting reduced the macro-nutrient content of the rooting zone. The composition of species which emerged after sod cutting reflected the poor soil seed bank, and establishment of target species was limited, even after 5 years, suggesting hardly any dispersal from elsewhere. Dispersal limitation was overcome by sowing seeds of target species. The introduced species thrived during the first year, but did not survive beyond 2 years, indicating that the abiotic conditions were unfavourable as the site had low cover after sod cutting. Flooding did not increase base saturation, as the water was poor in base-cations (Van Duren *et al.* 1998). It was concluded that raising the groundwater table locally can be carried out relatively easily, but subsequent restoration might be constrained by the composition of the groundwater. The emergence of base-rich seepage water depends on the infiltration of rainwater often at a distance of many kilometres. Therefore, these problems can only be solved at the level of the landscape by affecting the regional hydrological conditions in entire catchment areas (Grootjans *et al.* 1996; Roelofs *et al.* 1996).

Predicting plant biodiversity is an important issue in restoration ecology. As far as abiotic conditions are concerned, much progress has been made at the scale of the landscape. In particular, research on hydrological conditions has made much progress during the last decades (Grootjans *et al.* 1996; Roelofs *et al.* 1996). It is also now clear which nutrients and their interactions are limiting for plant production at the community or stand level. Nevertheless, we still do not understand the mechanisms that link nutrient availability and plant biodiversity at the species or individual level. We may understand the occurrence of dominant species, but to what extent the occurrence of subordinate species (Grime 1998) is related to heterogeneity in nutrient availability is not clear. Maybe we also have to focus on the structure of the canopy as governed by large-scale practices such as sod removal, cutting and especially the small-scale effects of grazing.

With respect to the availability of propagules we have a reasonable impression of seed longevity form existing databases (Thompson *et al.* 1997). Nevertheless, data on seed longevity of about half of the well-known flora of NW Europe are completely lacking, particularly of the rare and often endangered plant species that form the bulk of biodiversity. Moreover, experiments are needed on the effects of various soil conditions on seed longevity. Although a start has been made on building data bases on potential species dispersal by wind, water, machines and animals, much more work has to be done. It is necessary to know, for instance, the period of time in which 95% of a cohort of seeds will die, and the distance 95% will travel, in order to start modelling restoration processes. Experimental approaches are urgently needed (Bonn and Poschlod 1998; Poschlod *et al.* 1998) to reveal how potential dispersal may turn into realized dispersal after a propagule has found a safe site for establishment in often heterogeneous environments.

As the various factors contributing to plant biodiversity interact, it is difficult to elucidate their relative importance. Therefore, it is timely to set up and/or evaluate experiments that include interactions of various factors, such as nitrogen availability, soil moisture, and the amount of light reaching the soil. Such interactions should be studied at different scales and under a range of grazing regimes.

It is more and more important to set targets in restoration ecology (Hobbs and Norton 1996), including time paths. This procedure may enable the evaluation over the short- and long-term of the extent to which targets are fulfilled. When targets are met, it suggests that the ecosystem studied was an open book. More interesting therefore are the cases where targets failed. They open the way to new research and eventually better predictions of plant biodiversity after restoration.

Acknowledgments

The recordings of permanent plots used in the Figs 18.1, 18.2 and 18.3 were mostly done by Yzaak De Vries; Jelmer Elzinga carried out the data analyses. Frank Hoffmann collected the data shown in Fig. 18.6. The data for Tables 18.1 and 18.2 were derived from work by Renée Bekker, and that for Table 18.3 by Roel Strykstra. Dick Visser prepared the final version of the figures. An anonymous referee and Dr E. John greatly improved the text by their comments. Their contribution is gratefully acknowledged.

References

Aerts, R., Huiszoon, J.H., Van De Vijver, C.A.M.D. and Willems, J.H. (1995) The potential for heathland restoration on former arable field land at a site in Drenthe, the Netherlands. *Journal of Applied Ecology* **30**, 827–835.

Bakker, J.P. (1989) *Nature Management by Grazing and Cutting*. Kluwer, Dordrecht.

Bakker, J.P. (1998) The impact of grazing on plant communities. In: *Grazing and Conservation Management* (eds M.F. WallisDeVries, J.P. Bakker and S.E. Van Wieren), pp. 137–184. Kluwer Academic Publishers, Dordrecht.

Bakker, J.P., Leeuw, J. and Van Wieren, S.E. (1984) Micro-patterns in grassland vegetation created and sustained by sheep-grazing. *Vegetation* **55**, 153–161.

Bakker, J.P. and Olff, H. (1995) Nutrient dynamics during restoration of fen meadows by hay-making without fertilizer application. In: *Restoration of Temperate Wetlands* (eds B.D. Wheeler, S.C. Shaw, W.J. Foyt and R.A. Robertson), pp. 143–166. Wiley, Chichester.

Bakker, J.P., Bakker, E.S., Rosén, E., Verweij, G.L. and Bekker, R.M. (1996) Soil seed bank composition along a gradient from dry alvar grassland to *Juniperus* scrub. *Journal of Vegetation Science* **7**, 165–176.

Bakker, J.P., Esselink, P., Van Der Wal, R. and Dijkema, K.S. (1997a) Options for restoration and management of coastal salt marshes in Europe. In: *Restoration Ecology and Sustainable Development* (eds K.M. Urbanska, N.R. Webb and P.J. Edwards). Cambridge University Press, Cambridge.

Bakker, J.P., Bakker, E.S., Rosén, E. and Verweij, G.L. (1997b) The soil seed bank of undisturbed and disturbed dry limestone grassland. *Zeitschrift für Ökologie und Naturschutz* **6**, 9–18.

Bakker, J.P. and Berendse, F. (1999) Constraints in the restoration of ecological diversity in grassland and heathland communities. *Trends in Ecology and Evolution* **14**, 63–68.

Beaufoy, G., Baldock, G. and Clark, J. (1994) *The Nature of Farming: Low-Intensity Farming Systems in Nine European Countries*. Institute for European Environmental Policy, London.

Bekker, R.M., Verweij, G.L., Smith, R.E.N., Reine, R., Bakker, J.P. and Schneider, S. (1997) Soil seed banks in European grasslands: does land use affect regeneration perspectives? *Journal of Applied Ecology* **34**, 1293–1310.

Bekker, R.M., Bakker, J.P., Grandin, U., *et al.* (1998a) Seed shape and vertical distribution in the soil: indicators for seed longevity. *Functional Ecology* **12**, 834–842.

Bekker, R.M., Oomes, M.J.M. and Bakker, J.P. (1998b) The impact of groundwater level on soil seed bank survival. *Seed Science Research* **8**, 399–404.

Bekker, R.M., Knevel, I.C., Tallowin, J.B.R., Troost, E.M.L. and Bakker, J.P. (1998c) Soil nutrient input effects on seed longevity: a burial experiment with fen meadow species. *Functional Ecology* **12**, 673–682.

Bellemakers, M.J.S., Maesen, M., Verheggen, G.M. and Roelofs, J.G.M. (1996) Affects of liming on acidified shallow moorland pools. *Aquatic Botany* **54**, 37–50.

Berendse, F., Oomes, M.J.M., Altena, H.J. and Elberse, W.T. (1992) Experiments on the restoration of species-rich meadows in the Netherlands. *Biological Conservation* **62**, 59–65.

Berg, G., Esselink, P., Groeneweg, M. and Kiehl, K. (1997) Micropatterns in *Festuca rubra*-dominated salt-marsh vegetation induced by sheep grazing. *Plant Ecology* **132**, 1–14.

Bignal, E.M. and McCracken, D.I. (1996) Low-intensity farming systems in the conservation of the countryside. *Journal of Applied Ecology* **33**, 413–424.

Bonn, S. and Poschlod, P. (1998) *Ausbreitungs-biologie der Pflanzen Mitteleuropas*. Quelle und Meyer, Wiesbaden.

Bülow-Olsen, A. (1980) Nutrient cycling in grassland dominated by *Deschampsia flexuosa* and grazed by nursing cows. *Agro-Ecosystems* **6**, 209–220.

Burke, M.J.W. and Grime, J.P. (1996) An experimental study of plant community invasibility. *Ecology* **77**, 776–790.

Charles, W.N., McCowan, D. and East, K. (1977) Selection of upland swards by Red Deer (*Cervus elaphus* L.) on Rhum. *Journal of Applied Ecology* **14**, 55–64.

De Graaf, M.C.C., Verbeek, P.J.M., Bobbink, R. and Roelofs, J.G.M. (1998) Restoration of species-rich dry heaths: the importance of appropriate soil conditions. *Acta Botanica Neerlandica* **47**, 89–111.

De Mars, H., Wassen, M.J. and Peeters, W.H.M. (1996) The effect of drainage and management on peat chemistry and nutrient deficiency in the former Jegrznia-floodplain (NE Poland). *Vegetatio* **126**, 59–72.

Ehrlén, J. and Van Groenendael, J.M. (1998) Plants species diversity and the trade-off between dispersability and longevity. *Applied Vegetation Science* **1**, 29–36.

Ellenberg, H., Weber, H.E., Düll, R., Werner, W. and Paulissen, D. (1991) Zeigerwerte von Pflanzen in Mitteleuropa. *Scripta Geobotanica* **18**, 1–248.

Eriksson, O. (1993) The species-pool hypothesis and plant community diversity. *Oikos* **68**, 371–374.

Fischer, S., Poschlod, P. and Beinlich, B. (1995) Die Bedeutung der Wanderschäferei für den Artenaustausch zwischen isolierten Schaftriften. *Beihefte Veröfftlichungen Naturschutz und Landschaftspflege Baden-Württemberg* **83**, 229–256.

Fischer, S., Poschlod, P. and Beinlich, B. (1996) Experimental studies on the dispersal of plants and animals by sheep in calcareous grasslands. *Journal of Applied Ecology* **33**, 1206–1222.

Floate, M.J.S. (1970) Mineralization of nitrogen and phosphorus from organic materials and animal origin and its significance in the nutrient cycle in grazed uplands and hill soils. *Journal of the British Grassland Society* **25**, 295–302.

Galatowitsch, S.M. and Van Der Valk, A.G. (1996) Vegetation and environmental conditions in recently restored wetlands in the prairie pothole region of the USA. *Vegetatio* **126**, 89–99.

Grime, J.P. (1979) *Plant Strategies and Vegetation Processes*. Wiley, Chichester.

Grime, J.P. (1994) Role of plasticity in exploiting environmental heterogeneity. In: *Exploitation of Environmental Heterogeneity by Plants* (eds M.M. Caldwell and R.W. Pearcey), pp. 1–19. Academic Press, London.

Grime, J.P. (1998) Benefits of plant diversity to ecosystems: immediate, filter and founder effects. *Journal of Ecology* **86**, 902–910.

Grootjans, A.P. (1980) Distribution of plant communities along rivulets in relation to hydrology and management. In: *Epharmonie* (eds O. Wilmanns and R .Tüxen), pp. 143–170. Vaduz.

Grootjans, A.P., Van Wirdum, G., Kemmers, R. and Van Diggelen, R. (1996) Ecohydrology in the Netherlands: principles of an application-driven interdiscipline. *Acta Botanica Neerlandica* **45**, 491–516.

Handel, S.N. (1997) The role of plant animal-mutualism in the design and restoration of natural communities. In: *Restoration Ecology and Sustainable Development* (eds K. Urbanska, N.R. Webb and P.J. Edwards), pp. 111–132. Cambridge University Press.

Harrison, A.F. (1978) Phosphorus cycles of forest and upland grassland ecosystem and some effects of land management practices. In: *Phosphorus and the Environment: its Chemistry and Biochemistry* (eds R. Potter and D.W. Fitzsimmon), pp. 175–199. Elsevier, Amsterdam.

Hik, D.S. and Jefferies, R.L. (1990) Increases in the net above-ground primary production of a salt marsh forage grass: a test of the prediction of the herbivore optimization model. *Journal of Ecology* **78**, 180–195.

Hobbs, R.J. and Norton, D.A. (1996) Towards a conceptual framework for restoration ecology. *Restoration Ecology* **4**, 93–110.

Hunter, R.F. (1962) Hill sheep and their pasture: a study of sheep grazing in southeast Scotland. *Journal of Ecology* **50**, 651–680.

Huston, M. (1979) A general hypothesis of species diversity. *American Naturalist* **13**, 81–101.

Janssens, F., Peeters, A., Tallowin, J.B.R., *et al.* (1998) Relationship between soil chemical factors and grassland diversity. *Plant and Soil* **202**, 69–78.

Jefferies, R.L. (1999) Herbivores, nutrients and trophic cascades in terrestrial environments. In: *Herbivores: Between Plants and Predators* (eds H. Olff, V.K. Brown and R.H. Drent), pp. 301–330. Blackwell Science, Oxford.

Job, D.A. and Taylor, J.A. (1978) The production, utilization and management of upland grazings on Plynlimon, Wales. *Journal of Biogeography* **5**, 173–191.

Kiehl, K., Eischeid, I., Gettner, S. and Walter, J. (1996) The impact of different sheep grazing intensities on salt marsh vegetation in Northern Germany. *Journal of Vegetation Science* **7**, 99–106.

Kiviniemi, K. (1996) A study of adhesive seed dispersal of three species under natural conditions. *Acta Botonica Neerlandica* **45**, 73–83.

Klapp, E. (1965) *Grünlandvegetation und Ihre Standort*. Parey, Berlin.

Koerselman, W. and Verhoeven, J.T.A. (1995) Eutrophication of fen ecosystems: external and internal nutrient sources and restoration strategies. In: *Restoration of Temperate Wetlands* (eds B.D. Wheeler, S.C. Shaw, W.J. Fojt and R.A. Robertson), pp. 91–112. Wiley, Chichester.

Malo, J.E. and Suárez, F. (1995) Establishment of pasture species on cattle dung: the role of endozoochorous seeds. *Journal of Vegetation Science* **6**, 169–174.

Marrs, R.H. (1993) Soil fertility and nature conservation in Europe: theoretical considerations and practical management solutions. *Advances in Ecological Research* **24**, 241–300.

Miles, J. (1987) Soil variation caused by plants: a mechanism of floristic change in grassland? In: *Disturbance in Grasslands* (eds J. Van Andel, J.P. Bakker and R.W. Snaydon), pp. 37–49. Junk, Dordrecht.

Mitchell, R.J., Marrs, R.H. and Auld, M.H.D. (1998) A comparative study of the seed banks of heathland and successional habitats in Dorset, Southern England. *Journal of Ecology* **86**, 588–596.

Naveh, Z. and Whittaker, R.H. (1980) Structural and floristic diversity of shrublands and woodlands in northern Israel and other Mediterranean areas. *Vegetatio* **41**, 171–190.

Nicholson, I.A., Paterson, I.S. and Currie, A. (1970) A study of vegetational dynamics: selection by sheep and cattle in Nardus pasture. In: *Animal Populations in Relation to Their Food Resources Symposium British Ecological Society No. 10* (ed. A. Watson), pp. 129–143. Blackwell Scientific Publications, Oxford.

Olff, H. and Bakker, J.P. (1991) Long-term dynamics of standing crop, species richness and vegetation composition after the cessation of fertilizer application to hay fields. *Journal of Applied Ecology* **28**, 1040–1052.

Olff, H., Pegtel, D.M., Van Groenendael, J.M. and Bakker, J.P. (1994) Germination strategies during grassland succession. *Journal of Ecology* **82**, 69–77.

Olff, H. and Ritchie, M. (1998) Effects of herbivores on grassland plant diversity. *Trends in Ecology and Evolution* **13**, 261–265.

Olff, H., Vera, F.W.M., Bokdam, J., *et al.* (1999) Shifting mosaics in grazed woodlands mediated by sequential associational resistance of plants to herbivory. *Plant Biology* **1**, 127–137.

Oomes, M.J.M. and Mooi, H. (1985) The effect of management of succession and production of formerly agricultural grassland after stopping fertilisation. *Sukzession auf Grünlandbrachen* In: (ed. K.F. Schreiber), pp. 59–67. Münstersche Geographische Arbeiten 20.

Oomes, M.J.M., Olff, H. and Altena, H.J. (1996) Effects of vegetation management and raising the water table on nutrient dynamics and vegetation change in a wet grassland. *Journal of Applied Ecology* **33**, 576–588.

Ozinga, W.A., Van Andel, J. and McDonnell-Alexander, M.P. (1997) Nutritional soil heterogeneity and mychorriza as determinants of plant species diversity. *Acta Botanica Neerlandica* **46**, 237–254.

Pärtel, M., Zobel, M., Zobel, K. and Van Der Maarel, E. (1996) The species pool and its relation to species richness: evidence from

Estonian plant communities. *Oikos* **75**, 111–117.

Peet, R.K., Glenn-Lewin, D.C. and Walker Wolf, J. (1983) Prediction of man's impact on plant species diversity. In: *Man's Impact on Vegetation* (eds W. Holzner, M.J.A. Werger and I. Ikusima), pp. 41–54. Junk, Den Haag.

Pegtel, D.M., Bakker, J.P., Verweij, G.L. and Fresco, L.F.M. (1996) N, K and P deficiency in chronosequential cut summer-dry grasslands on gley podzol after the cessation of fertilizer application. *Plant and Soil* **178**, 121–131.

Perkins, D.F., Jones, V., Millar, R.O. and Neep, P. (1978) Primary production, mineral nutrients and litter decomposition in the grassland ecosystem. In: *Production Ecology of British Moors and Montane Grasslands* (eds O.W. Heal and D.F. Perkins), pp. 304–331. Springer, Berlin.

Pfadenhauer, J. and Klötzli, F. (1996) Restoration experiments in middle European wet terrestrial ecosystems: an overview. *Vegetatio* **126**, 101–115.

Prins, A.H., Dijkstra, G.A. and Bekker, R.M. (1998) Feasibility of target nature types in a Dutch stream valley system. *Acta Botanica Neerlandica* **47**, 71–88.

Poschlod, P. and Jackel, A.K. (1993) Untersuchungen zur Dynamik von generativen Diasporenbanken von Samenpflanzen in Kalkmagerrasen. I. Jahreszeitliche Dynamik des Diasporenregens und der Diasporenbank auf zwei Kalkmagerrasenstandorten der Schwäbischen Alb. *Flora* **188**, 49–71.

Poschlod, P., Kiefer. S., Tränkle, U., Fischer, S. and Bonn, S. (1998) Species richness in calcareous grassland is affected by dispersability in space and time. *Applied Vegetation Science* **1**, 75–90.

Ring, C.B., I.I. Nicholson, R.A. and Launchbaugh, J.L. (1985) Vegetational traits of patch-grazed rangeland in West-central Kansas. *Journal of Range Management* **38**, 51–55.

Roelofs, J.G.M., Bobbink, R., Brouwer, E. and De Graaf, M.C.C. (1996) Restoration ecology of aquatic and terrestrial vegetation on non-calcareous sandy soils in the Netherlands. *Acta Botanica Neerlandica* **45**, 517–541.

Rosén, E. (1973) Sheep grazing and changes of vegetation on the limestone heath of Öland. *Zoon Supplement* **1**, 137–151.

Silvertown, J., Lines, C.E.M. and Dale, M.P. (1994)

Spatial competition between grasses — rates of mutual invasion between four species and the interaction with grazing. *Journal of Ecology* **82**, 31–38.

Strykstra, R.J., Verweij, G.L. and Bakker, J.P. (1997) Seed dispersal by mowing machinery in a Dutch brook valley system. *Acta Botanica Neerlandica* **46**, 387–401.

Ter Heerdt, G.N.J., Schutter, A. and Bakker, J.P. (1997) Kiemkrachtig heidezaad in de bodem van ontgonnen heidevelden. *De Levende Natuur* **98**, 142–146.

Thalen, D.C.P., Poorter, H., Lotz, L.A. and Oosterveld, P. (1987) Modelling the structural changes in vegetation under different grazing regimes. In: *Disturbance in Grasslands* (eds J. Van Andel, J.P. Bakker and R.W. Snaydon), pp. 167–183. Junk, Dordrecht.

Thompson, K. and Grime, J.P. (1979) Seasonal variation in the seed banks of herbaceous species in ten contrasting habitats. *Journal of Ecology* **67**, 893–921.

Thompson, K., Band, S.R. and Hodgson, J.G. (1993) Seed size and shape predict persistence in soil. *Functional Ecology* **7**, 236–241.

Thompson, K., Bakker, J.P. and Bekker, R.M. (1997) *Soil Seed Banks of NW Europe: Methodology, Density and Longevity.* Cambridge University Press, Cambridge.

Thompson, K., Bakker, J.P., Bekker, R.M. and Hodgson, J.G. (1998) Ecological correlates of seed persistence in soil in the NW European flora. *Journal of Ecology* **86**, 163–169.

Tilman, D. (1988) *Plant Strategies and the Dynamics of Plant Communities.* Princeton University Press, Princeton.

Tilman, D. (1997) Community invasibility, recruitment limitation, and grassland biodiversity. *Ecology* **78**, 81–92.

Van Der Maarel, E. and Sykes, M.T. (1993) Small-scale plant species turnover in limestone grassland: the carousel model and some comments on the niche concept. *Journal of Vegetation Science* **4**, 179–188.

Van Der Woude, B.J., Pegtel, D.M. and Bakker, J.P. (1994) Nutrient limitation after long-term nitrogen fertilizer application in cut grasslands. *Journal of Applied Ecology* **31**, 405–412.

Van Duren, I.C., Pegtel, D.M., Aerts, B.A. and Inberg, J.A. (1997) Nutrient supply in undrained and drained Calthion meadows. *Journal of Vegetation Science* **8**, 829–838.

Van Duren, I.C., Strykstra, R.J., Grootjans, A.P., Ter Heerdt, G.N.J. and Pegtel, D.M. (1998) A multi-disciplinary evaluation of restoration measures in a degraded fen meadow (Cirsio-Molinietum). *Applied Vegetation Science* **1**, 115–129.

Van Wijnen, H.J., Van der Wal, R. and Bakker, J.P. (1999) The impact of small herbivores on soil net nitrogen mineralization rate: consequences for salt-marsh succession. *Oecologia* **118**, 225–231.

Vivier, J.P. (1997) Influence du pâturage sur la disponibilité de l'azote pour l'exportation dans un marais salé (baie du Mont Saint-Michel). PhD Thesis, University of Rennes.

WallisDeVries, M.F. (1998) Habitat quality and the performance of large herbivores. In: *Grazing and Conservation Management* (eds M.F. WallisDeVries, J.P. Bakker and S.E. Van Wieren), pp. 275–320. Kluwer Academic Publishers, Dordrecht.

Wedin, D. and Tilman, D. (1990) Species effects on nitrogen cycling: a test with perennial grasses. *Oecologia* **84**, 433–441.

Welch, D. (1985) Studies in the grazing of heather moorland in North-east Scotland. IV. Seed dispersal and plant establishment in dung. *Journal of Applied Ecology* **22**, 461–472.

Wielgolaski, F.E. (1975) Comparison of plant structure on grazed and ungrazed tundra meadows. In: *Fennoscandian Tundra Ecosystems. I. Plants and Microorganisms* (ed. F.E. Wielgolaski), pp. 86–93. Springer, Berlin.

Willems, J.H. and Huijsmans, K.G.A. (1994) Vertical seed dispersal by earthworms: a quantitative approach. *Ecography* **17**, 124–130.

Witte, J.P.M. (1998) *National water management and the value of nature.* PhD Thesis, Wageningen Agricultural University.

Zobel, M. (1997) The relative role of species pools in determining plant species richness: an alternative explanation of species coexistence? *Trends in Ecology and Evolution* **12**, 266–269.

Zobel, M., Van Der Maarel, E. and Dupré, C. (1998) Species pool: the concept, its determination and its significance for community restoration. *Applied Vegetation Science* **1**, 55–66.

Chapter 19

Concluding remarks: a review of some open questions

J.H. Lawton

Introduction

In drawing the symposium volume to a close I have chosen to concentrate on some open questions, making reference to earlier contributions as appropriate. I am going to say very little about temporal heterogeneity (e.g. Rees, this volume). Rather I have focused mainly on physical environmental heterogeneity (Wiens, this volume), broadly divided into two types—'spatial heterogeneity' that can be mapped in two dimensions and studied using spatial coordinates at many scales, and 'three-dimensional heterogeneity' that adds significant vertical structuring to habitats. The open questions and problems are these:

1 What are the links between spatial population dynamics and larger-scale macroecological patterns?

2 What is the role of heterogeneity in coupling loss of biological diversity to ecosystem processes?

3 How will climate change influence spatial (metapopulation) dynamics and shifts in species' geographical ranges?

4 How do evolutionary trade-offs drive the well-known, almost universal link between vertical habitat structure and local species richness?

5 What is the role of organisms themselves in altering the physical structure of their habitat—the problem of organisms as ecosystem engineers?

This is an eclectic, not to say idiosyncratic set of topics, linked loosely by two cross-cutting subthemes, namely global change issues (loss of biological diversity, habitat fragmentation and climate change), and a personal desire to see much closer integration between population and community ecology on the one hand, and ecosystem ecology on the other (Lawton 2000).

Spatial heterogeneity and macroecology

Macroecology is a rapidly emerging discipline that lies at the interface of ecology, biogeography and evolution (Brown and Maurer 1989; Brown 1995; Gaston and Blackburn 1999; Maurer 1999). Like all disciplines its boundaries are fuzzy, but first and foremost it is concerned with documenting and understanding large-scale

NERC Centre for Population Biology, Imperial College, Silwood Park, Ascot, Berkshire SL5 7PY, UK

patterns in the characteristics of organisms (e.g. body sizes), and in species' distributions and abundances, together with interrelationships between these and other variables. Since phenomena with a strong spatial component play a conspicuous role in macroecology, it makes sense to try to bridge thinking between macroecology and more traditional ecological work on spatial processes. I will do this primarily by concentrating on one example, but there are plenty of others to choose from and I will briefly describe a selection.

Ever since Huffaker's (1958) classic experiments, the role of spatial heterogeneity in population dynamics has been obvious, and there is now a rich body of theory, experiment and observation attesting to effects of spatial processes on everything from individual foraging behaviour to population and community structure, persistence and dynamics (Brown; Casper *et al.*; Godfray *et al.*; Rees, all this volume). We also know that destruction and fragmentation of habitats by humans (the great contemporary engine of global environmental change—Vitousek 1994) massively alters population persistence, abundance and species richness, even on surviving habitat patches (Dytham; Corlett, both this volume). Here I want to build on these insights, and forge links with macroecology.

The link between local population abundance and size of geographical range

On average, geographically widespread species tend to be locally more abundant at sites where they are found than geographically restricted species, generating a positive interspecific range-abundance correlation (Fig.19.1). The relationship is one of the most robust and regular patterns in ecology (Brown 1984; Hanski *et al.* 1993; Lawton 1993, 1996; Gaston *et al.* 1997; references therein). It is most clearly seen when a group of related species, breeding birds for example, is examined (it makes no sense to group very different taxa together). Although it has been described as 'almost without exception' (Hanski *et al.* 1993) there are a few exceptions. Gaston (1996) summarized over 90 range-abundance correlations and found that 80% were positive and statistically significant, 15% showed no significant relationship, and 5% were significant but negative. I will concentrate here on the positive correlations.

The pattern appears at many scales from landscapes to continents (Gaston 1996), is remarkably robust to the way in which geographical ranges are quantified (Gaston 1994, 1996) and to the number of sites used to measure local abundance. When more than one site is involved, abundances are averaged only where a species occurs; including the zeros automatically generates a statistically trivial positive range-abundance correlation. Instead of using estimates of local population density, one can also use total national or global populations for well-studied groups (birds and mammals: Gaston and Blackburn 1996; Blackburn *et al.* 1997), in which case plots of total population size vs. geographical range have slopes significantly bigger than unity on double-log axes.

In theory, there are at least nine mechanisms that can generate positive relationships between the local abundance and regional distribution of species (Gaston *et al.* 1997; Lawton 2000). As with several other major patterns in macroecology (for

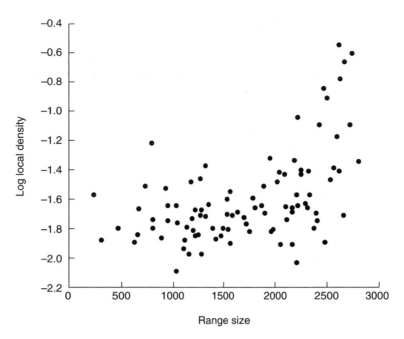

Figure 19.1 An example of a range-abundance correlation for British breeding farmland birds. Range is measured as the number of 10×10 km squares (out of a maximum of 2830) from which the species was recorded in the first British Trust for Ornithology (BTO) atlas (Sharrock 1976). Local densities are average local abundances (territories per hectare) at sites where the species occurred in Common Bird Census plots, also organized by the BTO. From Gaston *et al.* (1998)). (Figure kindly provided by Tim Blackburn.)

example the species-area relationship), it is extremely unlikely that there is a single correct underlying explanation. It will usually be more profitable to ask questions about the relative contributions of several processes, rather than seeking a single monolithic mechanism (Quinn and Dunham 1983; Lawton 1999). Here I will focus on the mechanism most pertinent to this symposium, namely metapopulation dynamics.

Metapopulation models generally predict a positive correlation between local population abundance and the geographical range of a species measured as the number of sites (patches) occupied, for two reasons. First, species with higher local carrying capacities will occupy more patches at equilibrium (because of reduced extinction rates and/or higher colonization rates). Second, because higher immigration rates from larger local populations reduce extinction rates (the 'rescue effect'), patch occupancy must also increase (Hanski and Gyllenberg 1997; Hanski 1998; references therein; Dytham, this volume). Both mechanisms are prime examples of spatial population processes operating in patchy, heterogeneous landscapes.

Gonzalez and colleagues tested the model using moss-covered rocks and their arthropod fauna (Gilbert *et al.* 1998; Gonzalez *et al.* 1998). The mites (Acari) and springtails (Collembola) that live in the moss cannot maintain populations on bare rock. After Gonzalez *et al.* fragmented these miniature mossy landscapes, species in the surviving moss patches 'slid down' the range-abundance regression, with many formerly scarce and local species going extinct, and the survivors becoming generally rarer (occurring at lower densities) and less widespread (found in fewer patches) (Fig. 19.2). This is exactly what the metapopulation model predicts as a consequence of reduced dispersal rates by the arthropods across the hostile environment of the bare rock. The effects were reduced by corridors linking the patches, but not by corridors with a barrier across them to prevent dispersal (pseudo-corridors). Assuming that real corridors increase migration rates between patches, this result is again exactly what the metapopulation model predicts via an enhanced rescue effect. In other words, here is an apparently direct and simple link between a macroecological pattern (the range-abundance correlation) and a series of well-known population processes that occur in spatially patchy, heterogeneous landscapes.

However, not all populations conform to the assumptions of classical metapopulation models, even in fragmented landscapes (Harrison *et al.* 1995; Harrison and Taylor 1996), so metapopulation dynamics cannot provide a universal explanation for the range-abundance correlation. It is also unlikely to explain continental (Bock and Ricklefs 1984; Bock 1987) or global (Gaston and Blackburn 1996) range-abundance correlations because it is difficult to imagine metapopulation dynamics working at such large scales. Positive range-abundance correlations are also found in laboratory microcosms of bacteria and protists, with or without dispersal between patches (Warren and Gaston 1997). For all these systems, one or more of the other mechanisms must be at work, and the challenge is to work out the relative contributions of spatial heterogeneity and metapopulation dynamics on the one hand, and all the other possible mechanisms on the other.

Other macroecological patterns and spatial population processes

Additional challenges lie in exploring further possible links between spatial population dynamics in heterogeneous landscapes and other macroecological patterns. Here is a brief list:

1 The range–abundance correlation and the species–area relationship both emerge as large-scale patterns from the same underlying metapopulation model (Hanski and Gyllenberg 1997). But as with the range–abundance correlation itself, metapopulation dynamics are by no means the only explanation for the species–area relationship (Rosenzweig 1995). What are the relative contributions of the various possible underlying mechanisms to these widespread, bold and important ecological patterns? How do the mechanisms vary with scale?

2 Another macroecological relationship, that between local and regional species richness (Cornell and Lawton 1992; Lawton 1999; Srivastava 1999) can take two extreme forms, and anything in between (Fig. 19.3). At one limit local richness is linearly related to, but usually less than, regional richness (the 'proportional sam-

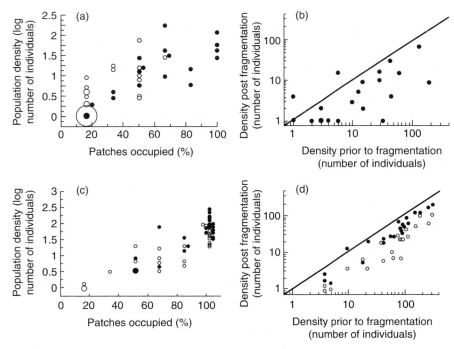

Figure 19.2 Effects of habitat fragmentation on range and abundance of moss-dwelling arthropods (Gonzalez *et al.* 1998). Ranges are local distributions, measured as the number of occupied habitat patches on moss-covered rocks. (a) Continuous moss cover was fragmented experimentally, and then distributions and abundances of arthropods were measured after 12 months. Overall there is a positive range-abundance correlation, but that for the fragmented habitat (open circles) lies to the left of that for the control (unfragmented) habitat (solid circles). Coincident points indicated by larger circles. (b) After fragmentation, surviving species in (a) were on average rarer than prior to fragmentation (the line is that for equal abundance before and after fragmentation). (c) A similar experiment to (a), but with two additional treatments—corridors connecting patches, and pseudocorridors of similar area and shape, but with a barrier preventing dispersal. After fragmentation, the range-abundance correlation for patches joined by pseudocorridors (open circles) still lies to the left of that for the control (solid circles). (d) However, corridors (solid circles) mitigate, but do not totally prevent, the decline in local abundance shown by surviving species in patches joined by pseudocorridors (open circles) (the line is that for equal abundance before and after fragmentation). Reproduced with permission from *Science* **281**, 2045–2047).

pling' or Type I model). At the other limit, local richness is a saturating function of regional richness (Type II model). Only a minority of ecological systems appear to be Type II (Lawton 2000). A simplistic interpretation of these extremes has it that species interactions (e.g. interspecific competition) are feeble and do not constrain local richness in Type I systems, but are strong and set hard limits to local richness in Type II systems. However, as contributors to this symposium have shown,

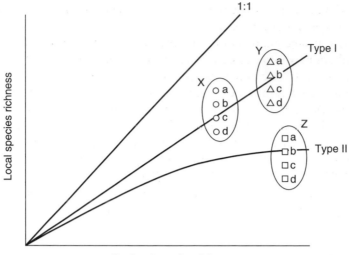

Figure 19.3 The relationship between regional and local species richness (Cornell and Lawton 1992). Because every species in the regional pool is unlikely to occur everywhere (1:1), local richness will usually be less than regional richness, but with two bounds defining the relationship. Type I systems show proportional sampling, in which local richness is, on average, a constant proportion of regional richness. Type II systems saturate with species, so that above a certain level of regional richness, on average local richness does not increase. Real systems may lie anywhere between Type I and Type II. These are average trends. Within any one region, local ecological processes may cause variation round the trend. To illustrate this, X–Z are three (hypothetical) regions, each with four local assemblages (a–d). If these local assemblages differ in habitat complexity, productivity, area, etc. (such that a > b > c > d), local richness will vary round the average trend-lines as illustrated (from Lawton 2000).

incorporating spatial heterogeneity into species interactions markedly alters population dynamics and species persistence (Godfray *et al.*; Rees, both this volume). In consequence, in a spatially heterogeneous world there may be no hard limits to local species richness even with very strong interspecific interactions (Cornell and Lawton 1992; Cornell and Karlson 1997; Lawton 1999; 2000). The importance of spatial heterogeneity in generating linear local *vs.* regional diversity plots, despite strong interspecific interactions, is virtually unexplored empirically.

3 The relationship between local and regional species richness is another way of expressing beta-diversity, the turnover and replacement of species across landscapes (Cornell and Lawton 1992; Harrison *et al.* 1992). Beta-diversity is basically the difference between the 1:1 line in Fig. 19.3, and average local richness expressed by the Type I and Type II curves in Fig. 19.3 (Cornell and Lawton 1992). Spatial heterogeneity in the physical environment (climate, topology, geology and soils) certainly generates beta-diversity, modulated by species' dispersal abilities. But beyond describing beta-diversity, ecologists have made essentially no progress in untangling and discovering useful rules and generalizations about what determines its magnitude (Harrison *et al.* 1992).

4 Finally, in an adjacent part of the macroecological rummage box, animal body-size distributions within taxa observed at large, continental scales may take a quite different form at local, community scales (Brown and Nicoletto 1991; Blackburn and Gaston 1994; Allen *et al.* 1999). In other words, beta-diversity appears to vary with body size. If this pattern is more than simple random sampling from a regional pool it implies that species of different body sizes are sorted and filtered in different ways across heterogeneous landscapes. But the problem remains virtually unexplored, with the exception of some highly speculative but stimulating work by Holling (1992) and colleagues (Allen *et al.* 1999).

I see great scope for more work at the interface of macroecological patterns and spatial population processes in heterogeneous landscapes.

Biodiversity and ecosystem processes

I want, now, to move to linkages between community ecology and ecosystem ecology. At first sight what I have to say appears to have very little to do with environmental heterogeneity, but bear with me. Of necessity this section deals with a rapidly growing subject in a very abbreviated way without, I hope, doing too much violence to the detailed arguments.

Ecologists have made great strides over the last decade in understanding the relationship between biodiversity (here used in the narrow sense of species richness) and ecosystem processes (for example primary production, or nutrient cycling) (Chapin *et al.* 1997, 1998; Lawton *et al.* 1998; Allison 1999; Lawton 2000). In a characteristically pioneering book, Ehrlich and Ehrlich (1981) were among the first to suggest that loss of species from ecosystems via local, regional or global extinctions may impair ecosystem processes. The loss of species observed in surviving habitat fragments by Gonzalez *et al.* (1998) (see above) is an example of one of the ways in which remnant natural and seminatural ecosystems all over the world are losing species (Terborgh *et al.* 1997).

Were Ehrlich and Ehrlich correct? Does loss of species impair ecosystem processes? Theory and data have, until very recently, focused on the relationship between plant species richness and ecosystem processes, and for reasons of space I will largely stick with this trophic level. The answer to the question is then 'yes'. Providing the species pool is reasonably large (thereby avoiding idiosyncratic effects of particular species, a single nitrogen-fixer for instance) the most likely theoretical relationship between loss of species and ecosystem processes is an accelerating decline in biomass production or nutrient cycling as species are lost from the system (Tilman 1997; Tilman *et al.* 1997b; Lawton *et al.* 1998; Loreau 1998a,b; Allison 1999). The fundamental underpinning mechanism is that species have different niches and differ in their ecologies. For plants these include differences in vertical habitat use, both above ground by leaves foraging for light, and below ground by roots foraging for water and nutrients. There are also inevitable differences in the horizontal, spatial and temporal distributions of species (Bakker, this volume), creating further opportunities for differences in the precise ways in which plants forage for, and divide up, above- and below-ground resources (Fitter *et al.* this volume; Hutchings and Wijesinghe, this volume; Watling and Press, this volume; Wilson, this volume). These differences between species mean lower and less efficient use of resources in communities that have lost species.

In brief, a set of interrelated problems that have been central to discussions by a number of authors in this symposium also have ecosystem-level consequences. Niche differences between plant species, illustrated by vertical and horizontal interspecific differences in resource-use, underpin the relationship between plant species richness and ecosystem processes.

Beyond this simple insight there are, however, some important and still poorly understood subtleties, because there are several ways in which the different ecological requirements and performance potentials of different species can generate richness-process relationships (Naeem *et al.* 1996; Lawton 2000), and they can be extremely difficult to disentangle experimentally (Allison 1999). I do not propose to discuss them here, and not everybody agrees with the basic theoretical arguments outlined above (Huston 1997; Tilman *et al.* 1997a; Hector 1998; Lawton *et al.* 1998; Loreau 1998b; Hector *et al.* 1999). Be that as it may, for herbaceous plant assemblages the magnitude of several ecosystem processes (primary production, nutrient cycling) does indeed decline with declining species-and/or functional group-richness (Naeem *et al.* 1994, 1996; Tilman *et al.* 1996; 1997a; Hooper and Vitousek 1997; Hector *et al.* 1999). Interestingly, most of the studies to date have not considered the potential effects of spatial and temporal heterogeneity. Field experiments have deliberately reduced spatial heterogeneity and have been carried out for relatively short periods of time, thereby avoiding major climatic fluctuations. Experiments are now beginning to address the 'insurance effects' of biodiversity (Naeem 1998; Tilman *et al.* 1998; Yachi and Loreau 1999) in increasing the reliability (Naeem and Li 1997) and predictability (McGrady-Steed *et al.* 1997) of ecosystem processes in temporally heterogeneous environments.

Finally, van der Heijden *et al.* (1998) have moved the problem to another trophic level in experimental herbaceous plant communities, and examined the influence of the diversity of arbuscular mycorrhizal fungae (AMF) on ecosystem productivity and soil phosphorus concentrations. Plant biomass, and efficiency of phosphorus uptake, again rise curvilinearly with increasing species richness of mycorrhiza. The authors explicitly explain their results in terms of niche complementarity by the mycorrhiza: 'increasing AMF biodiversity resulted in more efficient exploitation of soil phosphorus and to better use of the resources available in the system'.

Extensions to larger spatial scales

In a symposium on environmental heterogeneity it seems appropriate to consider two further aspects of the relationship between species richness and ecosystem processes, but by focusing now on larger spatial scales. The first is a point that appears to be causing increasing confusion in the literature. The second is a 'thought experiment' that arises from the first.

Landscapes are heterogeneous almost by definition. That is, landscapes are mosaics, patchwork quilts of more uniform habitats that differ in slope, geology, microclimate, soil fertility, water regimes, etc. Although patches blend into one another, ecologists for well over 100 years have recognized and worked with relatively homogeneous communities and ecosystems that join together in a mosaic to create landscapes.

What has this got to do with the relationship between biodiversity and ecosystem processes? It has to do with the distinction between the impacts of changes in biodiversity on ecosystem processes within a community (*within-system effects*), and comparisons between different communities (*across-system effects*) (Tilman *et al.* 1997c; Lawton *et al.* 1998). The experiments discussed in the previous section are within-system effects. An alternative approach is to resort to correlative field studies on natural vegetation (e.g. Wardle *et al.* 1997a,b), using different communities at different sites to examine the relationship between biodiversity and ecosystem processes—that is, to make across-system comparisons. This approach tests a fundamentally different problem, because it simultaneously examines changes in species richness and differences between environments. Models (Loreau 1998a) and empirical data (e.g. McNaughton 1993; Bulla 1996; Hector *et al.* 1999) show that unless environmental conditions are extremely similar, across-habitat or across-locality comparisons of the relationship between species richness and ecosystem processes give very different outcomes to experiments on within-site effects (Fig. 19.4). Wardle *et al.* (1997a), for example, find that across islands in the Baltic, productivity declines with increasing species richness, the opposite of the within-system results discussed above. There is nothing particularly unusual about this. Ecological patterns and processes are frequently scale-dependent (Wiens, this volume) but it is not helpful to confuse scales (Grime 1997; Wardle *et al.* 1997b).

Finally, consider the following 'thought experiment'. Imagine two kinds of communities that differ naturally in diversity, productivity and other ecosystem processes, embedded in a landscape. Does it make any difference to aggregated ecosystem processes over the whole landscape if the two patch-types are distributed in a fine-grained way across the area (like squares on a chess board), or placed in large blocks (half the area is a solid block of one type, and half the area is a solid block of the other)? We know for certain that population processes of many species in these two landscapes will be different (Kareiva and Wennergren 1995; Wijesinghe and Hutchings 1997, 1999; Gonzalez *et al.* 1998; Dytham, this volume; Corlett, this volume), but what about aggregated ecosystem properties, total productivity for instance? Common sense says it must matter. Landscape heterogeneity is known to play a crucial role in ecosystem processes (Power *et al.* this volume). There is, for example, considerably more edge habitat in the finely divided landscape, and edges (ecotones) affect ecosystems in many ways (Risser 1995). In patchy desert vegetation, the redistribution of water and nutrients from bare

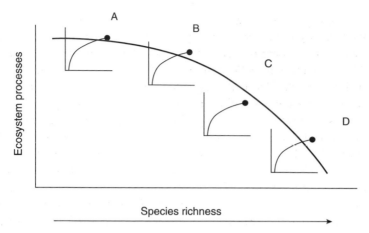

Figure 19.4 The difference between within-site and across-site effects of changes in species richness on ecosystem processes. This model imagines that there are four different sites (A–D) that differ in their natural species richness (A>B>C>D) and in their environments. But within each site (small, inset graphs, not to scale), declining species richness leads to a decline in ecosystem processes, as has now been shown by several field experiments (see text). Other across site relationships are obviously possible, including no, or positive correlations. The point is that within-site and across-site effects need not be similar and it is unwise to confuse the two (from Lawton 2000).

ground to patches with high cover increases overall ecosystem productivity (Aguiar and Sala 1999). But how similar patchiness might affect total landscape productivity, or nutrient cycling and leakage, in other ecosystems is a virtually unstudied problem.

Climate change, metapopulation dynamics and range changes

Staying with large-scale, landscape levels of spatial heterogeneity, I want to return to metapopulation dynamics and to heterogeneity in interspecific interactions in space, and consider a major consequence of global environmental change. How good are predictions about shifts in the geographical ranges of focal species (be they pests, beneficial organisms or species of conservation concern) under climate change?

The Quaternary record shows that migration has been the usual response of organisms to climate change (Huntley 1991, 1994; Bazzaz 1996; Shugart 1998). Crucially, we also know that species within assemblages respond individualistically, moving at different rates and in different directions (Coope 1978, 1995; Davis 1986; Foster *et al.* 1990; Elias 1991; Huntley 1991, 1994; Clark 1993; Buzas and Culver 1994; Graham *et al.* 1996; Jablonski and Sepkoski 1996; Shugart 1998). Communities do not move *en bloc*. They fall apart, and regroup in new combinations.

'Climate mapping' as the null hypothesis

Ecologists and biogeographers currently attempt to predict the future distributions of species by climate mapping (Rogers and Randolph 1993; Huntley 1994; Porter 1995; Sutherst *et al.* 1995; Jeffree and Jeffree 1996; Shugart 1998), based on the attractively simple idea that range and abundance are determined by the physiological tolerances of individual organisms. Knowing present climatic patterns, present distributions and predictions about future climates, species ranges are assumed to simply follow shifts in their characteristic climate envelopes. As Pacala and Hurtt (1993), Mack (1996) and Shugart (1998) amongst others have pointed out, this is tantamount to assuming that fundamental, physiologically based niches are sufficient to predict distributions. A more cautious view would be that climate envelopes predict potential ranges (Huntley 1994) and as such constitute the biological null hypothesis. And in most cases the null hypothesis will be wrong (Pacala and Hurtt 1993). How wrong is a major unresolved question, but there is no shortage of good reasons for coming to this conclusion.

First, climate envelopes assume that species interactions are not important in determining current ranges, which for most species seems unlikely. Or they assume that the target species and all the species with which it interacts significantly (enemies, competitors, food) move *en bloc*, leaving direct and indirect species interactions essentially unchanged. But we also know that this is extremely unlikely. Assemblages of species do not respond to environmental change as monolithic blocks (see references above). As ranges move, many existing species interactions will, in Root's (1993) words, be torn apart, and new interactions will form. If for either or both of these reasons mortality declines, then the future range and population abundance of the focal species will be bigger than its current range and abundance. Alternatively, if mortalities increase, populations and ranges will move but shrink.

Second, and central to this symposium, mountains, major rivers, the sea and highly fragmented, human-dominated landscapes may greatly hinder or totally prevent dispersal, stopping some species from getting to where models predict they ought to be. Other species may simply not be able to migrate fast enough to stay within tolerable limits, and will die out (Huntley 1991), and yet others will fail because species on which they depend do not make it. All these processes will further disrupt species associations and interactions.

Third, and again central to this symposium, at landscape scales the spatial configuration of metapopulations (patch number, size, and distance apart) has a major influence on patterns of patch occupancy by species, as well as on population abundances within patches, helping to generate the intraspecific range-abundance correlation discussed above. Since no two bits of the planet have identical physical geographies, it seems unlikely that the internal metapopulation structure of a current range will be exactly, or even closely reproduced somewhere else. Hence we do not expect range sizes and internal population structures to remain unchanged as ranges move.

Finally, climate envelopes assume that a relatively small number of climatic variables determine present, and hence future, ranges. There are several ways in which this could be wrong, including:

1 combinations and extremes of climatic variables in the future that have no exact extant equivalents (Graham and Grimm 1990; Huntley 1991; Clark 1993; Root 1993);

2 the modulation of plant responses to climate by rising atmospheric CO_2 concentrations (Clark 1993; Shugart 1998); and

3 the fact that diurnal to annual cycles in photoperiod are fixed at any one point on the globe, with the result that range-shifts expose organisms to novel combinations of climate and day length (Geber and Dawson 1993; Niemelä and Mattson 1996), with uncertain consequences for the timing of critical events in species' life histories (Leather *et al.* 1993).

Evidence that the null hypothesis is wrong

For all these reasons nobody seriously doubts that climate envelopes are bound to make the wrong predictions about future distributions, but there is considerable uncertainty about how wrong this approach might be. Common sense suggests that sometimes climate-space mapping will work and sometimes it will not, a view supported by case histories in the literature (Huntley 1994; Mack 1996; Shugart 1998) based, for example, on comparisons of the native and exotic geographical ranges of particular species, or on palaeoecological studies.

Some indication of how wrong climate envelopes might be is provided by experiments recently carried out by Davis *et al.* (1998a,b). Because it is impossible to do experiments with real ranges, they used laboratory microcosms consisting of sets of linked, controlled-temperature incubators simulating a climatic gradient ranging from 10°C at one end to 25°C at the other, in 5° steps. Inside the incubators were standard *Drosophila* cages connected by narrow tubes, allowing limited dispersal along the whole gradient, by up to three species of *Drosophila* and one of their larval parasitoids, *Leptopilina boulardi*. These four species co-occur in the wild in southern Europe and the Mediterranean basin. The cages were supplied with regularly renewed *Drosophila* medium. Basically the microcosms created replicated, sealed worlds in which the flies had real, long-term population dynamics and (most important in the present context) miniature geographical ranges along an environmental temperature gradient; the three species of *Drosophila* have different temperature preferences, and each performs best at a different point on the gradient.

Davis *et al.* then induced range-shifts by raising the temperature of entire replicate clines by 5°C (so that they now ranged from 15 to 30°C instead of 10–25°C) leaving others as controls. This is a much bigger increase in temperature than expected from global climate change over the next century, and it was not meant to mimic future climate change exactly. The question asked was whether the climate envelope model would make reliable predictions for this extremely simple community.

Notice that when Davis and colleagues raised the temperature they also significantly altered the metapopulation structure, because on the cool clines the 15°C incubators received immigrants from both the 10°C and the 20°C incubators, whereas in the hot clines the 15°C incubators were at the end of the temperature series, able to receive immigrants only from one side of the temperature gradient. Similarly, the 25°C incubators ceased to be at the end of the clines after warming. In other words, three of the processes outlined above that could lead to mistakes in attempting to predict the responses of communities to global warming (namely individualistic species responses, leading to alterations in species interactions, and changes in metapopulation structure) were present in these miniature worlds.

After running for several generations, each species of *Drosophila* occupied a unique slice of the environmental gradient, but this was not solely determined by physiological tolerances. The maximum extent of each species' geographical range (defined by incubators lacking a particular species) and peak population abundances were strongly influenced by migration (metapopulation dynamics), interspecific competition and parasitism, including clear evidence of apparent competition via the shared parasitoid. As a result, when Davis *et al.* warmed the clines the community did not simply move along the gradient as required by a model based on climate envelopes (Fig. 19.5). On the hot, two-species clines for example, *D. subobscura* disappeared completely at 25°C even though it was present at this temperature on the cool clines, and it became much more abundant at 15°C on the hot clines than it ever was at this temperature on the cool clines. Overall, simulated warming produced complex, counter-intuitive effects on the distributions and abundances of all three species of *Drosophila*, including complete reversals of rank abundances at some temperatures. Responses were also altered by interspecific interactions, differing markedly depending upon whether two or three species of *Drosophila* were involved.

Summarizing, this simple model world firmly rejects the null hypothesis that climatic matching is an adequate basis for predicting changes in the distributions and abundances of species under global warming. Most real assemblages of species involve many more interspecific interactions and more complex physical landscapes than were built into this model system. The real world also has other complications (outlined above) missing from this particular experiment. It is therefore difficult to see how climate matching can do a better job of forecasting changes in species' ranges in the real world than it did with these *Drosophila*. The magnitude of the likely errors is difficult to judge at the moment, but will depend critically on the degree to which current species associations and interactions unravel and new ones form in spatially heterogeneous landscapes. All the evidence points to these changes being substantial. Hence we have to conclude that substantial errors are likely. Ranges and abundances may change in some very unexpected ways in a rapidly warming world.

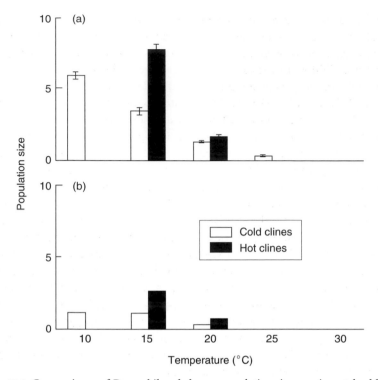

Figure 19.5 Comparisons of *Drosophila subobscura* populations in experimental cold and hot clines (see text for experimental details) (Davis *et al.* 1998a). Two-species clines (a) contain *D. subobscura* and *D. simulans*, three-species clines (b) these two plus *D. melanogaster*. Notice how both 'ranges' (the range of temperatures) supporting populations and abundances change markedly between two- and three-species clines, and that *subobscura* disappears completely at 25°C in the hot cline, even though it is present at this temperature on the cold cline. (Error bars are ± 1 SE, and are too small to show for the hot cline.) (Reproduced with permission from *Nature* **391**, 783–786 (1998), Macmillan Journals Ltd.)

The role of evolutionary trade-offs in generating habitat complexity-species richness relationships

I now want to move away from considerations of simple, two-dimensional heterogeneity and spatial processes, to heterogeneity involving more complex, three-dimensional physical structures. In this section I consider the role of evolutionary trade-offs in generating another widespread ecological pattern, namely the strong positive relationship that exists for many taxa between habitat complexity and species richness. With the exception of Boshier (this volume) the symposium has barely touched on problems at the interface of environmental heterogeneity, genetics and evolution, although unresolved problems abound in this area.

MacArthur's audaciously simple relationship between foliage height diversity and bird species diversity (MacArthur and MacArthur 1961) produced an avalanche of similar studies, for a wide variety of animal taxa. Almost without exception, more layers of habitat, more complex surfaces and more objects, particles or holes of different sizes and shapes are correlated with greater species richness in both contemporary and fossil assemblages (Bambach 1977; Spight 1977; Anderson 1978a,b; M'Closkey 1978; Reed 1978; Lawton 1983; Greenstone 1984; Bell *et al.* 1991; Etter and Grassle 1992; many others). The relationship holds for habitats of different complexities *within* a given regional pool of species (Fig. 19.3), just as larger patches harbour more species. All such patterns can be overridden by larger-scale, biogeographic differences in pool size. But within one biogeographic region, habitat complexity begets biological diversity. Why?

The obvious answer is that more complex habitats contain more niches — more places to feed, hide, nest and so on. Clearly that is true, but in part the answer is circular (we identify a potential niche only when it is occupied by a species) and anyway, how does it work? What are the underlying mechanisms? Most of the studies cited above are 10 or 20 years old, carried out at a time of intense interest in the problem, but when ecology was a less experimental science than it now is and basically relied on correlations (for an exception, see Reed 1978). Could we do experiments that might recreate and throw light on the evolution of species diversity in more complex physical habitats, whilst at the same time revealing important underlying principles? Surprisingly, the answer is 'yes', using bacteria and laboratory microcosms (Rainey and Travasino 1998).

Rainey and Travasino used the common aerobic, asexually reproducing bacterium *Pseudomonas fluorescens* to explore the effects of habitat heterogeneity on species diversity. *Pseudomonas* evolves rapidly under novel environmental conditions to yield mutants with very different growth forms. Although the mutants are clearly not species, they are good analogues of phenotypically different species. Rainey and Travasino exploited this feature of the biology of *Pseudomonas* by culturing populations in totally homogeneous habitats (6 mL of culture medium, continuously mixed by shaking) or heterogeneous habitats (6 mL of unshaken medium). Replicates of both types of tubes were seeded with a single bacterium of the ancestral morph, which forms simple, smooth colonies and hence is called the 'smooth morph' (SM). In the shaken tubes this remained the only phenotype, suspended in the culture medium. But in the stationary tubes, three phenotypes rapidly colonized the heterogeneous habitat: SMs in the body of the medium, 'wrinkly spreaders' (WS) on the surface of the medium, and 'fuzzy spreaders' (FS) on the bottom of the culture tube. These three phenotypes are highly distinct and partition the habitat between them. One might imagine a fourth niche, on the side-walls of the culture tubes, but no morph evolved to exploit it.

The remarkable thing about this little exercise in evolution is that it is repeatable and reversible. Diverse populations of the three morphs transferred to homogeneous (shaken) habitats lose phenotypic diversity; transferring this impoverished community back into the heterogeneous environment restores diversity.

All well and good. It is easy to see why lack of ecological opportunity only allows one phenotype to survive in the homogeneous environment, but why does one morph not come to dominate in the heterogeneous environment? The answer appears to be because of trade-offs. No morph can be best everywhere. Phenotypes are specialists, a phenomenon that Rainey and Travasino go on to show in a series of simple pair-wise competition experiments between the morphs. As they put it, the engine of adaptive radiation in this little system is competition. Within a matter of days, these *Pseudomonas* show 'adaptive radiation that has all the hallmarks of macroevolutionary dynamics, including rapid evolution and niche specialization' in physically heterogeneous habitats.

There is no reason to believe that the same general processes are not involved in other cases in nature where species diversity and habitat complexity are positively correlated. These systems do not have to have evolved together; species may come together by dispersal. Nor is interspecific competition essential (e.g. Strong *et al.* 1984), although when species do compete, habitat complexity can reduce interspecific competition (Petren and Case 1998). But positive correlations between habitat complexity and species richness must involve trade-offs, such that no one species performs best in all physical niches. I see considerable scope for further work in this area, both in laboratory microcosms and in the field.

Ecosystem engineering

Organisms do not just respond to their physical environment in the manner so elegantly demonstrated by Rainey and Travasino (1998). Some species physically modify their own environment, and hence the environment of other species, often with profound ecological consequences. Jones *et al.* (1994, 1997) call this modification physical ecosystem engineering. Formally defined, the organisms involved — the physical ecosystem engineers — are species that directly or indirectly control the availability of resources to other organisms by causing physical state changes in biotic or abiotic materials. Physical ecosystem engineering by organisms is the physical modification, maintenance or creation of habitats. The ecological effects of engineering on other species occur because the physical state changes directly or indirectly control resources used by these other species. These engineering activities inevitably result in changes to, and increases in, the physical heterogeneity of habitats (Pickett *et al.* this volume).

Some examples of engineering

Consider the example used by Jones *et al.* (1997), from where this material is taken. What does a tree do in a forest? The standard answer is that its living and dead tissues are eaten by many animals and microorganisms, and that it competes with other plants for light, water and nutrients. But a tree does much more than provide food and be a competitor. The branches, bark, roots, and living and dead leaves make shelter, resting locations and living space. Small ponds full of organisms form where rain water gets channelled into crotches (Kitching 1971, 1983;

Srivastava and Lawton 1998), and soil cavities form as roots grow, that make places where animals can live and cache food (Foster 1988; Vander Wall 1990). The leaves and branches cast shade, reduce the impact of rain and wind, moderate temperature extremes and increase humidity for organisms in the understorey and the soil (Holling 1992; Callaway and Walker 1996). Root growth aerates the soil, alters its texture and affects the infiltration rate of water (Tisdall and Oades 1982; Smiles 1988). Dead leaves fall to the forest floor altering raindrop impact, drainage, and heat and gas exchange in the soil habitat, and make barriers or protection for seeds, seedlings, animals and microbes (Facelli and Pickett 1991; Callaway and Walker 1996). The trunk, branches and leaves can fall into forest streams, creating debris dams and ponds for species to live in (Hedin *et al.* 1988). The roots can bind around rocks, stabilizing the substrate and ameliorating hurricane impacts on other species (Basnet *et al.* 1992). If the tree falls, the trunk, branches and resulting soil pit and mound create habitats for numerous organisms (Peterson *et al.* 1990).

It is likely that as many species, if not more, are affected by these things that a tree does than directly use the tree for food or compete with it for light, water and nutrients. Nor is the tree in the forest unique. All plants do the same or similar things to a greater or lesser extent, and many animals and microorganisms cause ecologically significant physical changes in their environments (Jones *et al.* 1994, 1997). A woodpecker or rot fungus may make holes in the tree that are then used by other species (Kitching 1971; Bradshaw and Holzapfel 1985; Daily *et al.* 1993), or beaver may cut it down to build a dam and pond in which hundreds of species live (Pollock *et al.* 1995).

Beyond description

Jones *et al.* (1994, 1997) took these and many other examples of ecosystem engineering by organisms, and first of all classified them into types. Autogenic engineers directly transform the environment via their own structures, and these living or dead structures remain as part of the engineered environment (trees and corals for example). Allogenic engineers change the environment by transforming living or non-living materials from one physical state to another (beaver and woodpeckers), but the 'body' of the engineer is not an integral part of the engineered environment. Some organisms work both ways, not least trees. Over and above these two broad divisions, there are other, more subtle differences between different kinds of engineering, just as there are various forms of interspecific competition (scramble, contest) and different types of enemy–victim interactions (predation, parasitism, herbivory). Sometimes the subtleties matter and sometimes they do not. I am not going to repeat them here; they are laid out in full in Jones *et al.* (1994, 1997).

In the context of this symposium, the question is: How important are engineers in creating habitat heterogeneity? Or more specifically, via changes in physical heterogeneity and the accompanying changes in the availability and fluxes of resources, how does engineering measure up as a major ecological player compared

417

with the more traditional concerns of ecologists (trophic and competitive interactions for example)? In my view engineering is every bit as important as trophic or competitive interactions. I know of no habitat on earth that is not created, or significantly modified by, ecosystem engineers (Jones *et al.* 1994, 1997; Lawton 2000). Nor are just big obvious things like elephants, beaver and trees involved. Some surprisingly obscure organisms can have major ecological consequences as engineers (Mazumder *et al.* 1990; West 1990; Townsend *et al.* 1992; Zaady and Shachak 1994; Thomas *et al.* 1998, 1999).

Interesting (and cheap!) experiments can be carried out by mentally eliminating the engineers. What would a valley look like with and without beaver? How would a forest work if trees had no physical structure? Or imagine a purely trophic world in which totally structureless entities floated around absorbing energy, complexing with chemicals and with each other. Whilst this may seem ghostly and unreal, it probably bears some similarity to the earliest scenes in the evolution of life on earth. In these mental experiments the formation of physical structures by organisms, and the effects of these structures on the rest of the world in both evolutionary (Bambach 1977; Thayer 1979; Jablonski and Sepkoski 1996) and ecological time (Naiman and Rogers 1997; Chauvel *et al.* 1999; Covich *et al.* 1999; Groffman and Bohlem 1999) seem both dramatic and fundamental (Alper 1998).

In a symposium devoted to the ecological consequences of environmental heterogeneity, I can think of no better way to close the discussion than by pointing out the huge ecological and evolutionary influence that physical ecosystem engineers have had, and continue to have, on the biosphere. Yet compared with other ecological interactions they remain very poorly studied in a formal sense. There are very few experiments where populations of engineers have been manipulated and the effects of such manipulations documented (Jones *et al.* 1997), or in which trophic vs. engineering effects have been partitioned, or situations in which models of the population and community dynamics of engineers have been built (Gurney and Lawton 1996). There is an urgent need for ecologists interested in heterogeneity to take ecosystem engineering much more seriously.

Acknowledgments

I am extremely grateful to the symposium organizers for asking me to participate in this exploration of the ecological consequences of environmental heterogeneity, not least for the privilege of having the last word. These ideas have been shaped by many collaborators, including Tim Blackburn, Andrew Davis, Kevin Gaston, Francis Gilbert, Andy Gonzalez, Andy Hector, Clive Jones, Michel Loreau, Shahid Naeem, Moshe Shachak, Bryan Shorrocks and Dave Tilman. Paul Rainey taught me about pseudomonads. Mark Fellowes, Andy Hector, Mike Hutchings, Alan Stewart and Doug Yu made helpful comments on the manuscript. All the mistakes and half-brained ideas are mine. The work was supported by the core NERC grant to CPB.

References

Aguiar, M.R. and Sala, O.E. (1999) Patch structure, dynamics and implications for the functioning of arid ecosystems. *Trends in Ecology and Evolution* **14**, 273–277.

Allen, C.R., Forys, E.A. and Holling, C.S. (1999) Body mass patterns predict invasions and extinctions in transforming landscapes. *Ecosystems* **2**, 114–121.

Allison, G.W. (1999) The implications of experimental design for biodiversity manipulations. *American Naturalist* **153**, 26–45.

Alper, J. (1998) Ecosystem 'engineers' shape habitats for other species. *Science* **280**, 1195–1196.

Anderson, J.M. (1978a) Inter- and intra-habitat relationships between woodland *Cryptostigmata* species diversity and the diversity of soil and litter microhabitats. *Oecologia* **32**, 341–348.

Anderson, J.M. (1978b) A method to quantify soil-microhabitat complexity and its application to a study of soil animal species diversity. *Soil Biology and Biochemistry* **10**, 77–78.

Bambach, R.K. (1977) Species richness in marine benthic habitats through the Phanerozoic. *Paleobiology* **3**, 152–167.

Basnet, K., Likens, G.E., Scatena, F.N. and Lugo, A.E. (1992) Hurricane Hugo: damage to a tropical rain forest in Puerto Rico. *Journal of Tropical Ecology* **8**, 47–55.

Bazzaz, F.A. (1996) *Plants in Changing Environments: Linking Physiological, Population, and Community Ecology.* Cambridge University Press, Cambridge.

Bell, S.S., McCoy, E.D. and Mushinsky, H.R. (1991) (eds). *Habitat Structure: the Physical Arrangement of Objects in Space.* Chapman and Hall, London.

Blackburn, T.M. and Gaston, K.J. (1994) Animal body size distributions: patterns, mechanisms and implications. *Trends in Ecology and Evolution* **9**, 471–474.

Blackburn, T.M., Gaston, K.J., Quinn, R.M., Arnold, H. and Gregory, R.D. (1997) Of mice and wrens: the relation between abundance and geographic range size in British mammals and birds. *Philosophical Transactions of the Royal Society of London B*, 352, 419–427.

Bock, C.E. (1987) Distribution-abundance relationships of some Arizona landbirds: a matter of scale? *Ecology* **68**, 124–129.

Bock, C.E. and Ricklefs, R.E. (1984) Geographical correlates of abundance vs. rarity in some North American songbirds: a positive correlation. *American Naturalist* **122**, 295–299.

Bradshaw, W.E. and Holzapfel, C.M. (1985) The distribution and abundance of treehole mosquitoes in eastern North America: perspectives from north Florida. In: *Ecology of Mosquitoes: Proceedings of a Workshop* (eds L.P. Lounibos, J.R. Rey and J.H. Frank), pp. 3–23. Florida Medical Entomology Laboratory, Vero Beach.

Brown, J.H. (1984) On the relationship between abundance and distribution of species. *American Naturalist* **124**, 255–279.

Brown, J.H. (1995) *Macroecology.* University of Chicago Press, Chicago.

Brown, J.H. and Maurer, B.A. (1989) Macroecology: the division of food and space among species on continents. *Science* **243**, 1145–1150.

Brown, J.H. and Nicoletto, P.F. (1991) Spatial scaling of species composition: body masses of North American land mammals. *American Naturalist* **138**, 1478–1512.

Bulla, L. (1996) Relationship between biotic diversity and primary productivity in savanna grasslands. In: *Biodiversity and Savanna Ecosystem Processes* (eds O.T. Solbrig, E. Medina and J.F. Silva), pp. 97–120. Springer-Verlag, Berlin.

Buzas, M.A. and Culver, S.J. (1994) Species pool and dynamics of marine paleocommunities. *Science* **264**, 1439–1441.

Callaway, R.M. and Walker, L.R. (1996) Competition and facilitation: a synthetic approach to interactions in plant communities. *Ecology* **78**, 1958–1965.

Chapin, F.S. III, Sala, O.E., Burke, I.C., Grime, J.P., Hooper, D.U. and Lauenroth, W.K. (1998) Ecosystem consequences of changing biodiversity. *Bioscience* **48**, 45–52.

Chapin, F.S. III, Walker, B.H., Hobbs, R.J., *et al.* (1997) Biotic control over the functioning of ecosystems. *Science* **277**, 500–504.

Chauvel, A., Grimaldi, M., Barros, E., *et al.* (1999) Pasture damage by an Amazonian earthworm. *Nature* **398**, 32–33.

Clark, J.S. (1993) Paleoecological perspective on modeling broad-scale responses to global change. In: *Biotic Interactions and Global Change* (eds P.M. Kareiva, J.G. Kingsolver and R.B. Huey), pp. 315–332. Sinauer, Sunderland, Mass.

Coope, G.R. (1978) Constancy of insect species versus inconstancy of Quaternary environments. In: *Diversity of Insect Faunas. Symposia of the Royal Entomological Society of London 9* (eds L.A. Mound and N. Waloff), pp. 176–187. Blackwell Scientific Publications, Oxford.

Coope, G.R. (1995) The effects of Quaternary climatic changes on insect populations: lessons from the past. In: *Insects in a Changing Environment* (eds R. Harrington and N.E. Stork), pp. 29–48. Academic Press, London.

Cornell, H.V. and Karlson, R.H. (1997) Local and regional processes as controls of species richness. In: *Spatial Ecology. The Role of Space in Population Dynamics and Interspecific Interactions* (eds D. Tilman and P. Kareiva), pp. 250–268. Princeton University Press, Princeton.

Cornell, H.V. and Lawton, J.H. (1992) Species interactions, local and regional processes, and limits to the richness of ecological communities: a theoretical perspective. *Journal of Animal Ecology* **61**, 1–12.

Covich, A.P., Palmer, M.A. and Crowl, T.A. (1999) The role of benthic invertebrate species in freshwater ecosystems. *Bioscience* **49**, 119–127.

Daily, G.C., Ehrlich, P.R. and Haddad, N.M. (1993) Double keystone bird in a keystone species complex. *Proceedings of the National Academy of Sciences USA* **90**, 592–594.

Davis, A.J., Jenkinson, L.S., Lawton, J.H., Shorrocks, B. and Wood, S. (1998a) Making mistakes when predicting shifts in species range in response to global warming. *Nature* **391**, 783–786.

Davis, A.J., Lawton, J.H., Shorrocks, B. and Jenkinson, L. (1998b) Individualistic species responses invalidate simple physiological models of community dynamics under global environmental change. *Journal of Animal Ecology* **67**, 600–612.

Davis, M.B. (1986) Climatic instability, time lags, and community disequilibrium. In: *Community Ecology* (eds J. Diamond and T.J. Case), pp. 269–284. Harper and Row, New York.

Ehrlich, P.R. and Ehrlich, A.H. (1981) *Extinction.*

The Causes and Consequences of the Disappearance of Species. Random House, New York.

Elias, S.A. (1991) Insects and climate change. *Bioscience* **41**, 552–559.

Etter, R.J. and Grassle, J.F. (1992) Patterns of species diversity in the deep sea as a function of sediment particle size diversity. *Nature* **360**, 576–578.

Facelli, J.M. and Pickett, S.T.A. (1991) Plant litter: its dynamics and effects on plant community structure. *Botanical Review* **57**, 1–32.

Foster, D.R., Schoonmaker, P.K. and Pickett, S.T.A. (1990) Insights from paleoecology to community ecology. *Trends in Ecology and Evolution* **5**, 119–122.

Foster, R.C. (1988) Microenvironments of soil microorganisms. *Biology and Fertility of Soils* **6**, 189–203.

Gaston, K.J. (1994) *Rarity.* Chapman and Hall, London.

Gaston, K.J. (1996) The multiple forms of the interspecific abundance-distribution relationship. *Oikos* **76**, 211–220.

Gaston, K.J. and Blackburn, T.M. (1996) Global scale macroecology: interactions between population size, geographic range size and body size in the Anseriformes. *Journal of Animal Ecology* **65**, 701–714.

Gaston, K.J. and Blackburn, T.M. (1999) A critique for macroecology. *Oikos* **84**, 353–368.

Gaston, K.J., Blackburn, T.M., Gregory, R.D. and Greenwood, J.J.D. (1998) The anatomy of the interspecific abundance-range size relationship for British birds: I. Spatial patterns. *Ecology Letters* **1**, 38–46.

Gaston, K.J., Blackburn, T.M. and Lawton, J.H. (1997) Interspecific abundance-range size relationships: an appraisal of mechanisms. *Journal of Animal Ecology* **66**, 579–601.

Geber, M.A. and Dawson, T.E. (1993) Evolutionary responses of plants to global change. In: *Biotic Interactions and Global Change* (eds P.M. Kareiva, J.G. Kingsolver and R.B. Huey), pp. 179–197. Sinauer, Sunderland, Mass.

Gilbert, F., Gonzalez, A. and Evans-Freke, I. (1998) Corridors maintain species richness in the fragmented landscapes of a microecosystem. *Proceedings of the Royal Society. London B*, 265, 577–582.

Gonzalez, A., Lawton, J.H., Gilbert, F.S., Blackburn,

T.M. and Evans-Freke, I. (1998) Metapopulation dynamics, abundance, and distribution in a microecosystem. *Science* 281, 2045–2047.

Graham, R.W. and Grimm, E.C. (1990) Effects of global climate change on the patterns of terrestrial biological communities. *Trends in Ecology and Evolution* 5, 289–292.

Graham, R.W., Lundelius, E.L. Jr, Graham, M.A., *et al.* (1996) Spatial response of mammals to late Quaternary environmental fluctuations. *Science* 272, 1601–1606.

Greenstone, M.H. (1984) Determinants of web spider species diversity: vegetation structural diversity vs. prey availability. *Oecologia* 62, 299–304.

Grime, J.P. (1997) Biodiversity and ecosystem function: the debate deepens. *Science* 277, 1260–1261.

Groffman, P.M. and Bohlen, P.J. (1999) Soil and sediment biodiversity. *BioScience*, 49, 139–148.

Gurney, W.S.C. and Lawton, J.H. (1996) The population dynamics of ecosystem engineers. *Oikos* 76, 273–283.

Hanski, I. (1998) Metapopulation dynamics. *Nature* 396, 41–49.

Hanski, I. and Gyllenberg, M. (1997) Uniting two general patterns in the distribution of species. *Science* 275, 397–400.

Hanski, I., Kouki, J. and Halkka, A. (1993) Three explanations of the positive relationship between distribution and abundance of species. In: *Species Diversity in Ecological Communities: Historical and Geographical Perspectives* (eds R.E. Ricklefs and D. Schluter), pp. 108–116. University of Chicago Press, Chicago.

Harrison, S., Ross, S.J. and Lawton, J.H. (1992) Beta diversity on geographic gradients in Britain. *Journal of Animal Ecology* 61, 151–158.

Harrison, S. and Taylor, A.D. (1996) Empirical evidence for metapopulation dynamics. Metapopulation Biology. In: *Ecology, Genetics, and Evolution* (eds I. Hanski and M.E. Gilpin), pp. 27–42. Academic Press, San Diego.

Harrison, S., Thomas, C.D. and Lewinsohn, T.M. (1995) Testing a metapopulation model of coexistence in the insect community on ragwort (*Senecio jacobaea*). *American Naturalist* 145, 546–562.

Hector, A. (1998) The effect of diversity on productivity: detecting the role of species complementarity. *Oikos* 82, 597–599.

Hector, A., Schmid, B., Beierkuhnlein, C., *et al.* (1999) Plant diversity and productivity experiments in European grasslands. *Science*, 286, 1123–1127.

Hedin, L.O., Mayer, M.S. and Likens, G.E. (1988) The effect of deforestation on organic debris dams. *Proceedings of the International Association for Theoretical and Applied Limnology* 23, 1135–1141.

van der Heijden, M.G.A., Klironomos, J.N., Ursic, M., *et al.* (1998) Mycorrhizal fungal diversity determines plant biodiversity, ecosystem variability and productivity. *Nature* 396, 69–72.

Holling, C.S. (1992) Cross-scale morphology, geometry, and dynamics of ecosystems. *Ecological Monographs* 62, 447–502.

Hooper, D.U. and Vitousek, P.M. (1997) The effects of plant composition and diversity on ecosystem processes. *Science* 277, 1302–1305.

Huffaker, C.B. (1958) Experimental studies on predation: dispersion factors and predator-prey oscillations. *Hilgardia* 27, 343–383.

Huntley, B. (1991) How plants respond to climate change: migration rates, individualism and the consequences for plant communities. *Annals of Botany* 67 (Suppl. 1), 15–22.

Huntley, B. (1994) Plant species' response to climate change: implications for the conservation of European birds. *Ibis* 137 (Suppl.) 127–138.

Huston, M.A. (1997) Hidden treatments in ecological experiments: re-evaluating the ecosystem function of biodiversity. *Oecologia* 110, 449–460.

Jablonski, D. and Sepkoski, J.J. Jr (1996) Paleobiology, community ecology, and scales of ecological pattern. *Ecology* 77, 1367–1378.

Jeffree, C.E. and Jeffree, E.P. (1996) Redistribution of the potential geographical ranges of mistletoe and Colorado beetle in Europe in response to the temperature component of climate change. *Functional Ecology* 10, 562–577.

Jones, C.G., Lawton, J.H. and Shachak, M. (1994) Organisms as ecosystem engineers. *Oikos* 69, 373–386.

Jones, C.G., Lawton, J.H. and Shachak, M. (1997) Positive and negative effects of organisms as ecosystem engineers. *Ecology* 78, 1946–1957.

Kareiva, P. and Wennergren, U. (1995) Connecting

landscape patterns to ecosystem and population processes. *Nature* **373**, 299–302.

Kitching, R.L. (1971) An ecological study of water-filled tree-holes and their position in the woodland ecosystem. *Journal of Animal Ecology* **40**, 281–302.

Kitching, R.L. (1983) Community structure in water-filled treeholes in Europe and Australia — comparisons and speculations. In: *Phytotelmata: Terrestrial Plants as Hosts for Aquatic Insect Communities* (eds J.K. Frank and L.P. Lounibos), pp. 205–222. Plexus, Medford, NJ.

Lawton, J.H. (1983) Plant architecture and the diversity of phytophagous insects. *Annual Review of Entomology* **28**, 23–39.

Lawton, J.H. (1993) Range, population abundance and conservation. *Trends in Ecology and Evolution* **8**, 409–413.

Lawton, J.H. (1996) Population abundances, geographic ranges and conservation: 1994 Witherby Memorial Lecture. *Bird Study* **43**, 3–19.

Lawton, J.H. (1999) Are there general laws in ecology? *Oikos* **84**, 177–192.

Lawton, J.H. (2000) *Community Ecology in a Changing World*. Ecology Institute. *Oldendorff/Luhe*.

Lawton, J.H., Naeem, S., Thompson, L.J., Hector, A. and Crawley, M.J. (1998) Biodiversity and ecosystem function: getting the Ecotron experiment in its correct context. *Functional Ecology* **12**, 848–852.

Leather, S.R., Walters, K.F.A. and Bale, J.S. (1993) *The Ecology of Insect Overwintering*. Cambridge University Press, Cambridge.

Loreau, M. (1998a) Biodiversity and ecosystem functioning: a mechanistic model. *Proceedings of the National Academy of Sciences* **95**, 5632–5636.

Loreau, M. (1998b) Separating sampling and other effects in biodiversity experiments. *Oikos* **82**, 600–602.

MacArthur, R.H. and MacArthur, J.W. (1961) On bird species diversity. *Ecology* **42**, 594–598.

Mack, R.N. (1996) Predicting the identity and fate of plant invaders: emergent and emerging approaches. *Biological Conservation* **78**, 107–121.

Maurer, B.A. (1999) *Untangling Ecological Complexity*. University of Chicago Press, Chicago.

Mazumder, A., Taylor, W.D., McQueen, D.J. and Lean, D.R.S. (1990) Effects of fish and plankton on lake temperature and mixing depth. *Science* **247**, 312–315.

McGrady-Steed, J., Harris, P.M. and Morin, P.J. (1997) Biodiversity regulates ecosystem predictability. *Nature* **390**, 162–165.

M'Closkey, R.T. (1978) Niche separation and assembly in four species of Sonoran desert rodents. *American Naturalist* **112**, 683–694.

McNaughton, S.J. (1993) Biodiversity and function of grazing ecosystems. In: *Biodiversity and Ecosystem Function* (eds E.-D. Schulze and H.A. Mooney), pp. 361–383. Springer-Verlag, Berlin.

Naeem, S. (1998) Species redundancy and ecosystem reliability. *Conservation Biology* **12**, 39–45.

Naeem, S., Håkansson, K., Lawton, J.H., Crawley, M.J. and Thompson, L.J. (1996) Biodiversity and plant productivity in a model assemblage of plant species. *Oikos* **76**, 259–264.

Naeem, S. and Li, S. (1997) Biodiversity enhances ecosystem reliability. *Nature* **390**, 507–509.

Naeem, S., Thompson, L.J., Lawler, S.P., Lawton, J.H. and Woodfin, R.M. (1994) Declining biodiversity can alter the performance of ecosystems. *Nature* **368**, 734–737.

Naiman, R.J. and Rogers, K.H. (1997) Large animals and system-level characteristics in river corridors. *Bioscience* **47**, 521–529.

Niemelä, P. and Mattson, W.J. (1996) Invasion of North American forests by European phytophagous insects. *Bioscience* **46**, 741–753.

Pacala, S.W. and Hurtt, G.C. (1993) Terrestrial vegetation and climate change: integrating models and experiments. In: *Biotic Interactions and Global Change* (eds P.M. Kareiva, J.G. Kingsolver and R.B. Huey), pp. 57–74. Sinauer, Sunderland, Mass.

Peterson, C.J., Carson, W.P., McCarthy, B.C. and Pickett, S.T.A. (1990) Microsite variation and soil dynamics within newly created treefall pits and mounds. *Oikos* **58**, 39–46.

Petren, K. and Case, T.J. (1998) Habitat structure determines competition intensity and invasion success in gecko lizards. *Proceedings of the National Academy of Sciences USA* **95**, 11739–11744.

Pollock, M.M., Naiman, R.J., Erickson, H.E., Johnston, C.A., Pastor, J. and Pinay, G. (1995) Beaver as engineers: influences on biotic and abiotic characteristics of drainage basins.

In: *Linking Species and Ecosystems* (eds C.G. Jones and J.H. Lawton), pp. 117–126. Chapman and Hall, New York.

Porter, J. (1995) The effects of climate change on the agricultural environment for crop insect pests with particular reference to the European corn borer and grain maize. In: *Insects in a Changing Environment* (eds R. Harrington and N.E. Stork), pp. 93–123. Academic Press, London.

Quinn, J.F. and Dunham, A.E. (1983) On hypothesis testing in ecology and evolution. *American Naturalist* **122**, 602–617.

Rainey, P.B. and Travasino, M. (1998) Adaptive radiation in a heterogeneous environment. *Nature* **394**, 69–72.

Reed, C. (1978) Species diversity in aquatic microecosystems. *Ecology* **59**, 481–488.

Risser, P.G. (1995) The status of the science examining ecotones. *Bioscience* **45**, 318–325.

Rogers, D.J. and Randolph, S.E. (1993) Distribution of tsetse and ticks in Africa: past, present and future. *Parasitology Today* **9**, 266–271.

Root, T.L. (1993) Effects of global climate change on North American birds and their communities. In: *Biotic Interactions and Global Change* (eds P.M. Kareiva, J.G. Kingsolver and R.B. Huey), pp. 280–292. Sinauer, Sunderland, Mass.

Rosenzweig, M.L. (1995) *Species Diversity in Space and Time.* Cambridge University Press, Cambridge.

Sharrock, J.T.R. (1976) *The Atlas of Breeding Birds in Britain and Ireland.* British Trust for Ornithology / Irish Wildbird Conservancy.

Shugart, H.H. (1998) *Terrestrial Ecosystems in Changing Environments.* Cambridge University Press, Cambridge.

Smiles, D.E. (1988) Aspects of the physical environment of soil organisms. *Biology and Fertility of Soils* **6**, 204–215.

Spight, T.M. (1977) Diversity of shallow-water gastropod communities on temperate and tropical beaches. *American Naturalist* **111**, 1077–1097.

Srivastava, D.S. (1999) Using local-regional richness plots to test for species saturation: pitfalls and potentials. *Journal of Animal Ecology* **68**, 1–16.

Srivastava, D.S. and Lawton, J.H. (1998) Why more

productive sites have more species: an experimental test of theory using tree-hole communities. *American Naturalist* **152**, 510–529.

Strong, D.R., Lawton, J.H. and Southwood, T.R.E. (1984) *Insects on Plants. Community Patterns and Mechanisms.* Blackwell Scientific Publications, Oxford.

Sutherst, R.W., Maywald, G.F. and Skarratt, D.B. (1995) Predicting insect distributions in a changed climate. In: *Insects in a Changing Environment* (eds R. Harrington and N.E. Stork), pp. 59–91. Academic Press, London.

Terborgh, J., Lopez, L., Tello, J., Yu, D. and Bruni, A.R. (1997) Transitory states in relaxing ecosystems of land bridge islands. In: *Tropical Forest Remnants* (eds W.F. Laurance and R.O. Bierregaard), pp. 256–274. Chicago University Press, Chicago.

Thayer, C.W. (1979) Biological bulldozers and the evolution of marine benthic communities. *Science* **203**, 458–461.

Thomas, F., Poulin, R., de Meeus, T., Guégan, J.-F. and Renaud, F. (1999) Parasites and ecosystem engineering: what roles could they play? *Oikos* **84**, 167–171.

Thomas, F., Renaud, F. and de Meeûs, T. and Poulin, R. (1998) Manipulation of host behaviour by parasites: ecosystem engineering in the intertidal zone? *Proceedings of the Royal Society London B*, **265**, 1091–1096.

Tilman, D. (1997) Distinguishing between the effects of species diversity and species composition. *Oikos* **80**, 185.

Tilman, D., Knops, J., Wedin, D., Reich, P., Ritchie, M. and Siemann, E. (1997a) The influence of functional diversity and composition on ecosystem processes. *Science* **277**, 1300–1305.

Tilman, D., Lehman, C.L. and Bristow, C.E. (1998) Diversity-stability relationships: statistical inevitability or ecological consequence? *American Naturalist* **151**, 277–282.

Tilman, D., Lehman, C.L. and Thomson, K.T. (1997b) Plant diversity and ecosystem productivity: theoretical considerations. *Proceedings of the National Academy of Sciences USA* **94**, 1857–1861.

Tilman, D., Naeem, S., Knops, J., *et al.* (1997c) Biodiversity and ecosystem properties. *Science* **278**, 1866–1867.

Tilman, D., Wedin, D. and Knops, J. (1996)

Productivity and sustainability influenced by biodiversity in grassland ecosystems. *Nature* **379**, 718–720.

Tisdall, J.M. and Oades, J.M. (1982) Organic matter and water-stable aggregates in soils. *Journal of Soil Science* **33**, 141–163.

Townsend, D.W., Keller, M.D., Sieracki, M.E. and Ackleson, S.G. (1992) Spring phytoplankton blooms in the absence of vertical water column stratification. *Nature* **360**, 59–62.

Vander Wall, S.B. (1990) *Food Hoarding in Animals.* University of Chicago Press, Chiacago.

Vitousek, P.M. (1994) Beyond global warming: ecology and global change. *Ecology* **75**, 1861–1876.

Wardle, D.A., Zackrisson, O., Hörnberg, G. and Gallet, C. (1997a) The influence of island area on ecosystem properties. *Science* **277**, 1296–1299.

Wardle, D.A., Zackrisson, O., Hörnberg, G. and Gallet, C. (1997b) Response. *Science* **278**, 1867–1869.

Warren, P.H. and Gaston, K.J. (1997) Interspecific abundance-occupancy relationships: a test of

mechanisms using microcosms. *Journal of Animal Ecology* **66**, 730–742.

West, N.E. (1990) Structure and function of micro-phytic soil crusts in wildland ecosystems of arid to semi-arid regions. *Advances in Ecological Research* **20**, 180–223.

Wijesinghe, D.K. and Hutchings, M.J. (1997) The effects of spatial scale of environmental heterogeneity on the growth of a clonal plant: an experimental study with *Glechoma hederacea.* *Journal of Ecology* **85**, 17–28.

Wijesinghe, D.K. and Hutchings, M.J. (1999) The effects of environmental heterogeneity on the performance of *Glechoma hederacea*: the interaction between patch contrast and patch scale. *Journal of Ecology,* **87**, 860–872.

Yachi, S. and Loreau, M. (1999) Biodiversity and ecosystem productivity in a fluctuating environment: The insurance hypothesis. *Proceedings of the National Academy of Sciences USA* **96**, 1463–1468.

Zaady, E. and Shachak, M. (1994) Microphytic crust and ecosystem leakage in the Negev Desert. *American Journal of Botany* **81**, 109.

Index

Page references to figures appear in *italic* type and those for tables appear in **bold** type.